Computer Communications and Networks

For other titles published in this series, go to
http://www.springer.com/series/4198

The **Computer Communications and Networks** series is a range of textbooks, monographs and handbooks. It sets out to provide students, researchers and nonspecialists alike with a sure grounding in current knowledge, together with comprehensible access to the latest developments in computer communications and networking.

Emphasis is placed on clear and explanatory styles that support a tutorial approach, so that even the most complex of topics is presented in a lucid and intelligible manner.

Aboul-Ella Hassanien · Jemal H. Abawajy
Ajith Abraham · Hani Hagras

Editors

Pervasive Computing

Innovations in Intelligent Multimedia and Applications

Springer

Editors

Prof. Aboul-Ella Hassanien
Cairo University
Fac. Computers & Information
Dept. Information Technology
5 Ahmed Zewal Street
Orman, Giza 12613
Egypt
a.hassanien@fci-cu.edu.eg

Dr. Jemal H. Abawajy
Deakin University
School of Engineering & Information
    Technology
Geelong VIC 3217
Australia
jemal.abawajy@deakin.edu.au

Prof. Dr. Ajith Abraham
Machine Intelligence Research
Labs (MIR)
Scientific Network for Innovation
    & Research Excellence
P.O.Box 2259
Auburn WA 98071-2259
USA
ajith.abraham@ieee.org

Prof. Hani Hagras
University of Essex
Dept. Computer Science and Electronic
    Engineering
Wivenhoe Park
Colchester
United Kingdom CO4 3SQ
hani@essex.ac.uk

Series Editor
Professor A.J. Sammes, BSc, MPhil, PhD, FBCS, CEng
Centre for Forensic Computing
Cranfield University
DCMT, Shrivenham
Swindon SN6 8LA
UK

ISSN 1617-7975
ISBN 978-1-4471-2514-3   e-ISBN 978-1-84882-599-4
DOI 10.1007/978-1-84882-599-4
Springer Dordrecht Heidelberg London New York

British Library Cataloguing in Publication Data
A catalogue record for this book is available from the British Library

Cover design: SPi Publisher Services

Printed on acid-free paper

Springer is part of Springer Science+Business Media (www.springer.com)

Preface

The main objective of pervasive computing systems is to create environments where computers become invisible by being seamlessly integrated and connected into our everyday environment, where such embedded computers can then provide information and exercise *intelligent control* when needed, but without being obtrusive. Pervasive computing and intelligent multimedia technologies are becoming increasingly important to the modern way of living. However, many of their potential applications have not yet been fully realized. Intelligent multimedia allows dynamic selection, composition and presentation of the most appropriate multimedia content based on user preferences. A variety of applications of pervasive computing and intelligent multimedia are being developed for all walks of personal and business life. Pervasive computing (often synonymously called ubiquitous computing, palpable computing or ambient intelligence) is an emerging field of research that brings in revolutionary paradigms for computing models in the 21st century. Pervasive computing is the trend towards increasingly ubiquitous connected computing devices in the environment, a trend being brought about by a convergence of advanced electronic – and particularly, wireless – technologies and the Internet. Recent advances in pervasive computers, networks, telecommunications and information technology, along with the proliferation of multimedia mobile devices – such as laptops, iPods, personal digital assistants (PDAs) and cellular telephones – have further stimulated the development of intelligent pervasive multimedia applications. These key technologies are creating a multimedia revolution that will have significant impact across a wide spectrum of consumer, business, healthcare and governmental domains.

Pervasive computers, networks and information are paving the road towards a smart world in which intelligent computational paradigms are distributed throughout the physical environment to provide trustworthy and relevant services to people. This intelligent pervasive computing environment will change the computing landscape because it will enable new breeds of applications and systems to be developed, and the realm of computing possibilities will be significantly extended by embedding intelligence in everyday objects.

This edited volume provides an up-to-date and state-of-the-art coverage of diverse aspects related to pervasive computing and intelligent multimedia technologies. It addresses the use of different computational intelligence-based approaches to various problems in pervasive computing such as video streaming, intelligent behaviour modelling and control for mobile manipulators, teleGaming, indexing video summaries for quick video browsing, Web service processes, virtual environments, ambient intelligence, prevention and detection of attacks to ubiquitous databases and so on.

This volume comprises 19 chapters including an overview chapter providing an up-to-date and state-of-the review of the current literature on computational intelligence-based approaches to various problems in pervasive computing, and some important research challenges.

The book is divided into 4 parts:

Part I: Intelligent Multimedia and Pervasive Systems

Part II: Ambient Intelligence and Ubiquitous Computing

Part III: Web services and Situation Awareness in Pervasive Computing

Part IV: Pervasive Networks and Ecommerce

Part I on Intelligent Multimedia and Pervasive Systems contains eight chapters. It discusses about pervasive computing approaches in the context of intelligent multimedia.

Chapter 1 by Peters et al. introduces a wireless, pervasive computing approach to adaptive therapeutic telegaming considered in the context of near set theory. Near set theory provides a formal basis for observation, comparison and classification of perceptual granules. A perceptual granule is defined by a collection of objects that are graspable by the senses or by the mind. The problem considered in this chapter is how to assess the performance of a handicapped player, e.g., an arthritis patient with pain and joint stiffness problems. In the proposed pervasive computing approach to telegaming, a handicapped person with limited hand, finger and arm function plays a video game by interacting with familiar instrumented objects such as cups, cutlery, soccer balls, nozzles, screw top-lids, spoons, so that the technology that makes therapeutic exercise game-playing possible is largely invisible. The basic approach to adaptive learning in the proposed telegaming environment is ethology-inspired and is quite different from the traditional approach to reinforcement learning. The telegaming system connects to the Internet and implements a store and feed-forward mechanism that transmits gaming session tables constructed and saved during each gaming session to a remote registry accessible to therapists and researchers. The telegaming module for this game makes it possible for the results of all exercise gaming sessions to be forwarded over the Internet to a rheumatoid arthritis (RA) Function PORTAL, as well as local rehabilitation centres and therapists to monitor and provide timely feedback to a client in a remote setting. A complete Automatic Tracking & Assessment (ATA) Exercise Gaming System for RA finger-hand function is explained.

In the last several years, *mobile manipulators* have been increasingly used and developed from a theoretical viewpoint, as well as for practical applications in space, underwater, construction and service environments. Chapter 2 by Elkady et al. deals with the problem of intelligent behaviour modelling and control of a mobile manipulator for the purpose of simultaneously following desired end-effectors and platform trajectories. A new algorithm for measuring manipulability index used for serial manipulators and implemented simulations supporting the methodology on different manipulators is presented. Furthermore, the chapter provides some simulations that are implemented on different serial manipulators such as the Puma 560 manipulator, a six DOF manipulator and the Mitsubishi Movemaster manipulator. Finally, they describe how mobile manipulator capabilities are a key to several robotic applications and how the manipulability measure is crucial in performing intelligent behaviour.

Video must be delivered to its consumers, but delivery over the Internet and other access networks will not be successful if the problem of network congestion is not solved. Computational intelligence offers a solution to this problem, and Chap. 3 by Fleury et al. demonstrates how higher quality video can be delivered across fixed and wireless networks to display devices in the home. In this way, video can follow the user wherever they are in a seamless and ubiquitous manner. The chapter also shows that this is one of the areas where type-2 fuzzy logic has significant potential outstripping the control offered by traditional type-1 logic.

Multimedia data are used in many fields. The problem is how to manipulate large volume of data. One of the proposed solutions is an intelligent video summarization system. Summarizing a video consists in providing another version, which contains pertinent and important items. The most popular type of summary is the pictorial summary. Chapter 4 by Karray et al. proposes a global architecture of a system, which helps users to navigate into news broadcast archive. It presents a concept of a digital video archive that offers three access levels, thereby making easier the search for video sequences. The first access level offers to the user a full access for the whole archive. The second access level allows the user to browse video archive by consulting video summaries. They contribute by adding a third access level, which accelerates the archive browsing by adding an indexing subsystem that operates on video summaries. Moreover, they propose to index video summaries to accelerate the research of desired sequences.

Virtual reality (VR) technology has matured to a point where humans can navigate in virtual scenes; however, providing them with a comfortable, fully immersive role in VR remains a challenge. Currently available sensing solutions do not provide ease of deployment, particularly in the seated position, because of sensor placement restrictions over the body, and optic-sensing requires a restricted indoor environment to track body movements. Chapter 5 by Gulrez and Tognetti presents a 52-sensor laden garment interfaced with VR, which offers both portability and encumbered user movement in a VR environment. Participants who navigated in a virtual art gallery using natural body movements were detected by their wearable sensor shirt, and the signals are then mapped to electrical control signals responsible for VR scene navigation. Experiments based on several different types of tasks demonstrate the necessity and effectiveness of proper coordination between the human operator and the VR system.

In Chap. 6, Sharda explores how innovative applications can be developed to meet the needs of the next generation hotels. Futuristic hotel rooms aim to be more than "home-away-from-home," and as a consequence, offer tremendous opportunities for developing innovative applications of pervasive computing and intelligent multimedia. Next generation hotels make use of increased use of technology products to attract new customers. High-end TV screens, changeable room ambiance, biometric guest recognition and electronic check-in facilities are some of the features already being implemented by some hotels. Entirely futuristic hotels in the sea, the stratosphere or the outer space are also being proposed. All of these provide many novel opportunities for developing innovative solutions using intelligent multimedia and ubiquitous computing.

Recently, human–computer interaction has shifted from traditional desktop computing to the pervasive computing paradigm where users are engaged with everywhere and anytime computing devices. Mobile virtual environment (MVE) is an emerging research area that studies the deployment of VR applications on mobile devices. In Chap. 7, Lazem et al. present MVEs as a real-time interactive distributed system and investigate the challenges in designing and developing a remote rendering perfecting application for mobile devices. Furthermore, test-bed architecture for MVEs was introduced to evaluate the remote rendering application through two implementation phases. The flexibility of the proposed architecture allowed for evaluating the system against different combinations of user, environment and network scenarios. The case study was used as a vehicle to illustrate the use of game theory to model, interactive, real-time distributed systems.

Part II on Ambient Intelligence and Ubiquitous Computing contains five chapters that describe several approaches in a ambient intelligent and ubiquitous environment, such as AI techniques in a context-aware ubiquitous environment, a distributed ambient intelligence-based multi-agent system for Alzheimer health care, and case study in pervasive computing including volcano monitoring, an agent-based architecture for preventing and detecting attacks to ubiquitous databases, hybrid multi-agent architecture for home care.

In Chap. 8, Coppola et al. propose MoBe: an approach for providing a basic infrastructure for pervasive context-aware applications on mobile devices, in which artificial intelligence techniques, namely, a principled combination of rule-based systems, Bayesian networks and ontologies, are applied to context inference. The aim is to devise a general inferential framework to fasten the development of context-aware applications by integrating the information coming from physical and logical sensors (e.g., position, agenda) and reasoning about this information in order to infer new and more abstract contexts.

Chapter 9 by Tapia et al. presents ALZ-MAS, an ambient intelligence-based multi-agent system aimed at enhancing the assistance and health care for Alzheimer patients. The system makes use of several context-aware technologies that allow it to automatically obtain information from users and the environment in an evenly distributed way, focusing on the characteristics of ubiquity, awareness, intelligence, mobility, etc., all of which are concepts defined by ambient intelligence. ALZ-MAS makes use of a services-oriented multi-agent architecture to distribute resources and enhance its performance.

In Chap. 10, Peterson et al. present a case study for developing a real-time pervasive computing system, called OASIS for optimized autonomous space In-situ sensor web, which combines ground assets (a sensor network) and space assets (NASA's Earth Observing (EO-1) satellite) to monitor volcanic activities at Mount

St. Helens. OASIS's primary goals are to integrate complementary space and in situ ground sensors into an interactive and autonomous sensor web, to optimize power and communication resource management of the sensor web and to provide mechanisms for seamless and scalable fusion of future space and in situ components. The OASIS in situ ground sensor network development addresses issues related to power management, bandwidth management, quality of service (QoS) management, topology and routing management, and test-bed design. The space segment development consists of EO-1 architectural enhancements, feedback of EO-1 data into the in situ component, command and control integration, data ingestion and dissemination and field demonstrations.

Chapter 11 by Pinzon et al. proposes the SiC architecture as a solution to the SQL injection attack problem. This is a hierarchical distributed multi-agent architecture, which involves an entirely new approach with respect to existing architectures for the prevention and detection of SQL injections. SiC incorporates a kind of intelligent agent, which integrates a case-based reasoning system. This agent, which is the core of the architecture, allows the application of detection techniques based on anomalies as well as detection techniques based on patterns, providing a great degree of autonomy, flexibility, robustness and dynamic scalability. The characteristics of the multi-agent system allow architecture to detect attacks from different types of devices, regardless of the physical location.

Home care (HoCa) is one of the main objectives of ambient intelligence. Nowadays, the dependent and elderly population, which represents a significant part of our society, requires novel solutions for providing home care in an effective way. Chapter 12 by Fraile et al. presents a hybrid multi-agent architecture that facilitates remote monitoring and care services for dependent patients at their homes. HoCa combines multi-agent systems and Web services to facilitate the communication and integration with multiple health care systems. In addition, HoCa focuses on the design of reactive agents capable of interacting with different sensors present in the environment, and incorporates a system of alerts through SMS and MMS mobile technologies. Finally, it uses RFID and Java Card technologies to provide advanced location and identification systems, as well as automatic access control facilities. Moreover, HoCa is implemented in a real environment and the results obtained are presented.

Web services and Situation Awareness in Pervasive Computing is Part III of the book. It contains two chapters discussing the issues in Web services and situation awareness in pervasive computing environment.

Chapter 13 by Di Pietro et al. proposes a new approach to the discovery, the selection and the automated composition of distributed processes in a pervasive computing environment, described as semantic Web services through a new semantic annotation. This approach has been tested in a real-world case study, where real Web services provided by Amazon, eBay and PayPal have been annotated with the language proposed in this chapter, and then, selected and composed. Furthermore, automated composition has been compared with hand-written composition made by an experienced programmer.

Ubiquitous applications such as health care monitoring applications need to analyze and process data streams that are generated at very high rates in real time. Therefore, it is of great importance for data stream mining techniques to be equipped with adapting strategies to promote the continuity and consistency of the running application. Current ubiquitous data stream mining approaches have limited levels of adaptations (mainly focusing on battery or memory). To enhance adaptation of data stream mining algorithms, there is a need to consider the contextual/situational information in the adaptation phase. Integrating data stream processing with situation awareness provides intelligent and cost-efficient analysis of data, and enables continuity and consistency of mining operations. In Chap. 14, Haghighi et al. present a novel approach for situation-aware adaptive processing (SAAP) of data streams for pervasive computing environments. This approach uses fuzzy logic principles for modelling and reasoning about uncertain situations and performs gradual adaptation of parameters of data stream mining algorithms in real-time according to availability of resources and the occurring situations.

The final part of the book deals with the Pervasive Networks and Ecommerce. It contains five chapters, which discuss the wireless network application, including mobile agents and e-commerce. Today, there are more applications than ever that require using the network, consuming the bandwidth, and sending packets far and wide. The service providers are actively upgrading the Internet backbone to fulfil the demand for high bandwidth applications such as multimedia communications. Chapter 15 by Ivan Lee illustrates the performance of a distributed video streaming framework, which utilized video source coding and distributed network adaptation schemes. An efficient video coding technique using multiple descriptions coding technique is applied, and the encoded sub-streams were transmitted over client/server, centralized P2P and decentralized P2P network infrastructures.

In Chap. 16, Agboma and Liotta introduce pervasive systems and services from the telecommunication perspective. They look at the enabling technologies and different pervasive services that are currently being provided to users. In view of this, the authors emphasize on why quality of experience (QoE) in telecommunication systems is important. Furthermore, they elaborate on the different requirements needed to provide pervasive services from the user's perspective. A case study is presented, illustrating how the sensitivity of different network parameters (such as bandwidth, packet loss and delay) for a pervasive service can affect QoE.

In Chap. 17, Al-Jaljouli and Abawajy describe robust security techniques that ensure a sound security of information gathered throughout agent's itinerary against various security attacks, as well as truncation attacks. A sound security protocol is described, which implements the various security techniques that would jointly prevent or at least detect any malicious act of intruders. Authors reason about the soundness of the protocol using STA (Symbolic Trace Analyzer), a formal verification tool that is based on symbolic techniques.

In Chap. 18, Liu et al. investigate a multi-swarm approach to the problem of neighbor selection in P2P networks. Particle swarm shares some common characteristics with P2P in the dynamic socially environment. Each particle encodes the upper half of the peer-connection matrix through the undirected graph, which reduces the search space dimension. They also attempt to theoretically prove that the multi-swarm optimization algorithm converges with a probability of 1 towards the global optima. The performance of the introduced approach is evaluated and compared with other two different algorithms. The results indicate that it usually requires shorter time to obtain better results than the other considered methods, especially for large-scale problems.

Mobile ad hoc networks (MANETs) are a fundamental element of pervasive networks, where users can communicate anywhere, anytime and on-the-fly. In fact, future advances in pervasive computing rely on advancements in mobile communication, which includes both infrastructure-based wireless networks and non-infrastructure-based MANETs. MANETs introduce a new communication paradigm, which does not require a fixed infrastructure – they rely on wireless terminals for routing and transport services. Because of highly dynamic topology, absence of established infrastructure for centralized administration, bandwidth constrained wireless links and limited resources in MANETs, it is challenging to design an efficient and reliable routing protocol. Qadri and Liotta in Chap. 19 review the key studies carried out so far on the performance of mobile ad hoc routing protocols. The authors discuss performance issues and metrics required for the evaluation of ad hoc routing protocols. This leads to a survey of existing work, which captures the performance of ad hoc routing algorithms and their behaviour from different perspectives and highlights avenues for future research.

Acknowledgements

We are very much grateful to the authors of this volume and to the reviewers for their tremendous service by critically reviewing the chapters. Most of the authors of the chapters included in this book also served as referees for chapters written by other authors. We thank all those who provided constructive and comprehensive reviews. The editors thank Dr. Wayne Wheeler, Springer, Germany, for the editorial assistance and excellent cooperative collaboration to produce this important scientific work. We hope that the reader will share our excitement to present this volume on pervasive computing and intelligent multimedia and will find it useful.

Giza, Egypt   *Aboul-Ella Hassanien*
Victoria, Australia   *Jemal H. Abawajy*
Trondheim, Norway   *Ajith Abraham*
Colchester, UK   *Hani Hagras*

Contents

Part I Intelligent Multimedia and Pervasive Systems

1 **Wireless Adaptive Therapeutic TeleGaming in a Pervasive Computing Environment** 3
James F. Peters, Tony Szturm, Maciej Borkowski,
Dan Lockery, Sheela Ramanna, and Barbara Shay

2 **Intelligent Behaviour Modelling and Control for Mobile Manipulators** 29
Ayssam Elkady, Mohammed Mohammed, Eslam Gebriel,
and Tarek Sobh

3 **Resource-Aware Fuzzy Logic Control of Video Streaming over IP and Wireless Networks** 47
M. Fleury, E. Jammeh, R. Razavi, and M. Ghanbari

4 **Indexing Video Summaries for Quick Video Browsing** 77
Hichem Karray, Mehdi Ellouze, and Adel Alimi

5 **Sensorized Garment Augmented 3D Pervasive Virtual Reality System** 97
Tauseef Gulrez, Alessandro Tognetti, and Danilo De Rossi

6 **Creating Innovative Solutions for Future Hotel Rooms with Intelligent Multimedia and Pervasive Computing** 117
Nalin K. Sharda

7 **Mobile Virtual Environments in Pervasive Computing** 135
Shaimaa Lazem, Ayman Abdel-Hamid, Denis Gračanin,
and Kevin P. Adams

Part II   Ambient Intelligence and Ubiquitous Computing

**8   AI Techniques in a Context-Aware Ubiquitous
      Environment** 157
      Paolo Coppola, Vincenzo Della Mea, Luca Di Gaspero,
      Raffaella Lomuscio, Danny Mischis, Stefano Mizzaro,
      Elena Nazzi, Ivan Scagnetto, and Luca Vassena

**9   A Distributed Ambient Intelligence Based Multi-Agent
      System for Alzheimer Health Care** 181
      Dante I. Tapia, Sara Rodríguez, and Juan M. Corchado

**10   Volcano Monitoring: A Case Study in Pervasive
      Computing**...201
      Nina Peterson, Lohith Anusuya-Rangappa,
      Behrooz A. Shirazi, WenZhan Song, Renjie Huang,
      Daniel Tran, Steve Chien, and Rick LaHusen

**11   SiC: An Agent Based Architecture for Preventing
      and Detecting Attacks to Ubiquitous Databases** 231
      Cristian Pinzón, Yanira De Paz, Javier Bajo, Ajith Abraham,
      and Juan M. Corchado

12   HoCaMA: Home Care Hybrid Multiagent Architecture.................259
      Juan A. Fraile, Javier Bajo, Ajith Abraham,
      and Juan M. Corchado

Part III   Web Service and Situation Awareness in Pervasive Computing

**13   Semantic Annotation for Web Service Processes
      in Pervasive Computing**..289
      Ivan Di Pietro, Francesco Pagliarecci, and Luca Spalazzi

**14   Situation-Aware Adaptive Processing (SAAP)
      of Data Streams** 313
      Pari Delir Haghighi, Mohamed Medhat Gaber,
      Shonali Krishnaswamy, and Arkady Zaslavsky

Part IV   Pervasive Networks and E-commerce

15   A Scalable P2P Video Streaming Framework 341
      Ivan Lee

16   QoE in Pervasive Telecommunication Systems...........................365
      Florence Agboma and Antonio Liotta

17 **Agents Based e-Commerce and Securing Exchanged
    Information**...383
    Raja Al-Jaljouli and Jemal Abawajy

18 **Neighbor Selection in Peer-to-Peer Overlay Networks:
    A Swarm Intelligence Approach**...405
    Hongbo Liu, Ajith Abraham, and Youakim Badr

19 **Analysis of Pervasive Mobile Ad Hoc Routing Protocols**...............433
    Nadia N. Qadri and Antonio Liotta

Index..455

Contributors

Jemal Abawajy School of Engineering and Information Technology, Deakin University, Australia, jemal@deakin.edu.au

Ayman Abdel-Hamid College of Computing and Information Technology, Arab Academy for Science, Technology, and Maritime Transport, Egypt, hamid@aast.edu

Ajith Abraham Norwegian Center of Excellence, Center of Excellence for Quantifiable Quality of Service, Norwegian University of Science and Technology, O.S. Bragstads Plass 2E, N-7491 Trondheim, Norway, ajith.abraham@ieee.org

Kevin P. Adams Naval Surface Warfare Center, Dahlgren, VA 22407, USA, Kevin.P.Adams@navy.mil

Florence Agboma Department of Computing and Electronic Systems, University of Essex, Wivenhoe Park, Colchester, CO4 3SQ, UK, Fagbom@essex.ac.uk

Adel Alimi Department of Electrical Engineering, REGIM: Research Group on Intelligent Machines, University of Sfax, ENIS, BP W-3038, Sfax, Tunisia, Adel.alimi@ieee.org

Raja Al-Jaljouli School of Engineering and Information Technology, Deakin University, Australia, ralj@deakin.edu.au

Lohith Anusuya-Rangappa School of Electrical Engineering and Computer Science, Washington State University, Pullman, WA 99163, USA

Youakim Badr National Institute of Applied Sciences, INSA de Lyon, F-69621, France, youakim.badr@insa-lyon.fr

Javier Bajo University of Salamanca, Plaza de la Merced s/n, 37008 Salamanca, Spain, jbajope@usal.es
Pontifical University of Salamanca, Compañía 5, 37002 Salamanca, Spain, jbajope@upsa.es

Maciej Borkowski Computational Intelligence Laboratory, University of Manitoba, Winnipeg, Manitoba R3T 5V6, Canada

Steve Chien Jet Propulsion Laboratory, M/S 301-260, 4800 Oak Grove Drive, CA 91109-8099, Pasadena

Paolo Coppola University of Udine, via delle Scienze 206, 33100 Udine, Italy, coppola@uniud.it

Juan M. Corchado Departamento Informática y Automática, Universidad de Salamanca, Plaza de la Merced s/n, 37008 Salamanca, Spain, corchado@usal.es

Vincenzo Della Mea University of Udine, Via delle Scienze 206, 33100 Udine, Italy, dellamea@dimi.uniud.it

Luca Di Gaspero University of Udine, Via delle Scienze 206, 33100 Udine, Italy, l.digaspero@uniud.it

Ayssam Elkady University of Bridgeport, Bridgeport, CT 06604, USA

Mehdi Ellouze Department of Electrical Engineering, REGIM: Research Group on Intelligent Machines, University of Sfax, ENIS, BP W-3038, Sfax, Tunisia, mehdi.ellouze@ieee.org

M. Fleury School of CSEE, University of Essex, Wivenhoe Park, Colchester CO4 3SQ, UK, fleum@essex.ac.uk

Juan A. Fraile Pontifical University of Salamanca, Compañía 5, 37002 Salamanca, Spain, jafraileni@upsa.es

Mohamed Medhat Gaber Faculty of Information Technology, Monash University, Level 7, Building H - Caulfield Campus - Caulfield East, Melbourne, Victoria, 3145, Australia, mmagdy555@yahoo.com

Eslam Gebriel University of Bridgeport, Bridgeport, CT 06604, USA egebriel@gmail.com

M. Ghanbari CES Department, University of Essex, Wivenhoe Park, Colchester CO4 3SQ, UK, ghan@essex.ac.uk

Denis Gračanin Department of Computer Science, Virginia Tech, Blacksburg, VA 24060, USA, gracanin@vt.edu

Tauseef Gulrez Department of Computer Engineering, College of Engineering and Applied Sciences, Al-Ghurair University, Dubai, UAE, gtauseef@ieee.org

Vitrual Interactive Simulations of Reality Labs, Department of Computing, Division of Information and Communication Sciences, Macquarie University, Sydney, Australia

Pari Delir Haghighi Centre for Distributed Systems and Software Engineering, Monash University, 900 Dandenong Rd, Caulfield East, VIC3145, Australia, Pari.DelirHaghighi@infotech.monash.edu.au

Renjie Huang School of Electrical Engineering and Computer Science, Washington State University, Vancouver, WA 98686, USA

E. Jammeh CES Department, University of Essex, Wivenhoe Park, Colchester CO4 3SQ, UK, emmanuel.jammeh@plymouth.ac.uk

Hichem Karray Department of Electrical Engineering, REGIM: Research Group on Intelligent Machines, University of Sfax, ENIS, BP W-3038, Sfax, Tunisia, hichem.karray@ieee.org

Shonali Krishnaswamy Centre for Distributed Systems and Software Engineering, Monash University, 900 Dandenong Road, Caufield East, VIC3145, Australia, Shonali.Krishnaswamy@infotech.monash.edu.au

Rick LaHusen USGS Cascades Volcano Observatory, Vancouver, WA 98660, USA

Shaimaa Lazem Department of Computer Science, Virginia Tech, Blacksburg, VA 24060, USA, shlazem@vt.edu

Ivan Lee University of South Australia, Mawson Lakes Campus, Mawson Lakes, South Australia 5095, Australia, Ivan.Lee@unisa.edu.au

Antonio Liotta Department of Electrical Engineering, Eindhoven University of Technology, P.O. Box 513, PT 11.29, 5600 MB Eindhoven, The Netherlands, a.liotta@tue.nl

Hongbo Liu School of Computer Science and Engineering, Dalian Maritime University, 116026 Dalian, China, lhb@dlut.edu.cn

Dan Lockery Computational Intelligence Laboratory, University of Manitoba, Winnipeg, Manitoba R3T 5V6, Canada, lockery@ee.umanitoba.ca

Raffaella Lomuscio University of Udine, Via delle Scienze 206, 33100 Udine, Italy, lomuscio@dimi.uniud.it

Danny Mischis University of Udine, via delle Scienze 206, 33100 Udine, Italy, mischis@dimi.uniud.it

Stefano Mizzaro University of Udine, via delle Scienze 206, 33100 Udine, Italy, mizzaro@dimi.uniud.it

Mohammed Mohammed University of Bridgeport, Bridgeport, CT 06604, USA

Elena Nazzi University of Udine, via delle Scienze 206, 33100 Udine, Italy, nazzi@dimi.uniud.it

Francesco Pagliarecci Università Politecnica delle Marche, Ancona, Italy, pagliarecci@diiga.univpm.it

Yanira De Paz University of Salamanca, Plaza de la Merced s/n, 37008 Salamanca, Spain, yanira@usal.es

James F. Peters Computational Intelligence Laboratory, University of Manitoba, Winnipeg, Manitoba R3T 5V6, Canada, jfpeters@ee.umanitoba.ca

Nina Peterson School of Electrical Engineering and Computer Science, Washington State University, Pullman, WA 99163, USA, npicone@eecs.wsu.edu

Ivan Di Pietro Università Politecnica delle Marche, Ancona, Italy,
dipietro@diiga.univpm.it

Cristian Pinzón University of Salamanca, Plaza de la Merced s/n, 37008
Salamanca, Spain, cristian_ivanp@usal.es

Nadia N. Qadri Department of Computing and Electronics Systems, University
of Essex, Wivenhoe Park, Colchester CO4 3SQ, UK, nnawaz@essex.ac.uk

Sheela Ramanna Department of Applied Computer Science, University
of Winnipeg, Winnipeg, Manitoba R3B 2E9, Canada, s.ramanna@uwinnipeg.ca

R. Razavi CES Department, University of Essex, Wivenhoe Park, Colchester CO4
3SQ, UK, rrazav@essex.ac.uk

Sara Rodríguez Departamento Informática y Automática, Universidad de
Salamanca, Plaza de la Merced s/n, 37008 Salamanca, Spain, srg@usal.es

Danilo De Rossi Interdepartmental Research Center E. Piaggio,
Faculty of Engineering, University of Pisa, Italy

Ivan Scagnetto University of Udine, via delle Scienze 206, 33100 Udine, Italy,
scagnett@dimi.uniud.it

Nalin K. Sharda Computer Science, Victoria University, PO Box 14428,
Melbourne, Victoria 8001, Australia, Nalin.Sharda@vu.edu.au

Barbara Shay Department of Physical Therapy, School of Medical Rehabilitation,
University of Manitoba, R106-771 McDermot Ave., Winnipeg, Manitoba R3E 0T6,
Canada, bshay@cc.umanitoba.ca

Behrooz A. Shirazi School of Electrical Engineering and Computer Science,
Washington State University, Pullman, WA 99163, USA

Tarek Sobh University of Bridgeport, Bridgeport, CT 06604, USA
sobh@bridgeport.edu

WenZhan Song School of Electrical Engineering and Computer Science,
Washington State University, Vancouver, WA 98686, USA

Luca Spalazzi Università Politecnica delle Marche, Ancona, Italy,
spalazzi@diiga.univpm.it

Tony Szturm Department of Physical Therapy, School of Medical Rehabilitation,
University of Manitoba, R106-771 McDermot Ave., Winnipeg, Manitoba R3E 0T6,
Canada, ptsturm@cc.umanitoba.ca

Dante I. Tapia Departamento Informática y Automática, Universidad de
Salamanca, Plaza de la Merced s/n, 37008 Salamanca, Spain, dantetapia@usal.es

Alessandro Tognetti Interdepartmental Research Center E. Piaggio,
Faculty of Engineering, University of Pisa, Italy, a.tognetti@ing.unipi.it

Daniel Tran Jet Propulsion Laboratory, M/S 301-260, 4800 Oak Grove Drive, CA
91109-8099, Pasadena

Luca Vassena University of Udine, via delle Scienze 206, 33100 Udine, Italy, vassena@dimi.uniud.it

Arkady Zaslavsky Centre for Distributed Systems and Software Engineering, Monash University, 900 Dandenong Road, Caufield East, VIC3145, Australia, Arkady.Zaslavsky@infotech.monash.edu.au

Part I
Intelligent Multimedia and Pervasive Systems

Chapter 1
Wireless Adaptive Therapeutic TeleGaming in a Pervasive Computing Environment

James F. Peters, Tony Szturm, Maciej Borkowski, Dan Lockery, Sheela Ramanna, and Barbara Shay

Abstract This chapter introduces a wireless, pervasive computing approach to adaptive therapeutic telegaming considered in the context of near set theory. Near set theory provides a formal basis for observation, comparison and classification of perceptual granules. A *perceptual granule* is defined by a collection of objects that are graspable by the senses or by the mind. In the proposed pervasive computing approach to telegaming, a handicapped person (e.g., stroke patient with limited hand, finger, arm function) plays a video game by interacting with familiar instrumented objects such as cups, cutlery, soccer balls, nozzles, screw top-lids, spoons, so that the technology that makes therapeutic exercise game-playing possible is largely invisible (Archives of Physical Medicine and Rehabilitation 89:2213–2217, 2008). The basic approach to adaptive learning (AL) in the proposed telegaming environment is ethology-inspired and is quite different from the traditional approach to reinforcement learning. In biologically-inspired learning, organisms learn to achieve some goal by durable modification of behaviours in response to signals from the environment resulting from specific experiences (Animal Behavior, 1995). The term *adaptive* is used here in an ethological sense, where learning by an organism results from modifying behaviour in response to perceived changes in the environment. To instill adaptivity in a video game, it is assumed that learning by a video game is episodic. During an episode, the behaviour of a player is measured indirectly by tracking the occurrence of gaming events such as a hit or a miss of a target (e.g., hitting a moving ball with a game paddle). An ethogram provides a record of behaviour feature values that provide a basis a functional registry for handicapped players for gaming adaptivity. An important practical application of adaptive gaming is therapeutic rehabilitation exercise carried out in parallel with playing action video games. Enjoyable and engaging interactive gaming will motivate patients to complete the rehabilitation process. Adaptivity is seen as a way to make action games more accessible to those who have physical and cognitive impairments. The telegaming

J.F. Peters (✉)
Computational Intelligence Laboratory, University of Manitoba, Winnipeg,
Manitoba R3T 5V6, Canada
e-mail: jfpeters@ee.umanitoba.ca

A.-E. Hassanien et al. (eds.), *Pervasive Computing: Innovations in Intelligent Multimedia and Applications*, Computer Communications and Networks, DOI 10.1007/978-1-84882-599-4_1, © Springer-Verlag London Limited 2009

system connects to the internet and implements a feed-and-forward mechanism that transmits gaming session tables after each gaming session to a remote registry accessible to therapists and researchers. The contribution of this chapter is the introduction of a framework for wireless telegaming useful in therapeutic rehabilitation.

Keywords Adaptive learning · Adaptive gaming · Automatic tracking · Assessment · Ethology · Near sets · Perceptual granule · Pervasive computing · Telegaming · Wireless

1.1 Introduction

In the proposed pervasive computing approach to telegaming, a handicapped person (e.g., stroke patient with limited hand, finger, arm function) plays a video game by interacting with familiar instrumented objects such as cups, cutlery, soccer balls, nozzles, screw top-lids, spoons (see, e.g., Fig. 1.2a), so that the technology that makes therapeutic exercise game-playing possible is largely invisible [47]. The problem considered in this chapter is how to assess the performance of a handicapped player, e.g., an arthritis patient with pain and joint stiffness problems. The term *adaptive* has a biologically-inspired connotation leading to a form of learning that is quite different from reinforcement learning [45]. In the observed behaviour of biological organisms, learning produces a durable modification of behaviour in response to information (e.g., intensity of perfume emitted by a female silk moth that leads to changing flight path of a male silk moth) acquired by an organism [1]. Hence, the term *adaptive* rather than *reinforcement* has been suggested to describe biologically-inspired learning by machines [21].

A framework for the proposed telegaming system is shown in Fig. 1.1. The current prototype for this system is available for experimentation at [15]. A complete automatic tracking and assessment (ATA) for rheumatoid arthritis (RA) finger-hand function during each exercise gaming session. In the overview of the telegaming system in Fig. 1.1, a client holds a top hat that has been instrumented to record hand movements while playing a video game. In this example, tipping the hat up or down leads to a corresponding up or down of a game paddle used to hit a moving target, e.g., an object representing a ping-pong ball. This ATA constructs an ethogram (tabular representation of player behaviour) concurrent with player movements during a game. After each gaming session, an ethogram is transmitted over a network to a secure RA function PORTAL.[1]

In this chapter, the term *adaptive* means that an entity (either a biological organism or a gaming system) adapts its behaviour relative to observed events in a changing environment. This approach to adaptivity is inspired by Oliver Selfridge's work on adaptive control in ill-defined systems [43] and Chris J.C.H. Watkins'

---

[1] PORTAL stands for *problem oriented registry of tags and labels* [51].

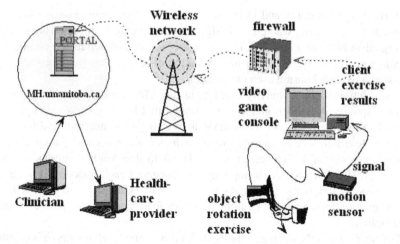

Fig. 1.1 Automatic tracking and assessment exercise gaming system

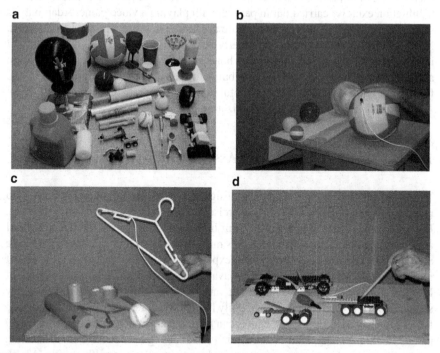

Fig. 1.2 (**a**) Sample gaming system objects; (**b**) soccer-based gaming system; (**c**) finger-hand rotation exercise; and (**d**) dexterity push–pull exercise

work on delayed rewards and Q-learning [55]. The term *behaviour* is used here
in an ethological sense, where knowledge about an organism results from observing organism behaviour [52,53]. In ethology, observed behaviours are recorded in
an ethogram [6,23,36], a tabular representation of feature values and assessments
(decisions) recorded during each observation.

The solution to the adaptivity problem in the ATA is biologically-inspired. To
instill adaptivity in a video game, it is assumed that learning by a video game is
episodic. During an episode, the behaviour of a player is measured indirectly by
tracking the occurrence of gaming events such as a hit or a miss of a target (e.g.,
hitting a moving ball with a game paddle). The Selfridge–Watkins run-and-twiddle
strategy provides the basis for a stopping mechanism for each episode. Also, during
each episode, ethograms (tabular representations of behaviour) are recorded. An
ethogram provides a record of gaming behaviour feature values that provide a basis
for adaptivity.

Consideration of the nearness of objects (in this context, behaviours) has recently
led to the introduction of what are known as near sets [33,34,40] and their applications [16–18,37,39]. The near set approach to observing player behaviour provides
an optimist's view of the approximation of sets of objects that are more or less near
each other. An important practical application of adaptive gaming is therapeutic rehabilitation exercise carried out in parallel with playing a video game. Adaptivity is
seen as a way to make video games more accessible to those who are handicapped.
Many studies in child, adults and elderly strongly suggest that many elements of
interactive action and learning games have tremendous potential as rehabilitation
and educational tools [2,3]. The contribution of this chapter is the introduction of a
framework for wireless telegaming useful in therapeutic rehabilitation.

This article has the following organization.

1.2 Automatic Tracking and Assessment System

The ATA reported in this chapter is designed to use any commercial game as a
means of motivating physiotherapy exercise and this is important for many reasons.
It is important to identify games that suit individual preferences; the wide range of
activities available in commercial games makes this possible. It is important to have
a large and ever changing variety of inexpensive games to maintain high levels of
motivation and interest. Commercially-available games do require a wide range of
levels of precision, and movements that vary in speed, amplitude and direction. By
selecting objects used in activities of daily living (see, e.g., Fig. 1.2), the therapy can
target specific tasks. Hence, the games can be graded to match a clients current level
of functioning. Finally, many commercially-available games involve multi-tasking.
Hence, the tasks also engage key attentional, perceptual and cognitive skills [13,14,
27,48]. The feasibility of the proposed therapeutic gaming system coupling object
manipulation with game-playing is presented in [47].

Through a variety of common objects, tools and utensils, the proposed therapeutic gaming system provides a basis for repetitive, task-specific therapy focused on

finger and hand function. A variety of objects have been used with the gaming system during interactive exercise (see, e.g., Fig. 1.2). Each of the objects in Fig. 1.2a can be instrumented for various finger-hand functions while playing a video game. For example,

1. Five different sized balls used for full-grip wrist rotation in Fig. 1.2b, where forward and backward and left and right rotations of the hand holding a round object such as a leather soccer ball provide motion signals used to control video game paddle (see Fig. 1.3a).
2. Seven different objects for two-finger grip, hand rotation in Fig. 1.2c, where up and down movements of the hand induce corresponding movements of a game paddle.
3. Four different objects for two-finger grip on a pencil and a push–pull action as shown in Fig. 1.2d. This requires considerable dexterity. Analogous to this, but on a more gross level, is the forward-backward movement of a hand on a roller (see Figs. 1.3b, c). The movements of the roller induce corresponding movements of a game paddle (see Fig. 1.3).

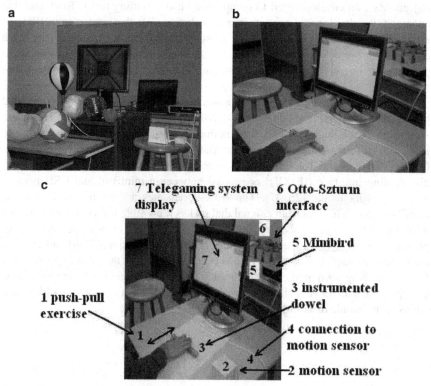

Fig. 1.3 Gaming system scenario. (**a**) Soccer-based gaming system; (**b**) wood dowel-based gaming system; and (**c**) rolling wood dowel exercise

Each exercise object is instrumented with the miniBird motion sensor. When the sports ball was rotated forward, the game sprite moved to the top of the monitor (bottom-left panel); when the ball was rotated to the right, the game sprite moved to the right edge of monitor (bottom-right panel). A short video is available, which demonstrates the interactive exercise gaming system [15].

1.2.1 Instrumenting Exercise Objects

Several studies have provided preliminary descriptions of the benefits of virtual reality and video games in rehabilitation training [5, 7, 10, 11, 20, 22, 24], especially recent studies using the interactive gaming described in this chapter [2, 3, 47]. The results of these studies suggest that many elements of interactive games have significant potential as rehabilitation tools. In their normal configuration, however, video games and computer systems do not employ a diverse range of objects as sources of inputs to video games. Piron and colleagues [41] developed a virtual reality training system that uses multi-axial motion sensors to instrument a small sample of common objects (e.g., an envelope used to complete a virtual mailing task). To extend this approach, we developed a custom interface device (ID) that uses a miniBIRD or microBIRD miniature motion tracking sensor to transform nearly any object into a computer mouse or joystick [47]. As a result, our approach allows participants to play any commercial video game by slaving the video game sprite to object motion signals.

The instrumented object in Fig. 1.3a is a soccer ball. An object is instrumented by attaching a miniature six degrees-of-freedom motion sensor (e.g., miniBird from Ascension Technologies[2]). This tiny motion sensor can be attached to many objects with different geometries and material properties useful in exercise therapy. Christopher Otto and Tony Szturm have designed an interactive educational exercise gaming interface (IEEGI)[3] connected between a miniBird and USB port on a gaming workstation [26, 47]. The IEEGI translates a motion signal from the miniBird into a game controller signal that makes it possible for a patient to interact with any video game by moving any instrumented object or body segment. Coupling exercise to appropriate action games is highly motivational (fun) and engages the patient in practice. The IEEGTS has been motivated by the need to provide extensive and long-term medical rehabilitation (interventions and outcome measures) and special needs for educational services for a growing population of children and adults with chronic disabilities.

---

[2] http://www.ascension-tech.com/products/minibird.php

[3] Teracade Patent pending, http://www.wipo.int/pctdb/en/wo.jsp?wo=2007030947

1.2.2 Task Variability

The proposed ATA uses video games that typically require random tasks with a wide range of adjustable movement amplitudes, speeds and precision levels. The end-result is task variability that is important for effective rehabilitation therapy. Task variability during practice is an important factor and studies have demonstrated that introducing variability (random practice) improves performance in subsequent sessions (retention) and is more effective than blocked repetition of a constant task [19, 27]. In addition, a diverse range of objects can be used, which will depend on the clients' needs and requirements. With this individualized approach, it is possible to maximize the rehabilitative effectiveness of training. It is the possibility of choosing among a wide variety of common household objects with varying geometries, sizes and weights that makes it possible for clients to gain experience over a wide spectrum of finger-hand manipulation tasks. It should also be observed that learning to restore function of fine and gross manual skills requires movement error reduction by the timely processing of tactile and proprioceptive sensory feedback [42, 44].

1.2.3 ATA PORTAL

To ensure cross-registry compatibility, problem-specific registries like the one in Fig. 1.4a are designed to comply with the requirements of a generic root registry within a PORTAL system like the one set up for Manitoba Health. During each physiotherapy session, the ATA automatically records and transmits tables of values to a PORTAL [51]. A sample architecture for a RA Function PORTAL is shown in Fig. 1.4a. This particular RA PORTAL is a by-product of a bioengineering joint research project with the Computational Intelligence Laboratory and Rehabilitation Hospital at the University of Manitoba. The specification for this PORTAL is an instance of what is known as a domain ontology. An *ontology* is a formal representation of a subject area and a *domain ontology* is a restriction of the specification to a particular topic [31], e.g., assessment of RA functional behaviour during physiotherapy. The PORTAL design in Fig. 1.4 is also an example of a health PORTAL that offers patient health information (for a detailed presentation of health portals, see [50]). An example of an extensive collection of health PORTALS is the National Library of Medicine (NLM).[4]

The registry information model (RIM)[5] defines the organization and types of objects that are stored in a PORTAL [8]. The semantics to be defined for a registry are prescribed by several RIM mechanisms.

---

[4] A facility that makes it possible for web users to conduct their own search of medical databases: http://www.nlm.nih.gov/

[5] ebXML Registry Information Model v2.5. http://www.oasis-open.org/committees/regrep/documents/2.5/specs/

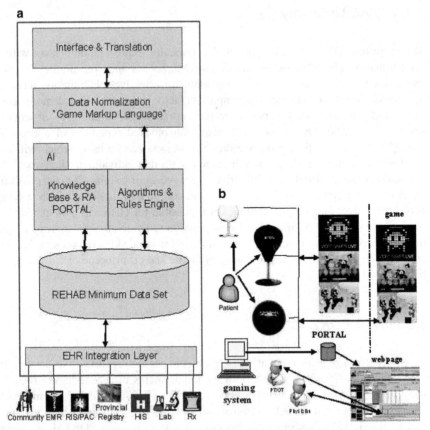

Fig. 1.4 Rheumatoid arthritis (RA) function problem oriented registry of tags and labels (POR-TAL) + gaming system environment [9]. (**a**) PORTAL architecture and (**b**) gaming system milieu

- Registry objects are defined via slots
- Metadata are stored in a registry using a classification mechanism, e.g., international classification of functioning, disability and health (ICF) developed by the World Health Organization (WHO) to describe health and handicaps in more detail in order to allow better classification and registration. In the RA Function PORTAL in Fig. 1.4a, the ICF is used in a data dictionary for all information stored on the PORTAL [38]
- ebRIM object external identifier is used for encoding registry semantics [8]

A framework for a motion-sensor based gaming milieu is shown in Fig. 1.4b. A suit of instrumented video games provide a basis for an ATA. This ATA was originally designed as a means of evaluating the performance of stroke patients while moving various instrumented objects like the ones shown in Fig. 1.4b. This ATA has recently led to the design of a specialized PORTAL used to store information about RA finger-hand function during each exercise session by RA patients (see Fig. 1.1). In sum, an RA Function PORTAL provides a basis for objective evaluation of finger-hand function for each RA client who has received physiotherapy.

1.3   Intellect of the ATA: Gaming System

The gaming system represented in Fig. 1.4b plays the role of an *intellect* (a specialized form of *computer model of the intellect that arrives at an assessment of player movements based on objective behavioural information recorded during each gaming session*) in the ATA. The gaming system is adaptive inasmuch as it learns to adjust the speed of a bullet, speed of a target and the number, shape and size of moving targets relative to the skill level of each player. For slower or beginning players, this adaptivity feature gaming system is intended to reduce the frustration level of handicapped players.

A multi-function action, adaptive video game has been recently designed for the ATA. This game includes moving targets and distracters with multiple shapes, colours, sizes and motions. The moving game sprite (horizontal or vertical) is used to shoot or intercept user-defined targets and avoid distracters. Cumulative scoring is visible for targets (positive outcomes) and distracters (negative outcomes). The game automatically logs a player-performance table for each exercise gaming session. This is useful in (a) client motivation, (b) statistical analysis of therapeutic effectiveness, (c) gaming adaptivity to match skill level of the client and (d) telegaming for feedback and therapy progression. Game logs also provide input to health information PORTAL. The telegaming module for this game makes it possible for the results of all exercise gaming sessions to be forwarded over the internet to PORTAL as well as local rehabilitation centres and therapists to monitor and provide timely feedback to a client in a remote setting.

In the proposed therapeutic exercise gaming environment, a patient moves a displayed video game sprite[6] or avatar (e.g., paddle) by moving an instrumented object (e.g., coat hanger, pencil, piece of styrofoam, Lego® car and soccer ball). A sample 2D game panel recently designed by Maciej Borkowski[7] is given in Fig. 1.5. Movements of the soccer ball in Fig. 1.3a result in corresponding movements of the paddle in Fig. 1.5. The paddle can be used to "collide" with a moving 2D projectile (shot). The 3D objects in the game panel in Fig. 1.5 serve as distractors intended to test discriminatory perception and cognition skills in distinguishing different types of objects during a gaming session.

---

[6] *Sprite*. A graphical figure that can be moved and manipulated as a single entity [25].
[7] This game downloadable from [4].

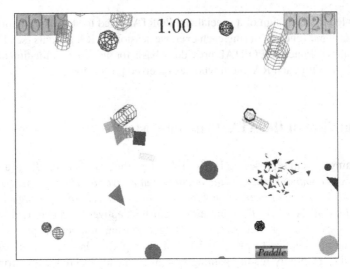

Fig. 1.5 Sample gaming system display

Fig. 1.6 Sample gaming
system display without
distractors

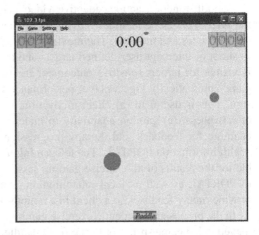

1.3.1 Targets and Distractors

The ATA gaming system is designed in terms of two types of randomly moving
objects: distractors and targets. A *distractor* is an object that distracts, i.e., prevents
someone from giving full attention to one type of object [25]. In the context of an
ATA, a therapeutic game distractor forces players to discriminate between moving
objects during a gaming session. The 3D objects shown in the sample game panel in
Fig. 1.5 are examples of distractors, moving objects that can be hit by a game sprite
but do not contribute to scoring, i.e., hitting a distractor does not increment the hits
counter in the upper righthand corner of Fig. 1.5. Hitting a distractor causes it to
explode into tiny fragments. It is possible to turn off the appearance of distractors to
simplify the game (see, e.g., Fig. 1.6).

In Fig. 1.6, the discs with varying diameters represent targets. Each time a player moves the game paddle so that it collides with a moving target, the game score is incremented by 1 (in the sample display in Fig. 1.5, a player has accumulated 21 hits and 11 misses). The total number of paddle misses during a gaming session is recorded with the counter in the upper lefthand corner of the game panel display.

1.3.2 Difficulty Level Controls

In the ATA gaming system, several parameters are used to control the difficulty level of a game.

- A speed of a bullet (a number from 0 to 10, where smaller number means slower)
- A speed of a target (a number from 0 to 10, where smaller number means slower)
- Number of targets that show up in one second of a game (possible values are 0.2, 0.25, 0.33, 0.5, 0.75, 1, 2, 3, 4 and 5)

To reduce the total number of all possible combinations of the three above parameters, some simplifications are introduced. The first two parameters are combined to form only one parameter. It is assumed that it is more difficult when the targets are moving faster and the bullets are moving slower. Therefore, quickly moving targets are combined with slowly moving bullets and vice versa. Possible values of two difficulty parameters are shown in Table 1.1.

For the third parameter (number of targets), only four values are used, e.g., 0.33, 1, 2 and 4. For example, for one game, the following three sets of difficulty levels are generated: {2, 7, 1}, {4, 6, 0.33} and {0, 8, 4}. Each of the possible settings would be used for 1 min. In the adaptive version of this game, a minimum scoring threshold is chosen and the difficulty levels are reduced until the scoring level either exceeds or is at the threshold. Adaptivity can either be turned on or off at the beginning of a gaming session.

1.3.3 Information Recorded by Gaming System

During each physiotherapy session with an RA client, the ATA automatically records and transmits two tables (statistics table and information table) to an RA Function PORTAL. A transmitted stats table includes (Table 1.2)

Table 1.1 Sample gaming system difficulty level settings

Parameter	Easiest	Easy	Normal	Harder	Hardest
Target speed	0	2	4	6	8
Bullet speed	8	7	6	5	4

Table 1.2 Sample Automatic tracking and assessment (ATA) statistics table

σ_1	σ_2	σ_3	σ_4	σ_5	σ_6	σ_7
0	5003	1	0	0	5	0.330
25010	5005	1	1	1	5	0.330

Table 1.3 Sample ATA information table

ι_1	ι_2	ι_3	ι_4	ι_5
56588	0.00000	C0000	0.67034	0.01186
56611	0.00000	C0000	0.67034	0.02163

- σ_1: Start time
- σ_2: Duration of system time (ms) to generate data in a row,
- σ_3: Number of shots
- σ_4: Number of targets hit
- σ_5: Number of targets missed
- σ_6: Shape speed or how fast targets move on screen
- σ_7: Frequency of targets appearing on screen

  A transmitted information table includes

- ι_1: Start time (in ms)
- ι_2: x-position of game sprite (a paddle), e.g., orientation is south in Table 1.3, where 0.00000 indicates the lefthand side of the display
- ι_3: Object number
- ι_4: x-coordinate of target, e.g., in a setup for a beginner, this does not change throughout a gaming session
- ι_5: y-coordinate of target, e.g., target moving from top of display to bottom, 0–1

For an RA Function PORTAL, pre- and post-exercise levels of pain and levels of joint stiffness are also recorded and transmitted at the end of each gaming session. This information makes it possible to determine the appropriate objects to use to maximize exercise therapy effectiveness and minimize consequent pain and joint stiffness levels.

1.4 Gaming System Adaptive Learning Methods

In the gaming system described in this chapter, two Adaptive Learning (AL) methods have been considered, namely, threshold-based AL and biologically inspired AL.

1.4.1 Threshold-Based Adaptive Learning

The threshold-based AL applies only to cases when the paddle moves around one edge of the screen and targets are being destroyed by a gun (not the paddle). There are two performance measurements:

Algorithm 1: Classical learning algorithm for Game1

Input : LT_1 lower threshold for the first measure
LT_2 lower threshold for the second measure
UT_1 upper threshold for the first measure
UT_2 upper threshold for the second measure
Output:

foreach *Episode End* **do**
   | Calculate PM_1 and PM_2
   | **if** $PM_1 \leq LT_1$ **and** $PM_2 \leq LT_2$ **then**
   | | IncreaseDifficultyLevel();
   | **end**
   | **else**
   | **if** $PM_1 > UT_1$ **or** $PM_2 > UT_2$ **then**
   | | DecreaseDifficultyLevel();
   | **end**
   | **end**
end

- PM_1 measures number of objects that made it through the screen (and the number of times the paddle was destroyed by distractors)
- PM_2 there are two versions of this measure:

  - measures the distance travelled by a target (before being hit)
  - measures the time for which the target lived (in milliseconds)

Learning is viewed as episodic. In general, an *episode* is a group of events [25]. In the context of the ATA gaming system, an episode has fixed duration and corresponds to a group of events before a change is made in the gaming difficulty level parameters. Algorithm 1 gives a capsule view of how the ATA gaming system adapts to a player skill level.

1.4.2   Ethology and the Ethogram

This section briefly introduces *ethology* and *ethogram* tables used in the biologically-inspired form of AL in the ATA gaming system. *ethology* is defined as the study of animal behaviour and an *ethogram* is a table containing a list of the different behaviours that an animal species can exhibit.

In the work of Tinbergen [53], *ethology* is a biological study of behaviour. There are four main aspects of behaviour to observe from an ethological perspective: causation, survival value, evolution, and ontogeny [53]. In the context of observed behaviour, causation, also known as *proximate cause*, refers to an event or situation leading up to a behaviour that has occurred. Next, *survival value* is the opposite of proximate cause, i.e., this quantity entails looking at the result or effect of a behaviour that has taken place already and how it has either improved or reduced the survival value of a species in question. The evolution of behaviours refers to how a species has evolved into a certain pattern of behaviours over time based on previous experience or conditions. Ontogeny is similar to evolution but on a life-time scale and refers to the development of a species over a lifetime. These four categories make up parts of an *ethogram* used to study animal species.

Ethology and the ethogram are relevant to adaptive gaming. The cause and effect pair corresponds to state and reward values in the context of gaming system learning. Also, an ethogram is generated during each gaming session to record and plot player behaviours. All the information regarding states, actions, rewards, selection preference and decisions are recorded in a table of behaviours. These tables are then to generate a performance metric (average rough coverage values) to adjust the gaming difficulty levels to facilitate improved player performance.

1.4.3 Biologically-Inspired Adaptive Learning

Biologically-inspired AL methods view a video game from an objective listener perspective. AL methods monitor user performance and take actions accordingly based on a preset optimum levels of play (for example, 80% target hit rate). Accordingly, states will be derived from features of game play over a span of time. Instead of using every sample as a separate state, it is more appropriate to use a period of time that will contain a number of events (e.g., targets appearing and being handled by the user). This will give a reasonable measure of user performance, so that we can develop a user profile based on similar features to what are used in the classical algorithm (they are readily available and a good starting point to develop states).

The threshold-based approach uses a fixed time frame for episodes (e.g., episodes with 10 s duration) before contemplating the need for adjusting game parameters. Game states will be based on performance measures already discussed and the subsequent actions will consist of making the game easier, harder or remain constant. The types of actions can be as varied as the game will allow (e.g., change of target speed, shape, size, also change paddle dimensions and sensitivity). The reward will be based on how close the user comes to achieving the desired performance level. More sophisticated features can be added including user movement trajectory (averages compared to a goal movement strategy), and overshoot and undershoot to determine if target hits are legitimate or how much a player is missing by (if they are really close but still missing, it might be better to keep the same difficulty level).

The biologically-inspired AL algorithm can be applied to any version of the game. Gaming states, actions and rewards will change accordingly. To begin with, the format of the algorithm will be kept similar to the appearance of the traditional actor-critic (AC) method.

1.4.4 Actor-Critic Method

Actor-critic (AC) methods are temporal difference (TD) learning methods with a separate memory structure to represent policy independent of the value function used (see Fig. 1.7). The AC method considered in this section is an extension of reinforcement comparison in [46]. The following notation is needed (here and in subsequent sections). Let S be a set of possible states, let s denote a (current) state and for each $s \in S$, and let $A(s)$ denote the set of actions available in state s. Put $A = \cup_{s \in S} A(s)$, the collection of all possible actions. Let a denote a possible action in the current state; let s' denote the subsequent state after action a (that is, s' is the state in the next time step); let $p(s, a)$ denote an action-preference (for action a in state s); let r denote the reward for an action while in state s.

Begin by fixing a number $\gamma \in (0, 1]$, called a *discount rate*, a number picked that diminishes the estimated value of the next state; in a sense, γ captures the confidence in the expected value of the next state. Let $C(s)$ denote the number of times the actor has observed state s. As is common (e.g., see [46, 55]), define the estimated value function $V(s)$ to be the average of the rewards received while in state s. This average may be calculated by

$$V(s) = \frac{C(s) - 1}{C(s)} V_{C(s)-1}(s) + \frac{1}{C(s)} r, \tag{1.1}$$

where $V_{C(s)-1}(s)$ denotes $V(s)$ for the previous occurrence of state s. After each action selection, the critic evaluates the quality of the selected action using

$$\delta \longleftarrow r + \gamma V(s') - V(s), \tag{1.2}$$

which is the error (labelled the TD error) between successive estimates of the expected value of a state. If $\delta > 0$, then it can be said that the expected return received from taking action a at time t is larger than the expected return in state s resulting

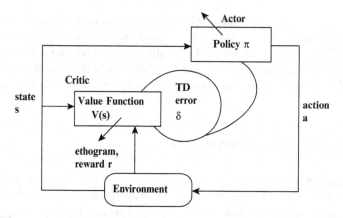

Fig. 1.7 Ethogram-based actor-critic learning

Algorithm 2: Actor-critic Method

Input : States $s \in S$, Actions $a \in A$, Initialized γ, β.
Output: Policy $\pi(s, a)$.
for (*all* $s \in S, a \in A(s)$) **do**

$\qquad p(s, a) \longleftarrow 0; \pi(s, a) \longleftarrow \dfrac{e^{p(s,a)}}{\sum_{b=1}^{|A(s)|} e^{p(s,b)}}; C(s) \longleftarrow 0;$

end
while *True* **do**
$\qquad$ Initialize s;
$\qquad$ **for** ($t = 0; t < T_m; t = t + 1$) **do**
$\qquad\qquad$ Choose a from $s = s_t$ using $\pi(s, a)$;
$\qquad\qquad$ Take action a, observe r, s';
$\qquad\qquad C(s) \longleftarrow C(s) + 1$;
$\qquad\qquad V(s) \longleftarrow \frac{C(s)-1}{C(s)} V(s) + \frac{1}{C(s)} \cdot r$;
$\qquad\qquad \delta = r + \gamma V(s') - V(s)$;
$\qquad\qquad p(s, a) \longleftarrow p(s, a) + \beta\delta$;
$\qquad\qquad \pi(s, a) \longleftarrow \dfrac{e^{p(s,a)}}{\sum_{b=1}^{|A(s)|} e^{p(s,b)}}$;
$\qquad\qquad s \longleftarrow s'$;
$\qquad$ **end**
end

---

in an increase in action preference $p(s, a)$. Conversely, if $\delta < 0$, the action a produced a return that is worse than expected and $p(s, a)$ is decreased [56].

The preferred action a in state s is calculated using

$$p(s, a) \leftarrow p(s, a) + \beta\delta, \qquad (1.3)$$

where β is the actor's learning rate. The policy $\pi(s, a)$ is employed by an actor to choose actions stochastically using the Gibbs softmax method (1.4) [12] (see also [46])

$$\pi(s, a) \longleftarrow \frac{e^{p(s,a)}}{\sum_{b=1}^{|A(s)|} e^{p(s,b)}}. \qquad (1.4)$$

Algorithm 2 gives the actor-critic method that is an extension of the reinforcement comparison method given in [46]. It is assumed that the behaviour represented by Algorithm 2 is episodic (with length T_m, an abuse of notation used in [49] for terminal state, the last state in an episode) and the while loop in the algorithm is executed continually over the entire learning period, not just for a fixed number of episodes.

1.4.5 Features and Measurements

It was Zdzisław Pawlak who proposed classifying objects by means of their attributes (features) considered in the context of an approximation space [29]. Explicit in the original work of Pawlak is a distinction between features of objects and

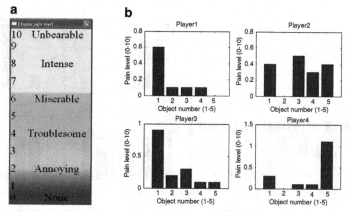

Fig. 1.8 Pain probe + sample RA measurements. (**a**) ATA pain gauge and (**b**) sample RA pain measurements

knowledge about objects. The knowledge about an object is represented by a measurement associated with each feature of an object. In general, a feature is an invariant property of objects belonging to a class [54]. The distinction between features and corresponding measurements associated with features is usually made in the study of pattern recognition (see, e.g., [28]). In this article, the practice begun by Pawlak [29] is represented in the following way. Let A denote a set of features for objects in a set X. For each $a \in A$, we associate a function f_a that maps X to some set V_{f_a} (range of f_a). The value of $f_a(x)$ is a measurement associated with feature a of an object $x \in X$. The function f_a is called a *probe* [28]. By $Inf_B(x)$, where $B \subseteq A$ and $x \in U$, we denote the *signature* of x, i.e., the set $\{(a, f_a(x)) : a \in B\}$. If $B = \{a_1, \ldots, a_m\}$, then Inf_B is identified with a vector $(f_{a_1}(x), \ldots, f_{a_m}(x))$ of probe function values for features in B.

Two examples of probe functions useful in assessing the results of physiotherapy using the ATA gaming system are pain and stiffness. The video game described in this chapter records pre- and post-gaming session pain and stiffness. Before and after physiotherapy session, an RA patient is asked to click on a pain gauge like the one shown in Fig. 1.8a. A comparison of estimated pain levels for four RA patients who manipulated five different objects is shown in Fig. 1.8b. Similarly, before and after each physiotherapy session, an RA patient is asked to click on a stiffness gauge like the one shown in Fig. 1.9a. A comparison of estimated stiffness levels for the same four RA patients is shown in Fig. 1.9b.

1.4.6 Approximation Spaces

This section briefly presents some fundamental concepts in rough set theory that provide a foundation for a new approach to reinforcement learning by collections

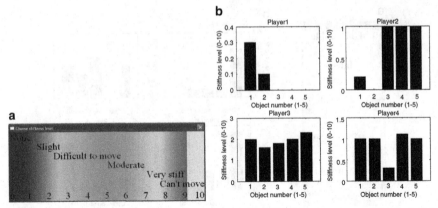

Fig. 1.9 Stiffness probe + sample RA measurements. (**a**) ATA stiffness gauge and (**b**) sample RA stiffness measurements

of cooperating agents. The rough set approach introduced by Pawlak [29] provides a ground for concluding to what degree a set of equivalent behaviours are *covered* by a set of behaviours representing a standard. The term "coverage" is used relative to the extent that a given set is contained in a standard set. Approximation spaces were introduced by Pawlak during the early 1980s [29], elaborated in [30]. The motivation for considering approximation spaces as an aid to reinforcement learning stems from the fact that it becomes possible to derive pattern-based rewards (see, e.g., [35]).

1.4.7 Rough Sets

Let U be a non-empty finite set (called a *universe*) and let $\mathcal{P}(U)$ denote the power set of U, i.e., the family of all subsets of U. Elements of U may be, for example, objects, behaviours, or perhaps states. A *feature* $\mathcal{F}$ of elements in U is measured by an associated probe function $f = f_{\mathcal{F}}$ whose range is denoted by $\mathcal{V}_f$, called the *value set* of f; that is, $f : U \rightarrow \mathcal{V}_f$. There may be more than one probe function for each feature. For example, a feature of an object may be its weight, and different probe functions for weight are found by different weighing methods; or a feature might be colour, with probe functions measuring, e.g., red, green, blue, hue, intensity and saturation. The similarity or equivalence of objects can be investigated quantitatively by comparing a sufficient number of object features by means of probes [28]. For present purposes, to each feature there is only one probe function associated and its value set is taken to be a finite set (usually of real numbers). Thus, one can identify the set of features with the set of associated probe functions, and hence, we use f rather than $f_{\mathcal{F}}$ and call $\mathcal{V}_f = \mathcal{V}_{\mathcal{F}}$ a set of feature values. If F is a finite set of probe functions for features of elements in U, the pair (U, F) is called a *data table*, or *information system* (IS).

For each subset $B \subseteq F$ of probe functions, define the binary relation $\sim_B = \{(x, x') \in U \times U : \forall f \in B, f(x) = f(x')\}$. Since each $\sim_B$ is an equivalence relation, for $B \subset F$ and $x \in U$, let $[x]_B$ denote the equivalence class, or *block*, containing x, that is,

$$[x]_B = \{x' \in U : \forall f \in B, f(x') = f(x)\} \subseteq U. \tag{1.5}$$

If $(x, x') \in \sim_B$ (also written $x \sim_B x'$), then x and x' are said to be *indiscernible* with respect to all feature probe functions in B, or simply, *B-indiscernible*.

Information about a sample $X \subseteq U$ can be approximated from information contained in B by constructing a *B-lower approximation*

$$B_* X = \bigcup_{x:[x]_B \subseteq X} [x]_B, \tag{1.6}$$

and a *B-upper approximation*

$$B^* X = \bigcup_{x:[x]_B \cap X \neq \emptyset} [x]_B. \tag{1.7}$$

The *B-lower approximation* $B_* X$ is a collection of blocks of sample elements that can be classified with full certainty as members of X using the knowledge represented by features in B. By contrast, the *B-upper approximation* $B^* X$ is a collection of blocks of sample elements representing both certain and possibly uncertain knowledge about X. Whenever $B_* X \subsetneq B^* X$, the sample X has been classified imperfectly, and is considered a rough set. In this chapter, only *B-lower* approximations are used.

1.4.8 Average Rough Coverage

An *ethogram* is a decision system representing observations of the behaviour of an agent interacting with an environment and provides a basis for the construction of a particular approximation space, which can be used to influence action preferences and a stochastic policy during reinforcement learning (see Fig. 1.10).

This section illustrates how to derive average rough coverage using an ethogram. An *episode* is a sequence of states that terminates. During an episode, an ethogram is constructed, which provides the basis for an approximation space and the derivation of the degree that a block of equivalent behaviours covers a set of behaviours representing a standard (see, e.g., [32, 36, 53]).

Define a *behaviour* to be a tuple $(s, a, p(s, a), r)$ at any one time t and let d denote a decision ($1 =$ choose action, $0 =$ reject action) for acceptance of a behaviour. Let $U_{\text{beh}} = \{x_0, x_1, x_2, \ldots\}$ denote a set of behaviours. Decisions to accept or reject an action are made by the actor during the learning process; let d denote a

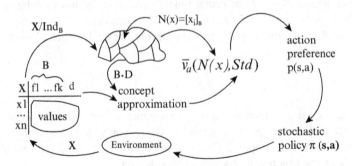

Fig. 1.10 Basic structures in approximation space-based learning

decision (0 = reject, 1 = accept). Often ethograms also include a column for "prox-imate cause" (see [53]); however, in the following example, this is considered as constant, and so such a column is redundant and does not appear.

Let B be the set of probe functions for state, action, action-preference and reward. The probe functions are suppressed, so identifying probe functions with features, write $B = \{s, a, p(s, a), r\}$. For each possible feature value j of a, (that is, $j \in V_a$), and $x \in U_{\text{beh}}$, put $B_j(x) = [x]_B$ if, and only if, $a(x) = j$, and call $B_j(x)$ an *action block*.

Put $\mathcal{B} = \{B_j(x) : j \in V_a, x \in U_{\text{beh}}\}$, a set of blocks that "represent" actions in a set E of sample behaviours. Setting $\nu = \nu_{SRC}$, define the *average* (lower) *rough coverage*

$$\bar{\nu} = \frac{1}{|\mathcal{B}|} \sum_{B_j(x) \in \mathcal{B}} \nu\left(B_j(x), B_* E\right). \tag{1.8}$$

Computing the average rough coverage value for action blocks extracted from an ethogram implicitly measures the extent that past actions have been rewarded.

1.4.9 Approximate Space-Based Actor-Critic Method

This section briefly introduces what is known as an approximation space-based actor critic (AAC) method. The AAC method estimates the value of a gaming state as shown in (1.9).

$$V(s) \longleftarrow V(s) + (1 - \bar{\nu})(r + \gamma V(s') - V(s)), \tag{1.9}$$

where $\bar{\nu}_a$ (average rough coverage derived from action a-blocks extracted from each ethogram at the end of each gaming session). Intuitively, this means action probabilities are now governed by the coverage of an action by a set of equivalent

---

Algorithm 3: Approximation Space-Based Actor-Critic

Input : States $s \in S$, Actions $a \in A(s)$, Initialize $\gamma, \bar{v}$.
Output: Policy $\pi(s, a)$ responsible for selecting action a in state s.
for $(all\ s \in S, a \in A(s))$ **do**
  $\quad p(s, a) \longleftarrow 0;$
  $\quad \pi(s, a) \longleftarrow \frac{e^{p(s,a)}}{\sum_{b=1}^{|A(s)|} e^{p(s,b)}};$
end
while *True* **do**
  $\quad$ Initialize s, data table;
  $\quad$ **for** *Repeat (for each step of episode)* **do**
    $\quad\quad$ Choose a from s using $\pi(s, a)$;
    $\quad\quad$ Take action a, observe r, s';
    $\quad\quad$ Record state, action and associated reward in data table;
    $\quad\quad \delta = r + \gamma V(s') - V(s);$
    $\quad\quad V(s) \longleftarrow V(s) + (1 - \bar{v})(r + \gamma V(s') - V(s));$
    $\quad\quad p(s, a) \longleftarrow p(s, a) + \beta \delta;$
    $\quad\quad \pi(s, a) \longleftarrow \frac{e^{p(s,a)}}{\sum_{b=1}^{|A(s)|} e^{p(s,b)}};$
    $\quad\quad s \longleftarrow s';$
  $\quad$ **end**
  $\quad$ Generate $\bar{v}$ from results recorded in data table for current episode;
  $\quad$ Update new value of $\bar{v}$;
  $\quad$ Clear data table;
end

---

actions which represent a standard. Algorithm 3 is the AAC one version of an AL algorithm used in an adaptive gaming system.

1.5 Sample Results from Physiotherapy Gaming Sessions

This section briefly presents sample results for different physiotherapy gaming sessions. For each of the sample plots given in this section, the shaded plane represents hits. Along the vertical, the scale represents downward or upward moves over roughly 30% of the screen. For example, in Fig. 1.11, client behaviour tends to favour either undershooting in moving the game sprite towards an incoming target (see Fig. 1.11a) or overshooting in trying to make the game sprite collide with an approaching target (see Fig. 1.11b).

The plot in Fig. 1.12a represents a player who tends to overshoot in trying to hit an incoming target, but really does fairly well in playing the game. By contrast, the plots in Figs. 1.12b and 1.14b represent a player who consistently overshoots in moving the game sprite to hit a target. A fairly balanced number of undershoot and overshoot cases are for each of the remaining cases represented by Figs. 1.13a, b and 1.14a, respectively.

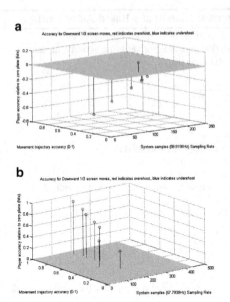

Fig. 1.11 Sample overshoot and undershoot cases. (**a**) Dominant undershoot case and (**b**) dominant overshoot case

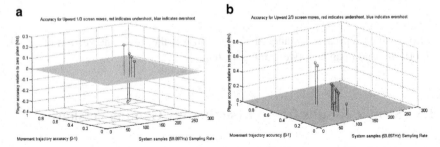

Fig. 1.12 Dominant overshoot cases. (**a**) Mixture case and (**b**) dominant overshoot case

1.6   Conclusion

This chapter gives a brief overview of an ATA that can be used for assessing the performance of patients during physiotherapy sessions. This ATA records movements of instrumented objects while playing a video game. The gaming system stores and feeds forward the results of each physiotherapy session to a health information registry. At this writing, the focus has been on the design of a telegaming system that sends object-movement hand function behaviour to a RA function PORTAL.

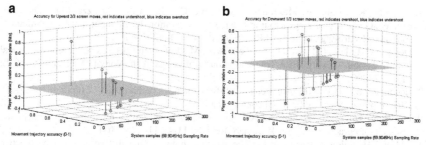

Fig. 1.13 Mixture of overshoot and undershoot cases. (**a**) Mixture case and (**b**) balanced case

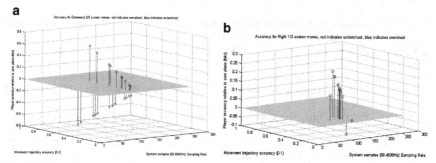

Fig. 1.14 Extreme cases. (**a**) Balanced case and (**b**) dominant overshoot case

Acknowledgments This research has been funded by grant SRI-BIO-05 from the Canadian Arthritis Network (CAN) and by discovery grant 185986 from the Natural Sciences and Engineering Research Council of Canada (NSERC).

References

1. Alcock, J.: Animal Behavior, 5th edn. Sinauer, Sunderland, MA (1995)
2. Betker, A., Desai, A., Nett, C., Kapadia, N., Szturm, T.: Game-based exercises for dynamic short-sitting balance rehabilitation of subjects with chronic spinal cord and traumatic brain injuries. Physical Therapy **87**(10), 1389–1398 (2007)
3. Betker, A.L., Szturm, T., Moussavi, Z.K., Nett, C.: Video game-based exercises for balance rehabilitation: A single-subject design. Archives of Physical Medicine and Rehabilitation **87**(8), 1141–1149 (2006)
4. Borkowski, M.: Therapeutic Game (2008). URL http://wren.ece.umanitoba.ca/
5. Broeren, J., Rydmark, M., Bjorkdahl, A., Sunnerhagen, K.: Assessment and training in a 3-dimensional virtual environment with haptics: A report on 5 cases of motor rehabilitation in the chronic stage after stroke. Neurorehabilitation and Neural Repair **21**(2), 180–189 (2007)
6. Brown, J.: The Evolution of Behavior. W.W. Norton, New York (1975)

7. Colombo, R., Pisano, F., Mazzone, A., Delconte, C., Micera, S., Carrozza, M.C., Dario, P., Minuco, G.: Design strategies to improve patient motivation during robot-aided rehabilitation. Journal of NeuroEngineering and Rehabilitation **4**(3), 1–12 (2007)

8. Dogac, A., Laleci, G.B., Aden, T., Eichelberg, M.: Enhancing the xds for federated clinical affinity domain support. IEEE Transaction on Information Technology in Biomedicine **11**(2), 213–222 (2007)

9. Eckhardt, B.: PORTAL Architecture. InfoMagnetics Technologies Corporation (2008). URL http://www.imt.ca. Personal communication

10. Fasoli, S., Krebs, H., Hogan, N.: Robotic technology and stroke rehabilitation: Translating research into practice. Top Stroke Rehab (Review) **11**(4), 11–19 (2004)

11. Gelfond, H., Salonius-Pasternak, D.: The plays the thing: A clinical-developmental perspective on video games. Child and Adolescent Psychiatric Clinics of North America **14**, 491–508, ix (2005)

12. Gibbs, J.: Elementary Principles in Statistical Mechanics. Dover, New York (1960)

13. Green, C., Bavelier, D.: Action video game modifies visual selective attention. Nature **423**, 534–537 (2003)

14. Green, C., Bavelier, D.: Enumeration versus multiple object tracking: The case of action video game players. Cognition **101**, 217–245 (2006)

15. Group, C.: Computational Intelligence Research Laboratory (2008). URL http://wren.ece.umanitoba.ca

16. Hassanien, A., Abraham, A., Peters, J., Schaefer, G.: Rough sets and near sets in medical imaging: A review. IEEE Transaction on Information Technology in Biomedicine (2008). submitted for publication

17. Henry, C., Peters, J.: Image pattern recognition using approximation spaces and near sets. In: Proc. Eleventh Int. Conf. on Rough Sets, Fuzzy Sets, Data Mining and Granular Computing (RSFDGrC 2007), Joint Rough Set Symposium (JRS 2007), Lecture Notes in Artificial Intelligence 4482. Heidelberg, Germany (2007, 475–482)

18. Henry, C., Peters, J.: Near set image segmentation quality index. In: GEOBIA 2008 Pixels, Objects, Intelligence. GEOgraphic Object Based Image Analysis for the 21st Century. University of Calgary, Alberta (2008, 1–6)

19. Jeremy, L., Emken, D., Reinkensmeyer, J.: Robot-enhanced motor learning: Accelerating internal model formation during locomotion by transient dynamic amplification. IEEE Transactions on Neural Systems **13**(1), 33–39 (2005)

20. Johnson, M., Feng, X., Johnson, L., Winters, J.: Potential of a suite of robot/computer-assisted motivating systems for personalized, home-based, stroke rehabilitation. Journal of NeuroEngineering and Rehabilitation **4**(6), 1–7 (2007)

21. Labella, T.H.: Division of labour in groups of robots. Ph.D. thesis, Universite Libre de Bruxelles(2007). URL http://iridia.ulb.ac.be/mdorigo/HomePageDorigo/thesis/phd/Labella-PhD.pdf

22. Lambercy, O., Dovat, L., Gassert, R., Burdet, E., Teo, C., Milner, T.: A haptic knob for rehabilitation of hand function. IEEE Transactions on Neural Systems and Rehabilitation Engineering **15**(3), 356–366 (2007)

23. Lehner, P.: Handbook of Ethological Methods. Cambridge University Press, Cambridge, UK (1996)

24. Merians, A., Poizner, H., Boian, R., Burdea, G., Adamovich, S.: Sensorimotor training in a virtual reality environment: does it improve functional recovery poststroke? Neurorehabilitation and Neural Repair **20**(2), 252–256 (2006)

25. Murray, J., Bradley, H., Craigie, W., Onions, C.: The Oxford English Dictionary. Oxford University Press, Oxford, UK (1933)

26. Otto, C.: Magnetic motion tracking system for interactive gaming. Master's thesis, Department of Electronic & Computer Engineering (2007). URL http://wren.ece.umanitoba.ca/

27. Patton, J., Musa-Ivaldi, F.: Robot-assisted adaptive training: Custom force fields for teaching movement reaching patterns. IEEE Transaction on Biomedical Engineering **51**(4), 636–646 (2004)

28. Pavel, M.: Fundamentals of Pattern Recognition, 2nd edn. Marcel Dekker, New York (1993)
29. Pawlak, Z.: Classification of objects by means of attributes. Polish Academy of Sciences **429** (1981)
30. Pawlak, Z., Skowron, A.: Rudiments of rough sets. Information Sciences **177**, 3–27 (2007)
31. Pekilis, B.: An ontology-based approach to concern-specific dynamic software structure monitoring. Ph.D. thesis, Department of Electronic & Computer Engineering. (2006). URL http://gp.uwaterloo.ca/files/2006-pekilis-phd-thesis.pdf
32. Peters, J.: Rough ethology: Towards a biologically-inspired study of collective behaviour in intelligent systems with approximation spaces. Transactions on Rough Sets (2005)
33. Peters, J.: Near sets. General theory about nearness of objects. Applied Mathematical Sciences **1**(53), 2609–2029 (2007)
34. Peters, J.: Near sets. Special theory about nearness of objects. Fundamenta Informaticae **75**(1–4), 407–433 (2007)
35. Peters, J., Henry, C., Ramanna, S.: Reinforcement learning with pattern-based rewards. In: Proc. Fourth Int. IASTED Conf. Computational Intelligence (CI 2005), pp. 400–406. IEEE, Compiegne Univ. of Technology, France (2005)
36. Peters, J., Henry, C., Ramanna, S.: Rough ethograms: Study of intelligent system behaviour. In: Proc. New Trends in Intelligent Information Processing and Web Mining (IIS05), pp. 117–126. Springer, Gdańsk, Poland (2005)
37. Peters, J., Ramanna, S.: Feature selection: A near set approach. In: ECML & PKDD Workshop on Mining Complex Data, pp. 1–12. Warsaw (2007)
38. Peters, J., Ramanna, S., Szturm, T., Shay, B.: Rheumatoid arthritis function portal. Technical report, University of Manitoba (2008). Research Report CI-2008-0010
39. Peters, J., Shahfar, S., Ramanna, S., Szturm, T.: Biologically-inspired adaptive learning: A near set approach. In: Frontiers in the Convergence of Bioscience and Information Technologies, pp. 1–8. IEEE Computational Intelligence Society, Korea (2007)
40. Peters, J., Skowron, A., Stepaniuk, J.: Nearness of objects: Extension of approximation space model. Fundamenta Informaticae **79**(3–4), 497–512 (2007)
41. Piron, L., Tonin, P., Piccioni, F., Iania, V., Trivello, E., Dam, M.: Virtual environment training therapy for arm motor rehabilitation. Presence-Teleoperators and Virtual Environments **14**(6), 732–740 (2005)
42. Scheidt, R., Dingwell, J., Mussa-Ivaldi, F.: Learning to move amid uncertainty. Neurophysiology **86**, 971–985 (2001)
43. Selfridge, O.: Some themes and primitives in ill-defined systems. Adaptive Control of Ill-Defined System. Plenum, New York (1984)
44. Shadmehr, R., Wise, S.: The computational neurobiology of reaching and pointing: a foundation for motor learning. The MIT Press, Cambridge, MA (2005)
45. Sutton, R., Barto, A.: Reinforcement Learning. An Introduction. The MIT Press, Cambridge, MA (1998)
46. Sutton, R., Barto, A.: Reinforcement Learning: An Introduction. The MIT Press, Cambridge, MA (1998)
47. Szturm, T., Peters, J.F., Otto, C., Kapadia, N., Desai, A.: Task-specific rehabilitation of finger-hand function using interactive computer gaming. Archives of Physical Medicine and Rehabilitation **89**(11), 2213–2217 (2008).
48. Takhutina, T., Foreman, N., Krichevets, A., Matikka, L., Narhi, V., Pylaeva, N., Vahakopus, D.: Improving spatial functioning in children with cerebral palsy using computerized and traditional game tasks. Disability and Rehabilitation **25**, 1361–1371 (2003)
49. Tang, T.T.: Temporal abstraction in reinforcement learning. Ph.D. thesis (2000). Ph.D. Thesis
50. Tang, T.T.: Quality-oriented information retrieval in a health domain. Ph.D. thesis (2006). URL http://cs.anu.edu.au/ Tim.Tang/Documents/thesis.pdf
51. Taswell, C.: Doors to the semantic web and grid with a portal for biomedical computing. IEEE Transaction on Information Technology in Biomedicine **12**(2), 191–204 (2008)
52. Tinbergen, N.: The Herring Gull's World. A Study of the Social Behavior of Birds. Collins, London (1953)

53. Tinbergen, N.: On aims and methods of ethology. Zeitschrift für Tierpsychologie **20**, 410–433 (1963)
54. Watanbe, S.: Pattern Recognition: Human and Mechanical. John Wiley & Sons, Cishester, UK (1985)
55. Watkins, C.: Learning from delayed rewards. Ph.D. thesis, King's College (May 1989). Ph.D. Thesis, supervisor: Richard Young
56. Wawrzyński, P.: Intensive reinforcement learning. Ph.D. thesis (2005). Ph.D. Thesis, supervisor: Andrzej Pacut

Chapter 2
Intelligent Behaviour Modelling and Control for Mobile Manipulators

Ayssam Elkady, Mohammed Mohammed, Eslam Gebriel, and Tarek Sobh

Abstract In the last several years, mobile manipulators have been increasingly utilized and developed from a theoretical viewpoint as well as for practical applications in space, underwater, construction and service environments. The work presented in this chapter deals with the problem of intelligent behaviour modelling and control of a mobile manipulator for the purpose of simultaneously following desired end-effector and platform trajectories. Our mobile manipulator comprised a manipulator arm mounted on a motorized mobile base wheelchair. The need for accurate modelling of the mobile manipulator is crucial in designing and controlling the motion of the robot to achieve the target precision and manipulability requirements. In this chapter, we propose a new method for measuring the manipulability index used for serial manipulators. Furthermore, we provide some simulations that are implemented on different serial manipulators, such as the Puma 560 manipulator, a six degrees of freedom (DOF) manipulator and the Mitsubishi Movemaster manipulator. We then extend the manipulability concept commonly used for serial manipulators to general mobile manipulator systems.

Keywords Mobile manipulator · Manipulability · Jacobian · Dexterity · Singular value decomposition · Singularities · Nonholonomic · Kinematics

2.1 Introduction

Studying the performance characteristics of the robot, such as dexterity, manipulability and accuracy, is very important to the design and analysis of a robot manipulator. The manipulability is the ability to move in arbitrary directions, while the accuracy is a measure of how close the manipulator can return to a previously taught point. The workspace of a manipulator is a total volume swiped out by the end effector when it executes all possible motions. The workspace is subdivided into the reachable workspace and the dexterous workspace. The reachable

A. Elkady (✉)
University of Bridgeport, Bridgeport, CT 06604, USA
e-mail: ayssam.elkady@gmail.com

A.-E. Hassanien et al. (eds.), *Pervasive Computing: Innovations in Intelligent Multimedia and Applications*, Computer Communications and Networks, DOI 10.1007/978-1-84882-599-4_2, © Springer-Verlag London Limited 2009

workspace is all point reachable by the end-effector. But the dexterous workspace consists of all points that the end-effector can reach with an arbitrary orientation of the end-effector. Therefore, the dexterous workspace is a subset of the reachable workspace. The dexterity index is a measure of a manipulator to achieve different orientations for each point within the workspace.

In this chapter, we present a new method for measuring the manipulability index, and some simulations are implemented on different manipulators, such as the Puma 560 manipulator, a six degrees of freedom (DOF) manipulator and the Mitsubishi Movemaster manipulator. In addition, we describe how the manipulability measure is crucial in performing intelligent behaviour tasks. The manipulability index is considered as a quantitative and performance measure of the ability for realizing some tasks. This measure should be taken into consideration in the design phase of a serial robot and also in the design of control algorithms. Furthermore, we use the proposed method for measuring the manipulability index in serial manipulators to generalize the standard definition of the manipulability index in the case of mobile manipulators.

2.2 Prior Work

Klein and Blaho [6] proposed some measures for the dexterity of manipulators, then they compared several measures for the problems of finding an optimal configuration for a given end-effector position, finding an optimal workpoint and designing the optimal link lengths of an arm. They considered four measures for dexterity: determinant, condition number, minimum singular value of the Jacobian and joint range availability. Salisbury and Craig [8] illustrated hand designs with particular mobility properties. In addition, they gave a definition of accuracy points within manipulator workspace. They used another performance index which is the condition number of the Jacobian. Yoshikawa [13] gave one of the first mathematical measures for the manipulability of any serial robot by discussing the manipulating ability of robotic mechanisms in positioning and orienting end-effectors. He introduced the term manipulability, which involves the Jacobian and its transpose; then the evaluation of the determinant of the Jacobian can be used to determine the manipulability measure. Gosselin [3] presented two dexterity indices for planar manipulations, the first one is based on a redundant formulation of the velocity equations and the second one is based on the minimum number of parameters. Then the corresponding indices were derived for spatial manipulators. These indices are based on the condition number of the Jacobian matrix of the manipulators. He considered the dexterity index, manipulability, condition number and minimum singular value, then he applied these indexes to a SCARA type robot. Van den Doel and Pai [12] introduced a performance measure of robot manipulators in a unified framework based on differential geometry. The measures are applied to the analysis of two- and three-link planar arm. In [5], the authors demonstrated that manipulability of a mechanism is independent of task space coordinates. Furthermore, they provided a proof of the independency of the manipulability index on the first DOF. In [7], the author examined two geometric tools for measuring the dexterousness of robot manipulators, manipulability ellipsoids and manipulability polytopes. He illustrated that the manipulability ellipsoid does not transform the exact joint velocity constraints into task space and so may fail to give exact dexterousness measure and optimal direction of motion in task space. Furthermore, he proposed a practical polytope method that can be applied to general 6-dimensional task space.

In [10], Sobh and Toundykov presented a prototyping software tool which runs under the mathematica environment and automatically computes possible optimal parameters of robot arms by applying numerical optimization techniques to the manipulability function, combined with distances to the targets and restrictions on the dimensions of the robot.

Nearly all of the above techniques start by getting the forward kinematics, then the Jacobian equation, which relates to the velocity of the end-effector and the joint velocities.

2.3 Manipulability Measure

2.3.1 Jacobian Matrix

The Jacobian matrix provides a transformation from the velocity of the end-effector in cartesian space to the actuated joint velocities as shown in equation (2.1)

$$\dot{x} = J\dot{q}, \tag{2.1}$$

where $\dot{q}$ is an m-dimensional vector that represents a set of actuated joint rates, $\dot{x}$ is an n-dimensional output velocity vector of the end-effector and J is the $m \times n$ Jacobian matrix. It is possible that $m \neq n$. As an example, a redundant manipulator can have more than six actuated joints, while the end-effector will at most have six DOF, so that $m > n$.

In the singular position, the Jacobian matrix J looses rank. This means that the end-effector looses one or more degrees of twist freedom (i.e., instantaneously, the end-effector cannot move in these directions). The mathematical discussion of singularities relies on the rank of the Jacobian matrix J, which, for a serial manipulator with n joints, is a $6 \times n$ matrix. For a square Jacobian, $\det(J) = 0$ is a necessary and sufficient condition for a singularity to appear.

2.3.2 Singular Value Decomposition Method

The singular value decomposition (SVD) method works for all possible kinematic structures (i.e., with every Jacobian matrix J with arbitrary dimensions $m \times n$). The SVD decomposition of any matrix J is on the form:

$$J_{m \times n} = U_{m \times m} \Sigma_{m \times n} V^t_{n \times n}, \tag{2.2}$$

with

$$\Sigma = \begin{pmatrix} \sigma_1 & 0 & 0 & \ldots & 0 & 0 & \ldots & 0 \\ 0 & \sigma_2 & 0 & \ldots & 0 & 0 & \ldots & 0 \\ 0 & 0 & \ddots & 0 & \ldots & 0 & \ldots & 0 \\ 0 & 0 & \ldots & \sigma_{m-1} & 0 & 0 & \ldots & 0 \\ 0 & 0 & \ldots & 0 & \sigma_m & 0 & \ldots & 0 \end{pmatrix}.$$

Such that U and V are orthogonal matrices. Thus,

$$U^t U = I_{m \times m}, \tag{2.3}$$

$$V^t V = I_{n \times n}, \tag{2.4}$$

where I is the identity matrix and the singular values are in descending orders $\sigma_1 \geq \sigma_2 \geq \cdots \geq \sigma_m$. The matrix has a zero determinant and is, therefore, singular (it has no inverse). The matrix has two identical rows (or two identical columns). In other words, the rows are not independent. If one row is a multiple of another, then they are not independent, and the determinant is zero. (Equivalently: If one column is a multiple of another, then they are not independent, and the determinant is zero.) The rank of a matrix is the maximum number of independent rows (or the maximum number of independent columns). A square matrix $A_{n \times n}$ is nonsingular only if its rank is equal to n. Mathematically, matrix J having a full rank means that the rank of $J = m$. In this case, $\sigma_m \neq 0$. When $\sigma_m \approx 0$, the matrix J does not have a full rank, which means that the matrix J looses one or more DOF. This happens physically, when the serial robot has two joint axes coinciding on each other.

2.3.3 Manipulability Measures

Yoshikawa [13] defined the manipulability measure μ as the square root of the determinant of the product of the manipulator Jacobian by its transpose

$$\mu = [\det(J \cdot J^t)]^{1/2}. \tag{2.5}$$

If the Jacobian matrix J is a square matrix, the manipulability μ is equal to the absolute value of the determinant of the Jacobian. Using the SVD, the manipulability can be written as follows:

$$\mu = \sigma_1 \sigma_2 \ldots \sigma_m. \tag{2.6}$$

Another method for the manipulability measure is the reciprocal of the condition number [termed the conditioning index] that was used in [11].

2.3.4   Optimizing the Manipulability Index of Serial Manipulators Using the SVD Method

Our current work addresses the manipulability index for every point within the workspace of some serial manipulators. The method provided promising results, since it is considered one of the crucial tasks required for designing trajectories or avoiding singular configurations. We propose a new method for measuring the manipulability, then we implemented simulations supporting our method on the Puma 560 manipulator, a six DOF manipulator and the Mitsubishi Movemaster manipulator. As mentioned in [11], the determinant of a Jacobian cannot be used for expressing the manipulability's index. It reaches zero when a manipulator reaches any singular configuration. Another method has been proposed, labelled the reciprocal of the Jacobian (as in [11]). In past researches, there was an argument about whether the minimum value of the σ's in (2.2) or the multiplication of all σ's exactly represents the manipulability's index [3].

In this work, we propose a new concept for measuring this index, then justify this concept by visualizing the bands of this index, resulting from our experiments. Moreover, a new relationship between the minimum rank of the Jacobian matrix and the order of one of these σ's (in (2.2)) can exactly express the manipulability's index.

2.3.4.1   The Puma 560 Manipulator: A Case Study

In case of the singular configuration of the Puma 560 manipulator at $Q = [0, 0, -\frac{\pi}{2}, 0, 0, 0]$, the following would be the J, U, Σ and V matrices as depicted in (2.2):

$$
J = \begin{bmatrix}
0 & 0 & 0 & 0 & 0 & 0 \\
20 & 0 & 0 & 0 & 0 & 0 \\
0 & 20 & 10 & 0 & 0 & 0 \\
0 & 0 & 0 & 1 & 0 & 1 \\
0 & 1 & 1 & 0 & 1 & 0 \\
1 & 0 & 0 & 0 & 0 & 0
\end{bmatrix},
$$

$$
U = \begin{bmatrix}
0 & 0 & 0 & 0 & 1 & -0.0034 \\
0 & -0.9988 & 0 & 0 & -0.0002 & -0.0499 \\
-0.9982 & 0 & 0 & 0.06 & 0 & 0 \\
0 & 0 & -1 & 0 & 0 & 0 \\
0.06 & 0 & 0 & 0.9982 & 0 & 0 \\
0 & -0.0499 & 0 & 0 & 0.0034 & 0.9987
\end{bmatrix},
$$

$$\Sigma = \begin{bmatrix} 22.401 & 0 & 0 & 0 & 0 & 0 \\ 0 & 20.025 & 0 & 0 & 0 & 0 \\ 0 & 0 & 1.4142 & 0 & 0 & 0 \\ 0 & 0 & 0 & 1.0935 & 0 & 0 \\ 0 & 0 & 0 & 0 & 0 & 0 \\ 0 & 0 & 0 & 0 & 0 & 0 \end{bmatrix},$$

$$V = \begin{bmatrix} 0 & -1 & 0 & 0 & 0 & 0 \\ -0.8939 & 0 & 0 & 0.1852 & 0.4074 & -0.027 \\ -0.4483 & 0 & 0 & -0.3638 & -0.8147 & 0.0539 \\ 0 & 0 & -0.7071 & 0 & -0.0467 & -0.7056 \\ -0.0027 & 0 & 0 & -0.9129 & 0.4074 & -0.027 \\ 0 & 0 & -0.7071 & 0 & 0.0467 & 0.7056 \end{bmatrix}.$$

It is obvious that in the singular matrix Σ, σ_5 and σ_6 assume the value zero with small tolerance. This is due to the fact that there are two singular cases in its configuration; the fourth and sixth joints are on same axis and it is in a singular arm configuration, and thus, σ_5 is zero.

2.3.5 Proposed Manipulability Measure Algorithm

To justify the proposed method, the following algorithm is proposed:

Algorithm 1: Calculate the manipulability index

1: Find the joint(s) that may lead to a singular configuration assuming that the number of these joints $= n$.

2: **for** $i = 1$ to n **do**

3:     Change the value of the ith joint from its initial to its final value using simulation software – Matlab robotic toolbox [2] is used in our case.

4:     Calculate the Jacobian (J) and singular (Σ) matrix.

5:     Plot every normalized σ and also the rank of the Jacobian matrix.

$$Normalized \sigma_i = \frac{\sigma_i}{Max\{\sigma_{i1}, \sigma_{i2}, \sigma_{i3}, \ldots\ldots, \sigma_{in}\}} \tag{2.7}$$

   Where: i is the order of the σ in the singular matrix and n is the number of steps during the simulation.

6:     Check the rank of the Jacobian matrix.

7: **end for**

2.4   Experiments

In this section, we will show and explain some results using serial manipulators with DH parameters illustrated in Tables 2.1–2.3. We have proposed some assumptions which can be summarized as follows:

- In our case study, we have dealt with the arm manipulability regardless of the orientation singularity.
- We study non-redundant manipulators only.

2.4.1   The Puma 560 Manipulator

In the Puma 560, we have experienced that the third joint is the cause of singularity. The sample trajectory of this manipulator from the initial position $Q_{\text{initial}} = [0, 0, -\frac{\pi}{2}, 0, 0, 0]$ to the final position $Q_{\text{final}} = [0, 0, \frac{\pi}{2}, 0, 0, 0]$ is shown in Fig. 2.1. The DH parameters of the Puma 560 are shown in Table 2.1.

Table 2.1   DH parameters of the Puma 560 manipulator

i	α	a	θ	d	Initial limit	Final limit	Joint's type
1	90	0	*	0	−170	170	R
2	0	0.4318	*	0	−225	45	R
3	−90	0.0203	*	0.15005	−250	75	R
4	90	0	*	0.4318	−135	100	R
5	−90	0	*	0	−100	100	R
6	0	0	*	0	−180	180	R

Table 2.2   DH parameters of a six degrees of freedom (DOF) serial manipulator

i	α	a	θ	d	Initial limit	Final limit	Joint's type
1	90	0	*	10	−170	170	R
2	0	10	*	0	−225	45	R
3	−90	0	*	0	−250	75	R
4	90	0	*	10	−135	100	R
5	−90	0	*	0	−100	100	R
6	0	0	*	0	−180	180	R

Table 2.3   Manipulability's bands of the Mitsubishi Movemaster manipulator in 2D workspace

i	α	a	θ	d	Initial limit	Final limit	Joint's type
1	90	0	*	300	−150	150	R
2	0	250	*	0	100	130	R
3	0	160	*	0	−110	0	R
4	−90	0	*	0	−90	90	R
5	0	0	*	72	0	0	R

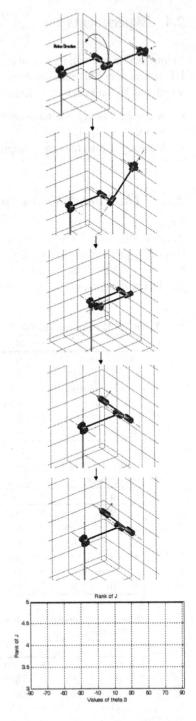

Fig. 2.1 Phases for the Puma
560 manipulator, changing
from the initial singular
configuration to the final
singular configuration with
the corresponding rank

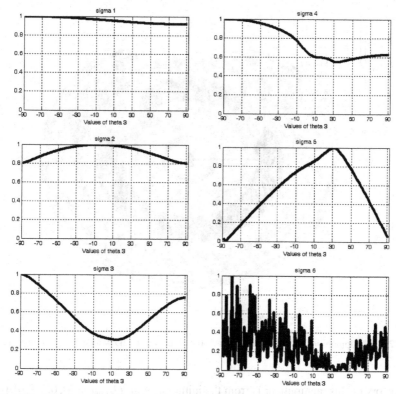

Fig. 2.2 The behaviour of σ_1 to σ_6 during the experiment

In Fig. 2.2, it is obvious that σ_5 is exactly expressing the manipulability's index. Furthermore, the rank of the Jacobian matrix during this experiment was constant at 5 because joints 6 and 4 were on same axis during the whole experiment. The manipulability index of every point within the whole workspace is represented in bands and each band is visualized using a different color as shown in Fig. 2.3.

Figure 2.3 is considered important in our research strategy since it provides a visual demonstration for the manipulability measure for the entire workspace for the Puma 560 manipulator. These results can strongly contribute in developing an intelligent mobile manipulator. For example, the positions with the highest manipulability index will have better dexterity compared with those of the lowest manipulability index.

2.4.2 A Six Degrees of Freedom Serial Manipulator

Similarly, we implemented the same procedure for the Mitsubishi Movemaster manipulator and a regular six DOF manipulator. In a six DOF manipulator, the sample

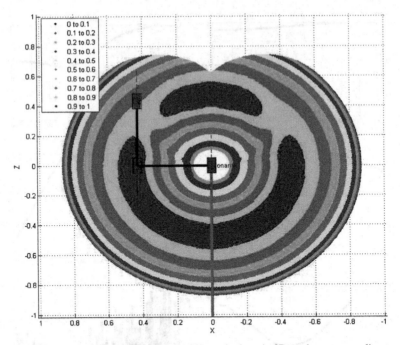

Fig. 2.3 Manipulability's bands of the puma 560 manipulator in 2D workspace according to σ_5

trajectory of this manipulator is from the initial position $Q_{\text{initial}} = [0, 0, -\frac{\pi}{2}, 0, 0, 0]$ to the final position $Q_{\text{final}} = [0, 0, \frac{\pi}{2}, 0, 0, 0]$. The DH parameters of this manipulator are shown in Table 2.2. The behaviour of σ_3 during the experiment is shown in Fig. 2.4. The visual demonstration of the manipulability index is shown in Fig. 2.5.

2.4.3 The Mitsubishi Movemaster Manipulator

The initial position is $Q_{\text{initial}} = [0, 0, -\frac{\pi}{2}, 0, 0, 0]$ and the final position $Q_{\text{final}} = [0, 0, \frac{\pi}{2}, 0, 0, 0]$. The DH parameters of this manipulator are shown in Table 2.3. The behaviour of σ_3 during the experiment is shown in Fig. 2.6. The visual demonstration of the manipulability index is shown in Fig. 2.7.

2.4.4 Experimental Results

It is obvious from Table 2.4 that we can suppose that the order of σ that is expressing the kinematics manipulability's index equals to the minimum rank of the Jacobian matrix.

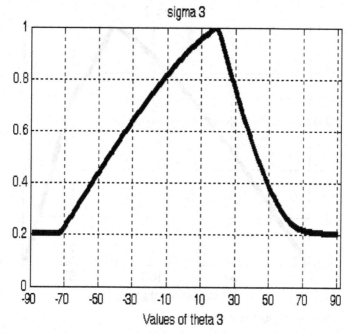

Fig. 2.4 The behaviour of σ_3 during the experiment

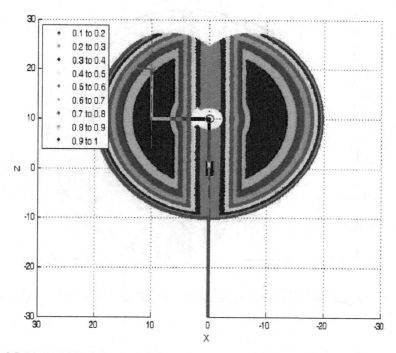

Fig. 2.5 Manipulability's bands of a six degrees of freedom (DOF) manipulator 2D

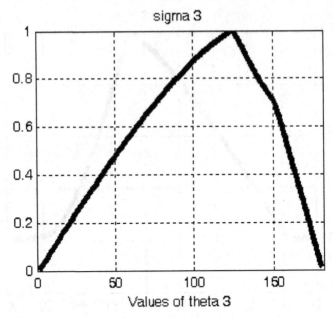

Fig. 2.6 The behaviour of σ_3 during the experiment

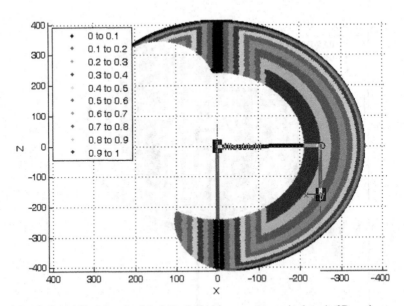

Fig. 2.7 Manipulability's bands of the Mitsubishi Movemaster manipulator in 2D workspace

Table 2.4 Summary of results

Manipulator	Order of σ expressing the manipulability	Min rank of the Jacobian matrix
Puma 560	5	5
Six DOF	3	3
Mitsubishi movemaster	3	3

2.5   Mobile Manipulator

A mobile manipulator is a manipulator mounted on a mobile platform with no support from the ground. A mobile manipulator offers a dual advantage of mobility offered by the platform and dexterity offered by the manipulator. For instance, the mobile platform extends the workspace of the manipulator. The DOF of the mobile platform also adds to the redundancy of the system. The mobile manipulator is required to perform complicated tasks and is potentially useful in dangerous and unpredictable environments, such as at a construction site, space, underwater, construction, service environments and in nuclear power station. Arai [1] suggested that the mobile manipulator system should be capable of both locomotion and manipulation when it is applied to various tasks in construction, agriculture, home, office and hospital services. Then he described why and how locomotion and manipulation should be integrated, what the benefits are and what problems must be solved in terms of practical application of the robot. In [9], a systematic modelling of the nonholonomic mobile manipulators is proposed. The derived models are used to generalize the standard definition of manipulability to the case of mobile manipulators. In addition, the effects of mounting a robotic arm on a nonholonomic platform were shown through the analysis of the manipulability.

In fixed based serial manipulators, manipulability depends on link lengths, joint types, joint motion limits and the structure of the manipulator. In mobile manipulator, the manipulability depends on the kinematics, geometric design, the payload and mass and mass distribution of the mobile platform. Thus, the manipulability measure in mobile manipulators is very complicated due to the coupling between the kinematic parameters and the dynamics effect.

We extend the manipulability concept commonly used for serial manipulators to general mobile manipulator systems. To study the manipulability and dexterity measure for a mobile manipulator, we first study those of the fixed base serial manipulator as discussed in the previous sections.

2.6   RISC Mobile Manipulator

We are developing and constructing the mobile manipulator platform RISC. The prototype of the RISC is shown in Fig. 2.8. The RISC mobile manipulator has been designed to support our research in algorithms and control for autonomous mobile

Fig. 2.8 A prototype of the RISC manipulator

manipulator. The objective is to build a hardware platform with redundant kinematic DOF, a comprehensive sensor suite and significant end-effector capabilities for manipulation. The RISC platform differs from any related robotic platforms because its mobile platform is a wheelchair base. Thus, the RISC has the advantages of the wheelchair, such as high payload, high speed motor package (the top speed of the wheelchair is 6 miles/h), Active-Trac and rear caster suspension for outstanding outdoor performance and adjustable front anti-tips to meet terrain challenges.

2.7 Modelling of the RISC

2.7.1 The Position of the Robot

In order to specify the position of the robot on the plane, we establish a relationship between the global reference frame of the plane and the local reference frame of the robot. The origin O of the global reference frame is selected at arbitrary on the plane as shown in Fig. 2.9. The point C is the centre of mass of the robot. The origin P of the local reference frame of the robot $\{X_p, Y_p\}$ is at the centre of the robot. The basis defines two axes relative to P on the robot chassis and is, thus, the robot's local reference frame. The position of P in the global reference frame is specified by coordinates x and y and the angular difference between the global and local reference frames is given by θ. The pose of the robot is described by a vector ξ.

$$\xi = \begin{bmatrix} x \\ y \\ \theta \end{bmatrix}. \tag{2.8}$$

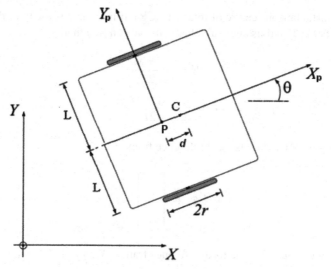

Fig. 2.9 Kinematic model of the RISC

To describe the robot's motion, it will be necessary to map the motion along the axes from the global reference frame to the robot's local reference frame. This mapping is accomplished using the orthogonal rotation matrix $R(\theta)$, where

$$R(\theta) = \begin{bmatrix} \cos(\theta) & \sin(\theta) & 0 \\ -\sin(\theta) & \cos(\theta) & 0 \\ 0 & 0 & 1 \end{bmatrix}.$$

This orthogonal rotation $R(\theta)$ is used to map the motion ξ in the global reference frame to motion $^P\xi$ in terms of the local reference frame $\{X_p, Y_p\}$. This operation is:

$$^P\xi = R(\theta)\xi \tag{2.9}$$

2.7.2 The velocity of the robot

Given that the spinning speed of left wheel is $\dot{\Phi}_l$ and the spinning speed of the right wheel is $\dot{\Phi}_r$, a forward kinematic model would predict the robot's overall speed in the global reference frame. The linear velocity of the centre of the right wheel is v_r, where

$$v_r = r\dot{\Phi}_r. \tag{2.10}$$

In addition, the velocity of the left one is v_l where

$$v_l = r\dot{\Phi}_l. \tag{2.11}$$

Using the instantaneous centre of rotation (ICR), if the linear velocity of the centre P of the robot is V and its angular velocity ω, we can find that:

$$V = \frac{v_r + v_l}{2},$$ (2.12)

$$\omega = \dot\theta = \frac{v_r - v_l}{2L}.$$ (2.13)

The velocity of point P in its local reference frame $^P\dot\xi_p$:

$$^P\dot\xi_p = \begin{bmatrix} V \\ 0 \\ \dot\theta \end{bmatrix}.$$ (2.14)

The velocity of point C in the local reference frame $\{X_p, Y_p\}$ is $^P\dot\xi_c$ where

$$^P\dot\xi_c = \begin{bmatrix} V \\ \dot\theta d \\ \dot\theta \end{bmatrix}.$$ (2.15)

The velocity of point P in the global reference frame $\dot\xi_p$ is

$$\dot\xi_p = R(\theta)^{-1}\,{}^P\dot\xi_p,$$ (2.16)

$$\dot\xi_p = \frac{r}{2} \begin{bmatrix} (\dot\Phi_l + \dot\Phi_r)\cos(\theta) \\ (\dot\Phi_l + \dot\Phi_r)\sin(\theta) \\ \frac{(\dot\Phi_r - \dot\Phi_l)}{l} \end{bmatrix}.$$ (2.17)

The velocity of point C in the global reference frame $\dot\xi_c$ is

$$\dot\xi_c = R(\theta)^{-1}\,{}^P\dot\xi_c.$$ (2.18)

Thus,

$$\dot\xi_c = \begin{bmatrix} \dot x_c \\ \dot y_c \\ \dot\theta \end{bmatrix} = \frac{r}{2} \begin{bmatrix} (\dot\Phi_l + \dot\Phi_r)\cos(\theta) + \frac{d}{l}(\dot\Phi_l - \dot\Phi_r)\sin(\theta) \\ r(\dot\Phi_l + \dot\Phi_r)\sin(\theta) + \frac{d}{l}(\dot\Phi_r - \dot\Phi_l)\cos(\theta) \\ \frac{(\dot\Phi_r - \dot\Phi_l)}{l} \end{bmatrix}.$$ (2.19)

2.7.3 Kinematic Constraints

However, several important assumptions will simplify this representation. First, the plane of the wheel always remains vertical and that there is, in all cases, one single point of contact between the wheel and the ground plane. Furthermore, there is no sliding at this single point of contact, so the wheel undergoes motion only under conditions of pure rolling and rotation about the vertical axis through the contact point.

The fixed standard wheel has no vertical axis of rotation for steering. Its angle to the chassis is fixed and it is limited to back and forth motion along the wheel plane and rotation around its contact point with the ground plane. The rolling constraint for this wheel enforces that all motions along the direction of the wheel plane must be accompanied by the appropriate amount of wheel spin. Thus, the first constraint is

$$\dot{y}_c \cos(\theta) - \dot{x}_c \sin(\theta) - \dot{\theta}d = 0. \tag{2.20}$$

Furthermore, there are two rolling constraints, i.e., the driving wheels do not slip,

$$\dot{x}_c \cos(\theta) + \dot{y}_c \sin(\theta) + \dot{\theta}l = r\dot{\phi}_r, \tag{2.21}$$
$$\dot{x}_c \cos(\theta) + \dot{y}_c \sin(\theta) - \dot{\theta}l = r\dot{\phi}_l. \tag{2.22}$$

Letting $q = [x_c\, y_c, \theta, \Phi_r, \Phi_l]^t$, the three constraints can be written in the form of:

$$A(q)\dot{q} = 0, \tag{2.23}$$

where

$$A(q) = \begin{bmatrix} \sin\theta & -\cos\theta & d & 0 & 0 \\ \cos\theta & \sin\theta & l & -r & 0 \\ -\cos\theta & -\sin\theta & l & 0 & r \end{bmatrix} \quad \text{and} \quad \dot{q} = \begin{bmatrix} \dot{x}_c \\ \dot{y}_c \\ \dot{\theta} \\ \dot{\phi}_r \\ \dot{\phi}_l \end{bmatrix}.$$

The last two equations are called the nonholonomic constraint because they are not integrable differential equations.

2.8 Conclusions and Future Work

In this chapter, we present a new algorithm for measuring manipulability, and then we implement simulations supporting our methodology on different manipulators. We describe how mobile manipulator capabilities are a key to several robotic applications and how the manipulability measure is crucial in performing intelligent behaviour tasks such as grasping, pulling or pushing objects with sufficient dexterity.

In our anticipated future work, there will be an ongoing effort for the development of multiple mobile manipulator systems and platforms, which will interact with each other to perform more complex tasks exhibiting intelligent behaviours utilizing the proposed manipulability measure.

References

1. T. Arai (1996) Robots with integrated locomotion and manipulation and their future. Proceedings of the 1996 IEEE/RSJ International Conference on Robots and Intelligent Systems, IROS 96, vol. 2, Osaka, pp. 541–545.
2. P.I. Corke (2002) Robotic toolbox.
3. C.M. Gosselin (1990) Dexterity indices for planar and spatial robotic manipulators. Proceedings of the International Conference on Robotics and Automation, vol. 1, May 1990, pp. 650–655.
4. C. Gosselin, J. Angeles (1988) The optimum kinematic design of a planar three-degree-of-freedom parallel manipulator. Journal of Mechanisms, Transmissions and Automation in Design 110, 35–41.
5. K. Gotlih, I. Troch (2004) Base Invariance of the Manipulability Index. Robotica archive. Cambridge University Press, New York, NY, USA, 22(4), pp. 455–462.
6. C.A. Klein, B.E. Blaho (1987) Dexterity measures for the design and control of kinematically redundant manipulators. The International Journal of Robotics Research 6(2), 72–83.
7. J. Lee (1997) A study on the manipulability measures for robot manipulators. Intelligent Robots and Systems 3(7–11), 1458–1465.
8. J.K. Salisbury, J.J. Craig (1982) Articulated hands. Force control and kinematic issues. The International Journal of Robotics Research 1(1), 4–17.
9. R. Siegwart, I.R. Nourbakhsh (2004) Intelligent Robotics and Autonomous Agents Series. MIT Press, Cambridge, MA, ISBN 0-262-19502-X.
10. T.M. Sobh, D.Y. Toundykov (2004) Optimizing the tasks at hand. IEEE Robotics and Automation Magazine 11(2), 78–85.
11. T. Tanev, B. Stoyanov (2000) On the Performance Indexes for Robot Manipulators. Problems of Engineering Cybernetics and Robotics.
12. K. van den Doel, D.K. Pai (1996) Performance measures for robot manipulators: A unified approach. The International Journal of Robotics Research 15(1), 92–111.
13. T. Yoshikawa (1985) Manipulability of robotic mechanisms. The International Journal of Robotics Research 4(2), 3–9.

Chapter 3
Resource-Aware Fuzzy Logic Control of Video Streaming over IP and Wireless Networks

M. Fleury, E. Jammeh, R. Razavi, and M. Ghanbari

Abstract Congestion control of real-time streaming a video clip or film across the Internet is vital, as network traffic volatility requires constant adjustment of the bit rate in order to reduce packet loss. Traditional solutions to congestion control are prone to delivery rate fluctuations and may respond only when packet loss has already occurred, while both fluctuations and packet loss seriously affect the end user's appreciation of the delivered video. In this chapter, fuzzy logic control (FLC) is newly applied to control of video streaming in fixed and wireless networks. In a fixed network, by way of congestion control the encoded video bitstream's rate is adjusted according to the available bandwidth. Compared to existing controllers, FLC's sending rate is significantly smoother, allowing it to closely track available bandwidth at a bottleneck on the video stream's path across a network. The chapter also shows that when multiple video streams are congestion controlled through FLC, the result is a fairer and more efficient sharing of the bandwidth capacity. Also considered is a pioneering application of FLC to wireless networks, where other resources, apart from available bandwidth, come into play. An FLC system has been designed that provides a modular solution to control of latency and energy consumption, which is important for battery-powered devices, but must be balanced against the quality of delivered video. The chapter concludes by presenting the potential of emerging type-2 fuzzy logic as a way of significantly improving the robustness of classical type-1 fuzzy logic.

Keywords Congestion control · Fuzzy logic · Networks · Video streaming

3.1 Introduction

Real-time video streaming applications, such as IPTV (TV distributed over an IP network), video-on-demand, video-clip-Web-click, and network-based video recorder, have high bit rates that risk overwhelming traditional networks if it is not

M. Fleury (✉)
School of CSEE, University of Essex, Wivenhoe Park, Colchester CO4 3SQ, UK
e-mail: fleum@essex.ac.uk

A.-E. Hassanien et al. (eds.), *Pervasive Computing: Innovations in Intelligent Multimedia and Applications*, Computer Communications and Networks, DOI 10.1007/978-1-84882-599-4_3, © Springer-Verlag London Limited 2009

possible to control their flows. In video streaming, a compressed video bitstream is transmitted across a network to the end user's decoder (prior to display) without the need for storage other than in temporary buffering. Such video services are attractive to end users because of their variety and flexibility compared to broadcast TV over the airwaves and they interest telecommunications companies because of their high bit rates. These companies are also interested in seamlessly extending video services across wireless networks because these networks have the advantages of mobility and convenience. However, wireless networks reintroduce many impediments to high-quality video delivery such as adverse channel conditions due to noise and interference, while mobility brings a need to preserve a device's battery power.

We have applied fuzzy logic control (FLC) of unicast video streaming across packet-switched internet protocol (IP) networks and wireless networks. Prior to our research, analytical methods have been almost exclusively applied to congestion control of video on the Internet. For example, the industry standard approach models the video stream's rate with a complex equation designed to replicate the average flow of other competing flows across network bottlenecks. In that way it is hoped that further network congestion will be avoided. Unfortunately, this approach may lead to unnecessary packet loss because of the need to probe the network using the video stream itself. Inevitably as the video rate is increased, packet loss occurs once the available bandwidth or capacity limit is reached. Based on fuzzy logic, we have devised a more flexible method that estimates traffic conditions without the need for probing. Though fuzzy logic has been applied to access control for prior networking technologies such as the asynchronous transfer mode (ATM), to the best of the authors' knowledge it has not or rarely been applied to congestion control over IP networks. In recent years, interval type-2 logic has grown in prominence [1] as an improvement on traditional type-1 FLC. We examine the possibility of employing interval type-2 logic to improve estimates of the network conditions into which the video stream is injected. Certainly, no other research has extended FLC to type-2 fuzzy logic congestion control for video streaming.

Within fixed networks, an FLC must compete with traditional solutions to congestion control. The main transport protocol within the Internet is the transmission control protocol (TCP). However, as TCP transport in order to ensure reliability may result in unbounded delay, the user datagram protocol (UDP) is normally preferred for video communication, while congestion control is done by a variety of application layer controllers. Both protocols are routed through the Internet by IP. IP is a best-effort protocol in the sense that packets may be lost if it proves impossible to deliver them through a variety of causes. Typically, buffer overflow occurs at a bottleneck link, but mis-routing may also occur and very occasionally in today's fixed networks, errors are detected within the packet. The traditional method of gauging congestion in the wired Internet is through packet loss, as is the case for TCP, though round-trip time plays its part. Packet losses certainly indicate congestion, but do not provide direct information on the level of network congestion or the available network bandwidth. In fact, packet loss does not signal the onset of congestion, but rather the presence of already full-blown congestion. While packet loss is acceptable in file transfer, as lost packets are simply retransmitted through TCP, playout and decode deadlines must be met when streaming video.

A compressed video stream must compete for buffer space and bandwidth across the fixed Internet, as other traffic flows continuously cross the video stream's path. Without a fixed Internet core, the mobile or pervasive Internet cannot exist. At the periphery of the fixed core network, access networks directly deliver the Internet over its final hop to the consumer. In a wireless access link, added competition for resources occurs, as energy and latency become important commodities and the wireless channel's capacity fluctuates according to the channel error conditions. Uncertainty exists in various forms: in the measured delay across a network path; in variations in the cross-traffic; and in volatile wireless channel conditions. With uncertainty comes the need to employ fuzzy logic rather than precise analytical methods.

We have found that fuzzy control is able to function in low packet loss environments, which is certainly necessary to preserve fragile compressed video streams, but is unavailable to traditional solutions as they mostly rely on packet loss to predict network conditions. Because of the predictive nature of video compression, the effect of packet loss is not confined to a single video frame but may have a repercussion across a group of pictures (GOP) within a video stream, which, in the standard codecs [2], normally consists of 12 or 15 frames. (Notice that the terms "picture" and "frame" are used interchangeably within this chapter, as they are equivalent in respect to progressive video, video without interlacing.) If packets forming an intra-coded frame (I-frame) are lost then all other frames within a GOP are affected, as all depend on motion estimation from this reference frame. If predictive frame (P-frame) packets are lost then all frames following that frame are affected until the next I-frame is transferred.

For us, FLC is a convenient tool for handling un-anticipated or unmodeled network congestion states. In respect to FLC over a fixed network, a sender-based system for unicast flows [3]. The receiver returns a feedback message that indicates time-smoothed and normalized changes to packet inter-arrival times. These allow the sender to compute the network congestion level. The sender subsequently applies a control signal either directly to an encoder in the case of live video or to an intermediate bit rate transcoder's [4] quantization level in the case of stored video. (A transcoder converts the bit rate of an encoded bitstream from the pre-encoded rate to a lower rate. To reduce delay this process may be performed in frequency space, as all encoded videos undergo a frequency transform to reduce spatial correlations in the contents.)

For reasons of cost, Bluetooth or IEEE 802.15.1 (Sect. 3.4.1) is widely available on cellular phones and laptops as a cable replacement technology. In British Telecom's plans for a next generation IP network, Bluetooth is a way of seamlessly moving between a cellular phone network and indoor wireless access network (Sect. 3.4). We take Bluetooth as an example of a centrally scheduled time division multiple access wireless system, which is the norm for multimedia traffic delivery as it avoids unbounded latencies. Effective automatic repeat request (ARQ) management is the key to both ensuring acceptable video quality at the receiver device in the event of packet error over the error-prone wireless channel and power management of the transmission.

Our pioneering development of FLC of ARQ [5] is a way of combining three factors: (1) channel state, (2) display/decode deadline, and (3) power budget. We have adopted a modular scheme whereby a two-input FLC stage with a single output is concatenated with a second FLC stage, with the output from the original FLC and an additional "remaining power" input. A modular scheme reduces the construction complexity of the design and enables future enhancements. Assuming a fixed power budget for the duration of a video clip streaming session, the declining power budget as the stream progresses has the effect of modulating the ARQ retransmission count.

Real-time delivery of video is delay-sensitive, as a frame cannot be displayed if its data arrive after their display or decode deadline [6]. In practice, a play-out buffer exists on a mobile device to account for start-up delay and also absorbs delay jitter (variation of delay). Therefore, the maximum delay permissible corresponds to the start-up delay deemed tolerable to the user. Error concealment at the decoder is implementation dependent, but to reduce decoder complexity, it often only consists of replacing the missing portion of the frame with a matching portion from the previous frame. The net result is poor quality video. Not only do packets arrive after their display deadline, but while retransmission takes place, other packets may either wait too long in the send buffer, or in the extreme case, arriving packets may find the send buffer full. ARQ adds to delay and, therefore, the number of retransmissions should be minimized even before taking into account their impact on the power budget.

In general, a fuzzy scheme is easily tuned by adjustment of its membership functions. A fuzzy scheme is also well suited to implementation on a mobile device because not only are the decision calculations inherently simple (and can be made more so by adoption of triangular membership functions), but also, by forming a look-up-table (LUT) from the fuzzy control surface, its operation can be reduced to simple LUT access. There is also a range of hardware designs [7] for FLC to aid real-time operation. Therefore, many practical reasons exist why of all the natural algorithms, fuzzy logic is most suited to real-time control.

3.2   Related Work on Fuzzy Logic in Telecommunications

Fuzzy logic is of course a form of computational intelligence. In a survey of congestion control through computational intelligence, the authors of [8] observe that little work has been reported on deploying natural algorithms including fuzzy logic within the Internet. ATM networks, which employ access control to virtual switched circuits, are one domain to which fuzzy logic has been more extensively applied [9, 10], but for the purpose of access control. In fact, [11] reports a type-2 FLC used for that purpose. However, it should be remarked that access control does not involve dynamically controlling a video stream once it is admitted to the network, unlike congestion control. This is because once a virtual circuit is established, it is assumed that sufficient capacity already exists within the network. Moreover, there is currently strong pressure from telecommunications manufacturers to move away from ATM and towards Ethernet framing on fixed networks. Consequently, ATM is losing its relevance to contemporary networks. Because of Bluetooth (IEEE 802.15.1)'s centralized scheduling, which resembles ATM admission control, fuzzy logic video bit rate control was applied in a similar manner to a Bluetooth wireless link [12]. An interesting modular design was employed, but the main input to the fuzzy models was the Bluetooth input buffer fullness, which does not account for a number of important factors in wireless transmission including energy consumption.

Again because the problem resembles ATM admission control, in a number of papers, the authors of [13] have explored fuzzy logic to improve the performance of the random early discard (RED) router queue algorithm, and in [14] fuzzy logic was applied to DiffServ buffer occupancy for each class of layered video packets. Both these systems control the quality-of-service of video streams at routers in the face of other competing traffic. These are not end-to-end solutions to the problem of network congestion, but rely on deployment of quality-of-service strategies that in practice are confined to particular internet service providers. In the case of RED, packets are dropped to signal to TCP controlled flows that congestion is about to occur. Even if TCP could be employed for video streaming, this implies packet loss with its destructive effect on video quality.

Within video coding, fuzzy logic has found an application [15, 16] in maintaining a constant video rate by varying the encoder quantization parameter according to the output buffer state, which is a complex control problem without an analytical solution. This is an open loop solution to the problem of controlling access to the network and should be compared to the ATM-based solutions previously discussed. In our work, we have preferred a closed loop solution in which feedback for the network state from the receiver serves as input to the FLC. This allows greater awareness of traffic conditions experienced by the video stream within the network itself. In [17], fuzzy logic determines the size of different video frame type sizes and classifies the video genre. The intention is to allow modeling of variable bit rate (VBR) video traffic without the need for video sources. However, there is no attempt at real-time control.

Wireless networks represent a promising application of fuzzy logic as not only are their uncertainties inherent in network traffic, but also the wireless channel is more error prone and takes a wider variety of forms than a wired link. Additionally, the need to conserve battery energy brings into play another set of factors. In [18], fuzzy logic was applied to modeling the lifetime of a wireless sensor network, though again no real-time control took place. In [19], the problem of fading wireless channels (ones in which multi-path interference causes mutual interference between simultaneously received versions of the signal) was tackled with fuzzy filters to equalize the signal response according to variation of the wireless channel. This is a physical layer technique, whereas our work with FLC is cross-layer between the application and data link layers of the standard model for the protocol stack.

Recent applications of fuzzy logic have been with type-2 logic, which are further discussed in Sect. 3.5. Though the possibility of type-2 fuzzy systems has been known for some time [20], only recently have algorithms become available [21] allowing calculation of an interval type-2 output control value at video frame rates. The first work on interval type-2 sets, which simplifies the calculation of type-2 logic, is due to Gorzalczany [22] and other pioneering work is given credit in [23]. A growing number of type-2 controllers for robotic and industrial applications are already surveyed in [1], demonstrating the effectiveness of the new algorithms for real-time control.

3.3 Fuzzy Logic Control on the Fixed Internet

Figure 3.1 shows a video streaming architecture in which fuzzy logic is utilized to control the bit rate. A video transcoder at the server is necessary for adaptation of stored pre-encoded video-rate adaptation, while a video decoder at the client decodes the received video stream in real time. (For live video, directly changing the quantization parameter of the encoder has the same effect.) The client-side timer unit monitors the dispersion of incoming packets and relays this information to the congestion level determination (CLD) unit. The CLD unit monitors the outgoing packet stream, especially the packet sizes, and combines this information with the receiver device feedback as a basis for determining the network congestion level, C_L. This unit also computes the congestion-level rate of change, δC_L.

Principally, the timer unit measures the arriving packet inter-packet gaps (IPGs) before finding a time-smoothed and normalized estimate of the packet dispersion. An IPG is the time duration between the receipt of the end of one packet and the arrival of the next. The FLC takes C_L and δC_L as inputs and computes a sending rate that reflects the network's state. The appropriate change in the transcoder

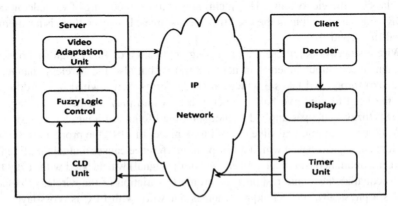

Fig. 3.1 Fuzzy logic control (FLC) video streaming architecture

quantization level is then calculated. Transported packets are received by the client, depacketized, decoded and displayed at video rate.

At the server, the video transcoder inputs the encoded video and reduces its bit rate in response to a control signal from the FLC. A lower bound to the sending rate is set to be 10% of the input sending rate. For an average input sending rate of 2 Mb/s, a lower limit of 200 kb/s is sufficient for an acceptable video quality. The transcoded video is packetized, with one slice per packet, and sent across the network within a UDP packet. European format source input format (SIF) at 25 frame/s Motion Picture Experts Group (MPEG)-2 encoded video can be partitioned into eighteen slices per frame, each slice consisting of a row of 22 macroblocks (a macroblock is a unit of motion estimation in standard codecs [2]). Apart from error resilience due to decoder synchronization markers, per-slice packetization also reduces delay at the server. Transcoded video packets are subsequently output with a constant IPG at the point of transmission. Ensuring a constant IPG reduces packet inter-arrival jitter at the client and also renders the streamed video more robust to error bursts. At 18 packets per frame, for 25 frame/s the IPG at the server before dispersion is 2.2 ms. The MPEG-2 codec was employed in this work as it has been adopted by the Digital Video Broadcasting consortium and is widely deployed by other major commercial broadcasters.

3.3.1   Calculation of the Congestion Level

Let the IPG of the packets be T_S and T_C for the packet entering the network and exiting the network, respectively. T_C will equal T_S when the available network bandwidth is equal to or more than the sending rate of the packets. In other words, as far as the application sending the packets is concerned, equality will apply when the network is not congested. A congested network will generally have a dispersive effect on the IPG, resulting in T_C being greater than T_S. The difference between T_C and T_S is, therefore, a measure of network congestion. The more congested the network, the more is the difference. The IPGs, T_C and T_S, apart from being dependent on the sending rate of the packets, are dependent on two variables: (1) the level of network congestion and (2) the size of the packets. Normalizing these variables by the packet sizes makes them only dependent on the network congestion level. Knowing the normalized values of T_C and T_S will then enable computation of the level of network congestion.

Thus, congestion level is determined without relying on packet loss, which is vital for video because, as previously mentioned in Sect. 3.1, any packet loss from an anchor or reference frame endures until the GOP completes. A mean packet transfer time G_S is found at the server and similarly G_C is found after measurements made at the client. G_S and G_C are calculated over the duration of one frame's transmission and subsequently act to estimate the level of network congestion. The sending rate is changed when and only when a feedback message arrives at the receiver. To ensure consistent quality within a frame, the change itself is only made at the beginning of a video frame.

The sending rate of the application into the network, and the receiving rate of the client from the network are calculated as R_S and R_C, respectively, in (3.1).

$$R_S = \frac{1}{G_S}; \quad R_C = \frac{1}{G_C}. \tag{3.1}$$

The difference between the two rates, Rd, can then be calculated as:

$$R_D = R_S - R_C. \tag{3.2}$$

The network congestion level, C_L, can subsequently be calculated as:

$$C_L = \frac{R_D}{R_S}, \tag{3.3}$$

$$C_L = 1 - \frac{G_S}{G_C}. \tag{3.4}$$

Finally, δC_L is also calculated as simply the difference between the present and previous value of C_L.

3.3.2 Fuzzy Logic Controller

The input variables were fuzzified by means of triangular-shaped membership functions, being the usual compromise between reduced computation time at the expense of a sharper transition from one state to another. Choosing the number of membership functions is important, since it determines the smoothness of the bit rate granularity. However, the number of membership functions is directly proportional to the computation time. The congestion level, the rate at which it changes and the control signals of the sample set were each partitioned into nine triangular membership functions.

Table 3.1 defines the linguistic variables for inputs C_L and δC_L. The defuzzified output has the same linguistic variables as δC_L in Table 3.2, but abbreviated with a prefix of S, e.g., SZ (zero). All the inference rules of a complete set used in simulations for a fixed Internet are given in Table 3.2.

The centre of gravity method was used for defuzzification [24]. From Table 3.2, a typical number of rules is 45 (total number of outputs). A few different rules map to the same outputs. The control signal resulting from defuzzification, CT, is normalized to the range (0, 1], subject to a minimum lower bound. For input bit rate R_{in}, the target output bit rate is $Rout = CT.Rin$ through multiplication. In steady state, to achieve sending rate $Rout$, the quantization scale of the transcoder is directly proportional to CT and the dynamic range of available quantizers. In order to

Table 3.1 Fuzzy logic control (FLC) linguistic variables for C_L and δC_L

C_L		δC_L	
Value	Meaning	Value	Meaning
CL	Low	NVH	Negative very high
CM	Medium	NH	Negative high
CH	High	NM	Negative medium
CVH	Very high	NL	Negative low
CEH	Extremely high	Z	Zero
		PL	Positive low
		PM	Positive medium
		PH	Positive high
		PVH	Positive very high

Table 3.2 FLC inference rules

$\delta C_L/C_L$	CL	CH	CH	CVH	CEH
NVH	SPH	SPM	SPL	SZ	SNL
NH	SPM	SPL	SZ	SNL	SNM
NM	SPL	SZ	SZ	SNM	SNM
NL	SPL	SZ	SNL	SNM	SNH
Z	SZ	SNL	SNM	SNH	SNH
PL	SNL	SNL	SNM	SNH	SNH
PM	SNL	SNM	SNH	SNH	SNVH
PH	SNM	SNH	SNH	SNVH	SNVH
PVH	SNM	SNH	SNVH	SNVH	SNVH

manage the combined transcoder and target decoder buffer occupancy [25] without increasing delay, a correction factor is applied in a picture dependent manner. As *CT* equates to α in Algorithm A of [26], the interested reader is referred to that paper for further details.

3.3.3   Testing FLC on a Fixed Network

The algorithm was simulated with the well-known ns-2 network simulator (v. 2.31 used). The simulated network, with a typical "dumbbell" topology, Fig. 3.2, had a tight link between two routers and all side link bandwidths were provisioned such that congestion would only occur at the tight link. A tight link is the link that instantaneously represents the link with minimum available bandwidth on a network path. In Fig. 3.2, the tight link's total bandwidth capacity can also be altered. The one-way delay of the tight link was set to 5 ms and the side links' delays were set to 1 ms. The tight link's queueing policy was defaulted to be drop-tail or FIFO and the queue

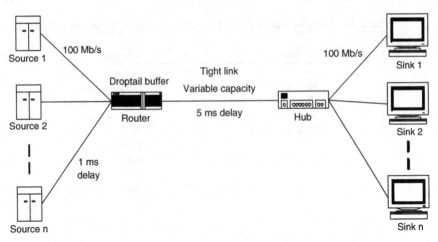

Fig. 3.2 Simulated network topology

size was set to twice the bandwidth-delay product, as is normal in such experiments to avoid packet losses from too small a buffer. An MPEG-2 encoded video "news clip" with GOP size of 12 pictures was selected as a generic input to the simulations. In live tests of 4,000 video clips [25], over 50% of clips were less than 200 s with a median of 180 s. Consequently, though the chosen news clip had a duration of 40 s, it was preferable for the experiments than a still shorter standard clip so as to provide information about the behaviour across more frames. The newsclip shows a newsreader against a moving backdrop, with moderate motion and by implication with moderate encoding complexity.

3.3.4 Calibration Experiments

Figures 3.3a, b illustrate a set of calibration experiments: simulating streaming of the MPEG-2 "news clip" encoded at a VBR with an average bit rate of 2.7 Mb/s against a constant bit rate (CBR) background cross traffic, with packet size 700 B. The bottleneck link was set to 2 Mb/s and then 3 Mb/s., which are typical of constrictions at the core network boundary before entering an edge local area network (LAN). The goal of the controller is to detect the available channel rate and make this the target bit rate of the video transcoder. The results in Fig. 3.3 show that the FLC clearly detects and adapts to the available network bandwidth. For example, in Fig. 3.3a for a 2 Mb/s capacity link, the average background traffic is initially 1.5 Mb/s and the FLC sending rate is at the 0.5 Mb/s level and when the average CBR rate steps down to 0.5 Mb/s, the FLC stream is at the 1.5 Mb/s level. The FLC rate retains some of the inherent "burstiness" in the instantaneous rate of the news

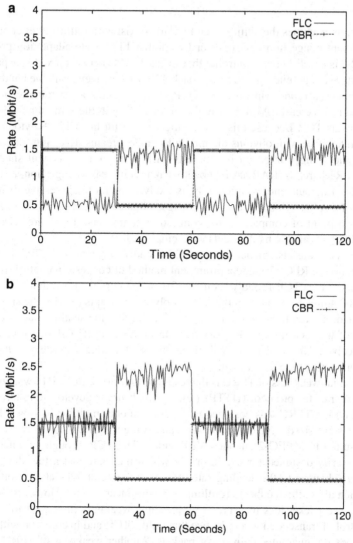

Fig. 3.3 FLC instantaneous sending rate of an MPEG-2 video stream in the presence of step-wise varying Constant Bit Rate cross traffic for a (**a**) 2.0 Mb/s and (**b**) 3.0 Mb/s bottleneck

clip, especially when a scene contains motion. Without adequate buffering, the FLC (or CBR) traffic may suffer packet loss. However, the intention of this set of experiments was primarily to demonstrate the ability to track the changing available bandwidth.

3.3.5 Comparison with Traditional Congestion Controllers

This Section examines the ability of an FLC to coexist with traffic either controlled by a different congestion controller or by another FLC. Rate adaptation protocol (RAP) [27] is a well-known controller that varies the IPG between fixed-size packets to allow its average sending rate to approach TCP's for a given available bandwidth. Every smoothed round trip time (RTT), RAP implements an arithmetic increase multiplicative decrease (AIMD)-like algorithm [28] with the same thresholds and increments as TCP. Because this would otherwise result in TCP's "sawtooth"-like sending rate curve with obvious disruption to video streams, RAP introduces fine-grained smoothing (turned on in our tests), which takes into account short- and long-term RTT trends. RAP has a known weakness in heavy congestion, as it does not employ timeouts and, consequently, is likely to be more aggressive than TCP. Because of its pioneering role and its close resemblance to TCP, RAP has frequently served as a point of comparison for congestion controllers. To ensure fairness to RAP, publicly-available ns-2 models were employed.

Comparison was also made with the TCP-friendly rate control (TFRC) protocol, the subject of an RFC [29] and a prominent method of congestion control from the originators of the "TCP-friendly" concept. To ensure fairness, the publicly available TFRC ns-2 simulator model (in the form of object tcl scripts to drive the simulator) was availed of from http://www.icir.org/tfrc/. In TFRC, the sending rate is made a function of the measured packet loss rate during a single RTT duration measured at the receiver. The sender then calculates the sending rate according to the TCP throughput equation given in [30].

A potential weakness of TFRC is the response to short-term TCP flows, typically hyper text transfer protocol (HTTP) traffic, which never develop long-term TCP flow behaviour. TFRC was designed to produce smooth multimedia flows, but assumes constant-sized large (or maximum transport unit (MTU)) packet sizes, which are not suited to MPEG-2 encoded VBR video. The TCP throughput equation is not necessarily designed for conditions in which there are just a few flows. This is because changes to the sending rate may alter the conditions at the bottleneck link, which affect the feedback, resulting in a non-linear system. However, TFRC's reliance on a packet loss measure is its principle weakness in respect to congestion control of transcoded video. Notice that unlike TCP, and in common with FLC, TFRC does *not* guarantee delivery of packets. Another weakness of TFRC is that rate change decisions are made every RTT. It appears that less frequent decisions would lead to a tendency for a TFRC controlled flow to dominate the bandwidth across a tight link [31]. Unfortunately, too frequent rate changes, as remarked earlier, can have a disturbing subjective effect upon the viewer of decoded video.

In intra-protocol fairness tests, a number of flows were simultaneously streamed over the shared tight link. The simulator was unable to set the feedback at exactly the same time for all the controllers and, therefore, as for live Internet sources, the output is not identical, even though the congestion controllers are. Figure 3.4 records the intra-protocol allocation of bandwidth for the three congestion controllers for a 2.0 Mb/s bottleneck over 120 s. Visual inspection indicates that the FLC flow is

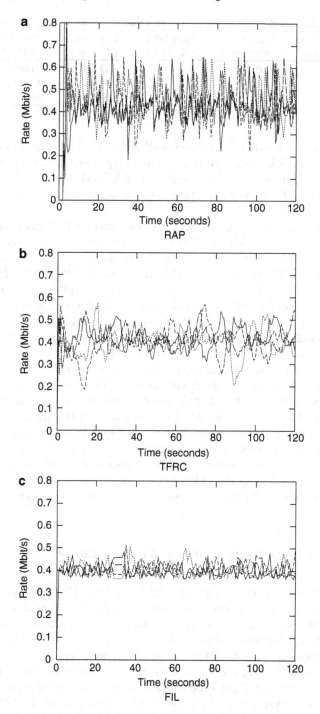

Fig. 3.4 Five simultaneous flows each with identical congestion controllers for a 2 Mb/s bottleneck with (**a**) rate adaptation protocol controllers, (**b**) TCP-friendly rate control (TFRC) controllers, and (**c**) with FLC

Table 3.3 Standard deviations (s.d.'s) for a sample of two flows over a 120 s test

Congestion controller	Bottleneck b/w (Mb/s)	Flow 1 (F1) s.d. (Mb/s)	Flow 2 (F2) s.d. (Mb/s)	Abs(F1–F2) s.d. (Mb/s)
TFRC	2.0	0.44849	0.63709	0.18860
RAP	2.0	1.35377	0.99761	0.37616
FLC	2.0	0.27979	0.28815	0.00836

certainly smoother than RAP and often smoother than TFRC, as is also shown quantitatively in Table 3.3. Though all flows, for each type of controller, cluster around the correct level, given the available bandwidth, RAP is visibly more "bursty" in its response. The RAP plot includes a large initial sending rate, which was discarded in subsequent analysis.

The issue is less easy to resolve between TFRC and the FLC and to do so standard deviations (s.d.'s) were taken. Table 3.3 tabulates the s.d.'s for a sample of two flows (the other flows were similar) taken at random from the five, for each of the congestion controllers in Fig. 3.4 (with bit rate around 0.4 Mb/s for the 2 Mb/s bottleneck). The FLC's s.d.'s are less than those of TFRC (and RAP), showing that in these circumstances the FLC's output is smoother. Moreover, there is more consistency in the FLC's behaviour for tight bottlenecks, as the absolute difference column in Table 3.3 indicates. It should be remarked that for less constricted bottlenecks, TFRC fares better in respect to smoothness, but these situations are not so critical.

Turning to inter-protocol allocation of bandwidth, when multiple flows compete, Fig. 3.5, then the average bandwidth of the TFRC flows is always above that of the FLC flows and above the ideal or equally-shared bottleneck bandwidth. This behaviour of TFRC, when exposed to a tight link without TCP traffic, would work to the disadvantage of other traffic. In fact, converged IP networks are just such networks, as these networks are under construction with multimedia traffic in mind [32]. If replicated in such a network, it is also likely that this behaviour would result in increased packet loss for the TFRC flows. It is postulated that the cause is oversensitivity on the part of TFRC's response to variation in packet loss and RTT.

3.4 Fuzzy Logic Control on the Wireless Internet

This Section considers using Bluetooth (IEEE 802.15.1) [33] for video streaming across an access network. Though Bluetooth was originally conceived as a Personal Area Network with a role in cable replacement, its centralized control means that it is potentially suitable for real-time applications such as video streaming. The master node responsible for scheduling acts as a wireless access point, connecting to the fixed Internet. Consequently, Bluetooth can act as an access network in wireless hot-spots such as at airports and on trains or coaches. The Enhanced Data Rate (EDR) of Bluetooth version 2.1 [34] now has a peak user payload of 2.2 Mb/s (gross air rate 3.0 Mb/s), which is the same average rate offered by some implementations

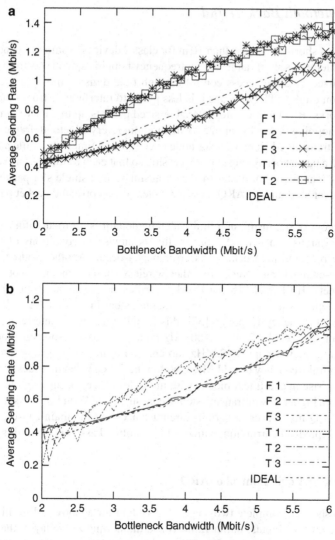

Fig. 3.5 Multiple competing flows with different controllers across a range of bottlenecks, compared to an ideal per-flow allocation of bandwidth (**a**) 3 FLC and 2 TFRC flows (**b**) 3 FLC and 3 TFRC flows

of IP-TV. Compared to IEEE 802.11 (Wi-Fi)'s [35] typical current usage of 100–350 mA, Bluetooth's consumption is 1–35 mA, implying that for mobile multimedia applications with higher bandwidth capacity requirements, Bluetooth is a preferred solution. Many cellular phones are also equipped with a Bluetooth transceiver and larger resolution screens of CIF (352×288) and QCIF (176×144) pixel size. Consequently, Bluetooth is part of the "Bluephone" solution to connectivity, whereby a user may wander seamlessly between a home access network and a telephony network [36].

3.4.1 Bluetooth Background

Bluetooth is a short-range (less than 10 m for class 2 devices), radio frequency interconnect. Bluetooth's short range, robust frequency hopping spread spectrum (FHSS)
and centralized medium access control through time division multiple access and
time division duplex (TDD) means it is less prone to interference from other Bluetooth networks. Bluetooth employs variable-sized packets up to a maximum of five
frequency-hopping time-slots of 625 μs in duration. Every Bluetooth frame consists
of a packet transmitted from a sender node over 1, 3 or 5 timeslots, while a receiver
replies with a packet occupying at least one slot, so that each frame has an even number of slots. Therefore, in master to slave transmission, a single slot packet serves
for a link layer stop-and-go ARQ message, whenever a corrupted packet payload is
detected.

The timeout or retransmission limit value by default is set to an infinite number
of retransmissions. On general grounds, this is unwise in conditions of fast fading caused by multi-path echoes, as error bursts occur. Another source of error
bursts is co-channel interference by other wireless sources, including other Bluetooth piconets, IEEE 802.11b,g networks, cordless phones, and even microwave
ovens. Though this has been alleviated to some extent in version 1.2 of Bluetooth
by Adaptive Frequency Hopping [37], this is only effective if interference is not
across all or most of the 2.402–2.480 GHz unlicensed band. However, both IEEE
802.11b and g may occupy a 22 MHz sub-channel (with 30 dB energy attenuation
over the central frequency at ±11 MHz) within the 2.4 GHz band. Issues of interference might arise in apartment blocks with multiple sources occupying the 2.4 GHz
band or when higher-power transmission occurs such as at WiFi hot-spots. For Bluetooth, an ARQ may occur in various circumstances but the main cause of packet
error [38] is payload corruption, which is the simplified assumption of this work.

3.4.1.1 Fuzzy Logic Control of ARQ

Figure 3.6 shows a complete two-stage FLC system for adaptive ARQ. In the first
stage, there are two inputs: buffer fullness and the normalized delay of the head of
the queue packet. Bluetooth buffer fullness is a preferable measure (compared to
delay or packet loss) of channel conditions and of buffer congestion, as was established in [39]. Buffer fullness is available to an application via the host controller
interface (HCI) presented by a Bluetooth hardware module to the upper layer software protocol stack. As an FLC input, buffer fullness is normalized to the size of
the send buffer. The retransmission count of the packet at the head of the Bluetooth
send queue will affect the delay of packets still to be transmitted. Retransmissions
not only overcome the effect of noise and interference, but also cause the send buffer
queue to grow, with the possibility of packet loss from send buffer overflow, which
is why it is necessary to also introduce an active buffer, as discussed in the next
Section. The second FLC input modulates the buffer fullness input by the already
experienced delay of the head of queue packet.

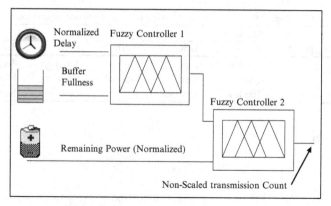

Fig. 3.6 Overview of the FLC of ARQ system

Table 3.4 FLC stage 1 If...then rules used to identify output fuzzy subsets from inputs

| | Delay/Deadline | | | | |
Buffer fullness	Too low	Low	Normal	High	Too high
High	Normal	Normal	Low	Too low	Too low
Normal	Too high	High	Normal	Low	Too low
Low	Too high	Too high	High	Low	Too low

The output of the first stage FLC forms the input to the second stage FLC. Though it might be possible to modify the first stage output by non-fuzzy logic means, the arrangement adopted neatly provides for an all FLC solution. The other input to the second stage is normalized remaining power, assuming a predetermined power budget for streaming of a particular video clip, which diminishes with time and retransmissions. The output of the second stage is a transmission count, which is subsequently scaled according to picture type importance. In other words, reference picture packets are allocated a greater allocation of power and of the reference frame packets I-frame packets are favoured over P-frame packets.

It is important to note that any packet in the send buffer is discarded if its deadline has expired. However, this takes place after fuzzy evaluation of the desired ARQ retransmission count. In practice, the inputs to the FLC were sampled versions of buffer fullness and packet delay deadline, to avoid excessive ARQ retransmission count oscillations. The sampling interval was every 20 packets. Table 3.4 shows the "if...then" rules that allow input fuzzy subsets to be combined to form an output from stage one and an input to stage two. Notice more than one rule may apply because of the fuzzy nature of subset membership. The output of stage one is combined with a fuzzy input for "remaining power," and the "if...then" rules resulting in the final non-scaled transmission count are in Table 3.5. Triangular membership functions were employed to model all inputs and outputs.

Table 3.5 FLC stage 2 If...then rules used to identify output fuzzy subsets from inputs

	Output 1				
Remaining power	Too low	Low	Normal	High	Too high
High	Too low	Low	High	Too high	Too high
Normal	Too low	Low	Normal	High	High
Low	Too low	Too low	Low	Low	Normal

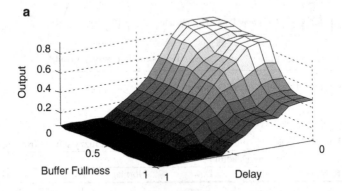

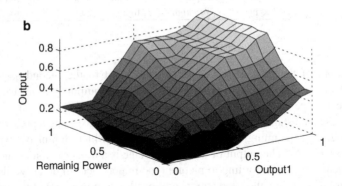

Fig. 3.7 (**a**) Stage 1 FLC control surface resulting from FLC ARQ (**b**) Stage two control surface giving the transmission count output (before subsequent scaling)

The inputs were combined according to the Mamdani model [24] to produce the output values for each stage. The standard centre of gravity method was employed to resolve a crisp output value. The fuzzy control surfaces are represented in Fig. 3.7, as derived from the Matlab Fuzzy Toolbox v. 2.2.4.

Clearly a packet can only be transmitted an integer number of times, but the final crisp output may result in a real-valued number. This difficulty was resolved by generating a random number from a uniform distribution. If the random number was less than the fractional part of the crisp output value, then that value was rounded up to the nearest integer, otherwise it was rounded down. The advantage of the randomization procedure over simple quantization is that, in the long term, the mean value of the output numbers of transmissions will converge more closely to a desired output level.

The crisp output after defuzzification of the FLC is scaled according to picture type. A simple scaling of 5:3:2 was applied respectively for I-, P-, B-pictures, given up to five maximum transmissions. (B-pictures are bi-predicted but themselves have no predictive role). For example, if the crisp output value was 0.7 and a P-picture packet was involved then the value after scaling is $0.7 \times 3.0 = 2.10$. Then, the random number-based resolution results in three transmissions, if the random number is less than or equal to 0.10 and two transmissions otherwise. It should be mentioned that a maximum value of five retransmissions was also adopted in the priority queueing tests in [40], albeit for an IEEE 802.11 wireless network.

3.4.2   Testing FLC on a Wireless Network

3.4.2.1   Buffer Specification

An important but sometimes neglected aspect of simulating a wireless link when multimedia is involved is the specification of the buffer. ARQ adds to delay and, therefore, the number of retransmissions should be minimized. To reduce the number of retransmissions, an active buffer or deadline-aware buffer (DAB) is possible. In a conservative send buffer discard policy, all packets of whatever picture type have a display deadline, which is the size of the playout buffer expressed as a time beyond which buffer underflow will occur. In a conservative policy, the deadline is set as the maximum time that the playout buffer can delay the need for a packet. In simulations, the display deadline was set to 0.10 s. In addition to the display deadline, all I-picture packets have a decode deadline, which is the display time remaining to the end of the GOP. For a 12-picture GOP, this is the time to display 11 frames, i.e., 0.44 s at 25 frame/s. For P-picture packets, the decode deadline will vary depending on the number of frames to the end of the GOP. For B-pictures, the decode deadline is set to zero (as B-pictures have no value to the decoding of future frames). The decode deadline is added to the display deadline and a packet is discarded from the send buffer after its total deadline expires.

3.4.2.2   Channel Specification

Unlike a fixed network, for which optical transmission at the Internet core makes channel errors very unlikely, the wireless channel characteristics are important, as errors are very likely to be introduced from various sources of noise and interference. A Gilbert-Elliott [41, 42] two state discrete-time, ergodic Markov chain is a standard model for the wireless channel error characteristics between a Bluetooth master and slave node. By adopting this model, it is possible to simulate burst errors of the kind that cause problems to an ARQ mechanism.

The mean duration of a good state, T_g, was set at 2 s and in a bad state, T_b was set to 0.25 s. In units of 625 μs (the Bluetooth time slot duration), $T_g = 3,200$ and $T_b = 400$, which implies from:

$$T_g = \frac{1}{1 - Pgg}, \qquad T_b = \frac{1}{1 - Pbb} \tag{3.5}$$

that, given the current state is good (g), Pgg, the probability that the next state is also g, is 0.9996875 and Pbb, and given the current state is bad (b), the probability that the next state is also b, is 0.9975. At 3.0 Mb/s, the BER during a good state was set to $a \times 10^{-5}$ and during a bad state to $a \times 10^{-4}$, where a is a scaling factor (of course, not the fuzzy output scaling factor) and is subsequently referred to as the channel parameter.

3.4.2.3 Simulations

The same "news clip," as was used for the fixed network, was employed in tests for the wireless access network. For these tests, the clip was encoded at a mean rate of 1.5 Mb/s. However, the packetization policy differed from the one slice per packet policy for the fixed network discussed previously in this chapter. In [43], fully filled Bluetooth packets were formed using maximal bandwidth five time-slot packets, regardless of slice boundaries. These packets carry a 1,021 B payload. While this results in some loss in error resilience (and added latency), as each MPEG-2 slice contains a decoder synchronization marker, in [43] it is shown that the overall de-livered video quality is superior to choice of smaller packet sizes.

Figure 3.8 shows the output of stage 1 of the FLC as the video clip was passed across a Bluetooth link with channel parameter a set to two. The high variability of the output is due to the repeated onset of bad states occasioned by the Gilbert-Elliott channel model.

The normalized power budget for the clip declines with the number of bits passed across the link and the loss is exacerbated by repeated retransmissions during bad states. As the power budget changes linearly, this has the effect of modulating the original input, as illustrated by Fig. 3.9 for the output of FLC stage 2, again with channel parameter set to two. As the power budget varies linearly over time, the envelope of the output from stage 2 also varies in a linear fashion over time. This is as required because as the sending device's power budget declines it must reduce the number of retransmissions in order to reduce its power usage.

After the removal of deadline expired packets, through operation of the DAB, the buffer fullness input to stage one of the send buffer oscillates around a level well-below the 50 packet maximum. Consequently, head-of-line packet delay acts as a typical trimming input to the FLC stage one unit, as its pattern resembles that of buffer fullness over time.

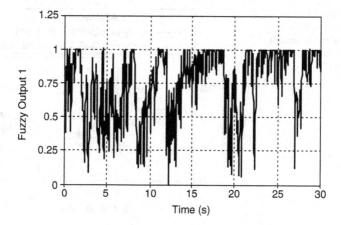

Fig. 3.8 Output from stage one of the FLC, with $a = 2$

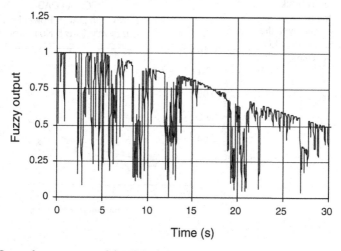

Fig. 3.9 Output from stage two of the FLC, with $a = 2$

3.4.2.4 Comparison with Default ARQ

A comparison was made between the default Bluetooth scheme of infinite ARQ and no power control with the FLC scheme with power control. That is the default scheme was allocated an infinite power budget. For fairness both schemes were compared with a DAB in place, though, of course, a DAB is not a feature of the Bluetooth standard. The channel parameter, a, was varied in the tests to show the impact of differing channel conditions. As an aid to comparison, the FLC scheme was also tested with an infinite power budget.

Figure 3.10 compares the ratio of packets lost to total packets arriving in the send buffer. Even though the FLC scheme is compensating for a diminishing power

Fig. 3.10 Packet loss during transmission of the News video clip, with the default scheme and the FLC power-aware scheme

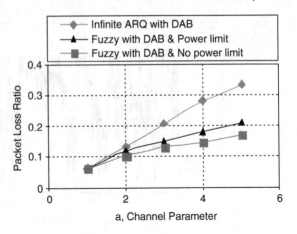

Fig. 3.11 Average packet delay during transmission of the News video clip, with the default scheme and the FLC power-aware scheme

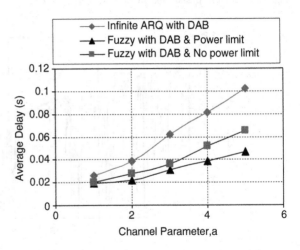

budget, it shows a clear superiority. The effect is more pronounced with worsening channel conditions. The average delay of successfully transmitted packets was also considerably reduced under the FLC scheme, Fig. 3.11, while the default ARQ scheme results in a more rapid climb to its peak average value. Larger average delay will impact start-up time in one-way streaming and add to overall delay in a two-way interactive video exchange, such as for a videophone connection. Notice that removing the power budget results in more delay for the FLC scheme than with a power budget because the scheme is not handicapped by the need to reduce transmissions for power budget considerations. Either way the scheme is superior to default ARQ in delay (and also in reduced packet loss). Crucially, the FLC is able to save power over the non-power-aware default ARQ scheme, Fig. 3.12. The impact is clearly greater as channel conditions worsen.

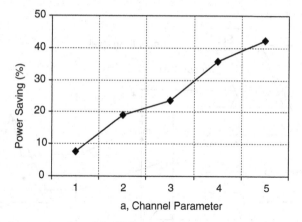

Fig. 3.12 Relative power saving of the FLC power-aware ARQ scheme compared to that of the default ARQ scheme

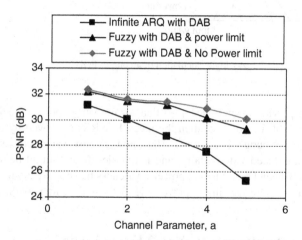

Fig. 3.13 Comparison of PSNR for the News video clip between the Bluetooth default and FLC ARQ schemes with DAB

Video quality is objectively measured by the peak signal-to-noise ratio (PSNR), which has logarithmic units of measurement, the decibel (dB). Provided PSNR comparisons are made across the same video [2], PSNR is a reliable measure of video quality, though other subjective effects also have a role. Considering the packet loss statistics of Fig. 3.10, it is not surprising, Fig. 3.13, that the mean PSNR of FLC ARQ is better than that of the default scheme and the relative advantage becomes more so as the channel conditions worsen. A significant part of that advantage is also due to the superiority of FLC ARQ and there is little difference between FLC ARQ with and without a power budget in better channel conditions. Notice that for power-aware control, averaged PSNR figures do not "show the whole story," as the achievable PSNR will deteriorate over time as the available power reduces.

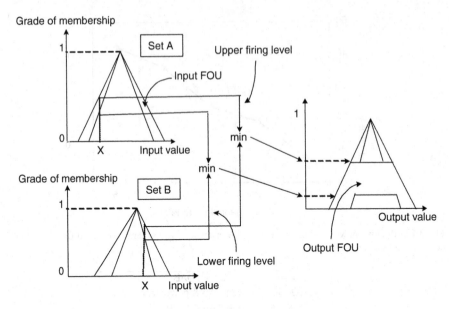

Fig. 3.14 Interval type-2 fuzzy logic calculation of an output FOU

This confirms previous experience [44] that for the very worst channel conditions shown in Fig. 3.14, i.e., $a = 5$, then the mean PSNR is improved by around 3 dB if an infinite power budget is assumed. Thus, power conservation comes at a cost to the receiver in reduced video quality and is a trade-off that might be open to user configuration. The end result is that power-awareness has been realistically factored in, resulting in over 40% saving in power, Fig. 3.12, in the same conditions.

3.5 Future Development: Type-2 Fuzzy Logic

A traditional, type-1 FLC is not completely fuzzy, as the boundaries of its membership functions are fixed. This implies that there may be unforeseen traffic scenarios for which the existing membership functions do not suffice to model the uncertainties in the video stream congestion control task. An interval type-2 FLC can address this problem by extending a footprint-of-uncertainty (FOU) on either side of an existing type-1or traditional membership function. In interval type-2 fuzzy logic, the variation is assumed to be constant across the FOU, and hence, the designation "interval."

Consider two type-2 sets A and B, then strictly an infinite number of membership functions (not all necessarily triangular) can exist within the FOUs of sets A and B. However, interval type-2 sets allow the upper and outer firing levels to be taken rather than the complete range of firing levels, as shown in Fig. 3.14. The minimum operator (min) acts as a t-norm on the upper and lower firing levels to produce a firing interval. The firing interval serves to bound the FOU in the output triangular membership function shown to the right in Fig. 3.14. The lower trapezium outlines the FOU, which itself consists of an inner trapezoidal region that is fixed in extent. The minimum operator, used by us as a t-norm, has the advantage that its implementation cost is less than a product t-norm. (A t-norm or triangular norm is a generalization of the intersection operation in classical logic.) Once the FOU firing interval is established, Centre-of-Sets type reduction was applied by means of the Karnik-Mendel algorithm, which is summarized in [21]. Type reduction involves mapping the interval output set to a type-1 set. In practice, defuzzification of this type-1 output fuzzy set simply consists of averaging maximum and minimum values. The result of defuzzification is a crisp value that determines the change in the video rate.

Results adapting an FLC for congestion control over the fixed Internet have been encouraging [45]. For example in Fig. 3.15, (a) News and (b) Football VBR sources

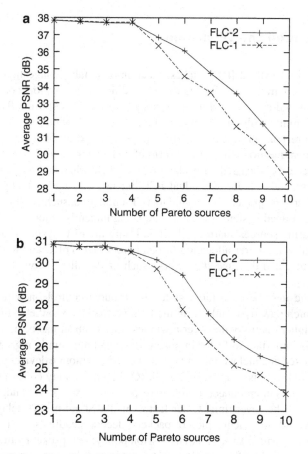

Fig. 3.15 Interval type-2 and type-1 FLCC showing resulting PSNR when tracking against an increasing number of Pareto sources for (**a**) news and (**b**) football video clips

are controlled against the same cross-traffic on the tight link of a dumbbell topology network. "Football" is a video clip with the same encoding characteristics as the News clip employed elsewhere in this chapter, with a mean rate of 1 Mbit/s. Where it differs is that there is considerable motion within the video sequence, increasing the encoded bitstream's complexity owing to motion estimation and compensation. A number of long-tailed, Pareto probability distribution function (pdf) with shape factor of 1.3 sources were configured. The heavy-tailed nature of Internet file sizes and the synchronization of TCP connections are two factors that give rise to this type of traffic source on the Internet. Each 500 kbit/s source was set with 500 ms for both idle and burst time. The resulting video quality varied from moderately good to weak as the number of sources sharing the tight link increased. For "Football," at lower background traffic intensities, the type-1 FLC at a few data points gave a little better quality owing to the pattern of losses' impact on the compressed stream. However, as the number of cross-traffic sources increased, the relative gain from interval type-2 FLC became apparent.

3.6 Conclusion and Discussion

The anticipated growth of IPTV makes selection of suitable congestion controllers for video stream traffic of vital concern. Traditional congestion controllers are strongly motivated by the need to avoid congestion collapse on the fixed Internet and, as such, mimic with UDP transport the average throughput behaviour of TCP, which is still responsible for transport of the great majority of fixed Internet traffic. It is an open question whether this form of congestion control is suited to video streaming because of the need for packet loss feedback, when no loss is preferred for video transport, and because of residual TCP-like rate fluctuations that persist when these controllers are applied. Compared to TCP-emulators, such as TFRC and RAP, a fuzzy logic trained system's sending rate is significantly smoother when multiple video-bearing sources share a tight link. Using the FLC system in this chapter similarly results in a fairer allocation of bandwidth than TFRC and RAP. It is also more suited to video dominated networks such as the all-IP networks now being constructed.

Fuzzy logic may be even more suited to resource control on wireless access networks, which now frequently form the final network hop to the end user. Transmission of higher quality video over a wireless interconnect has been long sought. However, it is important to factor in power usage and not simply regard a wireless channel as a fixed channel with the addition of errors, as mobile devices are typically battery powered. In this chapter, FLC of ARQ (in a case study concerned with the Bluetooth wireless interconnect) is able to respond to a fixed power budget that subsequently diminishes over time. Other factors included are packet delay deadlines (both display and, for anchor picture packets, decode deadlines) and send buffer congestion. FLC, which varies its transmission policy with packet picture type, still outperforms a default fully-reliable ARQ scheme, resulting in superior delivered video quality and reduced delay.

One problem with FLC has always been that compared to mathematically based analytic methods, it has always been possible to object that the response to unmodeled network states is difficult to predict. However, type-2 logic can now model uncertainty in network conditions to a still greater extent, and therefore, should increasingly find applications in video streaming over fixed and wireless networks.

Acknowledgments The authors gratefully acknowledge assistance from C. Wagner and H. Hagras in applying interval-type 2 fuzzy logic to an original type-1 controller.

This work was supported by the EPSRC, UK under grant no. EP/C538692/1.

References

1. Hagras, H.: Type-2 FLCs: A new generation of fuzzy controllers. IEEE Comput. Intell. **2(1)**, 30–43 (2007)
2. Ghanbari, M.: Standard codecs: Image compression to advanced video coding. The Institute of Electrical Engineering Press, London, (2003)
3. Jammeh, E., Fleury, M., Ghanbari, M.: Fuzzy logic congestion control of transcoded video streaming without packet loss feedback. IEEE Trans. Circuits Syst. Video Technol. **18(3)**, 387–393 (2008)
4. Assunção, A. A., Ghanbari, M.: A frequency domain video transcoder for dynamic bit-rate reduction of MPEG-2 bit streams. IEEE Trans. Circuits Syst. Video Technol. **8(8)**, 953–967 (1998)
5. Razavi, R., Fleury, M., Ghanbari, M.: Power-constrained fuzzy logic control of video streaming over a wireless interconnect. EURASIP J. Adv. Signal Process. 14 (2008). Available online at http://www.hindawi.com/journals/asp/2008/560749.html
6. Kalman, M., Ramanathan, P., Girod, B.: Rate-distortion optimized video streaming with multiple deadlines. Int. Conf. on Image Processing, 662–664, Singapore, Sept. (2003)
7. Baturone, I., Barriga, A., Sánchez-Solano, S., Jiménez, C., López, C.: Microelectronic design of fuzzy logic-based systems. CRC Press, Baton Rouge, FO, (2000)
8. Pitsillides A., Sekercioglu, A.: Congestion control. In W. Pedrycz and A. Vasiliakos, (eds.) Computational Intelligence in Telecommunications Networks, CRC Press, Boca Raton, FL, pp. 109–158 (2000)
9. Ghosh, S., Razouki, Q., Schumacher, H. J., Celmins, A.: A survey of recent advances in fuzzy logic in telecommunications networks and new challenges. IEEE Trans. Fuzzy Syst. **6(3)**, 443–447 (1998)
10. Şekercioglu, A., Pitsillides, A., Vasilakos, A.: Computional intelligence in management of ATM networks: A survey of current state of research. Soft Comput. J. **5(4)**, 257–263 (2001)
11. Liang, Q., Karnik, N., Mendel, J. M.: Connection admission control in ATM networks using survey-based type-2 fuzzy logic system. IEEE Trans. Syst. Man Cybern. C Appl. Rev. **30(3)**, 329–339 (2000)
12. Kazemian, H. B., Meng, L.: An adaptive control for video transmission over Bluetooth. IEEE Trans. Fuzzy Syst. **14(2)**, 263–274 (2006)
13. Rossides, L., Chrysostemou, C., Pitsillides, A., Şekercioglu, A.: Overview of Fuzzy-RED in Diff-Serv networks. Soft-Ware 2002, 2–14, Coleraine, April (2002)
14. Wang, X., D. Ye, D., Wu, Q.: Using fuzzy logic controller to implement scalable quality adaptation for stored video in DiffServ networks. 12th Int. PacketVideo workshop. Pittsburgh, PA, April (2002)
15. Leone, A., Bellini, A., Guerrieri, R.: An H.261 fuzzy-controlled coder for videophone se quences. IEEE World Conference on Computational Intelligence, 244–248 June (1994)

16. Grant, P. M., Saw, Y.-S., Hannah., J. M.: Fuzzy rule based MPEG video rate prediction and control. Eurasip ECASP Conference, 211–214 (1997)
17. Liang, Q., Mendel, J. M.: MPEG VBR video traffic modeling and classification using fuzzy techniques. IEEE Trans. Fuzzy Syst. **9(1)**, 183–193 (2001)
18. Shu, H., Liang, Q., Gao, J.: Wireless sensor network lifetime analysis using interval type-2 fuzzy logic systems. IEEE Trans. Fuzzy Syst. **16(2)**, 416–427 (2008)
19. Liang, Q., Mendel, J. M.: Equalization of time-varying nonlinear channels using type-2 fuzzy adaptive filters. IEEE Trans. Fuzzy Syst. **8(5)**, 551–563 (2000)
20. Zaddeh, L. A.: The concept of linguistic variable and its application to approximate reasoning. Inform. Sci. **8**, 199–249 (1975)
21. Mendel, J. M.: Type-2 fuzzy sets and systems: An overview. IEEE Comput. Intell. **2(1)**, 20–29 (2007)
22. Gorzalczany, M. B.: A method of inference in approximate reasoning based on interval-valued fuzzy sets. Fuzzy Sets and Systems **21**, 1–17 (1987)
23. John, R., Coupland, S.: Type-2 fuzzy logic: A historical view. IEEE Comput. Intell. **2(1)**, 57–62 (2007)
24. Jang, J.-S. R., Sun, C.-T., Mitzutani, E.: Neuro-fuzzy and softcomputing, Prentice Hall, Upper Saddle River, NJ, (1997)
25. Chun, J., Zhu, Y., Claypool, M.: FairPlayer or foulPlayer? – head to head performance of Re-alPlayer streaming video over UDP versus TCP. Worcester Polytechnic Institution, Worcester, MA, Tech. Rep. May (2002)
26. Assunção, P. A. A., Ghanbari, M.: Buffer analysis and control in CBR video transcoding. IEEE Trans. Circuits Syst. Video Technol. **10(1)**, 83–92 (2000)
27. Rejaie, R., Handley, M., Estrin, D.: RAP: An end-to-end rate-based congestion control mechanism for realtime streams in the Internet. IEEE INFOCOM, 1337–1345, New York, Mar. (1999)
28. Cai, L., Shen, X., Pan, J., Mark, J. W.: Performance analysis of TCP-friendly AIMD algorithms for multimedia applications. IEEE Trans. Multimed. **7(2)**, 339–335 (2005)
29. Handley, M., Floyd, S., Padyhe, S. J., Widmer, J.: TCP friendly rate control (TFRC): Protocol specification. IETF RFC 3448 (2003). Available online at http://www.ietf.org/rfc/rfc3448.txt
30. Padyhe, J., Firoiu, V., Towsley, D., Krusoe, J.: Modeling TCP throughput: A simple model and its empirical validation, ACM SIGCOMM'98, 303–314, Vancouver, Sept. (1998)
31. Rhee I., Xu, L.: Limitations of equation-based congestion control. IEEE/ACM Trans. on Networking **15(4)**, 852–865 (2007)
32. Greer, D.: Building converged networks with IMS technology. IEEE Comput. **38(11)**, 14–16 (2005)
33. Haartsen, J.: The Bluetooth radio system. IEEE Personal Comms. **7(1)**, 28–36 (2000)
34. Specification of the Bluetooth System – 2.1 + EDR. Nov. (2007) Available online at http://www.bluetooth.com
35. Ferro E., Potorì, F.: Bluetooth and Wi-Fi wireless protocols: A survey and a comparison. IEEE Wireless Communications **12(1)**, 12–26 (2005)
36. Reeve, M., Bilton, C. E., Holmes, M., Bross, M.: 21CN. IEEE Comms. Eng. Oct. (2005)
37. Golmie, N., Chevrolier, N., Rebala, O.: Bluetooth and WLAN Coexistence: Challenges and solutions. IEEE Wireless Commun. **10(6)**, 22–29 (2003)
38. Valenti, M. C., Robert, M., Reed, J. H.: On the throughput of Bluetooth data transmissions. IEEE Wireless Communication and Networking Conference, 119–123, Orlando, Florida, Mar. (2002)
39. Razavi, R., Fleury, M., Ghanbari, M.: Detecting congestion within a Bluetooth piconet: Video streaming response. London Comms. Symposium, 181–184 Sept. (2006)
40. Li, Q., van der Schaar, M.: Providing QoS to layered video over wireless local area networks through real-time retry limit adaptation. IEEE Trans. on Multimed. **6(2)**, 278–290 (2004)
41. Gilbert, E. N.: Capacity of burst-noise channel. Bell System Technical J. **39**, 1253–1265 (1960)
42. Elliott, E. O.: Estimates of error rates for codes on burst noise channels. Bell System Technical J. **42**, 1977–1997 (1963)

43. Razavi, R., Fleury, M., Ghanbari, M.: An efficient packetization scheme for Bluetooth video transmission. Electron. Lett. **42(20)**, 1143–1145 (2006)
44. Razavi, R., Fleury, M., Ghanbari, M.: Fuzzy control of adaptive timeout for video streaming over a Bluetooth interconnect. 2nd mediaWin Workshop at IEEE 12th Int. Symposium on Computers and Communications, Lisbon, Portugal, July (2007)
45. Jammeh, E. A., Fleury, M., Wagner, C., Hagras, H., Ghanbari, M.: Interval type-2 fuzzy logic congestion control of video streaming. IET Intelligent Environments Conference, Seattle, July (2008)

Chapter 4
Indexing Video Summaries for Quick Video Browsing

Hichem Karray, Mehdi Ellouze, and Adel Alimi

Abstract Multimedia data are used in many fields. The problem is how to manipulate the large quantity of these data. One of the proposed solutions is an intelligent
video summarization system. Summarizing a video consists in providing another
version that contains pertinent and important items. The most popular type of
summary is the pictorial summary. We propose in this chapter to index pictorial summaries in order to accelerate the browsing operation of video archives. The chapter
presents a conception of a digital video archive that offers three access levels making easier the search for video sequences. The first access level offers to the user
a full access for the whole archive. The second access level allows to the user to
browse video archive by consulting video summaries. We contribute by adding a
third access level that accelerates the archive browsing by adding an indexing sub-
system, which operates on video summaries. We propose to index video summaries
to accelerate the research of desired sequences. We treat the case of news broadcast video

Keywords News broadcast · Pictorial summary · Extraction text · Indexation
· Browsing

4.1 Introduction

Video is used in many domains and events. With the evolution of the technology, the
problems of acquisition and storage of video are solved. In fact, digital cameras have
invaded houses and they are equipped with high storage capacity. Besides, personal
video recorder has become popular as a large volume storage device for video/audio
content data.

H. Karray (✉)
Department of Electrical Engineering, REGIM: Research Group on Intelligent Machines,
University of Sfax, ENIS, BP W-3038, Sfax, Tunisia
e-mail: hichem.karray@ieee.org

A.-E. Hassanien et al. (eds.), *Pervasive Computing: Innovations in Intelligent
Multimedia and Applications*, Computer Communications and Networks,
DOI 10.1007/978-1-84882-599-4_4, © Springer-Verlag London Limited 2009

The growth of the quantity of video data has caused a new problem, the problem of browsing these data. The solution is to summarize video and offer it to users interfaces which can help them to browse video archives.

One of the most widespread types of summary is the pictorial summary. This type of summary consists of a set of concatenated pictures extracted from the original video. The pictures included in the summary represent important shots. The shots are selected according to some criteria (color, length, text presence, etc.).

As it is defined in [1], pictorial summaries must respond to three constraints. First, they must respect the video structure and the time order. In fact the viewers must have a clear idea of the whole structure of video.

The viewers must be able to locate persons and events in the right temporal order. Second, pictorial summaries must filter well the video content in order to preserve only pertinent information and to draw the viewer attention to the important topic. Finally, pictorial summaries must be well presented. Indeed, a summary without a good layout cannot be useful and cannot realize the principal goal, which helps users to judge if the video content is interesting or not.

In our work, we will try to generate pictorial summaries and index them in order to accelerate the browsing process. In fact, imagine that we have an archive with thousands of video sequences and we have for each one of them a pictorial summary. It is not practical to browse all the summaries one by one in order to select a video sequence. The problem becomes greater if we use mobile devices that are getting popular, such as mobile phone or PDA (personal, digital assistant). These devices are generally small and it is not practical to browse search archives with them.

The idea is to filter the summaries by identifying the user's needs. In fact, users who are browsing video summaries are searching special topics. The idea is to filter summaries and keep only summaries speaking about this topic.

For this reason, we imagine a digital archive with three access levels. The first access level is the full access level in which the user can consult the full video. The second level is the partial access level in which user can only consult summaries of video sequences. The third level is the quick access level in which user can consult only summaries of video containing desired topics (Fig. 4.1).

The choice of the suitable access level relies on the context. If we need to browse quickly the archive (importance of time parameter), we use the third access level

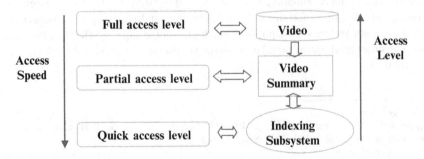

Fig. 4.1 An archive with three access levels

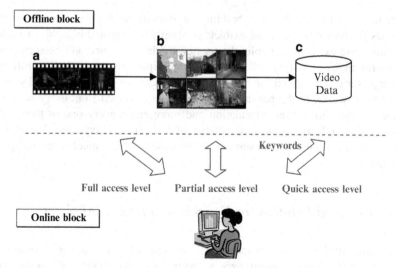

Fig. 4.2 The system overview, (**a**) the original sequence, (**b**) the summary, and (**c**) the indexes extracted from the summary

and if we need to browse the archive with a lot of precision (importance of the data precision parameter), we use the first access level. The choice of the access level relies on time and the precision parameter.

There are three major contributions in this chapter. The first contribution is an intelligent video summarization system in which we integrate low and high level features using genetic algorithms to produce pictorial abstracts. Indeed, there are several advantages of genetic algorithms. They are able to support heterogeneous criteria in the evaluation function and are naturally suited for doing incremental selection, which may be applied to streaming media as video. The second contribution is an intelligent system for extraction text in which a supervised learning method based on color and edge information is used to detect text regions. Thereafter, an unsupervised clustering for text segmentation and binarization is applied using color information. The third contribution is the fact of indexing the summaries to accelerate the browsing operation (Fig. 4.2). We treat the case of news broadcast video.

The rest of the chapter will be organized as follow: we present in Sect. 4.2 the partial access level and our intelligent video summarization system; in Sect. 4.3, firstly we present the quick access level, secondly, our intelligent system for extraction text and thirdly, how we index the summaries to accelerate the browsing operation; in Sect. 4.4, we evaluate our global system and finally, we conclude with direction for future works.

4.2 The Partial Access Level

In the full access level, there is no filtering or restriction. To validate our approach and to show its efficiency, we choose the work on news broadcast. This type of media has received great attention from the research community basically motivated by the interest of broadcasters in building large digital archives of their news programmes in order to reuse some extracts or simply to expose this archive to other companies and the general public. Every news video sequence will be segmented into stories, then every story will be summarized separately by a pictorial abstract.

Every user can watch all the news archive sequentially news sequence by news sequence. However, in the partial access level, we extracted from every news sequence the most important information and represented every one of them by a summary that reflects the general context of the original sequence. We choose to work the pictorial abstract summaries because of their small size and quick browsing.

4.2.1 Classical Solution for Generating Pictorial Abstract

Many solutions have been proposed in the field of video pictorial summary. Taniguchi et al. [2] have summarized video using a 2-D packing of "panoramas" which are large images formed by compositing video pans. In this work, key-frames were extracted from every shot and used for a 2-D representation of the video content. Because frame sizes were not adjusted for better packing, much white space can be seen in the summary results. Besides, no effective filtering mechanism was defined. Uchihachi et al. [3] have proposed to summarize video by a set of key-frames with different sizes.

The selection of key-frames is based on eliminating uninteresting and redundant shots. Selected key-frames are sized according to the importance of the shots from which they were extracted. In this pictorial summary the time order is not conserved due to the arrangement of pictures with different sizes.

Later, Ma et al. [1] have proposed a pictorial summary, called video snapshot. In this approach the summary is evaluated for four criteria. It must be visually pleasurable, representative, informative and distinctive. A weighting scheme is proposed to evaluate every summary. However this approach suggests a real filtering mechanism but uses only low level features (color, saturation, etc). Indeed, no high level objects (text, faces, etc) are used in this mechanism.

It is clear that all the summarization systems do not use high-level features to generate pictorial abstracts. For this reason, our contribution will be to integrate low and high level features to generate pictorial abstracts.

4.2.2 Our Solution

The news programme is a specific type of video. It is usually structured as a collection of reports and items. A story as it was defined by U.S. National Institute of Standards and Technologies (NIST) [4] is a segment of a news broadcast with a coherent news focus, which may include political issues, finance reporting, weather forecast, sports reporting, etc (Fig 4.3). Besides, every report is introduced by an

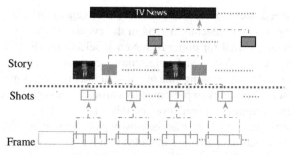

Fig. 4.3 Structure of a news program

anchor person. We adopt in our system this pattern: anchor shot, report, anchor shot, report, etc. We summarized and indexed each report separately because every report is semantically independent of other reports.

4.2.2.1   News Segmentation

Stories segmentation is an essential step in any work done on video news sequences. The story in every news programme is the most important semantic unit. Story segmentation is an active research field with a lot of categories of works. For this reason, we find a special session concerning video stories segmentation in TRECVID campaigns [5] (TREC video retrieval evaluation), which are the most challenging evaluation for video retrieval in the world. However, the majority of proposed works are based on detecting anchor shots. Indeed, the anchor shot is the only repetitive shot in a news programme. The first anchor shot detector dates back to 1995 and it was proposed by Zhang [6]. In these works, the anchor shot detection is based on classifying shots according to anchorperson shot models. The drawback of this method is the fact that it is impossible to define a standard model for all channels. Now, we speak about multimodal anchor shot detection pioneered by Informedia. In this project, Yang et al. [7] propose to use high level information (speech, text transcript and facial information) to classify persons appearing in the news programme into three types: anchor, reporter and person involving in a news event. This method has been proved effective on TRECVID dataset. However, analyzing different video modalities including speech, transcript text, video frames and combining them to extract stories can take a lot of time. In our approach [8], we used our previous work in which news programme is segmented by detecting and classifying faces to find group of anchor shots. It is based on the assumption that the anchors' faces are the only repetitive face throughout the entire programme.

4.2.2.2   Stories Summarization

The major contribution of our summarization process of key frames extraction is the integration of low and high level features in the selection process using genetic algorithms. Indeed, there are several advantages of genetic algorithms. First, they are able to support heterogeneous criteria in the evaluation. Second, genetic algorithms are naturally suited for doing incremental selection, which may be applied to streaming media as video. Genetic algorithms are a part of evolutionary computing [9], which is a rapidly growing area of artificial intelligence. A genetic algorithm begins with a set of solutions (represented by chromosomes) called the population. The best solutions from one population are taken and used to form a new population. This is motivated by a hope that the new population will be better than the old one. In fact, the selection operator is intended to improve the average quality of the population by giving individuals of higher quality a higher probability to be copied into the next generation.

We suggest generating randomly a set of summaries (initial population). Then, we run the genetic algorithm (crossing, mutation, selection, etc.) many times on this population with the hope of ameliorating the quality of summaries population. At every iteration, we evaluating the population through a function called fitness. Evaluating a given summary means evaluate the quality of selected shots. For this reason, we rely on three assumptions. First, long shots are important in news broadcast. Generally the duration of a story is between 3 and 6 min, which is not an important duration. So, the producer of the news programme must attribute to every shot the suitable duration. These long shots are certainly important and contain important information. Secondly, shots containing text are also crucial because text is an informative object. It is often embedded in news video and contains useful data for content description. For broadcast news video, text information may come in the format of caption text at the bottom of video frames. It is used to introduce the stories (War in Iraqand Darfour conflict) or to present a celebrity or an interviewed person (Kofi Anan, chicken traderand Microsoft CEO). Finally, to insure a maximum of color variability and a maximum of color coverage, the selected shots must be different in color space.

Number of Key Frames

The number of selected shots is computed through a rate called summary rate. If we raise the summary rate, the number of selected shots will be greater, then the summary size will be larger and so the browsing speed will decrease. The number of selected shots is computed as follows:

$$N_s = N * R \qquad (4.1)$$

For example, if the summary rate is 20% and the story is composed of 15 shots, then the number of selected shots will be equal to three shots.

Binary Encoding

We have chosen to encode our chromosomes (summaries) with binary encoding because of its popularity and relative simplicity. In binary encoding, every

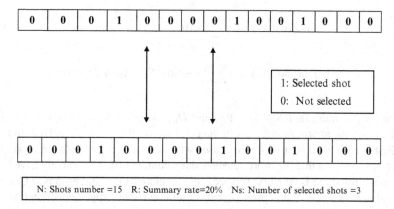

Fig. 4.4 Binary encoding of the genetic algorithm. The shots which are present in the summary are encoded by 1. The remaining shots are encoded by 0

chromosome is a string of bits (0, 1). In our genetic solution, the bits of a given chromosome are the shots of the story. We use 1's to denote selected shots (Fig. 4.4).

Evaluation Function

Let PS be a pictorial summary composed of m selected shots. PS $= \{S_i, 1 \leq i \leq m\}$. We evaluate the chromosome C representing this summary as follows:

$$f(C) = \frac{\text{AvgHist}(C) + \text{AvgText}(C) + \text{AvgDuration}(C)}{3} \qquad (4.2)$$

AvgHist(C) is the average color distance between selected shots. AvgHist is computed as follows:

$$\text{AvgHist}(C) = (\sum_{i=1}^{m} \sum_{i=j+1}^{m} \text{Hist}(S_i, S_j))/(m(m-1)/2) \qquad (4.3)$$

The distance between two shots A and B is defined as the complementary of the histograms intersection of A and B:

$$\text{Hist}(A, B) = 1 - (\sum_{k=1}^{256} \min(H_A(k), H_B(k))/\sum_{k=1}^{256} H_A(k)) \qquad (4.4)$$

AvgText and AvgDuration are respectively normalized average text score and normalized average duration of selected shots.

$$\text{AvgText}(C) = \left(\sum_{i=1}^{m} \text{Text}(S_i)\right)/(m * T_{\max}) \qquad (4.5)$$

$$\text{AvgDuration}(C) = \left(\sum_{i=1}^{m} \text{Duration}(S_i)\right)/(m * D_{\max}) \qquad (4.6)$$

Where $T_{\max} = \max\{\text{Text}(S_i), S_i \in \text{PS}\}$ and $D_{\max} = \max\{\text{Duration}(S_i), S_i \in \text{PS}\}$.

The more the shots are different in the color space, the more is AvgHist. In fact, AvgHist is related to Hist which increases when the compared shots are more different. It is obvious that the more selected shots contain text (respectively have long durations), the more is AvgText (respectively AvgDuration). The proposed Genetic Algorithm tries to find a compromise between the three heterogeneous criteria.

Computation of Parameters

Our genetic solution is based on three parameters: text, duration and color. To quantify these parameters for every shot, we define three measures. The first is the text score of the shot, the second is its duration and the third is its color histogram. The duration of a shot can be easily computed. Color and text parameters are computed for the middle frame of the shot. To compute the color parameter of a given shot, we compute the color histogram of its middle frame.

The computation of text parameter is more complicated. In our approach, we work only with artificial text, it appears generally as a transcription at the foot of the frame. To compute the text parameter, we select the middle frame of the shot, then we divide it into three equal parts and like in [10] we apply a horizontal and vertical Sobel filter on the third part of the frame to obtain two edge maps of the text. We compute the number of edge pixels (white pixels) and we divide it by the total number of pixels of the third part. The obtained value is the text parameter (Fig. 4.5).

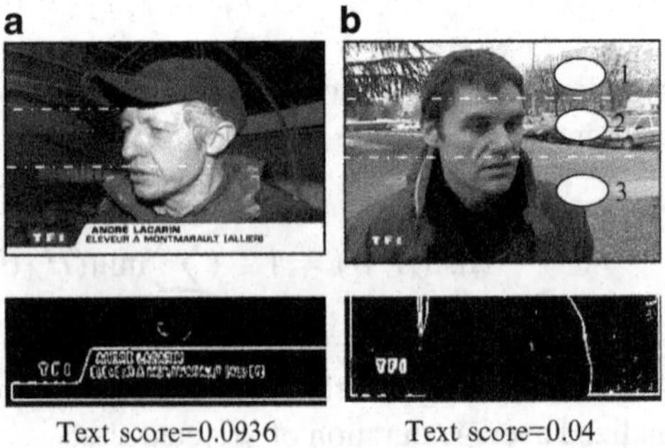

Fig. 4.5 (a) The text score of a frame containing text and (b) is greater than text score of a frame not containing text

Text score=0.0936   Text score=0.04

We have avoided computing the text parameters by the classic problems of text extraction, which may reduce the efficiency of our approach. We have been guided by the fact that frames containing text captions certainly contain more edge pixels than the others in their third part. So, their text scores will be greater.

Genetic Operations

The genetic mechanism works by randomly selecting pairs of individual chromosomes to reproduce for the next generation through genetic operations: the crossover and the mutation.

The crossover consists in exchanging a part of the genetic material of the two parents to construct two new chromosomes. This technique is used to explore the space of solutions with the proposition of new chromosomes to ameliorate the fitness function. In our genetic algorithm, the crossover operation is classic, but not completely random. In fact, like their parent, the produced children must respect the summary rate. For this reason, the crossing site must be carefully chosen (Fig. 4.6).

After a crossover is performed, a mutation takes place. Mutation is intended to prevent the falling of all solutions in the population into a local optimum. In our genetic solution, mutation must also respect the summary rate. For this reason, mutation operation must affect two genes of the chromosome. Besides, these genes must be different ("0"and "1") (Fig. 4.7).

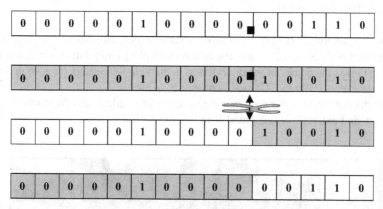

Fig. 4.6 Crossover operation. We must carefully select the crossover site to respect the summarization rate

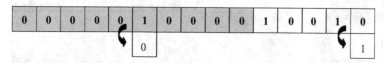

Fig. 4.7 Mutation operation. To respect the summarization rate, the mutation must affect two different bits

4.3 The Quick Access Level

After summarizing the news programme (Fig. 4.8) by a set of pictorial abstracts, we will extract from every one of them the context. The context will help viewers to filter and to have quickly the right story. We ignore low level features in our system because they are not semantically meaningful. In fact users who search in news broadcast archives are aiming generally parts of news speaking about a special topic as Iraqi war, Palestinian conflict and World cup 2066. Generally each news story is linked to a special event (Israeli-Palestinian conflict, Iraqi war, world cup, etc.), to special persons (Arafat, Sharon, Saddam Husseinand Blatter) and to special places where events have been taking place (UN New York, UNESCO Paris and Jerusalem).

That is why we use two mechanisms in indexing every news stories: the overlaid text extraction and the manual annotation.

4.3.1 The Indexation Part

In the indexation part of the partial access level, we have essentially three processes: the overlaid text extraction, the annotation and the storage of indexes.

4.3.1.1 Text Extraction

In news broadcast, Text is used to show several information about the shot being broadcasted such as the site where the action takes place (Iraq, Israel, United States, etc.), text gives the names of the interviewed in the video-viewed persons or presents important events (Olympic Games, hostage crisis, etc.).

For this reason, it will be interesting to segment overlaid text from every story summary and extract from obtained strings important keywords.

Fig. 4.8 An example of a news story summarized by our genetic algorithm

Works on text extraction may be generally grouped into four categories: connected component methods [11], texture classification methods [12], edge detection methods [13] and correlation based methods [14]. The connected component methods detect text by extracting the connected components of monotone colours that obey certain size, shape and spatial alignment constraints. The texture-based methods treat the text region as a special type of texture and employ conventional texture classification method to extract the text. Edge detection methods have been increasingly used for caption extraction due to the rich edge concentration in characters. The correlation based methods are those that use any kind of correlation in order to decide if a pixel belongs to a character or not.

In this chapter, we used our previous work [15] in which we combine color and edges to extract text. However, as the majority of approaches it includes four main tasks: detection, localization, segmentation and binarization.

Text Detection and Localization

In this step, we try to detect and localize text pixels from the remaining rows and columns clusters. Every window is represented by two frames. One is the frame of the window filtered along rows and the other is the frame filtered along the columns. For every frame, we achieve two operations. First, we realize a transformation from the RGB space to HSV space. Second, we generate using Sobel filters an edge picture.

For every cluster of these frames, we formulate a vector composed of ten features: five representing the HSV image and five representing the edge picture. These features are computed as follows:

$$f_1(E, I) = M(E, I)/M(I) \tag{4.7}$$

$$f_2(E, I) = \mu_2(E, I)/\mu_2(I) \tag{4.8}$$

$$f_3(E, I) = \mu_3(E, I)/\mu_3(I) \tag{4.9}$$

$$f_4(E, I) = \frac{c\_\mathrm{sup}(E, I)}{c\_\mathrm{sup}(E, I)} \tag{4.10}$$

$$f_5(E, I) = \frac{c\_\mathrm{inf}(E, I)}{c\_\mathrm{inf}(I)} \tag{4.11}$$

"E" represents rows clusters or columns clusters. "I" represents the HSV image or the edge picture.

$M(E, I)$ is the mean of color pixels of the cluster E in the picture I.

$$M(E, I) = \frac{1}{N} \sum_{i=0}^{N} E_I(i) \tag{4.12}$$

$\mu_2(E, I)$ is the second order moment

$$\mu_2(E, I) = \frac{1}{N} \sum_{i=0}^{N} (E_I(i) - M(E, I))^2 \tag{4.13}$$

$\mu_3(E, I)$ is the third order moment

$$\mu_3(E, I) = \frac{1}{N} \sum_{i=0}^{N} (E_I(i) - M(E, I))^3 \tag{4.14}$$

$c\_\mathrm{sup}(E, i)$ is the maximum value of the confidence interval

$$c\_\mathrm{sup}(E, I) = M(E, I) + \frac{1.96 * \sqrt{\mu_2(E, I)}}{\sqrt{N}} \tag{4.15}$$

$c\_\mathrm{inf}(E, i)$ is the minimum value of the confidence interval

$$c\_\mathrm{inf}(E, i) = M(E, I) - \frac{1.96 * \sqrt{\mu_2(E, I)}}{\sqrt{N}} \tag{4.16}$$

The generated vectors will be presented to a trained back propagation neural network containing ten inputs nodes, three hidden nodes and one output node. The training database contains 2,000 key frames with the dimension of 320×240. The results of the classifications are two images: an image containing rows considered as text rows and an image containing columns considered as text columns. Finally, we merge results of the two images to generate an image containing zones of text (Fig. 4.9).

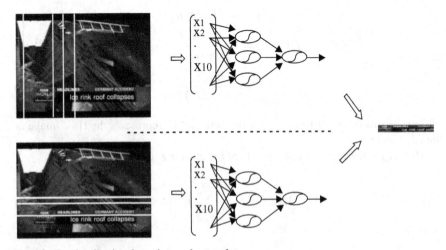

Fig. 4.9 Text localization through neural networks

Text Segmentation and Binarization

After localizing text in the frame, the following step consists in segmenting and binarizing text. First, we compute the gray levels image. Second, for each pixel in the text area, we create a vector composed of two features: the standard deviation and the entropy of the eight neighbourhood of pixels which are computed as follows:

$$\text{std}(p) = \left(\frac{1}{N * N} \sum_{i=1}^{N} \sum_{j=1}^{N} (f(i, j) - \overline{f})^2 \right)^{\frac{1}{2}} \tag{4.17}$$

$$\text{ent}(p) = - \sum_{i=1}^{N} \sum_{j=1}^{N} (f(i, j) * \log(f(i, j))) \tag{4.18}$$

where $f(i, j)$ indicates the gray level of the pixel in position (i, j). Third, we run the fuzzy C-means clustering algorithm to classify the pixels into "text" cluster and "background" cluster. Finally, we binarize the text image by marking text pixels in black.

This technique is motivated by two observations. First, text has usually a unique texture. Second, the border of text character results in high contrast edges. Some segmentation on results are show in Fig. 4.10.

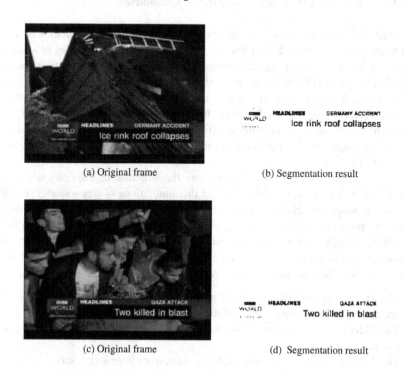

(a) Original frame   (b) Segmentation result

(c) Original frame   (d) Segmentation result

Fig. 4.10 Example of text extraction from video frames

4.3.1.2 Annotation Augmentation

Text embedded in news broadcast video usually provides brief and important information about the content, such as places, countries, locations, name, date (or time) etc. This kind of embedded text, referred to as closed caption, is a powerful keyword resource in building video annotation and retrieval system. However, text extraction is a difficult task because background, color and size of text strings may vary in a same image. Besides, it does not always offer the sufficient information to describe the audiovisual document.

For this reason, we choose to make our system opened and extensible to additions and annotations. Every annotation is related to a specific story in a news broadcast programme. The annotation may be either a sentence or a set of words. The text annotation is strongly required since it provides a description of the content directly usable at the application level for displaying information to the user for building (or answering to) queries. As far as annotations are concerned, MPEG-7 supports both free textual content and structured annotations in terms of action ("What"), people ("Who"), objects ("What Object"), action ("What Action"), places ("Where"), time ("When"), purposes ("Why") and manner ("How"). We provide to users an interface that helps them to annotate every summary.

4.3.1.3 MPEG7 to Describe News Stories Summaries

The MPEG-7 standard aims to satisfy the above operational requirements by defining a multimedia content description interface and providing a rich set of standardized tools to describe multimedia content [16]. MPEG-7 will specify a standard set of descriptors (Ds) that can be used to describe various types of multimedia information. It will also specify a rich set of predefined structures of descriptors and their relationships, as well as ways to define one's own structures; these structures are called description schemes (DSs). Defining new DSs is done using a special language, the description definition language (DDL), which is a part of the standard [17].

In this chapter, we are interested to store the structure of the news stories and to archive the extracted overlaid text and the annotations of news stories. For this reason we adopt the scheme created in the COALA project [18] in which the researchers propose TVN schema (Fig. 4.11), a TV news description schema based on MPEG-7, which allows the representation of TV news information in an environment that integrates the three processes of production, archiving and retrieval. The elements which are used in this schema are:

- The video segment description scheme represents the video segments as news programmes, news stories, presentations, reports, etc.
- The VideoText description scheme represents the Teletext subtitles and graphical overlay.
- The TextAnnotation description scheme represents Free text description.

```
<AudioVisual xsi:type="AudioVisualSegmentType">
  <SegmentDecomposition decompositionType="temporal" id="shots" >
    <!-- The Story number 1-->
    <Segment xsi:type="VideoSegmentType" id="ST1">
      <MediaLocator> (?) </MediaLocator>
      <TextAnnotation><FreeTextAnnotation>Introduction.</FreeTextAnnotation>
      </TextAnnotation>
    </Segment>
    <!-- The Story number 2-->
    <Segment xsi:type="VideoSegmentType" id="ST2">
      <MediaLocator> (?) </MediaLocator>
      <TextAnnotation>
        <FreeTextAnnotation>Game.</FreeTextAnnotation>
      </TextAnnotation>
    </Segment>
  </SegmentDecomposition>
</AudioVisual>
```

Fig. 4.11 An example of MPEG7 file related to a news program and to two stories

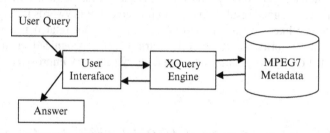

Fig. 4.12 The query part based on Xquery technology

4.3.2 The Querying Part

We created for users an easy-to-use interactive interface. It translates a user query (words query) to its corresponding form in XQuery and passes it to the XQuery Engine. The result in XML from the XQuery Engine, which is an XML fragment of MPEG-7 metadata, is returned to the user.

XQuery [19], which has been influenced from most of the previous XML query languages, is a forthcoming standard for querying XML data. Since MPEG-7 metadata are XML data, XQuery was a natural choice as a query language. Besides, we believe that the use of both a standard metadata and a standard query language would be essential for interoperability among multimedia digital library systems.

The system searches MPEG-7 metadata and returns the metadata that match the query to a varying extent. The architecture is depicted in (Fig. 4.12). The system consists of three main modules: MPEG-7 Metadata, User Interface and XQuery Engine.

4.4 Experiments

To validate our approach, we choose to work with French channels *"TF1"* and *"France2"* as general channels and the English Channel "BBC" as news broadcast channel. We have recorded 20 h of news from *"TF1"* and *"France2"* (night and midday news) and 10 h from "BBC." Our system is implemented with matlab and tested on a PC with 2.66 GHZ and 1 GB RAM.

4.4.1 Experimental Results of the Partial Access Level

Our work aims at producing summaries helping users to judge if the news sequence is interesting or not. To experiment our previous work, we have invited ten test users to search through summaries of news programmes four topics speaking about: "Avian flu," "Aids," "Iraqi war" and "Israeli-Palestinian conflict."

Table 4.1 shows the results of this experiment. Topics speaking about wars and conflicts, which are related to special key objects as tanks, victims, damage, bombing, soldier, present good results. And the improvement of keywords is very limited. However, topics like "Avian flu" and "Aids" that are not related to special objects need extra information to be easily retrieved and recognized in summaries. In fact, the list of keywords attached to every story summary improves the retrieval results.

4.4.2 Experimental Results of the Quick Access Level

To evaluate the performance of the quick access level part of the system, we have tested it through four test detection of the same concepts used to test the partial access level. The concepts are avian flu, Aids, Iraq war and Israeli-Palestinian conflict. A true detection is defined as detecting a concept in the story when it is present. A false alarm is defined as detecting a concept in a story when it is not present. It is clear that there is an important improvement in system performance. The results are obtained rapidly with a higher recall but with lower precision (Table 4.2).

4.5 Conclusion

In this chapter, we have proposed a global architecture of a system that helps users to navigate into news broadcast archive. We proposed a system with three access levels. The first access level is a full access level in which users have a sequential access to all news programmes. The second is a partial access level in which users have a

Table 4.1 Evaluation results of the partial access level for four topics on our dataset

Topics	Manual relevant stories	True/False detected stories	Mean (true/false)	Recall (%)	Precision (%)
Avian flu	8	6/2	6.7/1.4	83.75	82.71
		7/1			
		8/2			
		6/1			
		7/1			
		7/0			
		6/2			
		6/2			
		7/1			
		7/2			
Aids	5	3/1	3.6/1.3	72	73.46
		4/1			
		4/2			
		4/1			
		3/1			
		3/0			
		4/2			
		3/2			
		4/1			
		4/2			
Iraq war	17	14/2	14.7/1.6	86.47	90.18
		15/2			
		14/1			
		16/2			
		15/2			
		15/1			
		15/1			
		14/2			
		15/2			
		14/1			
Israeli-Palestinian conflict	13	12/2	12.1/1.6	93.07	88.32
		13/1			
		12/2			
		11/1			
		12/2			
		12/1			
		12/2			
		12/3			
		13/1			
		12/1			

Table 4.2 Evaluation results of the partial access level for four topics on our dataset

Topics	Used keywords	Manual relevant stories	True/False detected stories	Recall (%)	Precision (%)
Avian flu	Avian flu	8	7/3	87.5	70
Aids	Aids Epidemic	5	5/2	100	71.42
Iraq war	Iraq, Saddam	17	15/4	88.23	78.94
Israeli-Palestinian conflict	Israel Arafat Sharon	13	11/4	84.61	73.33

sequential access level to summaries of news programmes. The last one is quick access level in which users use keywords to filter the relevant news programmes. For this access level, we used the summaries as input for an indexation system that generates as the output MPEG7 files describing the every news story. We choose to use summaries as input because they contain the useful and the effective information without redundancy and because generated summaries contain a semantic information that is overlaid text. In fact to generate informative and semantically meaningful summaries, we relied on three basic aspects. First, long shots are important in news broadcast. Second, shots containing text are also crucial because text is an informative object. It is often embedded in news video and it is useful data for content description.

Finally, to insure a maximum of color variability and a maximum of color coverage, the selected shots must be different in color space. To find a compromise between all these criteria, we used the genetic algorithm that is dedicated to this kind of problems.

In fact the annotations and the overlaid text extracted from the news stories summaries help the users to detect rapidly the majority of the relevant news stories. However, many stories may be detected wrongly because the keywords used in the filtering process may belong to many concepts. For instance, the keyword "Iraq" may belong to the Iraq war concept, to economic Iraqi difficulties concept or to Saddam Hussein lawsuit concept. However, the wrong detections may not be a great problem because the user may filter the obtained results through the quick access level visually by showing the summary of every detected story. That is why the partial access level and the quick access level are complementary and we can use both of them to obtain rapidly the desired news stories.

The quality of generated summaries is evaluated and the results are promising. Besides, through the evaluation, we demonstrated the complementarity of the quick access level and the partial access level.

The encouraging results obtained for news broadcast corpus motivate us to think to use our system with other corpus. In fact, we have begun to investigate adapting the architecture to films and documentary videos. We began to investigate thinking in using other types of features semantically meaningful and especially faces.

Acknowledgments The authors want to acknowledge the financial support of this work by grants from the General Direction of Scientific Research and Technological Renovation (DGRST), Tunisia, under the ARUB programme 01/UR/11/02.

References

1. Y.F Ma, Zhang H.J: A Bird View of Video Sequence, In Proceedings of International Multimedia Modeling Conference 2005 page (94–101).
2. Y. Taniguchi, A. Akutsu, Y. Tonomura: Extracting and Packing Panoramas for Video Browsing, In Proceedings of ACM Multimedia 1997 page (427–436).
3. S. Uchihashi, J. Foo, A. Girgensohn, J. Boreczky: Generating Semantically Meaningful Video Summaries, In Proceedings of ACM Multimedia 1999 page (383–392).
4. NIST, 2004 http://www-nlpir.nist.gov/projects/tv2004/tv2004.html#2.2.
5. TRECVID, 2003, 2004, TREC Video Retrieval Evaluation:http://www-nlpir.nist.gov/projects/trecvid/.
6. H.J. Zhang, W. Smoliar, D. Zhong: An integrated and Content-Based Solution, In Proceedings of ACM Multimedia 1995 page (45–54).
7. J. Yang, A.G. Hauptmann: Multi-modal Analysis for Person Type Classification in News Video, In Proceedings of the Symposium on Electronic Imaging 2005 page (165–172).
8. M. Ellouze, H. Karray, W.B. Soltana, A.M. Alimi: Utilisation de la carte de Kohonen pour la détection des plans présentateur d'un journal télévisé, TAIMA'2007 2007 page (271–276).
9. D.E. Goldberg: Genetic algorithms in search, optimization, and machine learning Addison-Wesley, Reading MA 1989.
10. X. Chen, H. Zhang: Text area Detection from video frames, In Proceedings of the IEEE Pacific-Rim Conference on Multimedia 2001 page (222–228).
11. K. Jain, B. Yu: Automatic text location in images and video frames, Pattern recognition Vol. 31, No.12, 1998 page. (2055–2076).
12. H.P. Li, D. Doemann, O. Kia: Automatic text detection and tracking in digital video, IEEE Trans. on Image Processing Vol. 9, No.1, 2000 page (147–156).
13. S. Hua, X., X.-R. Chen L. Wenyin, H-J. Zhang: Automatic location of text in video frames, Workshop on Multimedia Information Retrieval (MIR2001, In conjunction with ACM Multimedia 2001).
14. H. Karray, A.M. Alimi: Detection and Extraction of the Text in a video sequence, In Proceedings IEEE 12 International Conference on Electronics, Circuits and systems 2005 page (474–478).
15. H. Karray, M. Ellouze, A.M. Alimi: Using Text Transcriptions For Summarizing News Video, In Proceedings of the International Conference' information and communication technologies International symposium (ICTIS) 2007.
16. ISO/IEC: Introduction to MPEG-7 (version 4.0). approved, N4675, March 2002.
17. B.S. Manjunath, P. Salembier, T. Sikora: Introduction to MPEG-7: Multimedia Content Description Interface. ISBN0471486787, Wiley 2002 page (335–361).
18. N. Fatemi, O. Abou-Khaled: Indexing and Retrieval of TV News Programs based on MPEG-7, IEEE International Conference on Consumer Electronics, Los Angeles, CA, June 2001.
19. W3C: XQuery 1.0: An XQuery Language. WorkingDraft, http://www.w3.org/TR/2003/WD-xquery-20030502 May 2003.

Chapter 5
Sensorized Garment Augmented 3D Pervasive Virtual Reality System

Tauseef Gulrez, Alessandro Tognetti, and Danilo De Rossi

Abstract [1] Virtual reality (VR) technology has matured to a point where humans can navigate in virtual scenes; however, providing them with a comfortable fully immersive role in VR remains a challenge. Currently available sensing solutions do not provide ease of deployment, particularly in the seated position due to sensor placement restrictions over the body, and optic-sensing requires a restricted indoor environment to track body movements. Here we present a 52-sensor laden garment interfaced with VR, which offers both portability and unencumbered user movement in a VR environment. This chapter addresses the systems engineering aspects of our pervasive computing solution of the interactive sensorized 3D VR and presents the initial results and future research directions. Participants navigated in a virtual art gallery using natural body movements that were detected by their wearable sensor shirt and then mapped the signals to electrical control signals responsible for VR scene navigation. The initial results are positive, and offer many opportunities for use in computationally intelligent man-machine multimedia control.

Keywords Virtual reality · Wearable sensor-shirt · Navigation · Pervasive computing · Body movements

5.1 Introduction

Personalized computing solutions are usually placed on the desks and users need full attention, area restriction and both hands to operate the device. Laptops are

T. Gulrez (✉)
Vitrual Interactive Simulations of Reality Labs, Department of Computing, Faculty of Science, Macquarie University, NSW 2109, Sydney, Australia
and
Department of Computer Engineering, College of Engineering and Applied Sciences, Al-Ghurair University, Dubai Academic City, P.O. Box 37374, Dubai, United Arab Emirates
e-mail: gtauseef@ieee.org

[1] This research has been approved by the ethical committee of Macquarie University Sydney Australia, under the humans research ethical act of New South Wales, Australia, in approval letter No.HE23FEB2007-D05008 titled Personal Augmented Reality and Immersive System based Body Machine Interface (PARIS based BMI).

A.-E. Hassanien et al. (eds.), *Pervasive Computing: Innovations in Intelligent Multimedia and Applications*, Computer Communications and Networks, DOI 10.1007/978-1-84882-599-4_5, © Springer-Verlag London Limited 2009

becoming smaller and weightless, and enabling users to work at any convenient place, but still users have to leave everything and use their both hands and fingers to operate the device. These computing solutions may restrict the facility to a larger disabled community, which is approximately 10% of the world's total population according to the United Nations' recent survey [4, 5, 38].

Wearable computing [23, 24, 32, 36] is determined to refute the preconceptions of computer usability laid over the last two decades. A trendy personal computer can be worn like a shirt or a trouser with different fashionable designs. A professional may check his emails and prepare his presentations using his thoughts while sitting in a bus or in his car, whereas computing is taking place in his shirt, trousers or jackets. These wearable devices can be augmented with human sensory system and enhance the human intelligence by facilitating the memory maps or by rather remapping of the brain pouring intelligence into it [15, 21, 28]. Imagine that you are sitting in a plane, bus, subway and a device interwoven in your clothing is capable of reading your mind, translating your speech into signals through your brain and transmitting wirelessly to your fellow sitting in an another continent. By the end of next decade, we are very likely to adapt to wearable computing. Unquestionably, over the time our culture is likely to absorb these technologies and a new culture will emerge, where people from different cultural backgrounds having same techno-clothings can become part of the community easily. Similarly, a new brain-language may emerge to connect the consciousness of human beings together, which may lay the foundation of an everlasting and pure relationship (in a pervasive distraction free environment). The wearable devices can be built in many ways, and the marketplace will determine which fashions and styles will prevail.

The pervasive computing technologies [2, 8, 9, 25] are evolving rapidly enabling the virtual reality (VR) applications to a new level of user participation. A platform for interactive virtual applications integrates a high-end VR system with smart wearable computers, facilitating and enhancing user navigation and visualization control and information exchange. More advanced, next-generation pervasive virtual applications exploit VR technology [6, 16, 18, 35] to give users immersive experiences such as archaeological site navigation, time and space travel and ancient artifact reconstruction in 3D. In this context, our work focuses on the post next-generation of pervasive virtual applications, which aim to provide an immersive and interactive user experience. Interactive pervasive VR has a long history, but its development has issues like the limited availability, poor usability and high expense of VR interface devices used in its early stages.

Pervasive computing technologies [8, 9, 16] have paved the path for the favorable conditions necessary for overcoming the limitations of early interactive VRs prototypes. In this chapter, we exploited portable and wearable computing device, a sensorized shirt, and software environments (3D WorldViz) to create highly interactive VR application. We have enabled the VR application user to interact in the VR environment with his or her own natural body movements without having to become familiar with a new I/O interface.

The chapter is organized such that in Sect. 5.2 the overall system has been described that is necessary to integrate the sensorized shirt with the pervasive VR system. In Sect. 5.3, the layout and stability analysis of the sensorized garments have been shown. Section 5.4 deals with the concept of pervasive virtual presence along with the software architecture and component modularity. Section 5.5 shows the user experience, rationale behind choosing the signal processing methodology and finally the results have been shown. The chapter concludes with Sect. 5.6.

5.2   System Overview

Our main goal is to manage interaction in a collaborative pervasive virtual environment shared by people visiting art gallery, it can further be exploited for archaeologists and cultural heritage experts (but also architects, virtual model designers, art experts, computer scientists and so on). However, we do not limit ourselves to simple interactions as in the case of a visitor in a virtual art gallery. We view the VR site as an active workplace, where users have ample of degrees of freedom to proactively interact with the environment and to cooperate with others in an unencumbered fashion. In order to achieve this level of autonomy, we need to satisfy fundamental technical requirements, i.e., user interactivity for longer periods, sense of presence and multimedia data support.

In this chapter, we have described a novel method for navigating in a VR environment using smart sensing garment technologies [12–15]. A wearable multi-sensor shirt is introduced as an interface device between a human and VR environment that can detect upper body (wrist, elbow and shoulder) movements. A combination of VR and signal processing methods was used to develop an effective body-machine interface to perform tasks. The experimental system is shown in Fig. 5.1 where the participant navigates in a VR environment through different body postures. The sensor shirt was worn by a participant (Fig. 5.2) showing the front side of the sensor

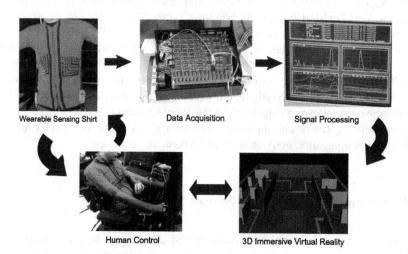

Fig. 5.1   A wearable computing system

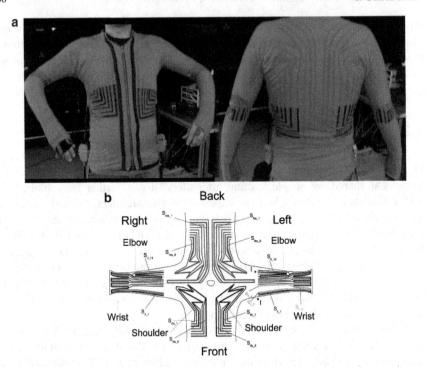

Fig. 5.2 (**a**) Sensor shirt's front and back view, as it was worn by the participant for experiment purposes. (**b**) The adhesive mask (sensor layout of the shirt) which is printed on the shirt, showing the front and back side of the sensor layout

shirt, and the analogue signals that originated from the shirt were converted into digital signals by a National Instruments' analogue-to-digital converter. The digital output was read in Matlab Realtime Windows Target [27] and the processed signals (as shown in Fig. 5.1) were sent as unified data protocol (UDP) packets to the VR software. From an initial starting point in the VR scene, the control signals generated by the participant's residual movements were used to move the participant in VR. The participant's trajectories are shown in figure. The sensor shirt was used with the VR system continuously for 1 h without recalibration, as shown in Fig. 5.1. Error measurements were calculated in the shoulder sensors outputs after 20 and 60 min intervals. The results show the complete stability of the system (for at least an hour without recalibration), ease of deployment and comfort.

5.3 Sensorized Garments – Sensor Shirt Layout

Bio-sensors that can be worn and allow measurement of higher-level cues to the state of the person are very useful for building a pervasive VR environment. These sensors will provide a mobile-interaction in the environment and allow user navigation control in the virtual environment. The advantage of these bio-sensors is that they can be worn on a human body in the usual way a person wears his/her cloths, thereby giving user a natural flavour of interaction while navigating in the VR.

Recently, new bio-sensors have been developed to measure biomedical data [14, 15, 23]. The users could wear these sensors and the data could be transmitted to the virtual environment's sensor-net for higher-level content interpretation. The sensorized garment used in the experiments shown in this chapter consists of 52-piezoresistive sensors, which generate analog signals upon the deformations that take place due to human body movement [22, 23, 36]. The sensor shirt Fig. 5.2a has been made by directly printing a Conductive Elastomer (CE) material (commercial product provided by Wacker LTD [7]) on a Lycra/cotton fabric previously covered by an adhesive mask Fig. 5.2b. The mask adopted to realize the sensor shirt is shown in figure. and it is designed according to the desired sensor and connection topology. In each shirt section, sensors are connected in series and are represented by the wider lines of Fig. 5.2b. Connections between sensors and electronic acquisition unit are represented by the thinner lines of Fig. 5.2b. Since connections are realized by the same material adopted for sensors, they have an unknown and unpredictable change in electrical resistance when the user moves. For this reason, the acquisition unit front-end has been designed to compensate connection resistance variations. The sensor series is supplied with a constant current I and the voltage falls across consecutive connections are acquired using high input impedance amplifiers (instrumentation amplifiers) following the methodology of [15, 36]. Let us consider the example of sensor S_{11_3} (the prototype electrical model and the acquisition strategy are shown in Fig. 5.3). This is a sensor placed in the left wrist region of the shirt and is represented by the light blue line in Fig. 5.2b. Connections of this sensor are represented in Fig. 5.3b by the two green lines. If the amplifier is connected between C_{11_3} and C_{11_4}, only a small amount of current flows through interconnections compared to the current that flows through S_3. In this way, if the current I is well dimensioned, the voltage read by the amplifier is almost equal to the voltage drop on the sensor that is proportional to the sample resistance. In conclusion, a generic sensor consists of a segment of the bold track between two consecutive thin track intersections. Sensor shirt was interfaced to a National Instruments' NI-DAQ SCB-100 PCI [26, 30, 33] card installed in a personal computer as shown in Fig. 5.3. For the testing purposes of the shirt, to ensure that all sensors are working properly and producing signals, the sensor shirt was worn by a participant while the shirt was connected to the PC running Matlab Real-time Windows Target [26, 27]. The participant was then asked to move his elbows and shoulders and relative signal obtained due to the body movements are shown in Fig. 5.3c, d. The signals, shown in Fig. 5.3d, show the 12 sensor reading covering the (right) shoulder of the participant from back to front. The signal peaks can be seen during every deformation made during this test trial. Similarly, Fig. 5.3c shows the 4 sensors attached to the (right) elbow of the participant. Elbow is a single degree of freedom joint of the human body, and the signals shown here are taken during the extension and abduction of the elbow.

Data acquisition blocks for left and right connec- A shirt testing system. The body originated sig-
tion of the sensor shirt. A National instruments nals can be seen on the monitor, due to the
analog to digital converter block DAQ SCB 100 deformations caused by upper limb movement.
is connected to the computer via a SH 100 pin
shielded cable connection.

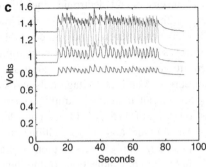 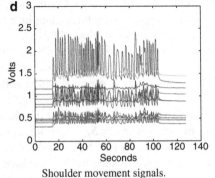

Elbow sensors signals originated in result of el-   Shoulder movement signals.
bow movement by the participant.

Fig. 5.3 Sensor shirt interface system

5.3.1 Sensor Shirt Stability Analysis

Sensor shirt's stability is a very important issue, since the performance of the VR
control depends mainly upon the similarity in the signal values generated from the
shirt over the different time periods. It is very likely that the patient wearing the
shirt uses the wheelchair for atleast 2–3 h continuously. The idea is that shirt should
not lose the calibration signals even after the 1 or 2 h since the first calibration was
done. Here in this section, we will show the analysis and results obtained during
sensor shirt's stability testing. In this process, I recorded the sensor output while
making postures at different time intervals; while looking at the stability data of
sensor values, one can also deduce the most effective posture for sensor shirt/VR
control based upon stability analysis.

Table 5.1 Sensor shirt layout

Body part	Left side	Right side
Front shoulder	6 sensors	6 sensors
fs	$S_{lfs\_1} - S_{lfs\_6}$	$S_{rfs\_1} - S_{rfs\_6}$
Back shoulder	8 sensors	8 sensors
bs	$S_{lbs\_1} - S_{lbs\_8}$	$S_{rbs\_1} - S_{rbs\_8}$
Limb	12 sensors	12 sensors
l	$S_{ll\_1} - S_{ll\_12}$	$S_{rl\_1} - S_{rl\_12}$
Total sensors	26	26

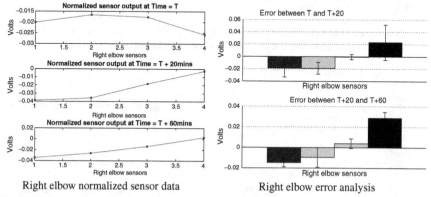

Right elbow normalized sensor data   Right elbow error analysis

Fig. 5.4 Elbow sensor data

The sensor shirt consists of 52-piezoresistive conductive CE sensors woven inside the garment, capable of producing signals upon the deformations produced in the CE material due to any posture made by human body. The sensors are divided into four sections as in Table 5.1 for each left and right side. In order to find out the stability of the shirt, I recorded the shirt signals in three different time intervals, i.e., t, $t + 20$ and $t + 60$ (at 20 and 60 min difference), given the same configuration of the human body (i.e., the subject wore the shirt continuously for that given period of analysis). Human shoulder movement is a complicated combination of many degrees of freedom bone joints (scapular movement, i.e., abduction and flexion). The shirt sensors overlay the shoulder portion from two sides, i.e., from the front and from the back; this division of sensors makes it easy to capture the front and back movement of the shoulder by tracing the front and back sensor deformation value into signals. The complexity of the human shoulder was kept in mind during the stability analysis, and hence, priority was given to the shoulder section and three different movements were recorded while our participant made three different shoulder movements. The sensor analysis of these positions can be seen in Figs. 5.4 and 5.5. The shirt has been divided into front and back shoulder sensors as can be seen in Fig. 5.2b, which made the acquisition of signals become more effective and stronger while the recording.

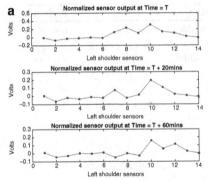

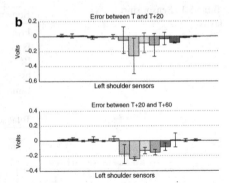

Left shoulder forward movement (while rest position is backward) normalized sensor data

Left shoulder forward movement (while rest position is backward) error analysis

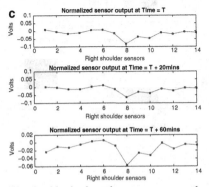

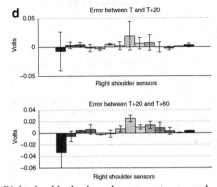

Right shoulder backward movement normalized sensor data

Right shoulder backward movement error analysis

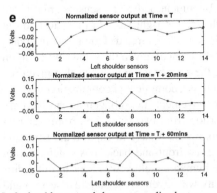

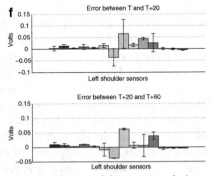

Left shoulder up and down normalized sensor data

Left shoulder up and down error analysis

Fig. 5.5 Up and down shoulder movement

Following are the different positions in which the sensing was recorded for both left and right portions of the shirt:

1. Elbow movement, up and down
2. Shoulder forward movement while rest position is backward
3. Shoulder backward movement while rest position is forward
4. Shoulder forward movement (while rest is normal zero position)
5. Shoulder backward movement (while rest is normal zero position)
6. Shoulder up and down position

We performed the stability analysis of the sensor shirt on a consented healthy participant. The participant wore the sensor shirt and was asked to perform above mentioned body postures. The sensing was recorded and plotted against the different time periods as shown in Figs. 5.4 and 5.5. In each of these results, left hand side plot shows the single sensor value, whereas the bar plot shows the difference between the rest position and the value of the sensor.

The stability of the shirt can be analyzed while looking at the graph shapes obtained through the sensor values or through the error barplot. It is very unlikely for humans to make identical postures, if they are asked to repeat some posture after a pause of 20 min. Hence in our analysis, posture made by the participant at t time will never exactly be repeated by the participant after $t + 20$ min or $t + 60$ min. In this case, a slight difference of upto 5% of the sensor value can cater inside the results while analysing the data. Also, an important thing to be noted here is that, data-fusion [11] methodology was used to remove noise and artifacts from the sensor values in our wheelchair navigation experiments. We used principal component analysis (PCA) as described in [17, 31] to reduce the dimensions of our sensor values, while retaining as much variance as possible between the two consecutive sensor dimensions.

5.4 Pervasive Virtual Sense of Presence

Pervasive virtual sense of presence is the main contribution of using interactive VR technologies. VR can simulate real environments with a realism with its interactive and experience characteristics. The important characteristic that really distinguishes VR from real-time 3D graphics is that it provides the illusion of being present inside a virtual world through immersivity and interaction. Moreover, the integration of immersivity in VR applications enables users to better understand and examine 3D models. This is particularly important in the case of reconstruction of objects and environments no longer available or accessible in the real world. To achieve effective immersivity and sense of presence, we must utilize the following subrequirements, i.e., firstly provide a projection system supporting stereoscopic vision as well as software and hardware for real-time processing; secondly, enable major interaction tasks; and thirdly and finally, integrate/introduce physical devices that do not divert from the sense of presence.

5.4.1 Virtual Reality Projection System

Currently, there are four forms of VR display systems, head mounted display, augmented reality, Fish Tank and projection-based display systems. We used an immersive semi-cylindrical projection system placed in our Virtual Reality Systems (VRS) Lab as shown in Fig. 5.6. The system consists of three projectors which display the virtual world onto a 6 m wide semi-cylindrical screen canvas. The user is positioned slightly off centre towards the canvas to allow a 160° field of view.

5.4.2 Virtual Reality Software

For interoperability, extendibility, maintenance and reusability purposes, we have taken a modular design approach where each component has separate roles and responsibilities and well-defined interfaces to allow other components to access their functionality. Also driving our modular design is the desire to (re)use existing third party components and swap components as required. Many of the components are provided by third party vendors such as the 3D modelling and animation package Coindesigner [3] and VR Software (WorldViz, open inventor scene graphs (OISG) and Cavelib) [19, 37].

In order to implement a modelling application with AR working planes, construction at a distance and user interface, a complex underlying infrastructure is required to simplify the development. In this work we have used CAVELib™ and WorldViz™ Application Programmer's Interface (API) for developing applications for immersive displays [19, 37]. The CAVELib and WorldViz APIs provide the building blocks to handle the intricacies of creating robust applications for Virtual Environments. These APIs are independent platforms enabling developers to create high-end VR applications on IRIX, Solaris, Windows and Linux operating systems. The applications built by these software are externally configurable at run-time,

Fig. 5.6 Virtual reality lab at department of computing, Macquarie University, Sydney

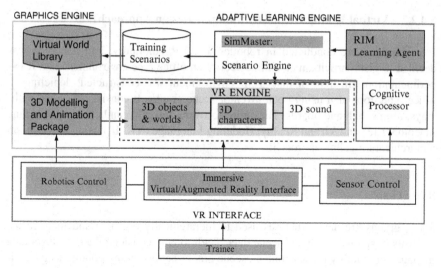

Fig. 5.7 System architecture of RIMS

making an application executable independent of the display system. So, without recompilation, the application can be run on a wide variety of display systems. And the cross-platform API of these software makes it possible to maintain a single code base, yet run on a variety of display systems and operating systems.

In this section, we will describe the components and agents of the Robotics Interface Multi-agent System (RIMS) software. RIMS has a hybrid system architecture that integrates a rapid response mechanism with the proactive behaviour enabled by planning. RIMS is composed of modules that separate the data modules and functionality. The major modules of our system are as follows (and are shown in Fig. 5.7):

- Graphics engine
- Virtual reality engine

5.4.2.1   Graphics Engine Module

In order to show VR user a natural flavour of life, VR objects and environment modeling plays a very critical role in VR scene building. The capability to touch and manipulate virtual objects according to natural patterns of body movements is a fundamental requirement for future applications of virtual environment technologies. Although in this work as a CAD package, Coindesigner rapid application development (RAD), Coin3D and Open Inventor libraries [3] have been used to make 3D models.

5.4.2.2 Virtual Reality Engine (A Modular Design Approach)

Experiments were conducted in robotics and VR laboratory, and hence, it was decided to give participants a similar feel of an office type environment in VR experimentations. In light of that, a 3D environment was constructed, depicting an office type floor plan using open inventor scene graphs. It consists of doors, pathways, rooms, hall and boards. The entire software designing and creation was done in Coin3D [3] and Virtual Reality Modeling Language (VRML) using scene graph hierarchical modeling approach.

Scene Graphs

Scene graphs are data structures used to hierarchically organize and manage the contents of spatially oriented scene data. Traditionally considered a high-level data management facility for 3D content, scene graphs are becoming popular as general-purpose mechanisms for managing a variety of media types. MPEG-4, for instance, uses the VRML scene graph programming model for multimedia scene composition, regardless of whether 3D data are part of such content.

Scene Graph Nodes

With the exception of the topmost root node (which defines the entry point into the scene graph), every node in a scene has a parent. Nodes containing other nodes are parent nodes, while the nodes they contain are the child nodes (children) of their parent. Nodes that can contain children are grouping nodes; those that cannot are leaf nodes. Subgraph structures as in Fig. 5.8 let a specific grouping of nodes exist as a discrete and independently addressed unit of data within the main scene graph structure. Operations on the scene can be performed on all nodes in the graph, or

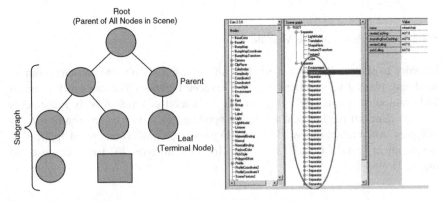

Fig. 5.8 Scene graph nodes

they may be restricted to a particular subgraph (scenes can therefore be composed of individual nodes as well as entire subgraphs that may be attached or detached as needed).

5.5   Experience Summary and Results

The preliminary results shown in this chapter were tested on consented participants after taking ethical approval from Macquarie University's Ethical Committee for Humans Research. We must mention here that the sensorized garment interfaced VR setup is still in its initial stages. We are improving the prototype setup in a more compact form, and hopefully by the end of next year, an improved version of the system will be introduced.

The sensorized upper garment was worn by the participant in a usual manner (Fig. 5.11). In order to capture the body movement signals, the participant was asked to perform different body movements. The body movements were captured by the sensors attached inside the garment; since the shirt contains several sensors at each joint, we examined the possibility of reducing the dimensionality of the shirt signals by applying PCA [1,10,17,20,31] Fig. 5.10 to the signals originating from the same joint. PCA was performed on data that were collected while the subject was moving his arms and shoulders in an uninstructed manner for a period of 10 s. We found that the first principal component (PC) of each joint captures 80–90% of the same jointsensors variance, that is why we selected the first PC of each right, left shoulder and elbow movement to control the navigation scheme for virtual reality walk.

Signal Processing

For removing possible drift and noise artifacts from the shirt signals, a derivative rectification algorithm was developed [15]. The time derivative of each of the four PC was calculated and a dead-zone was applied to each of them. The signals were only positively-rectified, as we are only interested in the rising part of each PC (see Fig. 5.10). The processed signals from the two elbows were then subtracted from each other to generate the transitional acceleration, while the processed signals from the two shoulders are subtracted from each other to generate the rotational velocity.

Rationale behind choosing PCA

In fact, the human joint movement is a combination of several degrees of freedom, for instance, the human shoulder has three degrees of freedom, i.e., 240° of pitch, 180° of yaw and 90° of roll. Whenever any shoulder movement takes place (as a control command to the virtual scene), it is equivalent to a direction movement vector, which is a linear combination of the pitch, yaw and roll. The sensors are placed

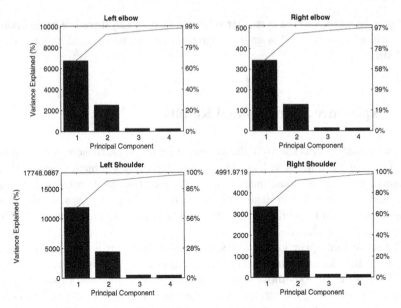

Fig. 5.9 Principal components of the multiple sensors attached to one body part

on the shirt such that each individual sensor captures the single degree of freedom, whereas the combined effect of the sensor may correlate the combined effect of the degrees of freedom of the shoulder or the single direction movement vector of the shoulder. The rationale behind choosing PCA is that the first PC captures 80% of the variance in the data (see Fig. 5.9), the second an additional 15%, the third an additional 3%, whereas the contribution of the fourth one drops below 3%. Our hypothesis is that the first PC of signals coming from one of the shirt areas of interest (right-elbow, left-elbow, right-shoulder and left-shoulder) is a good candidate as reference signal for the VR control scheme. Figure 5.10a–c shows first PC extraction from signals coming from right and left elbow sensors in consequence to four elbow extensions. Figure 5.10 depicts clearly PC due to the periodic change in signal by subject's body movements, and hence, the PCA makes it easier to reduce the dimensions of the large signal dataset.

Navigation Control in the Scene – An Interactive Task

Navigation, manipulation and system status changes refer to interaction with the interactive VR. At the same time, these tasks enhance the sense of presence and immersion inside the virtual world. Obviously, we must respect real-time constraints, and interaction techniques should not affect navigation smoothness or the virtual world's immediate reaction to user requests. One of the basic interaction tasks in a pervasive interactive VR is navigation. It lets users move from one place to another or helps the mental or cognitive process of guiding movement (wayfinding), which

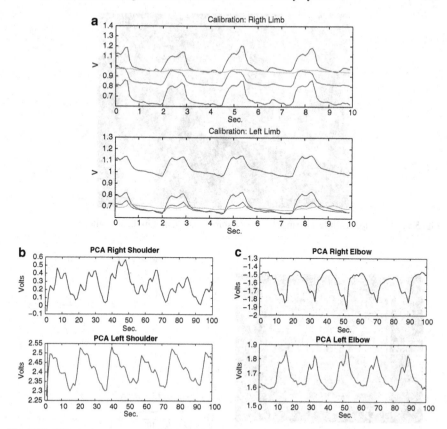

Fig. 5.10 Principal components of the multiple sensors attached to one body part

could be more difficult in a virtual world compared with the same process in the real world. Navigation is the aggregate task of the cognitive element and the motor element [29], wayfinding and travel.

The navigation control strategy of the virtual art gallery scene is based upon the dynamics of differential non-holonomic robot like vehicle as discussed in [34]. We tested our system-control in a virtual art gallery environment (Fig. 5.11), where the environment consisted of different rooms, walls (different paintings mounted on the wall) and floorplan. In order to measure the efficacy of the control scheme, the participant was asked to walk on a marked line designed on the floor of the art gallery from the starting point to the finish point. The idea behind walking on the marked line is to calculate the error, i.e., deviation of the participant's travel from the prescribed line. The participant moved around the art gallery scene using the natural body movements, i.e., moving upper limbs and shoulders in a comfortable and unencumbered movement fashion (Fig. 5.11). In the first trial, the subject began by familiarizing himself with the control strategy (through arm and shoulder movements) without following the prescribed trajectory. After completing this initial acquaintance step, he started following the prescribed path (shown in

Fig. 5.11 Participant while wearing the sensor shirt is navigating in the art gallery

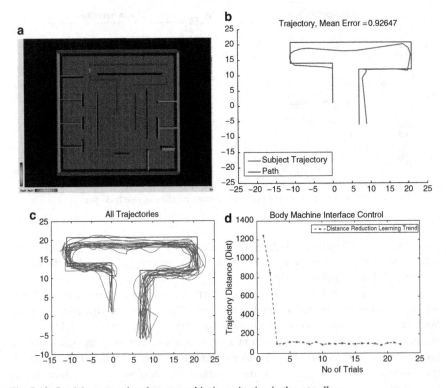

Fig. 5.12 Participant wearing the sensor shirt is navigating in the art gallery

Fig. 5.12c, d). He moved along different directions in the virtual environment, as shown in Fig. 5.12a, to learn the control criteria. As the subject spent more time moving in the virtual scene, the understanding of the control map improved and he was able to navigate the scene with greater accuracy.

The results (see Fig. 5.12b–d) describe the total distance travelled by the subject for each trial to reach the prescribed endpoint from the starting point. The drastic reduction in area and distance error between the first, second and third trials shows that the subject's initial mobility adjustments are significant. In subsequent trials, the participant's movement adjustments are more finely tuned as the familiarity of the sensor shirt-VR control plan improves, resulting in smaller distance errors.

5.6   Conclusion

This chapter throws light on the major challenges in the VR and ease of human interaction. We have developed a system where the human participant wears a sensor-shirt and becomes a part of the 3D VR. The sensor shirt is a very comfortable device and can be worn just in a usual manner; it captures the movements of the participant and the system translates the movements and sends the control commands to VR. In this way the participant feels like moving in the virtual space by just moving the body parts in a natural fashion. Experiments based on several different types of tasks demonstrate the necessity and effectiveness of proper coordination between the human operator and the VRS. Our system has several important distinctions. Firstly, it tracks the pose of the participant's body movements relative to the unified coordinate system of the virtual world, fusing together sensor information from all over the body. Secondly, it provides user a comfortable sensing solution where no indoor restriction or heavy sensor placement on the body is required.

References

1. E. Beltrami. Sulle funzioni bilineari. *Giornale di Mathematiche di Battaglini*, 11:98–106, 1873.
2. I. Carreras, I. Chlamtac, F. De Pellegrini, and D. Miorandi. Bionets: Bio-inspired networking for pervasive communication environments. *IEEE Transactions on Vehicular Technology*, 56(1):218–229, 2007.
3. Coin 3D Graphics Development Library, www.coin3d.org/lib/downloads
4. Disability and rehabilitation (dar) team – assistive devices/technologies. www.who.int/disabilities/technology/en/index.html, World Health Organisation. 2007.
5. Disability and rehabilitation who action plan 2006–2011. www.who.int/disabilities/, World Health Organisation, 2007.
6. M. Dollarhide. Pervasive computing helps fans get into the game. *IEEE Pervasive Computing*, 6(3):7–10, 2007.
7. Electrically conductive liquid silicone rubber, Elastocil LR 3162, www.wacker.com/cms/en/products-markets/products/product.jsp?product=9091
8. I.A. Essa. Ubiquitous sensing for smart and aware environments. *IEEE Personal Communications*, 7(5):47–49, 2000.
9. E. Farella, D. Brunelli, L. Benini, B. Ricco, and M.E. Bonfigli. Pervasive computing for interactive virtual heritage. *IEEE Multimedia*, 12(3):46–58, 2005.
10. R.A. Fisher and W.A. Mckenzie. Studies in crop variation ii. the manurial response of different potato varieties. *Journal of Agricultural Science*, 13:311–320, 1923.

11. T. Gulrez and S. Challa. Relevant opportunistic information extraction and scheduling in heterogeneous sensor networks. In *1st IEEE International Workshop on Computational Advances in Multi-Sensor Adaptive Processing (ICAMP 2005)*, Mexico City, 2005.

12. T. Gulrez and M. Kavakli. Precision position tracking in virtual reality environments using sensor networks. In *IEEE International Symposium on Industrial Electronics*, Vigo, 2007.

13. T. Gulrez and M. Kavakli. Sensor relevance establishment problem in shared information gathering sensor networks. In *IEEE International Conference on Networking Sensing and Control (ICNSC'07)*, London, 2007.

14. T. Gulrez, M. Kavakli, and A. Tognetti. Robotics and virtual reality: A marriage of two diverse streams of science. In *Computational Intelligence in Multimedia Processing: Recent Advances*, 99–118. Springer, Heidelberg, 2008.

15. T. Gulrez, A. Tognetti, A. Fishbach, S. Acosta, C. Scharver, D. DeRossi, and F.A. Mussa-Ivaldi. Controlling wheelchairs by body motions: A learning framework for the adaptive remapping of space. In *Proceedings of the International Conference on Cognitive Systems (CogSys 2008)*, Karlsruhe, 2008.

16. J. Hey and S. Carter. Pervasive computing in sports training. *IEEE Pervasive Computing*, 4(3):54, 2005.

17. H. Hotelling. Analysis of a complex of statistical variables into principal components. *Journal of Educational Psychology*, 24:417–444, 498–520, 1933.

18. K. Jegers and M. Wiberg. Pervasive gaming in the everyday world. *IEEE Pervasive Computing*, 5(1):78–85, 2006.

19. A. Johnson, D. Sandin, G. Dawe, Z. Qiu, and D. Plepys. Developing the paris: Using the cave to prototype a new vr display. In *Proceedings of IPT 2000*, Ames, Iowa, June 2000.

20. M.C. Jordan. Memoire sur les formes bilineaires. *Journal of Pure and Applied Mathematics*, 19:35–54, 1874.

21. H.I. Krebs, M. Ferraro, S.P. Buerger, M.J. Newbery, A. Makiyama, M. Sandmann, D. Lynch, B.T. Volpe, and N. Hogan. Rehabilitation robotics: Pilot trial of a spatial extension for mitmanus. *Journal of NeuroEngineering and Rehabilitation*, 1(5), 2004.

22. F. Lorussi. *Analysis and synthesis of human movement: Wearable kinesthetic interfaces*. PhD thesis, DSEA, University of Pisa, 2003.

23. F. Lorussi, W. Rocchia, E. P Scilingo, A. Tognetti, and D. De Rossi. Wearable redundant fabric-based sensors arrays for reconstruction of body segment posture. *IEEE Sensors Journal*, 4(6):807–818, 2004.

24. F. Lorussi, E.P. Scilingo, M. Tesconi, A. Tognetti, and D. De Rossi. Strain sensing fabric for hand posture and gesture monitoring. *IEEE Transactions On Information Technology In Biomedicine*, 9(3):372–381, September 2005.

25. D. Marculescu, R. Marculescu, N.H. Zamora, P. Stanley-Marbell, P.K. Khosla, S. Park, S. Jayaraman, S. Jung, C. Lauterbach, W. Weber, T. Kirstein, D. Cottet, J. Grzyb, G. Troster, M. Jones, T. Martin, and Z. Nakad. Electronic textiles: A platform for pervasive computing. *Proceedings of the IEEE*, 91(12):1995–2018, 2003.

26. MathWorks. xPC Target, www.mathworks.com/products/xpctarget/

27. Matlab simulink. www.mathworks.com

28. F.A. Mussa-Ivaldi, A. Fishbach, T. Gulrez, A. Tognetti, and D. De-Rossi. Remapping the residual motor space of spinal-cord injured patients for the control of assistive devices. In *Neuroscience 2006*, Atlanta, Georgia, 14–18, 2006.

29. F.A. Mussa-Ivaldi and L.E. Miller. Brain machine interfaces: Computational demands and clinical needs meet basic neuroscience. *Review, Trends in Neuroscience*, 26:329–334, 2003.

30. National Instruments, Multi-function Data Acquisition, www.ni.com/dataacquisition/

31. K. Pearson. On lines and planes of closest fit to systems of points in space. *Philosophical Magazine*, (6)2:559–572, 1901.

32. E.R. Post, M. Orth, P.R. Russo, and N. Gershenfeld. Design and fabrication of textile-based computing. *IBM System Journal*, 39(3–4), 2000.

33. R.W. Stevens. *TCP/IP Illustrated*. Addison-Wesley, ISBN 0201633469, 1994.

34. S. Takezawa, T. Gulrez, D. Herath, and G. Dissanayke. Environmental recognition for autonomous robot using slam real time path planning with dynamical localised voronoi division. *Transactions of the Japan Society of Mechanical Engineers (JSME)*, 3:904–910, 2005.

35. S. Teller, Jiawen Chen, and H. Balakrishnan. Pervasive pose-aware applications and infrastructure. *IEEE Computer Graphics and Applications*, 23(4):14–18, 2003.

36. A. Tognetti, F. Lorussi, R. Bartalesi, S. Quaglini, M. Tesconi, G. Zupone, and D. De Rossi. Wearable kinesthetic system for capturing and classifying upper limb gesture in post-stroke rehabilitation. *Journal of NeuroEngineering and Rehabilitation*, 2(8), 2005.

37. CAVELib[TM] for interactive 3D environments, www.mechdyne.com/integratedSolutions/software/products/CAVELib/CAVELib.htm

38. World report on disability and rehabilitation. Concept Paper, www.who.int/disabilities/, World Health Organisation, 2007.

Chapter 6
Creating Innovative Solutions for Future Hotel Rooms with Intelligent Multimedia and Pervasive Computing

Nalin K. Sharda

Abstract Pervasive computing and intelligent multimedia technologies are becoming increasingly important to the modern way of living. However, many of their potential applications have not been fully realized yet. This chapter explores how innovative applications can be developed to meet the needs of the next generation hotels. Futuristic hotel rooms aim to be more than "home-away-from-home," and as a consequence, offer tremendous opportunities for developing innovative applications of pervasive computing and intelligent multimedia. Next generation hotels will make increased use of technology products to attract new customers. High end TV screens, changeable room ambiance, biometric guest recognition, and electronic check-in facilities are some of the features already being implemented by some hotels. Entirely futuristic hotels in the sea, the stratosphere or the outer space, are also being proposed. All of these provide many novel opportunities for developing innovative solutions using intelligent multimedia and ubiquitous computing.

6.1 Introduction

This chapter articulates how innovation theory and practice can be applied to create novel ideas for future hotel rooms and services, using pervasive computing and intelligent multimedia.

Consistent innovation has become the hallmark of most successful business areas. Hotels and hotel rooms offer a great opportunity for being innovative and creative in providing new technology-based facilities to make the guest's stay easy, comfortable and enjoyable.

N.K. Sharda (✉)
Computer Science, Victoria University, PO Box 14428, Melbourne, Victoria 8001, Australia
e-mail: Nalin.Sharda@vu.edu.au

A.-E. Hassanien et al. (eds.), *Pervasive Computing: Innovations in Intelligent Multimedia and Applications*, Computer Communications and Networks, DOI 10.1007/978-1-84882-599-4_6, © Springer-Verlag London Limited 2009

Some hotel managers feel that, by and large, hotels have not yet used new media technologies to make any remarkable difference to the hotel room facilities; however, dramatic changes are in the offing with the advances being made in pervasive computing and multimedia technologies.

6.1.1   Pervasive Computing

The aim of pervasive computing systems "is to create an environment where the connectivity of devices is embedded in such a way that the connectivity is unobtrusive and always available [1]." Intelligent multimedia allow dynamic selection, composition and presentation of the most appropriate multimedia content based on a set of parameters. A variety of applications of pervasive computing and intelligent multimedia are being developed for all walks of personal and business lives, including hotel rooms.

6.1.2   Hotel Rooms of the Future

Hotel rooms offer a unique set of challenges and opportunities for applying pervasive computing concepts to fulfill the guests' requirements.

For most people, personal and business environments are two distinct spaces, each with its own connectivity, multimedia and communications requirements. Hotel rooms are different, in that they aim to provide an amalgam of personal and business spaces. They attempt to provide the guest a space better than "home-away-from-home," as well as a place to conduct business.

A European Union report on the future of hotels points out that: "Technology has been a primary driving force of change among consumers and in the (hospitality) sector, thereby helping to globalize it. While it creates opportunities, technology is also a major threat to small enterprises in the sector. Because of their small size, it is much harder for them to generate economies of scale and recover the cost of investment in new technologies. However, if they do not invest in new technologies, they are likely to lose out to those who have [2]."

Therefore, there is a tremendous opportunity for the pervasive computing and intelligent multimedia technologies to develop innovative solutions for the hotel industry, targeting large as well as small hotels. To create such innovative solutions, the technologists need to understand the needs of the futuristic hotels and use systematic models and processes for creating innovative solutions using their creativity.

6.1.3   Chapter Aim and Objectives

The main aim of this chapter is to investigate how hotels of the future and the rooms therein can use innovative ideas and applications based on pervasive computing, and combine these with intelligent multimedia to create features that will make these next generation hotels more technically superior providing seamless experience of high-end multimedia applications.

Some of the specific objectives of the chapter include:

- To investigate theories of innovation and their practical implementation models.
- To study some of the futuristic hotel room ideas presented in the literature.
- To articulate technology needs for the hotel rooms of the future.
- To present innovative ideas for hotels and hotel rooms of the future using pervasive computing and intelligent multimedia.

6.1.4   Chapter Layout

Section 6.1 introduced the motivations, aims and objects for this chapter. Section 6.2 presents theoretical models of innovation and some practical implementation methodologies. Section 6.3 presents some concept hotel rooms and how these use computing and multimedia technologies. Section 6.4 presents some futuristic hotels and their technology needs. Section 6.5 presents some innovative ideas for hotel rooms of the future.

6.2   Creativity and Innovation

We all have some understanding of what creativity and innovation are; however, most technologists have had little or no training in methods for enhancing their creativity, and in developing innovative solutions. Most people think that these come naturally to some people, while others cannot be creative. In fact, most of us can be creative and innovative if we use some systematic methodology [3]. In the following sections we investigate how creativity and innovation can be enhanced and pursued systematically.

6.2.1   Creativity

Generally the term creativity is applied to more artistic endeavours, e.g., differentiating between technical and creative writing; however, creativity can be used to develop innovative solutions for technical problems as well. Chris Stevens defines creativity as "the ability to generate and use insight"; and this description applies to technical areas, just as well it does to artistic areas. Everyone is capable of being creative; however, most people do not exploit their full creative potential, as they do not have a clear understanding and models to guide and sustain the flow of their "creative juices" [3].

Stevens identifies six ways to enhance creative potential [4]:

1. *Perspiration*: This implies working consistently, but without burning out.
2. *Egolessness*: This implies to "lose self," and thus minimize the negative effects often caused by self concern and ego.
3. *Switching consciousness*: This implies switching between two types of consciousness: (a) a "tighter mode" associated with more calculative and analytical left-brain thinking and (b) the "looser mode" associated with imaginative and innovative right-brain thinking.
4. *Intuitional capabilities*: Being resilient even in the face of some ambiguity by using intuition.
5. *Abstractive play*: Being able to use abstract thoughts, based on analogy and metaphor.
6. *Social factors*: Creating a "social space" conducive to creativity involving mentors, colleagues, managers/bosses, i.e., a Community of Practice that supports creativity [5].

One of the aims of this chapter is to inculcate creativity in technically oriented computer scientists and engineers, so that they can develop innovative solutions for the next generation hotels using pervasive computing and intelligent multimedia.

6.2.2 Innovation

In the past, much emphasis was placed on inventing new technologies; however, in the current internationally competitive world, innovations are more important. An innovation leads to improvement to something that already exists [6], and becomes the catalyst for the development of new products, or the creation of newer versions of an existing product. According to Joyce Wycoff, innovation is a "mental extreme sport" and requires "pulling unrelated things together [6]." Thus, to innovate, one must inculcate interest in a wide range of disciplines [3]; then, often, solutions in one domain can be seen as solutions to problems in another domain.

At times, a problem triggers an innovative solution in another area. The story of Velcro is particularly relevant as such an innovation. George de Mestral was a Swiss engineer who enjoyed hunting and walking through the countryside. "One morning in 1941, while returning from the fields with his dog, he noticed how difficult it was to detach the flowers of the mountain thistle from his trousers and his dog's fur [7]." He saw a potential solution in this problem and worked on it for many years; finally, he created a system of loops (velour in French) and hooks (crochet in French) to produce workable VELCRO® fastening tapes.

6.2.3 Incremental and Radical Innovations

Two types of innovations can be identified: incremental innovation and radical innovation. Incremental innovation makes a small change to an existing product or a process. A radical innovation leads to a dramatic change to the product or the process in question [8].

The effect of these innovations can be felt at two dimensions: internal and external (to the organization). The internal dimension relates to the organization's existing knowledge and resources. The external dimension relates to the changes taking place in the industry as a whole [9].

As for the internal dimension, for incremental innovation, the organization aims to build upon existing knowledge and resources. Therefore, incremental innovation is competence-enhancing, and thus, is also called sustaining innovation. Radical innovation requires completely new knowledge and/or resources; therefore, it can be competence-destroying, and thus, is also called disruptive innovation.

The external dimension is based on the overall technology market and the organization's competitiveness within the same. With regard to the external dimension, incremental innovation involves modest technological enhancements to keep existing products competitive. On the other hand, a radical innovation involves large technological advancement, and often makes the existing products non-competitive or obsolete.

6.2.4 Creating Innovations

Humanity has advanced through innovations from prehistoric times. However, some innovators have succeeded more than the others. Leonardo da Vinci was a prolific innovator. He made sure that as he got ideas, those were documented diligently in one of the three notebooks he always carried on the string of his gown. He jotted down thousands of ideas, even though only a few of those could be implemented in his lifetime. Today, we can use more advanced models and tools to support innovation.

Newhart and Joyce offer the Innovation Funnel model [6], shown in Fig. 6.1. "This model predicates that one needs to create a large number of ideas (1,000s), and record them systematically. Only some (100s) of these may be evaluated, even fewer (10s) would then be researched. This is because creating new ideas needs few

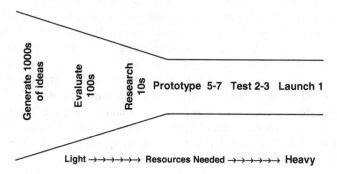

Fig. 6.1 The innovation funnel model [3, 6]

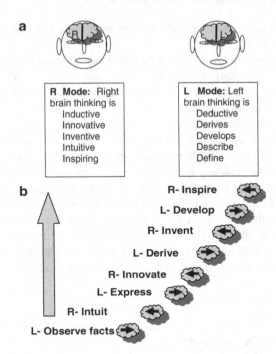

Fig. 6.2 (**a**) Right and left brain thinking and (**b**) The left/right brain transfer model [10, 11]

resources; but as we move to the right of the funnel, heavier investment in resources is required. Thus, one can build a prototype for just a few ideas, and test even fewer, to be able to launch but one product [3]."

Figure 6.2a shows a model that uses the two modes of human thinking, called the right brain (R-Mode) thinking and left brain (L-Mode) thinking [10]. "The L-Mode thinking is more deductive, and is better at deriving, developing, describing and defining. The R-Mode thinking is more imaginative, inductive, innovative, inventive, intuitive and inspiring [11]." These modes are similar to the tighter and looser modes of thinking described by Chris Stevens [4].

Figure 6.2b shows a Left/Right Brain Cognition Transfer model offered by Sharda [11]. This model points to the fact that we must make effective use of both hemispheres of the brain. "It shows how one can rise from observing facts to creating inspirational ideas. One should begin by using the left brain to observe facts, but then shift to the right brain and apply intuition to "read between the lines," i.e., develop an understanding that goes beyond the observed facts. The outcome of the observations and intuition must be expressed and documented using the left brain to ensure that these are not lost. This left to right and right to left transfer should continue: innovate with right brain, derive new models with left brain, invent new concepts using right brain, develop new systems using left brain and inspire others using the right brain [11]."

6.2.5 Sustaining Innovation

Denning and Dunham present a list of practices that can sustain innovation. They also articulate the following reasons which often lead to breakdown in an organization's ability to grasp the opportunity to innovate [12]:

1. *Sensing possibilities*: "Sensing and articulating opportunities and their value in a community. Seeing possibilities in breakdowns. Being sensitive to disharmonies [12]." Breakdowns are caused by: "Blindness. Inability to move from sensing to articulation, to hold the thought or to see opportunities in disharmonies [12]."
2. *Envisioning new realities*: "Speculating about new worlds in which an opportunity is taken care of; and means to get there [12]." Causes for breakdown include: "Inability to tell vivid, concrete, compelling stories or to design plans of action [12]."
3. *Offering new outcomes*: "Proposing new rules and strategies of play that produce the new outcomes. Listening to concerns, then modifying proposals for better fit. Establishing credibility in one's expertise to fulfill the offer [12]." Failures in this aspect can be caused by: "Missing awareness of and respect for customers. Inability to listen, to enroll people, to articulate value or to see people as fundamental in the process. Unwillingness to modify proposals in response to feedback [12]."
4. *Executing plans and actions*: "Building teams and organizations. Carrying out action plans for reliable delivery [12]." Breakdowns can be caused by: "Failure to manage commitments, satisfy customers, deliver on time or build trust [12]."
5. *Adopting new practice*: "Demonstrating value of proposed adoption, so that others can commit to it. Becoming aware of power structures and community interests to determine fit. Aligning action plans for coherence with existing practices, concerns, interests and adoption rates of community members. Developing marketing strategies for different groups. Recruiting allies. Overcoming resistance [12]." Reasons for the failure of this action can include: "Forcing adoption through compulsion. Failure to anticipate opposition, to anticipate differing adoption rates of segments of community or to articulate the value from adopting. Lack of enabling tools and processes for adoption [12]."
6. *Sustaining integration*: "Developing supporting infrastructure. Aligning new practices with surrounding environment, standards and incentives. Assessing related innovations for negative consequences. Abandoning bad innovations. Discontinuing after end of useful life [12]." Causes for breakdown can include: "Failure to plan for support and training, to change enabling tools and systems or to align incentives with the new practices [12]."
7. *Leading*: "Declaring new possibilities in ways that people commit to them. Moving with care, courage, value, power, focus, sense of larger purpose (destiny) and fluency of speech acts [12]." The leadership process can be caused by: "Inability to listen for concerns, offer value, work with power structures, maintain focus, operate from a larger purpose or perform speech acts skillfully [12]."

8. *Attending to somatics*: "Working with the somatic aspects of communication and commitment. Ascending the ladder of competence. Connecting with people. Producing trust. Developing an open and inviting "presence." Blending with concerns, energies and styles of others [12]." These somatic indicators, i.e., those based on body characteristics, can breakdown due to: "Inability to read and respond to body language, gesture, etc. Inability to connect and blend. Failure to recognize and overcome one's own conditioned tendencies, to appreciate differing levels of skill and their criteria or to engage in regular practice in the other practice areas [12]."

It is important to note that innovations are not always based on existing needs; some innovative ideas create new needs, while others meet an existing need better than the competing product, giving the organization a competitive advantage. We can extend a long-held belief that "need is the mother of invention," by adding that "competition is the father of innovation," i.e., competition spurs along innovation.

Thus, to create innovative products and systems for hotels of the future, one needs to combine the theoretical models of innovation presented in the preceding section, with the guest needs and futuristic possibilities, giving hotels a competitive advantage.

6.3   Concept Hotels of the Future

Over the recent years, the hotel industry has been busy thinking and dreaming of ideas that will be used in the hotels of the future. Some of these ideas have already been implemented, while others are just concepts. Nonetheless, these are presented here as possible triggers for creating innovative applications of intelligent multimedia and pervasive computing suitable for hotels of the future.

6.3.1   Hilton's Room of the Future

Hilton hotel's "Room of the Future" is housed in the Hilton University near Los Angeles International Airport, furnished with many next-generation products to cater for business activities, enhanced comfort and entertainment [13].

Some of the facilities included are just the latest technology, while others aim to be futuristic, including:

- Wall-mounted, 42-in. flat-screen HDTV Panasonic plasma television connected to a Technics receiver with surround-sound Bose speakers
- Philips DVD/CD player
- Second, smaller flat-screen LCD monitor next to the Jacuzzi bathtub
- Motion-detection lights that activate when guests enter the room
- Biometric room safe that uses a thumbprint as the lock and key

- Free broadband, accessible via laptop or the TV
- Panja touch-panel remote control that manages lighting levels and room climate; opens and closes the drapes; controls the TV, radio and DVD player; and even repositions the head and foot of the king-size bed
- Compressor-less mini-refrigerator that is completely silent
- Panasonic massage chair, a heated toilet seat/bidet, a computerized five-nozzle shower, and a defogging bathroom mirror

6.3.1.1   Test Results

Michael S. Lasky of PCWorld gave the following comments on Hilton's Room of the Future. He liked the fact that it allowed remote printing using PrinterOn, a remote printing service. After logging on to the PrinterOn site for Hilton Garden Inn, guests could send a print job to the hotel business centre's color printer, or to any other hotel in the chain where the printout would be kept in a secure location until the guest claims it. The new features were targeted not only to make it a utilitarian space, but also "a boy's playroom [13]."

6.3.1.2   Multimedia Facilities

A Smart Card reader allowed entry to the room with an enhanced credit card such as the American Express Blue card. However, the hotel-supplied card could be used as well. A TV camera by the front door could be used in conjunction with the room's Airphone to check out a visitor before opening the door.

The room safe was big enough to store a laptop. The safe worked with a thumb reader to store the belongings and open it later; much easier than remembering numbers and punching buttons.

A T-shaped wooden desk had adjustable lighting and a convenient Ethernet port for free Internet access. No computer was provided; however, one could use the wireless keyboard to surf the Internet, with the 42-in. plasma TV as the monitor.

Michael S. Lasky quipped that: "But it was difficult to sit behind a computer with so many other toys available to test. The Panasonic massage chair, a leather recliner with a remote control, seemed uncomfortable at first. After I started its massager, the stress of the day melted away. Wait – now the room was too bright! Using the Panja universal touch-screen remote, I closed the curtains and blinds, dimmed the lights, turned on the TV, and switched channels. I was all but ready to move in permanently [13]." It sure was a "boy's playroom."

6.3.1.3   High-Tech Bathing

The bathroom had a glassed-in shower with five nozzles and computerized water-temperature control; however, it turned out to be more annoying than enjoyable.

Lasky related his experience and evaluation as: "First, guests need 20/20 vision to deal with the plethora of controls. I don't usually wear my glasses into a shower. Since I couldn't see what buttons I was pushing, the crotch-level nozzle blasting 102° water came as a shock – and my attempts to shut it off only caused other nozzles to splash me as if I were in a penitentiary riot. (Hilton's plan to install a voice-activated control could be just the solution.) Another surprise: Despite all the high-end design, the shower lacks a soap dish."

The Jacuzzi had an overhead flat-panel TV. However, it showed the same channel as on the main TV in the bedroom; and it was not possible to change channels from the bathroom.

The king size bed did not use a mattress, but a system of air baffles over slats. One could raise or lower the head, foot and left and right sides of the bed via remote controls at each side; perfect for watching TV or reading.

"When I turned off the room lights – the whole dozen of them – with the remote, the room took on the look of a planetarium, what with all the glowing device LED lights scattered about. But I was too comfortable to let them bother me. I woke up the next morning in the same position I fell asleep in." In his conclusion, Lasky wrote: "This might be the room of the future, but after one stay, I want it now [13]."

6.3.2 Self Check-in Systems

To overcome customer frustration with issues such as slow check-in and inappropriate temperature setting, hotels are looking at new technologies. Already, Boston-based Nine Zero Hotel employs an iris scanner to control access to their Cloud Nine suite [14]. Holiday Inn's eCheck kiosk system lets guests check in themselves and skip the front desk.

Dave Ellis thinks that: "Whether it's iris-scanning technology, iPod docking stations or rooms that tailor themselves to your body temperature, the hotel of the future may only be a few reservations away [14]."

Since 2003 the hotel business in USA rebounded from the 9/11 attack led downturn, and technology products such as self-check-in kiosks have been used by hotel chains to "win new customers, keep old ones coming back and cut costs when they can [14]."

Holiday Inn chain has also tested an eCheck system that allows guests to print boarding passes as they leave for the airport. Prof. Richard Penner of Cornell University believes that self-check-in is finally gaining momentum, after a few false starts. Today's time starved guest is happy to bypass a personal smile, get to the room as quickly as possible. Richard Senechal, Senior Vice President of facilities for Loews Hotels, has even called the front desk "a dead duck."

A more useful extension to the eCheck systems is the ability to use one's own handheld device (mobile phone, PDA and iPOD) to check-in. This would also allow the hotel system to get the guest's preferences [14], and provide customized services.

6.4 Out-of-this-World Hotels

Who says that a hotel has to stand on a solid foundation? Ideas have been mooted to build hotels in the oceans, in the wilderness, in the stratosphere and even in the outer space. As these hotels are only concepts yet, and will be build by the time computing technology has advanced much further, these hotels will be an excellent "sand-box" to try new ideas for enhancing guest services with ubiquitous computing and intelligent multimedia.

6.4.1 Foldable Hotel Pods

Valhouli presents a novel concept for hotels of the future with designs that include undersea and space resorts [15]. These foldable hotel pods (Fig. 6.3) could even be moved from one location to another.

In the "Future Holiday Forum," a report entitled "2024: A Holiday Odyssey" predicted that in the future hotels will be a foldable pod that can be easily relocated to remote locations [15]. Guests will be able to choose the images they want to project on the walls, changing the ambiance to their personal choice. When a destination falls out of fashion, whether due to demand or terrorism, the pod can simply be folded up and moved. An added advantage of these pod hotels is that they will have minimal impact on the environment and will not require roads to get there, as helicopters can be used to bring in the guests.

Fig. 6.3 Foldable hotel pods (picture courtesy www.m3architects.com) [15]

6.4.2   Resort Hotels in the Stratosphere

Who does not dream of flying with arms spread out like wings? While such ideas can come true only in imagination or dreams, we can certainly build living spaces that will hover around in the stratosphere.

Geoff Manaugh introduces a flying hotel proposed by Wimberley Allison Tong & Goo (WATG), an architectural firm based in London [16]. WATG has challenged the old ideas about how to design new resorts and where to place them. In a recent competition co-sponsored by WATG, entitled "Hospitality Transformed: Resort Hotels in 2055," architecture students around the world presented futuristic ideas ranging from "environmentally sensitive resorts in pristine remote locations to highly sophisticated technological wonders in dense urban settings.

WATG has also partnered with Worldwide Aeros Corp, the Aeroscraft manufacturer and world leader in manufacturing of the FAA-certified lighter-than-air vehicles, to design the interiors of a new generation of airborne cruise ships [17]."

6.4.3   Space Hotels

Space tourism is coming. The Genesis module (Fig. 6.4) launched on 12 July 2006 using the Russian Dnepr (SS-18) rocket is a tangible step in the ongoing development of the space tourism [18]. The most important aspect of this mission is that it shows that the space tourism industry is not only developing vehicles for suborbital and eventually orbital flight, but also that future space tourists will have a place to

Fig. 6.4 Genesis 1 a step towards space tourism (courtesy Bigelow Aerospace) [18]

stay when they get up there. Having an experimental module in orbit is essential in order to show investors that this industry is going to be in business for a long time to come.

Future space tourists may not be content with a short ride into orbit inside a cramped capsule. A "space hotel" is the minimum needed to attract space tourists beyond some adventurers. One of the essential facilities will be windows for viewing the Earth. Cramped space and weight limitations will stretch the technology at all levels. Therefore, wireless ubiquitous computing will be required for multimedia and other communication applications.

These space hotels will include technology such as dosimeters to record the cumulative radiation received by the traveler, and microphones, and cameras to record the antics of items sent by people using Bigelow's "Fly Your Stuff" programme [18]. The company is hoping that this will catch on and generate some cash flow even before paying hotel guests make the trip.

6.4.4 Fanciful Hotels

David Neilsen presents a number of ideas for fanciful hotels; some already made, some under construction and some just fanciful ideas. Some of these hotels do not use technology as their attraction, while others will rely on technical gizmos to attract guests [19]. With the amorphous nature of most such hotels, they will be fertile ground for the use of wireless ubiquitous computing and intelligent multimedia systems.

6.4.4.1 Ice Hotel, Quebec, Canada

Jacques Desbois has built an Ice Hotel in Quebec, Canada (http://www.icehotel-canada.com/en/). He said: "People thought I was crazy, but I had to make an ice hotel. . . ." "And so he did. A five-suite hotel in Northern Canada built entirely out of ice. North America's first ice hotel (There is already one in existence in Sweden) . . . the temperature may climb as high as −4 °C (26 °F) and guests must be regularly thawed out of bed [19]."

6.4.4.2 L'Hotel Machet, Paris, France

L'Hotel Machet is the world's first hotel to be made out of Paper Mache. It includes "readable walls in multiple languages, an all-mache pastry shop and free paste for the kids! Hotel will be equipped with wheels for use as a float in local parades and comes with a smiling, waving "Princess Paper" in the lobby [19]."

6.4.4.3   Tinker-Toys Hotel, Wichita, Kansas

Hutch Duggle wanted to tap into people's nostalgia for "Tinker-Toys!" He conceived of the world's first hotel made entirely with tinker toys. According to him: "Bring your whole family! No matter the size, we've got a room for them! Heck, if needed, you can adjust your room yourself! It's Tinker-Toys! [19]."

6.4.4.4   Hotel-O, Sydney, Australia

Hotel-O is made entirely out of Jell-O. "Special features include Bill Cosby permanently sitting in the lobby and cost-efficient fire escape exits – you simply walk through the walls. Guests desiring true privacy may want to ask for the darker-flavoured rooms [19]."

6.4.4.5   Disney's Pyramid on Ice, Cairo, Egypt

Disney does theme parks bigger and better than anyone else. They announced plans to build "Disney's Pyramid on Ice!" outside of Cairo, Egypt. "Special features include ice-skating bellboys dressed as your favourite Disney characters, monorail service to The Sphinx and David Blaine frozen for your enjoyment in the lobby. Opens 6 June 2001, melts itself closed 3 h later [19]." Did it really?

6.4.4.6   Invisible Hotel, Central Park, New York

Sam Smilky announced his plans for the world's first invisible hotel in the middle of Central Park, New York [19]. "They told me I was crazy, but I had a dream," said Sam. It is meant to be an entirely invisible 3-story luxury hotel accommodating over 100 guests. "People will walk by, and think you're lying on the ground, but that's only because they won't be able to see the luxurious accommodations surrounding you!" said Smilky, "Plus I'm making it out of walls you can walk right through! As if they're not even there! How much would you pay for that? [19]." Now that is a fanciful idea, but one full of opportunities for innovative solutions using ubiquitous computing.

6.4.5   Technology Needs of Hotel Room of the Future

Despite the technology upgrades of the recent past, most hotel rooms are still using wires for various functions. "All too often travelers find themselves crawling around on their hotel room floor looking for telephone jacks, waiting ages for room service, stumbling in the dark during late-night trips to the bathroom or puzzling for hours over setting the alarm on the clock radio [20]."

These inconveniences provide a fertile ground for innovations using intelligent multimedia, wireless communications and pervasive computing to develop innovative solutions. Some such ideas include [20]:

- Handheld computers for curb-side check-in
- Mini-bars that know your likes and dislikes
- Thermostats that adjust the temperature based on guest presence in the room
- Digital movies and other multimedia on demand
- Biometric scanners for tighter security
- Electronics that alter everything from the firmness of the mattress to the art on the walls based on guest's preferences

Together, these features would aim to deliver a personalized experience to the guest. "One product making it easy to accommodate guests' personal preferences is the Bartech e-fridge^{TM} ... [it] has sensors that detect when a beverage has been removed. The front desk is alerted, your bill is updated and room service knows what to replace in the morning. The e-fridge can also be programmed to change drink prices throughout the day, lowering them during happy hour. In the future, hotel guests could find their minibars stocked only with their favourite drinks and preferences gleaned from past selections [20]."

Already cards that use radio frequency identification (RFID) technology have been developed. These can not only open the room doors, but can also be linked to pay for dinner. The challenge is make them do more, e.g., luggage transfer: "Place the card in your bag and when the luggage comes off the conveyor belt, the airline can retrieve it, scan it and send it straight to your hotel [20]."

Furthermore, it can contain a biometric record letting the guest check in easily not only at the hotel, but also on a plane, as being trialed at London's Heathrow Airport for British Airways and Virgin Atlantic frequent travelers. Imagine: simply by looking at the check-in gates the guests can pass through. Using handheld devices such as mobile phones and PDAs for check-in is possible now; however, these are not yet being used widely. Motion detectors can avoid annoying mid-shower knocks at the door by telling housekeeping that the guest is in. However, new technologies require innovative deployment and economies of scale to work in their favour before they are adopted widely.

6.5 Innovative Ideas for Hotel Rooms

This section explores how some of the ideas proposed by the hotel industry can be combined with intelligent multimedia and pervasive computing systems.

6.5.1 Intelligent Systems in Future Hotels

Glen Hiemstra of www.futurist.com predicts that the future hotel rooms will make extensive use of robotics, nanotechnology and biometric recognition, including retina scans. Retina scan is already used in high-security offices, banks and the military; however, soon these will be used in the hotel industry [15].

We can envision hotels where robotic devices will do a majority of the tasks like check-in and room service. Highly futuristic possibility can be realized with nanotechnology. By 2025 or 2030, it may be possible for rooms to reconfigure (in fact almost rebuild) themselves to the guest's whim and fancy [15].

However, the more automated services are made, the less personal they become. Loosing human touch is not always popular as we have learnt from automated phone answering services. However, intelligent multimedia systems, using three dimensional holographic images, can provide a more humanistic experience, if the guests can feel that they are interacting with a human being's Avatar.

6.5.1.1   Opportunities in the Future

The need for hotel chains to distinguish themselves will provide many opportunities for the development of innovative products and processes using intelligent multimedia and ubiquitous computing systems.

Andrew Zolli, president of Z Plus Partners, New York, focused on aging baby boomers, and predicted the need for "health-monitoring" rooms in the years to come [14]. Such rooms may include:

- Sensors in the toilet that measure blood sugar in urine
- Infrared cameras that track body temperature and send a message to regulate the thermostat and humidity in the room even as the guests sleep; or call a doctor

With the concern for global warming or climate change, many guests may like to stay in "carbon-neutral" hotels. This will require not only eco-friendly products and organic food, but also minimization of energy and water waste. According to Zolli: "The boomers want to keep up with the Jones, and the Jones are realigning their chakras and driving hybrid cars [14]."

Some of the new gadgets may come from standard product range and some from novel products and services. The deployment of these products is where the hotels will try to differentiate their services and gain some competitive advantage. How will the cost of all these innovations be absorbed? "That depends on the hotel," said Hospitality Technology's Paul, and "Luxury brands might absorb some of the costs, but in two- and three-star properties, the guest may foot the bill [19]."

Hotels have to find a compromise between raising rates and providing new services. "It's much easier to charge for individual services than to raise room rates," said Paul. "That's the ultimate goal in a lot of ways – to find ways to generate more revenue without raising rates [19]."

6.5.1.2   Multimedia Delivery Technology

Many hotels still have the old Cathode Ray Tube (CRT)-based TV sets. Prof. Tom Lattin of University of Houston believes that all the major hotel chains will replace old TVs with flat-screen ones in the near future. Flat screen TVs will provide improved picture quality while freeing up living space; additionally, these TVs will become the display device for the delivery of a variety of intelligent multimedia content.

Reid Paul, editor of Hospitality Technology, suggests that these flat screen TVs will provide a greater variety of content: from local news to international sports coverage. Moreover, the room will be outfitted to cater for variety of wireless devices such as a docking station for iPod right on the bedside table.

The aim of such technology upgrades would be to make the hotel experience more seamless and customized for the individual guest. Many experts predict that free Internet access will become standard and telephone calls will use Voice over IP (VoIP) technology, provided at much reduced cost.

At the St. Martin's Lane Hotel, Covent Gardens, London, the walls are painted white, so that guests have the choice of "altering the color of their room anywhere from deep violet to a jungle green [14]."

The Mandarin Oriental Hotel Group, including its New York location, has outfitted rooms to remember regular guests' preferences. Consequently, as a regular guest walks into the room, "the lights, room temperature and speed dial on the phone are set to their specifications." Danielle DeVoe of Mandarin Oriental hotels claims that such features help to distinguish their hotels from the competition. "Advanced in-room technology is critical in how we attract guests to our hotels and hideaway properties," claims DeVoe [14].

6.6   Conclusions

Next generation hotels will provide a fertile ground for creating innovative applications of pervasive computing and intelligent multimedia. However, creating innovative applications needs systematic models and processes to enhance creativity and support innovation. Innovation funnel model and the Left-Right brain cognition models can be used towards this end. Proposals for futuristic hotel rooms aim to provide the guest more than "home-away-from-home." Next generation hotels are being proposed with features such as high-definition flat TV screens, changeable room ambiance, biometric guest recognition and electronic check-in facilities. Proposals are also afoot for hotels in the sea, in the stratosphere and the outer space. These proposed features provide a fertile ground for developing innovative solutions for next generation hotels using intelligent multimedia and ubiquitous computing.

References

1. Pervasive Computing, Webopedia, http://www.webopedia.com/TERM/p/pervasive _computing.htm, Accessed July 2008.
2. What future? Visions of the future: Policies, issues and the future references, European Foundation for the Improvement of Living and Working Conditions, www.eurofound.eu.int, Accessed July 2007.

3. Sharda, N., Creating innovative new media programs: Need, challenges, and development framework, ACM Workshop on Educational Multimedia and Multimedia Education (in conjunction with ACM Multimedia 2007), Augsburg, Germany, 28 September 2007.
4. Stevens, C.D., Coming to insight, eventually. Screenhub, March 2007, http://www. screenhub.com.au/news/newsarticle_sendfriend.asp?newsID = 14910, Accessed May 2007.
5. Nickols, F., Communities of practice: An overview, 2003, http://home.att.net/~discon/KM/CoPOverview.pdf, Accessed June 2008.
6. Newhart, R.L., Joyce, C., Free radicals of innovation [video recording], Innovation Center, Star Thrower Distribution, 2005. Center, Star Thrower Distribution, 2005.
7. History of Velcro, http://www.velcro.co.uk/cms/History.6.0.html?&L = 0http://www.velcro.co.uk/cms/History.6.0.html?&L = 0, Accessed July 2008.
8. Trauffler, G., Tschirky, H., Sustained Innovation Management: Assimilating Radical and Incremental Innovation Management, Palgrave MacMillan, Hampshire, UK, 2007.
9. Scocco, D., Innovation Management Theory – Round Up, http://innovationzen. com/blog/category/innovation-theory/, Accessed July 2008.
10. Von Wodtke, M., Design with Digital Tools, McGraw Hill, 2000.
11. Sharda, N., Authoring educational multimedia content using learning styles and story telling principles, ACM Workshop on Educational Multimedia and Multimedia Education, Augsburg, Germany, 28 September 2007.
12. Denning, P.J., Dunham, R., Innovation as language action, Commun ACM 49(5);2006:47–52.
13. Lasky, M.S., A Night in the Hotel of the Future: PC World tests the gadgets and gizmos of a traveling techie's dreams, 06 June 2003, http://www.pcworld.com/article/id,111042-page,1/article.html, Accessed July 2007.
14. Ellis, D., Get ready for the hotel of the future, http://money.cnn.com/2006/02/14/news/companies/hotels_future/index.htm, Accessed July 2008.
15. Valhouli, C., Hotels of the future: Designs include undersea and space resorts, 7 June 2004, Forbes.com, http://www.msnbc.msn.com/id/5077355/, Accessed July 2007.
16. Manaugh, G., Resort hotels of the stratospheric future, http://bldgblog.blogspot.com/2006/03/resort-hotels-of-stratospheric-future.html, Accessed July 2008.
17. Wimberley, Allison, Tong, & Goo, WATG Looks to the Future, http://www.watg.com/index.cfm?view = story_ideas&theme = WATG%20Looks%20to%20the%20Future, Accessed July 2008.
18. Dinerman, T, Genesis and the future space hotel, July 2006, http://www.thespacereview.com/article/660/1, Accessed July 2008.
19. Neilsen, D., The future of hotels, http://www.brunching.com/newhotels.html, Accessed July 2008.
20. Stanford, K., High Wired: The Hotel Room of the Future, Hospitality Upgrade, Spring, 2004, http://www.hotel-online.com/News/PR2004_2nd/Apr04_HighWiredRoom.html, Accessed July 2008.

Chapter 7
Mobile Virtual Environments in Pervasive Computing

Shaimaa Lazem, Ayman Abdel-Hamid, Denis Gračanin, and Kevin P. Adams

Abstract Recently, human computer interaction has shifted from traditional desktop computing to the pervasive computing paradigm where users are engaged with everywhere and anytime computing devices. Mobile virtual environments (MVEs) are an emerging research area that studies the deployment of virtual reality applications on mobile devices. MVEs present additional challenges to application developers due to the restricted resources of the mobile devices, in addition to issues that are specific to wireless computing, such as limited bandwidth, high error rate and handoff intervals. Moreover, adaptive resource allocation is a key issue in MVEs where user interactions affect system resources, which, in turn, affects the user's experience. Such interplay between the user and the system can be modelled using game theory. This chapter presents MVEs as a real-time interactive distributed system, and investigates the challenges in designing and developing a remote rendering prefetching application for mobile devices. Furthermore, we introduce game theory as a tool for modelling decision-making in MVEs by describing a game between the remote rendering server and the mobile client.

Keywords Mobile Virtual Environments · Game theory · Adaptive resource allocation · Decision-making

7.1 Introduction

Distributed virtual environment (DVE) systems are complex, interconnected, computer generated, interactive, distributed virtual worlds that provide a shared *place* for interactions and collaboration [32]. DVE systems can be deployed on networks ranging from small-scale to global ones. The DVE users can interact in real-time (e.g., multi-player online games) and their number could reach hundreds or thousands in a single application (e.g., SecondLife™).

S. Lazem (✉)
Department of Computer Science, Virginia Tech, Blacksburg, VA 24060, USA
e-mail: shlazem@vt.edu

A.-E. Hassanien et al. (eds.), *Pervasive Computing: Innovations in Intelligent Multimedia and Applications*, Computer Communications and Networks, DOI 10.1007/978-1-84882-599-4_7, © Springer-Verlag London Limited 2009

The expansion of broadband wired and wireless network services, combined with recent advances in commodity computing and graphics hardware, especially mobile devices, is making it possible to deploy persistent and pervasive virtual worlds as large-scale DVE systems shared by hundreds of thousands of users.

The pervasive nature of such systems, combined with new ways to enable and analyze interactions (augmented reality (AR) and sensors) requires new thinking. In order to provide support for transparent, adaptive and intelligent DVE systems, we need a good understanding of the *traditional* DVE technologies and of the enabling technologies like sensor networks, web services and agent architectures. Providing users with effective and consistent 3D interactions and 3D user interfaces requires a lot of work *behind the user interface* to address DVE system-related practical and theoretical issues. There are many important research problems such as physical integration and spontaneous interoperation [17] that provide exciting opportunities for new discoveries and advancements.

Mobile, hand-held devices, such as PDAs and smart phones, can serve as an *entry* point into a shared virtual world, thereby providing for mobile virtual environments (MVEs). The use of location and related services for mobile devices will further bridge the gap between the virtual world and the real world to provide for pervasive virtual environments (VEs). Such pervasive VEs could bring social aspects of everyday life into a virtual world. For example, pervasive gaming can integrate the social quality of traditional non-computer games into the game play [5, 15].

Characteristics of MVEs are manifestations of complex interactions between the user, application and network levels. The qualitative nature of user experience makes it difficult to relate the user level experience with quantitative network level characteristics. We explore the use of game theory as a way to model these complex interactions and provide a better user experience.

Section 7.2 provides an overview of related work. Section 7.3 defines mobile MVEs as an emerging research field and discusses the potential challenges in designing and evaluating MVE applications. In addition, we describe a remote-rendering application as an MVE case study. Section 7.4 proposes a test-bed architecture for evaluating MVEs applications. Section 7.5 presents game theory related concepts, and introduces a game theory model for the remote rendering application. Finally, Sect. 7.6 outlines the chapter conclusions and discusses directions for future work.

7.2 Related Work

Recently, the rapid evolution of the pervasive computing paradigm [13] and the increased production of portable devices have enabled large scale deployment of virtual reality applications on mobile devices.

Pervasive computing allowed complex VEs, e.g., virtual heritage, to step beyond specialized interfaces and reach larger population of users [11]. Similarly, it enabled large scale deployment of AR applications. Wagner et al. [37] introduced a system architecture for multi-user AR applications running on handheld devices, while

Kimura, Tokunaga and Nakajima [16] propose a pervasive computing framework was proposed for developers to build and deploy AR applications.

Broll et al. [5] introduced the technological challenges and requirements to achieve pervasive AR games. Tracking technologies are needed for determining user position, especially orientation tracking to specify user's field of view.

AR pervasive games inherit the challenges of distributed systems, such as consistency, reliability and persistence, in addition to mobility problems, such as signal failure and disconnected intervals. Moreover, the wide range of end user devices raises additional interoperability issues.

Pervasive games or mixed reality games are another by-product for encompassing pervasive computing features into virtual worlds [8,14,15,25]. Pervasive games employ pervasive and mobile computing technologies either to augment traditional games or to create new games that are impossible to realize with traditional media [15].

A mixed reality version of the traditional *Capture the Flag* game was introduced by Cheok et al. [8]. The interaction between physical and virtual world players improved the game by adding social aspects to the play. Herbst et al. [14] is another example of pervasive game, where players interact with the city of Cologne and explore its temporal changes. This time mixed reality is used to add the temporal dimension for game players.

MVEs illustrate a typical example for dynamic, interactive, real-time distributed systems. A general trend of real-time resource management moves away from static open-loop approaches to dynamic and adaptive closed-loop approaches. While classical real-time scheduling is concerned with absolute guarantees in highly predictable environments, we need adaptive and efficient solutions to handle unpredictable environments [23].

Many such problems can be described as optimization problems and solved using optimization techniques. That assumes a complete description of the optimization problem, which may not work when faced with the uncertainty of future values. Optimality requires clairvoyance.

Dynamic, interactive, real-time distributed systems requiring this near real-time clairvoyant control need the simplicity, linearity and stability of the transformation function in open-loop solutions. While the optimization of values based on future values is not possible, it may be possible to find a good quality heuristic solution.

For optimization strategies without derivatives, four general techniques are employed [1]: direct search methods, simulated annealing (SA), derivative free optimization (DFO) and genetic algorithms (GAs). Often the SA and GAs are combined.

Classical direct search methods (e.g., conjugate direction, simplex and complex searches, adaptive random searches, etc.) are based on well-defined search methods that require only objective function values for unconstrained minimization. SA is derived from a class of heuristics with analogies to the motion of molecules in the cooling and solidification of metals [18]. DFO takes advantage of the availability of parallel computing and reconsiders the classical direct search approaches.

GAs usually represent solutions for chromosomes with bit coding (genotype) and searches for the better solution candidates in the genotype space using GA operations of selection, crossover and mutation. The GA uses the fitness values to select current possible solutions used to determine the next searching points. The offspring in the next generation is generated by applying the GA operations, crossover and mutation to the selected parent solution. This process is iterated until the GA search converges to the required searching level.

GAs have been used to solve distributed real-time scheduling problems by replacing the prominent rule-based heuristic schedulers [30, 38].

Lee and Hsu [21] developed a methodology to approximately solve optimization problems in near real-time using a neural network. They first formulate the problem's constraints and desired optima by a specific mathematical function that characterizes the desired problem and has the characteristic that the stable states of the network model correspond to the *best* solutions of the problem. They map the problem to a neural network model and select an appropriate activation function that can make the mathematical function converge in the neural network model. Finally, they adjust the parameters of the mathematical function.

Adams et al. [1, 2] propose an approach to real-time decision making for quality of service-based scheduling of distributed asynchronous data replication. They address uncertainty and variability in the quantity of data to replicate over low bandwidth fixed communication links. A dynamic stochastic knapsack models the acceptance policy with dynamic programming optimization employed to perform offline optimization. Offline processing is used to establish the initial acceptance policy and to verify that the system continues to perform near-optimally.

Game theory, founded by Von Neumann, studies and analyzes interaction strategies between a number of interacting agents (players) in mathematically well-defined competitive situations called games [26].

Traditionally, the goal is to find an equilibrium in the game. The equilibrium is defined as a set of strategies where a player is unlikely to change behavior. Game theory can be used to adaptively address uncertainties in users' and system behavior.

Game theory has been applied in economics, sociology, psychology and biology [35] and recently in computer science and engineering applications [28, 29].

Game theory concepts have been applied to wireless communication [12, 24, 39] for analyzing wireless ad hoc networks [34] in addition to modelling admission control and bandwidth allocation [22, 27].

Furthermore, game theory models have been used for resource sharing in Peer-to-Peer systems [6] and optimizing rate control in video coding [3].

7.3 Mobile Virtual Environments

DVE is a software system in which multiple users interact with each other in real-time, even though those users may be located around the world [33]. DVEs are challenging applications for several reasons. First, they are multimedia-rich environments that include 3D graphical objects as well as audio and video streams. Second, users interact in real-time, with the number of users reaching hundreds or thousands in a single application as in multi-player online games. Third, users can compete or collaborate individually or in groups. That, in turn, implies high variations in users' requirements.

The increased availability of wireless networks and production of mobile devices has introduced novel forms of interaction between users and computing devices or the so-called pervasive computing paradigm.

Pervasive computing technologies have allowed traditional virtual reality systems to overcome some of its limitations such as restricted availability and high cost interfaces [11]. Virtual museums, guiding malls and online mobile games are becoming prevalent.

It provides intuitive interface for AR applications, instead of the heavy bulky wearable AR systems [37]. Furthermore, pervasive computing has added the social dimension to user collaboration by introducing mixed reality games [8, 15].

Still, pervasive computing creates a new set of challenges in designing and testing VEs applications. The existing DVE challenges are now augmented by the device scarce resources in addition to issues related to wireless networking. MVEs are an emerging research paradigm that aims at addressing these challenges.

MVEs should cope with the limited power, storage and display capabilities of mobile devices. In addition, it is necessary to consider innovative approaches to handle situations special to wireless connection, such as limited bandwidth, high error rate and handoff intervals.

Moreover, system evaluation has to span large combinations of VEs and network effects, which is difficult to achieve using regular network simulation or usability studies independently.

MVEs are dynamic, interactive, real-time distributed systems. Such systems are characterized by the runtime uncertainties due to the application environment and system resource states [10]. The large variability of the temporal and execution characteristics, such as event distributions and execution time bounds, makes the classical static real-time objective of always meeting all timing constraints very difficult or even impossible.

Resource management in dynamic real-time systems represents a typical example where an optimal solution is not feasible simply because we do not know future demands. Therefore, our approach must be adaptive to handle the variations in the available device and network resources. For example, as the device power decreases, its ability to send or receive network messages decreases accordingly. Ignoring this fact will misuse network bandwidth and shorten the device battery life.

Decisions made by the system are strongly interrelated with the interaction decisions taken by system users. A change in the user's behavior will result in the change of resource allocation, which, in turn, changes the user experience and use of the system.

The rest of this section describes a remote-rendering walkthrough application that demonstrates typical MVEs device and network challenges. The application deals with mobile devices with graphics card unable to render 3D models. Instead, they connect to a remote server that performs the rendering task and streams the images to the client device. Prefetching techniques are introduced to lessen the effect of network latency on the user experience.

7.3.1 MVE Case Study: Client-Server Remote-Rendering Application

We consider the problem of deploying VEs on mobile devices with limited graphics card capabilities that cannot render 3D models. Image-based remote rendering is an attractive solution due to its low storage requirements. It was first introduced on mobile devices by Chang et al. [7], where they extended the technique for a client-server framework. The server constructs the model dynamically and the client runs a 3D wrapping algorithm.

Boukerche et al. [4] introduced a remote rendering client-server architecture for virtual walkthrough applications. The client sends periodic updates with its position inside the virtual scene to the server, which employs scheduling mechanisms to stream the rendered images according to their priority.

In previous work [20], we introduced a server-side prefetching scheme that predicts the client's next movement and streams the corresponding images ahead to the client. The client sends its position inside the VE to a remote server. The server then renders the scene and streams the corresponding images back to the mobile client. Our study considered the walkthrough class of applications, where the client navigates inside a static VE (i.e., the client cannot change object properties in the environment).

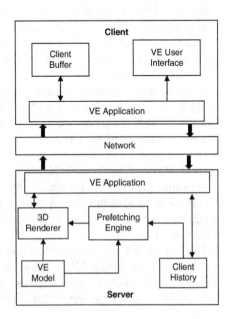

Fig. 7.1 Remote rendering system architecture

Figure 7.1 depicts the architecture used for the remote rendering client-server system. The client navigates in the VE through the user interface component, while the VE model is stored on the remote server. The client sends position updates to the server, which renders the 3D model and streams the equivalent image to be stored in the client local buffer.

To enhance the system resilience to changes in wireless connection, we introduced a server-side prefetching scheme, where the server prefetches images most likely required in the client's next steps and sends them a priori to the client. The client's next movement is predicted based on the client movement history. Two prediction schemes were adopted, the average window and the weighted average window [9].

Assume that P_i is the client's ith movement vector, while $\bar{P}_j$ is the estimated jth movement vector. In the average window scheme, the client's estimated movement is computed as the average of the previous w steps, where w is the window size (7.1). The second scheme uses a weighted average window, where the recent movement has α weight, and the average of the remaining window movements has $(1 - \alpha)$ weight, $0 < \alpha \leq 1$ (7.2).

$$\bar{P}_{n+1} = P_n + \frac{1}{w}(P_n - P_{n-w}), \quad n > w, \tag{7.1}$$

$$\bar{P}_{n+1} = P_n + \alpha(P_n - P_{n-1}) + (1 - \alpha)\frac{1}{w-1}(P_{n-1} - P_{n-w-1}), \quad w > 1. \tag{7.2}$$

In order to evaluate the introduced prefetching schemes, we were faced by numerous challenges. The evaluation has to span large combination of VEs, user navigation patterns and network scenarios that mimic typical wireless network situations. That augmented functionality was difficult to achieve using regular network simulation or user studies independently.

In Sect. 7.4, we report our experiences in developing a test-bed architecture for our system. A VE simulator is used to simulate VEs with different levels of detail. In addition, a system prototype was implemented for usability studies. An emulation mode has been added to handle preconfigured input scenarios and to mock up network effects.

7.4 Test-Bed Architecture for Mobile Virtual Environments

In this section, we describe an MVE test-bed architecture for the image-based remote-rendering application (Sect. 7.3.1). However, we argue that the adopted approach is general enough to be beneficial for other MVE applications.

The test-bed is designed to operate in two modes. The prototype mode that supports user studies and the simulation mode that runs using predefined user input or user models. For both modes, the system can operate on either a wireless network or emulated network effects. The final system provides the following abstractions for MVE developers:

- Prototype implementation for remote rendering server and client.

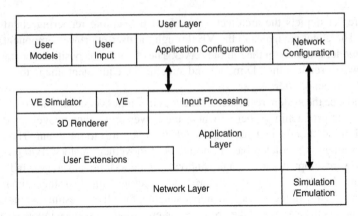

Fig. 7.2 Test-bed software architecture

- The ability to import 3D models and customize it according to the mobile device screen size.
- Operating on either a wireless connection or writing network scenario to test certain situations. Network scenarios allow the user to set specific variables such as average network delay, client update interval and disconnection period.
- Take input from real users as well as predefined movement paths. The latter allow for repeating the same experiments with different setup conditions.

Figure 7.2 shows the test-bed software architecture. The architecture consists of three layers: user layer, application layer and network layer.

User Layer

The user layer is responsible for handling user inputs in the test-bed configuration. The system input is either taken from user models or users in the prototype mode. User models are synthetic movement models that mimic user navigation patterns, such as random or circular walks [9], inside the virtual scene. By that, the system is evaluated for several classes of users before conducting expensive user studies.

The user input component is responsible for handling user interaction during the prototype mode. It maps the input from a certain device to corresponding actions such as changing the navigation speed or the avatar orientation and so forth.

Application configuration states the operation mode of the system (simulation/prototype), 3D input model, the mobile device screen size, the number of prefetched images per client update and the input device.

As for network configuration, users can pre-configure the network to create network scenarios by setting network parameters, network delay or the client update rate (client delta) to certain values during the navigation session. That allows for testing the effect of the sudden changes in network parameters on the users.

Server	Client
server	client
1	1 // prefetch count
40	40 //average delay
200	200 //client delta
	1
	4
	4
	2
	2
	d100 // change Average delay
	3
	2
	2
	...
	c150 // change client delta
	p
	P
	P // generate movement from model
	P
	...
	999 // end of pre-defined input, take input from users

Client log
00:00:00.1666670
00:00:00.0833335
00:00:00.0833335
00:00:00.0833335
...
00:00:00.0000012
hitratio=39.50617,
totalReceived=146,
receivedPrefetched=103,
totalUsed=33

Server log
client requests=7,
totalsentimages=28,
totalprefetched=14

Fig. 7.3 Test-bed: sample application and network configuration scripts and log files

Figure 7.3 shows sample application and network configuration scripts and log files for the server and the client. The script file identifies the node (server or client), the average network delay and client update rate (client delta). The client script describes the input scenario, where client delta and network delay are changed in the middle of a synthetic navigation path.

Application Layer

The application layer processes the input either from users or user models and renders the VE 3D model. VE is either imported to the system or created using the VE simulator component. Simulated VEs are synthesized VE database descriptions generated according to specific properties [20].

The user extensions component is used by the system developers to identify new data structures, intercept the simulation loop or add special functionality, such as the prefetching engine and client local buffer.

Network Layer

The Network layer is responsible for the communication between system nodes. The network operates in three modes as follows:

- Normal mode: the users communicate using physical connections.
- Network simulation mode: network simulators are used to simulate network architectures.
- Network emulation mode: software or hardware emulation is used.

Network modes and system operation modes are mutually independent, which provides system developers with large combinations of evaluation scenarios. It is worth mentioning here that this view has been evolved during two implementation phases. Therefore, our implementation does not adhere completely to the proposed architecture. In the first phase, a VE simulator was designed with minor emphasis on the network layer. The second phase, however, focused on prototype implementation and emulating network effects.

7.4.1 Simulation

An event-driven simulator was designed and implemented using the C++ programming language. The simulation phase has focused on developing user navigation models and the VE simulator. Our design choices for simulating the VE are influenced by our interest in evaluating the impact of prefetched images, in addition to the fact that we are dealing only with navigation tasks.

The VE was modelled as a two-dimensional matrix of squared cells. Each cell is represented by 12 panoramic images as a fine-grained representation of the VE.

Two parameters were used to characterize the level of details in VE content, cell size and step size. The cell size is the size of matrix cells, while the step size is the maximum distance the client can move in a single step.

A cell size greater than the step size, Fig. 7.4, indicates that the modelled VE has a low level of detail since the surrounding images do not change as the client moves in the same cell. Conversely, a cell size smaller than step size, Fig. 7.5, reflects a high level of details in the VE, since at every step, the client moves to a new cell and requests new images.

This phase of implementation did not include user studies, and user models were employed instead. Two movement patterns were generated, the random walk and the circular movement [9, 19]. Experiments were conducted to study the impact

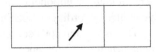

Fig. 7.4 Cell size ≥ step size

Fig. 7.5 Step size ≥ cell size

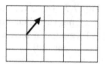

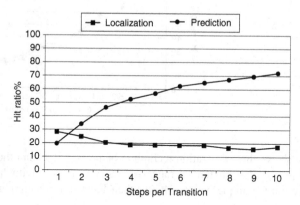

Fig. 7.6 The effect of increasing (S) on the random walk movement [20]

of prefetching on the quality perceived by the user. In addition, sensitivity of prefetching mechanisms to different types of movements as well as VEs is explored.

Moreover, the proposed technique, prediction-based prefetching, is compared to another prefetching mechanism, the localization-based prefetching. In the former technique, the server sends the image corresponding to the current position in addition to one predicted image, while in the latter, it sends the current image in addition to two panoramic images to the right and the left of the user's field of view. The effectiveness of the prefetching techniques is measured using the client *hit ratio* as it represents the ratio of the images that are rendered from the client local buffer.

Simulation experiments have shown that choosing the prefetching scheme depends on the user movement pattern and the type of the VE. The prediction scheme outperformed the localization counterpart in random walk as well as circular movement patterns. The localization technique, however, performs better in VEs with low level of details in the circular movement pattern. Figures 7.6 and 7.7 show part of our experimental results. The interested reader is referred to [19, 20] for more details.

Figure 7.6 shows the effect of the maximum number of steps the client takes in one movement path (S) on the *hit ratio*. When $S = 1$, the localization technique performs better than the prediction technique. This is due to the fact that the client position changes every step, which results in reducing the prediction efficiency in the prediction technique.

As S increases, the prediction method outperforms the localization counterpart since the linear prediction conforms now with client movements. Prediction is shown to perform better than localization with mean 34.83 and confidence interval 90% [22.85, 46.82].

Fig. 7.7 The effect of
changing virtual environment
(VE) model on the circular
movement [20]

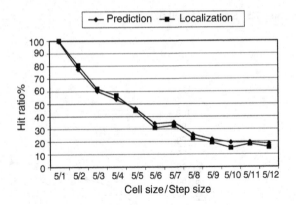

Figure 7.7 shows the localization technique behaves better than the prediction-based technique by 2% on the average. As for VE models with high level of details, prediction technique behaves better than localization technique by 3% on the average.

The simulation phase has enabled us to evaluate the system using a different mixture of VEs as well as client navigation patterns. The promising results argued for the effectiveness of the proposed approach and motivated us to implement a prototype for the system.

7.4.2 Prototype

A prototype for the system was implemented using XNA game engine. The prototype adopts a thin-client architecture as shown in Fig. 7.8. The client implements the user, application and network layers as shown in Fig. 7.2. The user layer accepts user inputs from the keyboard or from scripts describing user path according to a certain movement model. The application layer is responsible for input processing and managing the client local buffer in which streamed images are stored.

The server implements the application and network layers. The 3D model, either generated using VE simulator or imported from user file, is stored at the server. The server renders the model according to the client position, prefetches look-ahead images and streams the images to the client. Figure 7.9 shows a snapshot of the client view in the implemented prototype. The VE represents a 3D urban city [36].

Simulation phase was important to show the significance of the introduced approach. Prototype experiments, however, are essential to evaluate the system by actual users. Parameters such as client *hit ratio* seem to be good indication of user experience. However, prototype experiments have shown that in certain situations, when the network delay is very small, the hit ratio is small yet the user perception is not affected. With further investigations, we concluded that the time between requesting and receiving an image is another significant factor that affects the end-user experience.

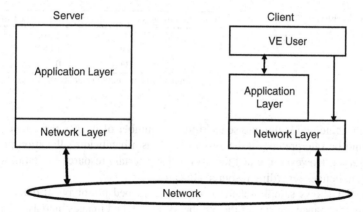

Fig. 7.8 Test-bed: prototype system architecture

Fig. 7.9 Remote-rendering
system prototype: snapshot of
the client view

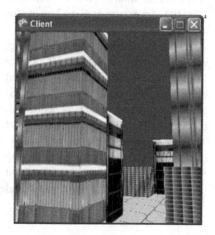

The work on the prototype is in progress, though our goal has shifted from evaluating a single application to explore the interaction between the users, networks and systems using the information from the test-bed experiments. Such analysis will be beneficial for resource allocation in MVEs. Section 7.5 discusses the test-bed results and proposes using game theory to model client-server interaction in the remote rendering application.

7.5 Modelling Decision-Making in MVEs Using Game Theory

Simulation results have proven a high dependency between prefetching mechanisms, user movement patterns and VE type. That, in turn, implies the need for an adaptive mechanism that selects the proper prefetching method according to VE and the user's interactions within it.

Table 7.1 Prototype sample results

Prefetched images	Use ratio (%)	Response time (ms)
0	0	166
1	49	133
2	33	0

Client delta = 300 ms, network delay = 40 ms

Each prefetching technique sends different number of images per client update that would be interpreted, on the system level, as a bandwidth allocation problem for the server. However, the fact that MVEs have certain resource limitations poses a set of challenges regarding resource allocation.

Table 7.1 shows sample results from the developed prototype. It demonstrates system performance metrics as the number of prefetched images increases. The *use ratio* is the ratio between the number of prefetched images that were used by the client and the total number of prefetched images. It indicates the resource utilization from the server perspective. The average response time, defined in Sect. 7.4, points to the quality perceived by the user.

As the number of prefetched images increases, the average response time decreases. The *use ratio*, however, decreases reaching 33% for two prefetched images. In other words, 67% of the prefetched images were useless for the client. On the other hand, the client might trade small response time by a longer battery life. Such a closed loop and the interdependent nature of the decisions between the client and the server provide a strong motivation for using game theory.

Game theory is the formal study of decision-making where several players must make choices that potentially affect the interests of the other players [35]. Section 7.5.1 gives an overview about game theory, while Sect. 7.5.2 proposes a game theory model for the remote rendering application.

7.5.1 Game Theory Basic Definitions

A *game* consists of two or more *players*, each with a set of *strategies*, and for each combination of strategies, there is a numerical *payoff* for each player. Players rationality is a central assumption in game theory, where players are rational and seek to maximize their payoffs. The concepts of game theory provide a language to formulate, structure, analyze and understand strategic scenarios [35].

In 1950, John Nash demonstrated that games with finite strategy space always have an equilibrium point [35], where neither player will unilaterally change strategy and get a higher payoff.

A *Pure Strategy* defines a specific move or action that a player will make in any situation in a game. A *Mixed Strategy* is a probability distribution over his/her pure-strategy choices, where every finite strategic form game has a mixed-strategy Nash equilibrium [12].

NonCooperative Games describe strategic choices, where the players have conflicting interests. In contrast, *Cooperative Games* describe coalition between game players and the payoffs each group can obtain by the cooperation of its members.

The *strategic form* (normal form) is the basic type of games in noncooperative game theory. A game in strategic form lists each player's strategies and the outcomes that result from each possible combination of choices. The *extensive form* or the game tree describes how the game is played over time, the order of player's action and the information they have at the time they take those actions.

We formally describe a game in the strategic form $G = (P, S, U)$, where P is the set of game players. S_i is the strategy space of ith player and $S = S_1 \times \cdots \times S_n$ is the joint set of all strategy spaces for all players.

The payoff function of player i is defined by the utility functions $u_i : S_1 \times \cdots \times S_n \to R$; $i = 1, \ldots, n$, which assign a payoff for each player for every combined strategy choices. $U = \{u_1(s), \ldots, u_n(s)\}, s \in S$.

The *best response strategy* of player i is the strategy $s_i \in S_i$ that maximizes the player's utility. Nash equilibrium can be defined as the strategy profile for which $u_i(x_1, \ldots, x_i, \ldots, x_n) \geq u_i(x_1, \ldots, x_i', \ldots, x_n), \forall x_i' : x_i' \in S_i, i = 1, \ldots, n$.

In terms of the *best response* strategies, Nash equilibrium is the strategy profile in which a player's strategy is the best response to other players.

7.5.1.1 Game Examples

Table 7.2 describes a famous game, the *prisoner's dilemma* [29], introduced by A. Tucker in 1940s. The game analyzes a situation, where two prisoners were arrested for corruption. Each of them can collaborate with each other or defect and testify against the other. Table 7.2 shows the game in strategic form. The table rows and columns are the strategies for player 1 and 2, respectively, where "C" refers to the *Collaborate* strategy, while "D" corresponds to the *Defect* strategy. The payoffs for players 1 and 2 are shown as an ordered pair in the table cells. It is considered a dilemma because based on the rationality assumption, the strategy pair (D,D) is the equilibrium point. However, they get higher payoff if both of them collaborate (C,C).

Table 7.3 is the game model of the matching pennies game. If the outcome matches player 1 wins, otherwise player 2 wins. Matching pennies is an example of a zero-sum game, where the sum of the all players payoff equals zero. In other words, if one wins the other will lose.

Table 7.2 Prisoner's dilemma game model	C	D
C	(3,3)	(0,4)
D	(4,0)	(1,1)

Table 7.3 Matching pennies
game model

	H	T
H	(1, −1)	(−1, 1)
T	(−1, 1)	(1, −1)

7.5.2 Client-Server Game

We start by describing the game from the client and the server perspectives. We then
discuss each player's rational, strategies and payoff function.

Client view: Rendering most of the images from the local buffer hides the network latency and improves the application responsiveness. Hence, the client benefits
from prefetching images that cover as much as possible the upcoming movements.
However, the client has restricted resources, e.g., power, CPU and memory, which
should not be consumed in receiving and manipulating images that might not be
used later.

Server view: The server, on the other hand, has to prefetch a certain number of
images so that it serves the client's needs without exceeding certain resource limitations, i.e., CPU and bandwidth. The number of prefetched images varies according
to the client movement. For example, increasing the number of prefetched images
using linear prediction is practical if the client moves on straight lines (e.g., driving
on a high way), but not in the circular movement case.

7.5.2.1 Client

The client rational is to maximize the quality perceived by adopting interaction
strategies that cope with wireless network variations. At the same time, the client
aims at maintaining the usage of the mobile device resources.

Client Strategies

The client strategy space manifests the ways in which the client interacts with the
VE. We assume the existence of three interaction modes (high (H), medium (M) and
low (L)) that vary in the navigation speed or the number of client movements per
time interval. The client uses the interaction decisions to adapt to network problems
by changing its navigation speed.

Client Payoff

We propose to use the response time and the cache hit ratio parameters to represent
client satisfaction of the game. The response time will represent client satisfaction
for images that were not found in the buffer and retrieved from the server, while the
hit ratio represents images that were found directly in the cache. The mapping of the

two parameters to a single satisfaction value could be performed using the function introduced in [31].

7.5.2.2   Server

The second player in our game model is the remote rendering server. The server aims at supporting the client interaction requirements by providing the prefetching service. Such service is constrained by the resources available for each client, e.g., the server bandwidth in order to avoid dedicating server resources to one client.

Server Strategies

The server decides on the number of images the server prefetches per client movement. We assume that the client can receive prefetched images until the next image requested from the server. This is due to the fact that the new client request will correct any prefetching errors.

Assume that λ is the average time between client consecutive movements. Then, given the round trip time (RTT) for one image, the client might receive maximum number of prefetched images $m = 2\lambda/RTT$. Accordingly, the server strategies are prefetch i images where $1 \leq i \leq m$.

Server Payoff

We introduce the *use ratio*, the ratio between the number of prefetched images that were used by the client and the total number of prefetched images, as the server payoff function. Use ratio reflects the resource usage from the server perspective.

Use ratio could be computed over long or short time intervals according to the server goal, *maximize the server use ratio during the whole navigation session or during the next time interval*. We assume that the client is not revisiting positions she/he has visited earlier. Therefore, previously prefetched images do not affect use ratio in the upcoming time interval, and hence, the server reactions aim at maximizing the use ratio per time interval.

The client decision is based either on the task inside the environment or as a response to wireless connections conditions. For example, high latency in the system response or discontinuities in the displayed image are indications for low bandwidth or weak wireless signal. The client then might try to slow down the navigation speed. On the server side, the server has to decide the number of prefetched images that maximizes the *use ratio* given the client's decision.

7.6   Conclusion and Discussion

Pervasive computing has enabled large scale deployment of MVE applications on mobile devices. MVEs present additional challenges to application developers due to the issues specific to wireless computing and the limited device resources. A more general approach to developing such applications and related software architectures needs to be flexible and adaptive.

MVE users continuously make real-time decisions of how to use the system, while the system makes real-time decisions of how to use available resource to respond to user decisions. This strategic interaction and the corresponding decision-making process can be studied using game theory.

An MVE application, a remote rendering problem, was presented as a case study. While relatively simple to develop, it provided a wealth of information and experience regarding the interaction between the network, system and users, as well as the user's experience.

Moreover, a test-bed architecture for MVEs was introduced to evaluate the remote rendering application through two implementation phases. The flexibility of the proposed architecture allowed for evaluating the system against different combinations of user, environment and network scenarios.

The case study was used as a vehicle to illustrate the use of game theory to model interactive, real-time distributed systems. We plan to conduct further experiments to explore and develop more general guidelines concerning how such a model could be constructed for a specific application. Those experiments will also help us to further refine our understanding of how game theory can be used and incorporated into architectures for MVE applications and provide better experiences to the users.

References

1. Adams, K.P.: An approach to real time adaptive decision making in dynamic distributed systems. Ph.D. thesis, Virginia Polytechnic Institute and State University. Blacksburg, VA (2005)
2. Adams, K.P., Gračanin, D., Teodorović, D.: A near optimal approach to quality of service data replication scheduling. In: Proceedings of the 2004 Winter Simulation Conference, vol. 2, pp. 1847–1855. Washington, DC (2004)
3. Ahmad, I., Luo, J.: On using game theory to optimize the rate control in video coding. IEEE Transactions on Circuits and Systems for Video Technology 16(2), 209–219 (2006). DOI 10.1109/TCSVT.2005.856899
4. Boukerche, A., Pazzi, R.W.N.: Scheduling and buffering mechanisms for remote rendering streaming in virtual walkthrough class of applications. In: WMuNeP '06: Proceedings of the 2nd ACM International Workshop on Wireless Multimedia Networking and Performance Modeling, pp. 53–60. ACM, New York, NY (2006). DOI http://doi.acm.org/10.1145/1163698.1163708
5. Broll, W., Ohlenburg, J., Lindt, I., Herbst, I., Braun, A.K.: Meeting technology challenges of pervasive augmented reality games. In: NetGames '06: Proceedings of 5th ACM SIGCOMM Workshop on Network and System Support for Games, p. 28. ACM, New York, NY (2006). DOI http://doi.acm.org/10.1145/1230040.1230097

6. Buragohain, C., Agrawal, D., Suri, S.: A game theoretic framework for incentives in p2p systems. In: P2P '03: Proceedings of the 3rd International Conference on Peer-to-Peer Computing, p. 48. IEEE Computer Society, Washington, DC (2003)
7. Chang, C.F., Ger, S.H.: Enhancing 3d graphics on mobile devices by image-based rendering. In: PCM '02: Proceedings of the Third IEEE Pacific Rim Conference on Multimedia, pp. 1105–1111. Springer, London (2002)
8. Cheok, A.D., Sreekumar, A., Lei, C., Thang, L.N.: Capture the flag: Mixed-reality social gaming with smart phones. IEEE Pervasive Computing 5(2), 62–69 (2006). URL http://dx.doi.org/10.1109/MPRV.2006.25
9. Chim, J.H.P., Green, M., Lau, R.W.H., Leong, H.V., Si, A.: On caching and prefetching of virtual objects in distributed virtual environments. In: MULTIMEDIA '98: Proceedings of the Sixth ACM International Conference on Multimedia, pp. 171–180. ACM, New York, NY (1998). DOI http://doi.acm.org/10.1145/290747.290769
10. Dua, V., Papalexandru, K., Pistikopoulos, E.: Global optimization issues in multiparametric continuous and mixed-integer optimization problems. Journal of Global Optimization 30, 59–89 (2004)
11. Farella, E., Brunelli, D., Benini, L., Ricco, B., Bonfigli, M.: Pervasive computing for interactive virtual heritage. IEEE Multimedia 12(3), 46–58 (2005). DOI 10.1109/MMUL.2005.54
12. Felegyhazi, M., Hubaux, J.P.: Game theory in wireless networks: A tutorial. Technical Report LCA-REPORT-2006-002, EPFL-Switzerland (2006)
13. Hagras, H.: Embedding computational intelligence in pervasive spaces. IEEE Pervasive Computing 6(3), 85–89 (2007). DOI 10.1109/MPRV.2007.54
14. Herbst, I., Braun, A.K., McCall, R., Broll, W.: Multi-dimensional interactive city exploration through mixed reality. IEEE Virtual Reality Conference, 2008. VR '08, pp. 259–260 (2008). DOI 10.1109/VR.2008.4480790
15. Hinske, S., Lampe, M., Carsten Magerkurth, C.R.: Classifying Pervasive Games: On Pervasive Computing and Mixed Reality, vol. 1. Shaker Verlag, Aachen (2007)
16. Kimura, H., Tokunaga, E., Nakajima, T.: Building mobile augmented reality services in pervasive computing environments. 2006 ACS/IEEE International Conference on Pervasive Services, pp. 285–288 (2006)
17. Kindberg, T., Fox, A.: System software for ubiquitous computing. IEEE Pervasive Computing 1(1), 70–81 (2002)
18. Laarhoven, P., van Aarts, E.: Simulated Annealing: Theory and Applications. Reidel, Dordrecht (1987)
19. Lazem, S., Elteir, M., Abdel-Hamid, A.: Prediction-based prefetching for remote rendering streaming in mobile virtual environments. Technical Report TR-07-24, Computer Science Department, Virginia Polytechnic Institute and State University (2007)
20. Lazem, S., Elteir, M., Abdel-Hamid, A., Gracanin, D.: Prediction-based prefetching for remote rendering streaming in mobile virtual environments. IEEE International Symposium on Signal Processing and Information Technology, pp. 760–765 (2007). DOI 10.1109/ISSPIT.2007.4458059
21. Lee, H., Hsu, C.: Neural network processing through energy minimization with learning ability to the multiconstraint zero-one knapsack problem. In: Proceedings of the IEEE International Workshop on Architectures, Languages and Algorithms: Tools for Artificial Intelligence, pp. 548–555 (1989)
22. Lin, H., Chatterjee, M.: Arc: An integrated admission and rate control framework for competitive wireless cdma data networks using noncooperative games. IEEE Transactions on Mobile Computing 4(3), 243–258 (2005). DOI http://dx.doi.org.ezproxy.lib.vt.edu:8080/10.1109/TMC.2005.35
23. Lu, C., Xiaorui, W., Xenofon, K.: Feedback utilization control in distributed real-time systems with end-to-end tasks. IEEE Transactions on Parallel and Distributed Systems 16(6), 550–561 (2005)
24. MacKenzie, A., Wicker, S.: Selfish users in aloha: a game-theoretic approach. Vehicular Technology Conference, 2001. VTC 2001 Fall. IEEE VTS 54th, vol. 3, pp. 1354–1357 (2001). DOI 10.1109/VTC.2001.956417

25. Magerkurth, C., Cheok, A.D., Mandryk, R.L., Nilsen, T.: Pervasive games: Bringing computer entertainment back to the real world. Computers in Entertainment 3(3), 4 (2005). DOI http://doi.acm.org/10.1145/1077246.1077257

26. Neumann, J.V., Morgenstern, O.: Theory of Games and Economic Behavior. Princeton University Press, Princeton, NJ (1944). URL http://jmvidal.cse.sc.edu/library/neumann44a.pdf

27. Niyato, D., Hossain, E.: A game-theoretic approach to bandwidth allocation and admission control for polling services in ieee 802.16 broadband wireless networks. In: QShine '06: Proceedings of the 3rd International Conference on Quality of Service in Heterogeneous Wired/Wireless Networks, p. 51. ACM, New York, NY (2006). DOI http://doi.acm.org/10.1145/1185373.1185439

28. Papadimitriou, C.: Algorithms, games, and the internet. In: STOC '01: Proceedings of the Thirty-Third Annual ACM Symposium on Theory of Computing, pp. 749–753. ACM, New York, NY (2001). DOI http://doi.acm.org/10.1145/380752.380883

29. Papadimitriou, C.H., Yannakakis, M.: On complexity as bounded rationality (extended abstract). In: STOC '94: Proceedings of the Twenty-Sixth Annual ACM Symposium on Theory of Computing, pp. 726–733. ACM, New York, NY (1994). DOI http://doi.acm.org/10.1145/195058.195445

30. Pu, W., Zou, Y.: Using GASA to solve distributed real-time scheduling problem. In: Proceedings of the First International Conference on Machine Learning and Cybernetics, pp. 958–961 (2002)

31. Richards, A., Rogers, G., Antoniades, M., Witana, V.: Mapping user level QoS from a single parameter. In: International Conference on Multimedia Networks and Services (MMNS '98) (1998). URL citeseer.ist.psu.edu/richards98mapping.html

32. Roehl, B.: Distributed virtual reality: An overview. In: Proceedings of the First Symposium on Virtual Reality Modeling Language (VRML '95), pp. 39–43. ACM, New York, NY (1995). DOI http://doi.acm.org.ezproxy.lib.vt.edu:8080/10.1145/217306.217312

33. Singhal, S., Zyda, M.: Networked Virtual Environments: Design and Implementation. ACM Press/Addison-Wesley, New York, NY (1999)

34. Srivastava, V., Neel, J., Mackenzie, A., Menon, R., Dasilva, L., Hicks, J., Reed, J., Gilles, R.: Using game theory to analyze wireless ad hoc networks. IEEE Communications Surveys and Tutorials 7(4), 46–56 (2005)

35. Turocy, T.L., von Stengel, B.: Game theory. In: Encyclopedia of Information Systems (2002)

36. Tutorials, R.X.: URL http://www.riemers.net/eng/Tutorials/XNA/

37. Wagner D., Pintaric T., Ledermann F., Schmalstieg D.: Towards massively multi-user augmented reality on handheld devices. In H. W. Gellersen, R. Want, and A. Schmidt (eds.), Proceedings of the Third International Conference on Pervasive Computing (PERVASIVE 2005), Lecture Notes in Computer Science, Berlin, Springer 3468, 208–219 (2005)

38. Watanabe, M., Furukawa, M., Mizoe, M., Watanabe, T.: Ga applications to physical distribution scheduling problem. IEEE Transactions on Industrial Electronics 48(4), 724–730 (2001)

39. Yeung, M., Kwok, Y.K.: A game theoretic approach to power aware wireless data access. IEEE Transactions on Mobile Computing 5(8), 1057–1073 (2006). DOI 10.1109/TMC.2006.107

Part II
Ambient Intelligence and Ubiquitous Computing

Chapter 8
AI Techniques in a Context-Aware Ubiquitous Environment

Paolo Coppola, Vincenzo Della Mea, Luca Di Gaspero, Raffaella Lomuscio,
Danny Mischis, Stefano Mizzaro, Elena Nazzi, Ivan Scagnetto,
and Luca Vassena

Abstract Nowadays, the mobile computing paradigm and the widespread diffusion
of mobile devices are quickly changing and replacing many common assumptions
about software architectures and interaction/communication models. The environment, in particular, or more generally, the so-called user context is claiming a central
role in everyday's use of cellular phones, PDAs, etc. This is due to the huge amount
of data "suggested" by the surrounding environment that can be helpful in many
common tasks. For instance, the current context can help a search engine to refine the set of results in a useful way, providing the user with a more suitable and
exploitable information. Moreover, we can take full advantage of this new data
source by "pushing" active contents towards mobile devices, empowering the latter with new features (e.g., applications) that can allow the user to fruitfully interact
with the current context. Following this vision, mobile devices become dynamic
self-adapting tools, according to the user needs and the possibilities offered by the
environment. The present work proposes MoBe: an approach for providing a basic
infrastructure for pervasive context-aware applications on mobile devices, in which
AI techniques (namely a principled combination of rule-based systems, Bayesian
networks and ontologies) are applied to context inference. The aim is to devise
a general inferential framework to make easier the development of context-aware
applications by integrating the information coming from physical and logical sensors (e.g., position, agenda) and reasoning about this information in order to infer
new and more abstract contexts.

Keywords Context-aware browser · CAB · MoBe · Mobile · Bayesian · Inference
and wireless systems

8.1 Introduction

Due to the appearance and widespread diffusion of new and more powerful mobile
devices (PDAs, smartphones, etc.), the traditional notion of computing is quickly

P. Coppola (✉)
University of Udine, Via delle Scienze 206, 33100 Udine, Italy
e-mail: coppola@uniud.it

A.-E. Hassanien et al. (eds.), *Pervasive Computing: Innovations in Intelligent
Multimedia and Applications*, Computer Communications and Networks,
DOI 10.1007/978-1-84882-599-4_8, © Springer-Verlag London Limited 2009

fading away, giving birth to new computational paradigms and new non-trivial problems. Hence, the scientific community is searching for models, technologies and architectures to suitably describe and guide the implementation of this new computing scenario. In this situation, the notion of "context" (whether physical or virtual or a mixture of both) plays a fundamental role since it influences the computational capabilities of the devices that are in it.

Context-aware computing is a computational paradigm that has faced a rapid growth in the last few years, especially in the field of mobile devices. One of the promises of context-awareness in this field is the possibility of automatically adapting the functioning mode of mobile devices to the environment and the current situation the user is in, with the aim of improving both the device efficiency (using the scarce resources in a more efficient way) and effectiveness (providing better services to the user).

The work we present directly addresses the need for new computational paradigm presenting a novel architecture for a pervasive computing environment that allows a proactive acquisition of digital contents (applications, web pages, multimedia content, etc.) on mobile devices on the basis of the current context the user is in. This is an interdisciplinary work: mobile agent community, context-aware computing, artificial intelligence, software engineering and middleware, interaction with mobile devices applications, information retrieval and filtering, and privacy and security management are all disciplines that are deeply involved in this project.

Most previous context-aware applications focused almost exclusively on time and/or location and other few data, while the same contexts inference was limited to preconceived values. Our approach differs from previous works since we do not focus on particular contextual values, but rather have developed an architecture where managed contexts can be easily replaced by new contexts, depending on the different needs. In this way the solution we propose allows to trigger multimedia (and in general digital) content based not only on the user location, but also on more complex information, like user activity, future needs, etc.

In the present work, after presenting some related works (Sect. 8.2), we first present the architecture we have developed highlighting both the structure and the main ideas behind it (Sect. 8.3); then we focus on a particular component of the architecture aimed at inferring and managing the current user context (Sect. 8.4). We want to describe a novel approach for providing a basic infrastructure for context-aware applications on mobile devices, in which AI techniques (namely a principled combination of rule-based systems, Bayesian networks and ontologies) are applied to context inference. The aim is to devise a general inferential framework to ease the development of context-aware applications by integrating the information coming from sensors of both physical (e.g., location, time, temperature, surroundings, etc.) and logical (e.g., user profile, user history, agenda, etc.) kind, and reasoning about this information in order to infer new and more abstract contexts.

8.2   Related Work

Several research fields are relevant to our approach. We briefly survey the work that has been done on context awareness and frameworks for context-based applications.

8.2.1   Context-Awareness

8.2.1.1   Context

The concept of context is still a matter of discussion and through the years several different definitions have been proposed. They can be divided into extensional and intensional definitions.

Extensional definitions present the context through a list of possible context dimensions and their associated values. In the first work that introduces the expression *context-aware* [20], the context is represented by the location of the user and the surrounding objects. In a similar way, Brown et al. [6] define context as location, proximity to other people, temperature, daytime, etc. In [21] the concept of context is divided in three categories: computing context (network, display, etc.), user context (profile, people nearby, social situation, etc.) and physical context (light, noise, etc.). Chen et al. [8] add two other categories: time context (day, month, etc.) and history.

Intensional definitions present the concept of context more formally. In [1] the context is defined as "any information that can be used to characterize the situation of an entity. An entity is a person, place, or object that is considered relevant to the interaction between a user and an application, including the user and applications themselves." For Brazire and Brezillion [3], "the context acts like a set of constraints that influence the behaviour of a system (a user or a computer) embedded in a given task." This definition moves from the analysis of a collection of 150 context definitions from several fields of application as sociology, computer science, etc.

Extensional definitions seem to be useful in practical applications, where the abstract concept of context has to be made concrete. However, from a theoretical point of view, they are not fully correct as the context cannot be outlined just by some of its aspects. On the other hand, intensional definitions are of little use in the practice, despite they are theoretically satisfying.

8.2.1.2   Context-Aware Computing

Context-aware computing can be defined as the use of context in software applications, where the applications adapt to discovered contexts by changing their behaviour [8]. From an extensional point of view, a context-aware application presents the following features [1, 18]: context sensing, presentation of information and services to a user, automatic execution of a service, and tagging of context to information for later retrieval.

In most earlier context-aware applications, the notion of context included just a small amount of data. Most researches, for example, focused on time and/or location and few other data [22, 25]. More complex approaches tend to combine several contextual values to generate new contextual information. Abowd et al. [1] define *primary* contexts as location, entity, activity and time, which act as indices into other sources of contextual information. Similarly, in the TEA Project [23] Schmidt et al. use a resolution layer to determine a user's activity starting from basic contextual information.

As in the previously cited works, we intend to combine contexts to determine new, more abstract contexts. Differently from them, however, we do not want to limit the inferences only on an a priori defined set of contextual dimensions, but we aim to develop an inferential infrastructure that is able to work in a general way.

8.2.2 Frameworks

8.2.2.1 Stick-e Notes

Stick-e Notes [5, 6] is a framework developed around the idea of the electronic equivalent of Post-its: the user can associate notes (texts, HTML pages, sounds, videos, programs, etc.) to different contexts (location, daytime, etc.) in such a way that when the event will happen again, the relative note will be activated. This framework was conceived as the basis to build context-aware applications in an easier way.

8.2.2.2 Cooltown

The Cooltown project [14] aims at establishing a context model based upon the Web and, in particular, upon the concept of "Web Presence"; the main idea is to associate virtual services to physical entities. This approach is motivated by the fact that many databases and web pages contain a huge amount of information about the physical world. However, such information remains "detached from the latter." So, physical entities are classified into people, places and things (since, a person during his everyday life can meet people, move to different places and interact with things) and their relative access modality is expanded to a virtual world of web contents, where people, places and things are represented by means of the "Web Presence" context. This essentially amounts to the idea of being accessible in the Web, connecting the advantages of information systems with the physical world and vice versa.

8.2.2.3   Context Toolkit

The Context toolkit [11] is the result of several research activities at GeorgiaTech with the aim of building an architecture supporting the development of context-aware applications. The overall approach is object-oriented, being characterized by three kinds of objects, namely, widgets, servers and interpreters. Context widgets are essentially software components isolating applications from the activities bound to context sensing. They are reusable components defined by attributes ("pieces" of contextual information available to other components) and callback methods (representing the kind of events that can be notified by the widget). Context servers are collectors used to gather the whole context of a particular entity, e.g., the user; they must register themselves with each widget they are interested in, acting as proxies for applications. Finally, Context Interpreters manage the interpretation of contextual data, allowing one to present such information in different formats and to combine several contextual data in new pieces of information.

8.2.2.4   Sparkle

Sparkle [24] is a platform for context-aware application-level state management. It is based on context-aware state capturing and restoring mechanism that can achieve context-aware application migration. In the Sparkle system, applications are composed of facets. Facets are pure functional units that are independent of data or user interface. Facets do not interact with the user and do not maintain any application state. Hence, every application is associated with a container. The container contains the user interface and stores the data and execution state. It also stores the set of functionalities that the application can offer. Facets are housed on facet servers on the network. An application, during execution, will request for a certain functionality. There may be more than one facet which fulfill the same functionality. At run-time, the facet that is most suitable for the run-time environment is brought in and executed.

8.2.2.5   Hydrogen

Hydrogen [13] is a framework for distributed context-aware applications, based on the idea of not having a centralized component to depend on. Hydrogen is an architecture, which not only contains the context of the location device, but is also open to represent the context of remote devices. In case of encountering another device, context information can be mutually exchanged (via WLAN, Bluetooth, etc.), enabling a local representation of the remote device's context. This exchange of context information among client devices is called "context sharing."

8.3   The MoBe Approach

8.3.1   Motivations

We envisage a world in which the mobile devices that everybody currently uses (cellular phones, smart phones, PDAs and so on) constantly and frequently change their functioning mode, automatically adapting their features to the surrounding environment and to the current context of use. For instance, when the user enters a museum, the mobile phone can provide him/her with applications that suggest a tour according to the user preferences and needs, or can show multimedia material related to the artworks according to the interests of the users, etc.

Even if it is well known that current mobile devices can be used as computers, since they have computational and communication capabilities similar to computers of a decade ago, how to achieve this goal is not clear. One approach might be to have an operating system continuously monitoring sensors on the mobile device, thereby adapting backlight, volume, orientation, temperature, etc. to the changing environment.

We propose a different approach in which servers continuously push digital contents to mobile devices, depending on the current context of use. Inspired by the Nicholas Negroponte's "Being Digital" locution, we name our approach MoBe (Mobile Being).

8.3.2   General Architecture

MoBe [9] is a general architecture for context-aware distributed applications on mobile devices, which is based on the dynamic and automatic download, configuration, execution and unload of applications on the basis of the user's context. Rather than having the applications rigidly installed on a mobile device, the user and device context is used to obtain and start useful applications and to discard the ones not useful anymore. This way, a device is not limited to a set of predetermined functionalities, but allows to adopt those which are (probably) more useful for the user at a given time.

We use the idea of application for conveying digital content as it is the most general concept: an application can just show textual data, but it can also allow to manage multimedia material to interact with the surrounding environment, etc.

For example, when a person enters his/her home, the device provides automatically the application to control the household appliances. This application can be discarded (or just stopped) when the person leaves home. The device can turn into a TV remote controller while the user is watching TV or it can turn into a cooking book while the user is cooking and so on.

MoBe architecture is presented in Fig. 8.1 and is composed of the following three layers (from bottom to top):

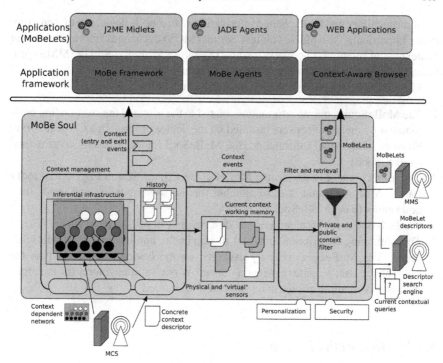

Fig. 8.1 General architecture of MoBe platform

MoBeSoul: It is the middleware on the mobile device whose basic responsibilities are to sense the surrounding environment, to perform the context inferences, to determine the context likelihood (as the contextual information are not certain) and to manage the retrieval of applications.

Application framework: It consists of the software infrastructure for building the concrete mobile applications. Since the MoBeSoul component is completely general and can be adapted to different implementations, we currently have developed and tested three implementations based on (1) MoBe framework, an ad hoc J2ME middleware, (2) MoBeAgents, the extensions of a Multi-Agent framework and (3) a *Context-Aware* browser, a browser extension that allows the development of contextual web applications.

MoBeLets: It is a basic context-aware application built upon this architecture.

The applications, called MoBeLets, reside on the MoBeLet Server and migrate transparently to the user on his/her mobile device. Each MoBeLet presents a descriptor that holds the most important information related to the application in order to make the retrieval easier (e.g., the type of task carried out) and decide whether it is suitable or not for the mobile device of the user (e.g., information about the minimal CPU/memory requirements or the kind of needed peripherals/communication media).

Some ancillary servers exchange information with mobile devices in that environment. In particular, the MoBe Context Server (MCS) exchanges information about contexts (and inferential networks), while the MoBe MoBeLet Server (MMS) provides MoBeLets' related information and the actual MoBeLets.

The workflow managed in the MoBe architecture is the following:

1. The MoBeSoul acquires information related to the user and the surrounding environment by means of sensors installed on the device or through a Context Server
2. From this contextual information, the MoBeSoul infers the user's context (and its likelihood)
3. The user's context is sent to the MoBeLet Descriptor Search Engine that looks for the MoBeLets that is most suitable for the user's context and sends their descriptors to the MoBeSoul
4. On the basis of user preferences, the descriptors can be filtered again
5. The remaining descriptors are used to obtain the applications from MoBeLet server. The MoBeLets currently executed on the device are managed on the basis of the user's context: when a context is not valid anymore, for example, the associated application can be stopped or discarded

8.3.3 Main Activities and Modules

While in the previous section we have described the general MoBe architecture, in this section we provide a more detailed description of the three main modules in the MoBeSoul.

8.3.3.1 Context Management

The process starts with context data received through:

- Physical sensors: Almost all mobile devices are equipped with some form of wireless network technologies (GSM, GPRS, Edge, UMTS, Bluetooth, Wi-Fi, Radio Frequency, IrDA, etc.) and can, therefore, sense if there is a network connection around them (and the strength of the corresponding electromagnetic field). Moreover, the device might be equipped with sensors capable of sensing data about the physical world surrounding the mobile device (e.g., noise, light level, temperature, etc.), some of which might be sent to the device by surrounding sensors.
- Virtual sensors: MoBeSoul might receive data from other processes running on user's mobile device, like an agenda, a timer, an alarm clock and so on.
- MoBeContext sensors: MoBeSoul is capable of receiving context information provided by an ad hoc MCS. The MCS pushes information about the current context to the users' devices, with the aim of providing a more precise and complete context description. MCS might be implemented by a Wi-Fi antenna, a RFID tag

sensed by the mobile device or other technologies. The MCS also broadcasts a Concrete Context Descriptor, which might contain a brief declarative description of the current context and a context ID (that, in the case of a Wi-Fi antenna might be the network SSID and/or its MAC address).

- Explicit user actions: The user can explicitly communicate, via the user interface, data about the current context. For instance, he/she might choose a connection/network provider, set the alarm clock, select the silent mode and so on.

All these sensors data are processed by the MoBeSoul Context submodule. It is responsible for producing, storing, maintaining and updating a description of the current context(s) the user is in. A detailed description of the inferential techniques exploited is given in Sect. 8.4.

8.3.3.2   Filter and Retrieval

The Filter and Retrieval submodule is in charge of selecting which MoBeLets to retrieve and to download their code. Its activity is triggered by notifications of context entry and exit events, received from the Context submodule. The Filter component receives these notifications, and on the basis of its internal criteria and depending on user's preferences, decides when to request the current public context descriptors for the Context submodule and on their basis, how to express a contextual query (i.e., a query that might contain also elements of the current public context) to be sent to a MoBe Descriptors Search Engine (MDSE). Furthermore, the MDSE can be also provided with explicit MoBeLet queries directly formulated by the user. The MDSE is in charge of selecting, on the basis of the received contextual query, those MoBeLets that are more relevant to the current user's context.

Since not all the MoBeLets selected by the MDSE will be actually downloaded (nor executed), the MDSE does not store and send MoBeLet code, but just MoBeLets descriptors. Each descriptor is a simple XML file that contains several structured and unstructured data about the corresponding MoBeLet: a unique identifier, a textual description, a manifest declaring which resources the MoBeLet will need and use while executing, a download server from which the actual MoBeLet can be downloaded and so on.

The received MoBeLet descriptors are filtered once again by the Filter component on the basis of the private context descriptors. As a result of this step, the probability that the user will desire to run each MoBeLet is determined. Then the Download component retrieves, on the basis of its own internal criteria, the MoBeLets code from the MMS specified in the corresponding descriptors. The stream of MoBeLets is then passed to the Execution submodule (see the following subsection).

There are many benefits of this design, such as:

- To encapsulate inside the Filter component adequate strategies to send to the MDSE the contextual queries for a more efficient resource usage: the Filter might send a new query containing the new context descriptors at each context change or rather it might collect a certain number of context descriptors (perhaps removing those corresponding to context exit events received meanwhile) before sending a new query. Other possible strategies include sending contextual queries at fixed time points and so on.

- To separate public and private context data: only the public data are considered to form the queries to be sent to MDSE, but both public and private are used to filter the MoBeLet descriptors received.
- To cache in a straightforward way both MoBeLet descriptors and code in order to minimize bandwidth usage.
- To have the user controlling the whole process and to participate in MoBeLets filtering and selection: the user might proactively stop an undesired MoBeLet or be requested a preference to a rather resource demanding MoBeLet and so on. On the other side, the two stage filtering allows a lower cognitive load to the user.

8.3.3.3 Personalization

The Personalization submodule consists of two components:

- The Personal Data Gathering component collects data about user's preferences and habits and stores them into an internal User Profile database. The database contains several different kinds of data directly related to the user, like user's demographic information (age, gender, etc.), preferences about real world activities (e.g., restaurants, friends, etc.), habits (working hours, typical trips, etc.) and so on. In addition, the User Profile database contains data about the behaviour of the user with respect to the MoBeLets. For example, the database keeps track of which MoBeLets have been downloaded and executed in the past, for how much time, which resources have been used and so on. User's data are collected both automatically (monitoring user's behaviour) and manually by explicit user intervention.
- The Personalized Context Generation component interacts with the Context submodule, affecting the inference process with the aim of making it more tailored to individual needs. The Personalization layer is specific to the single user, has a higher priority and is capable of changing the underlying (and more general) context network. The personalization layer can remove (hide) nodes and arcs and change arcs weights (probabilities) either in an absolute way (by specifying a new value) or in a relative way (by increasing or decreasing the underlying weight of a given amount). This also allows to modify in a seamless way the Context network, being an activity that would allow to include unforeseen contexts and inferences even after the system is deployed.

The clear separation between context and personalization has important benefits: independent modification of the Context network, independent usage of well established techniques from both the personalization and context-awareness fields, initial development of a non-personalized version of the MoBeSoul and so on.

8.4 Context Inference System

In the previous section, we have described the general architecture we propose for distributing context-aware digital content on mobile devices. In this section, we focus on a particular component of the architecture aimed at managing the current user context, highlighting the artificial intelligence techniques exploited for the context inference [7].

8.4.1 Inferring Abstract Contexts from Concrete Contexts

The current user's context is composed of an undefined number of contextual values. Each value is described by two elements: an unambiguous ID and a probability value. We divide contextual values into two categories:

Concrete contexts: They represent the information obtained by a set of sensors. These contexts can be read from the surrounding environment through physical sensors (e.g., temperature sensor) or can be obtained by other software (e.g., calendar) through logical sensors. Some examples are: "temperature: 20 °C," "12:30," "meeting at 14:30" and so on. Concrete contexts are returned by the sensors and represent the input of the inferential mechanism.

Abstract contexts: They represent everything that can be inferred from concrete contexts, for example, "user at home," "user is shopping," etc.

The problem we are facing is, therefore, the definition of an inferential system capable to derive the abstract contexts from the concrete ones. Concrete and abstract contexts are the inferential system input and output, respectively. From a theoretical point of view, this difference is faded since the contexts cannot be unambiguously assigned to one or the other category: the context "temperature 90 °C" can be a concrete context as it is obtained from a sensor or it can be inferred by other contexts (e.g., "user in sauna"). The aim of the inferential system it to combine concrete contexts to determine abstract contexts and to combine abstract contexts to obtain new, more abstract contexts.

8.4.2 Two Approaches for the Inferential System

To develop our inferential system, we have analyzed several approaches. Two of them seem intuitively adequate and have been taken into consideration: rule-based systems and Bayesian networks.

8.4.2.1 Rule-Based Systems

As it is well known, a rule-based system [17] is a general mechanism for the knowledge representation and management.

It presents a set of rules, a working memory and an interpreter. Each rule is composed of two facts (left and right or condition and action) and it is in the form *IF ⟨ condition ⟩ THEN ⟨ action ⟩*. The working memory stores the facts known by the system. The interpreter, until it terminates, tries to match the known facts with the rules' conditions in order to infer new facts. For example: given the rules *IF ⟨ x is a penguin ⟩ THEN ⟨ x is a bird ⟩* and *IF ⟨ x is a bird ⟩ THEN ⟨ x has wings ⟩* and given the fact *Pingu is a penguin*, the system infers the knowledge *Pingu is a bird* and *Pingu has wings*.

Although rule-based systems are a relatively simple model, they can be naturally adapted to the context-aware field. The left and right sides of a rule can represent two contextual values and the rule suggests a connection between them, e.g., *IF ⟨ I'm in the bathroom ⟩ and ⟨ there is an high humidity level ⟩ and ⟨ there is a continuous sound ⟩ THEN ⟨ I'm having a shower ⟩*. Let us remark that rule-based systems allow to use variables, a feature that simplifies knowledge management.

Indeed, rule-based systems have already been used in the context-aware field. Bacon and colleagues [2] describe a multimedia system based on user location, where contextual information is represented as facts in a rule-based system. Zhang [26] proposes a framework for allowing user to program his context-aware application: a user can visually create the rules that are then combined with sensors data to adapt the application to user context. In [12] a rule-based system is used to trigger the actions depending on the registered contexts.

8.4.2.2 Bayesian Networks

Bayesian networks [19] represent a model for the execution of inferences based on probability, and they can be easily adapted to the context-aware field as well. Each node can represent a contextual value, the edges representing dependence relationships between different contexts, while the probability distributions indicate the certainty related to contexts.

A Bayesian network is a direct and acyclic graph composed of:

- A set of nodes, one for each variable.
- A set of oriented edges, where each edge connects two nodes. If there is an edge from node X to Y, X is called Y *parent* and Y is directly conditioned by X.
- Each node X has an associated conditional probability distribution that assesses the effect of parents on the node $P(X | P(\text{parents}(X))$.

Bayesian networks have been used in the context-aware field mainly as systems to determine the uncertainty of contexts. In [4] a Bayesian network is used to measure the efficiency of contexts derivation from rough sensors data, while in [15] Bayesian networks are used to classify contexts related to a user's everyday activities.

8.4.2.3 Considerations

Even if the use of rule-based systems is reasonable in context-aware computing, it presents a remarkable limit: they manage certain knowledge, whereas almost everything related to contexts is characterized by uncertainty. Because of the uncertainty management, Bayesian networks are more suitable than rule-based systems for contextual inferences. On the other hand, a rule-based system allows the use of variables, which allow to limit the dimension of the same inferential mechanism. For example, instead of managing all temperature values, we can simplify them to the three abstract values, *temperature high, low, and normal,* and use rules generalized with variables to map the real sensed temperature value on the three abstract ones. In our opinion, both the approaches are important and needed for a complete and functional system.

8.4.3 The Inferential Infrastructure

We design a two-stage inferential mechanism, where both rules and Bayesian networks are used. We define the combination of rules and Bayesian network as the *inferential infrastructure.*

The input to the inferential infrastructure is represented by concrete contexts. Concrete contexts are processed by a rule-based system in order to simplify the information and map them on the starting node of the Bayesian network, which represents the second and main stage of the inferential infrastructure where abstract contexts are transformed into concrete ones. This represents the container of all the knowledge needed for context inferences.

The combination of concrete and inferred abstract contexts is the current user's context (Fig. 8.2).

The following is a simple example. A concrete context is "sound 60 dB." Through the first rule-based stage, this information is mapped into the Bayesian network starting nodes. In this way we simplify the contextual information: instead of managing all the possible sound volume values, we create an abstraction (i.e., "sound low," "sound high"). Without the rules (and the variables), when the management of all the single sound values is needed, we should introduce in the Bayesian network a node for each sound volume value. Then the Bayesian network starts from this point to infer abstract contexts like "user is listening to music."

8.4.4 Critical Issues

We can identify four main limits of the basic inferential infrastructure that we have presented so far.

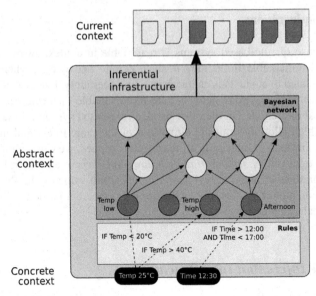

Fig. 8.2 Inferential infrastructure model

The first limit concerns the size of the inferential network. Since we do not want to limit the inferences only on an a priori defined set of contextual dimensions, the network, in principle, should be omniscient and include information and inferential mechanisms for every possible situation. The possible contextual values that should be managed in such a case are innumerable, and as they have to be built into the inferential network, this would lead to a universal network, which would be unmanageable in practice.

The solution we adopt consists in splitting the inferential network into several subnetworks on the basis of a single dimension of concrete context. For example, a hypothetical universal network can be split using location as an index: in this way we obtain several networks, each of them relevant to a particular location (e.g., one for home, office, car, etc.). These specialized networks have a smaller size, so they are more manageable. Furthermore, if they are still too complex, they can be partitioned further.

Single inferential networks are acquired automatically on the basis of the value of the contextual dimension used for the partitioning. The mobile device will receive one or more networks from a remote server and will combine them to infer more precisely the user abstract context. For example, when the user enters her home, if the user location is selected as the partitioning dimension, the device will obtain the inferential network specialized on the contexts related to the home.

Location is just one of the dimensions that can be used to partition the inferential network; other dimensions could be time (e.g., a set of applications related to work is downloaded during working hours or according to an agenda) or a combination of location and time.

The second problem concerns the potential mismatch between concepts in the inferential networks and the concrete contexts (e.g., a network could execute inferences starting from a contextual value expressed as "temperature in Celsius degrees" while the temperature sensor on the device manages information in Fahrenheit degrees). These incoherences would of course lead to erroneous contexts inference. To avoid that, we define an ontology of concrete contexts, which provides a shared model for situations, sensors, provided values and relationships among them. In this ontology, the sensors are categorized on the basis of the contextual information they provide. Similarly, in the development of the inferential network, its concrete nodes (or the starting ones) must also be categorized in the ontology. In this way the inferential engine is able to obtain the information needed by the inferential network through the appropriate sensors.

The third problem is a consequence of the previous two and it concerns the agreement on contexts representations. Indeed, it is possible to represent the same context in many different ways, leading to a troublesome matching between the context descriptions in the inferential network and those in the specific application descriptors. Again, a shared ontology allows to link related contexts by explicitly associating them through the common concepts they share, even when they are expressed in different ways.

Therefore, we extended the ontology previously suggested, so that all contextual values (not only the concrete ones) are classified in it. In this way we formalize the contexts definitions and representations, regulating their use. Our ontology is based on Wordnet (http://wordnet.princeton.edu), which is both a terminology and a constitutive ontology that supports multilanguages and implements a set of semantic relations between concepts (e.g., synonymy, part-set, etc.).

WordNet must be extended since it only provides a basic terminology and a first group of semantic relations. However, the definition of relations specific to the contextual aspects is required to obtain an ontology of contexts. To this aim, we devise a domain ontology that includes concepts and basic relations for sensors and contexts and can be extended by more specific ontologies. For example, to define the concepts related to "house," we refer to the basic relations and extend the generic concepts from a previously defined "building" ontology.

A fourth problem concerns subjectivity: since a "one-size-fits-all" approach will most likely be inadequate for users with different needs, we have introduced some other functionalities that allow users to personalize their inferential system. A user can associate to each context of interest in the network two values, called *privacy* and *importance*. These values refer to two thresholds managed by the user. The first one refers to the sensibility of the contextual information; contexts with privacy value higher than the privacy threshold will not be diffused outside the mobile device. The importance value acts somehow in the opposite direction: it allows a context to be made public to remote servers even if its probability is lower than the filtering threshold. Moreover, the user has the possibility to modify and personalize the network by adding or removing nodes (contexts) and changing the probability relations between contexts. This feature is crucial in order to make the network more suitable to model the current user's situation.

Finally, although the inferential system's main goal is to infer abstract contexts from the concrete contexts, the prototype could also execute the opposite inference: the user can define manually his abstract contexts (e.g. "watching TV") and from this the other contexts probability will be determined.

8.5 Context-Aware Browser

With the emergence of AJaX technology on desktop web browsers and on mobile devices browsers as well, it has been natural to think of adapting the previously described MoBe framework to a web-oriented paradigm. Among the aims, reducing the technological gap needed for using such a kind of system was one of the most crucial as the web browser is now a daily use tool for most people, while mobile software applications like midlets are still somewhat unconventional. Moreover, with a web-oriented approach, the currently existing web contents could be re-used (whereas MoBeLets have to be designed from scratch). Finally, we believe that also the developers, in these days, are more familiar with web applications.

Looking at such a web-oriented MoBe, one can realize that it is a new kind of system that we named Context-Aware Browser. In other terms, the main idea behind CAB is to empower a generic mobile device with a browser being able to automatically and dynamically load web pages, services and applications selected according to the current context the user is in. Despite the apparent simplicity of this approach, a more thorough definition has to take into account several features; thus, we can say that the Context-Aware Browser is best described by the sum of the following parts (Fig. 8.3 shows a schematic representation).

Web browser: CAB is able to interpret and render in a sound way (X)HTML code, to interpret client side (e.g., JavaScript) code and to fully exploit AJaX implemented applications (moreover, a browser is the standard way of representing the web contents interface to the user).

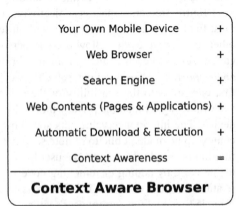

Fig. 8.3 Context-aware browser definition

Software application for mobile devices: Indeed, the latter are the main target of CAB (a device tied to a fixed location cannot fully exploit the context-awareness of our browser, since a fixed location entails a more static context).

Context-aware application: CAB is able to automatically retrieve and constantly update the contextual information gathered from the surrounding environment (this feature allows CAB to provide contents varying in dependence of the current context of the user).

Search engine: CAB is able to search both for "traditional" web pages and applications on the Web and for specifically tailored applications as we will see in the following.

Application able to automatically load contents: The resources retrieved by the search engine are automatically filtered against user's preferences and several other parameters in order to reduce the cognitive load imposed on the user by automatically selecting the most appropriate contents.

Application providing web pages and applications: CAB is able to manage both static resources (e.g., plain (X)HTML pages) and dynamic ones requiring user interaction (e.g., web applications).

All the above mentioned parts are needed and equally important in the characterization of the Context-Aware Browser; as a consequence, if we left out even only one of those, we cannot speak of CAB, but of something significantly different and more limited.

This new web-based approach makes easier the porting of the system on different architectures: for example, we have developed versions for Windows Mobile, IPhone, Android and for common PCs' browsers like Google Chrome (although it is not executable on mobile devices, it is likely that it will be included in the next versions of Android).

8.6 Usage Scenarios

We describe here two scenarios chosen as application examples of our prototype. The first one refers to a domotic/automotive environment and its aim is to demonstrate the feasibility of our ideas. The second one, on the contrary, presents an application built on the proposed system, currently under development, representing a pervasive multimedia social guide. All the presented applications are built upon the MoBe and Context-Aware Browser platform.

8.6.1 Implementation

We focused our efforts only on the implementation of the main modules of our architecture and on our inferential approach and thus, the sensors information is simulated by an external application in order to avoid low level details and to concentrate ourselves just on the context inferences and on the retrieval, manipulation and presentation of the digital content.

On the server side, prototypes for MDS, MMS and MCS have been realized in Java. On the client side, for mobile devices (smartphones and PDAs), the MoBeSoul has been realized using J2ME Personal Profile and the browser Opera Mobile; a porting to Google Android and Apple IPhone has also been done. For other devices, such as notebooks and netbooks, the MoBeSoul has been realized using Java Standard Edition and the browser can be both Firefox and Opera and Google Chrome.

The inferential system is composed of networks and an inferential engine that manages the acquisition of contextual values from sensors, the acquisition of networks and the execution of the inferences on them. This one has been implemented in Java using the package JavaBayes (www.cs.cmu.edu/javabayes) for Bayesian networks and JESS (http://herzberg.ca.sandia.gov) for the rule-based stage.

8.6.2 Domotics and Automotive Scenario

This scenario models an everyday situation: a user in his/her home and car. Three inferential networks are related to this scenario: the first manages home contexts, the second manages car contexts and the third manages highway contexts.

We have chosen these environments as they are limited enough to avoid complexity issues and to be explicitly managed, but, at the same time, they present a quite heterogeneous set of situations. Also, it is well known that the definition of the rules and the relations between contextual values in the Bayesian network and their probabilities can be generated taking as examples our everyday life.

At first, the user is at home and his mobile device acquires automatically the home inferential network. In this network, we take into account the following concrete contextual information (which we consider the most meaningful in the domestic field): user location within the house, time of the day, user movement, light level, sound level, temperature and humidity. Starting from the concrete contexts, the system infers the abstract contexts. In Fig. 8.4, an example of the home inferential network is showed.

For instance, when a user is in his/her home, his device will receive an application to control the domotics system; when a user is watching TV, his device will turn into a TV remote; when the user is having a shower, his/her device will play a list of mp3.

Also, context and application filtering can be performed on the basis of the probability value. For example, if the user could define an 80% threshold to discard all the contexts with a lower probability, and to retrieve the most suitable applications or web pages (MoBeLets) on the basis of the higher probability contexts. Then, knowing that "the user is in kitchen" and "it's lunch time" and "the user is not in movement," the system can infer with a certain probability that "the user is having lunch," and with a lower probability "the user is preparing lunch."

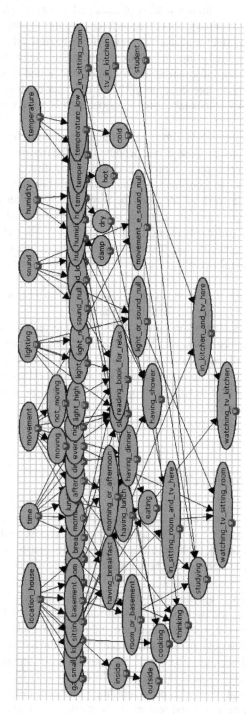

Fig. 8.4 Home network example

It is worth to notice that a higher number of managed concrete contextual values correspond to a more probabilistically correct inference of the abstract contexts. For instance, it is possible to infer the abstract context "user is having a shower" from the concrete context "user in the bathroom." However, increasing the concrete contexts number and also managing information like humidity and sound level, the system can provide a more correct representation of the current user context. Anyway, the set of concrete contextual values taken into consideration is more than enough for the purposes of this prototype.

This network is simple and its aim is just to demonstrate the feasibility of our approach; as the system we propose is independent from the networks in it, this one can be substituted with other more complex and closer to reality.

Then the user moves out from his home and enters his/her car: his/her mobile device receives the car network and discards the home one. When he/she drives into the highway, the device receives the highway network, and the system integrates it with the other networks (the car network, in this example). As the networks are obtained according to the user location, they are integrated according to the following criterion: the more general network receives in input the contexts inferred by the less general network.

The car network receives concrete context values from car sensors (e.g., oil and water condition, etc.) and infers the current car status.

The highway network receives in input the contexts inferred by the car network and uses several concrete contexts: weather, location, traffic information, speed limits, etc. The integration of the two networks allows a more precise description of the current user's context: for example, the "user at gas station" context, inferred by the highway network, acquires different meanings if the "car broken" context has been inferred by the car network.

Figure 8.5 shows two screenshots of our prototypes.

8.6.3 Pervasive Multimedia Social Guide

In this second scenario, we present an application built on the proposed system, currently under development. The main idea is to have a pervasive multimedia guide that allows tourists to interact with the digital content related to artworks in the museum in a social way: a person can be both a user of the content and a producer. We want to extend the philosophy of social Web or Web 2.0 with mobile, pervasive and context-aware features, adapting it to the cultural heritage sector [10].

Entering the museum the user receives on his mobile device the inferential networks that manage the contexts in the museum and the main application related to the museum. The main contextual information is obviously the location of the tourist inside the museum, but we take into consideration also other information like tourist profile, history, needs and social context around the tourist.

The application is first of all a guide. According to the user position, the system provides the tourist with audio and textual description, videos, etc. related to the

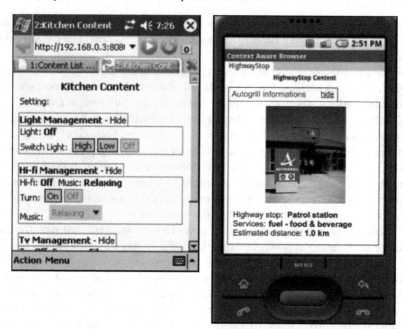

Fig. 8.5 Home and highway examples (Windows Mobile/Android)

Fig. 8.6 Example screenshots of our pervasive social guide based on MoBe-CAB architecture

artworks in the proximity (Fig. 8.6). The tourist can be also the producer of the content: he/she can capture content at the point of inspiration and upload it in real-time on system. Content can be of different kinds: photos, videos, audios, text about an artwork (comments or posts), drawings, etc. The tourist can also tag, using his/her mobile device, the artwork he/she is looking at in order to provide a classification of the artwork.

In this way the tourists are true content providers, uploading information that can be viewed by other tourists. This is a break with the actual situation in museums and cultural institutions, where professional curators are the only content authority.

Collaboration and participation features involve evaluation mechanisms, and for this reason, we propose the adoption of social evaluation. Following [16], all contents can be judged by users (e.g., according to accuracy, comprehensibility, etc.). The score assigned to a content item will depend on the combination of the score given by a user and the user's actual score. In addition, every content provider has a dynamic reliability score that depends on the scores of contents she produced. In this way, the crowd is the reviewer of its own contents.

Moreover, a tourist can rate every artwork. This rating, combined with the user profile, contributes to improve the artwork profile. In this way the system can suggest to tourists the artworks closer to their preferences.

The system can also help tourists by suggesting a tour. The tourist can request to the system an ideal tour according to her preferences, and/or she can select on her mobile device a tour criterion. There are three main kinds of tours: custom, dynamic and contextual tours. By custom tour, we mean that system can detect user information keeping track of her actions (e.g. visited places or artworks, commented posts) or it can evaluate user's profile to set her preferences, then system processes these information in order to create the user's ideal tour. A dynamic tour does not relate to user's personal information, but depends on all users' actions; thus, user can decide to visit the most viewed, most commented or most voted artworks. In other words, she can visit all the artworks that the crowd (community) advises to see. Finally, in a contextual tour, user can decide to visit only artworks about a specific topic or artworks belonging to the same artist and so on.

8.7 Conclusions and Future Work

In this work, we have presented a new architecture for ubiquitous and context-aware computing on mobile devices and have shown the general approach to context inference. In particular, we have proposed an approach based on the combination of rule-based systems, Bayesian networks and ontologies; we have shown how these three AI tools can be exploited in real-world context-aware ubiquitous systems. Differently from past works in the context-aware field, we have not focused only on particular contextual values as our inferential infrastructure is able to work in a more general way; our aim was to combine contexts to determine new, more abstract contexts.

The novelty of the proposed approach is twofold. Firstly, we take into account the information provided by the surrounding environment in order to carry out a more refined search of digital contents (applications, web pages and multimedia).

Secondly, information is not only automatically pushed towards the mobile device and then filtered, rather our approach involves a two-stage retrieval plus filtering process that minimizes bandwidth and maximizes privacy and security risks. As an overall outcome, the effort required on behalf of the user is minimized as well.

The work presented is just a preliminary work. Although it demonstrates the feasibility of our approach, several questions have to be answered. The following step concerns a more robust and complete implementation of our prototype in order to perform a complete user testing.

In particular, we want to complete the development of our pervasive multimedia social guide to test how the combination of ubiquitous computing, context-aware computing, mobile and social interaction can affect the user experience. In particular, we aim at verifying if our "pushing" approach reduces the negative feeling about the use of graphical interfaces and input systems of mobile devices in complex information seeking tasks. Indeed, the latter are rather cumbersome for the final user both from a cognitive viewpoint (thinking of the right query to submit, checking the obtained results) and a practical one (lots of keystrokes, screen scrolls: in general many interactions with the user interface). If this can be acceptable in the everyday use of a desktop system by a computer scientist or by people familiar with such interactions, it becomes a serious issue when the same task has to be carried out on a PDA or a mobile phone. Indeed, the graphical user interfaces and the input/output peripherals of such devices are rather limited when compared to their counterparts on a classical PC; moreover, the user is often a person not very familiar with digital applications and mobile technology.

References

1. Abowd, G.D., Dey, A.K., Brown, P.J., Davies, N., Smith, M., Steggles, P.: Towards a better understanding of context and context-awareness. In: Proceedings of the 1st International Symposium on Handheld and Ubiquitous Computing (HUC'99), pp. 304–307. Springer, 1999.
2. Bacon, J., Bates, J., Halls, D.: Location-oriented multimedia. IEEE Personal Communications, 4(5), 48–57 (1997).
3. Bazire, M., Brezillon, P.: Understanding context before using it. In: Proceedings of 5th International Conference CONTEXT 2005, pp. 29–40. Springer, 2005.
4. Biegel, G., Cahill, V.: A framework for developing mobile, context-aware applications. In: Proceedings of 2nd IEEE International Conference on Pervasive Computing and Communication (PerCom 2004), 2004.
5. Brown, P.J.: The stick-e document: A framework for creating context-aware applications. In: Proceedings of Electronic Publishing '96 (EP'96), pp. 259–272, 1996.
6. Brown, P.J., Bovey, J.D., Xian, C.: Context-aware applications: From the laboratory to the marketplace. IEEE Personal Communications, 4(5), 58–64 (1997).
7. Bulfoni, A., Coppola, P., Della Mea, V., Di Gaspero, L., Mischis, D., Mizzaro, S., Scagnetto, I., Vassena, L.: Ai on the move: Exploiting ai techniques for context inference on mobile devices. In: Proceedings of 5th Prestigious Applications of Intelligent Systems (PAIS 2008), Colocated with ECAI08, pp. 668–672, 2008.
8. Chen, G., Kotz, D.: A survey of context-aware mobile computing research. Technical Report TR2000-381, Department of Computer Science, Dartmouth College, 2000.

 9. Coppola, P., Della Mea, V., Di Gaspero, L., Mizzaro, S., Scagnetto, I., Selva, A., Vassena, L., Zandegiacomo Riziò, P.: MoBe: A framework for context-aware mobile applications. In: Proceedings of Workshop on Context Awareness for Proactive Systems (CAPS 2005), pp. 55–65. HIT, 2005.
10. Coppola, P., Lomuscio, R., Mizzaro, S., Nazzi, E., Vassena, L.: Mobile social software for cultural heritage: A reference model. In: 2nd Workshop on Social Aspects of the Web (SAW 2008), pp. 69–80, 2008.
11. Dey, A.K., Abowd, G.D.: A conceptual framework and a toolkit for supporting the rapid prototyping of context-aware applications. Human-Computer Interaction Journal, 16, 97–166 (2001).
12. Di Flora, C., Riva, O., Raatikainen, K., Russo, S.: Supporting mobile context-aware applications through a modular service infrastructure. In: Proceedings on the 6th International Conference on Ubiquitous Computing (UbiComp 2004), 2004.
13. Hofer, T., Schwinger, W., Pichler, M., Leonhartsberger, G., Altmann, J., Retschitzegger, W.: Context-awareness on mobile devices – the hydrogen approach. In: Proceedings of the 36th Annual Hawaii International Conference on System Sciences (HICSS'03), p. 292.1. IEEE Computer Society, 2003.
14. Kindberg, T., Barton, J., Morgan, J., Becker, G., Caswell, D., Debaty, P., Gopal, G., Frid, M., Krishnan, V., Morris, H., Schettino, J., Serra, B., Spasojevic, M.: People, places, things: Web presence for the real world. Mobile Networks and Applications, 7(5), 365–376 (2002).
15. Korpipää, P., Koskinen, M., Peltola, J., Makela, S.M., Seppanen, T.: Bayesian approach to sensor-based context awareness. Personal Ubiquitous Computing, 7(2), 113–124 (2003).
16. Mizzaro, S.: Quality control in scholarly publishing: A new proposal. Journal of the American Society for Information Science and Technology, 54(11), 989–1005 (2003).
17. Newell, A., Simon, H.A.: Computer Augmentation of Human Reasoning. Spartan Books, 1965.
18. Pascoe, J.: Adding generic contextual capabilities to wearable computers. In: Proceedings of the 2nd International Symposium on Wearable Computers. IEEE Computer Society Press, 1998.
19. Pearl, J.: Probabilistic reasoning in intelligent systems: Networks of plausible inference. Morgan Kaufmann Publishers, 1988.
20. Schilit, B., Theimer, M.: Disseminating active map information to mobile hosts. IEEE Network, 8(5), 22–32 (1994).
21. Schilit, B., Adams, N., Want, R.: Context-aware computing applications. In: IEEE Workshop on Mobile Computing Systems and Applications, pp. 85–90, 1994.
22. Schmidt, A., Beigl, M., Gellersen, H.W.: There is more to context than location. In: Proceedings of the International Workshop on Interactive Applications of Mobile Computing (IMC98). Springer, 1998.
23. Schmidt, A., Aidoo, K.A., Takaluoma, A., Tuomela, U., Laerhoven, K.V., De Velde, W.V.: Advanced interaction in context. In: Proceedings of 1st International Symposium on Handheld and Ubiquitous Computing (HUC'99), pp. 89–101. Springer, 1999.
24. Siu, P., Belaramani, N., Wang, C., Lau, F.: Context-aware state management for ubiquitous application. In: Embedded and Ubiquitous Computing (EUC), pp. 776–785, 2005.
25. West, D., Apted, T., Quigley, A.: A context inference and multi-modal approach to mobile information access. In: Artificial Intelligence in Mobile Systems (AIMS 2004) in Conjunction with UbiComp 2004, 2004.
26. Zhang, T.: An architecture for building customizable context-aware applications by end-users. In: Pervasive 2004 Doctoral Colloquium, 2004.

Chapter 9
A Distributed Ambient Intelligence Based Multi-Agent System for Alzheimer Health Care

Dante I. Tapia, Sara Rodríguez, and Juan M. Corchado

Abstract This chapter presents ALZ-MAS (*Alzheimer multi-agent system*),[1] an ambient intelligence (AmI)-based multi-agent system aimed at enhancing the assistance and health care for Alzheimer patients. The system makes use of several context-aware technologies that allow it to automatically obtain information from users and the environment in an evenly distributed way, focusing on the characteristics of ubiquity, awareness, intelligence, mobility, etc., all of which are concepts defined by AmI. ALZ-MAS makes use of a services oriented multi-agent architecture, called *flexible user and services oriented multi-agent architecture*, to distribute resources and enhance its performance. It is demonstrated that a SOA approach is adequate to build distributed and highly dynamic AmI-based multi-agent systems.

Keywords Multi-agent systems · Ambient intelligence · Services oriented architectures · Health care · Radio frequency identification · Wireless sensors

9.1 Introduction

The continuous technological advances have gradually surrounded people with devices and technology. It is necessary to develop intuitive interfaces and systems with some degree of intelligence, with the ability to recognize and respond to the needs of individuals in a discrete and often invisible way, considering people in the centre of the development to create technologically complex and intelligent environments.

Ambient intelligence (AmI) is an emerging multidisciplinary area based on ubiquitous computing, which influences the design of protocols, communications, systems, devices, etc., proposing new ways of interaction between people and

D.I. Tapia (✉)
Departamento Informática y Automática, Universidad de Salamanca, Plaza de la Merced s/n, 37008 Salamanca, Spain
e-mail: dantetapia@usal.es

[1] The system presented in this paper is an improved version of ALZ-MAS released on Q3 – 2006 by the BISITE Research Group (http://bisite.usal.es/) at the University of Salamanca, Spain.

technology and adapting them to the needs of individuals and their environment [38]. It offers a great potential to improve quality of life and simplify the use of technology by offering a wider range of personalized services and providing users with easier and more efficient ways to communicate and interact with other people and systems [12, 38]. However, the development of systems that clearly fulfil the needs of AmI is difficult and not always satisfactory. It requires a joint development of models, techniques and technologies based on services. An AmI-based system consists of a set of human actors and adaptive mechanisms that work together in a distributed way. Those mechanisms provide on demand personalized services and stimulate users through their environment according to specific situation characteristics [38].

This paper describes ALZ-MAS (*Alzheimer multi-agent system*), an AmI-based multi-agent system aimed at enhancing the assistance and health care for Alzheimer patients. ALZ-MAS makes use of a *flexible user and services oriented multi-agent architecture* (FUSION@), an experimental architecture that has been developed by the BISITE Research Group (http://bisite.usal.es) at the University of Salamanca, Spain. This architecture presents important improvements in the area of AmI [38]. One of the most important characteristics is the use of intelligent agents as the main components in employing a service oriented approach, focusing on distributing the majority of the systems' functionalities into remote and local services and applications. FUSION@ proposes a new and easier method of building distributed multi-agent systems, where the functionalities of the systems are not integrated into the structure of the agents, rather they are modelled as distributed services and applications, which are invoked by the agents acting as controllers and coordinators. This paper also demonstrates that a distributed SOA-based approach is adequate for developing dynamic multi-agent systems for improving health care in geriatric residences, focusing on the AmI paradigm.

Agents have a set of characteristics such as autonomy, reasoning, reactivity, social abilities, pro-activity, mobility, organization, etc., which allow them to cover several needs for AmI environments, especially ubiquitous communication and computing and adaptable interfaces. Agent and multi-agent systems have been successfully applied to several AmI scenarios such as education, culture, entertainment, medicine, robotics, etc. [12, 33, 34, 38]. The characteristics of the agents make them appropriate for developing dynamic and distributed systems based on AmI, as they possess the capability of adapting themselves to the users and environmental characteristics [21]. The continuous advancement in mobile computing makes it possible to obtain information about the context and also to react physically to it in more innovative ways [21]. The agents in ALZ-MAS are based on the deliberative belief, desire, intention (BDI) model [6, 22, 30], where the agents' internal structure and capabilities are based on mental aptitudes, using beliefs, desires and intentions [5, 16, 18]. Nevertheless, AmI developments need higher adaptation, learning and autonomy levels than pure BDI model [6]. This is achieved by modelling the agents' characteristics [39] to provide them with mechanisms that allow solving complex problems and autonomous learning. An essential aspect in this work is the use of a set of technologies that provides the agents automatic and real time information of the environment, and allow them to react upon it.

In the next section, the problem description that motivated the development of ALZ-MAS is presented. Section 9.3 introduces some related work regarding agents and multi-agent systems in health care scenarios and their integration with SOA-based approaches. Section 9.4 describes the basic components of ALZ-MAS and shows how FUSION@ has been used to distribute its functionalities. Section 9.4 also briefly describes the main technologies used to provide the agents in ALZ-MAS with context-aware capabilities. Finally, Sect. 9.5 presents the results and conclusions obtained.

9.2   Problem Description

Dependence is a permanent situation in which a person needs important assistance from others in order to perform basic daily life activities, such as essential mobility, object and people recognition, and domestic tasks [14]. There is an ever growing need to supply constant care and support to the disabled and elderly, and the drive to find more effective ways of providing such care has become a major challenge for the scientific community [28]. The World Health Organization has determined that in the year 2025, there will be one billion people in the world over the age of 60 and twice as many by 2050, with nearly 80% concentrated in developed countries [40]. Spain will be the third "oldest country" in the world, just behind Japan and Korea, with 35% of its citizens over 65 years of age [33]. In fact, people over 60 years old represent more than 21% of the European population [40], and people over 65 are the fastest growing segment of the population in the United States of America [1]. Furthermore, over 20% of those people over 85 have a limited capacity for independent living, requiring continuous monitoring and daily assistance [16]. The importance of developing new and more reliable ways of providing care and support for the elderly is underscored by this trend, and the creation of secure, unobtrusive and adaptable environments for monitoring and optimizing health care will become vital. Some authors [28] consider that tomorrow's health care institutions will be equipped with intelligent systems capable of interacting with humans. Multi-agent systems and architectures based on intelligent devices have recently been explored as supervision systems for medical care for dependent people. These intelligent systems aim to support patients in all aspects of daily life [9], predicting potential hazardous situations and delivering physical and cognitive support [3].

AmI-based systems aim to improve quality of life, offering more efficient and easy ways to use services and communication tools to interact with other people, systems and environments. Among the general population, those most likely to benefit from the development of these systems are the elderly and dependent persons, whose daily lives, with particular regard to health care, will be most enhanced [11,36]. Dependent persons can suffer from degenerative diseases, dementia or loss of cognitive ability [14]. In Spain, dependency is classified into three levels: [14] Level 1 (moderated dependence) refers to all people that need help to perform one or several basic daily life activities, at least once a day; Level 2 (severe dependence) consists of people who need help to perform several daily life activities two or three times a day, but who do not require the support of a permanent caregiver; and finally, Level 3 (great dependence) refers to all people who need support to perform several daily life activities numerous times a day, and because of their total loss of mental or physical autonomy, need the continuous and permanent presence of a caregiver.

9.3 Related Work

Agents and multi-agent systems in dependency environments are becoming a reality, especially in health care. Most agents-based applications are related to the use of this technology in the monitoring of patients, treatment supervision and data mining. Lanzola et al. [23] present a methodology that facilitates the development of interoperable intelligent software agents for medical applications, and propose a generic computational model for implementing them. The model may be specialized in order to support all the different information and knowledge-related requirements of a hospital information system. Meunier et al. [26] propose the use of virtual machines to support mobile software agents by using a functional programming paradigm. This virtual machine provides the application developer with a rich and robust platform upon which to develop distributed mobile agent applications, specifically when targeting distributed medical information and distributed image processing. While an interesting proposal, it is not viable due to the security reasons that affect mobile agents, and there is no defined alternative for locating patients or generating planning strategies. There are also agents-based systems that help patients to get the best possible treatment, and that remind the patient about follow-up tests [27]. They assist the patient in managing continuing ambulatory conditions (chronic problems). They also provide health-related information by allowing the patient to interact with the on-line health care information network. Decker and Li [15] propose a system to increase hospital efficiency by using global planning and scheduling techniques. They propose a multi-agent solution that uses the generalized partial global planning approach, which preserves the existing human organization and authority structures while providing better system-level performance (increased hospital unit throughput and decreased inpatient length of stay time). To do this, they use resource constraint scheduling to extend the proposed planning method with a coordination mechanism that handles mutually exclusive resource relationships. Other applications focus on home scenarios to provide assistance to elderly and dependent persons. RoboCare presents a multi-agent approach that covers several research areas, such as intelligent agents, visualization tools, robotics and data analysis techniques to support people with their daily life activities [29]. TeleCARE is another application that makes use of mobile agents and a generic platform in order to provide remote services and automate an entire home scenario for elderly people [7]. Although these applications expand the possibilities and stimulate research efforts to enhance the assistance and health care provided to elderly and dependent persons, none of them integrate intelligent agents, distributed and dynamic applications and services approach or the use of reasoning and planning mechanisms into their model.

The integration and interoperability of agents and multi-agent systems with SOA and Web Services approaches have been recently explored [2]. Some developments are centred on communication between these models, while others are centred on the integration of distributed services, especially Web Services, into the structure of the agents [4, 24, 25, 32, 35, 37]. There are also frameworks, such as Sun's Jini and IBM's WebSphere, which provide several tools to develop SOA-based systems. Jini uses Java technology to develop distributed and adaptive systems over dynamic environments. WebSphere provides tools for several operating systems and programming languages. However, the systems developed using these frameworks are not open at all because the framework is closed and services and applications must be programmed using a specific programming language that supports their respective proprietary APIs.

Although these developments provide an adequate background for developing distributed multi-agent systems integrating a service oriented approach, most of them are in early stages of development, so it is not possible to actually know their potential in real scenarios. FUSION@ has an advantage regarding development because we have already implemented it into ALZ-MAS. This system is presented in the next section.

9.4   ALZ-MAS

ALZ-MAS [11, 12] is a distributed multi-agent system designed upon AmI and aimed at enhancing the assistance and health care for Alzheimer patients living in geriatric residences. The main functionalities in the system include reasoning and planning mechanisms [19] that are embedded into deliberative BDI agents, and the use of several context-aware technologies to acquire information from users and their environment. In the later part of this section, the main characteristics of ALZ-MAS are described, followed by a description of the new ALZ-MAS system developed by means of the FUSION@ architecture.

ALZ-MAS structure has five different deliberative agents based on the BDI model (BDI Agents), each one with specific roles and capabilities:

- *User agent*: This agent manages the users' personal data and behaviour (monitoring, location, daily tasks and anomalies). The *user agent* beliefs and goals applied to every user depend on the plan or plans defined by the super-users. *User agent* maintains continuous communication with the rest of the system agents, especially with the *scheduleuser agent* (through which the scheduled-users can communicate the result of their assigned tasks) and with the *superuser agent*. The *user agent* must ensure that all the actions indicated by the SuperUser are carried out, and sends a copy of its memory base (goals and plans) to the *admin agent* in order to maintain backups. There is one agent for each patient registered in the system.

- *Superuser agent*: This agent runs on mobile devices (PDA) and inserts new tasks into the *admin agent* to be processed by a reasoning mechanism [12]. It needs to interact with the *user agents* to impose new tasks and receive periodic reports, and with the *scheduleuser agents* to ascertain the evolution of each plan. There is one *superuser agent* for each doctor connected to the system.
- *Scheduleuser agent*: It is a BDI agent with a planning mechanism embedded in its structure [12]. It schedules the users' daily activities and obtains dynamic plans depending on the tasks needed for each user. It manages scheduled-users profiles (preferences, habits, holidays, etc.), tasks, available time and resources. Every agent generates personalized plans depending on the scheduled-user profile. There is one *scheduleuser agent* for each nurse connected to the system.
- *Admin agent*: It runs on a Workstation and plays two roles: the security role that monitors the users' location and physical building status (temperature, lights, alarms, etc.) through continuous communication with the *devices agent*; and the manager role that handles the databases and the task assignment. It must provide security for the users and ensure the efficiency of the tasks assignments. There is just one *admin agent* running in the system.
- *Devices agent*: This agent controls all the hardware devices. It monitors the users' location (continuously obtaining/updating data from sensors), interacts with sensors and actuators to receive information and control physical services (temperature, lights, door locks, alarms, etc.) and also checks the status of the wireless devices connected to the system (e.g., PDA or Laptops). The information obtained is sent to the *admin agent* for processing. This agent runs on a Workstation. There is just one *devices agent* running in the system. The technologies associated with this agent are presented in Sect. 9.3.2.

In previous versions of ALZ-MAS, each agent integrates its own functionalities into their structure. If an agent needs to perform a task that involves another agent, it must communicate with that agent to request it. So, if the agent is disengaged, all its functionalities will be unavailable to the rest of agents. This has been an important issue, since agents running on PDA are constantly disconnecting from the platform and consequently crashing, making it necessary to restart (killing and launching new instances) those agents. Another important issue is that complex mechanisms are integrated into the agents [12]. These mechanisms are busy almost all the time, overloading the respective agents. Because these mechanisms are essential in the system, they must be available at all times. The system depends on these mechanisms to generate all decisions, so it is essential that they have all processing power available in order to increase overall performance. The problem is solved in a distributed way, so that if a component (i.e., agent) fails, the rest of the agents continue working. Moreover, the agents have certain responsibilities through which an agent looks for the overall integrity within the system.

In the version of ALZ-MAS presented in this paper, these mechanisms have been modelled as services, so any agent can make use of them. As can be seen in Fig. 9.1, the entire ALZ-MAS structure has been modified according to FUSION@ model, separating most of the agents' functionalities from those to be modelled as services.

ALZ-MAS 2.0

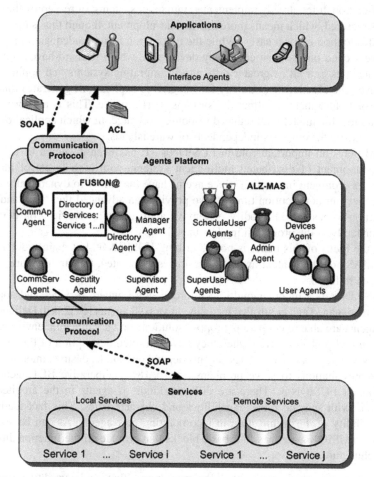

Fig. 9.1 ALZ-MAS basic structure

Next, the main components of FUSION@ are briefly described. It is also explained why it is necessary to use a new architecture.

9.4.1 Using FUSION@ to Distribute Resources

The development of AmI-based software requires creating increasingly complex and flexible applications, so there is a trend towards reusing resources and share compatible platforms or architectures. In some cases, applications require similar functionalities already implemented into other systems that are not always compatible. At this point, developers can face this problem through two options: reuse functionalities already implemented into other systems; or re-deploy the capabilities required, which means more time for development, though this is the easiest and safest option in most cases. While the first option is more adequate in the long run, the second one is most chosen by developers, which leads to have replicated functionalities as well as greater difficulty in migrating systems and applications. Moreover, the absence of a strategy for integrating applications generates multiple points of failure that can affect the systems' performance. This is a poorly scalable and flexible model with reduced response to change, in which applications are designed from the outset as independent software islands.

AmI plays an important role in FUSION@. It has been designed to facilitate the development of distributed multi-agent systems with high levels of human-system-environment interaction, since agents have the ability to dynamically adapt their behaviour at execution time. It also provides an advanced flexibility and customization to easily add, modify or remove applications or services on demand, independently of the programming language.

As the focus of this paper is not describing FUSION@, but mainly describing ALZ-MAS and the context-aware technologies associated, this architecture is just briefly introduced.[2]

FUSION@ is a modular multi-agent architecture, where services and applications are managed and controlled by deliberative BDI agents [6,22,30]. Deliberative BDI agents are able to cooperate, propose solutions on very dynamic environments and face real problems, even when they have a limited description of the problem and few resources available. These agents depend on beliefs, desires, intentions and plan representations to solve problems [5, 16, 18]. Deliberative BDI agents are the core of FUSION@. There are different kinds of agents in the architecture, each one with specific roles, capabilities and characteristics. This fact facilitates the flexibility of the architecture in incorporating new agents. As can be seen on Fig. 9.2, FUSION@ defines four basic blocks that provide all the functionalities of the architecture.

1. *Applications*, which represent all the programmes that can be used to exploit the system functionalities. They can be executed locally or remotely, even on mobile devices with limited processing capabilities, because computing tasks are largely delegated to the agents and services.
2. An *Agents Platform* as the core of FUSION@, integrating a set of agents, each one with special characteristics and behaviour. These agents act as controllers and administrators for all applications and services, managing the adequate functioning of the system, from services, applications, communication and performance to reasoning and decision-making.
3. *Services*, which are the bulk of the functionalities of the system at the processing, delivery and information acquisition levels. Services are designed to be invoked locally or remotely.

---

[2] Further information about FUSION@ can be obtained at http://bisite.usal.es/

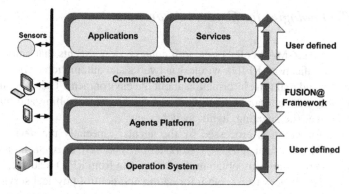

Fig. 9.2 FUSION@ framework

4. And finally a *communication protocol,* which allows applications and services to communicate directly with the agents platform. The protocol is based on simple object access protocol (SOAP) specification and is completely open and independent of any programming language [8].

These blocks are managed by means of pre-defined agents that provide the basic functionalities of FUSION@:

- *Commapp agent* is responsible for all communications between applications and the platform.
- *Commserv agent* is responsible for all communications between services and the platform.
- *Directory agent* manages the list of services that can be used by the system; Supervisor Agent supervises the correct functioning of the other agents in the system.
- *Security agent* analyzes the structure and syntax of all incoming and outgoing messages.
- *Manager agent* decides which agent must be called by taking into account the services performance and users' preferences; Interface Agents are designed to be embedded in users' applications (e.g., programmes running into PDA or mobile phones). Interface agents communicate directly with the agents in FUSION@, so there is no need to employ the communication protocol, rather the FIPA ACL specification [17].

FUSION@ also facilitates the inclusion of context-aware technologies that allow systems to automatically obtain information from users and the environment in an evenly distributed way, focusing on the characteristics of ubiquity, awareness, intelligence, mobility, etc., all of which are concepts defined by AmI. The goal in FUSION@ is not only to distribute services and applications, but also promote a new way of developing AmI-based systems focusing on ubiquity and simplicity.

Next, the most important technologies used in ALZ-MAS to provide the agents with context-aware capabilities are presented.

9.4.2 Technologies for Context-Awareness

The agents in ALZ-MAS collaborate with context-aware agents that employ radio frequency identification (RFID), wireless networks and automation devices providing automatic and real time information about the environment. These technologies also allow the users interacting with their surroundings, controlling and managing physical services (i.e., heating, lights, switches, etc.).

All the information is processed by the agents, especially the *devices agent*, which is a BDI agent that runs on a Workstation. The *devices agent* monitors the users' location (continuously obtaining/updating data from RFID readers), interacts with the ZigBee devices to receive information and control physical services, and also checks the status of the wireless devices connected to the system (e.g., PDA). The information obtained is sent to the *admin agent* to be processed. All hardware is some way integrated to agents, providing automatic and real time information about the environment that is processed by the agents to automate tasks and manage multiple services. Next, these technologies are described.

An RFID technology is a wireless communications technology used to identify and receive information about humans, animals and objects on the move. An RFID system contains basically four components: tags, readers, antennas and software. Tags with no power system (e.g., batteries) integrated are called passive tags or "transponders," these are much smaller and cheaper than active tags (power system included), but have shorter read range. The transponder is placed on the object itself (e.g., bracelet). As this object moves into the reader's capture area, the reader is activated and begins signalling via electromagnetic waves (radio frequency). The transponder subsequently transmits its unique ID information number to the reader, which transmits it to a device or a central computer where the information is processed. This information is not restricted to the location of the object, and can include specific detailed information concerning the object itself. Its most use is in industrial/manufacturing, transportation, distribution, etc., but there are other growth sectors including health care [10].

The configuration used in ALZ-MAS consists of a transponder mounted on a bracelet worn on the user's wrist or ankle, and several sensors installed over protected zones, with an adjustable capture range up to 2 m, and a central computer where all the information is processed and stored. Figure 9.3 shows the RFID infrastructure used in ALZ-MAS.

Figure 9.4 shows two Sokymat's Q5 chip 125 KHz RFID wrist bands and a RFID USB Desktop Reader used in ALZ-MAS for people identification and location monitoring.

Wireless LAN (local area network), also known as Wi-Fi (wireless fidelity) networks, increases the mobility, flexibility and efficiency of the users, allowing programmes, data and resources to be available, no matter the physical location. These networks can be used to replace or as an extension of wired LANs. They provide reduced infrastructure and low installation cost, and also give more mobility and flexibility by allowing people to stay connected to the network as they roam among covered areas, increasing efficiency by allowing data to be entered and accessed on

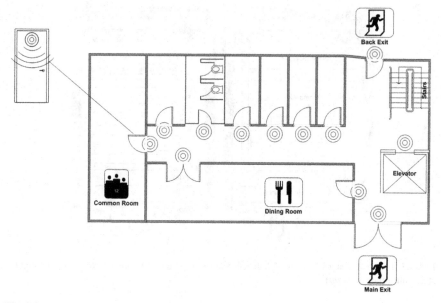

Fig. 9.3 RFID infrastructure in ALZ-MAS

Fig. 9.4 RFID technology
used in ALZ-MAS: two RFID
wrist bands (*up*); a USB
desktop reader (*down*)

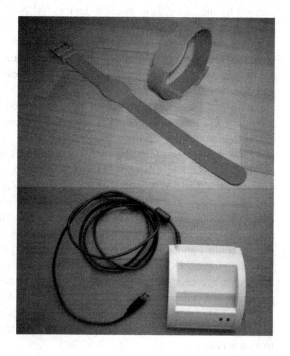

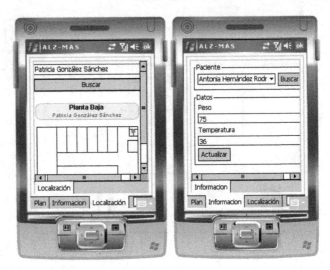

Fig. 9.5 PDA user interface in ALZ-MAS. Location of patients and nurses (*left*); and a patient's status information (*right*)

site [20]. New handheld devices facilitate the use of new interaction techniques, for instance, some systems focus on facilitating users with guidance or location systems [13, 31] by means of their wireless devices. ALZ-MAS incorporates "lightweight" agents that can reside in mobile devices, such as cellular phones, PDA, etc., and therefore, support wireless communication, which facilitates the portability of a wide range of devices. Figure 9.5 shows the user interface executed in a PDA emulator. The Wi-Fi infrastructure in ALZ-MAS supports a set of PDA for interfaces and users' interaction, a Workstation where all the high demanding CPU tasks (e.g., planning and reasoning mechanisms) are processed, and several access points for providing wireless communication between distributed agents.

ZigBee is another significant technology used in ALZ-MAS. ZigBee is a low cost, low power consumption, two-way wireless communication standard, developed by the ZigBee alliance [41]. It is based on IEEE 802.15.4 protocol, and operates at 868/915 MHz and 2.4 GHz spectrum. ZigBee is designed to be embedded in consumer electronics, home and building automation, industrial controls, PC peripherals, medical sensor applications, toys and games, and is intended for home, building and industrial automation purposes, addressing the needs of monitoring, control and sensory network applications [41]. ZigBee allows star, tree or mesh topologies. Devices can be configured to act as: network coordinator (control all devices); router/repeater (send/receive/resend data to/from coordinator or end devices); and end device (send/receive data to/from coordinator). Figure 9.6 shows a Silicon Laboratories' C8051 chip-based 2.4 GHz development board that controls heating, lights, door locks, alarms, etc. A mesh of these boards is necessary to control all services.

Fig. 9.6 A ZigBee device
used in ALZ-MAS

9.5   Results and Conclusions

ALZ-MAS is an AmI-based multi-agent system aimed at enhancing the assistance
and health care for Alzheimer patients. ALZ-MAS takes advantage of the cooperation among autonomous agents and the use of context-aware technologies
providing a ubiquitous, non-invasive, high level interaction among users, system
and environment.

Figure 9.7 shows the main user interface of ALZ-MAS. The interface displays
basic information about nurses and patients (name, tasks that must be accomplished,
schedule, location inside the residence, etc.) and the building (outside temperature,
specific room temperature, lights status, etc.).

One of the most important features in ALZ-MAS is the use of complex reasoning
and planning mechanisms. These mechanisms dynamically schedule the medical
staff daily tasks.

Figure 9.8 shows a window with the general planning process result. It contains
the date, time to initiate the task, task description, priority of the task, length of
the task, and the patient associated with each task. To generate a new plan, a *sched-*
uleuser agent (running on a PDA) sends a request to the *agents platform*. The request
is processed by the *manager agent*, which decides creating a new plan. Then, the
solution is sent to the platform that delivers the new plan to all *scheduleuser agents*
running. The planning mechanism creates optimal paths and scheduling in order
to facilitate the completion of all activities defined for the nurses connected to the
system.

As can be seen in Fig. 9.9, the information is provided to all nurses and doctors in
a user-friendly format using mobile devices (PDA) to see their corresponding tasks.

Several tests have been done to demonstrate the efficiency of ALZ-MAS after
improving its structure and functionalities in this release. The tests were similar
to those performed in the past [11], which consisted of collecting data regarding
the time spent by the nurses on routine tasks and the number of nurses working
simultaneously. The ALZ-MAS version presented in this paper was adopted on June
12, 2007.

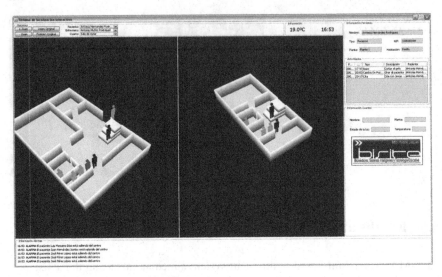

Fig. 9.7 ALZ-MAS main user interface

Fecha	H...	Tarea	Descripción	Prioridad	Durac...	Paciente
2007/06/21	18:21	Medicación Especial	Suministrar suero	1	5	María González Pérez
2007/06/21	23:01	Medicación Especial	Suministrar dosis de Rivastigmina	1	5	Luis Manzano Díaz
2007/06/22	00:06	Medicación Especial	Suministrar dosis de Tacrina	1	5	Luis Manzano Díaz
2007/06/22	01:06	Medicación Especial	Suministrar dosis de Donepizilo	1	5	Francisco López López
2007/06/21	18:11	Cita	Cita con Jesús Santos Marcos	2	30	José Pérez López
2007/06/21	23:01	Cita	Cita con Rosa Benito Gómez	2	30	Sara Díaz Fernández
2007/06/22	00:31	Cita	Cita con Jesús Santos Marcos	2	30	Patricia González Sánchez
2007/06/21	23:21	Medicación Oral	Suministrar Glimepirida	3	3	Miguel Sánchez Pérez
2007/06/21	20:26	Visita	Visita de familiares	3	10	Patricia González Sánchez
2007/06/21	18:11	Medicación Oral	Suministrar Miglitol	4	3	Juan Hernández Santos
2007/06/21	22:26	Visita	Visita de un amigo	4	10	Francisco López López
2007/06/21	19:36	Cambio De Postura	Inclinar la cama	5	10	Sara Díaz Fernández
2007/06/21	21:06	Alimentación	Pieza de fruta (plátano)	5	10	José Pérez López
2007/06/21	21:16	Cambio De Postura	Girar al paciente	6	10	Juan Hernández Santos
2007/06/21	21:46	Ejercicio	Rehabilitación	6	10	María González Pérez
2007/06/22	00:46	Cambio De Postura	Mover al paciente	6	10	Fernando Benito Iglesias
2007/06/21	19:36	Ejercicio	Dar un paseo	7	10	Miguel Sánchez Pérez
2007/06/21	18:51	Alimentación	Pieza de fruta (manzana o pera)	8	10	Francisco López López
2007/06/21	20:11	Limpieza	Dar un baño	9	10	Luis Manzano Díaz
2007/06/21	18:51	Aseo	Cortar el pelo	10	23	Antonia Hernández Rodríguez
2007/06/21	20:36	Aseo	Cortar las uñas	10	23	Fernando Benito Iglesias
2007/06/21	22:01	Limpieza	Lavar las manos	10	10	Antonia Hernández Rodríguez

ALZ-MAS   PLAN

Fig. 9.8 A result of a general planning

The tasks executed by nurses were divided in two categories, direct action tasks and indirect action tasks. Direct action tasks are those which require the nurse acting directly on the patient during the whole task (e.g., medication, posture change, toileting, feeding, etc.). In the indirect action tasks, the nurses do not need to act

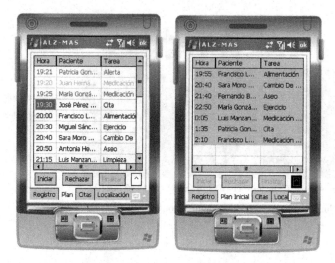

Fig. 9.9 PDA user interface showing a nurse planning: A current plan which must be completed by the nurse (*left*); and an initial plan where the nurse can compare the daily progress (*right*)

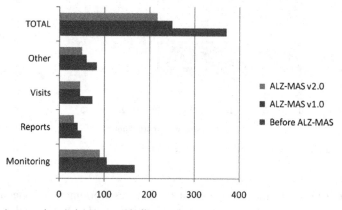

Fig. 9.10 Average time (min) spent on indirect tasks

directly on the patients all the time (e.g., reports, monitoring and visits). Once again we focused on indirect tasks because ALZ-MAS can handle most of them, so nurses can increase their productivity and the quality of health care.

Figure 9.10 shows the average time spent on indirect tasks by all nurses before implementation, with the previous release of ALZ-MAS and finally the release presented in this paper. ALZ-MAS continues reducing the time spent on indirect task. For example, the average number of minutes spent by all nurses on monitoring patients has been reduced from more than 150 daily minutes (before ALZ-MAS implementation) to approximately 90 daily minutes (after ALZ-MAS implementation). Furthermore, this new release of ALZ-MAS performed slightly better than the previous release.

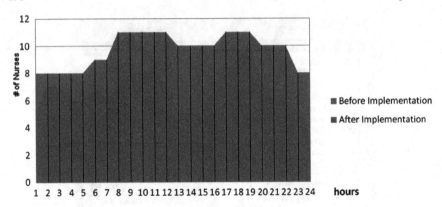

Fig. 9.11 Number of nurses working simultaneously

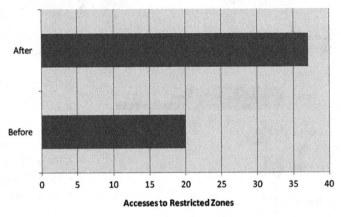

Fig. 9.12 Number detected accessed to restricted zones

Figure 9.11 shows the average number of nurses working simultaneously each hour of a day before and after the implementation of ALZ-MAS. In these sets of tests, 50 patients and 12 nurses were selected. According to the times spent by the nurses carrying out their tasks before the implementation, it can be seen how ALZ-MAS facilitates the more flexible assignation of the working shifts. The number of nurses working simultaneously before and after the implementation of the system is reduced substantially, especially at peak hours in which the indirect action tasks are more prone to overlap with the direct action tasks. For instance, from 13:00 to 15:00, there is a reduction of five nurses working simultaneously. This is achieved because there is an optimal distribution of tasks using ALZ-MAS.

The security of the centre has also been improved in two ways: the system monitors the patients and guarantees that each one of them is in the right place, and secondly, only authorized personnel can gain access to the residence protected areas. Figure 9.12 shows the number of accesses to restricted zones detected before and after the implementation of ALZ-MAS. As can be seen, almost twice unauthorized accesses were detected. This is an important information because it can be assumed that several accesses were not detected in the past and most of them could have led to risky situations.

It is demonstrated that ALZ-MAS can improve the security and health care efficiency through monitoring and automating medical staff's work and patients' activities, facilitating working shifts organization and reducing time spent on routine tasks. RFID, Wi-Fi and ZigBee technologies supply the agents with valuable information about the environment, contributing to a ubiquitous, non-invasive, high level interaction among users, system and the environment.

ALZ-MAS makes use of a services oriented multi-agent architecture called FUSION@, distributing resources and enhancing its performance. It is demonstrated that a SOA approach is adequate to build distributed and highly dynamic AmI-based multi-agent systems. Future work consists of improving ALZ-MAS by adding more features and increasing its performance.

Acknowledgments This work has been partially supported by the FIT-350300-2007-84 project.

References

1. Anderson R N (1999) A method for constructing complete annual U.S. life tables. Vital Health Statistics, National Center for Health Statistics, vol. 2(129), pp. 1–28
2. Ardissono L, Petrone G, Segnan M (2004). A Conversational Approach to the Interaction With Web Services. Computational Intelligence, 20(4):693–709. doi: 10.1111/j.0824-7935.2004.00261.x
3. Bahadori S, Cesta A, Grisetti G, Iocchi L, Leone R, Nardi D, Oddi A, Pecora F, Rasconi R (2003) RoboCare: An integrated robotic system for the domestic care of the elderly. In: Proceedings of Workshop on Ambient Intelligence, Pisa, Italia
4. Bonino da Silva L O, Ramparany F, Dockhorn P, Vink P, Etter R, Broens T (2007) A service architecture for context awareness and reaction provisioning. IEEE Congress on Services (Services 2007), pp. 25–32
5. Bratman M E (1987) Intentions, plans and practical reason. Harvard University Press, Cambridge, MA
6. Bratman M E, Israel D, Pollack M E (1988) Plans and resource-bounded practical reasoning. In: Computational Intelligence, vol. 4. Blackwell Publishing, Oxford, pp. 349–355
7. Camarinha-Matos L, Afsarmanesh H (2002) Design of a virtual community infrastructure for elderly care. In: PRO-VE'02 – 3rd IFIP Working Conference on Infrastructures for Virtual Enterprises, Sesimbra, Portugal
8. Cerami E (2002) Web services essentials distributed applications with XML-RPC, SOAP, UDDI & WSDL, 1st edn. O'Reilly & Associates, Inc
9. Cesta A, Bahadori S, Cortellesa G, Grisetti G, Giuliani M, Locchi L, Leone G, Nardo D, Oddi A, Pecora F, Rasconi R, Saggese A, Scopelliti M (2003) The RoboCare Project, cognitive systems for the care of the elderly. In: Proceedings of International Conference on Aging, Disability and Independence (ICADI), Washington, DC, USA
10. CE RFID (2006) Position paper: General guidelines for promoting RFID in Europe. Coordinating European efforts for promoting the European RFID value chain. http://www.rfid-in-action.eu/public/papers-and-documents/guidelines.pdf
11. Corchado J M, Bajo J, Abraham A (2008a) GERAmI: Improving the delivery of health care. In: IEEE Intelligent Systems, Special Issue on Ambient Intelligence – Mar/Apr '08, vol. 23(2), pp. 19–25

12. Corchado J M, Bajo J, Paz Y D, Tapia D I (2008b). Intelligent environment for monitoring Alzheimer patients, agent technology for health care. Decis. Support Syst., 44(2), pp. 382–396
13. Corchado J M, Pavón J, Corchado E, Castillo L F (2005) Development of CBR-BDI agents: A tourist guide application. In: Seventh European Conference on Case-based Reasoning. LNAI 3155, Springer, Berlin, pp. 547–559
14. Costa-Font J, Patxot C (2005) The design of the long-term care system in Spain: Policy and financial constraints. In: Social Policy and Society, vol. 4(1). Cambridge University Press, Cambridge, pp. 11–20
15. Decker K, Li J (1998) Coordinated hospital patient scheduling. In: Y Demazeau (Ed.), Proceedings of ICMAS98, Paris, France, pp. 104–111
16. Erickson P, Wilson R Shannon I (1995) Years of healthy life. US Department of Health and Human Services, CDC, National Center for Health Statistics, Hyattsville, Maryland. Statistical Notes No. 7
17. FIPA (2005) Foundation for Intelligent Physical Agents. Retrieved July 14, 2006, from http://www.fipa.org
18. Georgeff M, Rao A (1998) Rational software agents: From theory to practice. In: Agent Technology: Foundations, Applications, and Markets. In: N R Jennings, M J Wooldridge (Eds.). Springer, New York
19. Glez-Bedia M, Corchado J M (2002) A planning strategy based on variational calculus for deliberative agents. In: Computing and Information Systems Journal 10(1):2–14
20. Hewlett-Packard (2002) Understanding Wi-Fi. http://www.hp.com/rnd/library/pdf/
21. Jayaputera G T, Zaslavsky A B, Loke S W (2007) Enabling run-time composition and support for heterogeneous pervasive multi-agent systems. Journal of Systems and Software 80(12):2039–2062
22. Jennings, N R, Wooldridge M. (1995) Applying agent technology. Applied Artificial Intelligence. Taylor & Francis, vol. 9(4), pp. 351–361
23. Lanzola G, Gatti L, Falasconi S, Stefanelli M (1999) A framework for building cooperative software agents in medical applications. Artificial Intelligence in Medicine 16(3):223–249
24. Li Y, Shen W Ghenniwa H (2004) Agent-based web services framework and development environment. In: Computational Intelligence. Blackwell Publishing, vol. 20(4), pp. 678–692
25. Liu X (2007) A multi-agent-based service-oriented architecture for inter-enterprise cooperation system. In Proceedings of the Second International Conference on Digital Telecommunications (ICDT'07). IEEE Computer Society, Washington, DC
26. Meunier J A (1999) A virtual machine for a functional mobile agent architecture supporting distributed medical information. In: Proceedings of CBMS '99. IEEE Computer Society, Washington, DC
27. Miksch S, Cheng K, Hayes-Roth B (1997) An intelligent assistant for patient health care. In: Proceedings of Agents'97, ACM Press, New York, pp. 458–465
28. Nealon J, Moreno A (2003) Applications of software agent technology in the health care domain. In: Whitestein Series in Software Agent Technologies, Birkhauser
29. Pecora F, Cesta A (2007). Dcop for smart homes: A case study. In: Computational Intelligence, vol. 23(4). Blackwell Publishing, pp. 395–419
30. Pokahr A, Braubach L, Lamersdorf W (2003) Jadex: Implementing a BDI-Infrastructure for JADE Agents. In: EXP – in search of innovation (Special Issue on JADE), Department of Informatics, University of Hamburg, Germany, pp. 76–85
31. Poslad S, Laamanen H, Malaka R, Nick A, Buckle P, Zipl A (2001) CRUMPET: creation of user-friendly mobile services personalised for tourism. IEE Conference Publications, 2001(CP477), pp. 28–32. doi: 10.1049/cp:20010006
32. Ricci A, Buda C, Zaghini N (2007) An agent-oriented programming model for SOA & web services. In: Fifth IEEE International Conference on Industrial Informatics (INDIN'07), Vienna, Austria, pp. 1059–1064
33. Sancho M, Abellán A, Pérez L Miguel J A (2002) Ageing in Spain: Second World Assembly on Ageing. IMSERSO, Madrid, Spain
34. Schön B, O'Hare G M P, Duffy B R, Martin A N, Bradley J F (2005) Agent Assistance for 3D World Navigation. In: Lecture Notes in Computer Science. Springer, vol. 1, pp. 499–499

35. Shafiq M O, Ding Y, Fensel D (2006) Bridging multi agent systems and web services: towards interoperability between software agents and semantic web services. In: Proceedings of the 10th IEEE International Enterprise Distributed Object Computing Conference (EDOC'06). IEEE Computer Society, Washington, DC, pp. 85–96
36. Van Woerden K (2006) Mainstream developments in ICT: Why are they important for assistive technology? In: Technology and Disability, vol. 18(1). IOS Press. pp. 15–18
37. Walton C (2006) Agency and the Semantic Web. Oxford University Press
38. Weber W, Rabaey J M, Aarts E (2005) Ambient Intelligence.Springer, New York
39. Wooldridge M, Jennings N R (1995) Intelligent agents: Theory and practice. In: The Knowledge Engineering Review, Cambridge University Press, vol. 10(2), pp. 115–152
40. WHO (2007) Global Age-friendly Cities: A Guide. World Health Organization. http://www.who.int/ageing/publications/Global_age_friendly_cities_Guide_English.pdf
41. ZigBee Standards Organization (2006) ZigBee Specification Document 053474r13. ZigBee Alliance

Chapter 10
Volcano Monitoring: A Case Study in Pervasive Computing

Nina Peterson, Lohith Anusuya-Rangappa, Behrooz A. Shirazi, WenZhan Song, Renjie Huang, Daniel Tran, Steve Chien, and Rick LaHusen

Abstract Recent advances in wireless sensor network technology have provided robust and reliable solutions for sophisticated pervasive computing applications such as inhospitable terrain environmental monitoring. We present a case study for developing a real-time pervasive computing system, called OASIS for optimized autonomous space in situ sensor-web, which combines ground assets (a sensor network) and space assets (NASA's earth observing (EO-1) satellite) to monitor volcanic activities at Mount St. Helens. OASIS's primary goals are: to integrate complementary space and in situ ground sensors into an interactive and autonomous sensorweb, to optimize power and communication resource management of the sensorweb and to provide mechanisms for seamless and scalable fusion of future space and in situ components. The OASIS in situ ground sensor network development addresses issues related to power management, bandwidth management, quality of service management, topology and routing management, and test-bed design. The space segment development consists of EO-1 architectural enhancements, feedback of EO-1 data into the in situ component, command and control integration, data ingestion and dissemination and field demonstrations.

Keywords Wireless sensor networks · Pervasive computing · Environment monitoring · Quality of service · Situation awareness

10.1 Introduction

New emerging technological advances have opened the door for more sophisticated pervasive computing applications to integrate more robust and reliable techniques. These advancements have led to the development of more powerful physical hardware available at a cheaper price, allowing for greater expansion of the applications.

N. Peterson (✉)
School of Electrical Engineering and Computer Science, Washington State University, Pullman, WA 99163, USA
e-mail: npicone@eecs.wsu.edu

A.-E. Hassanien et al. (eds.), *Pervasive Computing: Innovations in Intelligent Multimedia and Applications*, Computer Communications and Networks, DOI 10.1007/978-1-84882-599-4_10, © Springer-Verlag London Limited 2009

Our optimized autonomous space – in situ sensor-web (OASIS) application is designed to monitor Mount St. Helens, an active volcano in the state of Washington and provide feedback to Earth scientists, so they have the required information to make crucial decisions (for example, ordering evacuations and air traffic routing). Through the development of our earth-hazard-monitoring sensor-web, we will be able to demonstrate the ability to mitigate volcano hazards through the first "smart" in situ network. In order to accomplish this, we are integrating a continuous feedback loop between two primary components: a ground in situ component and a space component. The in situ ground sensor network is composed of tiny Imote2 sensor motes that collect data from five different sensors: GPS, seismic, infrasonic, RSAM and lightning. We dealt with systems issues, such as power management, bandwidth management, QoS management, topology and routing management and test-bed design issues. The space component currently consists of NASA's earth observing (EO)-1, though we hope to expand to other spacecrafts as well. EO-1 is a satellite that will monitor the volcano from space, providing additional science data in conjunction with the data gathered from the ground component. It is currently operational, and to support the OASIS requirements, several architectural enhancements were made. These include a continuous feedback loop between EO-1 and the in situ component allowing for command and control integration and data ingestion and dissemination. The combined OASIS will have two-way communication capability between the ground and the space assets, using both space and ground data for optimal allocation of limited power and bandwidth resources on the ground, and use smart management of competing demands for the limited space assets.

This case study is a 3 year project with a full scale implementation to be complete in 2009. By August 2008, we expect the first field deployment to occur. This deployment will consist of a self-configuring, self-healing wireless sensor network that will be deployed on Mount St. Helens and linked to the command and control of the EO-1 satellite. The ground sensor-web element will use in situ observations (seismic, gas and ground deformation) to trigger high-resolution data taken by EO-1, which will be down-linked back to the ground sensor-web control centre. These data will be automatically processed and analyzed where the results are ingested into a dynamic and scalable communication bandwidth allocation scheme to optimize communication and power usage.

An active volcano provides a challenging environment to examine and advance in situ sensor-web technology. The crater at Mount St. Helens is a dynamic three-dimensional communication environment, with batteries as the only reliable energy source. Various geophysical and geochemical sensors generate continuous high-fidelity data, whose priority depends on volcanic status. There is a compelling need for real-time data with sensors occasionally destroyed by falling rocks. Hence, an in situ network must be self-configuring and self-healing, with a smart power and bandwidth management scheme and autonomous in-network processing. In order to accomplish this, we have assembled a multidisciplinary team involving sensor-network experts, space scientists and Earth scientists, who are developing this prototype dynamic and scaleable hazard monitoring sensor-web for applying it to volcanic monitoring.

10.2   Literature Review

Wireless sensor network research has been growing rapidly in recent years [1–3]. Existing applications include habitat monitoring, infrastructure surveillance and environmental monitoring [4–9]. To meet the unique challenges of the volcanic environment, OASIS will significantly advance topology management [10], power and bandwidth management, real-time data gathering and autonomous in-network processing technologies. At present, topology management typically makes use of hierarchical architecture, which enables scalable management [11–14], and flat architecture, which enables better fault-tolerance and more concurrent communications [15,16]. OASIS will introduce a new topology management scheme combining hierarchical control structure with flat routing topology to enable a fully self-configuring and self-healing network. To prolong network lifetime, a smart power adjustment and role rotation algorithm will also be developed. At present, bandwidth [17] and power management schemes [18] typically use contention-based medium access control (MAC) protocols [19,20] and non-priority-differentiated normal routing protocols [19, 21, 22]. OASIS will develop a time-optimal and energy-efficient packet scheduling algorithm to coordinate the traffic, in which sensor nodes autonomously determine communication packet priorities based on mission needs and local bandwidth information. Bayesian network techniques will be applied here. In addition, a data aggregation algorithm will be developed to reduce bandwidth demand. OASIS will also, for first time, take advantage of in situ situation awareness strategies to capture subtle environmental changes in real-time, with the aid of smart bandwidth management. In addition, OASIS will apply a new interactive protocol at the sensor nodes and control centre, as part of integration of both space and in situ sassets.

Automated scheduling and planning environment (ASPEN's) extension to request assets and re-plan in cases where requests are not granted will leverage the negotiation methods used in distributed coordination using the SHAC (shared activity coordination) protocol [23]. This is a generalization of existing re-planning capabilities in ASPEN used to automatically negotiate ground contacts for the EO-1 mission. However, this negotiation approach will utilize a general sensor capability tasking structure and use SensorML (sensor markup language) descriptions of potentially relevant sensors to drive the request generation and backtracking when observation requests are not granted. The existing EO-1 sensor-web demonstrated crude aspects of sensor-web automated response [24]. All of the existing triggers use static combinations of sensors thresholds mapped onto response sensors that are manually defined by scientists. This will significantly extend the capability to distributed control centres and request oriented protocols and capability-based matching of sensors to requests based on SensorML.

10.3   Ground Component

Our ground component is composed of a suite of wireless sensor nodes, each connected to an array of deformation monitoring sensors. These deformation monitoring sensor arrays consist of GPS (global positioning system), seismic, infrasonic, RSAM (real-time seismic-amplitude measurement) and lightning sensors. In order to protect the sensors from the harsh elements, each suite and its sensor array are housed in a box. Each box, shown below in Fig. 10.1, will be dropped by helicopter on Mount St. Helens. In order to allow for proper placement of the boxes on the crater, each is equipped with a metal tripod-like structure, called a spider designed and created by earth scientists at cascades volcanic observatory.

Although the wireless sensor nodes are tiny compact devices, each is equipped with a complex yet lightweight software architecture. This architecture is composed of a link layer, network layer, transport layer and application layer. The lowest level is the link layer that is responsible for maintaining proper connectivity and link quality between nodes. Next, the network layer ensures that the routing of packets, including sensor to sink and sink to sensor, is executed according to the appropriate algorithms. The network layer also implements the smart-broadcasting algorithm, discussed in detail in Sect. 10.3.4.2. On top of the network layer lies the transport layer, which is responsible for the transportation of all packets including both reliable transport as well as best-effort transport. The type of transportation depends on the situation and the goals of the transport. Lastly, the application layer is the top-most layer which is composed of the sub-components: the data sensing module, the network management module and the situation awareness module. The sensing module, discussed in more detail in Sect. 10.3.6, is vital to the overall reliability

Fig. 10.1 Spider being deployed by helicopter

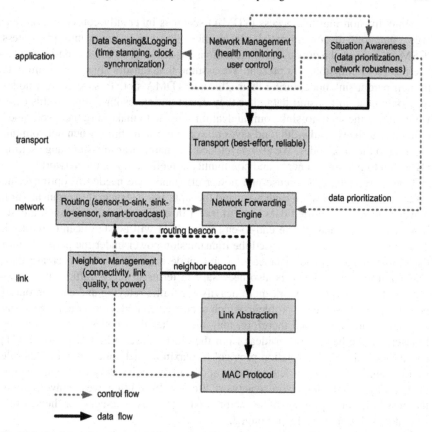

Fig. 10.2 In situ node software architecture graph

of the network as it controls the clock synchronization and timestamping of packets, making sure that the network is in sync. It is necessary that the Earth scientists be able to both monitor and control the network. In order to accomplish this, the scientists interact with the network management module that enables them to monitor the current status of the network as well as make any adjustments to network parameters such as the priority of a particular type of data, as necessary. Fig. 10.2 shows the architectural arrangement of the sensor node's software. Different components of this software architecture will be discussed in detail.

10.3.1   Power Management

The main challenge facing the power management of almost all wireless networks and in particular a volcano sensor-web is striking a balance between the need for high-rate data and the desire for network longevity. The OASIS smart sensor nodes have the built-in ability to adjust transmission power according to local density.

Time-division multiple-access (TDMA) schemes inherently conserve more energy compared to contention-based schemes like carrier sense multiple access (CSMA), because the duty cycle of the radio is reduced and no contention-introduced overhead and collisions are present. We assume that sensors always transmit data to their parent/sink node during their allocated TDMA slot. To save energy, nodes may only need to transmit data after they detect an interesting event. In this case, we optimize the node-to-sink communication scheme to make sure that every node efficiently utilizes bandwidth (and saves power at the same time) when not communicating to the sink nodes. We also developed a dynamic transmission range setting algorithm to maximize energy and communication efficiency in the network.

Considering the space-reuse and power efficiency, we needed to optimize the distance (in hops) between each node and the sink. For instance, if the transmission power is low, the acquired data have to travel through more hops; in such a case, if we use single channel, the end-to-end throughput will be significantly reduced. To handle this issue, we increased the transmission power under the permission of the power budget. If the distance to a sink node is small, we can decrease their transmission power, which is also necessary in terms of relay traffic – the nodes close to the sink usually work more heavily for traffic relaying and can run out of power earlier. To solve the problem, which occurs when nodes closer to the gateway consume more power and therefore, may die earlier than nodes further from the basestation, we have built on ideas from the cluster-based LEACH protocol [21] and developed a cluster rotation protocol to maximize network lifetime. This role rotation algorithm aims at letting every node to have equal duty to deliver data to the gateway, in order to maximize network lifetime. In addition, we are investigating the possibility of deploying some "actor" nodes to relay messages for the sensors, so that their lifetime can be prolonged.

Moreover, the OASIS bandwidth management scheme has the added benefit that it establishes a time-optimum communication schedule, as well as a cooperative power schedule of sensors. Since each node alternates between reception/transmission and sleep states, the wasted energy associated with idle listening and contention is eliminated during normal operation.

10.3.2 Bandwidth Management

Due to the inherent limitations of the wireless capacities of the sensors used in environmental monitoring, bandwidth management is crucial to the overall successful transmission of data from the acquisition point to the basestation. The limited bandwidth between the gateway and the sensor network constrains the high-fidelity operations and the real-time acquisition requirements.

We made use of the "many-to-one" network scenario by applying a time-optimal scheduling algorithm [25]. In this algorithm, each node locally calculates its duty cycle after the initial network deployment, and continuously adjust its schedule if the network topology changes. Every node either sends/receives messages or goes to sleep, which eliminates the energy waste of idle listening. Another advantage of this scheduling algorithm is the mitigation of interference between concurrent communication pairs. Consequently, both energy and communication efficiency are maximized. A GPS receiver at every node accommodates both synchronization and deformation measurements.

During active periods when bandwidth demands are highest, the network will prioritize the information flow in the network and reserve bandwidth for high-priority data, based on mission-needs. Every node has a buffer management mechanism to differentiate the priorities of different kinds of traffic, and schedule the time slots allocated for each type of traffic. For instance, if during volcanic activity, gas measurements are deemed the highest priority, other data may be buffered to make more bandwidth available for gas data. Cluster coordinators are able to automatically identify and select the minimum set of sensors that will provide mission critical data. Bayesian network techniques were applied to address the sensor selection problem [26].

To further optimize bandwidth utilization, in situ data reduction, compression and aggregation are driven by science requirements. For example, when necessary, seismic data, typically recorded at 100 Hz, will be reduced by two orders of magnitude at the node level by reporting an average real-time seismic amplitude monitor (RSAM) parameter, which is an established measurement of both earthquakes and volcanic tremors [27]. In addition, continuous seismic data will be streamed into a buffer at each node, and when seismic events are triggered, the buffered waveform with precise time markers will be compressed and delivered to the control centre for higher level processing.

10.3.3   QoS Management

The middleware layer provides communication, quality of service (QoS) and bandwidth management for the wireless sensor network. This is accomplished through situation awareness, prioritization and robustness.

10.3.3.1   Situation Awareness

The functionality that the situation awareness component within the middleware layer provides is to ensure that the network is conscious of its environment and responds dynamically to changes. If a physical phenomenon such as an eruption occurs within a particular geographic region of the network, that region is categorized as an area of interest. The categorization of physical phenomenon will take place both automatically as well as manually. Automatic categorization is done through a set of predefined situations described by the Earth scientists. However, in addition to this automated detection, it is also possible for the Earth scientists to manually determine that a physical phenomenon is occurring by examining the data and categorizing it as a region of interest. Therefore, the sensor nodes within the region of interest are given a higher priority, guaranteeing that data and communication from those sensors are processed promptly and without loss. For example, if lava is emitted from a portion of the volcano, that area of the network is classified as high priority. Since the network is aware that this is a particular area of interest, it makes certain that all data collected from that region are communicated in a timely manner and without loss or delay, even in the presence of network saturation and/or congestion. It is important to note that an area can be categorized as an area of interest due to physical changes detected either by the ground sensors or another external source, such as EO-1. Additionally, the combination of both the ground and space component provides the most sophisticated and accurate representation of the physical phenomena being detected.

10.3.3.2   Prioritization

Prioritization of data and communication within the middleware layer is based on both the context and the situation of the wireless sensor network. The context of the network pertains to the congestion within the network, as well as management of the assignment of priorities to data and communication from each of the individual nodes. In addition, the prioritization component is also conscious of the situation in which the network lies as described in the previous section. Thus, prioritization within the middleware component is twofold, incorporating both the context of the network and the current situation of the network. In order to accomplish this prioritization scheme, the middleware layer implements Tiny-DWFQ.

Tiny-DWFQ is our newly designed tiny-dynamic weighted fair queuing scheduling algorithm, which responds to an automated feedback in order to continually adjust to the current environment and dynamically reconfigure its algorithm in order to reflect the current state of the network. Dynamic adjustments allow Tiny-DWFQ to accomplish its ultimate goal of ensuring high level QoS for the most significant data, while still maintaining QoS requirements for less significant data.

One of the major obstacles in fulfilling this requirement is designing and implementing a lightweight algorithm, specifically for resource constrained wireless sensors, which is robust enough to handle continuous real-time data flows. Due to the limited computational capacity of wireless sensor networks (including memory, processor speed and communication bandwidth), our algorithm is designed specifically to meet these demanding requirements. Bandwidth limitations [28] in any wireless network provide a restricted amount of resources to be shared amongst competing data flows. Thus, in order to maximize the available resources, we designed a congestion reactive scheduling algorithm, Tiny-DWFQ, which addresses the extremely limited memory and computational requirements in its design of the scheduling of packets.

In order to meet the overall needs of many different types of networks, it is necessary for data to be categorized based on its importance or priority level within the network. For example, in our network scenario (OASIS), we are deploying wireless sensors on the crater of Mount St. Helens for volcanic monitoring and predication. The scientists who monitor the data do not view each data type as equally important, rather specific data (e.g., Lightning) are significantly more important than other data (e.g., GPS). Ideally we are able to transmit all of the data all of the time; however, when network congestion occurs due to bandwidth constraints, a decision must be made as to which data should be sent and in which order. If, due to the large number of packets, it is not possible to send or buffer all of the data, we must also determine which packets should be dropped. These decisions are the responsibility of our Tiny-DWFQ scheduling algorithm.

Within the design of Tiny-DWFQ, there are several critical items which factor into the algorithms execution: data priority, node priority, current congestion and available resources. In our model, we take into consideration both the importance of the type of data and the importance of the node where the data originated. This allows for a fine-grained granularity in our prioritization scheme, which gives the user a more powerful tool to utilize. For example, if activity is detected on the volcano, the data from the nodes within that area are considered more important and the data from those nodes are given a higher priority, than the data from nodes outside the region. However, all of the data from the nodes within the region of interest are not equally important (the lightning data are still more important than the GPS data). Thus, in order to capture this, we need to distinguish between data priority and node priority. In order to accomplish this, we assign a dynamic weighted priority (DWP), which incorporates both data and node priorities.

10.3.3.3   Link Layer Prioritization

Besides implementing prioritization of data and communication within the middleware layer based on network traffic, we also enhance prioritization in the link layer to guarantee QoS. We want to ensure that high priority packets can correspondingly have a higher packet delivery rate towards the sink. The hidden terminal problem in wireless networks can force concurrent transmissions, which cause received packets to become corrupt. We refer to this as the channel failure so that we can distinguish it from buffer failures, which cause packet loss due to buffer overflow. Without any optimizations, the probability of transmission failure with one-hop communication can be up to 50%. Additionally, if the communication is multi-hop, the situation can be much worse. For example, if the one-hop packet loss is p and a mote is of depth k within the communication tree, then its packet loss rate is $1 - (1 - p)^k$. If $p = 50\%$, $k = 5$, packet loss rate can be as high as 97%, which is unacceptable and results in a waste of both network and power resources. Consider communication that must traverse four-hops, if the transmission of the first three hops succeeds but last hop fails, then all of the energy that was consumed in the transmission of the first three hops is wasted. Thus, in order to provide a remedy, it is necessary for hop-by-hop retransmissions to be carried out in order to reduce the packet loss ratio and conserve the limited energy resources. Moreover, since the priority of each individual packet is different, we have a higher obligation to ensure the successful delivery of higher priority packets. Thus, in order to accomplish this, we correlate the number of retries for each packet with its priority. For some ordinary packets, one retry is enough; but for those that report certain important events, more retries are necessary. In our algorithm design, we have implemented a mapping that contains a static table for the mapping from priority to the number of retransmissions. The number of retransmissions is predefined based on empirical results obtained through simulations. When transmission failure occurs, the look up table is used to determine whether or not the current retry count has exceeded the maximum retry count for that packet's priority, if it has the transmissions stop; otherwise another transmission occurs.

10.3.3.4 Robustness

The QoS of the system includes, but is not limited to, ensuring fault tolerance within the network. Thus, failure of sensor nodes should and does not hinder other nodes' functionality. A minimal set of sensor nodes is determined to ensure that the network is capable of maintaining functional communication within the wireless sensor network. In addition, the system is able to dynamically recover from node failures exhibiting self-healing mechanisms. Polling and hinting relationships within the routing protocols ensure the desired robustness as well as the service provisions provided.

There are two types of node behaviours which must be addressed in order to ensure QoS: misbehaving nodes and failed (dead) nodes. A misbehaving node is any node that is communicating invalid or erroneous data. These data may be for one particular data type or for all data types. If erroneous data are detected at a node, two things must take place. First, we do not want the limited bandwidth to be consumed by the erroneous data. In order to accomplish this, we must adjust the priority of the bad data flow(s) so that it(they) will be given the lowest priority and be transmitted only if there is no congestion. Second, if a node dies and is, thus, no longer collecting and transmitting data, we still want to be able to predict the data values, which would have been collected by the node if it were functioning. Additionally, if a node is misbehaving, we want to be able to artificially generate accurate data as if the node were functioning correctly.

Currently, complex artificial intelligence algorithms are capable of implementing machine learning techniques, which can predict future behaviour based on past observations. However, it is not feasible to implement these algorithms on each individual sensor due to their limited resources. Instead, we are designing and implementing an algorithm that will be primarily housed at the control centre (a more powerful laptop computer) and will only need to send update messages to individual nodes. Our algorithm is based on the physical characteristics of the environment and the physical properties of the data, the relationship between the nodes and the past behaviours of the nodes. Due to the innate physical characteristics of the data being collected, such as seismic data waves, we can utilize these physical properties and the determined distance between the failed or misbehaving node and its neighbours to estimate the missing or erroneous data. However, some physical phenomena such as lightning cannot be estimated based on physical relationships between node. Thus, historical data and the relationship between the historical data of neighbouring nodes must be used to approximate the missing data.

10.3.4   Topology and Routing Management

The in situ sensor-web is a *self-organizing* and *self-healing* network capable of responding to environmental changes (such as eruption progression) and dynamically restructuring the communication topology, so that all nodes are able to find alternative energy-efficient paths of reaching the gateway in the presence of node failures. To maximize both the flexibility and efficiency of the network, we combine hierarchical logical control with flat routing topology. The hierarchical control architecture allows us to enable scalable management, while routing can take advantage of all of the physical network connections in order to maximize efficiency.

The routing module provides the logical backbone upon which sensor samples are disseminated to the U.S. geological survey (USGS) data management systems, also known as sensor to sink routing, while command and control elements address and communicate with individual sensors, referred to as sink to sensor routing.

A coordinator in each logical control cluster is responsible for network management and situation awareness. Unlike other hierarchical control architectures, the coordinator does not control routing in clusters. The coordinator role rotates among all of the nodes in the cluster, so that the energy consumption of each node is balanced.

The routing algorithm was developed based on all network connections, without being restricted by a logical control cluster, making concurrent communication within a cluster possible. Under normal circumstances, the data flow follows a many-to-one routing paradigm and forms a data diffusion tree [4], with the gateway as the sink. In a data diffusion tree, each node periodically monitors its parent's status. If its parent dies, it broadcasts a *join request* and waits for other upper level node to accept it as a child. This idea also applies to integration of newly joining sensors, eliminating the need to reconfigure the network as it grows. The routing protocol of command and control flows (e.g., network management and situation awareness) was developed based on geocasting protocols [29, 30], which enable interaction according to geographical positions and boundaries.

One key aspect of the routing module is its ability to adapt autonomously to both changing conditions within the sensor network, such as topology updates and link-quality changes, and application concerns, for example, increased network activity due to event detection. Another key component of the routing module is its ability to balance application network demands with overall network service level. Additionally, the routing module also provides a consistent interface to the OASIS application modules in order to minimize the need for cross-layer network programming.

The routing module is responsible for autonomous network formation and network topology maintenance over the life of the sensor network, referred to as self-organizing. Upon deployment, a sensor node detects that its routing table is empty and begins interaction with the MAC module to determine its neighbours and potential paths towards the sinks. Probes are then sent towards the sinks in order to verify that such a path is available. The sinks acknowledge the probes, thereby completing the network initialization for that sensor node and populating the sink's routing table with the information required for sink to sensor routing. Network formation is complete once all of the sensor nodes within the network have determined at least one path to a sink, which indicates that all sensor nodes can be addressed by the sinks.

The routing module autonomously constructs a stable routing topology, both from any initial state and when additional nodes are deployed. Nodes may join the network at any time, and upon joining they are incorporated into the routing topology. Node removal is also handled autonomously. The only a priori logical or geographical information required during network formation is the identification of sink nodes. In order to avoid contention and make efficient use of the available bandwidth, the routing topology makes use of multiple paths whenever available.

Once the routing topology has been established, the routing module provides three different types of routing to the application layer: sink to sensor, sensor to sink and reliable broadcast. The type of routing to be used is requested by the application layer when a packet is sent. All routing types employ multi-hop routing techniques as needed to achieve successful packet delivery. Nodes between the source and destination, referred to as intermediate nodes, are responsible for the appropriate prioritization of traffic based on both the traffic type and the bandwidth considerations.

Sink to sensor routing is an explicit one-to-one routing, using the MAC address of the sensor as the destination address. Sensor to sink routing is a logical routing algorithm wherein the sending application only designates the destination as its sink. The determination of which of the potentially multiple sinks will be used is done by the routing module. Sensor to sink paths are weighted initially by the neighbours' signal strength and number of hops to the sink. These weights are continually adjusted based on interactions with the MAC module in order to ensure that new and missing neighbours are detected and an optimized route is available. When the first hop of the primary sink-path is determined to have insufficient bandwidth, the routing module employs multiple paths to deliver sensor traffic to the sinks. Because sink routing is logical, this mechanism is transparent to the application layer.

Reliable broadcast requires guaranteed delivery by the routing module; whether guaranteed delivery is supported for the other routings is to be determined based on design considerations within the MAC module and the application layer. Reliable broadcast provides a multicast mechanism that addresses all sensor nodes. Packet delivery is guaranteed to ensure coherent command and control.

In addition to being self-organizing, the routing module is also responsible for assuring that the network is self-healing. Thus, the network must continue to function for as long as a network path is available. The routing module must appropriately select new routing neighbours to overcome temporary environmental conditions, which affect link quality. Additionally, the routing module must react according to the permanent loss of a network node.

The routing module plays an active role in the environmentally aware nature of the OASIS project's in situ network by cooperating with the sensing and data-delivery applications to deliver the highest service level possible given the current network conditions. Application data prioritization rules are encapsulated in order to make autonomous decisions about discarding data to preserve the overall health of the network and provide fair queuing to all sensor nodes. The routing module exposes an interface to the command and control elements to allow for explicit prioritization rules to be established, for example, providing preferential treatment for a specific node or subset of nodes. The routing module's policy interface enables command and control overrides of autonomous bandwidth management decisions. Bandwidth management requires that the routing module be cognizant of the nodes states, the network state and of the nature of the traffic being routed. Intermediate nodes have to make traffic prioritization decisions based on local congestion and memory considerations. The semantics of application interaction, for example, whether to queue locally or throttle the sender, are determined. In order to provide the desired QoS, the routing module can request reduction in transmission power from the MAC module as appropriate when full radio power is unnecessary. The routing module facilitates interactions between the MAC module and the application layer in order to conserve the limited power resources whenever possible. One mechanism for accomplishing this is through packet queuing, which allows for a reduced radio duty cycle. This also facilitates bandwidth management and congestion management provided by the MAC module. Packet queueing is employed both at the source and at intermediate nodes.

10.3.4.1   Sensor to Sink Routing

In order to enhance our system's performance, we have optimized the routing protocol MultihopLQI, which is employed for sensor to sink routing in our system. MultihopLQI is distance vector routing protocol. It is contained in the TinyOS-1.x distribution using a link quality indicator (LQI) as its routing metric. The LQI measurement is a characterization of the strength and quality of a received packet. The LQI value is generated using a combination of the received signal strength indicator (RSSI) and the correlation values for the first eight symbols of each frame used with the CC2420 radio. Once the LQI value has been generated, an additional formula is used to correlate this into the one-hop cost for each link. The total path cost for each node is the sum of the path cost for its parent and the one-hop cost to its parent. MultihopLQI uses Bellman Ford's algorithm to discover the ideal path to the sink, which is the one with the lowest total cost.

Fig. 10.3 Count-to-infinity problem

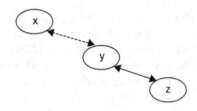

Count-to-Infinity Problem

MultihopLQI as implemented in TinyOS1.x has the inherent count-to-infinity problem typical of distance vector routing protocols. The count-to-infinity problem occurs when a link is broken between two nodes, say x and y, shown below in Fig. 10.3.

If node y, which is linked to node z, looks in its routing table, it sees that node z has a path to node x which is two hops. However, node y has no way to know that this path is through itself, and thus, when its link to node x was broken, so was node z's link to node x. Not knowing this, node y updates its routing table to reflect its new hopcount of three (two hops to from node z to node x and one hop from node y to node z). When node z sees this update, it will update (increase) its hop count to node x, since its path is through node y. This will continue resulting in the count-to-infinity problem.

Destination-sequenced distance-vector (DSDV) routing is a protocol that can be used to avoid this path looping problem. However, DSDV has the problem of slower convergence because a delay of advertising routes is introduced to dampen topology fluctuation. In order to address this, we have developed a method that uses time to live (TTL) in conjunction with both the sequence number and source address to detect loops which are occurring. When a packet is initially sent out from the first hop, the TTL field (5 bits) in the routing layer header is initialized to 31. The TTL value is decreased by one each time a packet traverses an intermediate node. When the TTL value becomes zero, the packet is discarded. Each sensor node maintains a history queue, which records the source address, the sequence number and the TTL of all forwarded packets in its history. Before forwarding a packet, the node refers to its history queue. If there already exists an entry that has the same source address and sequence number, but a different TTL, then it is flagged as a loop. The TTL portion is necessary in order to distinguish between an actual loop and the retransmission of a packet. For example, if for some reason a sender fails to receive an acknowledgement (ACK) for a packet, the sender will retransmit the packet. If TTL was not employed, there would be no way to distinguish this scenario (which is not a loop) from an actual loop (such as count-to-infinity). However, with the implementation of TTL, this misjudgment of loops can be avoided. If a loop is detected, MultihopLQI breaks it by invalidating the path to the sink and proactively discovers a new path.

Link Metric Estimation Enhancement

MultihopLQI uses LQI as its link metric. Through our own experimentation, we confirmed the widely reported belief that LQI has high variation in its time scale. More specifically, our experiments showed that instead of using a simple LQI, if the average LQI is taken, it is able to more accurately reflect the packet delivery rate (PDR). Thus, we accomplished this by applying the exponentially weighted moving-average (EWMA) to the neighbour management module in order to smooth out the values of the LQI within each time frame (window). We choose 0.25 for α. Hence, when a beacon arrives, instead of using the LQI value of that packet, the routing layer requests and receives the average LQI cost for the entire path from the neighbour management module. This calculation is shown below in (10.1)

Average LQI path cost

$$\text{LinkEst}(t) = (1 - \alpha) \times \text{LinkEst}(t - 1) + \alpha \times \text{LinkEst}(t) \qquad (10.1)$$

Alternative Path Backup

Sometimes particular sensor nodes within the network become overloaded or congested. Additionally, environmental conditions may cause interference, for example, ash cover for particular nodes. In these instances, not only will the node experience temporary loss, but their children will also be confronted with successive transmission failure because their buffer queues will quickly become full and forwarding packets will not be able to be inserted. This situation is extremely serious because the node may still be able to receive beacons from its parent in spite of transmission failure, and assume that its current link quality is good (when in fact it is not). We have addressed this problem by using the cooperation of the neighbour management module in order to back up all of the available paths. But we acknowledge that many sensor nodes are RAM-strict. Thus, in a network with high density, a node could potentially have more neighbouring nodes than the neighbour table can accommodate. If this is the case, it is necessary to apply a replacement strategy. In our replacement strategy if the table is full, then the table's entry, which contains the lowest link quality value, is replaced with entry containing the higher link quality.

Another important situation in which we must determine a backup path is if link failure occurs due to the parent node being "dead." In our design, if ten successive packets fail to be sent out successfully, the link is judged as dead. The backing up of this path is accomplished by the neighbour management module. When a beacon message is received, the path cost and source address of that message are passed into and stored in a table in the neighbour management module. Thus, when the network layer needs an alternate path, it makes an inquiry to the neighbour management module for a new parent. If there is a new parent available, it is returned.

Fast Network Self-Organizing and Updating

When a node detects that a loop has occurred, it will invalidate its current parent. Next, the node must wait until the new beacons from other nodes arrive in order to discover a new path. The length of time that the node must wait for the discovery of a new path is directly proportional to the length of the beacon period, in most cases, beacon packets are issued periodically. A comparatively longer beacon period can reduce extra communication traffic, but it also makes nodes in the network insensitive to links, which have become broken, and results in latency in the route discovery of new paths. A long beacon period will cause the node to remain in a waiting state in which it will experience high packet loss. However, a short beacon period also has the disadvantage of introducing additional overhead through increased traffic. Thus, a balance must be achieved in choosing the proper beacon period that is neither too fast nor too slow in order to speed up the network's self-organizing process.

In order to accomplish this, we disseminate good route information. This means that if a sensor node changes parents (from TOS_BCAST_ADDRESS to a valid node address), it will send out a beacon immediately to notify its neighbours of the new route information. In this way, it takes only a short time for the network to form. This reduction in self-organization and updating of the network is particularly effective during the initialization phase of the network formation. Just as it is necessary to disseminate good route information to neighbouring nodes, it is also desirable to update, in a timely manner, bad route information to neighbouring nodes. When a node does not receive a route beacon from its parent for more than three successive beacon periods or its transmission for ten successive packets fails, then the routing module begins the process of switching parents. If the process of switching parents fails, then the node's parent is set to TOS_BCAST_ADDRESS (which is the default upon initialization) and it proceeds to immediately send out a beacon with its infinite path cost. Additionally, if a node receives a beacon from its current parent while its grandparent is TOS_BCAST_ADDRESS, then it also sets its parent to be TOS_BCAST_ADDRESS and sends out a beacon message to notify the other nodes.

10.3.4.2 Reliable Broadcasting

Disseminating common information to all or a subset of the nodes in the network is often an integral part of many wireless network operations. Examples of situations that require reliable broadcasts include code updates, query of interested events, network maintenance and resource discovery. The reliability and speed of data dissemination are important aspects of protocol behaviour in wireless networks.

In environmental monitoring applications, absolute reliability in disseminating data, including both code updates and user command and control, throughout either the entire network or subsets of the network is required. Additionally, the delivery of both data and retasking commands must be accomplished within an acceptable period of time, as determined by the specific application. Due to the important role that each individual sensor plays in the overall network operations, it is vital that all of the sensors receive all of the data within a relatively short period of time (in terms of cycles per period). For instance, in a volcanic monitoring application, scientists might want to change the agent software so that all of the seismic sensors sampling rates are updated from 100 to 120 Hz. It is vital that this command reaches all target stations in a short time period; otherwise it will result in a system failure, as the network is not satisfying the user's needs. Network code updates are another important application that demands reliable and fast data dissemination.

Data dissemination in wireless networks is achieved via each node broadcasting the data to its neighbours, thereby taking advantage of the shared wireless media. A straightforward approach for broadcasting is blind flooding, in which each node is required to rebroadcast the packet whenever it receives the packet for the first time. Blind flooding is, therefore, simple and easy to implement. However, it may generate many redundant transmissions, which can cause serious broadcast storm congestions. Furthermore, it cannot guarantee broadcast reliability. Reliability of dissemination can be defined as the percentage of all nodes that successfully receive the information. Data dissemination losses can result in performance problems for flooding, and ultimately in routing and applications. Unreliable flooding can result in slow setup for query-response applications, slow discovery of new routes, creation of inferior data collection trees and incomplete information for target tracking and signal processing. Additionally, unreliable data dissemination is unacceptable for code updates and user command and control operations. Thus, reliable unicasts in wireless networks are often implemented via link-layer automatic repeat-requests (ARQ) (via an RTS-CTS-data-ACK exchange) in order to protect unicast traffic from collisions and corruptions; however, ARQ for broadcasted traffic causes control traffic implosion.

Sink-initiated data dissemination usually carries the user's command and control or code updates. Hence, it is necessary to ensure 100% reliability in a short time period. Otherwise, from a user or external system viewpoint, it results in a system failure. Motivated by this need, we invented the cascades protocol as the first-known reliable and fast data dissemination protocol in sensor networks. The cascades protocol leverages portions of the existing data gathering routing protocols, such as multihopLQI and drain, by utilizing their data gathering tree structure to implement effective routing dissemination.

Cascade implements the parent-monitor-children analogy within its tree structure to ensure 100% reliability: each (parent) node monitors whether or not its children have received the disseminated messages through implicit listening (e.g., snoop child's broadcast) or explicit ACKs. Each parent will rebroadcast periodically until successful receipt of each of its messages is confirmed. Cascades is also a smart opportunistic routing protocol, and thus, data flows do not necessarily follow the routing tree structure and a node does not necessarily wait for disseminated messages from its parent. Instead, in order to speed up the dissemination process, a node may snoop a message from nearby nodes rather than wait to receive its own copy. For example, in Fig. 10.4, node a is the parent of nodes b and f. However, node a's data only reache node b. Then b rebroadcasts the data to its neighbours (also as an implicit ACK to node a). At the same time, node h receives data from

Fig. 10.4 Illustration of opportunistic broadcast flow in a tree with Cascades protocol. The *solid lines* sketch the tree structure, and the *dashed lines* show the other network links

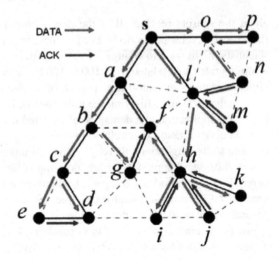

node l (though l is not node h's parent), and rebroadcasts the data to its neighbours, which includes its parent, node f. Thus, the speed of the dissemination process is increased. It should be noted that the cascades protocol does not necessarily need a specific data gathering routing tree to be successfully implemented, rather it can be executed with any connected spanning tree. The reason that cascades does not require a data gathering routing tree is because it only utilizes the parent-children relationship within the tree to ensure reliability, and thus, any tree will suffice. Additionally, cascade's dissemination flow is opportunistic and nondeterministic for different sessions. Cascades is a unified solution for sink-initiated reliable data dissemination, including broadcast, multicast and unicast.

10.3.4.3 Pipelined Sending and Receiving Between Layers for Optimization

TinyOS is an even-driven system that does not support multithreading. As recommended by TinyOS, an upper-layer component should not send another message to a low-layer component until it receives a sendDone event indicating that the previous message has been received. The sendDone event lets the upper-layer know that the lower-layer has successfully received its message. Figure 10.5a illustrates one of the timing issues of this simplex approach, which can cause a large gap between two consecutive sends. We propose the pipelined sending approach to mitigate this gap. It is illustrated in Fig. 10.5b. Similarly, for message receiving, a low-layer component cannot receive another message before the upper-layer component returns the previous message (or swaps it for a free message space).

Our proposed pipelined sending/receive approach is realized through buffering messages in sending/receiving queues at each component. Pipelined sending/receiving helps to improve the performance of the communication stack, since

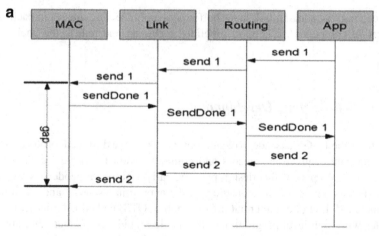

Time sequence of simplex sending

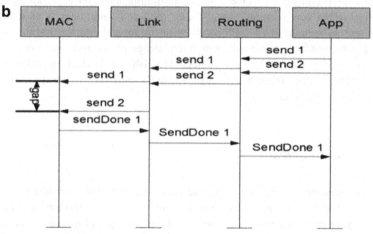

Time sequence for pipelined sending

Fig. 10.5 TinyOS communication stack optimization: (**a**) Time sequence of simplex sending and (**b**) Time sequence for pipelined sending

when using a TDMA protocol, once a node gets allocated a time slot, the node should use the entire time slot efficiently, especially when high throughput is demanded. However, in the simplex approach, when the MAC layer sends a packet, the MAC module will signal up a sendDone message, usually via posting a task. Thus, only after the original sender processes the sendDone event, it will make another send request to MAC component. Because of this, the resource constrained channel's time is wasted. However, in our design, we overcome this problem by adding queues to each communication component. By doing this once the MAC module finishes sending out one packet, it will immediately fetch the next packet in the queue, instead of waiting for the upper-layers to send down a new packet.

For receiving, we added a link layer buffer pool and receiving queues in each communication component to support pipelined receiving and reduce the packet loss ratios.

10.3.5 Sensor Node Development

The staff at the USGS cascades volcano observatory have designed, prototyped and tested the data acquisition, sensors and communication hardware for the in situ sensor nodes. As part of this design process, early input from geodesists and seismologists was incorporated to ensure that the appropriate sensors and capabilities were included. Use of commercial off-the-shelf (COTS) embedded microcontroller modules with high level programmability enabled rapid development and application of an affordable platform. An expansion circuit and printed wiring board were designed and produced to include power conditioning and control, sensor input multiplexing, signal conditioning, signal digitization and communications interfaces. COTS sensors include an L1 GPS receiver for timing and deformation monitoring, seismic accelerometer, microphone or microbarograph for infrasonic detection of explosions and emissions, lightning detector for ash cloud detection. Telemetry between nodes is either IEEE 802.15.4 or 900 MHz ISM spread spectrum given the specific link requirements.

10.3.6 Smart Sensing

Our sensing module is the first step in acquiring data from the environment. When working in harsh environments such as volcanic monitoring, the long-term continuous running of the network and the high frequency sampling scenarios make it particularly challenging for the sensing module which, if not designed properly, can become the weak point of the entire system. A broken sensing module will cause the network to do unnecessary work resulting in useless data transmissions. In order to satisfy the requirements of the seismologists of USGS and NASA JPL (jet propulsion laboratory), the in situ network as a part of our OASIS project was designed with a sensing module that supports real-time high frequency data monitoring for an extended period of time. Below we will discuss our design principles and implementation in the development of our sensing module.

10.3.6.1 Sensing Module Challenges

Due to the nature of our project, many of the challenges that we faced are unique to our project. For example, until recently in traditional wireless sensor networks, the limited resources of the sensor devices have prohibited both high sampling rates and real-time data streaming. However, through recent advances in technology this challenge is now overcome. Thus, we have implemented high sampling rates and real-time data streaming into our sensing module. Now we will delve further into the design principles that we employed when we faced the following five major obstacles: high sampling rates and real-time data streaming, synchronized sampling, event detection, multiple sensors and a harsh environment.

High Sampling Rates and Real-Time Data Streaming

In contrast with low-data-ratio applications, we have the requirement of sampling at 100 Hz (a very high data rate) with 16-bits of data resolution. This brings a high workload to the system. High frequency sampling also faces competition for processor resource from real-time data streaming transmissions. Additionally, sensor sampling and data processing (analyzing, saving and packaging) must be finished within a short period.

Synchronized Sampling

Synchronized sampling is necessary in order for seismologists to make comparisons across the whole network. It is the desire of the seismologists, and thus, one of the requirements of our project to have all of the nodes samples with a particular sensor, say infrasonic, at the same time. In order for the comparisons to be accurate, the difference between timesamples must be less than 1 ms. Although each node is equipped with GPS for time synchronization, we still cannot guarantee that all nodes will perform synchronized sampling due to multiple time delays that occur within the network. We did not adopt a time synchronization protocol into our system because in addition to time synchronization, geologists also wanted to be able to obtain the position information of each node in order to monitor the movement on different portions of the volcano. Since we are already implementing real-time data transmissions, it is necessary for the system to reduce other types of network communications, and adding a time synchronization protocol to our system would greatly increase network communications. Instead, we have implemented low power consuming GPS sensors and a high quality battery supply, which can guarantee long-term system health and extend the lifetime of the network.

Time Synchronization

In this section, we describe the implementation of our time synchronization protocol as one key component of our smart sensing module. Our OASIS time synchronization protocol is a GPS receiver based generic protocol. It can be implemented on any sensor node equipped with a GPS receiver. In general, GPS based synchronization removes the uncertainty problem that arises with radios; however, we cannot claim that the high accuracy synchronization is achieved unless we address the uncertainty

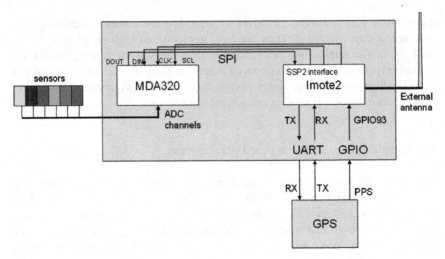

Fig. 10.6 Hardware components connection

resulted from interrupt handling, clock accuracy, mote clock drift, long-term running and environmental changes. In addition, OASIS's time synchronization protocol was not developed solely for time stamping, rather it is also used as the timer driver for the sensing module, as shown below in Fig. 10.6.

In order to fully comprehend this architecture, it is necessary to have a brief overview of the construction of an Imote2 sensor node. The Imote2 sensor node is a newly developed sensor node, which contains a powerful CPU and a relatively large memory space. Each sensor node is capable of running either the TinyOS operating system or a Linux operating system. The processor of Imote2 is an Intel PXA27x processor that provides multiple timer channels and general purpose input/output (GPIO) resources. Both the operating system timer and the GPIO interface are necessary for the implementation of time synchronization. The operating system timer, PXA27x, provides eleven clock channels in which the clock resolution can be adjusted from 1 μs to 1 s. In order to generate a low granularity clock, we use the OS Timer channel 10 as clock source, with the resolution set to 1 μs. Although there are many GPIO interfaces provided through the PXA27x, we can only use three of them for our customized application due to the design of the Imote2 sensor node. In our implementation, we use the GPIO 93, shown in Fig. 10.6, to capture PPS (Pulse Per Second) signal.

Now that we have an understanding of the architecture of the Imote2 sensors, we will discuss the design of our OASIS time synchronization protocol, shown below in Fig. 10.7. Our protocol is a three phase synchronization protocol. In phase 1, the GPS readings and coordinated universal time (UTC) preparation are performed. Phase 2 consists of real-time setting. Finally, phase 3 is responsible for ensuring that the errors associated with the time are self-keeping.

The time synchronization protocol is composed of two components, the real-time timer and the GPS sensor. The realtime timer is a timer that is fired every one

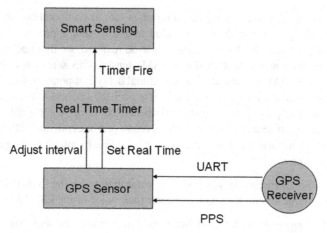

Fig. 10.7 Synchronization process

thousand microseconds. After each fired event, the UTC time, maintained by the re-altimetimer module, will be updated. It should be noted that UTC time is formatted hour:minute:second:millisecond. In addition to updating the UTC time, the timer interval may also be adaptively changed according to the offset value in the time fire event. The GPS sensor acts as the GPS data receiving agent and PPS capturing agent. GPS data are configured to arrive every 10 s and the PPS signals are configured to arrive every 1 s. The PPS signals are nanosecond accurate. GPS data arrive several milliseconds later then PPS. Thus, it is not wise to immediately set the UTC time after getting the GPS data. After the first PPS event is detected, the application moves into a synchronous waiting state. The next incoming GPS data packet will only be processed if the application is in the synchronous waiting state. After the GPS data processing has taken place, when each successive PPS event arrives, the UTC time in the Realtime Timer module will be incremented by 1 s.

Event Detection

Event detection is crucial to the overall system performance since, at times in order to reduce the network traffic, it is necessary for the system to stop real-time data transmissions for a short period of time. However, during this period, the system still needs to detect and transmit all of the big events back to the base station. In order to accomplish this, our event detection algorithm was implemented. Within our algorithm, it is necessary to achieve fast in-node data analysis to accomplish event detection, while helping to reduce the data transmission by only sending out the data from big events and remaining silent when insignificant events take place.

Initially, we decided to use the following method to implement event detection. Every time an RSAM value was sampled, we would compare it to the average of the last 400 samples. If the ratio was over some event threshold, we would consider it to be an event. However, this schema requires lots of computation and disobeys our fast sampling principle, thus we decided to use another approach that employs hardware support. In order for this approach to be realized, we first had to introduce a new sensor, the long-term RSAM (LRSAM) sensor. This sensor is composed of one short term RSAM sensor and some additional delay components. Readings from this sensor give us an average sensing value for each 20 s period. By simply reading this value and comparing it to the short-term RSAM value, we are able to greatly reduce the necessary calculation. LRSAM is read every second, and SRSAM is read every 10 ms. Therefore, we define the occurrence of an event, either large or small, using two lemmas:

- Lemma 1 Small Event: SRSAM is not greater than twice the LRSAM value.
- Lemma 2 Large Event: SRSAM is greater than twice of the LRSAM value.

Note that if a large event is detected, one period of data must be sent. After detecting this event, the application sends out the timestamped sensed data plus the two previous seconds worth of data. This additional 2 s ensure that the data being transmitted capture the entire earthquake.

Multiple Sensors

OASIS requires the simultaneous sampling of multiple sensors. Our sensing module is required to process multiple sensors data without any data fusion, which introduces resource competition for memory allocation, timer allocation and the sequence of processing and transmitting the acquired data. For OASIS, the following sensors and sampling rates are required:

1. Seismic sensor: 100 samples per second (100 Hz sampling rate), 16 bytes per sample (200 Bps)
2. Infrasonic sensor: 100 samples per second (100 Hz sampling rate), 16 bytes per sample (200 Bps)
3. RSAM sensor: 1 sample per second (1 Hz sampling rate), 2 bytes per sample (1 Bps)
4. GPS sensor: 1 sample per 10 second, 200 bytes per sample (20 Bps)
5. Lightning sensor: 10 samples per 1 second, 2 bytes per sample (20 Bps)

Thus, the total size of the raw data being sampled and transmitted is 440 bytes per second, not including network message headers.

In order to accommodate the multiple sensors, we will sample synchronically from all of the required sensors. Additionally, the earth scientists will have easy interactive control of the network, which will be achieved through a centralized command and control centre. This will allow the user to adjust the sampling rate and priority of individual sensors as well as temporarily turn sensors on and off.

Harsh Environmental Conditions

The harsh environment produced from the networking being deployed on an active volcano provides an additional challenge for the sensing module. Due to the harsh conditions, it is not unusual for sensors to be destroyed. Additionally, debris from broken sensors can cause interference. Thus, it is necessary to implement an error detection scheme and a self-healing scheme in order to reduce these adverse effects. If an error is detected, depending on the type of error, either the self-healing scheme needs to be executed or else a report of the errors must be sent to the base station.

Error Detection

In order to accomplish error detection, one timer will be dedicated to periodically checking the sensor data. This timer will continually check the last fifty data samples and get following information: the maximum value, the minimum value, the average value, the maximum deviation and the average standard deviation. The combination of these five values will indicate the type of error that has occurred. There are four main types of errors that we will detect: a sensor board disconnection error, a sensor disconnected from the sensor board error, a broken sensor error and a battery offset error.

In order to detect that a sensor board has been disconnected, the maximum and minimum values are examined. If both of these values are the same, and more specifically 0xffff, then it is determined that the sensor board has become disconnected. If we detect that the sensor board is disconnected, we will turn off the node and send an event report packet to the control centre.

It can be determined that a sensor node has become disconnected from its sensor board if the ADC channel is sampling noisy data, which will be in accordance with the current time, and whether or not the volcano is experiencing activity. However, the noisy data must also follow a pattern. The maximum deviation value and the maximum average deviation value must both exceed the maximum threshold. Additionally, the maximum and minimum sampling values must also exceed the normal range. When it is detected that a sensor is disconnected from its sensor board, the node will be turned off and an event report packet will be sent to the control centre.

If a sensor is broken, the value will either jump to an extreme value, high or low, because of the destroyed resister or the error will be similar to that experienced when a sensor-disconnected error occurs. Additionally, if a sensor is broken, its average value may drop below the minimum threshold value. If a broken sensor is detected, the sensor will not be closed immediately, instead we will change the value of the detected count and then, if this count goes over the predefined threshold, the sensor will be closed and a report will be sent to control centre. However, even if a broken sensor error is detected in a node, it is still possible that it is a false positive detection. Thus, centralized detection calculations will also be added after analyzing the data. Note that if the scientists decide to continue running that sensor and later errors are detected, the sensor cannot be turned off again.

Battery offset detection cannot be detected in-node because the drop will also affect the reference voltage in the node. This error can only be detected in the control centre by comparing the sensed data with other neighbouring nodes' sensed data.

10.4 Space Component

One of the primary goals of OASIS is to implement a two-way communication channel between the ground and space components. The motivation for this two-way communication channel is optimal allocation of the limited power and bandwidth ground resources, while also providing smart management for the competing demands. Just as we would like to have unlimited power and bandwidth resources available for the ground sensors, it would be ideal to have space assets available to meet every demand and desire of the Earth scientists, such as providing a continuous streaming of data products from space assets. However, given the multiple demands on satellites, this is not feasible. Thus, it is crucial that resources are used strategically. Some of the questions asked by Earth scientists requiring satellite data are:

- What is happening?
- Where is it happening?
- What is the magnitude of the event?
- What is the change, or rate of change?

The space component consists of JPL sensorweb ground software and the EO-1 satellite, shown below in Fig. 10.8.

The EO-1 satellite is the first mission of NASA's new millennium program earth observing series, managed from Goddard Space Flight Center. Designed as a testbed for the next-generation of advanced land imaging instruments, EO-1 was launched on a Delta 7320 from Vandenberg Air Force Base on 21 November 2000 into a 705 km circular sunsynchronous orbit at a 98.7° inclination.

EO-carries three instruments: the advanced land imager (ALI), the hyper-spectral Hyperion Imager and the atmospheric corrector (AC). The ALI combines novel wide-angle optics with a highly integrated multispectral and panchromatic spectrometer to demonstrate spatial and spectral resolution comparable or improved from Landsat at substantial mass, volume, and cost savings. The Hyperion is a high-resolution imager capable of resolving 220 spectral bands (from 0.4 to 2.5 μm) with a 30-m spatial resolution. The instrument typically images a 7.5 km by 42 km land area per image, and provides detailed spectral mapping across all 220 channels with high radiometric accuracy (ASE uses the products from the Hyperion instrument for onboard science processing). Finally the EO-1 AC provides the first space-based test of an AC that is – designed to compensate for atmospheric absorption and scattering, allowing for increased accuracy of surface reflectance estimates.

The requirements of the space component are twofold. First, it is responsible for responding to inquiries regarding general capabilities. These are inquiries regarding generic sensor capabilities such as providing information on the data pedigree, the

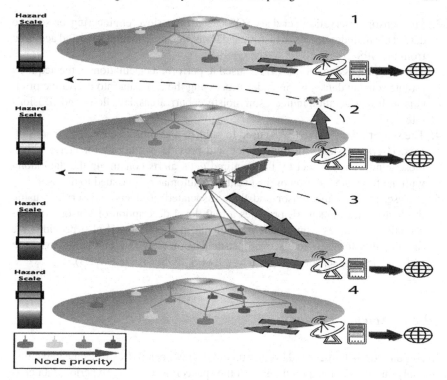

Fig. 10.8 Optimized autonomous apace in situ sensorweb

number of frequency bands, the spectral resolution of the image, the spatial resolution of the image, the wavelength range of the data and the signal-to-noise ratio of the data. Second, it is also responsible for tasking all requests made by Earth scientists for data acquisition, processing the data and generating any alerts derived from the data. Specifically, the space component receives alerts from the in situ sensors. Upon receipt of an alert, the space component attempts to issue a request to EO-1 to acquire data of the region of interest. Observation contention is resolved by first determining if the priority of the new request is greater than the existing observation requests in the schedule. If the priority is greater, the new request is uploaded to EO-1 for execution. Once the data has been acquired onboard EO-1, analysis searching for features of interest, e.g., thermal activity, is executed. The results of the analysis are later downlinked in an engineering telemetry stream, while onboard they may have generated a follow-up observation activity.

In order to support these requirements, we have adopted the open geospatial consortium sensor web enablement initiative to develop generalized service orient interfaces. These include the following:

1. The sensor planning service (SPS) used to determine if the sensor is available to acquire requested data. For example, using the SPS, an observation request to EO-1 can be issued to acquire science data, determine the status of an existing request and cancel a previous request.

2. The sensor observation service (SOS) used to retrieve engineering or science data. This includes access to historical data as well as data requested and acquired from the SPS.
3. The web processing service (WPS) used to perform a calculation on the acquired remote sensing data. This includes processing the raw data into derivative products such as vegetation indices, soil moisture, burn areas, lava flows and effusions rates, etc.
4. The sensor alert service (SAS) used to publish and subscribe to alerts from sensors. Users register with this service and provide conditions for alerts. When these conditions are met by the acquired data, alerts containing the data along with the time and location of the events are automatically issued to the user.
5. A description of the sensor and their associated products and services using the SensorML. SensorML provides a high level description of sensors and observation processes using an XML schema methodology. It also provides the functionality for users to discover instruments on the web along with services to task and acquire sensor data (such as the SPS, SOS, SAS and WPS).

10.4.1 Science Products

In conjunction with the standard instrument data collected, EO-1 has the capability of analyzing the data acquired onboard the spacecraft. Custom Hyperion data classification algorithms were uploaded to EO-1 in late 2003, which include thermal, snow/water/ice/land, flood, cloud and sulfur detection (cite each classifier author). In the context of OASIS, the thermal detection algorithm analyzes all acquisitions of Mount St. Helens. This algorithm is able to generate an onboard thermal summary products containing the radiance values of each hot pixel at 12 specific wavelengths. A hot spot is classified as an area of intense heat that is emitted from the volcano. Additionally, the hot and extreme pixels are another important product. Integrated hot spot energy, which is the summation of all of the hot pixels within the cluster, provides a useful summary data to the Earth scientists for evaluation.

Full data products nominally are downlinked 6–15 h after data acquisition, depending on when the ground contact was scheduled. However, a thermal summary product can be available with a couple of hours of the acquisition. This thermal summary product identifies both the line and the sample of thermally-active pixels; however, due to downlink constraints; its size is limited to 20 KB.

These summary products are used to generate alerts that are broadcast to interested entities, completing two-way communications with sensor peers. For OASIS, the alerts from the results of the thermal detection algorithm will automatically be ingested by the in situ command-and-control centre and autonomously trigger ground-based data collections.

10.5   Conclusion and Discussion

We have designed and are currently implementing and testing OASIS. Once our field tests are complete, we will deploy the sensor network on Mount St. Helens where it will run continuously for 1 year. Our deployment will be the first to integrate space and ground components into a continuous feedback loop, which will be constantly updating and optimizing the network's performance in order to obtain the maximum possible performance.

Acknowledgment This work is partially supported by NASA AIST Grant #106269, NSF-ITR grant IIS-0326505 and NSF-ITR grant IIS-0324835.

References

1. Pottie G, Kaiser W (2000) Wireless sensor networks. Commun ACM 43(5):51–58
2. Asada G, et al. (1998) Wireless integrated network sensors: low power systems on a chip, ESSCIRC
3. Eynde FO, et al. (2001) A fully-integrated single-chip SOC for Bluetooth, ISSCC 2001, vol. 446, pp. 196–197
4. Cerpa A, Elson J, Estrin D, Girod L, Hamilton M, and Zhao J (2001) Habitat monitoring: application driver for wireless communications technology. ACM SIGCOMM Workshop on Data Communications in Latin America and the Caribbean
5. Mainwaring A, Polastre J, Szewczyk R, and Culler D (2002) Wireless sensor networks for habitat monitoring. ACM Workshop on Sensor Networks and Applications
6. Estrin D, Culler D, Pister K, and Sukhatme G (2002) Connecting the physical world with pervasive networks. IEEE Pervasive Comput 1(1):59–69
7. Fang Q, Zhao F, and Guibas L (2003) Lightweight sensing and communication protocols for target enumeration and aggregation. ACM MobiHoc, pp. 165–176
8. Werner-Allen G, Johnson J, Ruiz M, Lees J, and Welsh M (2005) Monitoring volcanic eruptions with a wireless sensor network. In Proc. Second European Workshop on Wireless Sensor Networks (EWSN'05)
9. Delin KA, Jackson SP, Johnson DW, Burleigh SC, Woodrow RR, McAuley JM, Dohm JM, Ip F, Ferre TPA, Rucker DF, and Baker VR (2005) Environmental studies with the sensor web: principals and practice. J Sens 5:103–117
10. Kok T, Seah WKG, and Wong WC (2006) An Energy Efficient Topology Management Scheme for Underwater Acoustic Sensor Network Using Connected Dominating Sets. OCEANS 2006 – Asia Pacific, pp. 1–7
11. Yarvis M, Ye W (2004) Tiered architectures in sensor networks. In Mohammed Ilyas (ed.), Handbook of Sensor Networks: Compact Wireless and Wired Sensing Systems. CRC Press, Boca Raton, FL, USA
12. Kottapalli V, Kiremidjian A, Lynch JP, Carryer E, Kenny T, Law K, and Lei Y (2003) A two-tier wireless sensor network architecture for structural health monitoring. In Proceedings of SPIE's 10th Annual Symposium on Smart Structures and Materials, San Diego, CA
13. Govindan R, Kohler E, Estrin D, Bian F, Chintalapudi K, Gnawali O, Rangwala S, Gummadi R, and Stathopoulos T (2005) Tenet: An Architecture for Tiered Embedded Networks. CENS Technical Report 56
14. Bluetooth SIG, Inc. http://www.bluetooth.org Accessed 28 May 2008
15. Rodoplu V, Meng TH (1999) Minimum energy mobile wireless networks. IEEE JSAC 17(8):1333–1344

16. Intanagonwiwat C, Govindan R, and Estrin D (2000) Directed diffusion: a scalable and robust communication paradigm for sensor networks. In Proceedings of the International Conference on Mobile Computing and Networking

17. Hwang I-S, Hwang B-J, Ku L-F, and Chang P-M (2008) Adaptive bandwidth management and reservation scheme in heterogeneous wireless networks. IEEE International Conference on Sensor Networks, Ubiquitous and Trustworthy Computing, SUTC '08, pp. 338–342

18. Zhu M, Reid A, Finney S, and Judd, M (2008) Energy scavenging technique for powering wireless sensors. International Conference on Condition Monitoring and Diagnosis, pp. 881–884

19. Woo A, Culler D (2001) A transmission control scheme for media access in sensor networks. In Proceedings of Seventh Annual International Conference on Mobile Computing and Networking (MobiCom). ACM, Rome, Italy, pp. 221–235

20. Ye W, Heidemann J, and Estrin D (2002) An energy-efficient mac protocol for wireless sensor networks. In IEEE INFOCOM

21. Heinzelman W, Chandrakasan A, and Balakrishnan H (2000) Energy-efficient routing protocols for wireless microsensor networks. In Proceedings of Hawaii International Conference on System Sciences

22. Sankarasubramaniam Y, Akan OB, and Akyildiz IF (2003) Esrt:event-to-sink reliable transport in wireless sensor networks. In The 4th ACM International Symposium on Mobile Ad Hoc Networking and Computing(MobiHoc)

23. Clement B, Barrett A (2003) Continual coordination through shared activities. 2nd International Conference on Autonomous and Multi-Agent Systems (AAMAS 2003), Melbourne, Australia

24. Chien S, Cichy B, Davies A, Tran D, Rabideau G, Castano R, Sherwood R, Mandel D, Frye S, Shulman S, Jones J, and Grosvenor S (2005) An Autonomous Earth-Observing Sensorweb. Intelligent Systems, IEEE, May–June, 20(3):16–24

25. Song W-Z (2005) Real-time data gathering in wireless sensor networks. Technical Report 2005-S001. Washington State University, Vancouver

26. Alex H, Kumar M, and Shirazi B (2005) Collaborating agent communities for information fusion and decision making. International Conference on Knowledge Integration and Multi Agent Systems (KIMAS 05)

27. Murray TL, Ewert JW, Lockhart AB, and LaHusen RG (1996) The integrated mobile volcano-monitoring system used by the Volcano Disaster Assistance Program (VDAP). Monitoring and Mitigation of Volcano Hazards

28. Tai S, Benkoczi RR, Hassanein H, and Akl SG (2007) QoS and data relaying for wireless sensor networks. J Parallel Distribution Computing, pp. 715–726

29. Karp B, Kung HT (2000) GPSR: Greedy perimeter stateless routing for wireless networks. ACM Mobicom

30. Seada K, Helmy A (2005) Efficient and robust geocasting protocols for sensor networks. Elsevier Computer Commun J, Special Issue on Dependable Wireless Sensor Networks

Chapter 11
SiC: An Agent Based Architecture for Preventing and Detecting Attacks to Ubiquitous Databases

Cristian Pinzón, Yanira De Paz, Javier Bajo, Ajith Abraham, and Juan M. Corchado

Abstract One of the main attacks to ubiquitous databases is the structure query language (SQL) injection attack, which causes severe damages both in the commercial aspect and in the user's confidence. This chapter proposes the SiC architecture as a solution to the SQL injection attack problem. This is a hierarchical distributed multiagent architecture, which involves an entirely new approach with respect to existing architectures for the prevention and detection of SQL injections. SiC incorporates a kind of intelligent agent, which integrates a case-based reasoning system. This agent, which is the core of the architecture, allows the application of detection techniques based on anomalies as well as those based on patterns, providing a great degree of autonomy, flexibility, robustness and dynamic scalability. The characteristics of the multiagent system allow an architecture to detect attacks from different types of devices, regardless of the physical location. The architecture has been tested on a medical database, guaranteeing safe access from various devices such as PDAs and notebook computers.

Keywords SQL injection · Security database · Intrusion detection system · Multiagent · Case based reasoning

11.1 Introduction

New technologies have provided ubiquitous working environments without time and location constraint. Nowadays, users handle several mobile devices such as a notebook computers, PDAs or intelligent phones. These devices manage information in immediate way, independently of the physical location and time instant. These new

A. Abraham (✉)
Norwegian Center of Excellence, Center of Excellence for Quantifiable Quality of Service, Norwegian University of Science and Technology, O.S. Bragstads Plass 2E, N-7491 Trondheim, Norway
e-mail: ajith.abraham@ieee.org

A.-E. Hassanien et al. (eds.), *Pervasive Computing: Innovations in Intelligent Multimedia and Applications*, Computer Communications and Networks, DOI 10.1007/978-1-84882-599-4_11, © Springer-Verlag London Limited 2009

computing environments are supported by the growth of the network computing, especially wireless networks [26]. Furthermore, it is necessary taking into account a distributed database in a strategic mode. Databases provide information to user applications on the different devices.

Information systems are based on a back-end database system. The database is a critical piece both in daily operations and decision making [10]. Information systems have great impact in each aspect of the daily life (e.g. bank accounts registers, medical registers, retirements, payrolls, phone registers, tax registers, vehicle registers, supermarket purchases and school registers). Any meaningful data of the daily life is stored on a database system [32]. Due to this situation, very often the databases are a target of great number of attacks. The current solutions have been unable to provide enough confidentiality and integrity of the stored data. Firewalls, intrusion detection system (IDS), antivirus software and other security measures are limited and cannot protect from new threats and zero day attacks.

The effort carried out to detect and stop the attacks targeted to the information systems seems to be not very sound. However, the cyber attack problem acquires more importance if recent technologies are taken into account. Nowadays, the users use mobile devices with wireless access. These devices have a great capability to access data in a ubiquitous way. As a consequence of these new computing environments, the information should be distributed to fulfil the requests of different users independently of the location, platform or physical devices. The distribution of information supports ubiquitous databases, where the data are partitioned according to the autonomy degree and efficiency required. The distribution of information and new technologies makes it possible for an increase of complex attacks directed to databases. One of the weak points of new working environments is that the data transfer is done through insecure communication channels, such as local networks and Internet. This weakness is exploited by a malicious user who scans the traffic for eavesdropping and can steal, change or delete sensitive information.

The structure query language (SQL) injection represents a potential attack for the database systems. The SQL injection attack is at the top of the list of latest threats in recent years. The damages caused by a SQL injection attack involve financial losses and loss of reliance of the consumers, providers and trading partners. In addition, such attacks disrupt the development of outside and inside activities of the organization [13]. The architecture presented in this chapter, named SiC (Agent based architecture for preventing and detecting attacks to ubiquitous database), is targeted at solving the problem of the SQL injection attacks on databases. This proposal is oriented for ubiquitous environments, but is not limited only for this scenario. SiC proposes a novel strategy to block SQL injection attack through a distributed approach based on the capacities of the agents and multiagent systems [49]. The philosophy of multiagent systems allows dealing with the SQL injection attacks from a perspective of the communication elements, ubiquity and autonomous computation and from a viewpoint of a global coordinated system. Every component in SiC interacts to achieve a global common goal. SiC presents a hierarchical organization structured by levels or layers of agents. The agents of each level have specific tasks assigned, which can be executed independently to their physical location. The complexity of the agents is incremented with the advance by the hierarchy pyramid. This hierarchical structure allows a distribution of roles and tasks for the detection and prevention of SQL injection attacks. Additionally, it has a great capacity for errors recovery.

The use of agents with advanced capabilities to reason and predict situations is the main feature of this architecture. SiC makes use of case-based reasoning-believe, desire, intention (CBR-BDI) agents [15], which are characterized by the integration of a CBR mechanism [1]. This mechanism provides the agents a greater level of adaptation and learning capacity. CBR systems make use of past experiences to solve new problems [22]. Thus, it is possible to generate new solutions from the results obtained in problems with similar characteristics taken place in the past. CBR systems are characterized by executing a reasoning cycle to solve each new problem. This reasoning cycle is able to make a feedback from each new experience and modify the case memory and the reasoning capacity according to new changes. The latter is very suitable to block SQL injection attacks by anomaly detection [29, 35]. A CBR system learns and predicts behaviours or events that disclose a particular signature of a SQL injection attack. CBR-BDI agents have a predictive capacity by means of a mixture of neural network within the adaptation stage of the CBR cycle.

Agents can be characterized through their capacities in areas such as autonomy, reasoning, reactivity, social abilities, proactivity and mobility, among others. These capacities provide great advantage for offering solutions at highly dynamic and distributed environment. Many activities in areas as networks security, e-commerce, telecommunications, among others are carried out by multiagent systems implemented successfully [2, 7, 19]. The capacity of the agents to be executed by mobile devices makes them particularly suitable to detect SQL injection attacks on ubiquitous databases. The agents integrated in SiC are based on the BDI deliberative model [21, 48]. The internal structure of these agents and the capacities are based on mental aptitude using beliefs, desires and intentions [12].

In summary, a distributed hierarchical multiagent architecture is presented as a solution to SQL injection attacks. The main feature of SiC is the use of CBR-BDI agents with detection and prediction capabilities to classify and block this type of threats. CBR systems are especially suitable to solve classification problems, similar to the SQL injection attacks. CBR-BDI agents incorporate a mixture of neural networks in the adaptation phase of the CBR cycle to predict new attacks. Finally, the architecture handles misuse detection, which accomplishes all the strategies of detection and prevention proposed.

The preliminary results obtained after the implementation of the initial prototype show the effectiveness of the strategy to minimize attacks; the highest performance through the distribution of the workload among the available nodes into the architecture; the scalability, offering an easy way to incorporate new nodes in monitored environments; a great learning and adaptation capacity, which is provided by the CBR mechanism and the mixture of neural networks and the flexibility to be adapted to many sensitive scenarios of SQL injection attacks. The ultimate goal of this work is the presentation of an effective and novel solution, designed for working in new environments, mainly in those where the mobility of the information is essential.

The remainder of this chapter is structured as follows: Sect. 11.2 presents the problem that has prompted most of this research work; Sect. 11.3 describes the SiC architecture, different agents incorporated to the architecture and the communication among them; Sect. 11.4 explains in detail the most important agent of the SiC architecture, the CBR-BDI classifier agent. Section 11.5 describes a study case using a medical database and presents the results and discussion. Finally, in Sect. 11.6, conclusions are presented.

11.2 Database Threat and Security Revision

Data is usually stored in a ubiquitous database in order for the applications to have access to them from any location and any time. A ubiquitous system is necessarily distributed [52], claiming that data have to be present everywhere for the authorized user. This feature is achieved when the databases are partitioned, so that data are distributed in several local databases strategically located on different geographic nodes.

A ubiquitous database allows any user to access its data through custom applications. The source of these data does not need to be known by the user. The development of a ubiquitous model has two determining factors, the rising tide of Internet and the World Wide Web. These factors had been made into a means for the global spreading and the data interchange. In this sense, databases have played a crucial role for the storage of a huge volume of data. On the other hand, the access via wireless has enabled a great interconnection among devices and unrestricted data accesses.

As a result of the decentralization of the information, new issues about the privacy and the information security have been addressed. In recent years, large companies have opted by transferring the management control through service outsourcing of a specialized supplier for specific tasks. One of the most notable outsourcing services is database outsourcing where organizations outsource the data storage and management to third-party service supplier [51]. This management model has generated discussions about the issue of sharing sensitive data that might endanger private information of clients and the organization itself. In the same vein, the knowledge extraction through rules of data mining has caused hard criticism. The tools used to discover unknown patterns can extract unauthorized information that put in risk the privacy of individuals and the confidentiality of their data [45]. The ongoing threats targeted against the information system and databases are the viruses and worms. The worms are considered a particularly dangerous threat because of its evolution towards complex techniques to avoid the security mechanisms. They can carry an explosive charge to be executed according to fixed conditions by the hacker. New sophisticated variants of worms are expected to become more prevalent in short term such as SQL injecting attacks through the application layer [6]. Because of the increase of incidents, the information security is considered a critical issue within the strategic policies of organizations. In the commercial sector and the research centres, more resources and human capital are devoted to research new security solutions that can face new attacks and to protect corporate databases.

Security measures to protect information systems and databases of outsider attacks include firewalls, filters, authentication, communication transport encryption, intrusion detection, auditing, monitoring, honeypots, security tokens, biometric devices, sniffers, active blocking, file level security analysis or Demilitarized Zone [36]. In the particular case of the database security, it is necessary to have a closer look from a outlook of mechanisms such as access control policies, authentication and identification mechanisms. In a multilevel secure database management system (MLS/DBMS), authorized users at different security levels access share a database at different security levels without violating security. The security policy of MSL/DBMS includes a policy for mandatory access control (MAC) and discretionary access control (DAC). Mandatory security controls restrict access to data depending on the sensitivity levels of the data and the authorization level of the user. Discretionary Security measures are usually in the form of rules, which specify the type of access that users or groups of users may have to different kinds of data [10]. Additionally, other approaches have arisen, such as the Hippocratic Databases inspired in the Hippocratic Oath [3] and the use of cryptography techniques to protect the confidentiality of data [33].

The current databases security measures seem insufficient and less if it is examined from the perspective of the threats targeted to the new working environments. Nowadays, the attacks are addressed to the application layer and the database systems in such a way that the protection mechanisms cannot detect them. A decade or more ago, databases were usually kept physically secure in a central data centre and accessed mostly by applications into the corporate borders. However, now applications and databases may be distributed in business units to meet local needs. Even more critical is the fact that these applications and databases are increasingly available to suppliers, customers and business partners in order to carry out business over the Web [5]. Organizations are hit hard when a malicious user bypass or violates protective measures to steal, modify or destroy sensitive information.

SQL injection attacks are a potential threat at the application layer. The SQL forms the backbone of many Database Management Systems, especially relational databases. It allows carrying out information handling and databases management, but also facilitates building a type of attack that is extremely lethal. The SQL injection is not a new attack, but has not been removed of the threat list for databases.

A SQL injection attack brings harm to the organizations such as financial losses, affects customer confidence, suppliers and business partners and disrupts the outside and inside activities of the organization. A SQL injection attack takes place when a hacker changes the semantic or syntactic logic of a SQL text string by inserting SQL keywords or special symbols within the original SQL command that will be executed at the database layer of an application [4, 24, 31]. The response capacity after carrying out a SQL injection attack depends on the type of technique used and the caused damage grade. This response can take hours, days and even weeks. Web applications are the main target of this type of attack. In the case of these applications, the static chain is concatenated with user inputs. If the user inputs are tainted, an injection attack is carried out when the query is executed on database. However, even though the most common attack method is through request via HyperText Transport Protocol (HTTP), other methods are vulnerable to a SQL injection attack. Applications on wireless mobile devices execute SQL queries on the database. These queries are transmitted through insecure transmission channel allowing that it can be monitored, captured and changed by a hacker. Finally, a recent vulnerability has arisen in the pervasive computing applications by the use devices or sensors vulnerable [40–42]. This new technology has presented security hole, and therefore, it can be exploited by a SQL injection attack causing great damage.

The cause of the SQL injection attacks is relatively simple. This attack is caused by inadequate input validation on user interface. As a result of this attack, a hacker can carry out an unauthorized data handling, retrieval of confidential information, and in the worst possible case, take over control of the application server. The main features to give a detailed description of a SQL injection attack are the attack mechanism used and the attack intention [25].

The most common Database Management Systems such as Microsoft SQL Server, Oracle, MySQL, Informix, Sybase have been targets of SQL injection attacks during recent years [32]. The problem of the SQL injection attack increases with the use of technologies designed to offer new working environments, especially in sectors such as e-commerce, healthcare system, industry, e-government, among other. The benefits offered by the new devices such as the full interconnection and corporate database access from any location can give space to SQL injection attacks. The new working environments require information at any location and time for all the authorized users. This fact forces decentralization of data and a strategic location of databases into the working environments. In the case of the SQL injection attacks, this setting is special to exploit new vulnerabilities.

SQL injection attacks have led up to a significant number of research works, both in the sector commercial as at academic research centres. Unfortunately the advances in the detection and prevention measures have not achieved the required level to overcome this type of attack. The current security products found at the market are vital for the defense of information security; nevertheless, the results against the SQL injection attacks are poor enough. The low efficacy is due to the fact that security measures are not intended for a specific type of attack, but on the contrary, are diversified to many threats. These security products are not intended for SQL injection attacks exclusively.

Regarding the proposed academic approaches as a solution to the SQL injection attacks, a wide revision is carried out. Some artificial intelligence techniques have been proposed as solution to the SQL injection attack. Among the approaches revised is Web Application Vulnerability and Error Scaner (WAVES) [27]. This solution is based on a black-box technique. WAVES is a web crawler that identifies vulnerable points, and then builds attacks that target those points based on a list of patterns and attack techniques. WAVES monitors the response from the application and uses a machine learning technique to improve the attack methodology. WAVES cannot check all the vulnerable points like the traditional penetration testing. The strategy used by the IDSs have been implemented in the SQL injection attacks. Valeur [46] presents an IDS approach that uses a machine learning technique based on a dataset of legal transactions. These are used during the training phase prior to monitoring and classifying malicious accesses. Generally, IDS systems depend on the quality of the training set; a poor training set would result in a large number of false positives and negatives. Rietta [43] proposed an IDS system at the application layer using an anomaly detection model, which assumes certain behaviour of the traffic generated by the SQL queries, i.e., elements within the query (sub-queries, literals and keyword SQL). It also applies general statistics and proposes grouping the queries according to SQL commands and then comparing them against a previously built model. The SQL query that deviates from the normal profile is rejected. The proposals based on intrusion detection depend on the database, which requires a continue updating in order to detect new attacks. Finally, Skaruz [44] proposed the use of a recurrent neural network (RNN). The detection problem becomes a time series prediction problem. This approach leads to a large number of false alarms.

Another strategy based on techniques of string analysis and the generations of dynamic models has been proposed as solution to the SQL injection attacks. The Java string analysis (JSA) library [16] provides a mechanism for generating models of Java strings. JSA performs a conservative string analysis of an application and creates automata that express all the possible values a specific string can have at a point in the application. This technique is not targeted to SQL injection attacks, but is important because other approaches use the library to generate middle forms of models. JDBC Checker [23] is a technique for statically checking the type correctness on SQL queries dynamically generated. This technique was not intended to detect and prevent general SQL injection attacks, but can be used to prevent attacks that take advantage of type mismatches in a dynamically generated query string. Wassermann and Su [47] proposed an approach that uses a static analysis combined with automated reasoning. The technique verifies that the SQL queries generated in the application usually do not contain a tautology. The technique detects only SQL injections that insert a tautology in the SQL queries, but cannot detect other types of SQL injections attacks. Halfond and Orso [24] propose Analysis and Monitoring for Neutralizing SQL Injection Attacks (AMNESIA). This approach uses a static analysis to build the models of the SQL queries that an application generates at each point of access to the database. In the dynamic phase, AMNESIA captures all the SQL queries before they are sent to the database and checks each query against the statically built models. Queries that violate the model are classified as SQL injection attacks. AMNESIA depends on accuracy static analysis. With only slight variations of accuracy, it generates a large number of false positive and negatives. SQLGuard [14] is an approach that checks queries at runtime to analyze if these queries conform to a model of expected queries. In this approach, the model is expressed as a grammar that only accepts legal queries. The model is deduced at runtime by examining the structure of the query before and after the addition of user input. The approach uses a secret key to delimit user input during parsing by the runtime checker. The security of this approach depends on an attacker not being able to find the key. Additionally, it requires that the programmer rewrites the code to use a special middle library. Kosuga et al. [28] proposed SANIA (Syntactic and

Semantic Analysis for Automated Testing against SQL Injection), which captures queries between Web application and database. It automatically generates crafted attacks according to the syntax and semantic of vulnerable points. SANIA uses a syntactic analysis tree of the query to evaluate the security of the points. SANIA presents a drawback; it has a significant rate of false positive.

Other main query development paradigms proposed as solution to SQL injection attacks are discussed below. SQLrand [11] provides a framework that allows developers to create SQL queries using randomized keywords instead of the normal SQL keywords. A proxy between the web application and the database server captures SQL queries and de-randomizes the keywords. The SQL keywords injected by an attacker would not have been constructed by the randomized keywords, so the tainted SQL strings would have syntax error. SQLrand depends on secret key to modify keywords; its security relies on hackers not being able to discover this key. Additionally, it requires the application developer to rewrite code. SQL DOM [34] and Safe Query Objects [17] use encapsulation of database queries to avoid SQL injection attacks. These techniques are changing the process to build SQL string to one systematic way that uses a type-checked API. API is able to systematically apply coding best practices such as input filtering and close-fitting type checking of user input. Although effective, these techniques have the drawback that requires developers to both learn and use a new programming paradigm or query development process.

A great interest has existed to overcome the SQL injection attacks through new solutions. However, the approach addressed for this type of attack has been limited to centralized models with little flexibility, scalability and a low efficacy. If the use of new technologies such as mobile technology is considered , many of these solutions are not easy to implement or they require changes to adapt to this environments. In this sense a solution has been proposed to work at scenarios where the protecting of the database and the information is carried out into a ubiquitous environment. The proposal is based on a distributed hierarchical multiagent architecture, using autonomous agents organized by levels. It is an innovative solution to stop the SQL injection attacks. The special design allows incorporating two main techniques used in the IDS Systems, such as anomaly detection and misuse detection. Both techniques are integrated inside SiC architecture.

With a well-structured architecture, each component knows its roles and has the necessary resource to do its job. SiC as solution to SQL injection attack is effective, presents a great performance and provides flexibility, adaptability and scalability for new computation environments. Detailed architecture of SiC is presented in the following section, describing the role of each component, type of agents, interaction, communication and tasks.

11.3   An Architecture Based on Multiagent System

The agents handle capacities such as autonomy, social abilities, reasoning, learning, mobility, among others [49]. One of the main features of agents is their ability to carry out cooperative and collaborative work, when they are grouped into multiagent systems to solve problems in form distributed [18]. These features make the agents suitable to deal with the SQL injection attacks. A distributed hierarchical multiagent architecture presents a great capacity for the distribution of task and responsibilities, such as failure recovering, adaptation to new changes and high level of learning. These factors are important to achieve a robust and efficient solution. One of the main novelties of the architecture is the use of CBR-BDI agent [30], which presents a great capacity of learning and adaptation. The agents BDI have a deliberative structure based on the BDI model [49]. Moreover, a BDI agent integrates a CBR mechanism [1] that allows to solve problems through the use of past experiences. As the core of the strategy for the classification of SQL queries is founded in detection by anomaly, it seems appropriate to use a CBR mechanism [1] that leverages past experience to detect anomaly. This CBR mechanism additionally incorporates a mixture of neural networks [38] in its reuse phase. This mixture of neural networks provides a capacity for the prediction of SQL injection attack.

The SiC presents an additional advantage through the use of wireless mobiles device, which can execute mobile agents. These devices have experimented a great growth in recent years, and it is common to find SQL queries that can be originated from different mobile devices including personal digital assistants (PDA), mobile phones, computer notebooks and workstations. The agents based on misuse detection and anomaly detection can be organized in a distributed way to leverage available resources and improve the performance of the classification process, regardless of the nature of the physic device. The approach is based on an organizational design that is obtained through a multi-hierarchical architecture. The agents are distributed so that at the time of initiating a classification task, each type of agent knows its responsibilities, the data it needs to do its job and where to send the results. The interaction and communication between the agents are crucial to achieve the goal of classification and detection of SQL injection attacks.

Function of each type of agent within the architecture is described below:

- Sensor agents: They are incorporated at each device with access to the database. Their functions consist of capturing datagrams, ordering of TCP fragments for extracting the SQL query string and syntactic analysis. The tasks of the Sensor agents end when the results (the SQL string transformed by the analysis, the result of the analysis of the SQL string and the user data) are sent to the next agent at the hierarchy of the classification process.
- FingerPrint agents: The numbers of FingerPrint agents depend on the workload at a given time. A FingerPrint agent receives the information of a Sensor agent and executes a searching process and matching with well-known patterns stored in a previously built database. The FingerPrint agents works in coordination with the Pattern agents to search and save SQL string patterns in the database. The FingerPrint agent finishes its task when it sends its results together with the results of the Sensor agent to the Anomaly agent. The results of the FingerPrint agent consist of the SQL string transformed by the analysis, the result of the analysis of the SQL string, the user data and the search results.
- Pattern Agent: It is responsible to save the new SQL string patterns in the database and search for patterns when the FingerPrint agent requests it.

- Anomaly agents: They are the core of the classification process. Their strategy is founded in a CBR mechanism that incorporates a mixture of neural networks. These agents retrieve those similar past cases with respect to the new cases, and then train the neural networks with the recovered cases and generate the final classification. The number of Anomaly agents depends on the workload at a given time. The result of the classification is sent to the Manager agent for the evaluation. This agent works in coordination with the LogUser agent.
- LogUser agent: This agent records the actions of the user and searches for the user profile (the historical profile and the user statistics) when it is requested by the Classifier agent.
- Manager agent: This agent allows an expert to evaluate the classification process and situations that have not been solved in the classification process such as a suspicious classification. Moreover, it allows adjustment of the configuration of the architecture, carries a record and control of the active agents in each level and coordinates the distribution of the workload among the agents. Finally, it coordinates the alerts with the Interface agent and required actions to take over an attack when it has been detected. Avoiding the risk to compromise the architecture to a fault, an anomaly agent can be promoted to be Manager agent. This agent is selected by means of a voting method [50] between the Anomaly agents.
- Interface agent: This agent allows the interaction of the user of the security system with the architecture. The interface agent communicates the details of an attack to the security personnel when an attack is detected. It has the ability to work on mobile devices. This capacity allows ubiquitous communication to attend the alerts immediately.
- DB agent: It is in charge of executing the query in the database. When the query has been classified as legal, it executes on the database and the results are send to the user owner of the request.
- Response agent: This agent delivers a response to the user once a classification solution is obtained. If the query has been classified as legal, the results of the query are sent to the user interface. Otherwise, if the query has been classified as illegal, a warning message is sent to the user interface.

Figure 11.1 presents the abstract multiagent architecture showing different types of agents in charge of the classification of SQL queries.

11.3.1 Communication Among Agents

In distributed environments, it is essential to provide necessary mechanisms for the coordination and cooperation among the agents, so they can efficiently develop their tasks. The SiC architecture incorporates agents to work on mobile device such as PDAs, Smart phones, computer notebooks and also on workstations. The communication between the devices is carried out via wireless and LAN. The wireless mobile devices allow taking advantage of the portability.

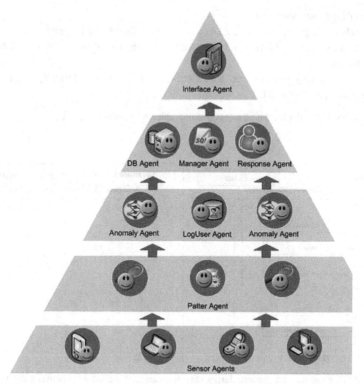

Fig. 11.1 Multiagent architecture for the classification of structure query language (SQL) queries

The communication among the type of agents is carried out using a standard recommended by Foundation for Intelligent Physical Agents (FIPA) [8]. The standard is named Communicative Act Library (CAL), which includes a set of performative to build the message format. The platform to build SiC architecture has been Java Agent Development Framework (JADE) [9], which is an implementation extended of the FIPA standard, and as such, it provides a set of libraries for the development of the agents. The communication of the agents by remote device is through an extension HTTP of JADE. In the case of the mobile agents, it uses Jade-Leap [9], which is another available extension of the framework. The Content specification language used is FIPA-SL [20], which allows defining the messages semantically according to the type of contents of the message defined for SiC. Figure 11.2 shows an example of the messages communicated between two agents of the architecture.

Figure 11.2 presents a message format transmitted by an agent to other. Once captured the SQL query by a Sensor agent, this sends a message inform type to a FingerPrint agent to carry out a detection based on pattern matching. The message includes data of the captured SQL string, such as transformed SQL string, data of the SQL string analysis and user data owner of the query.

The types of messages used in the multi-agent architecture are request, agree, cancel, inform, query-if, subscribe, propose, reject-proposal, accept-proposal, failure

```
:( Performative inform
 :sender (agent-identifier :   name SensorO1Agent
 :receiver(set (Agent-identifier : name FingerPrintO1Agent
 :Content
        String_Analizer(ParserSQL, ParserAnalysis, UserData)
 :Language FIPA-SL
```

Fig. 11.2 Example of a format of message communicated among the agents

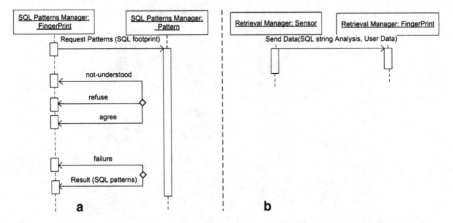

Fig. 11.3 Communications pattern during the interchange of the message between the agents

and not-understood. The protocols used for the communication and negotiation are defined by FIPA: FIPA-request protocol, FIPA-query protocol and FIPA-ContractNet protocol. The agents need to interact and negotiate continuously to fulfill the assigned task. Figure 11.3 presents two examples of the communication between two agents through a protocol diagram.

Figure 11.3a shows the communication between the FingerPrint agent and the Pattern agent to request stored SQL patterns when is applied for misuse detection. Figure 11.3b shows the message sent by the FingerPrint agent when it sends the results generated by the capture of the SQL query, string analysis and user data.

The security is a primordial element in the agents communication. This resource has been provided by a secured channel through the protocol Hy-pertext Transfer Protocol Secure (HTTPS) [39]. HTTPS is an Internet Protocol that provides a SSL layer of security. This protocol uses SSL and HTTP to protect the communication channel between the client and the server on a network. When HTTP is used to access the data on the Internet, HTTPS provides strong authentication. For the internal communication between the agents, the solution applied was by means of JADE-S [9]. JADE-S is a plug-gin that supports user authentication and agents, encryption and signature of message, but JADE-S is limited for working with mobile agents.

11.4   Classifier Model of SQL Injection Attacks

The classifier CBR-BDI agent [37] incorporates a CBR system that allows the prevention and detection of a SQL injection attack. The prevention and detection are supported by a prediction model based on neural networks, configured for short-term predictions of intrusions. This mechanism uses a memory of cases, which identifies past experiences with the corresponding indicators that characterize each of the attacks. This chapter presents a novel classification system that combines the advantages of the CBR systems, such as learning and adaptation, with the predictive capabilities of a mixture of neural networks. These features make the architecture appropriate for using it in dynamic environments. For working with CBR mechanism, the key concept is that of "case." A case is defined as a previous experience and is composed of three elements: a description of the problem; a solution; and the final state. To introduce a CBR motor into a BDI agent, we represent CBR system cases using BDI and implement a CBR cycle. This CBR cycle consists of four steps: retrieve, reuse, revise and retain.

The elements of the SQL query classification problem are described as follows:

- Problem Description: Describes the initial information available for generating a classification. As evident in Table 11.1, the problem description consists of a case identification, user session and SQL query elements.
- Solution: Describes the action carried out in order to solve the problem description. As evident in Table 11.1, it contains the case identification and the applied solution.
- Final State: Describes the achieved state after the solution has been applied. It takes three possible values: attack, not attack and suspicious. The multi-agent architecture incorporates the Manager agent, which allows an expert to evaluate the classification.

The proposed mechanism is responsible to classify SQL database queries made by users. When a user makes a new request, it is checked by a pattern matching. These patterns are stored in a database that handles a significant number of signatures that are not allowed on user level, such as symbol combination, binary and hexadecimal encoding and reserved statement of language (union, execute, drop, revoke, concat, length, asc, chr among others). If the FingerPrint agent detects some known signature, it is automatically identified as an attack. In order to identify the rest of the SQL attacks, the Anomaly agent uses a CBR mechanism, which must have a memory of cases dating back at least 4 weeks, with the structure described in Table 11.1. The problem description of a case is obtained by means of a string analysis technique over the SQL query. This process can be understood easily through the following example: It receives a query with the following syntax: Select field1, field2, field3 from table1 where field1 = input1 and field2 = input2.

If the fields input1 and input2 are used to bypass the authentication mechanism with the following input data: Input1 = "or 9876 = 9876 – and Input2 = (blank). The result of these input data would alter the SQL string as follows: Select field1, field2, field3 from Table 11.1 where field1 =" or 9876 = 9876 – "and field2="

Table 11.1 Structure of the problem definition and solution for a case of structure query language (SQL) query classification

Problem description fields		Solution fields	
IdCase	Integer	Idcase	Integer
Sesion	Session	Classification_Query	Integer
User	String		
IP_Adress	String		
Query_SQL	Query_SQL		
Affected_table	Integer		
Affected_field	Integer		
Command_type	Integer		
Word_GroupBy	Boolean		
Word_Having	Boolean		
Word_OrderBy	Boolean		
Number_And	Integer		
Number_Or	Integer		
Number_literals	Integer		
Number_LOL	Integer		
Length_SQL_String	Integer		
Cost_Time_CPU	Float		
Start_Time_Execution	Time		
End_Time_Execution	Time		
Query_Category	Integer		

Table 11.2 SQL String transformed through the string analysis

c1	c2	c3	c4	c5	c6	c7	c8	c9	c10	c11	c12	c13
1	3	0	0	0	0	1	1	2	81	1	2.91	0

The analysis of the SQL string would generate the result presented in Table 11.2 with the following fields: Affected_table$^{(c1)}$, Affected_field$^{(c2)}$, Command_type$^{(c3)}$, Word_GroupBy$^{(c4)}$, Word_Having$^{(c5)}$, Word_OrderBy$^{(c6)}$, Number_And$^{(c7)}$, Number_Or$^{(c8)}$, Number_literals$^{(c9)}$, Length_SQL_String$^{(c10)}$, Number_LOL$^{(c11)}$, CostTime_CPU$^{(c12)}$ and Query_Category$^{(13)}$. The fields Command_type and Query_Category have been encoded with the following nomenclature Command_Type: 0 = select, 1 = insert, 2 = update, 3 = delete; Query_Category: -1= suspicious, 0 = illegal, 1 = legal.

The first phase of the CBR cycle consists of recovering past experience from the memory of cases, specifically those with a problem description similar to the current request. In order to do this, a cosine similarity-based algorithm is applied, allowing the recovery of those cases which are at least 90% similar to the current request. The cases recovered are used to train the mixture of neural networks implemented in the reuse phase. The neural network with the sigmoidal function is trained with the recovered cases that were either an attack or not, whereas the neural network with hyperbolic function is trained with all the recovered cases (including the suspects). A preliminary analysis of correlations is required to determine the number of neurons of the input layer of the neuronal networks. Additionally, it is necessary to normalize the data (i.e., all data must be values in the interval [0,1]). The data used to train the mixture of networks must not be correlated. With the cases stored after deleting correlated cases, the inputs for training the mixture of networks are normalized. It is considered to be two neural networks. The results obtained using a mixture of the outputs of the networks provide a balanced response and avoid individual tendencies (always taking into account the weights that determine which of the two networks is more optimal).

Figure 11.4 shows the four steps of the CBR cycle including the mixture of the neural networks through an algorithm. This strategy of classification is carried out inside an Anomaly CBR-BDI agent. This Anomaly CBR-BDI agent is located on a strategic level of the architecture.

11.4.1 Neural Network Learning Algorithm

As is indicated earlier, an essential element is the mixture of neural networks that is used in the reuse stage of the CBR cycle by the Anomaly CBR-BDI agent to predict attacks. This section describes in detail the operation of the mixture of neural networks. The mixture uses two neural networks, and both of them are multilayer perceptrons, but use different types of activation functions. Each of these networks obtains an individual solution for the problem. Then, the solutions provided are combined to find the optimal classification. Figure 11.5 illustrates a GUI of the neural networks architecture.

The new case is presented to both neural networks and then each neural network provides its independent opinions about the classification. The neural network based on a sigmoidal function gives two results (illegal or legal) and the neural network through a hyperbolic tangential function produces three results (illegal, legal or suspicious). In the following paragraphs, we describe the learning algorithm for the neural networks, explaining the differences for each type of network. The advantages of the classification method provided by each of the individual networks are discussed. Finally, the mixture is presented and formalized. The equations are presented in the order they should be executed.

1. To present the input vector to the input layer.

$$X^P = (x_1^P, \ldots, x_i^P, \ldots, x_N^P)^\mathrm{T}. \tag{11.1}$$

2. To calculate the value of the levels of excitation for the neurons from the hidden layer

$$\mathrm{net}_j^P = \sum_{i=1}^{N} W_{ji}^P(t) X_i^P(t) + \theta_j^P, \tag{11.2}$$

```
 2    Begin
 3        cases:=Retrieve(new_case)    {case retrieval function}
 4        assessment:=Reuse(cases[], new_case) {result of the classifi
 5        decision:=Revise(new_case, assessment) {revision of the clas
 6        If decision then  {If decision is accepted}
 7            Retain(new_case, solution) {update of the memory base}
 8        End if
 9    End
10    Algorithm_Retrieve(new_case)  {Retrieve Algorithm}
11    Begin
12        SQL_Query:=Select cases from Tb_Cases Where
13        If [User] and [Ip_adress] then    {If User and Ip Adress is
14        SQL_Query+="user=[user]and IP_Adress=[IP_adress] and Comm
15        [Command_type] and Affected_table=[Content(Affected_table
16        Else
17                If [User] then {If only one User is recognized}
18                SQL_Query+="User=[User] and Command_type=[Command_typ
19                Affected_table=[Content(Affected_table)]"
20                Else
21                    If [Ip_adress] then {If only one Ip Adress is recog
22                        SQL_Query+="IP_adress=[IP_adress] and Command_t
23                        [Command_type] and Affected_table=[Content(Affe
24                    Else  {If user and Ip Adress are not included in th
25                        SQL_Query+="Command_type=[Command_type] and
26                        Affected_table=[Content(Affected_table)]"
27                    End If
28                End If
29            End If
30        cases[]:=executeQuery(SQL_Query) {recovering of the cases i
31        cases[]:=fsimilirity_cosine(cases[]) {cosine similarity-bas
32        cases[]:=fcorrelation(cases[]) {eliminating correlated case
33    End
34    Algorithm_Reuse(cases[], new_case) {Reuse Algorithm}
35    Begin
36        blnew_case=false
37        If description_new_case<>descripcion_previous_case then
38            blnew_case=true   {If user or Ip_adress are different of p
39        End If
40        If blnew_case then    {If is true then training neural networ
41            Input:=Retrieve_Input(cases[]) {Retrieval of input}
42            Output:=Retrieve_Output(cases[]) {Retrieval of ouput}
43            {Training of the neural network}
44            error_training:=Training_Neural_Network(Input, Output)
45            if (error_training)=low then
46                {Classification by mixture of neural network}
47                assessment:=Classification_Neural_Network(new_case)
48            Else
49                Exception(Error_Code, Description) {Imposible to classi
50            End If
51        Else
52            {Classification by mixture of neural network}
53            assessment:=Classification_Neural_Network(new_case)
54        End If
55    End
56    Algorithm_Revise(new_case, assessment)  {Revise Algorithm}
57    Begin
58        Boolean decision
59        If new_case=complete and assessment=optimal then {Evaluatic
60            decision:=true
61        End If
62    End
63    Algorithm_Retain(new_case, solution) {Retain Algorithm}
64    Begin
65        executeUpdate(new_case, solution) {Update case memory with
66    End
```

Fig. 11.4 Algorithm of the cycle case-based reasoning for classifying SQL query

where W_{ji}^{P} is the weight that connects the neuron "i" from the input layer with the neuron "j" from the hidden layer, according to a "p" pattern (Fig. 11.5). θ_{j}^{P} is the threshold or bias associated to the neuron "j" from hidden layer, according to a "p" pattern.

3. To calculate the outputs of the neurons from the hidden layer.

$$Y_{j}^{p} = f_{j}(\text{net}_{j}^{p}), \tag{11.3}$$

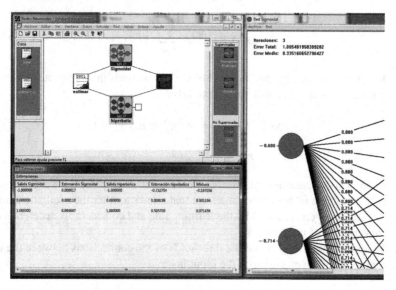

Fig. 11.5 Capture of the mixture of the neural networks

where f_j is the deactivation function of the neurons "j" from the hidden layer.

4. To calculate the value of the levels of excitation for the neurons at the output layer.

$$\text{net}_k^p = \sum_{j=1}^{H} W_{kj}^p(t) y_j^p(t) + \theta_k^p, \tag{11.4}$$

where W_{kj}^P is the weight that connects the neuron "k" from the output layer with the neuron "j" from the hidden layer according to a "p" pattern (Fig. 11.5). θ_k^P is the threshold or bias associated to the neuron "k" from output layer, according to a "p" pattern.

5. To calculate the output of the neural network.

$$Y_k^p = f_k(\text{net}_k^p), \tag{11.5}$$

where f_k is the activation function of the neuron "k" from the output layer.

6. To calculate the sensitivity of the neurons from the output layer based on error showed at the output with the targeted output vector is defined as

$$d^p = (d_1^p, \ldots, d_k^p, d_M^p)^{\mathrm{T}}, \tag{11.6}$$

$$\delta_k^p = -\frac{\partial E^p}{\partial(\text{net}_k^p)} = (d_k^p - y_k^p) = \frac{\partial f_k(\text{net}_k^p)}{\partial \text{net}_k^p}. \tag{11.7}$$

7. To calculate the sensibility of the neurons from the hidden layer is given by

$$\delta_j^p = f_j'(\text{net}_j^p) \sum_{k=1}^{M} \delta_k^p w_{kj}^p. \tag{11.8}$$

8. To update the weights and the bias of the connections that connect the neurons from the hidden layer with the output layer

$$\Delta w_{kj}^p(t+1) = \eta \delta_k^p y_j^p + \mu \Delta w_{kj}^p(t), \tag{11.9}$$

$$\Delta \theta_k^p(t+1) = \eta \delta_k^p + \mu \Delta \theta_k^p(t), \tag{11.10}$$

where η is the learning rate controls the size of the change of the weights in each iteration and μ is the momentum term that allows to filter the oscillations in the surface of the error caused by the learning rate and considerably accelerates the convergence of the weights.

9. To upgrade the weights and the thresholds of the connections between the neurons of the hidden layer with the input layer

$$\Delta w_{ji}^p(t+1) = \eta \delta_j^p x_i^p + \mu \Delta w_{ji}^p(t), * \tag{11.11}$$

$$\Delta \theta_j^p(t+1) = \eta \delta_j^p + \mu \Delta \theta_j^p(t). \tag{11.12}$$

10. To calculate the error

$$E^p = \frac{1}{2} \sum_{k=1}^{M} (d_k^p - y_k^p)^2, \tag{11.13}$$

where d_k^p is the desired output of the neuron "k" from the output layer, according to a "p" pattern. Since this term reflects the adaptation capacity of the neural network, it is necessary to keep it in mind to determine if the neural network learns in a satisfactory way or not. As previously explained, the mixture is composed of two multilayer perceptrons, one of them uses sigmoidal function and the other tangential function. In this sense, the algorithm has been adapted by considering the activation functions, the sigmoidal or the tangential function.

- The Sigmoidal activation function has its range within the interval [0,1]. It is used to detect if the request is an attack or not. The value 0 represents an illegal request and 1 a legal request. The Sigmoidal activation function is the activation function most used for classifications between two groups. This function has drawbacks that it works well for binary classifications. That is:

$$f(x) = \frac{1}{1 + e^{-ax}}, \tag{11.14}$$

where $a = 1$. For the weights used to connect a hidden layer with an output layer, the updating formula of the weights in series is given by "p" pattern as follows:

$$\Delta w_{kj}^P(t+1) = \eta \delta_k^P y_j^P + \mu \Delta w_{kj}^P(t) = \eta(d_k^P - y_k^P)(1 - y_k^P)y_k^P y_j^P + \mu \Delta w_{kj}^P(t).$$
$$(11.15)$$

For the bias associated to the neurons from the output layer, given a "p" pattern, the updating formula of the weights in series is given by

$$\Delta \theta_k^P(t+1) = \eta \delta_k^P + \mu \Delta \theta_k^P(t) = \eta(d_k^P - y_k^P)(1 - y_k^P)y_k^P + \mu \Delta \theta_k^P(t).$$
$$(11.16)$$

For the weights used to connect the input layer with the hidden layer, the updating of the weights in series given by a "p" pattern is

$$\Delta w_{ji}^P(t+1) = \eta(1 - y_j^P)y_j^P \left(\sum_{k=1}^M \delta_k^P w_{kj}\right) x_i^P + \mu \Delta w_{ji}^P(t)$$

$$= \eta(1 - y_j^P)y_j^P \left(\sum_{k=1}^M (d_k^P - y_k^P)(1 - y_k^P)y_k^P w_{kj}\right) x_i^P$$

$$+ \mu \Delta w_{ji}^P(t). \qquad (11.17)$$

For the bias associated to the neurons from the hidden layer, given "p" pattern, the update is given by

$$\theta_j^P(t+1) = \theta_j^P(t) + \eta(1 - y_j^P)y_j^P \left(\sum_{k=1}^M \delta_k^P w_{kj}\right) + \mu(\theta_j^P(t) - \theta_j^P(t-1))$$

$$= \theta_j^P(t) + \eta(1 - y_j^P)y_j^P \left(\sum_{k=1}^M (d_k^P - y_k^P)(1 - y_k^P)y_k^P w_{kj}\right)$$

$$+ \mu(\theta_j^P(t) - \theta_j^P(t-1)). \qquad (11.18)$$

- The hyperbolic tangential function has its range in the interval $[-1,1]$. It is used to detect if the request is an attack, not attack or suspicious. The hyperbolic tangential function allows more possible cases than the sigmoidal function. The value 0 represents illegal request, value 1 represents legal request and value -1 suspicious requests. Hyperbolic tangential function is suitable for classifying in three groups. Hyperbolic tangential activation function is given by

$$f(x) = \tanh(x) = \frac{e^x - e^{-x}}{e^x + e^{-x}}. \qquad (11.19)$$

For the weights used to connect a hidden layer with an output layer, the updating formula of the weights in series given by a "p" pattern is

$$\Delta w_{kj}^P(t+1) = \eta \delta_k^P y_j^P + \mu \Delta w_{kj}^P(t) = \eta(d_k^P - y_k^P)(1 - y_k^P)y_k^P y_j^P + \mu \Delta w_{kj}^P(t).$$
$$(11.20)$$

For the bias associated to the neurons from the output layer, given a "p" pattern, the updating formula of the weights in series is defined as

$$\Delta\theta_k^P(t+1) = \eta\delta_k^P + \mu\Delta\theta_k^P(t) = \eta(d_k^P - y_k^P)(1 - (y_k^P)^2) + \mu\Delta\theta_k^P(t).$$

(11.21)

For the weights used to connect the input layer with the hidden layer, the updating of the weights in series given by a "p" pattern is defined as

$$\Delta w_{ji}^P(t+1) = \eta(1 - y_j^P)y_j^P\left(\sum_{k=1}^{M}\delta_k^P w_{kj}\right)x_i^P + \mu\Delta w_{ji}^P(t)$$

$$= \eta(1 - y_j^P)y_j^P\left(\sum_{k=1}^{M}(d_k^P - y_k^P)(1 - y_k^P)y_k^P w_{kj}\right)$$

$$\times x_i^P + \mu\Delta w_{ji}^P(t).$$

(11.22)

For the bias associated to the neurons from the hidden layers, given a "p" pattern, the updating in series is defined as

$$\theta_j^P(t+1) = \theta_j^P(t) + \eta(1 - (y_j^P)^2)\left(\sum_{k=1}^{M}\delta_k^P w_{kj}\right) + \mu(\theta_j^P(t) - \theta_j^P(t-1))$$

$$= \theta_j^P(t) + \eta(1 - (y_j^P)^2)\left(\sum_{k=1}^{M}(d_k^P - y_k^P)(1 - (y_k^P)^2)w_{kj}\right)$$

$$+ \mu(\theta_j^P(t) - \theta_j^P(t-1)).$$

(11.23)

It is intended to detect attacks, so if only one network with a sigmoidal activation function was used, then the result provided by the network would tend to be an attack or not, and no suspects would be detected. On the other hand, if only one network with a hyperbolic tangent activation was used, then a potential problem could exist in which the majority of the results would be identified as a suspect, though they were clearly an attack or not. The mixture provides a more efficient configuration of the networks, since the global result is determined by merging the two filters. This way, if the two networks classify the user request as an attack, so will be the mixture; and if both agree that it is not an attack, the mixture will as well be. If there is no concurrence, the system uses the result of the network with the least error in the training process or classifies it as a suspect. In the reuse phase, the two networks are trained by a back-propagation algorithm for the same set of training patterns, using a Sigmoidal activation function (which will take values within [0,1], where 0 = Illegal and 1 = legal) for a Multilayer Perceptron and a hyperbolic tangent activation function for the other Multilayer Perceptron (which take values within

[−1,1], where −1 = Suspect, 0 = illegal and 1 = legal). The response of both networks is combined to obtain the mixture of networks denoted by y^2, where the superscript indicates the number of mixtured networks.

$$y^2 = \frac{1}{\sum_{r=1}^{2} e^{-|1-r|}} \sum_{r=1}^{2} y^r e^{-|1-r|}. \tag{11.24}$$

The number of neurons in the output layer for both networks is 1, and is responsible for deciding whether or not there is an attack. The error of the training phase for each of the neural networks can be quantified using (11.24), where P is the total number of training patterns.

$$\text{Error} = \frac{1}{P} \sum_{i=1}^{P} \left| \frac{\text{Forecast}_P - \text{Target}_P}{\text{Target}_P} \right|. \tag{11.25}$$

11.5   Experimental Results and Discussion

A case study has been proposed to test the effectiveness of a SiC prototype. The prototype has been evaluated by means of a previously developed multiagent system, installed in a geriatric residence [18]. The implemented multiagent system improves the security of the patients, facilitates the carers' activity and guarantees an adequate level of efficiency. The system has been developed in a distributed environment containing devices, such as PDA, notebook computers and accessed via wireless. A back-end database stores and supplies information. The database manager is Oracle. The actors in the scenario such as nurses, doctors, patients, worker social and other employees can be seen in Fig. 11.6. The medical staff in charge of patients' care was integrated by 2 doctors, 10 nurses and 1 social worker. The number of patients under the monitoring and attention of the multi-agent system was 30. In the case of the nurses, each nurse was equipped with a PDA, thus a total of 10 PDAs execute queries on the database during the working day. With these data, we prepared the attack scenario. The performance of the test required to incorporate equipments and mobile devices with connection via wireless and LAN. Equipments include 2 workstations and 3 PDAs. The test has been carried out during 30 working days without interruption.

During the execution of the multiagent system, several types of SQL queries were carried on the database. The queries were related to the patients' treatments, the scheduling of the working day of the nurses, etc. Most of the queries were executed from PDAs. The PDAs are used by doctors and nurses to accomplish their tasks. To facilitate the evaluation of the prototype, we focused on the role of the nurse. The main volume of queries were generated each time a plan was assigned to a nurse. The plans changed due to different reasons during their execution and these changes increased the number of queries on the database. When a nurse starts and

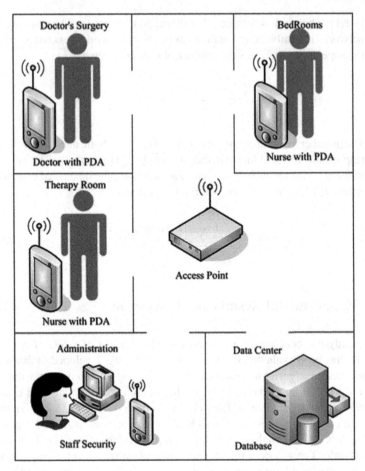

Fig. 11.6 Abstract scenario of the real environment (geriatric residence)

finalizes a task, a response is send through a SQL query. The nurses have direct
access to the database system by means of the application interface on the PDAs.
The strategy was based on the execution of crafted queries from 2 PDAs. These
PDAs were fixed with a similar user interface with the nurses' PDAs, but these
have capacity to execute tainted queries. When a query is executed from the PDA
of attack, this query carries out a type of SQL injection that has to be captured,
analyzed and classified as legal, illegal or suspicious. The FingerPrint agents and
Anomaly agents were distributed in the 2 workstations. As the test was carried out
on the real medical database, a special mechanism has been built to guarantee the
integrity of the database. All the queries executed both by the nurses' PDA and the
attack PDAs are examined and classified. The test was conducted with a total of
12 PDAs available, 10 PDAs assigned to the active nurses and 2 PDAs to execute
attacks, a total of 10,200 queries were sent to the medical database. Each nurse's
PDA executed around 30 daily queries and, during the 30 days of the test, 9,000 legal

queries were carried out. In the case of the two attack PDAs, each PDA executed 20 illegal daily queries. These PDAs sent 40 events of attack during a working day. Throughout the 30 days of the test, a total of 1,200 events of attack were targeted to the medical database. The volume of queries during the test period allows building a case memory to validate the strategy proposed.

To check the validity of the proposed model, we elaborated a series of tests, which were executed on a memory of cases, specifically developed for these tests, and which generated attack consults. The results obtained are promising, improving in many cases that are obtained with other existing techniques, which let us conclude that SiC can be considered as a serious alternative to detect and predict SQL injection attacks. The classification system integrated within the Anomaly agent provides the results illustrated in Table 11.3, which are promising. It is possible to observe different techniques for predicting attacks at the database layer and the errors associated with misclassifications. All the techniques presented in Table 11.3 have been applied under similar conditions to the same set of cases, taking the same problem into account in order to obtain a new case common to all the methods. Note that the technique proposed in this article provides the best results, with an error of only 0.5% of the cases.

As shown in Table 11.3, the Bayesian method is the most accurate statistical method, since it is based on the likelihood of the events observed. But it has the disadvantage of determining the initial parameters of the algorithm, though it is the fastest of the considered statistical methods. Taking into account the errors obtained using different methods, after the neural networks and Bayesian methods, we found that the regression models could also be used. Due to the non-linear behaviour of the hackers, linear regression offers the worst results, followed by the polynomial and exponential regression. This can be explained by looking at hacker behaviour: as the hackers break security measures, the time for their attacks to obtain information decreases exponentially.

The empirical results show that the best methods are those that involve the use of neural networks and if we consider a mixture of two neural networks, the predictions are notably improved. These methods are more accurate than statistical methods for detecting attacks to databases because the behaviour of the hacker is not linear, dynamic and chaotic.

Table 11.3 Results obtained after testing different classification techniques

Forecasting techniques	Successful (%)	Approximated time (s)
Anomaly CBR-BDI agent (mixture NN)	99.5	2
Back-propagation neural networks	99.2	2
Bayesian forecasting method	98.2	11
Exponential regression	97.8	9
Polynomial regression	97.7	8
Linear regression	97.6	5

Table 11.4 Successful (%) depending on the number of training patterns

Number of patterns of training	Successful (%)
1,000	99.5
900	99.1
700	98.5
500	98.6
300	96.8
100	89

The advantage of using a mixture of neural networks improves performance that provides other classification techniques, but also improves performance that can provide the neural networks on an individual basis. The mixture has the advantage that the number of cases where the classifier agent could not decide is smaller, and in few cases, the mediation by a human expert was required. We could check the decision of the mixture of networks with the verdict of a human expert for those cases in which a single network did not decide and both the mixture of networks and the human expert were in agreement on 99% of cases. Figure 11.7 depicts the effectiveness of the classification schemes both for the networks with distinct activation function work on an individual basis and the effectiveness of the mixture of networks.

Figure 11.8 shows the success of the predictions for the number of training patterns presented in Table 11.4. As observed, with a large number the training patterns, percentage of successful prediction could be also improved.

When the number of patterns for training the neural network increases, the prediction error decreases. It is to be noted that the number of training patterns is the result after applying filters, such as the similarity based algorithm and the corre-

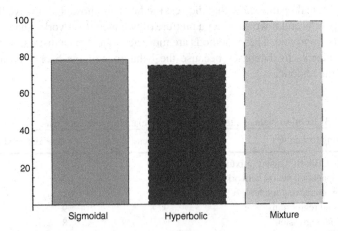

Fig. 11.7 Effectiveness in the classification of the networks on an individual basis and the mixture of networks

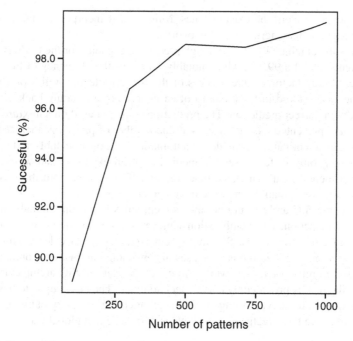

Fig. 11.8 Successful percentage vs. number of patterns

lation function. These filters reduce the quantity of cases meaningfully in order to improve the performance during the training stage.

11.6   Conclusions

The problem of SQL injection attacks on databases presents a serious threat against information systems. This chapter has presented a novel solution consisting of a new hierarchical multiagent architecture for detecting SQL injection attacks, which combines the advantages of multiagent systems, such as autonomy and distributed problem solving, with the adaptation and learning capabilities of the CBR systems. The SiC architecture proposed a new perspective in the strategies for detecting and predicting SQL injection attacks, since the existing approaches are based on centralized strategies. The SiC architecture provides a distributed hierarchical structure, which allows a more efficient balance and distribution of the tasks involved in the problem of detecting and classifying attacks to databases by means of SQL injection. The core of the architecture is a special type of CBR-BDI agent, which assures great capacities for learning and adaptation. This agent is a classifier agent that, supported by the philosophy of the CBR mechanisms, proposes a new strategy, based on the use of past experiences, to classify SQL injection attacks. This strategy differs in its conception from the existing ones. Moreover, it incorporates the prediction capabilities that characterize neural networks.

The results obtained illustrated a high prediction capacity for the CBR-BDI classifier agents, about a 99.5%, which notably improves the efficiency of the existing solutions. A key factor for the success of the SiC architecture relies on the quality of the cases stored in the memory of cases, requiring a dating back of at least 4 weeks for a correct prediction. The prediction strategy based on a mixture of neural networks presented a clear advantage: the number of problems analyzed where the classifier agent cannot provide an automatic decision is notably reduced and, consequently, only in few cases the mediation of an expert human was required. The experimental results indicate that around 99% of cases, both the mixture of networks and the human expert were in agreement.

Finally, the SiC architecture combines techniques based on anomaly detection and misuse detection. This combination achieves a robust solution to block any type of SQL injection attack. The SiC multiagent architecture provides flexibility and scalability to protect ubiquitous databases in new computational environments. The results are promising and it is worthy to conclude that the SiC architecture could improve the results provided by current technologies. The next step is to have a full solution where all the types of agents in the architecture can carry out their tasks in order to improve the effectiveness and the performance in a global way.

Acknowledgments This development has been partially supported by the Spanish Ministry of Science project TIN2006-14630-C03-03.

References

1. Aamodt A, Plaza E (1994) Case-based reasoning: Foundational issues, methodological variations, and system approaches. AI Communications. Vol. 7, pp. 39–59.
2. Abraham A, Jain R, Thomas J, Han SY (2007) D-SCIDS: Distributed soft computing intrusion detection system. Journal of Network and Computer Applications. Vol. 30(1), pp. 81–98.
3. Agrawal R, Kiernan J, Srikant R, Xu Y (2002) Hippocratic databases. In: 28th International Conference on Very Large Data Bases. Hong Kong, pp. 143–154.
4. Anley C (2002) Advanced SQL Injection in SQL Server Applications. NGS Software http://www.nextgenss.com/papers/advanced sql injection.pdf. Accessed 10 April 2007.
5. Application Security Inc (2005) Protecting the Crown Jewels. http://www.appsecinc.com/cgi-bin/search.pl?Terms=crown. Accessed 12 April 2008.
6. Application Security Inc (2007) Introduction to Database and Application Worms. http://www.appsecinc.com/presentations/Database_Application_Worms.pdf. Accessed 10 April 2008.
7. Bajo J, De Luis A, González A, Saavedra A, Corchado JM (2006) A shopping mall multiagent system: Ambient intelligence in practice. In: 2nd International Workshop on Ubiquitous Computing & Ambient Intelligence, pp. 115–125.
8. Bellifemine F, Poggi A, Rimassa G (1999) Jade: A FIPA-compliant agent framework. In: Proceedings of PAAM-1999, pp. 97–108.
9. Bergenti F, Poggi A (2001) LEAP: A FIPA platform for handheld and mobile devices. In: Proceedings of the ATAL 2001 Conference. Seattle.

10. Bertino E, Sandhu R (2005) Database security-concepts, approaches, and challenges. In: IEEE Computer Society, Los Alamitos. Vol. 2, pp. 2–9.
11. Boyd SW, Keromytis AD (2004) SQLrand: Preventing SQL injection attacks. In: Applied Cryptography and Network Security. Vol. 3089, pp. 292–302.
12. Bratman ME (1987) Intention, Plans, and Practical Reason. Harvard University Press, Cambridge, MA.
13. Breach Security, Inc (2007) The Web Hacking Incidents Database. http://www.breach.com/. Accessed 02 April 2008.
14. Buehrer G, Weide BW, Sivilotti PAG (2005) Using parse tree validation to prevent SQL injection attacks. In: 5th International Workshop on Software Engineering and Middleware. ACM, New York, pp. 106–113.
15. Carrascosa C, Bajo J, Julian V, Corchado JM, Botti V (2008) Hybrid multi-agent architecture as a real-time problem-solving model. Expert Systems with Applications. Vol. 34(1), pp. 2–17.
16. Christensen AS, Moller A, Schwartzbach MI (2003) Precise analysis of string expressions. In: 10th International Static Analysis Symposium. Springer, pp. 1–18.
17. Cook R, Rai S (2005) Safe query objects: Statically typed objects as remotely executable queries. In: 27th International Conference on Software Engineering. ACM, St. Louis, pp. 97–106.
18. Corchado JM, Bajo J, Abraham A (2008) GerAmi: Improving healthcare delivery in geriatric residences. IEEE Intelligent Systems. Vol. 23, pp. 19–25.
19. Corchado JM, Bajo J, De Paz Y, Tapia D (2008) Intelligent environment for monitoring Alzheimer patients, agent technology for health care. In: Decision Support Systems. Vol. 34(2), pp. 382–396.
20. Foundation for Intelligent Physical Agents. http://www.fipa.org. Accessed 15 August 2007.
21. Georgeff MP, Lansky AL (1987) Reactive reasoning and planning. In: American Association of Artificial Intelligence. Seattle, pp. 677–682.
22. Glez-Bedia M, Corchado JM (2002) A planning strategy based on variational calculus for deliberative agents. Computing and Information Systems Journal. Vol. 10(1), pp. 2–14.
23. Gould C, Su Z, Devanbu P (2004) JDBC Checker: A static analysis tool for SQL/JDBC applications. In: 26th International Conference on Software Engineering. IEEE Computer Society, Washington, DC, pp. 697–698.
24. Halfond W, Orso A (2005) AMNESIA: Analysis and monitoring for neutralizing SQL-injection attacks. In: 20th IEEE/ACM International Conference on Automated Software Engineering. ACM, New York, pp. 174–183.
25. Halfond WG, Viegas J, Orso A (2006) A classification of SQL-injection attacks and countermeasures. In: IEEE International Symposium on Secure Software Engineering. Arlington.
26. Hayat Z, Reeve J, Boutle C (2007) Ubiquitous security for ubiquitous computing. In: Elsevier Advanced Technology Publications, Oxford, pp. 172–178.
27. Huang Y, Huang S, Lin T, Tsai C (2003) Web application security assessment by fault injection and behavior monitoring. In: 12th International Conference on World Wide Web. ACM, New York, pp. 148–159.
28. Kosuga Y, Kono K, Hanaoka M, Hishiyama M, Takahama Y (2007) Sania: Syntactic and semantic analysis for automated testing against SQL injection. In: 23rd Annual Computer Security Applications Conference. IEEE Computer Society, pp. 107–117.
29. Kruegel C, Vigna G (2003) Anomaly detection of web-based attacks. In: 10th ACM Conference on Computer and Communications Security. ACM, New York, pp. 251–261.
30. Laza R, Pavón R, Corchado JM (2003) A reasoning model for CBR_BDI agents using an adaptable fuzzy inference system. In: 10th Conference of the Spanish Association for Artificial Intelligence. Springer. Vol. 3040, pp. 96–106.
31. Litchfield D (2005) Data Mining with SQL Injection and Inference, NGS Software. http://www.ngssoftware.com/research/papers/sqlinference.pdf. Accessed 10 April 2007.
32. Litchfield D, Anley C, Heasman J, Grindlay B (2005) The Database Hacker's Handbook: Defending Database Servers. Wiley, New York.
33. Maurer U (2004) The role of cryptography in database security. In: ACM SIGMOD International Conference on Management of Data. ACM, New York, pp. 5–10.

34. McClure RA, Krger IH (2005) SQL DOM: Compile time checking of dynamic SQL statements. In: 27th International Conference on Software Engineering. ACM, New York, pp. 88–96.
35. Mukkamala S, Sung AH, Abraham A (2005) Intrusion detection using an ensemble of intelligent paradigms. Journal of Network and Computer Applications. Vol. 28(2), pp. 167–182.
36. Pervasive Software Inc (2003) Implementing Security Best Practices for HIPAA with Pervasive.SQL. http://www.msmiami.com/custom/downloads/Pervasive_HIPAASecurity_Paper.pdf. Accessed 10 April 2008.
37. Pinzón C, De Paz Y, Cano R (2008) Classification agent-based techniques for detecting intrusions in databases. In: 3rd International Workshop on Hybrid Artificial Intelligence Systems.
38. Ramasubramanian P, Kannan A (2004) Quickprop neural network ensemble forecasting a database intrusion prediction system. Neural Information Processing. Vol. 5, pp. 847–852.
39. Rescorla E, Schiffman A (1999) The Secure HyperText Transfer Protocol RFC Editor, United States. http://www.rfc-editor.org/rfc/rfc2660.txt. Accessed 10 January 2008.
40. Rieback MR, Crispo B, Tanenbaum AS (2006) Is your cat infected with a computer virus?. In: Fourth Annual IEEE International Conference on Pervasive Computing and Communications. IEEE Computer Society, Washington, DC, pp. 169–179.
41. Rieback MR, Crispo B, Tanenbaum AS (2006) RFID Malware: Truth vs. Myth. IEEE Security and Privacy. Vol. 4(4), pp. 70–72.
42. Rieback MR, Simpson PN, Crispo B, Tanenbaum AS (2006) RFID malware: Design principles and examples. Pervasive and Mobile Computing. Vol. 2(4), pp. 405–426.
43. Rietta F (2006) Application layer intrusion detection for SQL injection. In: 44th Annual Southeast Regional Conference. ACM, New York, pp. 531–536.
44. Skaruz J, Seredynski F (2007) Recurrent neural networks towards detection of SQL attacks. In: 21st International Parallel and Distributed Processing Symposium. IEEE International, pp. 1–8.
45. Thuraisingham B (2002) Data mining, national security, privacy and civil liberties. ACM, New York. Vol. 4(2), pp. 1–5. http://portal.acm.org/citation.cfm?id=772862.772863.
46. Valeur F, Mutz D, Vigna G (2005) A learning-based approach to the detection of SQL attacks. In: Proceedings of the Conference on Detection of Intrusions and Malware and Vulnerability Assessment. Vienna, Austria, pp. 123–140.
47. Wassermann G, Su Z (2004) An analysis framework for security in web applications. In: FSE Workshop on Specification and Verification of Component-Based Systems, pp. 70–78.
48. Wooldridge M, Jennings NR (1995) Intelligent agents: Theory and practice. Knowledge Engineering Review. Vol. 10(2), pp. 115–152.
49. Woolridge M, Wooldridge MJ (2002) Introduction to Multiagent Systems. Wiley, New York.
50. Wu J, Wang C, Wang J, Chen S (2006) Dynamic hierarchical distributed intrusion detection system based on multi-agent system. In: EEE/WIC/ACM International Conference on Web Intelligence and Intelligent Agent Technology. IEEE International, pp. 89–93.
51. Xiong L, Chitti S, Liu L (2007) Preserving data privacy in outsourcing data aggregation services. In: ACM Transactions on Internet Technology. New York, Vol. 7(3), pp. 17.
52. Zaidenberg S, Reignier P, Crowley, JL (2007) An architecture for ubiquitous applications. In: 1st International Joint Workshop on Wireless Ubiquitous Computing. Vol. 1, pp. 86–95.

Chapter 12
HoCaMA: Home Care Hybrid Multiagent Architecture

Juan A. Fraile, Javier Bajo, Ajith Abraham, and Juan M. Corchado

Abstract Home Care is one of the main objectives of Ambient Intelligence. Nowadays, the disabled and elderly population, which represents a significant part of our society, requires novel solutions for providing home care in an effective way. In this chapter, we present HoCaMA, a hybrid multiagent architecture that facilitates remote monitoring and care services for disabled patients at their homes. HoCaMA combines multiagent systems and Web services to facilitate the communication and integration with multiple health care systems. In addition, HoCaMA focuses on the design of reactive agents capable of interacting with different sensors present in the environment, and incorporates a system of alerts through SMS and MMS mobile technologies. Finally, it uses Radio Frequency IDentification and JavaCard technologies to provide advanced location and identification systems, as well as automatic access control facilities. HoCaMA has been implemented in a real environment and the results obtained are presented within this chapter.

Keywords Ambient intelligence · Home care · Multiagent system · Ubiquitous computing

12.1 Introduction

Nowadays, there is a considerable growth in the development of automation technologies as well as intelligent environments as demonstrated by the relevance acquired by the ambient intelligence (AmI) [1, 9]. One of the main objectives of AmI is to look after the user's well-being and obtain friendly, rational, productive, sustainable and secure relationship for users within their environments. Several architectures based on multiagent systems have emerged and thanks to their appro-

A. Abraham (✉)
Norwegian Center of Excellence, Center of Excellence for Quantifiable Quality of Service, Norwegian University of Science and Technology, O.S. Bragstads Plass 2E, N-7491 Trondheim, Norway
e-mail: ajito.abraham@ieee.org

A.-E. Hassanien et al. (eds.), *Pervasive Computing: Innovations in Intelligent Multimedia and Applications*, Computer Communications and Networks, DOI 10.1007/978-1-84882-599-4_12, © Springer-Verlag London Limited 2009

priateness to be applied in the development of intelligent spaces and the integration of devices that are programmable via computer networks [23]. Moreover, they contribute to the development of ubiquitous computation [15], which notably helps to resolve the challenge of defining strategies that can allow the early detection and prevention of problems in an automated environment.

The ubiquitous environments require the improvement of the services offered to the users as well as the way they can be accessed. Moreover, it is necessary to adopt the trends already tested and proven in technological environments. Ubiquitous environments are focused on the user, since the user is the centre of the new technological facilities and demands access to unified services. In this sense, every user interacts in a personal way for the enjoyment of services. An ubiquitous environment is constituted by devices sensitive to the presence of the user, and is able to automatically identify and recognize the user preferences. There are several benefits provided by AmI services [22]: users get easier access to services that are contracted, access to services is independent of the terminal that is used and use of services is simpler, allowing a rapid assimilation by the user. In addition, users can receive personalized services entirely, so they have quick access to what they call their personal needs.

The high growth of the sector of the population requiring AmI solutions in home care environments, as well as commitments that are being acquired to meet the needs of this sector suggest that it is necessary to modernize the current solutions. Multiagent systems [34] and architectures based on the use of intelligent devices have been recently explored as monitoring systems for medical care services [2] for the elderly and people with Alzheimer's disease [9]. Multiagent systems can provide continued support in the daily life of disabled people [7], predicting potentially dangerous situations and hanging over a cognitive and physical support to the medical staff [4].

This work uses the possibilities provided by the new technologies to develop an open multiagent architecture, which can integrate video surveillance techniques, artificial intelligence, intelligent agents, wireless and mobile technology. The use of these technologies facilitates new functionalities that allow optimizing the management and efficiency of services and applications, improving the quality of life of users and facilitating the work of the care givers.

The main objective of this paper is to define a hybrid MultiAgent architecture, HoCaMA, for the control and the supervision of open environments. HoCaMA involves functionalities that allow automated identification, localization, alarms management and control of movement. The users of solutions based on HoCaMA are able to gain wireless access to all the information that they need to perform their work. A novel real time communication protocol at the core of the architecture allows secure and rapid communication between the reactive agents and the system sensors. The reactive agents, whose response time is critical, are influenced by deliberative BDI agents, which are located inside the platform. Additionally, the HoCaMA architecture integrates an alert system across the agents' platform, specifically designed to work with mobile devices. The alert system contains different levels of emergency, and the alert level is determined by a deliberative agent who, depending on the alert level, emits the alarm to the appropriate agent, either a reactive agent or a deliberative agent.

Rest of the chapter is organized as follows: Sect. 12.2 presents the problem that prompted this work; Sect. 12.3 presents the proposed architecture; Sect. 12.4 deals with the scenario in which the architecture is applied to a real case and Sect. 12.5 illustrates the results and conclusions obtained after applying the proposed architecture to a real case in an environment of dependence.

12.2   General Description of the Problem

The use of intelligent agents is an essential component for analyzing information on distributed sensors [27, 33]. These agents must be capable of both independent reasoning and joint analysis of complex situations in order to be able to achieve a high level of interaction with humans [4]. Although multiagent systems already exist and are capable of gathering information within a given environment in order to provide medical care [18], there is still much work to be done.

It is necessary to continue developing systems and technology that focus on the improvement of services in general. After the development of the internet, there has been continual progress in new wireless communication networks and mobile devices such as mobile telephones and personal digital assistants (PDAs). This technology can help to construct more efficient distributed systems capable of addressing new problems [10]. The PROSAFE project [8] attempts to automatically identify the daily activities of the monitored person. The processing of collected data is carried out on doctor's request with an adapted interface. The final operational objective is to detect any abnormal behaviour such as a fall, a runaway or an accident.

The research objective is to gather characteristic data about the night or daily activities of the patient. The AILISA project [20] (Intelligent Apartments for effective longevity) is an experimental platform to evaluate remote care and supportive technologies in gerontology. This ambitious project regroups specialists of smart homes, networks and computing, electronics and signal processing. The e-Vital project [24] (cost-effective health services for interactive continuous monitoring of vital signs parameters) is a modular and ambulatory telemedicine platform. Its objective is to increase patient's feeling of safety concerning their health. Patients and care givers feed a central database with some measuring equipment. The developed device allows staff to take measurements and data collected to be sent to the resident doctor. This doctor can remotely diagnose whether there is a problem that needs them to visit or that requires the resident to receive hospital treatment. By way of a PDA, the e-Vital server connects monitoring devices produced by several manufacturers. The server is a multiagent system where each agent focuses on a specific task related to the medical stored data. For example, an alert manager (specialized people in their own homes) is a multiagent framework in which agents use a restricted cooperation protocol to collectively perform classifications.

We choose a multiagent approach because these systems proved their adequacy in many health problems. Multiagent architecture is particularly adequate if the problem-solving implies the coordination of various specialized people (e.g., units of a hospital must collaborate to establish patient scheduling). Then, the agents have cooperative skills to communicate and to build together a solution. Moreover, many medical problems are complex and often standard solutions are not easy to find. A multiagent problem-solving is based on decomposition in sub-problems. Multiagent technology also proved its reliability in medical information retrieval.

12.2.1 The Pervasive Services in Home Care

According to Weiser [32], more entrenched technologies are those that disappear and are intermingled in the reality of everyday life to become invisible. Weiser's motivation was to find a way to make easier the use of computers. Today, the main purpose of pervasive computing is to improve the user experience when it comes to interaction with computer technology. Weiser quoted that pervasive systems refer to a mixture of digital and physical environments that are inhabited by computer components and communications, and integrated seamlessly with human users and their needs. Such systems make the technology transparent and allows users to concentrate on their tasks and experience. While designing pervasive services, it is necessary that the users can operate them in a enjoyable manner. Currently, pervasive systems can be found in environments such as automobiles, offices, public buildings and, of course, in our homes. Several requirements are to be met so that such systems cover a multitude of services [31] in areas such as multimedia, communications or automation, and these systems use hardware devices to provide these services. Want [30] describes that mobile devices are becoming brokers of the person and their activities, improving their efficiency during the movement. A mobile phone is experiencing almost all physical parameters that a person travelling at the same speed may experience, is exposed to the same temperature, the same sound and pollution levels and is close to the same people and equipment as its owner. Through a network of sensors registered at all the mobile owners, all users can share experiences and act accordingly.

The users can interact with the pervasive environment using different devices (PDAs, laptops, PCs, mobile, etc.). Moreover, the environment can modify its behaviour depending on the user context. As the computing and communication capabilities of the environment increase, newer service lines in mobility are achieved, either through wired or wireless access [26]. Aiming to give users the best experience possible, all devices which are surrounded must be transformed or abstracted into a communications environment that can be accessed easily and that could be used by someone without technological experience. This requires the designer to hide the terminal capabilities complexity as well as the communications variety, thereby promoting the acceptance of new terminals and new services for users, without any prior training phase. Taking into account the wide variety of communication tools available today and the diversity of contexts in which they can be used, there are innovative services that can respond to users' expectations [19]. These new and innovative services have to be smart enough:

- Understanding the context linked to a person or group of persons.
- Behave accordingly, both reactively (the service detects a change of context and adapts) and proactively (service predicts something that user does not know yet and intends to adapt their behaviour).
- Exploiting optimally communications capabilities available to the user.
- It has to be easy to use.

To implement all these concepts, pervasive services should behave according to the scheme described in Fig. 12.1. Under this scheme, services are able to learn the context of the user through a series of concepts such as location, presence, mood, sensor networks, type of terminal access, etc. Moreover, users define a profile based on their preferences [19]. By combining information on the context and the user profile, a series of rules are obtained that serve as input to the personalization process, where the service is provided to user so it is personalized and contextualized [11].

The blocks that define the pervasive services behaviour are:

- The block user context. One of the main information sources to customize services to users comes from their environment or context. The term "context awareness" refers to the ability of services to capture information from very diverse nature that is in the user environment. Some of the information sources that constitute the user context are:

  - *The location.* Important information data that can determine the service behaviour is the place where the user is at any given moment.

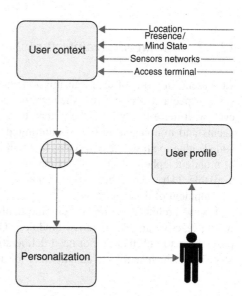

Fig. 12.1 Pervasive services behaviour

- *The presence/mind state.* The ability to report on our state is known as presence, even though the user itself determines about this information. This information can be enriched with details on our mood in a pervasive services context, which may come as determined by various sensors that analyze our behaviour and properties of the environment in which we find ourselves.
- *The access terminal.* Clearly, the terminal or terminals through which we access to services largely determine the format, quantity and quality of content they can offer.
- *The sensor networks.* The characteristics of our environment can be picked up by sensors networks, which revolutionize the way to understand and manage complex contexts. The terminals interact with the environment to obtain information from the user. They process and store without user participation that only delivered the data abstract, which leads to a better understanding of environment and better alignment of services to the context in which they are developing.

- *The user profile block.* Another information source in which a ubiquitous service must be supported to adapt to the user is the user's profile. This profile includes information that facilitates the user itself, classified into categories on their preferences and habits. Logically, the user profile information is very sensitive and must be adequately protected, so as to ensure its confidentiality. This leads us to the need to users identify, which may be done using a microchip.
- *The personalization block.* Combining information from the proper context with the user profile, we get a set of rules that allow customized services to the environment and user preferences, or even a combination of both. Some of the actions that can be carried out during this services personalization process are adapting graphical interfaces, the content adaptation and discovery and services composition.

12.2.2 Multiagent Architecture: State-of-the-Art

At present, in terms of data transmission and security, there are many problems to solve, especially derived from the technology used in their development. However, even with these limitations, the potential of wireless systems in combination with agents and multiagent systems is unlimited. The multiagent systems can provide added value to all wireless services that will be generated with the third generation of mobile telephony, so that a user can interact with a "personal agent" that will be available 24 h a day. The current technology provides the necessary basis for the development of these systems.

Hybrid architectures try to combine deliberative and reactive aspects by combining reactive and deliberative modules. The reactive modules are in charge of processing stimuli that do not need deliberation, whereas the deliberative modules determine which actions to take in order to satisfy the local and cooperative aims of the agents. The services centralization adversely affects the system functionality by limiting their capabilities. The classical architectures are characterized by modularity and structure that is oriented with the system that applies.

The aim of modern architectures like service oriented architecture (SOA) is to be able to interact among different systems by distributing resources or services without needing to consider which system they are designed for. An alternative to the SOA architectures are the multiagent systems, which can help to distribute resources and reduce the centralization of tasks. Unfortunately the complexity of designing multiagent architecture is great since there are not many tools to either help programme needs or to develop agents.

Multiagent systems combine aspects of both classical and modern architectures. The integration of multiagent systems with SOA and web services has been recently investigated [3]. Some investigators focus on the communication among both models, whereas others focus on the integration of distributed services, especially web services, in the agents' structure [5, 21, 29]. Bonino da Silva et al. [5] proposed to merge multiagent techniques with semantic web services to enable dynamic, context-aware service composition. They focus on SOA to design a multiagent service composition as an intelligent control layer, where agents discover services and adapt their behaviour and capabilities according to semantic service descriptions. Ricci et al. [21] developed a Java based framework to create SOA and Web Services compliant applications, which are modelled as agents. Communication between agents and services is done using what they call "artifacts" and Web Service Definition Language (WSDL). Shafiq et al. [25] proposed a gateway that allows interoperability between Web Services and multiagent systems. This gateway is an agent that integrates Foundation for Intelligent Physical Agents (FIPA) and W3C (The World Wide Web Consortium) specifications, translating Agent Communication Language (ACL), SOAP and WSDL messages, and combines both directories from agents' platforms and web services. Li et al. [16] proposed a similar approach, but focus on the representation of services. They used SOAP and WSDL messages to interact with agents. Liu [17] proposed a multiagent architecture to develop inter-enterprise cooperation systems using SOA and Web Services components and communication protocols. Walton [29] presented a technique to build multiagent systems using Web Services, defining a language to represent the dialogues of agents. There are also frameworks, such as Sun's Jini and IBM's WebSphere, which provide several tools to develop SOA-based systems. Jini uses Java technology to develop distributed and adaptive systems over dynamic environments. Rigole et al. [23] used Jini to create agents on demand into a home automation system, where each agent is defined as a service in the network. WebSphere provides tools for several operating systems and programming languages. However, the systems developed using the mentioned frameworks are not open at all because the framework is closed and services and applications must be programmed using a specific programming language that supports their proprietary APIs.

The works illustrated in this section provide a good base for the development of multiagent systems. However, because the majority of them are in the development stage, their full potential in a real environment is still unknown. HoCaMA has been implemented in a real environment and not only does it provide communication and integration among distributed agents, services and applications, but also provides a new method for facilitating the development of multiagent systems, thereby allowing the agents and systems to function as services. Another feature is the security, which HoCaMA manages in the multiagent framework. All communications are through agents and services cannot share resources unless the designer allows the agents. The services defined must be always available and are not shared with other systems unless otherwise specified. HoCaMA implements an alert and alarm system across the agent's platform, specially designed to be used by mobile devices. The platform agents manage this service and determine the level of alert at every moment, so that they can decide who will receive the alert and when. In order to identify each user, HoCaMA implements a system based on Java Card [34] Radio Frequency IDentification (RFID) microchip technology in which there are a series of distributed sensors that provide the necessary services to the user.

12.3   HoCaMA Architecture

The HoCaMA architecture uses a model with a series of components to offer a solution that includes different levels of service for heterogeneous systems. The model incorporates intelligent agents, identification and localization technology, wireless networks and mobile devices. Additionally, it provides access mechanisms to multiagent system services through mobile devices, such as mobiles phones or PDA. The ubiquitous access is provided via Wi-Fi wireless networks and the notification and alarm management module is based on SMS and MMS technologies. The user identification and localization system in HoCaMA are based on Java Card and RFID technologies. The system proposed within this work is dynamic, flexible, robust and very adaptable to changes of context. All these make it an open system, easy to integrate into complex environments and that it does not depend on a specific programming language.

HoCaMA architecture describes four basic blocks as depicted in Fig. 12.2: Applications, Services, Agents Platform and Communication Protocol. These four blocks constitute the whole functionality of the architecture.

12.3.1   Applications

Represent all programmes that can be used to exploit the system functionalities. Applications are dynamic and adaptable to context, reacting differently according to certain situations and the service invoked. They can be executed locally or remotely, even on mobile devices with limited processing capabilities because computing tasks are largely delegated to the agents and services.

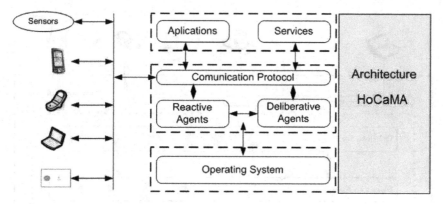

Fig. 12.2 HoCaMA framework

12.3.2 Agents Platform in HoCaMA

The Agents platform is the core of the architecture and integrates two types of agents, each of which behaves differently for specific tasks, as shown in Fig. 12.3.

The first group of agents is made up of deliberative BDI agents, which are in charge of the management and coordination of all system applications and services. They are able to modify their behaviour according to the preferences and knowledge acquired in previous experiences, thereby making them capable of choosing the best solution. Deliberative agents constantly deal with information and knowledge. Because they can be executed on mobile devices, they are always available and provide ubiquitous access for the users.

The second group is made up of reactive agents. Most of the research conducted within the field of multiagent systems focuses on designing architectures that incorporate complicated negotiation schemes as well as high level task resolution, but does not focus on temporal restrictions. In general, the multiagent architectures assume a reliable channel of communication and while some establish deadlines for the interaction processes, they do not provide solutions for limiting the time the system may take to react to events.

It is possible to define a real-time agent as an agent with temporal restrictions for some of its responsibilities or tasks [14]. From this definition, we can define a real-time multiagent system (RT-MAS) as a multiagent system in which at least one of the agents is a real-time agent. The use of RT-MAS makes sense within an environment of critical temporal restrictions, where the system can be controlled by autonomous agents that need to communicate among themselves in order to improve the degree of system task completion. In this kind of environments, every agent requires autonomy as well as certain cooperation skills to achieve a common goal. In addition, it is necessary to ensure system response in real time, and avoid establishing too bulky communications between agents.

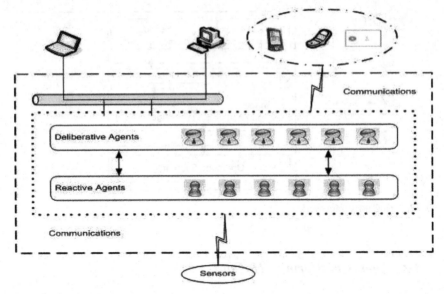

Fig. 12.3 Agents platform structure in the HoCaMA architecture

There are different kinds of agents in the architecture, each one with specific roles, capabilities and characteristics. This fact facilitates the flexibility of the architecture to incorporate new agents. However, there are predefined agents which provide the basic functionalities of the architecture.

12.3.2.1 CoAp Agent

This agent is responsible for all communications between applications and the platform. It manages the incoming requests from the applications to be processed by services, and responses from services to applications. CoAp Agent is always on "listening mode." Applications send XML messages to the agent requesting for a service, then the agent creates a new thread to start communication using sockets. The agent sends all requests to the Manager Agent, which processes the request. The socket remains open until a response to the specific request is sent back to the application using another XML message. All messages are sent to the Security Agent to analyze their structure and syntax.

12.3.2.2 CoSe Agent

It is responsible for all communications between services and the platform. The functionalities are similar to CommApp Agent, but backwards. This agent is always on "listening mode" waiting for responses of services. Manager Agent indicates

CommServ Agent the service that must be invoked. Then, CommServ Agent creates a new thread with its respective socket and sends an XML message to the service. The socket remains open until the service returns a response. All messages are sent to the Security Agent to analyze their structure and syntax. This agent also checks periodically the status of all services to know if they are idle, busy or crashed.

12.3.2.3   Directory Agent

Manages the list of services that can be used by the system. For security reasons, the list of services is static and can only be modified manually. However, services can be added, erased or modified dynamically. The list contains the information of all trusted available services. The name of the service, description of the service, parameters required and IP address of the computer where the service is running are some of the information stored in the list of services. However, there is dynamic information that is constantly modified: the service performance (average time to respond requests), the number of executions and the quality of the service. This last data is very important, assigning a value between 0 and 1 to all services. All new services have a quality of service (QoS) value set to 1 and this value decreases when the service fails (e.g. service crashes, no service found, etc.), or have a subpar performance compared to similar executions in the past. QoS is increased each time the service processes the tasks assigned efficiently. Information management is especially important in AmI environments because of the sensitivity of the personal data processed. Thus, security must be a major concern when developing AmI-based systems and this is the main reason why HoCaMA does not implement a service discovery mechanism, so that systems must employ only the specified services at a trusted list of services. However, agents can select the most appropriate service (or group of services) to accomplish a specific task.

12.3.2.4   Supervisor Agent

This agent supervises the correct functioning of the agents in the system. Supervisor Agent verifies periodically the status of all agents registered in the architecture by means of sending ping messages. If there is no response, the agent kills the agent and creates another instance of that agent.

12.3.2.5   Security Agent

This agent analyzes the structure and syntax of all incoming and outgoing XML messages. If a message is not correct, the Security Agent informs the corresponding agent (CoAp or CoSe) that the message cannot be delivered. This agent also informs the problem to the Directory Agent, which modifies the QoS of the service where message was sent.

12.3.2.6   Manager Agent

Decides which agent must be called taking into account the QoS and users' preferences. Users can explicitly invoke a service, or can let the Manager Agent decide which service is better to accomplish the requested task. If there are several services that can resolve the task requested by an application, the agent selects the optimal choice. An optimal choice has higher QoS and better performance. Manager Agent has a routing list to manage messages from all applications and services. This agent also checks if services are working properly. It requests the CoSe Agent to send regularly ping messages to each service. If a service does not respond, CoSe informs Manager Agent, which tries to find an alternate service and informs the Directory Agent to modify the respective QoS.

12.3.2.7   Interface Agent

This kind of agent has been designed to be embedded in users' applications. Interface agents communicate directly with the agents in HoCaMA, so there is no need to employ the communication protocol, but FIPA ACL specification. The requests are sent directly to the Security Agent, which analyzes the requests and sends them to the Manager Agent. The rest of the process follows the same guidelines to call any service. Interface agents must be simple enough to allow them execute on mobile devices, such as cell phones or PDAs. All high demanding processes must be delegated to services.

12.3.3   Services

Represent the activities that the architecture offers. They are the bulk of functionalities of the system at processing, delivery and acquire information level. Services are designed to be invoked locally or remotely. Services can be organized as local services, web services, GRID services or even as individual stand alone services. Services can make use of other services to provide the functionalities that users require. HoCaMA has a flexible and scalable directory of services, so they can be invoked, modified, added or eliminated dynamically and on demand. It is absolutely necessary that all services follow the communication protocol to interact with the rest of the architecture components.

HoCaMA measures and collects data through sensors and mobile devices, as illustrated in Fig. 12.4. A simple case depicted in Fig. 12.4 can better demonstrate the basic functioning of HoCaMA when it is requesting a service. A user needs to calculate the sum of two numbers and wants to do it through a PDA remotely connected to the system. The user executes a mathematical tool kit, which provides him/her with a large set of formulas from which the user selects the sum function, introduces a set of values and clicks a button to get the results. When the user clicks

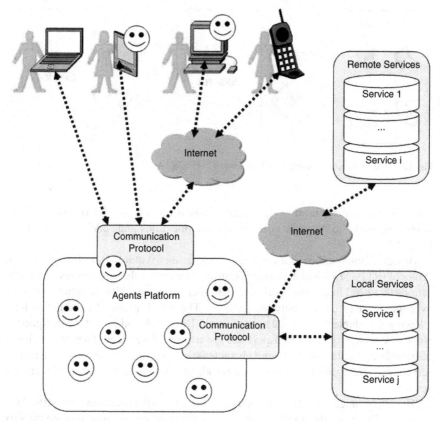

Fig. 12.4 Request a service by an application

the button, the application sends a request to the platform to find a service that can process that request. The agents invoke the appropriate service and send the request. The service processes the request and sends the result back to the agents, which, in turn, send it to the application. It is obvious that invoking a remote service to execute a sum is not the best choice. But imagine a large scale process that uses complex AI techniques, such as genetic algorithms, data mining tools, neural networks, etc., where the limited processing capacity of the PDA makes it impossible to calculate. In this case, the service may be provided by a powerful computer and could be remotely invoked by the PDA.

12.3.4   HoCaMA Communication Protocol

Communication protocol allows applications, services and sensors to be connected directly to the platform agents. The protocol presented in this work is open and

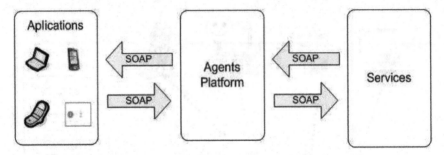

Fig. 12.5 Communication using SOAP messages in HoCaMA

independent of programming languages. It is based on the SOAP standard and allows messages to be exchanged between applications and services as shown in Fig. 12.5.

However, interaction with environmental sensors requires Real-time Transport Protocol (RTP) [13], which provides transport functions that are adapted for applications that need to transmit real-time data such as audio, video or simulation data, over multicast or unicast network services. The RTCP protocol is added to RTP, allowing a scalable form of data supervision. Both RTP and RTCP are designed to work independently of the transport and lower network services. They are in charge of transporting data with real-time characteristics, and of supervising the quality of service and managing the information for all the entities taking part in the current session.

The communications between agents within the platforms follow the FIPA ACL standard. This way, the applications can use the platform to communicate directly with the agents.

12.3.5 Location and Identification System in HoCaMA

The location and identification system in HoCaMA incorporates Java Card [34] and RFID [12, 28] technologies. The primary purpose of the system is to convey the identity of an object or person, as with a unique serial number, using radio waves. Java Card is a technology that permits small Java applications (applets) to be run safely in microchip smart cards and similar embedded devices. Java Card gives the user the ability to programme applications that can be run off a card so that it has a practical function in a specific application domain.

12.3.5.1 Identification System, Features and Operation

Java virtual machine (JVM) is seen as part of the operating system, called memory ROM in a smart card Java. The JVM is divided into two parts: the converter and

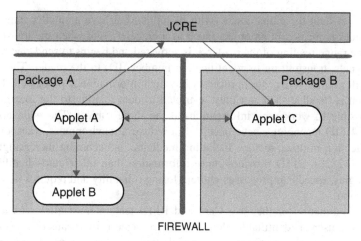

Fig. 12.6 "Firewall Model" for security in Java Card

runtime (JCRE). The converter, located in the external reader that connects to the card, makes the verification and translates byte code (compiled code) to a code inserted into the card. The JCRE, called on the card, manages the installation process, selection, deselect, execution and removal of an applet.

The main features of Java Card are portability and security as described in ISO 7816. Portability because the definition of standard Java Card applet allows the same function in different microchip, much like a Java applet running on different computers. The security is determined by various aspects such as an applet that is a state machine that only processes commands received via the device reader sending and responding with status codes and data. The different applications (applets) are also separated from each other by a firewall, as shown in Fig. 12.6, which limits access and control of data elements of a subprogramme to another. Each instance of AID or applet has its unique identifier through which they are selected. The applet is responsible for their data processing commands, elements which publishes and security in the data sharing. As shown in Fig. 12.6, the applet A and B share the same applet context and data, while the applet A shares data with the applet C at different context. The data are stored in the application and the Java Card applications are executed in an isolated environment, separate from the operating system and from computer that reads the card. The most commonly used algorithms, such as DES, 3DES, AES, and RSA, are cryptographically implemented in Java Card. Other services such as electronic signature or key generation are also supported.

RFID technology is grouped into the so-called automatic identification technologies. The RFID [12] is a wireless communication technology used to identify and receive information on humans, animals or objects in motion [28]. An RFID system consists principally of four elements: tags, readers, antennas and radios and Processing Hardware. The labels or RFID chips are passive (without batteries) and are called transponders [28]. The transponders are much cheaper and have a size smaller than the chips assets (with batteries), but have a smaller range. The transponder is located in an object (such as a bracelet), and when the transponder enters the range reading of the reader, it is activated and begins to send electromagnetic signals, transmitting its identification number (ID) to the reader. The reader relays information to a central processor in which information is processed. The information is handled; it is not only restricted to data relating to the location, but it is possible to work with information on the same subject. The main applications of RFID technology have occurred in industrial environment, transport, etc. Its application in other sectors, including medicine, is becoming increasingly important [12, 28]. RFID provides more information than other auto-identification technologies, speeds up processes without losing reliability and requires no human intervention.

The combination of the Java Card and RFID technologies allows us to both identify the user or identifiable element, and to locate it by means of sensors and actuators within the environment, at which time we can act on it and provide services. The microchip, which contains the identification data of the object to which it is adhered, generates a radio frequency signal with these data. The signal can be picked up by an RFID reader, which is responsible for reading the information and sending it in digital format to the specific application. In this sense, RFID is an automated data-capture technology that can be used to electronically identify, track and store information about patients. It is most frequently used in industrial/manufacturing, transportation, distribution and warehousing industries; however, there are other growth sectors including health care. HoCaMA uses microchips mounted on bracelets worn on the patient's wrist or ankle, and sensors installed over protected zones with an adjustable capture range up to 2 m. The microchips or transponders help locate the patients, which can be ascertained by consulting the deliberative agents.

12.3.6 Alert System in HoCaMA

The alert system is integrated into the HoCaMA architecture and uses mobile technology to inform users about alerts, warnings and information specific to the daily routine of the application environment. It aims to improve the service quality of communication and control at all times the performance of services that are implemented in architecture.

This is a very configurable system that allows users to select the type of information they are interested, and to receive it immediately on their mobile phone or PDA. It places the information to be sent into information categories. The users determine the information they are interested in. The system automatically sends the information to each of the users as soon as it is available.

12.3.6.1 Alert System Features

The user wishing to be entered in this service must register indicating his/her phone number and email address and giving the designer's permission to send messages to him/her. It can do so through the application that implements the service validated as users of the same.

From the application perspective, users can select which categories of information they wish to receive, so that they only receive the information that are really useful.

The alert system is proactive, i.e., users should not bother to monitor the environment in which the service is implemented to see if there is information that is interesting for them. It alerts the system itself, which cares for users to get information immediately on their mobile devices, with the benefits that this entails, so that they can get all these information without having to meet. The application also automatically generates alert messages and warnings, which can also send information on time or as scheduled. The application define a number of operators and reviewers of information that are responsible for inserting and sending messages to users who wish to receive such information.

The service alerts and warnings are composed as a sub-application within architecture HoCaMA, but can operate independently of this. The application is implemented with the Struts. It is based on pattern model-view-controller (MVC). This pattern of development allows us to completely detach three layers that make up the entire web. A model of this type allows the application fully scalable. As shown in Fig. 12.7, the bold lines indicate a direct association and dashed lines represent an indirect association.

- Model. This layer represents the data model of the application. This is for communication at all levels with the database.
- View. This is the presentation layer to the user. This is where the data are joined with the design chosen for the user accessing the information. In this layer, one can detect a type of client accessing data to personalize their presentation giving rise to language versions or versions for different channels such as PDA, SMS, WAP, etc.

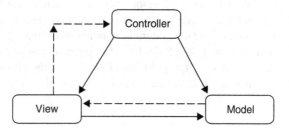

Fig. 12.7 Relationship between the model/view/controller in the model model-view-controller

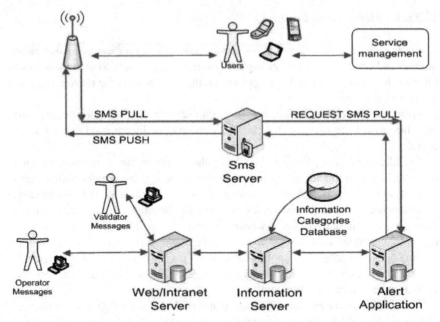

Fig. 12.8 Alert system framework

- Controller. Here comes the user communication with the application. Every action required by the user is reflected in a flood of calls to data model from the control layer.

Within the application as shown in Fig. 12.8, there are three profiles clearly differentiated, but not exclusive. The application profiles types are: users or subscribers, issuers and reviewers messages. Subscribers have to accept the conditions of the subscription service to introduce or modify their personal data and subscribe to categories wished. Issuers are responsible for writing messages and confirmation for subsequent validation. Each issuer sends information only to categories assigned to it. The reviewers are responsible for validating, if necessary, the messages issued by issuers. The reviewers only review messages of assignment categories.

On the other side, as shown in Fig. 12.8, system also handles requests for information by the user via mobile devices, which are called SMS PULL. The messages are sent to a special issue with a specific text, which depends on the information you want to ask, and the system is responsible for managing and providing the information requested. The SMS PUSH is generated by the system automatically without the user's explicit request. Fig. 12.9 depicts the options available for a reviewer of user messages on the alerts system described.

Fig. 12.9 Alert system implemented in HoCaMA

12.4   Using HoCaMA to Develop a MultiAgent System for a Home Care Environment

AmI-based systems aim to improve people's quality of life, offering more efficient and easy to use services and communication tools to interact with other people, systems and environments. One of the most benefited segments of population with the development of AmI-based systems is elderly and disabled people.

Agents and multiagent systems in environments for disabled people are becoming a reality, especially on health care. Most agents-based applications are related to the use of this technology in patients monitoring, treatment supervision and data mining.

HoCaMA has been employed to develop a multiagent system to enhance assistance and care for low dependence patients at their homes. As shown in Fig. 12.10, a series of detectors are installed to monitor presence and mechanisms for opening doors that interact with the microchip Java Card users to offer services in real time. This sensor network through a system of alerts is responsible for generating alarms comparing the user's current state with the parameters of the user's daily routine, which is stored in the system. The system can generate alarms if it is determined that the parameters, for example, if the user in a non-working day stands before a certain hour, or if the user spends more time than specified on the door of one's home without entering, or the user is a long time motionless in the hallway, etc.

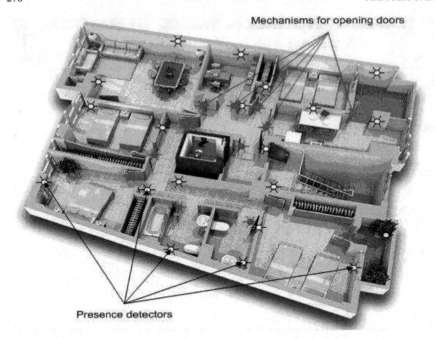

Fig. 12.10 Home plane

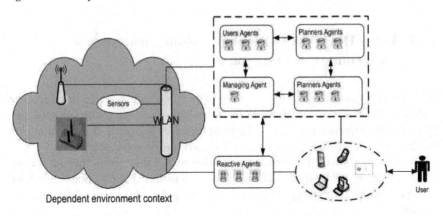

Fig. 12.11 HoCaMA structure in a home care environment for handicapped persons

Main functionalities of the system include reasoning, planning mechanisms, management alerts and responses in execution time offered to certain stimuli, as shown in Fig. 12.11. These functionalities allow the system the use of several context-aware technologies to acquire information from users and their environment. Among the technologies used are mobile systems for alerts service managing across PDA and mobile phones, Java Card elements for identification and presence detectors and access control.

Each agent in the system has its own functionalities. If an agent needs to develop a task in collaboration with other agent, a request form is send. There are priority tasks that a set of agents can perform. This ensures that the priority tasks are always available.

There are four types of new deliberative BDI agents, which have been defined in this case study:

- User Agents. This agent manages the users' personal data and behaviour (monitoring, location, daily tasks and anomalies). The beliefs and goals used for every user depend on the plan or plans defined by the super-users. User Agent maintains continuous communication with the rest of the system agents, especially with the ScheduleUser Agent (through which the scheduled-users can communicate the result of their assigned tasks) and with the SuperUser Agent. The User Agent must ensure that all the actions indicated by the SuperUser are carried out, sending a copy of its memory base (goals and plans) to the Manager Agent in order to maintain backups. There is one agent for each patient registered in the system.

- SuperUser Agent. It also runs on mobile devices (PDA) and inserts new tasks into the Manager Agent to be processed by a case-based reasoning (CBR) mechanism. It also needs to interact with the User Agents to impose new tasks and receive periodic reports, and with the ScheduleUser Agents to ascertain plans' evolution. There is one agent for each doctor connected to the system.

- ScheduleUser Agent. It is a BDI agent with a case-based planning (CBP) mechanism embedded in its structure. It schedules the users' daily activities obtaining dynamic plans depending on the tasks needed for each user. It manages scheduled-users profiles (preferences, habits, holidays, etc.), tasks, available time and resources. Every agent generates personalized plans depending on the scheduled-user profile. There are as many ScheduleUser Agents as nurses connected to the system. Fig. 12.12 shows the algorithm for plans generation and promotes interaction between actors and sensors. In the algorithm shown in Fig. 12.12, plans are generated when an existing plan is not currently being executed and when actions are executed. When a plan is executed, actions are suppressed and plans are executed to completion. Actions and plans are selected on the basis of respective utility functions. It is part of a state and an action generated by the agent. It changes the objectives if there is no plan of action in implementing the plan of selecting optimal action. If the plan being implemented is associated with an action, the plan can be added or create a new action plan to save the platform agents. Finally runs action.

- Manager Agent. It runs on a Workstation and plays two roles: the security role that monitors the users' location and physical building status (temperature, lights, alarms, etc.) through a continuous communication with the Devices Agent; and the manager role that handles the databases and the tasks assignment. It must provide security for the users and ensure the tasks assignments are efficient. This assignment is carried out through a CBR mechanism, which is incorporated within the Manager Agent. When a new assignment of tasks needs to be

```
program generatePlan ()


    for each state (s), action (A) generate by ag-BDI
    do
        //modify the set of objectives (O) (pe.
        //goals regarding the current situation,
        //denote by (s, A) associated with a plan
        //to the state denoted by (Ps))
        modifyTarget(s, A);
        for each target asset (Oa)
        do
            Calculate Utility(a) y Utility(Ps)
            if there is no running a plan then
                Select a plan Ps: Ps ={A1,A2,…,Ac,…,Af}
                where Ac is the current step Ps y Af is the
                last step Ps
            end if;
            if Utility(Ps) > Utility(Af) and there is
            running a plan then
                Running Ac, where Ac is in Ps;
            else Utility(Ps) < Utility(Af) if then
                if There is a plan Pe which can be added
                    Af (Pe,Af) then
                    add Af with step of Pe;
                else
                    create a new plan Pn;
                    add Af to Pn: Pn = {Af};
                end if;
                running Af;
            end if;
        end for;
    end for;

end;
```

Fig. 12.12 Algorithm for plan generation in HoCaMA

carried out, both past experiences and the needs of the current situation are re-called, allocating the respective and adequate task. There is just one Manager Agent running in the system.

On the other hand, there are a number of reactive agents that work in collabo-ration with the deliberative agents. Reactive agents are in charge of control devices interacting with sensors (access points, lights, temperature, alarms detection, etc.). They receive information, monitor environment services and also check the devices status connected to the system. All information is treated by the reactive agent and sent to the manager agent to be processed.

In Fig. 12.13, it is possible to see an example corresponding to a warning gen-erated by the system. The system generates the alert after detecting that the user is motionless in the hallway of his home longer than as determined by the parameters of a normal situation. The sensors determine all the time the patient's condition at

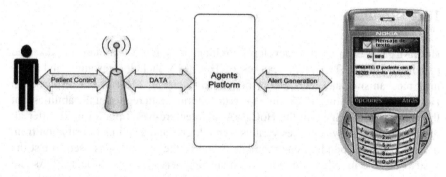

Fig. 12.13 Alert SMS example sent by the system

```
program sendAlert()

   sms = 0;
   for each sms Ready to send(s)
   do
      cat = getCategory(s);
      if thereareSubscribed(cat) then
         for each suscribe in the category(sus)
            mov = dataSuscribe(sus);
            sendSms(mov, s);
            sms = sms + 1;
         end for;
         //modify state sms to send
         modifyState(s);
      else
         // inform manager that there is no subscriber
         //in the category
         informAdmin(cat);
      end if;
   end for;

   //add sms send
   addData(sms);
end;
```

Fig. 12.14 Algorithm form sending alerts in HoCaMA

home and communicate this information to a reactive agent, identified as the user agent. The user agent is in charge to send all the sensor information to the central system and determines if it is necessary to generate an alert. When the user agent detects a warning, it automatically communicates the situation to the manager agent. Finally the manager agent, through the SMS alert system available, sends the warning SMS message to the health care centre and to the patient's family. This warning is recorded in the system for security reasons and for future statistical controls. The steps are illustrated in Fig. 12.14, which shows the action of sending a warning by the agent manager.

12.5 Results

HoCaMA has been used to develop a multiagent system for monitoring disabled patients at home. The main features of HoCaMA include reasoning and planning mechanisms, and alert and response management. Most of the responses in HoCaMA are reactions in real time to certain stimuli, and represent the abilities that the reactive agents have in the HoCaMA architecture-based platform. To offer all these features, the system uses various technologies and acquires information from users and the surrounding environment. Some of the technologies used to test the system include mobile technology for managing service alerts through PDAs and mobile phones, and Java Card technology for identification and access control.

One of the main contributions of the HoCaMA architecture is the alert system. We implemented several test cases to evaluate the management of alerts integrated into the system. This allowed us to determine the response time for warnings generated by the users, for which the results were very satisfactory, with response times shorter than those obtained prior to the implementation of HoCaMA. The system studies the information collected and applies a reasoning process, which allows alerts to be automatically generated. For the alerts, the system not only takes response time into account, but also the time elapsed between alerts, and the user's profile and reliability in order to generalize reactions to common situations. The results show that HoCaMA fits perfectly within complex systems by correctly exploiting services and planning mechanisms.

Table 12.1 presents the results obtained after comparing the HoCaMA architecture to the previously developed ALZ-MAS architecture [6] in a case study on medical care for patients at home. The ALZ-MAS architecture allows the monitoring of patients in geriatric residences, but home care is carried out through traditional methods. The case study presented in this work consisted of analyzing the functioning of both architectures in a test environment. The HoCaMA architecture was implemented in the home of five patients and was tested for 30 days. The results were very promising. The data shown in Table 12.1 are the results obtained from the test cases. They show that the alert system improved the communication between the user and the handicapped care services providers, whose work performance improved, allowing them to avoid unnecessary movements, such as travels and visits simply oriented to control or supervise the patient. The user identification and location system in conjunction with the alert system have helped to notably reduce the percentage of incidents in the environment under study. Moreover, in addition

Table 12.1 Comparison between the HoCaMA and the ALZ-MAS architectures

Factor	HoCaMA	ALZ-MAS
Average response time to incidents (min)	8	14
Assisted incidents	12	17
Average number of daily planned tasks	12	10
Average number of daily services completed	46	32
Time employed to attend and alert (min)	75	90

to a reduction in the number of incidents, the time elapsed between the generation of a warning and solution decreased significantly. Finally, due to the many improvements, the level of user satisfaction increased with the introduction of HoCaMA architecture, since patients can live in their own homes with the same level of care as those offered at the hospital.

12.6   Conclusions

The growing number of elderly population imposes an urgent need to develop new approaches to care provision. The convergence of a number of technologies, such as multiagent systems, federated information management, safe communications, hypermedia interfaces, rich sensorial environments, increased intelligence of home appliances, and collaborative virtual environments, represents an important enabling factor for the design and development of virtual elderly support community environments. In particular, a platform based on agents, combined with federated information management mechanisms, provides a flexible infrastructure on top of which specialized care services can be built. Participants in this community include the elderly people, their relatives, and care centre personnel as shown in Fig. 12.15. We chose to tackle the home-monitoring issue in a more global way, rather than in an only individual-centred way. This collective vision makes it possible to release individuals' patterns that will allow the system answering current health problems. This large-scale and global solution requires the setting up of a strongly distributed and dynamic system. Since conventional classification methods are not adapted to this context, we had to propose a new distributed classification method.

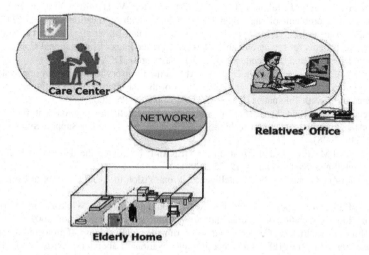

Fig. 12.15 Actors' communications in HoCaMA

The HoCaMA architecture presented in this paper is a step ahead in the development of AmI environments for Home Care. The architecture proposes novel systems for alert management and patient location and identification. However, there is still too much work to be done, for example, focusing on patients' attention and safety. That is our next step.

Acknowledgments This work has been partially supported by the Spanish Ministry of Science and Technology project TIN2006-14630-C03-03, the UPSA project U05EIA-07L01 and the Spanish Ministry of Labor and Social Security project "Plataforma inteligente para la gestión integral de residencia geriátricas."

References

1. Anastasopoulos M., Niebuhr D., Bartelt C., Koch J. and Rausch A.: Towards a reference middleware architecture for ambient intelligence systems. In: ACM Conference on Object-Oriented Programming, Systems, Languages, and Applications (2005)
2. Angulo C. and Tellez R.: Distributed intelligence for smart home appliances. In: Giráldez R., Riquelme J.C. and Aguilar-Ruiz J.S. (Eds.). Tendencias de la minería de datos en Espaa. Red Española de Minería de Datos, pp. 1–12 (2004)
3. Ardissono L., Petrone G. and Segnan M.: A conversational approach to the interaction with Web Services. In: Computational Intelligence, Blackwell Publishing, Malden, vol. 20, 693–709 (2004)
4. Bahadori S., Cesta A., Grisetti G., Iocchi L., Leone R., Nardi D., Oddi A., Pecora F. and Rasconi R.: RoboCare: pervasive intelligence for the domestic care of the elderly. Artificial Intelligence 1(1), 16–21 (2003)
5. Bonino da Silva L.O., Ramparany F., Dockhorn P., Vink P., Etter R. and Broens T.: A service architecture for context awareness and reaction provisioning. In: IEEE Congress on Services, Salt Lake City, UT, pp. 25–32 (2007)
6. Carrascosa C., Bajo J., Julián V., Corchado J.M. and Botti V.: Hybrid multi-agent architecture as a real-time problem-solving model. Expert Systems with Applications 34(1), 2–17 (2008)
7. Cesta A., Bahadori S., Cortellesa G., Grisetti G., Giuliani M., et al.: The RoboCare project, cognitive systems for the care of the elderly. In: Proceedings of International Conference on Aging, Disability and Independence (ICADI), Washington, DC (2003)
8. Chan M., Campo E. and Estéve D.: PROSAFE, a multisensory remote monitoring system for the elderly or the handicapped. In: Proceedings of the 1st International Conference on Smart Homes and Health Telematics (ICOST '03), Paris, pp. 89–95 (2003)
9. Corchado J.M., Bajo J., de Paz Y. and Tapia D.: Intelligent environment for monitoring Alzheimer patients, agent technology for health care. Decision Support Systems 34(2), 382–396 (2008)
10. Corchado J.M., Bajo J. and Abraham A.: GERAmI: improving the delivery of health care. IEEE Intelligent Systems 23(2), 19–25 (2008)
11. IST Advisory Group: Ambient Intelligence: From Vision to Reality. European Commission (2003)
12. ITAA: Radio Frequency Identification. RFID...coming of age. In: White Paper, Information Technology Association of America. http://www.itaa.org/rfid/docs/rfid.pdf (2004)
13. Jacobsen V., Fredrick R., Casner S. and Schulzrinne H.: RTP: a transport protocol for real-time applications. In: RFC 1889. Lawrence Berkeley National Laboratory, Xerox PARC, Precept Software Inc., GMD Fokus, January 1996. Online. Internet. Available via DIALOG. http://www.connect.org.uk./teckwatch/cgi-bin/rfcshow?1889

14. Julián V. and Botti V.: Developing real-time multi-agent systems. Integrated Computer-Aided Engineering **11**(2), 135–149 (2004)
15. Kleindienst J., Macek T., Seredi L. and Sedivy J.: Vision-enhanced multi-modal interactions in domotic environments. In: 8th ERCIM Workshop "User Interfaces for All." Available via DIALOG. http://www.ui4all.gr/workshop2004/ (2004)
16. Li Y., Shen W. and Ghenniwa H.: Agent-based web services framework and development environment. Computational Intelligence **20**(4), 678–692 (2004)
17. Liu X.: A multi-agent-based service-oriented architecture for inter-enterprise co-operation system. In: Proceedings of the Second International Conference on Digital Tele-communications (ICDT'07). IEEE Computer Society, Washington, DC (2007)
18. Mengual L., Bobadilla J. and Triviño G.: A fuzzy multi-agent system for secure remote control of a mobile guard robot. In: Second International Atlantic Web Intelligence Conference, AWIC 2004. Lecture Notes in Computer Science, vol. 3034, Springer, Heidelberg, pp. 44–53 (2004)
19. Moreno A. and Garbay C.: Special issue on software agents in health care. Artificial Intelligence in Medicine **27** (2003)
20. Noury N., Villemazet C., Barralon P. and Rumeau P.: Ambient multi-perceptive system for residential health monitoring based on electronic mailings experimentation within the AILISA project. In: Proceedings of the 8th IEEE International Conference on e-Health Net-working, Applications and Services (HEALTHCOM '06), New Delhi, pp. 95–100 (2006)
21. Ricci A., Buda C. and Zaghini N.: An agent-oriented programming model for SOA and web services. In: 5th IEEE International Conference on Industrial Informatics, pp. 1059–1064 (2007)
22. Richter K. and Hellenschmidt M.: Interacting with the ambience: multimodal interaction and ambient intelligence. In: Position Paper to the W3C Workshop on Multimodal Interaction, pp. 19–20 (2004)
23. Rigole P., Holvoet T. and Berbers Y.: Using Jini to integrate home automation in a distributed software-system. In: 4th International Workshop on Distributed Communities in the Web. Lecture Notes in Computer Science, vol. 2468, Springer, Heidelberg, pp. 291–304 (2002)
24. Sakka E., Prentza A., Lamprinos I.E., Leondaridis L. and Koutsouris D.: Integration of monitoring devices in the e-Vital service. In: Proceedings of the 26th Annual International Conference of the IEEE Engineering in Medicine and Biology Society (IEMBS '04), vol. 4, San Francisco, CA, pp. 3097–3100 (2004)
25. Shafiq M.O., Ding Y. and Fensel D.: Bridging multi agent systems and web services: towards interoperability between software agents and semantic web services. In: Proceedings of the 10th IEEE International Enterprise Distributed Object Computing Conference (EDOC'06). IEEE Computer Society, Washington, DC, pp. 85–96 (2006)
26. Tafazolli R. and Saarnio J.: eMobility: Mobile and Wireless Communications Technology Platform. Strategic Research Agenda. Versin 4 (2005)
27. Tapia D.I., Bajo J., De Paz F. and Corchado J.M.: Hybrid multiagent system for Alzheimer health care. In: Bajo J., Corchado E.S., Herrero Á. and Corchado J.M. (Eds.). Hybrid Artificial Intelligence Systems. HAIS 2006. Universidad de Salamanca, pp. 1–18 (2006)
28. U.S. Department of Commerce: Radio Frequency Identification. Opportunities and Challenges in Implementation. Available via DIALOG. http://www.technology.gov/ reports/2005/ (2005)
29. Walton C.: Agency and the Semantic Web. Oxford University Press, Oxford (2006)
30. Want R.: You are your cell phone. IEEE Pervasive Computing **7**(2), 2–4 (2008)
31. Want R., Pering T., Borriello G. and Farkas K.I.: Disappearing hardware. IEEE Pervasive Computing **1**(1), 36–47 (2002)
32. Weiser M.: The computer for the twenty-first century. Scientific American **265**, 94–104 (1991)
33. Wooldridge M.: An Introduction to MultiAgent Systems. Wiley, Chichester (2002)
34. Zhiqun C.: Java Card Technology for Smart Cards. Prentice-Hall, Boston (2000)

Part III
Web Service and Situation Awareness in Pervasive Computing

Chapter 13
Semantic Annotation for Web Service Processes in Pervasive Computing

Ivan Di Pietro, Francesco Pagliarecci, and Luca Spalazzi

Abstract In this chapter, we propose a new approach to the discovery, the selection and the automated composition of distributed processes in a pervasive computing environment, described as semantic web services through a new semantic annotation. In our approach, we map a process in a pervasive computing environment into a state transition system (STS) and semantically annotate it with a minimal set of ontological descriptions. This novel approach allows us to separate reasoning about processes and reasoning about ontologies. As a consequence, we can perform a limited, but efficient and still useful semantic reasoning for verifying, discovering, selecting and composing web services at the process level. The key idea is to keep separate the procedural and the ontological descriptions and link them through semantic annotations. We define the formal framework, and propose a technique that can exploit simple reasoning mechanisms at the ontological level, integrated with effective reasoning mechanisms devised for procedural descriptions of web services.

Keywords Pervasive computing · Web service · Semantic annotation

13.1 Introduction

Pervasive computing is defined as a set of devices and applications designed to be integrated into everyday life [23, 29]. Pervasive computing implies distributed and decentralized computing, and as a consequence, we have a set of decoupled computational resources. Until now, the software component of pervasive computing has featured a variety of incompatible solutions, each tailored for a specific niche. Furthermore, pervasive computing raises numerous challenges regarding discovery, selection and composition. In this respect, web services represent for pervasive computing the opportunity to mitigate these interoperability problems [3, 12]. Nevertheless, from one hand, the current approaches to automatically discover,

I. Di Pietro (✉)
Università Politecnica delle Marche, Ancona, Italy
e-mail: dipietro@diiga.univpm.it

A.-E. Hassanien et al. (eds.), *Pervasive Computing: Innovations in Intelligent Multimedia and Applications*, Computer Communications and Networks, DOI 10.1007/978-1-84882-599-4_13, © Springer-Verlag London Limited 2009

select and compose web services do not take into account semantics, and on the other hand, the current approaches to semantic web services are too complex for a practical use in pervasive computing. The objective of our work is to integrate semantical and procedural descriptions of web services in an efficient and still effective way. Therefore, the contribution of this chapter consists of a new minimalist (and thus efficient) approach to semantic annotation of web services.

The importance of describing web services at the *process-level* is widely recognized, a witness being the standard languages for describing business processes, like Business Process Execution Language (BPEL) [2], and the most popular standards for semantic web services, like Ontology Web Language for Services (OWL-S) [9] and Web Service Modelling Ontology (WSMO) [25]. In a process-level description, a web service is not simply represented as an "atomic" component – with its inputs, outputs, preconditions and effects – that can be executed in a single step. Instead, the interface of the service describes its behaviour, i.e., a process that interacts with other services in different steps and can have different control constructs, e.g., sequence, condition and iteration. BPEL is going to become a *de facto* standard in process representation. It does not deal with semantic web services, but provides us with the behavioural description of a web service in terms of basic control structures, service invocations and message exchanging. In OWL-S, an ontology about services written in Ontology Web Language (OWL) [17], even processes are described as ontologies, and therefore, there is no way to separate reasoning about processes and reasoning about ontologies. In WSMO, proccesses are represented as Abstract State Machines, a well known and general formalism to describe dynamic behaviours. The underlying idea is that variables of Abstract State Machines are all defined in terms of the WSMO ontological language. Once we have a behavioural model of a service, we can exploit it to perform verification, discovery, selection and composition tasks and to express requirements at process level (e.g., see [1]). This is especially true for composition as witnessed by [4, 14, 15, 18]. Some approaches do not deal with semantic web services and cannot, thus, exploit the ability to do reasoning about what services do. This is the case of techniques for composing BPEL processes [15] and of theoretical frameworks for the composition of services represented as finite state automata [4, 14]. From the other side, the approaches that have been proposed so far to exploit semantics (see, e.g., [18,25]) describe processes with comprehensive ontologies. They have the practical disadvantage to require long descriptions that are time- and effort- consuming, and that are very hard to propose in practice for industrial applications. Such semantic descriptions of web services are based on expressive languages, such as OWL or WSMO [25], which require complex reasoning mechanism. Indeed, for instance, the OWL family of languages is based on the description logics $\mathcal{SHIQ}$ and $\mathcal{SHIOQ}$, which have reasoning services that are EXPTime and NEXPTime, respectively [26].

We have proposed a selection algorithm [11, 20] and a composition algorithm [22] that exploit a minimalist semantic annotation of web services. In this chapter, we formally define the notion of enriching the representation of web services with a semantically annotated behavioural description and the grounding algorithm that is needed for discovery, selection, verification and composition. According to the line described in [11, 20, 22], the key idea is to keep separate the procedural description of processes and their ontological descriptions, and adding semantic annotations that link the two. Therefore, the main aspects of this chapter are the following:

- The procedural behaviour of a web service is described with languages that have been designed to describe processes; in this chapter, we refer to BPEL [2]. A BPEL process can be formally modelled as a state transition system (STS) [15].
- The data exchanged among processes are described in a standard file Web Service Description Language (WSDL).
- The semantics of exchanged data are described in a separate ontological language. The language we use is Web Service Modelling Language (WSML) [25] that belongs to the Description Logic family [26].
- We define an annotation language that allows us to link data (WSDL) and behavioural (BPEL) definitions of the process with ontology elements (WSMO). The language is based on XML and from a theoretical point of view, it belongs to the assertional part of the a Description Logic. Annotations are necessary to give semantics to the exchanged data (e.g., what relations exist between the data given in input to the service and the data received as answers from the service), as well as to define the effects and outcomes of the service executions (e.g., to identify the successful executions of the service and distinguish them from the failures, and to describe the effects associated to the successful executions). This approach allows us to annotate only what we need and leave to BPEL the duty of describing the behaviour.
- We define a language that can express requirements on the behaviour of the service that has to be verified, selected or composed. The language is a temporal logic based on Computation Tree Logic (CTL) [13], enriched with concept and role assertions of a Description Logic.
- We propose a grounding algorithm that includes semantic annotations in the STS that models the web services. This allows us to obtain an STS model processable by existing model checkers (e.g.,[8]) and planners (e.g., [5]) to solve verification, selection and composition problems.

The chapter is structured in the following manner. In Sect. 13.2, we provide an overview of our approach and a brief introduction to the case study that is used along all the chapter. Section 13.3 contains the schema (XSD) of the annotation file and some examples. In Sect. 13.4, we define semantically annotated state transition systems (ASTSs) that describe BPEL processes and semantically annotated conditions. In Sect. 13.5, we show an algorithm for the tranformation of ASTS and temporal specifications into their propositional versions, and we apply this algorithm to the case study. Finally, Section 13.6 reports some concluding remarks.

13.2   Overview of the Approach: The Methodology

A web service can be characterized in terms of its data and behaviour. Data description is the definition of the data types used within the service and this can be done by means of the standard language WSDL. This is not enough as WSDL only represents the static part of a service. With WSDL, we are not aware of the actual control and data flows in the process: we only know the interface of the web service and the data structures it uses. The behavioural aspects of a service can be represented with several languages; we will refer to BPEL in our running example.

WSDL plus BPEL are the "classical," purely syntactical representation of a process. This provides us with a set of powerful tools to solve several problems, but we need to add semantics to this representation. The use of semantics allows us to use some reasoning techniques that help us solving several problems related to services in a pervasive computing environment, such as selection, discovery and composition.

All these problems have in common the need of verifying certain conditions over the behaviour and the semantics of a given service. For instance, let us consider process selection: given a set of processes and a user specification, it consists in recognizing what processes satisfy the given specification. Thanks to the use of semantics, we can express both processes and specifications as semantically enriched models.

Our approach can be described in four steps:

1. Annotation
2. Model translation
3. Grounding
4. Model checking

Annotation: it is the phase in which both data and behavioural definitions of the process are enriched with links to a given ontology. The ontology should be a commonly accepted formalization of a certain domain. It is difficult to have such an ontology; indeed every organization may have its own one. Ontology matching is a parallel problem and we will not delve into it, and therefore, we assume we have a general shared ontology for our domain.

There are different approaches to process annotation (e.g., see SAWSDL [28]). We propose a novel one that aims mainly at preserving the original syntax of the BPEL and WSDL files. Therefore, in our approach, the annotation is put in a different file with links to BPEL and WSDL through XPath expressions.

Model Translation: it consists in expressing our process in a different form that can be model checked easily and automatically. As model checkers usually deal with some kind of STS, we translate an annotated BPEL process into an ASTS. This step can be done automatically.

Grounding: it is the procedure by which the semantic annotations are "lowered" to a purely syntactic form; roughly speaking, concept and role assertions must be transformed into propositions. From a technical point of view, each annotated state is a knowledge base, and therefore, we need to use the *query answering service* [19] of Description Logics in order to know what assertions hold in that state. This ensures that our annotations can be treated by existing model checkers that work only with propositions. The grounding algorithm receives as input an ASTS and a goal specification, which is expressed in *annotated CTL*. After its execution, the algorithm returns a gound (propositional) STS and a ground (propositional) CTL specification.

Model checking: it consists in checking whether the ground CTL specification is verified by the ground STS; in the case it does not, we get a counter-example. In our experiments, we used NuSMV ([8]), a well-known state-of-the-art model checker.

In order to describe our methodology, let us consider as case study an e-commerce company that exposes web services for online transactions. The interaction protocol between the site and users reflects what actually happens in real-world major e-commerce sites. At first, the user can perform a search based on some parameters like keywords. If the search succeeds, it returns a set items satisfying user's parameters, and thus, the user may order a certain quantity of them and go through a checkout process. Normally, several payment methods are available. In our case, the user has the possibility to pay either through an online account (this is a common scenario in modern e-commerce sites) or in an alternative way (by means of credit card or bank transfer). Once the payment method has been selected, the checkout operation is completed. In this process, there are two operations that may produce an error: the search, where no item might be returned, and the checkout, where errors might occur during the execution of the transaction.

As previously stated, the process description is composed of the service interface (WSDL) and the process behaviour (BPEL).

In our approach, the process interfaces defining the interaction of services are defined in *abstract* BPEL. BPEL provides an operational description of the (stateful) behaviour of web services on top of the service interfaces defined in their WSDL specifications. An abstract BPEL description identifies the partners of a service, its internal variables and the operations that are triggered upon the invocation of the service by some of the partners. Operations include assigning variables, invoking other services and receiving responses, forking parallel threads of execution and nondeterministically picking one among different courses of actions. Standard imperative constructs, such as if-then-else, case choices and loops, are also supported.

For the sake of readability, let us represent the abstract BPEL of the case study graphically (see Fig. 13.1). The annotation boxes will be explained in Sect. 13.3.4.

At the beginning, after the request operation (*searchRequest*), the service performs the *search*. The way in which information is obtained is not disclosed and published by the *abstract* BPEL we used: the sources of data, assigned to the variables by the *Assign*, are "opaque." The opaqueness mechanism allows us to present an abstract view of the business logic to the external world, which hides the portions that the designer does not intend to disclose, and that are robust to changes with respect to the actual way in which the internal business logic is defined.

Depending on its internal availability (the first *Switch* instruction), the e-commerce service can either send the information that no items match the keyword-based search and terminate (the *Sequence* on the right side), or prepare (*Assign*) and send (*searchResponse*) the information regarding found items. In the rest of the left side sequence, the service provides the *checkout* and the most interesting part, the payment.

The payment (the *payMe* operation) can be performed over two branches. Let us suppose that on the left the payment is done with an online account, whereas on the right one it is done by means of alternative methods.

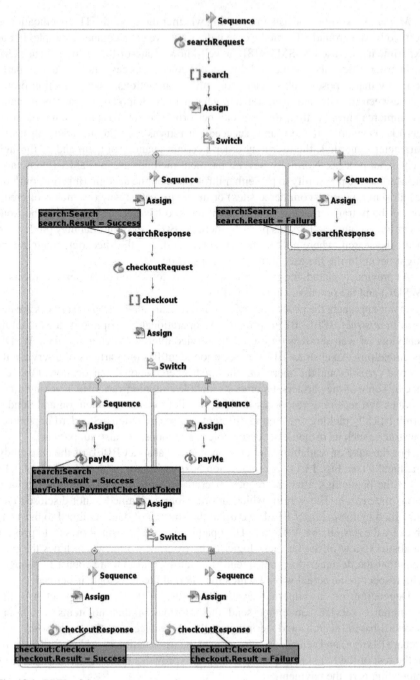

Fig. 13.1 BPEL of the e-commerce service

How can we express the fact that we have two different payment methods and what are these methods? This information can be needed for selecting or compositing this service. Can this information be derived from data types? Generally speaking, the answer is no. Data type definition does not constrain to avoid to use the same term with different meanings. In our example, this means that the same variables can be used for both the payment methods, creating an ambiguity for selection or composition. This is one of the motivations for semantic annotation.

Finally, the service sends a response (*checkoutResponse*) about the transaction condition (failure or success) and the process ends.

A complete description of the case study and all the source codes that we will use in this chapter can be downloaded at http://jeap.diiga.univpm.it/SWS.

13.3   Annotation Technique

The semantic annotation we propose in this chapter is based on the following technologies:

- WSDL: the "stateless" description of a web service. It gives information about the data used by the service and the exposed interface.
- BPEL: the procedural description of a web process.
- WSML: the language used to build up an ontology.

Our approach is driven by several requirements, namely:

- To annotate web processes with semantics.
- To keep the schema of the technologies safe and computable by existing tools.
- To develop an annotation strategy to cope both with static ("data oriented") and procedural ("process oriented") annotations.

All these requirements can be accomplished by keeping the annotation separate from WSDL and BPEL. Therefore, we will use an annotation file and link it to the related files through XPath queries. Our annotation file is defined over XML syntax, so we are going to come up with an XML schema for annotation.

According to Description Logic jargon, within a given ontology, we have a terminological component (called *T-BOX*) and an assertional component (called *A-BOX*). The *T-BOX* contains concept definitions as well as generalization and aggregation relationships among them. This part of the ontology is directly provided by a WSML file. The T-BOX simply matches the set of the declared concepts and their structure (i.e., their attributes/roles).

On the other hand, the *A-BOX* contains assertion definitions of two different types:

- Concept assertions
- Role assertions

Fig. 13.2 Annotation core
components

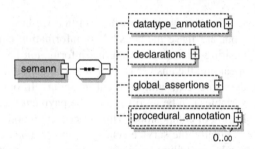

Concept assertions have the form *a:C*. Such an expression tells us that the individual *a* is an instance of the concept *C*. For example, *joe:Person* states that Joe is a (instance of) Person.

Role assertions specify the value that a certain role of an individual has. They have the form *a.R=b*. Intuitively, such an expression means that the value of the attribute *R* of the individual *a* is *b*, where *b* is another individual or a literal. For example, *joe.Mother = mary* states that Joe has a mother whose name is Mary. Mary is the identifier of another individual. As second example: *joe.Surname = "Smith"* states that the surname of Joe is "Smith," where "Smith" is a string.

The roles used in role assertions are defined in the terminological part of the ontology. For example, if the two assertions *joe:Person* and *joe.Surname = "Smith"* hold, this means that the concept *Person* has a role *Surname* whose type is string (formally: *Person* = ∀ *Surname . String* ⊓ ...).

Basically, in our approach, we have a T-BOX for all the services we have to annotate in our domain – it contains all the concepts we need to represent our application domain – and we associate an A-BOX for each state of each service – it describes what are the effects of a given action in terms of concept and role assertions. Nevertheless, there are some assertions that do not depend on any action, but hold everywhere. For example, we could say that *male* and *female* are individuals of the concept *Gender*. This is always true, no matter how our process evolves. This will become clearer with the introduction of global assertions in our annotation.

Let us now analyze the schema of an annotation file. The core components are shown in Fig. 13.2.

13.3.1 Datatype Annotation

In this section of an annotation file, there are several assertions that map WSDL elements into WSML concepts. There is no direct mapping between data and concepts at structural level. In other words, it is perfectly legal to annotate an element with a concept whose attributes do not match with those of the element, neither in number nor in type.

Data type annotations simply impose some restrictions on the procedural annotations, i.e., the A-BOXes related to the STS . As shown in Fig. 13.3, datatype annotation is composed of two elements. Source node is an XPath string pointing

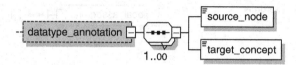

Fig. 13.3 Datatype annotation

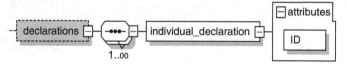

Fig. 13.4 Declarations

to a WSDL part (message, element, complex type, simple type or one of their sub-parts). Target concept is a WSML identifier pointing to a concept.

An example of datatype annotation is the following:

$< source\_node > /definitions/message[7] < /source\_node >$

$< target\_concept >$

   $http://www.diiga.univpm.it/ontologies/virtualStore\#Checkout$

$< /target\_concept >$

13.3.2 Declarations

We make this assumption: *individuals with the same name (id) refer to the same object.* So, if we had a pair of assertions like:

$god.Exists = True$
$god.Exists = False$

we would refer to the same instance "god," no matter if the A-BOX would be inconsistent. In the declarations section, we simply list all the individuals used in the assertions.

13.3.3 Global Assertions

Global assertions are concept and role assertions that hold in every state of our process. They are a sintactic sugar as they have been inserted here just to avoid to repeat them in every state (i.e., in the procedural annotations – see further). Instances directly declared in a WSMO ontology are mapped into global assertions. This is the case of the instances of the concept *Gender*.

Fig. 13.5 Global assertions

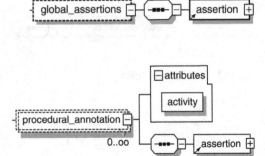

Fig. 13.6 Procedural
annotation

13.3.4 Procedural Annotation

A procedural annotation (see Fig. 13.6) contains sets of concept and role assertions. A procedural annotation is always referred to a BPEL activity. This activity is identified by the activity attribute, whose value is an XPath expression pointing into the BPEL. Intuitively, a procedural annotation contains all the assertions that hold after the related BPEL activity has been executed.

13.3.5 Assertions

Let us now delve into the structure of concept and role assertions. Assertions are used both in global assertions and procedural annotations. An assertion is composed of a set of concept assertions and role assertions (Fig. 13.7).

A *concept assertion* tells us that in a given activity (state of the STS), there exists an individual of a certain concept. Figure 13.8 shows the structure of a concept assertion within the proposed XML schema.

The individual can be a brand new one, with a name chosen by the user. In the other case, a new individual is associated to a BPEL variable. The variable is identified by its name. It is also possible to refer to a part of a variable, and in case the part is a complex type, we can use an XPath query to delve into it. In this case, datatype annotations play their role because they specify a constraint on this type of annotation. If a datatype annotation has previously mapped variable x into a concept C, then a concept assertion over the same variable x must have the concept C or one of its derived concepts as the right part. In every case, the individual used in the assertion is identified by the value of the id attribute, which refers to a previously declared individual in the declaration section.

Role assertions express a relation between an attribute (role) of a certain individual and another individual.

Fig. 13.7 Assertions

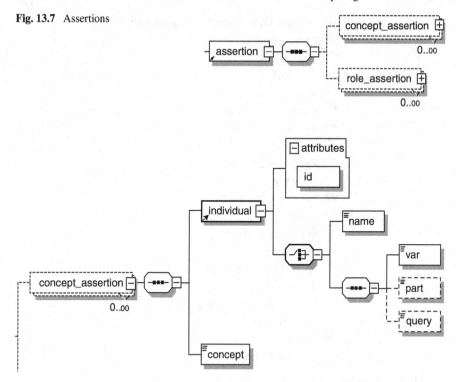

Fig. 13.8 Concept assertion

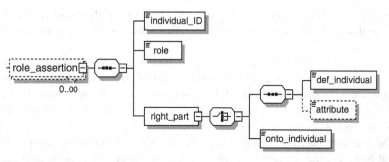

Fig. 13.9 Role assertion

The left part is an individual previously declared. The role points to one of the attributes of the concept to which the individual belongs to. The role is identified by a WSML URI. The right part of a role assertion may be another individual. The optional attribute element is not currently supported and is intended for future use. It would allow us to create role assertions like the following one:

$$x.R = y.S$$

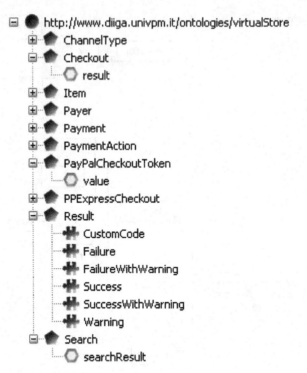

Fig. 13.10 WSMLe-commerce ontology

where S is one of the attributes of y's concept. Alternatively, the right part may be an individual directly declared in the ontology. This kind of individuals are considered as global ones.

Let us explain the annotation language with an example from our case study (the complete source code can be downloaded http://jeap.diiga.univpm.it/SWS). In the following, as already mentioned, we assume that the ontologies provided by the different services have been mapped into a common ontology that defines all the relevant concepts of the scenario.

Our ontology (see Fig. 13.10) is very simple, but it expresses the main concepts useful to model the domain (e-commerce) and to check our requirements. In the definition of *Checkout* and *Search*, we have the attributes *result* and *SearchResult*, respectively, whose values are restricted to belong to the concept *Result*. The possible values (instances) of *Result* are *CustomCode, Failure, Success, Warning*, ..., as depicted in Fig. 13.10.

As second step, we annotate the significant variables and activities of our process. For the sake of space, let us skip the annotation of the WSDL file (annotation of data types) and go directly to the annotation of the BPEL file (annotation of behaviour).

Let us consider the BPEL process described in Fig. 13.1.

Let us suppose we have to say that, after activity *searchResponse*, a search has been performed with a successful result. This means adding the following concept and role assertions to that activity:

- *search : Search*
- *search.Result = Success*

Similarly, in the other branches of the BPEL process, we have to annotate a failure.

For the activities named *checkoutResponse* in the final two branches of the BPEL process, the annotation is similar; indeed, in the left branch of Fig. 13.1 we have:

- *checkout : Checkout*
- *checkout.Result = Success*

whereas, in the right branch we have:

- *checkout : Checkout*
- *checkout.Result = Failure*

An important annotation must be associated to the payment action. Let us consider the left branch, where the payment is done by an online account. This is specified by using an individual of the concept *ePaymentCheckoutToken*.

13.4 Model Translation

We encode BPEL processes (extended with semantic annotations) as *ASTSs*. STS describe dynamic systems that can be in one of their possible *states* (some of which are marked as *initial states*) and can evolve to new states as a result of performing some *actions*. We distinguish actions in *input actions*, *output actions* and τ. *Input actions* represent the reception of messages, *output actions* represent messages sent to external services and τ is a special action, called *internal action*, which represents internal evolutions that are not visible to external services. In other words, τ represents the fact that the state of the system can evolve without producing any output, and without consuming any input (this is a consequence of the fact we use *abstract* BPEL, where the internal actions are "opaque"). A *transition relation* describes how the state can evolve on the basis of inputs, outputs or of the internal action τ.

In an ASTS, we associate to each state a set of *concept assertions* and *role assertions*. This configures a state as the assertional component (or ABox) of a knowledge representation system based on a given description logic where the ontology plays the role of the terminological component (or TBox). Therefore, *concept assertions* are formulas of the form $a{:}C$ (or $C(a)$) and state that a given individual a belongs to the interpretation of the concept C. *Role assertions* are formulas of the form $a.R = b$ (or $R(a,b)$) and state that a given individual b is a value of the role R for a. As a consequence, each action can be viewed as a transition from a state consisting in an ABox to a different state consisting in a different ABox.

Definition 1. Annotated State Transition System
An ASTS defined over a STS Σ is a tuple $\langle \Sigma, \mathcal{T}, \Lambda \rangle$ where:

- $\Sigma = \langle \mathcal{S}, \mathcal{S}^0, \mathcal{I}, \mathcal{O}, \mathcal{R}, \mathcal{P}, \mathcal{X} \rangle$ is the state transition system,
- $\mathcal{S}$ is the finite set of states
- $\mathcal{S}^0 \subseteq \mathcal{S}$ is the set of initial states
- $\mathcal{I}$ is the finite set of input actions
- $\mathcal{O}$ is the finite set of output actions
- $\mathcal{R} \subseteq \mathcal{S} \times (\mathcal{I} \cup \mathcal{O} \cup \{\tau\}) \times \mathcal{S}$ is the transition relation
- $\mathcal{P}$ is the set of propositions that in an annotated STS is empty ($\mathcal{P} = \emptyset$)
- $\mathcal{X} : \mathcal{S} \rightarrow 2^{\mathcal{P}}$ is the observation function, that in an Annotated STS is undefined
- $\mathcal{T}$ is the terminology (TBox) of the annotation
- $\Lambda : \mathcal{S} \rightarrow 2^{\mathcal{A}_{\mathcal{T}}}$ is the annotation function, where $\mathcal{A}_{\mathcal{T}}$ is the set of all the concept assertions and role assertions defined over $\mathcal{T}$

As an example, consider the annotated BPEL process of our case study; here we report a partial description of the corresponding STS: namely we report the set of states

$\mathcal{S} = \{$START, sequence, searchRequest, search, assign, switch, sequence2, assign2, assign2_1,
assign2_2, assign2_3, searchResponse, checkoutRequest, checkout, assign3, switch2, sequence3,
assign4, assign4_1, assign4_2, payMe_Sync, sync_invoke_lock, sequence4, assign5, assign5_1,
assign5_2, payMe_Sync2, sync_invoke_lock2, assign6, switch3, sequence5, assign7,
checkoutResponse, sequence6, assign8, assign8_1, assign8_2, checkoutResponse2, sequence7,
assign9, assign9_1, assign9_2, searchResponse2, END$\}$;

and the annotation of the state *payMe_Sync*

Λ(payMe_Sync) = {
```
        Failure : Result,
        Success : Result,
        Warning : Result,
        SuccessWithWarning : Result,
        FailureWithWarning : Result,
        CustomCode : Result,
        Sell : PaymentAction,
        Authorization : PaymentAction,
        Order : PaymentAction,
        eVendorItem : ChannelType,
        search : Search,
        search.searchResult = Success,
        payToken : ePaymentCheckoutToken
    }
```

Note that the last three assertions have been added during the annotation phase, whereas the other ones are derived directly from the ontology and are present in every state, since they are global.

In order to express process-level verification, selection and composition requirements, we need to express conditions on *ASTSs*, i.e., conditions on concept and role

assertions that hold in given states. In order to do that, we first give some definitions. Let us start with the definition of conjunctive query over a description logic
as reported in [19].

Definition 2 (Conjunctive Query).
A *conjunctive query* q over $\langle \mathcal{T}, \Lambda(s) \rangle$ is a set of atoms $\{p_1(\overline{x_1}), \dots, p_n(\overline{x_n})\}$
where each $p_i(\overline{x_i})$ is either $p_i(x_i)$ or $p_i(x_{i,1}, x_{i,2})$ and $\overline{x_i}$ is a tupla of variables
or individuals:

$$p_i(x_i) = x_i : C_i \qquad\qquad p_i(x_{i,1}, x_{i,2}) = x_{i,1}.R_i = x_{i,2}$$

$V(q)$ denotes the set of variables of q and $C(q)$ denotes the set of individuals of q.
Therefore, $VC(q) = V(q) \cup C(q)$ denotes the set of variables and individuals of q.
When $V(q) = \emptyset$, we have a ground conjunctive query, i.e., each x_i, $x_{i,1}$, or $x_{i,2}$ is
an individual. A concept assertion in a propositional condition intuitively denotes a
typical description logic problem: the *retrieval inference problem*. Let $x : C$ a goal
concept assertion, the retrieval inference problem is the problem of finding for each
state s all individuals mentioned in the ABox $\Lambda(s)$ that are an instance of the concept
C with respect to the given TBox $\mathcal{T}$. A non-optimized algorithm for a retrieval
can be realized by testing for each individual occurring in the ABox whether it
is an instance of the concept C. Once we have retrieved a set of instances $\{a\}$ for
the concept assertion $x{:}C$, we can substitute x in the propositional condition with the
retrieved instances and check whether the condition holds. Therefore, *a conjunctive
query denotes in fact a set of specifications* to be checked instead of a single one.

A temporal specification for an ASTS is a CTL formula containing conjunctive
queries, as defined in the following:

Definition 3 (Temporal Specification of ASTS).
A *Temporal Specification* $\phi(q_1, \dots, q_m)$ over $\langle \Sigma, \mathcal{T}, \Lambda \rangle$ is a formula defined over
the set of conjunctive queries $\{q_1, \dots, q_m\}$ as follows:

$$\phi = q_i \mid \phi \wedge \phi \mid \phi \vee \phi \mid \neg\phi \mid \mathsf{AF}\,\phi \mid \mathsf{AG}\,\phi \mid \mathsf{EF}\,\phi \mid \mathsf{EG}\,\phi \mid \mathsf{AX}\,\phi \mid \mathsf{EX}\,\phi \mid$$
$$\mathsf{A}\,(\phi\,\mathcal{U}\,\phi) \mid \mathsf{E}\,(\phi\,\mathcal{U}\,\phi) \mid \mathsf{A}\,(\phi\,\mathcal{B}\,\phi) \mid \mathsf{E}\,(\phi\,\mathcal{B}\,\phi)$$

We can extend to temporal specifications the definition of V as follows: $V(\phi(q_1, \dots, q_m)) = V(q_1) \cup V(q_2) \cup \dots V(q_m)$. The definition of C and VC can be extended
in a similar way. A ground temporal specification is a formula without variables,
i.e., such that $V(\phi(q_1, \dots, q_m)) = \emptyset$. Obviously, we can annotate other temporal
languages, e.g., EAGLE [10], but for the goal of this chapter, the annotation of CTL
formulas is enough.

CTL is a propositional, branching-time, temporal logic. Intuitively, according to
our extension, a temporal condition must be verified along all possible computation
paths (state sequences) starting from the current state. Concerning the temporal operators (i.e., AF, EF, AX, and so on), they maintain the same intuitive meaning that
they have in standard CTL. In other words, $\mathsf{EX}\phi$ is true in a state s if and only if s
has at least a successor t, such that ϕ is true at t. $\mathsf{E}[\phi\mathcal{U}\psi]$ is true in a state s if and
only if there exists a path starting at s and an initial prefix of the path, such that ψ
holds at the last state of the prefix and ϕ holds at all other states along the prefix.

EGϕ is true at state s if there is at least a path starting at s, such that ϕ holds at each state on the path. As a consequence of the fact that a temporal specification has concept and role assertions, *a temporal condition denotes a set of specifications* to be checked instead of a single one, as well as for a conjunctive query.

The semantics of a temporal specification are defined in three steps: first, we define the semantics of a ground conjunctive query (for the sake of space, we refer the reader to [19] for details); then, we define the semantics of a ground temporal specification; and finally, we define the semantics of temporal specification with variables.

Definition 4 (Semantics of Ground Temporal Specifications of ASTS).

Let $\langle \Sigma, \mathcal{T}, \Lambda \rangle$ be an *annotated state transition system*. Let q be a ground conjunctive query over $\langle \mathcal{T}, \Lambda(s) \rangle$. Let ϕ and ψ be ground temporal specifications. Then defined

- $\langle \Sigma, \mathcal{T}, \Lambda \rangle, s \models q$ iff $\langle \mathcal{T}, \Lambda(s) \rangle \models q$
- $\langle \Sigma, \mathcal{T}, \Lambda \rangle, s \models \phi \wedge \psi$ iff $\langle \Sigma, \mathcal{T}, \Lambda \rangle, s \models \phi$ and $\langle \Sigma, \mathcal{T}, \Lambda \rangle, s \models \psi$
- $\langle \Sigma, \mathcal{T}, \Lambda \rangle, s \models \neg\phi$ iff $\langle \Sigma, \mathcal{T}, \Lambda \rangle, s \not\models \phi$
- $\langle \Sigma, \mathcal{T}, \Lambda \rangle, s \models \text{EX} \, \phi$ iff $\exists t \in S, \exists \alpha \in \mathcal{I} \cup \mathcal{O} \cup \{\tau\}$ such that $R(s, \alpha, t)$ and $\langle \Sigma, \mathcal{T}, \Lambda \rangle, t \models \phi$
- $\langle \Sigma, \mathcal{T}, \Lambda \rangle, s \models \text{EG} \, \phi$ iff $\langle \Sigma, \mathcal{T}, \Lambda \rangle, s \models \phi$ and $\langle \Sigma, \mathcal{T}, \Lambda \rangle, s \models \text{EX EG} \, \phi$
- $\langle \Sigma, \mathcal{T}, \Lambda \rangle, s \models \text{E} \, \phi \mathcal{U} \psi$ iff $\langle \Sigma, \mathcal{T}, \Lambda \rangle, s \models \psi$ or
  $[\, \langle \Sigma, \mathcal{T}, \Lambda \rangle, s \models \phi$ and $\langle \Sigma, \mathcal{T}, \Lambda \rangle, s \models \text{EX E} \, \phi \mathcal{U} \psi \,]$

Definition 5 (Semantics of Temporal Specifications of ASTS).

Let $\phi(q_1, \ldots, q_m)[\overline{x}]$ be a temporal specification such that $V(\phi(q_1, \ldots, q_m)) = \{\overline{x}\}$ is the corresponding set of variables. Then

$$\phi(q_1, \ldots, q_m)[\overline{x}]^{\mathcal{I}}(s) = \{\overline{a} \mid \langle \Sigma, \mathcal{T}, \Lambda \rangle, s \models \phi(q_1, \ldots, q_m)[\overline{x}/\overline{a}]\}$$

is the interpretation of the temporal specification.

Now, let us suppose we want to check some extra requirements over the services we found. These requirements may help us select the most suitable service among the services returned by a preliminary, keyword-based search. This is the so-called *service selection*.

Requirement: I want to find an e-commerce service that makes me perform a search and then, if some items are returned, it allows me paying *only* by means of an online account.

In this requirement, we can find something different from the classical search engine-fashion query. Indeed, we have a *procedural specification* that looks for a payment *after* a search has been successfully performed. It is clear that we need the concept of time or sequence of actions to express the concept "after."

Second, we have a *semantic component* that lets us refer to an online account as described in an appropriate e-commerce ontology. The use of semantics eliminates possible misunderstanding about the terms we used. As long as we refer to a commonly accepted ontology, what we mean with search, checkout and account is clear.

We can express our requirement in annotated CTL:

```
AF (!(x:Search & x.searchResult=Failure) ->
   (x:Search & x.searchResult=Success & y:ePaymentCheckoutToken))
```

13.5 Grounding and Model Checking

A temporal specification can be efficiently checked by means of model checking [6, 8]. Concerning annotated temporal specifications, the basic idea consists of using model checking as well. However, the traditional model checkers cannot be used, as they are not able to deal with the ontological reasoning necessary to cope with state annotations. In this section, we discuss an approach that makes it possible to reuse existing model checkers (e.g., NuSMV [8]), in order to exploit their very efficient and optimized verification techniques. This approach is based on the idea to solve the problem of knowing in which states the assertions contained in the temporal specification hold *before the model checking task*. The algorithm is based on the query answering service (e.g., the algorithm reported in [19]). Therefore, the algorithm consists of the three following steps:

Ground process generation (see Fig. 13.11): it aims to map assertions (of the ASTS) into propositions in order to obtain a ground STS. It consists of applying the conjunctive query answering service for each conjunctive query in the temporal specification and for each state of the ASTS. Therefore, for each conjunctive query, we have a set of assertions to map into state propositions. The complexity of this algorithm is polynomial in the complexity of the query answering algorithm. The query answering algorithm has been shown to be PTIME-Hard with respect to data complexity for extended *DL-Lite* languages [7]. The result is that the ground process

```
Algorithm: Ground Process Generation
input : Γ = ⟨⟨S, S⁰, A, R, -, -⟩, T, Λ⟩
        φ = φ(q₁, ..., qₘ)
output: Σₒ = ⟨S, S⁰, A, R, P, X⟩
        Φ /* Set of ground CTL formulae */
{
    P = ∅
    for each qᵢ (1 ≤ i ≤ m) do Asser(qᵢ) = ∅;
    for each s ∈ S do }
        X(s) = Λ(s);
        for each qᵢ (1 ≤ i ≤ m) do {
            X(s) = X(s) ∪ cq_answer(qᵢ, ⟨T, Λ(s)⟩);
            P = P ∪ cq_answer(qᵢ, ⟨T, Λ(s)⟩);
            Asser(qᵢ) = Asser(qᵢ) ∪ cq_answer(qᵢ, ⟨T, Λ(s)⟩);
        }
    }
    Φ = ground_ts( {q₁, ..., qₘ}, φ(q₁, ..., qₘ),
                   {Asser(q₁), ..., Asser(qₘ)});
    return Σₒ , Φ;
}
```

```
Algorithm: ground_ts
/* Ground Spec. Generation */
input : L /* Set of conjunctive queries */
        φ /* Partially ground CTL formula */
        A /* Set of sets of assertions */
output: Φ /* Set of ground CTL formulae */
{
    Φ := ∅;
    if L ≠ ∅ {
        a := head(L);
        for each aı ∈ Asser(a) do {
            φ := substitute a with aı in φ;
            Φ := Φ∪
                ground_ts(rest(L), φ, rest(A));
        }
    }
    return Φ
}
```

Fig. 13.11 The algorithm for building a ground STS and related set of ground specifications

generation has a polynomial complexity with respect to data complexity.

Ground specification generation (Fig. 13.11): it aims to transform assertions contained in the annotated temporal specification into conditions on state propositions in order to obtain a ground temporal specification. It consists of generating a set of specifications by setting variables in the temporal specification with instances retrieved in the previous step.

Model checking: it consists of applying the model checking algorithm to each ground temporal specification generated in the previous step.

Now, let us explain this algorithm by means of the case study reported in this chapter. We would like to check whether our e-commerce service (see Fig. 13.1) satisfies the CTL requirement reported in Sect. 13.4. Let us separate the conjunctive queries that compose it:

$$q_1 = \{x{:}Search, x.searchResult{=}Failure\}$$

$$q_2 = \{x{:}Search, x.searchResult{=}Success, y{:}ePaymentCheckoutToken\}$$

Therefore, the corresponding sets of variables and the individuals are:

$V(\phi(q_1, q_2)) = \{search, payToken\}$

$C(\phi(q_1, q_2)) = \{Success, Failure\}$.

If we apply the query answering algorithm to the previous conjunctive queries and to our ASTS, we obtain in which states the assertions reported in the temporal condition hold, as reported in Table 13.1.

After the execution of the grounding algorithm in the state *payMe_Sync*, the $\mathcal{A}sser$ components are the following:

Asser(q1) = {}
Asser(q2) = {search:Search, search.searchResult=Success, payToken:ePaymentCheckoutToken}

In the State *searchResponse2*, the situation is the following:

Asser(q1) = {search:Search, search.searchResult=Failure}
Asser(q2) = {search:Search, search.searchResult=Success, payToken:ePaymentCheckoutToken}

The execution of the algorithm in the other states does not add any elements to our $\mathcal{A}sser$ sets. Therefore, the resulting ground CTL specification is the following:

$$\text{AF(!(search : Search\&search.searchResult} = \text{Failure)}{-}> \qquad (13.1)$$

$$\text{(search : Search\&search.searchResult} = \text{Success\&payToken : ePaymentCheckoutToken))}$$

Furthermore, a second result of the grounding algorithm is a ground STS. Roughly speakling, the ground STS does not have (concept and role) assertions, but Boolean propositions. In order to distinguish assertions from propositions, in our example,

Table 13.1 The states in which q_1 and q_2 hold

Conjunctive query	States
q_1	searchResponse2
q_2	payMe_Sync

we call a proposition with the name of the corresponding concept (or role) assertion and the prefix GCA (or GRA, respectively). Therefore, the set $\mathcal{P}$ of the ground STS of our case study is the following:

$\mathcal{P} = \{$GCA_Failure_Result, GCA_Success_Result, GCA_Warning_Result, GCA_SuccessWithWarning_Result

GCA_FailureWithWarning_Result, GCA_CustomCode_Result, GCA_Sell_PaymentAction

GCA_Authorization_PaymentAction, GCA_Order_PaymentAction, GCA_eVendorItem_ChannelType

GCA_search_Search, GCA_payToken_ePaymentCheckoutToken,

GRA_search_searchResult_Success GRA_search_searchResult_Failure $\}$

Concerning the transition relation $\mathcal{R}$, the grounding algorithm does not change it. Λ is empty as it is the goal of the grounding algorithm to remove semantic annotations, but we have the observation function χ. For the sake of space, here we report only the following fragment of χ:

$\chi(\text{START}) = \{$GCA_Failure_Result, GCA_Success_Result, GCA_Warning_Result,

GCA_SuccessWithWarning_Result, GCA_FailureWithWarning_Result,

GCA_CustomCode_Result, GCA_Sell_PaymentAction, GCA_Authorization_PaymentAction,

GCA_Order_PaymentAction, GCA_eVendorItem_ChannelType, ! GCA_search_Search,

! GCA_payToken_ePaymentCheckoutToken, ! GRA_search_searchResult_Success,

! GRA_search_searchResult_Failure $\}$

$\chi(\text{checkoutRequest}) = \chi(\text{searchResponse}) \cup$

$\{$GCA_search_Search, GRA_search_searchResult_Success $\}$

$\chi(\text{payMe_Sync}) = \chi(\text{assign4\_2}) \cup$

$\{$GCA_search_Search, GRA_search_searchResult_Success,

GCA_payToken_ePaymentCheckoutToken $\}$

$\chi(\text{searchResponse2}) = \chi(\text{assign9\_2}) \cup$

$\{$GCA_search_Search, GRA_search_searchResult_Failure $\}$

The last step of the selection process is model checking. In our experiments, we use NuSMV [8]. Generally speaking, a model checker takes in input a finite STS and a temporal condition, and verifies whether the finite STS satisfies the condition. If not, the model checker returns a counter-example. The presentation of the model checking algorithm is out of the scope of this chapter; the reader can refer to other works [6, 8].

In the case study reported in this chapter, the Condition (13.1) does not hold, and thus, we obtain a counter-example that involves the alternative payment method in our e-commerce process (see Fig. 13.12).

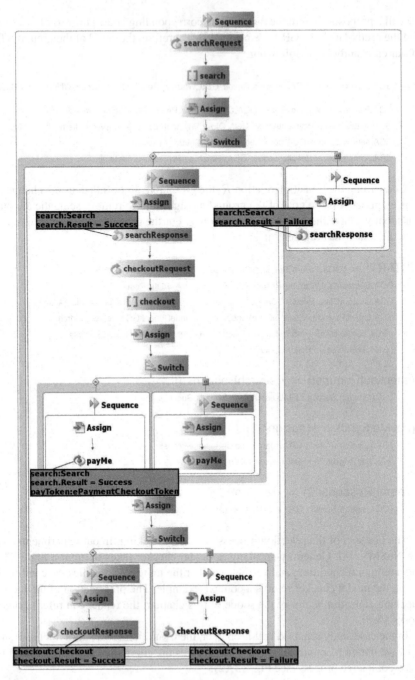

Fig. 13.12 Counter-example generated by NuSMV

13.6 Conclusions and Discussion

This work is based on and extends the work reported in [11, 20, 22]. In this chapter, we focused on the semantic annotation and the grounding process, whereas [11, 20, 22] focus on selection and composition algorithms. This approach has been tested in a real world case study [11] where real web services provided by Amazon, eBay and PayPal have been annotated with the language proposed in this chapter and then, selected and composed. In another test [15], automated composition has been compared with hand-written composition made by an experienced programmer. The quality of the resulting services is similar, but automatic composition required around 10 min, instead of around 20 h required by the programmer. Concerning the overhead required for semantically annotating a process, we are developing a user-friendly graphical interface. Thanks to this interface, a programmer can obtain a graphical representation of both the ontology and the process. As a consequence, the programmer can annotate the process by means of a simple "drag-and-drop" approach.

Finally, let us discuss our approach to semantic annotation in comparison with other approaches reported in literature. The WSMO [25] framework recognizes the importance of interfaces that describe behaviours of services, and proposes the use of mediators to match service behaviours against (discovery) goals. However, the WSMO framework includes services representations in its ontological model. We chose to use a bottom-up approach, not dismissing the existing and widespread technologies like BPEL. Indeed, BPEL provides us with the behavioural features of a service, whereas in WSMO we would need to express them in the orchestration and the coreography properties. The work on Web Service Description Language – Semantics (WSDL-S) and METEOR-S [21, 24, 27] provides semantic annotations for WSDL (the file dealing with the data description of a web service). It is close in spirit to ours, but does not deal with semantically annotated (BPEL) process-level descriptions of web services (i.e., with the procedural description of web services). The work in [16] is also close in spirit to our general objective of bridging the gap between the semantic web framework and the business process technologies. However, [16] focuses on the problem of extending BPEL with semantic web technology to facilitate web service interoperation only, while the problem of automated composition is not addressed.

Recently, an increasing amount of work is dealing with the problem of composing semantic web services taking into account their behavioural descriptions [18, 25, 30]. In this context, research is following two related but different main approaches: OWL-S [9] and WSMO [25]. Approaches based on OWL-S [18, 30] are different from the one proposed in this chapter, since, in OWL-S, even processes are described as ontologies. In our approach, we can separate reasoning about processes and reasoning about ontologies. In the approach undertaken in WSMO, processes are represented as Abstract State Machines and all the variables of an Abstract State Machine are defined in terms of the WSMO ontological language. Our processes work instead on their own state variables, some of which can be mapped to a separated ontological language, allowing for a minimalist and practical approach to semantic annotations and for effective reasoning to discover, select or compose services automatically. Indeed, the aim of the work on WSMO is to propose a general language and representation mechanism for semantic web services, while we focus on the practical problem of providing effective techniques for selecting and composing semantic web services automatically. It would be interesting to investigate how our approach can be applied to WSMO Abstract State Machines, rather than BPEL processes, and how the idea of minimalist semantic annotations can be extended to work with the rest of the WSMO framework. This task is in our research agenda. Concerning the language for requirements, in [1] the author proposes combination of the $\mathcal{SHIQ}$(D) DL and μ-calculus. In our approach, we use CTL to express temporal specifications. CTL is subsumed by μ-calculus, according to the minimalist nature of our approach.

References

1. Agarwal, S.: A goal specification language for automated discovery and composition of web services. In: International Conference on Web Intelligence (WI '07). Silicon Valley (2007). URL http://www.aifb.uni-karlsruhe.de/WBS/sag/papers/Agarwal- A Goal Specification Language For Automated Discovery And Composition Of Web Services-WI07.pdf
2. Andrews, T., Curbera, F., Dolakia, H., Goland, J., Klein, J., Leymann, F., Liu, K., Roller, D., Smith, D., Thatte, S., Trickovic, I., Weeravarana, S.: Business Process Execution Language for Web Services (version 1.1) (2003)
3. Ben-Natan, R., Sherman, D.: Web services in a pervasive computing environment. WebSphere Developer's Journal 1(3) (2002)
4. Berardi, D., Calvanese, D., Giacomo, G.D., Lenzerini, M., Mecella, M.: Automatic composition of E-Services that export their behaviour. In: Proc. ICSOC'03 (2003)
5. Bertoli, P., Cimatti, A., Pistore, M., Roveri, M., Traverso, P.: MBP: a model based planner. In: IJCAI-2001 workshop on Planning under Uncertainty and Incomplete Information (2001)
6. Burch, J.R., Clarke, E.M., McMillan, K.L., Dill, D.L., Hwang, L.J.: Symbolic model checking: 10^{20} states and beyond. Information and Computation 98(2), 142–170 (1992)
7. Calvanese, D., De Giacomo, G., Lembo, D., Lenzerini, M., Rosati, R.: Data complexity of query answering in description logics. AAAI (2006)
8. Cimatti, A., Clarke, E.M., Giunchiglia, F., Roveri, M.: NUSMV: a new symbolic model checker. International Journal on Software Tools for Technology Transfer 2(4), 410–425 (2000)
9. Coalition, T.O.S.: OWL-S: semantic markup for web services (2003)
10. Dal Lago, U., Pistore, M., Traverso, P.: Planning with a language for extended goals. In: Proc. AAAI'02 (2002)
11. Di Pietro, I., Pagliarecci, F., Spalazzi, L., Marconi, A., Pistore, M.: Semantic web service selection at the process level: the eBay/Amazon/PayPal Case Study. In: 2008 IEEE/WIC/ACM International Conference on Web Intelligence (WI'08). IEEE Computer Society (2008)
12. Doan, E.: Middleware extensions for pervasive computing. In: IEEE International Conference on Portable Information Devices (PORTABLE07). IEEE Press (2007)
13. Emerson, E.A.: Temporal and modal logic. In: J. van Leeuwen (ed.) Handbook of Theoretical Computer Science, vol. B: Formal Models and Semantics, chap. 14, pp. 996–1072. Elsevier Science Publishers B.V.: Amsterdam, The Netherlands, New York (1990)
14. Hull, R., Benedikt, M., Christophides, V., Su, J.: E-Services: A Look Behind the Curtain. In: Proc. PODS'03 (2003)
15. Marconi,A., Pistore,M., Poccianti,P., Traverso,P.: Automated web service composition at work: the Amazon/MPS Case Study. In: IEEE International Conference on Web Services (ICWS 2007), pp. 767–774. IEEE Computer Society (2007)

16. Mandell, D., McIlraith, S.: Adapting BPEL4WS for the semantic web: the bottom-up approach to web service interoperation. In: Proc. of 2nd International Semantic Web Conference (ISWC03) (2003)
17. McGuinness, D.L., F. van Harmelen, E.: OWL Web ontology language overview. W3C Recommendation (2004). http://www.w3.org/TR/2004/REC-owl-features-20040210/
18. Narayanan, S., McIlraith, S.: Simulation, verification and automated composition of web services. In: Proc. WWW'02 (2002)
19. Ortiz, M., Calvanese, D., Eiter, T.: Characterizing data complexity for conjunctive query answering in expressive description logics. AAAI (2006)
20. Pagliarecci, F., Pistore, M., Spalazzi, L., Traverso, P.: Web service discovery at process-level based on semantic annotation. In: Proc. of Fifteenth Italian Symposium on Advanced Database Systems (SEBD 2007), 17–20 June, Torre Canne, BR (2007)
21. Patil, A., Oundhakar, S., Sheth, A., Verma, K.: METEOR-S Web service annotation framework. In: WWW04 (2004)
22. Pistore, M., Spalazzi, L., Traverso, P.: A minimalist approach to semantic annotations for web processes compositions. In: Proc. of the 3rd European Semantic Web Conference (ESWC 2006). Springer, Berlin, Budva (Montenegro), 11–14 June (2006)
23. Satyanarayanan, M.: Pervasive computing: vision and challenges (2001)
24. Sheth, A., Verna, K., Miller, J., Rajasekaran, P.: Enhacing web service descriptions using WSDL-S. In: EclipseCon (2005)
25. The Web Service Modeling Framework - http://www.wsmo.org/
26. Tobies, S.: Complexity results and practical algorithms for logics in knowledge representation. Ph.D. thesis, RWTH Aachen (2001)
27. Verma, K., Mocan, A., Zarembra, M., Sheth, A., Miller, J.A.: Linking semantic web service efforts: integrationg WSMX and METEOR-S. In: Semantic and Dynamic Web Processes (SDWP) (2005)
28. W3C Semantic Annotations for Web Service Description Language Working Group: Semantic Annotations for WSDL and XML Schema (2007)
29. Weiser, M.: The computer for the 21st century. Scientific American, **265**(3), 66–75 (1991)
30. Wu, D., Parsia, B., Sirin, E., Hendler, J., Nau, D.: Automating DAML-S web services composition using SHOP2. In: Proc. ISWC'03 (2003)

Chapter 14
Situation-Aware Adaptive Processing (SAAP) of Data Streams

Pari Delir Haghighi, Mohamed Medhat Gaber, Shonali Krishnaswamy, and Arkady Zaslavsky

Abstract The growth and proliferation of technologies in the field of sensor networking and mobile computing have led to the emergence of diverse applications that process and analyze sensory data on mobile devices such as a smart phone. However, the real power to make a significant impact on the area of developing these applications rests not merely on deploying the technologies, but on the ability to perform real-time, intelligent analysis of the data streams that are generated by the various sensors. In this chapter, we present a novel approach for Situation-Aware Adaptive Processing (SAAP) of data streams for pervasive computing environments. This approach uses fuzzy logic principles for modelling and reasoning about uncertain situations, and performs gradual adaptation of parameters of data stream mining algorithms in real-time according to availability of resources and the occurring situations.

Keywords Data stream mining · Resource-aware computing · Pervasive computing · Fuzzy logic

14.1 Introduction

There is a range of emerging applications that use mobile devices for data analysis and processing of data streams in ubiquitous computing environments. Examples of such applications include mobile fieldworkers (e.g., healthcare professionals, firefighters, police, etc.), intrusion detection and Intelligent Transportation Systems. A very significant challenge for these applications is to process and analyze the vast amounts of data streams that are typically generated at very high rates with mobile devices such as a PDA in real-time and in a smart and cost-efficient way. Lightweight and one-pass data stream mining algorithms, such as LWC and LWCLass [1,2] that are developed for Ubiquitous Data Stream Mining (UDM) [3],

P.D. Haghighi (✉)
Centre for Distributed Systems and Software Engineering, Monash University, 900 Dandenong Rd, Caulfield East, VIC3145, Australia
e-mail: Pari.DelirHaghighi@infotech.monash.edu.au

A.-E. Hassanien et al. (eds.), *Pervasive Computing: Innovations in Intelligent Multimedia and Applications*, Computer Communications and Networks, DOI 10.1007/978-1-84882-599-4_14, © Springer-Verlag London Limited 2009

are able to perform real-time analysis on-board small/mobile devices while considering available resources, such as battery charge and available memory. However, to perform smart and intelligent analysis of data on mobile devices, it is imperative for adaptation strategies to go beyond mere computational resources and factor in contextual/situational information.

Context can be any information related to a network, environment, application, process, user or device. Here we consider context as the information used for representing real-world situations [4] in pervasive computing environments. Contextual information collected from every single sensor or data source represents a partial view of the real-world. Aggregation of data from multiple sensors and sources provides a wider and more general view of surrounding environment and situations of interest [5]. For example, in a smart room scenario, rather than monitoring sensed context from light, noise and motion sensors individually, this information can be used to reason about situations, such as "meeting," "presentation" or "study," which provides a better understanding of the environment. As a meta-level concept over context, we define the notion of a situation that is inferred from contextual information [5]. Situation-awareness provides applications with a more abstract view of their environment, rather than focusing on individual pieces of context.

Reviewing recent works in mobile data stream mining reveals that most of these projects [1–4] have limited levels of adaptations or mainly focusing on the battery or memory usage. A general approach for smart and cost-efficient analysis of data that is under-pinned using situation-aware adaptation has not been introduced in the current state-of-the-art and is still an open issue.

To incorporate situation-awareness into ubiquitous data stream mining, we have introduced a general approach called Situation-Aware Adaptive Processing (SAAP) of data streams. This chapter is devoted to introduce the architecture of SAAP and the techniques we apply to achieve situation-awareness and adaptation of data stream mining algorithms. The main contributions of the SAAP architecture are as follows:

- Modelling and reasoning about situations are achieved using a Fuzzy Situation Inference (FSI) model that is based on the Context Spaces (CS) model [5], a general and formal approach for reasoning about context under uncertainty. The FSI technique incorporates the CS model's underlying theoretical basis for supporting context-aware and pervasive computing environments while using fuzzy logic to model and reason about imperfect context and vague situations.
- Parameterized adaptation of data stream mining algorithms is performed in real-time and according to the occurring situations and available resources. This approach maximizes the benefits of adaptation and improves data stream mining operations in an intelligent and cost-efficient manner. Situation-aware adaptation leverages the full potential of UDM and can enable, if not guarantee, the continuity and consistency of the running application.

This chapter is organized as follows: Sect. 14.2 describes the SAAP architecture; Sect. 14.3 discusses the Fuzzy Situation Inference Engine (FSIE) that enables situation-awareness using fuzzy logic principles; Sect. 14.4 discusses parameterized adaptation of data stream mining algorithms factoring in situations and resources;

Sect. 14.5 describes implementation and evaluation of the architecture and finally, Sect. 14.6 provides the summary of the chapter.

14.2 Situation-Aware Adaptive Processing (SAAP) of Data Streams

The architecture for Situation-Aware Adaptive Processing (SAAP) of data streams consists of two main components of Fuzzy Situation Inference (FSI) and Adaptation Engine (AE) as shown in Fig. 14.1. FSI enables situation-awareness by combining fuzzy logic principles with the Context Spaces (CS) model. The second component, AE, is responsible for gradual and parameterized adaptation of data stream mining algorithms in real-time according to the occurring situations and available resources.

Resource Monitor (RM) is a software component that continuously monitors available resources, such as available memory and battery usage, and reports their availability to the adaptation engine. The SAAP layer is built on the top of the data stream mining algorithms running on mobile devices and provides them with situation-aware adaptation.

14.3 Fuzzy Situation Inference (FSI)

The Fuzzy Situation Inference (FSI) is a situation modelling and reasoning approach that integrates fuzzy logic into the Context Spaces model [5]. The strengths of fuzzy logic for modelling and reasoning of imperfect context and vague situations are

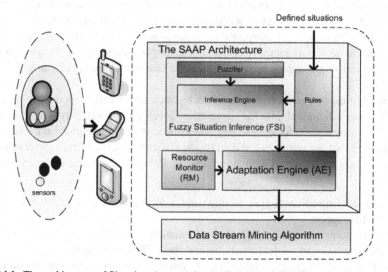

Fig. 14.1 The architecture of Situation-Aware Adaptive Processing (SAAP) of data streams

combined with the CS model's underlying theoretical basis for supporting context-aware pervasive computing scenarios.

One of the main challenges in enabling situation-awareness in pervasive applications is managing uncertainty. Uncertainty can be related to context imperfection, such as sensors' inaccuracy, missing information or imperfect observations [6]. However, there is another dimension of uncertainty that is inherent in human concepts and every day situations. In real-world, situations evolve and change into other situations (e.g., "walking" changes to "running"). Changes that occur between situations of "walking" and "running" are also good indicators of situations that may emerge, albeit with some vagueness and uncertainty. These uncertain situations can be of high importance to certain applications such as a health monitoring application that needs to monitor details of changes in a patient's health situation. The CS model mainly deals with uncertainty associated with sensors' inaccuracy. In order to model real-world situations and reflect this aspect of uncertainty in the situation reasoning results, we combine the CS modelling and reasoning techniques with fuzzy logic principles. The next subsection introduces the Context Spaces (CS) model and its main concepts.

14.3.1   The Context Spaces (CS) Model

The CS model represents contextual information as geometrical objects in multi-dimensional space called situations [5]. The basic concepts of the CS model are the *context attribute, application space, context state* and *situation space*. A *context attribute* describes any data used in the situation reasoning. The term *application space* defines the universe of discourse and *context state* refers to a collection of context values in CS. The concept of a *situation space* is characterized by a set of regions. Each *region* is a set of acceptable values of a context attribute that satisfies a predicate. A region is a crisp or conventional set of context attribute values such that any element is its member or not. For example, in a situation, a region of temperature can be the values between 15 and 25 that satisfy two predicates of ">15" and "<25".

In addition to basic concepts and techniques for situation modelling and reasoning, the CS model provides heuristics developed specifically for addressing context-awareness under uncertainty. These heuristics are integrated into reasoning techniques that are utility-based data fusion algorithms and compute the confidence level in the occurrence of a situation [5]. Main heuristics of the CS model are as follows:

- Individual significance (i.e., weight) and contribution of context attributes in the situation space.
- Inaccuracies of sensory originated information.
- Characteristics of context attributes and their effect on reasoning.
- Partial and complete containment of context-attributes' values in the situation space.

Each of the above-mentioned heuristics is used in a reasoning technique of CS to compute the confidence level in the occurrence of a situation. To enable situation-awareness in pervasive applications, it is imperative to address the issue of uncertainty. The CS deals with uncertainty mainly associated with sensors' inaccuracies. Yet there is another aspect of uncertainty in human concepts and real-world situations that needs to be represented in a context model and reflected in the results of situation reasoning. Fuzzy logic has the benefit of representing this level of uncertainty using membership degree of values. The next section describes situation modelling in FSI.

14.3.2   Situation Modelling

Definitions of "application space" and "context state" are applied similarly to the FSI model, but the "situation space" is differently defined. In FSI, a situation is defined by a set of fuzzy sets that are expressed as a FSI rule. In a fuzzy set, unlike a region, membership of an item is gradual and is represented by a membership degree between 0 and 1 [7]. Using fuzzy sets allows a context value to be represented both qualitatively as fuzzy terms and quantitatively using membership functions. The FSI consists of three subcomponents of fuzzifier, rules and inference engine. The following subsections discuss these parts in more detail.

14.3.2.1   Fuzzifier

In FSI, crisp inputs are context attribute values such as temperature degree or light level that are obtainable by the application. Fuzzifier, as a software component, uses membership functions to map crisp inputs (i.e., context attribute values) into fuzzy sets. Prior to fuzzification, we need to define linguistic variables and their terms and then select appropriate membership functions for mapping crisp inputs into fuzzy sets.

- Defining *Linguistic variables*: Zadeh [8], the founder of the field of fuzzy logic, defines linguistic variables as:

  "variables whose values are not numbers but words or sentences in a natural or artificial language."

In the FSI model, the term linguistic variable is used to express a "context attribute." Unlike context attributes, values that linguistic variables take are not numeric and are called *terms* (also known as fuzzy variables) [9]. Each term of a linguistic variable represents a fuzzy set that takes a pair of numeric values (i.e., a value and its membership degree). For a situation of "hyperthermia," linguistic variables can be "heart-rate," "room temperature" and "age."

- Breaking linguistic variables into terms: after defining linguistic variables, we need to break them into terms or fuzzy variables. Each term of a linguistic

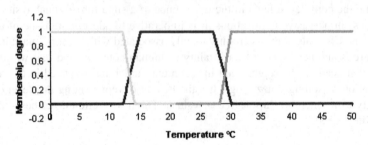

Fig. 14.2 An example of a trapezoidal membership function

variable is characterized by a fuzzy set. For example, the terms of the linguistic variable "heart rate" could be {"slow," "normal" and "fast"}.

- Selecting *membership functions*: a fuzzy set is characterized by a membership function that assigns to each object a grade of membership [7, 9]. Let A be a fuzzy set defined on a universe of U and x be an element of the universe. A membership function denoted as $\mu_A(x)$ maps x to a membership grade between 0 and 1 [7, 9]. If "heart rate" is 87 bpm, then we could have $\mu_{normal}(87) = 0.3$ and $\mu_{fast}(87) = 0.8$.

There are many different varieties of membership functions, such as trapezoidal, Gaussian and Bell. Selecting a membership function is subjective [7] and is based on the application requirements and expected membership degree for the values. We consider the trapezoidal membership function the most fitting function for characterizing our fuzzy sets with the following format:

$$\text{trapmf}(x; a, b, c, d) = \max\left(\min\left(\frac{x-a}{b-a}, 1, \frac{d-x}{d-c}\right), 0\right) \quad (14.1)$$

The parameters passed into the trapezoidal function determine the membership degree of elements. The greater the membership degree of elements, the greater confidence and evidence that the situation will occur. As shown in Fig. 14.2, the parameters "a" and "d" represent the "feet" and "b" and "c" locate the "shoulders" of the trapezoid. The membership degree of values across the "shoulders" is 1 and the membership degree of values towards the "feet" reduces from 1 to 0.

14.3.2.2 Rules

In fuzzy logic, rules are "if-then" statements whose return values are not restricted to "true" or "false" and can be a value between 0 and 1. In FSI, we use fuzzy rules to represent situations of interest. Each FSI rule consists of multiple conditions/antecedents joined with the AND operator, but a condition can itself be a disjunction of conditions [10]. An example of a FSI rule for a health-related situation with variables of RT (room temperature), heart rate (HR) and age can be expressed as follows:

Rule1: if RT is 'hot' and HR is 'fast' and (age is 'middle-aged' or 'old) then situation is 'heat-stroke'

In many cases, there are some fuzzy variables that are more important than others in describing a situation. For example, low blood pressure is a strong indication of "hypotension" in a person, while heart rate may not be equally important. To model the importance of fuzzy variables and conditions, we assign a pre-defined weight w to each condition with a value ranging between 0 and 1. The sum of weights is 1 per rule. A weight represents the importance of its assigned condition relative to other conditions in defining a situation.

In pervasive environments, an application's knowledge about its environment is partially based on the information that it collects from sensors. However, due to sensor faults or inaccuracies, this information can be incomplete or unavailable. This requires the situation modelling and reasoning approaches to provide more flexibility such that if one of the existing sensors fails or a new sensor is added, the system still performs reasoning based on the available information. *Representing a situation with different types or cardinality* of context provides an application with more flexibility to reason about situations. The FSI model supports definition of a situation with multiple rules. Each rule can consist of dependent or overlapping conditions to represent a certain situation as follows.

Rule 1: If A and B and C then situation is Z
Rule 2: If A and C and D then situation is Z
Rule 3: If E and F then situation is Z
Rule 4: If E and F and G then situation is Z

where A, B, C, D, E, F, G are conditions and Z represents a situation. Each rule represents situation Z with different combinations of conditions. The results of evaluation of all the rules for a situation are aggregated using maximum function to produce a single result per situation.

14.3.3 Situation Reasoning

To reason about a situation, rules need to be evaluated to produce a single output that determines the membership degree of the consequent. The conditions joined with the OR operator are evaluated using the *maximum* function [7]. To evaluate the conditions joined with the AND operator, FSI provides four reasoning techniques. These techniques integrate fuzzy logic principles into the reasoning methods of CS to provide another aspect of uncertainty (i.e., uncertainty of situations and delta changes of context) in the computation of confidence value for the occurrence of a situation. The degree of confidence is a measure reflecting how many and to what extent indicative events are supportive of the specific situation.

The CS model has based its reasoning techniques on four heuristics that deal with uncertainty in pervasive computing environments. The following subsections discuss these heuristics and their corresponding reasoning methods in CS and FSI.

14.3.3.1 Weights and Contribution Level

The first heuristic of CS deals with the weights of context attributes and the level of confidence of attributes' values. Weights are values between 0 and 1 that are assigned to context attributes and represent relative importance of each context attribute for inferring a situation. Level of confidence is assigned to each element and reflects how that element relates to the modelled situation. This heuristic is integrated into the first reasoning technique of CS that computes the confidence level (i.e., a value between 0 and 1) in the occurrence of a situation as follows.

$$\text{Confidence} = \sum_{i=1}^{n} w_i c_i \tag{14.2}$$

where w_i and c_i denote the weight and contribution level of context attributes of a situation, respectively. The contribution function that assigns the confidence values is proposed at a conceptual level and its implementation is later introduced in the second reasoning method based on sensors' inaccuracy.

In FSI, the concept of weights is associated with the conditions of a rule, but the concept of a contribution level is implemented in a different way. The FSI equivalent to the equation (14.2) is a rule evaluation method that computes a level of confidence using membership functions and is presented as follows.

$$\text{Confidence} = \sum_{i=1}^{n} w_i \mu(x_i) \tag{14.3}$$

where $\mu(x_i)$ denotes the membership degree of the element x_i and w_i represents a weight assigned to a condition. The result of $w_i \mu(x_i)$ represents a weighted membership degree of x_i and n represents the number of conditions in a rule ($1 \leq i \leq n$).

To improve cost-efficiency aspect of the evaluation process of the FSI rules, multiple rules are rearranged in an ascending order. The order is based on the weights of conditions because weights are the main indicators of importance of each condition in a rule. For example, if rules 1, 2 and 3 consist of three conditions with weights of (0.36, 0.32, 0.32), (0.5, 0.4, 0.1) and (0.4, 0.4, 0.2), respectively, these rules are rearranged as rule 2, 3 and 1. Table 14.1 illustrates an example of representing "heat-stroke" with multiple rules rearranged in an ascending order. The variables are RT, HR (i.e., represented by bepm), age and RR (respiratory rate represented by brpm) with the values of 36 °C, 89 bpm, 63 and 26 brpm, respectively.

Table 14.1 shows aggregation of rules when all the information about HR, RR, RT and age are obtainable. However, if one of the sensors, for example, heart rate

Table 14.1 An example of a situation defined by multiple rules

Rules for 'Heatstroke'
Rule1: If RT is hot and HR is fast and (age is middle-aged or old) then situation is hypothermia $(1 \times 0.5) + (0.9 \times 0.4) + \max((0.4 \times 0.1), (0.6 \times 0.1)) = 0.92$
Rule2: If RT is hot and RR is fast and (age is middle-aged or old) then situation is hypothermia $(1 \times 0.5) + (0.75 \times 0.4) + \max((0.4 \times 0.1), (0.6 \times 0.1)) = 0.86$
Rule3: If RT is hot and HR is fast and RR is fast then situation is hypothermia $(1 \times 0.36) + (0.9 \times 0.32) + (0.75 \times 0.32) = 0.888$
Aggregation result max $= 0.92$

sensor, fails (and even if heart rate is considered as a symmetric context attribute), the system is still able to reason about the situation and the result of aggregation would be 0.86. If we had used only one rule (i.e., rule 1) for representing "heat-stroke" and the sensor providing heart rate data failed, the result of inference would have been reduced to the confidence value of 0.56 that indicates a less accurate value compared to 0.86.

14.3.3.2   Sensors' Inaccuracy

To provide automatic computation of the contribution level at run-time, the second reasoning technique of CS incorporates the heuristic of sensors' inaccuracy. The impact of sensor inaccuracies and unreliability is used as a determining factor to compute the contribution level in the following reasoning method:

$$\text{Confidence} = \sum_{i=1}^{n} w_i \cdot \Pr(\widehat{a}_i^{\,t} \in A_i). \tag{14.4}$$

where $\Pr(\widehat{a}_i^{\,t} \in A_i)$ presents the confidence level of a context attribute value by computing the probability of a context attribute correct value $\widehat{a}_i^{\,t}$ being contained in the region A_i. To compute the probability value based on the reliability of a sensor, the reliability of reading (e.g., 95%) is used to represent the probability value (i.e., $\Pr(\widehat{a}_i^{\,t} \in A_i) = 0.95$).

The second option to compute the probability value is to integrate the sensors' inaccuracy of reading rather than the reliability of reading. Using this option, the probability value is calculated in the following format:

$$\Pr(e_j \leq a_i^t - \min(A_i^j)) - \Pr(e_j \leq a_i^t - \max(A_i^j)) \tag{14.5}$$

where a_i^t denotes the sensed value of the context attribute, e_j denotes the sensor reading error (i.e., a_i^t-$\widehat{a}_i^{\,t}$) and $\min(A_i^j)$ and $\max(A_i^j)$ represent minimum and maximum values of the region, respectively.

The CS equation (14.4) deals with uncertainty factoring in inaccuracies of sensors; however, this equation does not reflect delta changes of values in the equation and is not adequate to reason about vague situations. The FSI equivalent to the CS equation (14.4) not only incorporates the contribution level associated with sensors' inaccuracy, but includes the membership of the values as another factor affecting the contribution level. In FSI, we first calculate the correct value based on the reliability or error rate and then pass it to the membership function as follows:

$$\text{Confidence} = \sum_{i=1}^{n} w_i \mu(f(x_i, e_i)) \tag{14.6}$$

where w_i represents a weight assigned to a condition and $\mu(f(x_i, e_i))$ denotes the membership degree of the element x_i. The function f calculates the correct value of the context based on the inaccuracy value e_i. If e_i is a reliability rate, the sensed value is multiplied by it and if it is an error rate (i.e., $\pm$), it is added to the sensed value.

14.3.3.3 Symmetric and Asymmetric Attributes

The third reasoning technique of CS introduces the concepts of symmetric context attribute CA_S and asymmetric context attribute CA_A. A symmetric context attribute increases the confidence in inferring a situation if its value is within the corresponding region and decreases the confidence if it is outside that region (e.g., reasoning about the "hypertension" situation based on "blood pressure"). An asymmetric context attribute increases the confidence in inferring a situation if its value is within the corresponding region, but would not decrease the confidence if it is outside that region (e.g., reasoning about the "heat stroke" situation based on "age"). Whenever an asymmetric attribute is not contained within its region, the redistribution method assigns 0 to the weight of the attribute and recalculates the relative weights for the remaining attributes as follows:

$$\hat{w}_i = w_i / \sum_{i=1}^{n} w_i \tag{14.7}$$

The above-mentioned characteristic of context attributes is integrated into the following reasoning technique of CS:

$$\text{Confidence} = \sum_{i=1}^{n} \hat{w}_i \cdot \Pr(\hat{a}_i^t \in A_i) \tag{14.8}$$

where $a_i \in CA_S \cup CA_A$ and $\hat{w}$ denotes the recalculated weight.

The concept of symmetric and asymmetric context attributes and its corresponding reasoning techniques are applied to FSI as follows:

$$\text{Confidence} = \sum_{i=1}^{n} \hat{w}_i \mu(f(x_i, e_i)) \qquad (14.9)$$

where $x_i \in FS$ and $FS \in LV_S \cup LV_A$. Since values that linguistic variables take are not numeric (i.e., these values are called terms that represent fuzzy sets), the concept of symmetric and asymmetric concepts is applied to the values of fuzzy sets associated with linguistic variables.

14.3.3.4   Partial and Symmetric and Asymmetric Attributes

The fourth reasoning technique of CS is based on the notion that there is a trade-off between complete containment of all symmetric context attributes (i.e., when all values of symmetric attributes are contained in their corresponding regions) and their individual contribution using the third reasoning technique (i.e., when some of values of attributes are contained). This heuristic does not apply to asymmetric attributes because they do not decrease the confidence for the occurrence of a situation. The reasoning technique based on partial and complete containment is as follows:

$$\text{Confidence} = q_1 \sum_{i=1}^{n} \hat{w}_i . \Pr(\hat{a}_i^t \in A_i) + q_2 \prod_{k=1}^{m} \Pr(\hat{a}_k^t \in A_k) \qquad (14.10)$$

where $a_i \in CA_S \cup CA_A, a_k \in CA_S$ and $q_1 + q_2 = 1$. q_1 and q_2 denote the utility weights used to represent each aspect of containment with a dimension. Applying these dimensions addresses the trade-off between complete and partial containment and combines them towards inferring the occurrence of a situation. The utility weights of two dimensions determine which aspect of containment is more important (i.e., complete or partial).

The concept of partial and complete containment and its reasoning technique are applied to FSI and similar to the third reasoning method, FSI maps values of symmetric context attributes into the values of fuzzy sets corresponding to symmetric linguistic variables as follows:

$$\text{Confidence} = q_1 \sum_{i=1}^{n} \hat{w}_i . \mu(f(x_i, e_i)) + q_2 \prod_{k=1}^{m} \mu(f(x_k, e_k)) \qquad (14.11)$$

where $q_1 + q_2 = 1$, $x_i \in FS$ and $FS \in LV_S \cup LV_A$, $x_k \in FS$ and $FS \in LV_S$.

Results of computation of the above-mentioned reasoning techniques suggest the degree of confidence in the occurrence of a situation. In FSI, if the output of a rule evaluation for the "hypertension" situation yields a degree of 0.885, we can suggest that the level of confidence in the occurrence of "hypertension" is 0.885. This value can be compared to a confidence threshold ε between 0 and 1 (i.e., pre-defined by the application's designers) to determine whether a situation is occurring.

$$\mu_{s_i}(x) \geq \varepsilon \qquad (14.12)$$

Although the CS model's heuristics and reasoning techniques deal with sensors' inaccuracy and characteristics of context attributes, they are inadequate to represent the uncertainty associated with real-life and human concepts, which tend to be vague and uncertain. Changes that occur between situations are also indicators of vague and uncertain situations that need to be reflected in the situation inference results. A fuzzy approach has the strength to represent this level of uncertainty as well as minor and delta changes of context that can be important in certain applications.

The next section discusses the adaptation engine and describes how parameters of data stream mining algorithms are adjusted according to occurring situations and available resources.

14.4   Adaptation Engine (AE)

The AE (Adaptation Engine) is responsible for gradual tuning of data stream processing parameters according to the occurring situation/s and available resources in real time. AE provides three adaptation strategies including resource-aware, situation-aware and integrated strategies. The Controller is a subcomponent of AE that constantly monitors occurring situations that are inferred by FSI and availability of resources reported by RM. The Controller makes decisions on which strategy needs to be performed. AE and its components are shown in Fig. 14.3.

Lightweight data stream mining techniques such as LWC, LWCLass, LWF, RA-Cluster [11, 12] are adaptive to availability of resources via adjusting the algorithm parameters. These parameters control output, input and/or the process of the algorithm. The adaptation process is done through Algorithm Granularity (AG) approach. AG has three different variations. The first and most commonly used in our work is Algorithm Output Granularity (*AOG*) [13]. AOG controls the algorithm output rate via changing the data stream mining algorithm parameters to encourage or discourage the creation of new output structures. Similarly, Algorithm Input Granularity (*AIG*) [12] and Algorithm Processing Granularity (*APG*) [12] control the input rate and consumption of processing power, respectively.

LWC, LWCLass and LWF algorithms are based on the AOG approach that controls the output of the data stream mining according to the available memory. We have been inspired by the concept of AOG for developing our adaptation strategies.

To perform different strategies of adaptation, we need to pre-assign two thresholds for criticality of resources and occurring situations and specified by application designers. As depicted in Fig. 14.4, the thresholds of S_THRESHOLD_SAFE and R_THRESOLD_SAFE indicate the normal or safe level and S_THRESHOLD_CRITICAL and R_THRESOLD_CRITCIAL separate the medium and critical levels

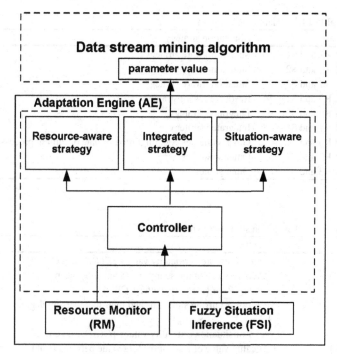

Fig. 14.3 Adaptation strategies of data stream mining algorithm

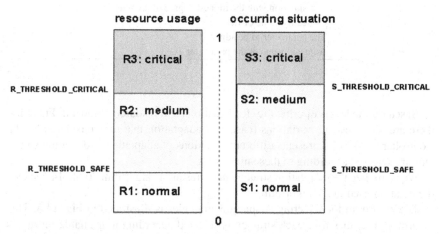

Fig. 14.4 Levels of criticality for resources and situations

for situations and resource usage. For example if we have three situations of "normal", "pre-hypertension" and "hypertension", we can assign the criticality values of 0.25, 0.6, 0.9 to these situations respectively. The thresholds assigned to computational resources show the level of their criticality regarding their usage. The higher the value, the higher is the usage.

Table 14.2 Adaptation cases

Cases	Adaptation strategy
If R1 and S1	Situation-aware strategy
If R1 and S2	Situation-aware strategy
If R1 and S3	Situation-aware strategy
If R2 and S1	Resource-aware strategy
If R2 and S2	Integrated strategy
If R2 and S3	Integrated strategy
If R3 and S1	Other strategies e.g., migration of data or mining process
If R3 and S2	Other strategies
If R3 and S3	Other strategies

Table 14.3 Adaptation strategies symbols

Symbol	Meaning
RC	Vector of resource criticality values $\{C(R_1), \ldots, C(R_n)\}$
$C(R_i)$	Criticality value of a resource R_i (a value between 0–1) where $R_i \in \{\text{memory}, \text{battery}, \text{CPU}\}$
IS	Vector of occurring situations and their membership degree $(\{S_1, \mu_1\}, \ldots, \{S_n, \mu_n\})$
SC	Vector of situation criticality values $\{C(S_1), \ldots, C(S_n)\}$
$C(S_i)$	Criticality value of a situation S_i (a value between 0 and 1)
$S(\max(\mu_i))$	Function returning a situation with the highest membership degree
HS	The situation with the highest degree of membership
$C(HS)$	Criticality value of HS
P_i	The parameter to be adjusted
PA_i	Adjusted value of the parameter P_i

Based on the levels of criticality for situations and resources shown in Fig. 14.4, there are nine possible variations (cases) of adaptation that are considered by the Controller. Table 14.2 presents different variations of adaptation. Adaptation strategies are selected according to these nine cases.

We formalize the adaptation strategy and present its algorithm. Table 14.3 shows the notation used in the algorithm.

The algorithm for selecting adaptation strategies is illustrated in Fig. 14.5. This algorithm describes how each strategy is selected according to available resources and occurring situations.

When resources are critical (R3) it means that the mobile device cannot continue the mining operations and the adaptation strategies that we provide are not adequate to address the issue. These cases require other strategies such as migration of the data or the process that are out of the scope of this project. Therefore, the algorithm depicted in Fig. 14.5 does not deal with this issue.

The next subsection discusses the resource-aware adaptation strategy that factors in available resources in the adaptation phase.

```
Start adaptation(Pᵢ)
   Repeat
     Get RCᵢ from RM
     Get IS from FSI
        If (C(Rᵢ)<=R_THRESHOLD_SAFE)
            PAᵢ=Do situation-aware strategy
          Else If (C(Rᵢ)>R_THRESHOLD_SAFE AND C(Rᵢ)<=R_THRESHOLD_CRITICAL)
            HS=S(max(μᵢ))
            If (C(HS)<=S_THRESHOLD_SAFE)
                PAᵢ=Do resource-aware strategy
            Else
                PAᵢ=Do Integrated strategy
        End If
        Return PAᵢ
   Until done.
End
```

Fig. 14.5 The algorithm for adaptation of parameters

14.4.1   Resource-Aware Strategy

Resource-aware adaptation strategy occurs when the situation is at normal level, but resource availability is at medium level. This is because normal situations do not require frequent monitoring and the results of resource-aware adaptation do not contradict the requirements of normal situations. Resource-awareness is inspired by the AOG approach. One of the AOG-based clustering algorithms is called LightWeight Clustering (LWC) [11]. LWC considers a threshold distance measure for clustering of data. Increasing this threshold discourages forming of new clusters and in turn, reduces resource consumption.

AOG is a three-stage, resource-aware distance-based mining data streams approach. The process of mining data streams using AOG starts with a mining phase. In this step, a value of threshold distance measure is determined. This threshold has the ability to control the output rate of the running mining algorithm. The second stage in AOG-mining approach is the adaptation phase. In this phase, the threshold value is adjusted to cope with the data rate of the incoming stream, available memory and time constraints to fill the memory with generated knowledge (data mining output). The last stage in AOG approach is the knowledge integration phase. This stage represents the merging of generated results when the memory is full. This integration allows the continuity of the mining process on resource-constrained devices. Figure 14.6 shows how AOG is applied to the LWC.

The details of how data stream mining algorithms are adjusted according to occurring situations are given in the next subsection.

14.4.2   Situation-Aware Strategy

Situation-aware adaptation in AE is performed when resources are available and at normal level. Situation-aware adaptation occurs based on occurring situations

Fig. 14.6 Light-weight
clustering algorithm based
on AOG

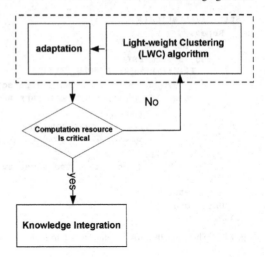

inferred by FSI. These results are multiple situations with different level of confidence. To provide a fine-grained adaptation and reflect the level of confidence of each situation in the adaptation phase, we compute weighted average of the data mining parameter value based on confidence values of situations and the pre-specified value of the parameter for each situation. The situation-aware adaptation enables reflecting all the results of situation inference in the adaptation of parameter values and is represented as follows:

$$\hat{p}_j = \sum_{i=1}^{n} \mu_i p_j / \sum_{i=1}^{n} \mu_i \tag{14.13}$$

where p_j represents the set value of a parameter for a pre-defined situation S_i, μ_i denotes the membership degree of situation S_i where $1 \leq i \leq n$ and n represent the number of pre-defined situations, and $\hat{p}_j$ represents aggregated value of the parameter. Figure 14.7 shows an example of situation-aware adaptation of LWC for three pre-defined situations of "normal," "hypertension" and "hypertension" at the time t. To start the adaptation phase, the threshold parameter values are pre-set for each situation accordingly.

Situation-aware adaptation itself results in cost-efficiency because when a situation is at normal level, the set value of parameter for a normal situation (e.g., a higher LWC threshold value) will be used and this reduces the use of resources.

The next subsection describes how integrated adaptation strategy combines resource-aware and situation-aware strategies and deals with the trade-off.

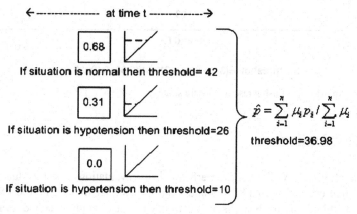

Fig. 14.7 An example of situation-aware adaptation strategy

14.4.3 Integrated Strategy

When criticality value of resources is at medium level and situation criticality value is at medium or critical level (i.e., R2S2 or R2S3), it is imperative to consider both resource availability and occurring situations in the adaptation phase.

When the adaptation cases R2S2 or R2S3 occur, resource-aware and situation-aware adaptation strategies compute different values for parameters. This is because resource-aware strategy reduces resource consumption to deal with resource criticality (i.e., at medium level) and situation-aware strategy intends to increase accuracy of mining results by increasing output that is typically required in critical situations. This causes a trade-off between the adjusted values of parameters.

As an example, consider the criticality value of memory is 0.62 and the criticality value of occurring situation (i.e., with highest level of confidence) is 0.9. To adjust the LWC's threshold parameter, the resource-aware strategy computes a higher threshold value (e.g., 32) to produce fewer results and conserve the memory, but the situation-aware strategy computes a lower value (e.g., 12) to increase the output. The integrated strategy addresses this issue by computing the average value of parameter based on the results of the two strategies (i.e., $\hat{p}_R$ and $\hat{p}_S$) and criticality values as follows:

$$\hat{p}_I = \frac{(\hat{p}_R.\text{criticality}_R) + (\hat{p}_S.\text{criticality}_S)}{\text{criticality}_R + \text{criticality}_S} \tag{14.14}$$

Figure 14.8 shows how the integrated strategy can be used to deal with the above-described problem/trade-off.

To validate SAAP, we have performed evaluation of the reasoning technique of FSI and situation-aware adaptation. The next section describes these evaluations.

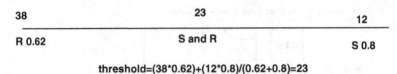

threshold=(38*0.62)+(12*0.8)/(0.62+0.8)=23

Fig. 14.8 An example of using resource-aware strategy

14.5 Evaluation

For evaluation of SAAP, we have performed two evaluations. First evaluation is a comparative evaluation of FSI, CS and Dempster-Shafer to validate the FSI technique and highlight its benefits in dealing with uncertainty. Second evaluation focuses on adaptation of threshold parameter according to occurring situations.

14.5.1 FSI Evaluation

To evaluate the FSI model, we have compared the FSI situation reasoning technique to the CS and Dempster-Shafer (hereafter DS) reasoning approaches. The purpose of this evaluation is first to validate the FSI model against a well-known reasoning technique such as DS and a context model developed for pervasive computing environments such as the CS model.

The second objective of the evaluation is to highlight the benefits of the FSI to deal with uncertain context and situations. In this evaluation, we consider three situations of "hypotension," "normal" and "hypertension" that are defined using context attributes of systolic (SBP) and diastolic blood pressure (DBP) with the scale of 40–170 and 20–150 mm Hg, respectively, and heart rate (HR) with the range of 20–150 bpm.

Table 14.4 depicts modelling of the three situations in the CS model including the weights of attributes and their corresponding regions of values. Unlike FSI, the CS model uses crisp boundary for regions. To provide a similar and balanced range of data for evaluation of these approaches, the boundaries of regions are selected in a way that they match the values of fuzzy sets with membership degree of 0.5.

Although FSI can represent a situation with multiple rules and each condition can be joined by the OR operator, we use one rule to define a situation and do not include the OR operator, so that both models can be closely compared. The modelling of the situations in FSI is presented in Table 14.5. Weights of conditions for the FSI rules conform to the weights specified for the context attributes in CS.

To model situations of Hypotension (L), Normal (N) and Hypertension (H) with DS, we first define propositions and events. Since all three situations are incompatible, we include a proposition of Unknown (U) that would consist of three situations. Then we identify the events and mass values that reflect the association of an event with the occurrences of each proposition. Mass values are assigned in a way that

Table 14.4 Situation definitions in the CS model

Situation	Context attribute	Region of values	Weight
Hypotension	1 = SBP	≤ 85	0.4
	2 = DBP	≤ 60	0.4
	3 = HR	≤ 45	0.2
Normal	1 = SBP	>85 and ≤ 135	0.4
	2 = DBP	>60 and ≤ 110	0.4
	3 = HR	>45 and ≤ 85	0.2
Hypertension	1 = SBP	>135	0.4
	2 = DBP	>110	0.4
	3 = HR	>85	0.2

Table 14.5 Situation definitions in the FSI model

Situation	Linguistic variable	Terms	Fuzzy set
Represented below via FSI rules	1 = SBP	Low, normal, high	Trapezoidal membership functions used
	2 = DBP	Low, normal, high	
	3 = HR	Slow, normal, fast	
Rule1: If SBP is low and DBP is low and HR is low then situation is hypotension			
Rule2: If SBP is normal and DBP is normal and HR is normal then situation is normal			
Rule3: If SBP is high and DBP is high and HR is high then situation is hypertension			

Table 14.6 Definitions of events and mass values

Event	Mass values for Normal	Mass values for Hypotension	Mass values for Hypertension	Mass values for unknown	Total mass
SBPLow (40–85)	0	0.7	0	0.3	1
SBPMed (86–135)	0.7	0	0	0.3	1
SBPHigh (136–180)	0	0	0.7	0.3	1
DBPLow (20–60)	0	0.7	0	0.3	1
DBPMed (61–110)	0.7	0	0	0.3	1
DBPHigh (110–130)	0	0	0.7	0.3	1
HRSlow (20–45)	0.2	0.4	0	0.4	1
HRMed (46–85)	0.4	0.2	0.2	0.2	1
HRFast (86–130)	0.2	0	0.4	0.4	1

they reflect to what degree each event indicates a situation. Table 14.6 depicts the events and mass values using the DS technique.

To apply the DS algorithm for situation reasoning, we use the Dempster's rule of combination. If R represents a situation, considering all existing propositions, the intersection of some of these propositions denoted as P and Q results in the proposition R (i.e., $P \cap Q = R$) and the intersection of other combinations of propositions results in an empty set. The normalized version of the combination rule of DS is as follows:

$$m(R) = \frac{\sum_{P \cap Q = R} m_i(P).m_j(Q)}{1 - \sum_{P \cap Q = \varphi} m_i(P).m_j(Q)} \tag{14.15}$$

where $m(R)$ denotes the mass value computed for a proposition R given the evidences i and j.

Since we have based our situations on three context attributes, we define three mass functions of m_1, m_2 and m_3 corresponding to each context attribute. Then we apply DS combination over all propositions and available evidence. For example, if we have the context values of 82 for SBP, 52 for DBP and 58 for HR, we combine evidence for the occurrence of hypotension (L) as follows:

$$
\begin{aligned}
m_{12}(L) &= \frac{\sum_{Q \cap R = L} m_1(A).m_2(B)}{1 - \sum_{Q \cap R = \phi} m_1(A).m_2(B)} \\
&= \frac{m_1(L).m_2(L) + m_1(L).m_2(U) + m_1(U).m_2(L)}{1 - m_1(L).m_2(H) - m_1(H).m_2(L) - m_1(L).m_2(N) - m_1(N).m_2(L)} \\
&= \frac{0.7 \cdot 0.7 + 0.7 \cdot 0.3 + 0.3 \cdot 0.7}{1 - 0.7 \cdot 0 - 0 \cdot 0.7 - 0.7 \cdot 0 - 0 \cdot 0.7} \approx 0.91
\end{aligned}
$$

$$
\begin{aligned}
m_{12}(H) &= \frac{\sum_{Q \cap R = H} m_1(A).m_2(B)}{1 - \sum_{Q \cap R = \phi} m_1(A).m_2(B)} \\
&= \frac{m_1(H).m_2(H) + m_1(H).m_2(U) + m_1(U).m_2(H)}{1 - m_1(H).m_2(L) - m_1(L).m_2(H) - m_1(H).m_2(N) - m_1(N).m(H)} \\
&= \frac{0 \cdot 0 + 0 \cdot 0.3 + 0.3 \cdot 0}{1 - 0 \cdot 0.7 - 0.7 \cdot 0 - 0 \cdot 0 - 0 \cdot 0} = 0
\end{aligned}
$$

$$
\begin{aligned}
m_{12}(N) &= \frac{\sum_{Q \cap R = N} m_1(A).m_2(B)}{1 - \sum_{Q \cap R = \phi} m_1(A).m_2(B)} \\
&= \frac{m_1(N).m_2(N) + m_1(N).m_2(U) + m_1(U).m_2(N)}{1 - m_1(N).m_2(L) - m_1(L).m_2(N) - m_1(N).m_2(H) - m_1(H).m(N)} \\
&= \frac{0 \cdot 0 + 0 \cdot 0.3 + 0.3 \cdot 0}{1 - 0 \cdot 0.7 - 0.7 \cdot 0 - 0 \cdot 0 - 0 \cdot 0} = 0
\end{aligned}
$$

$$
\begin{aligned}
m_{12}(U) &= \frac{\sum_{Q \cap R = U} m_1(A).m_2(B)}{1 - \sum_{Q \cap R = \phi} m_1(A).m_2(B)} \\
&= \frac{m_1(U).m_2(U)}{\begin{array}{c} 1 - m_1(H).m_2(L) - m_1(L).m_2(H) - m_1(N).m_2(H) \\ -m_1(H).m(N) - m_1(N).m_2(L) - m_1(L).m_2(N) \end{array}} \\
&= \frac{0.3 \cdot 0.3}{1 - 0 \cdot 0.7 - 0.7 \cdot 0 - 0 \cdot 0 - 0 \cdot 0 - 0.0.7 - 0.7.0} \approx 0.09
\end{aligned}
$$

$$m_{123}(L) = \frac{\sum_{Q \cap R=L} m_1(A).m_2(B)}{1 - \sum_{Q \cap R=\phi} m_1(A).m_2(B)}$$

$$= \frac{m_{12}(L).m_3(L) + m_{12}(L).m_3(U) + m_3(U).m_{12}(L)}{1 - m_{12}(L).m_3(H) - m_{12}(H).m_3(L)}$$
$$\frac{}{-m_{12}(L).m_3(N) - m_{12}(N).m_3(L)}$$

$$= \frac{0.91 \cdot 0.2 + 0.91 \cdot 0.2 + 0.09 \cdot 0.2}{1 - 0.91 \cdot 0.2 - 0 \cdot 0.2 - 0.91 \cdot 0.4 - 0 \cdot 0.2} = \frac{0.382}{0.454} \approx 0.841$$

The same DS reasoning computation presented above is used in our evaluation. Although the DS theory has the strength of representing unknown or uncertainty, determination of mass values for propositions can be a difficult task, particularly that they can have impact on the other situations. For evaluation of CS and FSI, we use the equations 14.1 and 14.2 (discussed in subsect. 14.4.2). These techniques do not include the sensor's inaccuracy and could be compared to the DS method more accurately.

The dataset used for evaluation is generated continuously (data rate is 30 records/minute) in ascending order to model the changes of situations. For this set of experiments, we have used our data synthesizer to represent the seven different situations based on the description in Table 14.6. This categorization shows the data scales that contribute to the occurrence of each pre-defined situation as well as the uncertain situations. Table 14.7 depicts a snapshot of 131 context states that is used along with their scales.

The results of the comparative evaluation of CS, DS and FSI for situations of "hypotension," "normal" and "hypertension" in Fig. 14.9 show that three approaches of CS, DS and FSI have a relatively similar trend according to context changes. When the data correspond to a pre-defined situation, the results of three approaches almost overlap. This overlapping is more noticeable with the CS and FSI models as they are based on similar heuristics. However, when changes of data indicate the occurrence of an unknown and uncertain situation, differences of reasoning results between CS, DS and FSI are more apparent.

Compared to FSI, the results of situation reasoning by the CS and DS methods show sudden rise and fall with sharp edges when situations change, which do not

Table 14.7 The dataset used for the evaluation

Context attribute scales	Corresponding DS events
SBP:40–65, DBP: 20–45, HR: 20–45	SBPLow, DBPLow, HRSlow
SBP:66–80, DBP: 46–60, HR: 46–60	SBPLow, DBPLow, HRMed
SBP:81–85, DBP: 61–65, HR: 61–65	SBPLow, DBPMed, HRMed
SBP:86–105, DBP: 66–85, HR: 66–85	SBPMed, DBPMed, HRMed
SBP:106–130, DBP: 86–110, HR: 86–110	SBPMed, DBPMed, HRHigh
SBP:131–135, DBP: 111–115, HR: 111–115	SBPLow, DBPHigh, HRHigh
SBP:136–170, DBP: 116–150, HR: 116–150	SBPHigh, DBPHigh, HRHigh

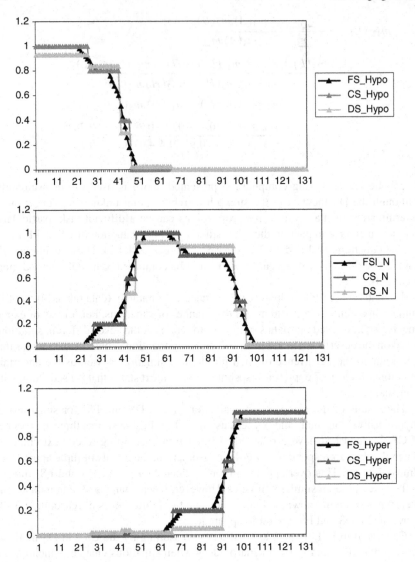

Fig. 14.9 The results of the comparative evaluation

match the real-life situations. This is because the DS and CS approaches do not deal with delta changes of the values and are not able to reflect the gradual evolution of one situation to another situation.

When the value of context attributes decreases or increases, its membership degree also increases and decreases accordingly and gradually. This enables FSI to provide more accurate situation reasoning results in terms of reflecting very minor changes of context.

The evaluation validates the accuracy of the FSI model for situation modelling and reasoning and it also shows that FSI is able to reflect very minor changes of context in situation inference and represents changes in a more gradual and smooth manner. The evaluation shows that the FSI model is a more appropriate approach for representation of human concepts and for reasoning about the real-world situations that are defined by continuous values. Health-related situations are examples of these types of scenarios where FSI can prove to be more fitting approach compared to the DS and CS reasoning approaches.

14.5.2   Evaluation of Situation-aware Adaptation

Data mining algorithm that we have used for evaluation is LightWeight Clustering (LWC) [9]. The threshold distance parameter of the LWC algorithm determines the distance between the centre of a cluster and a new incoming data record. In our evaluation, we have set the threshold value for the situation of "normal" to 42, "pre-hypotension" to 36, "hypotension" to 26, "pre-hypertension" to 18 and "hypertension" to 10. For critical situations, the threshold needs to be decreased and for normal situations, it needs to be increased. This is because these values are acceptable given a variation of 12 (i.e., 42 divided by 3) as none of the context attributes of SBP, DBP and HR has significant impact on a healthy individual, while a variation of 3 for "hypertension" can be significant.

To analyze the results of situation reasoning and adaptation for all the situations, we have simulated a 5-day scenario for a patient who experiences fluctuations of blood pressure. The scenario is described in Table 14.8. The dataset used for the evaluation is drawn from uniform distribution with different ranges for each context attribute (i.e., SBP, DBP and HR). The date is generated at a rate of 30 records/minute. The rate was chosen according to the application needs. This rate could be customized to meet the different requirements of various applications.

Figure 14.10 illustrates the results of this evaluation. The top graph shows changes of context attribute values for each day and the bottom graph shows the

Table 14.8   A 5-day scenario

Day	Patient's health state
1	Vital signs are normal and RT is mild
2	Morning: RT is gradually rising and SBP, DBP and HR are decreasing
	Afternoon: SBP, DBP and HR are very low (necessary medical treatment provided)
	Evening: SBP, DBP and HR are gradually increasing and RT is dropping
3	Vital signs are normal and RT is mild
4	Morning: SBP, DBP and HR are increasing
	Afternoon: SBP, DBP and HR are very high (necessary medical treatment provided)
	Evening: SBP, DBP and HR are gradually decreasing
5	Vital signs are normal and RT is mild

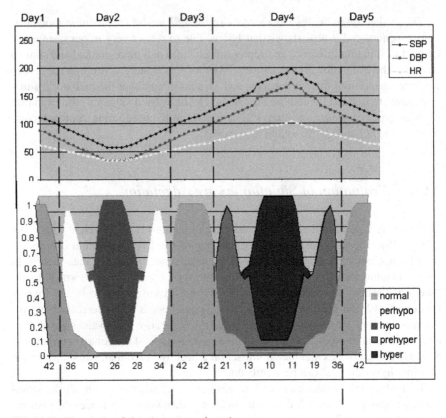

Fig. 14.10 The results of situation-aware adaptation

corresponding fuzzy situations. As the values of SBP, DBP and HR decrease (i.e., day 2), the membership degrees of "hypotension" and "pre-hypotension" situations increase and as these values increase (i.e., day 4), the membership degrees of "hypertension" and "pre-hypertension" increase. Furthermore, the results of situation inference for day 2 and 4 also reflect vague situations when the patient is recovering or moving towards a situation (e.g., "more or less normal" and "slightly pre-hypertension").

The bottom graph in Fig. 14.10 shows how the results of situation inference are used for gradual adjusting of the distance threshold value. The value of the threshold is automatically adjusted according to the fuzziness (i.e., membership degree) of each situation in run-time. Decreasing the threshold value increases the number and accuracy of the output (clusters) that is required for closer monitoring of more critical situations such as hypertension. Alternatively, increasing the threshold value for normal situations decreases the mining output and also provides cost-efficiency of resources.

14.6 Conclusion

Ubiquitous applications such as healthcare monitoring applications need to analyze and process data streams that are generated at very high rates in real-time. Therefore, it is of great importance for data stream mining techniques to be equipped with adapting strategies to promote the continuity and consistency of the running application. Current ubiquitous data stream mining approaches have limited levels of adaptations (mainly focusing on battery or memory). To enhance adaptation of data stream mining algorithms, there is a need to consider the contextual/situational information in the adaptation phase. Integrating data stream processing with situation-awareness provides intelligent and cost-efficient analysis of data and enables continuity and consistency of mining operations.

In this chapter, we proposed and validated a general approach for situation-aware adaptive processing (SAAP) of data streams that incorporates situation-awareness into data stream processing using fuzzy logic. The fuzzy situation inference model allows modelling and reasoning about real-world. The SAAP architecture enables real-time analysis of data emanating from multiple sensors onboard mobile devices while factoring in contextual/situational information and resource availability. This approach significantly enhances a range of ubiquitous applications that perform data stream mining on mobile devices.

In the future, we intend to investigate other strategies of adaptation that can deal with criticality of resources and situations such as migration of data or mining process to neighboring devices. We also aim to explore and model relationships between situations and extend FSI with learning capabilities, so that the system can predict future situations.

References

1. Gaber MM, Krishnaswamy S, Zaslavsky A (2005) Resource-Aware Mining of Data Streams. Journal of Universal Computer Science. 11(8): 1440–1453
2. Gaber MM, Zaslavsky A, Krishnaswamy S (2004) A Cost-Efficient Model for Ubiquitous Data Stream Mining, Proceedings of the Tenth International Conference on Information Processing and Management of Uncertainty in Knowledge-Based Systems, Perugia Italy
3. Kargupta H, Bhargava R, Liu K, Powers M, Blair P, Bushra S, Dull J, Sarkar K, Klein M, Vasa M, Handy D (2004) VEDAS: A Mobile and Distributed Data Stream Mining System for Real-Time Vehicle Monitoring, Proceedings of the SIAM International Data Mining Conference, SDM'04, Lake Buena Vista FL
4. Galan M, Liu H, Torkkola K (2005) Intelligent Instance Selection of Data Streams for Smart Sensor Applications. SPIE Defense and Security Symposium, Intelligent Computing: Theory and Applications III: 108–119
5. Padovitz A, Zaslavsky A, Loke S (2006) A Unifying Model for Representing and Reasoning About Context under Uncertainty, 11th International Conference on Information Processing and Management of Uncertainty in Knowledge-Based Systems (IPMU), Paris, France
6. Anagnostopoulos CB, Ntarladimas Y, Hadjiefthymiades S (2007) Situational Computing: An Innovative Architecture with Imprecise Reasoning. The Journal of Systems and Software. 80: 1993–2014

7. Jang JR, Sun Ch, Mizutani E (1997) Neuro-Fuzzy and Soft Computing: A Computational Approach to Learning and Machine Intelligence. Prentice-Hall: Upper Saddle River, NJ
8. Zadeh L (1975) The Concept of a Linguistic Variable and Its Application to Approximate Reasoning. Information Systems. 199–249
9. Zimmermann H (1996) Fuzzy Set Theory - and Its Applications. Kluwer Academic Publishers: Norwell, Massachusetts
10. Bruce G, Buchanan BG, Shortliffe ED (1984) Rule-based expert systems: the MYCIN experiments of the Stanford Heuristic Programming Project. Reading, Mass: Addison-Wesley
11. Gaber MM, Krishnaswamy S, Zaslavsky A (2005) On-board Mining of Data Streams in Sensor Networks, A Book Chapter in Advanced Methods of Knowledge Discovery from Complex Data, (Eds.) S. Badhyopadhyay, U. Maulik, L. Holder and D. Cook, Springer Verlag
12. Phung N, Gaber MM, Roehm U (2007) Resource-aware Distributed Online Data Mining for Wireless Sensor Networks, Proceedings of the International Workshop on Knowledge Discovery from Ubiquitous Data Streams (IWKDUDS07), in conjunction with ECML and PKDD 2007, Warsaw, Poland
13. Gaber MM, Krishnaswamy S, Zaslavsky A (2003) Adaptive Mining Techniques for Data Streams Using Algorithm Output Granularity, The Australasian Data Mining Workshop (AusDM 2003), Held in conjunction with the 2003 Congress on Evolutionary Computation (CEC 2003), Canberra, Australia, Springer Verlag, Lecture Notes in Computer Science (LNCS)

Part IV
Pervasive Networks and E-commerce

Chapter 15
A Scalable P2P Video Streaming Framework*

Ivan Lee

Abstract Peer-to-peer (P2P) networking technique represents a vast potential to overcome many constraints in the conventional content distribution networks, especially for the real-time applications such as P2P streaming. In this chapter, a P2P streaming system is examined, and the proposed system combines multiple-description source coding technique and a scalable streaming infrastructure. The proposed system aims to gradually offload congested traffic from a centralized bottleneck to the under-utilized P2P networks and hence, provides seamless transitions from client/server streaming to centralized P2P streaming and to decentralized P2P streaming. The performance of the proposed framework is evaluated in terms of video frame loss rate, which reflects the probability of freeze video frames.

Keywords Peer-to-peer network · Video Streaming · Multiple-description coding

15.1 Introduction

The explosive growth of the internet over the last decade has led to a revolution of information exchange. The advances in wired and wireless communication have changed the way we live, work, learn and play. The growth of the internet is driven by the blossom of network applications to increase the productivity while reducing the cost of operation. Today, there are more applications than ever that require to use the network, consume the bandwidth and send packets far and wide. The service providers are actively upgrading the internet backbone to fulfil the demand for high bandwidth applications such as multimedia communications.

I. Lee (✉)
University of South Australia, Mawson Lakes Campus, Mawson Lakes,
South Australia 5095, Australia
e-mail: Ivan.Lee@unisa.edu.au

* This chapter is the extended version of a manuscript submitted to the 2008 International Symposium on Ubiquitous Multimedia Computing.

A.-E. Hassanien et al. (eds.), *Pervasive Computing: Innovations in Intelligent Multimedia and Applications*, Computer Communications and Networks, DOI 10.1007/978-1-84882-599-4_15, © Springer-Verlag London Limited 2009

With the advances in multimedia consumer electronics, high-tech gadgets are popularized with affordable prices. Today, multimedia content production is no longer a specialized job for movie producers and photographers. An average person can easily create digitized media content using standard equipments, such as computers, digital cameras, digital video camcorders and scanners.

Video streaming is the method of video delivery over the Internet (or intranet) to end-users who are playing back the content in real time. The video can either be pre-recorded or live streamed. The major challenge posed in video streaming is its timing requirement, and a packet will be considered lost if the transmission fails to meet a real-time constraint. This differs significantly from a play-after-download approach where transmission delays are not considered as a factor of error. Another challenge for video streaming is the best-effort nature of today's Internet, where a successful data delivery is not guaranteed. To resolve these problems, numerous techniques on transmission feedback control, adaptive source encoding algorithm, efficient packetization, resource allocation and error control coding have been proposed to improve the quality of video communication [17, 18]. In [4], Chow et al. propose a variation of Gilbert model [20] where the loss parameters of a path depend on an application's transmission rate. Using this model, the authors optimize the load distribution among multiple paths to achieve better streaming quality. In [3], the authors propose an optimization framework to minimize the aggregate distortion for multiple video streams transmitted over a shared communication channel. In [2], the authors study the distributed video streaming from multiple servers to a single receiver. The servers independently partition the media packets based on the bandwidth information, such that the resulting video quality at the receiver is maximized.

Among different approaches proposed for video streaming to resolve the challenges on packet-based and best-effort internet today, distributed streaming over collaborative peer-to-peer (P2P) overlay networks has attracted increased attentions recently from both research and industrial communities. Unlike conventional client/server infrastructures commonly used for content distribution networks (CDN), in P2P networks, each node acts both as a client and as a server. This approach yields a high throughput and a good tolerance to loss and delay caused by network congestion [15]. P2P multimedia streaming and caching services also reduce initial delays for playback and hence, minimize jitters during playback [7]. Tran et al. [16] investigated application-layer multicast tree and proposed ZIGZAG, which possesses features on short end-to-end delay, low control overhead, efficient join and failure recovery and low maintenance overhead. Another study that utilizes advantage of the strong buffering capabilities of end hosts is oStream [5], which is a tree-based overlay that is specifically designed for one-to-many on-demand media distribution.

An alternative approach to reduce traffic loss for video communication is to adopt advanced source coding techniques. Erasure codes [1] have been proposed to improve the availability of archived data over distributed storage. Layered coding techniques, such as fine granularity scalable (FGS) coding [13] and progressive fine granularity scalable (PFGS) coding [19], divide the video bitstream with different priorities, which is best applied with DiffServ. If DiffServ is unavailable on the backbone, it is also possible to feedback the statistical loss patterns from the receiver to the sender for flow control. Major drawbacks of this approach are the round-trip feedback delay and the capability of adapting bandwidth to varying channels. To overcome these drawbacks, combined source coding and distributed streaming infrastructure were proposed in [10, 11], with a layered coding technique applied to the video bitstream and a collaborative streaming infrastructure. Another promising video coding technique, multiple descriptions coding (MDC) [6], emerges as an alternative way to improve the performance for streaming video. MDC encodes a media stream into multiple complementary descriptions. These descriptions serve the property that a baseline video quality can be reconstructed upon receiving any one description, and an improved quality video can be decoded upon receiving more descriptions. MDC, therefore, becomes a popular technique for real-time applications as it provides graceful video quality degradation without the need for retransmission. For example, in [8], Kim et al. present a distributed video streaming framework using unbalanced MDC and unequal error protection (UEP). The proposed algorithm minimizes the overall video distortion by optimally allocating the transmission rates and the channel coding rates for all senders.

This chapter examines a spatial domain MDC [12] technique and evaluates its performance under a collaborative streaming environment. Different approaches are presented to offload the bottleneck traffic by applying the MDC compressed video over the P2P network infrastructure. Three different streaming infrastructures, client/server, centralized P2P streaming and decentralized P2P streaming, are examined. To extend from traditional network performance analysis in terms of packet loss rate, this chapter further investigates the impacts of the loss traffic to the reconstructed video quality due to drifting error. The frame loss rate, which indicates the un-reconstructable video frames at the receiver, is analyzed in this chapter.

The remainder of this chapter is organized in the following manner. In Sect. 15.2, three different video streaming frameworks are examined: client/server, centralized P2P streaming and decentralized P2P streaming. The frame loss rates are analyzed for three video streaming frameworks respectively in Sect. 15.4. The experiments are presented in Sect. 15.5, and the conclusions are drawn in Sect. 15.6.

15.2 Centralized and Decentralized Video Streaming

Conventional video streaming applications using the client/server architecture face the scalability constraints. In this section, different video streaming approaches are presented, including client/server, centralized P2P streaming and decentralized P2P streaming. The different streaming infrastructures are designed for different subscriber populations. When a new video is newly brought to the internet, the client/server streaming model can be used to serve a limited number of subscribers. When the subscriber population grows, centralized P2P streaming model can be applied to offload part of the traffic from the bottleneck link to the P2P network. Once the centralized P2P streaming model reaches its capacity, decentralized P2P streaming can be applied to offload the entire traffic to the P2P network.

15.2.1   Client/Server Streaming

As illustrated in Fig. 15.1a, a centralized server is responsible for serving all the client requests. The aggregation link, thus, represents the bottleneck since the entire video traffic to all clients is carried on a single link. That is, the client/server model faces a scalability problem when the number of clients increases.

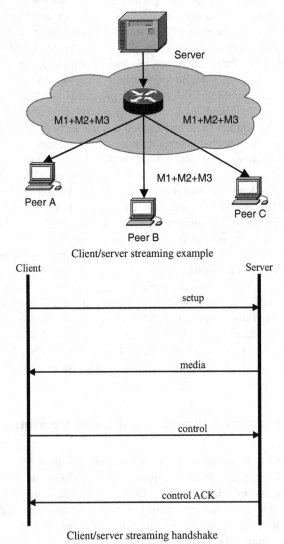

Client/server streaming example

Client/server streaming handshake

Fig. 15.1   Client/server video streaming. (**a**) Client/server streaming example and (**b**) client/server streaming handshake

Figure 15.1b summarizes the protocol handshake between the client and the server. The client initiates a setup request to a predetermined server port to open up a connection. The server is capable of performing authentication, authorization and accounting services to reinforce security. The video content is solely distributed from the server, and the centralized control mechanism helps reducing the content piracy in the streaming sessions. VCR-like control features such as fast forwarding can be requested by the client via the control request. The server will process the control requests and deliver different video streams as requested.

Two popular approaches are used for today's Internet to resolve scalability issues: (1) using cache engines or (2) applying multicast. Cache engines are typically located at the edge of the network, and they temporally store duplicated data traffic designated to different clients. Thus, a download request may be retrieved from a close-by cache engine instead of the far-away server, thereby decreasing the download time and reducing the load on the bottleneck link. However, since the video traffic in general demands a much higher bandwidth than conventional text and image-based traffic (such as the webpage applications), the storage space required on the cache engines will be substantially increased, making this approach impractical for video applications. Multicast eliminates duplicated traffics transmitted over network links, and it is best for broadcasting applications. However, the multicast may not fit the requirements for video on-demand applications where end-users may not download video simultaneously. In addition, multicast is not widely deployed on today's internet backbone, and the cost for upgrading the Internet backbone also represents a barrier for its popularity.

In this chapter, multiple-description coding technique is chosen to compress video signals. Different P2P infrastructures will be examined. In the subsequent subsections, an overview of centralized P2P streaming and decentralized P2P streaming will be discussed. The cache engine and the multicast techniques could both be applied to these P2P streaming models; however, the study is beyond the scope of this chapter. This chapter will focus on the comparisons without caching or multicast.

15.2.2   Centralized P2P Streaming

Applications over the P2P framework offer promising alternatives to resolve many problems existing in the conventional client/server framework, with a cost of centralized manageability. Besides, P2P nodes do not serve with high availability, which may result in a severe service degradation, especially for real-time applications such as video streaming.

In this chapter, a centralized P2P streaming framework is proposed, and it benefits from centralized manageability while offloading the traffic from the bottleneck bandwidth to under-utilized access networks. Centralized P2P streaming is controlled with a management server, which keeps track of the peer topology and manages the transmission of multimedia download sessions. The management server is in general a highly reliable source and it is used to deliver prioritized data; the P2P nodes are less reliable and therefore, it is responsible for forwarding low prioritized data. Centralized P2P streaming was designed with layered video codec [9], but the same arrangement may be applied with MDC. This arrangement guarantees a minimum quality level with the multimedia data delivered from the reliable server and a best-effort enhancement from the unreliable peers.

As illustrated in Fig. 15.2a, centralized P2P streaming offloads part of the video traffic from the bottleneck link to under-utilized P2P networks. In the client/server

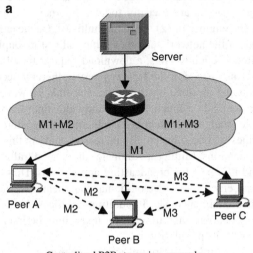

Centralized P2P streaming example

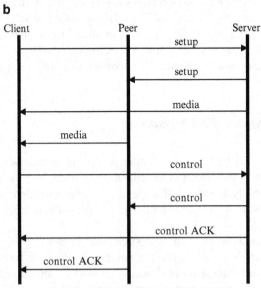

Centralized P2P streaming handshake

Fig. 15.2 Centralized peer-to-peer (P2P) video streaming. (**a**) Centralized P2P streaming example and (**b**) centralized P2P streaming handshake

streaming framework illustrated in Fig. 15.1a, the entire MDC substreams (M1+M2+M3) are transmitted to each individual end-user. For centralized P2P streaming, multiple peers may forward the missing MDC substreams. The server may arrange to transmit different MDC-streams into multiple peer-nodes, and these peer-nodes act as the forwarding peers. Therefore, there are multiple forwarding peers within a P2P cluster. The proposed framework is illustrated in Fig. 15.2a.

Figure 15.2b shows the protocol handshake of the centralized P2P streaming system. A new client will send the setup request to the server; thus, authentication, authorization and accounting services will take place at the centralized server. The server will forward the setup request to nearby peers of the client that already possess video under request. Centralized P2P streaming makes the server forwarding a video substream to guarantee a minimal video quality, while offloading enhanced video traffic among neighbouring peers. Like the setup request, the control requests will also be coordinated by the central server, and hence, that VCR-like operations may be processed securely.

Centralized P2P streaming offloads part of the MDC bitstreams to the P2P network. Let M denote the number of MDC substreams, and each substream with bit rate r_i where $i \in \{1, \ldots, M\}$, $r_i \in R$ and $r_i \geq 0$. Let n denote the number of peers within a P2P cluster, $n \in Z^+$ where Z^+ is the set of all positive integers. There is one forwarding peer for each P2P cluster. The bottleneck bandwidth requirement for client/server streaming framework is $n \sum_{i=1}^{M} r_i$, and bottleneck bandwidth for centralized P2P streaming framework is $\sum_{i=1}^{M} r_i + (n-1)r_1$. Thus, the bandwidth reduction by upgrading from client/server streaming to centralized P2P streaming is $(n-1) \sum_{i=2}^{M} r_i$. Since $(n-1) \geq 0$ and $r_i \geq 0, \forall i$. The bandwidth requirement for centralized P2P streaming is always equal to or less then that of client/server streaming.

For live streaming, the centralized P2P streaming may suffer from additional delays from the forwarding peers. A delay buffer may be applied at the destination as a workaround. For video on demand applications, assuming the video has been populated in the P2P network, the nodes which already downloaded the video will be nominated as the forwarding peers, instead of live download and forward. In this paper, we assume a living streaming system with the workaround described above or a video-on-demand scenario, and hence, the delay jitter will be ignored in the analysis.

15.2.3   Decentralized P2P Streaming

Centralized P2P streaming partially offloads video traffic from the bottleneck link; it extends the threshold of the client size, but is still constrained to a certain population. In other words, it is not fully scalable. Decentralized P2P streaming is the next phase

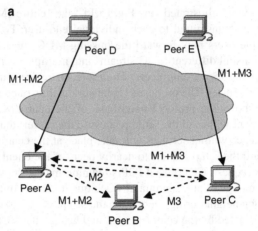

Decentralized P2P streaming example

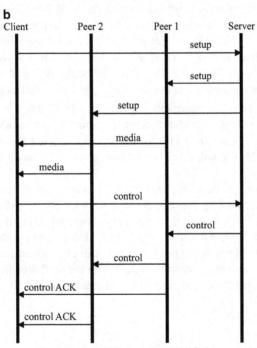

Decentralized P2P streaming handshake

Fig. 15.3 Decentralized P2P video streaming. (**a**) Decentralized P2P streaming example and (**b**) decentralized P2P streaming handshake

after centralized P2P streaming, which aims to resolve the scalability issue when centralized P2P streaming faces the critical point where traffic congestions occur on the bottleneck traffic.

Figure 15.3a illustrates the scenario of the decentralized P2P streaming. Decentralized P2P streaming assumes that there are a significant number of peers who receive the MDC substreams from the previous phase (i.e., centralized P2P streaming phase). When the bottleneck link observes traffic loss, any new peer requesting the video will be joining the decentralized P2P streaming framework, where the entire video substreams are transmitted from the P2P network. In decentralized P2P network, a central server is no longer required to guarantee the video delivery. Thus, decentralized P2P streaming is highly scalable with the trade-off in the guaranteed service. The reliability of the video stream, in terms of the frame loss probability, will be the main focus of discussion in this chapter.

Figure 15.3b shows the protocol handshake, and it maintains the benefit of centralized setup requests, authentication, authorization, accounting and control requests. Unlike client/server and centralized P2P streaming, video contents are entirely transmitted among the peers. Thus, setup and control requests are forwards to all peers responsible for providing the video.

15.3 Multi-Description Video Coding

Internet consists of an arbitrary interconnection of sources and links with heterogeneous propagation delays. In multi-path transmission, video can be transmitted over multiple paths. Most of the routing protocols today select the best path for data transmission, and a path handover will take place whenever transmission errors or network congestions occur. The major drawback for such an approach is the delay for updating the routing table during path handover, which can introduce a severe performance impact for real-time applications such as video streaming.

The multiple-description coding technique attempts to resolve the drawback caused by single path transmission with single description coding (SDC). MDC consists of an encoder E_{MDC} and a decoder D_{MDC}. The MDC encoder E_{MDC} maps a given video frame F_k into multiple description codes C_k^i, where $i = \{1, \ldots, M\}$

$$E_{\mathrm{MDC}} : F_k \mapsto \left\{ C_k^1, \ldots, C_k^M \right\}. \tag{15.1}$$

The MDC decoder D_{MDC} maps a subset of $\{x_1, \ldots, x_n\} \subset \{1, \ldots, M\}$ codes into a reconstructed frame, $\hat{F}_k^n$:

$$D_{\mathrm{MDC}} : \left\{ C_k^{x_1}, \ldots, C_k^{x_n} \right\} \mapsto \hat{F}_k^n \tag{15.2}$$

with the property that

$$d(F_k, \hat{F}_k^i) \leq d(F_k, \hat{F}_k^n) \quad \forall i < n, \tag{15.3}$$

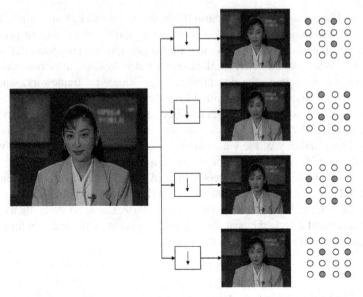

Fig. 15.4 Down-sampling process

where the distortion metric $d(F_1, F_2)$ evaluates the similarities between the two
video frames F_1 and F_2, for example, mean squared error (MSE). A lower $d(F_1, F_2)$
value indicates higher similarities between F_1 and F_2.

An efficient MDC codec with spatial diversity [12] is applied. This codec assumes strong inter-pixel similarities between adjacent pixels inside a video frame.
In the encoding stage, E_{MDC} is the spatial sub-sampling for each individual frame
in the video sequence, as illustrated in Fig. 15.4.

The down-sampled video sequences are encoded using a conventional video
codec. In our experiment, the advanced video codec standard using H.264 is chosen.
The decoded sequences by H.264 are used to reconstruct the video. Received MDC
streams are used to predict the missing MDC streams with cubic-spline interpolation. If there are more than one received MDC streams, the mean of the predicted
frame will be used. Figure 15.5 shows the block diagram of the proposed D_{MDC}
process.

Modern video codecs such as MPEG-1/2/4 and H.264 apply motion compensation technique to improve video coding efficiencies. Such technique applies different
encoding scheme for video frames, such as intra-prediction for I-frames, motion
prediction for P-frames and bi-directional predictions for B-frames. While P-frames
and B-frames improve the coding efficiency, they are dependent on the availability
of their reference frames: if the reference frames are lost, P-frames and B-frames
cannot be reconstructed properly. This is known as the drift error. To ensure that
the video sequence can recover from the loss, I-frames are forced to occur after a
certain duration to ensure a video *reset* will take place. This duration is known as
the group of picture (GOP). Figure 15.6 shows an example of frame loss patterns
among MDC substreams at the receiver end. Blocks with a cross sign indicate that
the substream video frame is lost, and blocks with a slash indicate that the substream

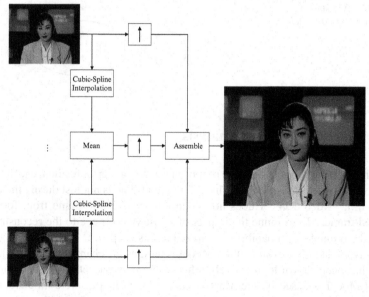

Fig. 15.5 Output video reconstruction using cubic spline interpolation

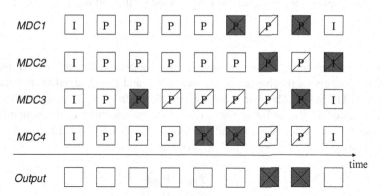

Fig. 15.6 Drifting error and reconstructed video frames

video frame is not decodable due to drifting error. The reconstructed output video is shown at the bottom of the figure, and as long as one substream delivers the video frame, an output video frame will be reconstructed (nevertheless the quality may be lower if the number of MDC substreams that reconstruct this output video frame is low). The frame loss rate indicates the number of output video frames that cannot be reconstructed at the receiver, and its value is the same as the one for the best delivered MDC substream within a GOP.

Fig. 15.7 Two-state
Markovian Gilbert model

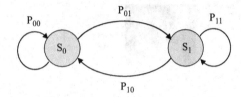

15.4   Video Frame Loss Analysis

To highlight the performance of the proposed framework, error resilience techniques
of the video codecs are disabled. Thus, if a video frame is not lost during the transmission, the video decoder does not attempt to recover the frame from formerly
received frames. To examine the impact of a lost video frame to the reconstructed
video, the frame loss probability is analyzed in this chapter.

The two-state Markovian Gilbert Model is used as the channel model [20]. This
model has been shown to effectively reflect the bursty packet loss behaviour. The
Gilbert Model is based on the Markov chain, which is a discrete-time stochastic
process with the Markov property: the state at the current time is decided only by the
immediately preceding one, and is not influenced by the state at any other previous
time. This property can be statistically represnted by the following equation:

$$P(x_{t+1}|x_0, x_1, x_2, \ldots, x_t) = P(x_{t+1}|x_t). \tag{15.4}$$

As shown in Fig. 15.7, the two states of this model are denoted as P_{S0} (good)
where the packets are received correctly and timely, and P_{S1} (bad) where the packets
are assumed to be lost. The state transition probability from P_{S0}-to-P_{S1} and P_{S1}-to-
P_{S0} is denoted as P_{01} and P_{10}, respectively. The probabilities of the remaining in
the same state are denoted as P_{00} and P_{01} where $P_{00} = 1 - P_{01}$ and $P_{11} = 1 - P_{00}$.
$P_x \in \Re$ and $0 < P_x < 1, \forall x \in \{00, 01, 10, 11\}$

$$P = \begin{bmatrix} P_{00} & P_{10} \\ P_{01} & P_{11} \end{bmatrix}. \tag{15.5}$$

The steady state probability of being in state Good and Bad can be formulated in
(15.6).

$$P \begin{bmatrix} P_{S0} \\ P_{S1} \end{bmatrix} = \begin{bmatrix} P_{S0} \\ P_{S1} \end{bmatrix}. \tag{15.6}$$

The steady state analysis indicates that P_{S0} and P_{S1} satisfy the criteria addressed
in (15.7).

$$\begin{bmatrix} P_{00} & 1 - P_{11} \\ 1 & 1 \end{bmatrix} \begin{bmatrix} P_{S0} \\ P_{S1} \end{bmatrix} = \begin{bmatrix} P_{S0} \\ 1 \end{bmatrix}. \tag{15.7}$$

Solving (15.7), the probabilities of successful and unsuccessful packet transmissions are

$$P_{S0} = \frac{P_{11} - 1}{P_{00} + P_{11} - 2} \tag{15.8}$$

and

$$P_{S1} = \frac{P_{00} - 1}{P_{00} + P_{11} - 2}, \tag{15.9}$$

respectively.

15.4.1   Packet Loss Analysis in Client-Server Streaming

In video streaming, the video bitstreams are encapsulated into data packets. A packet loss during the transmission will result in corruptions for the reconstructed video frames. Considering drifting errors, each lost video frame will impact its subsequent video frames, and the error will propagate until the end of the GOP. Take the extreme case, for example, if an I-frame is corrupted, the remaining P-frames cannot be reconstructed due to the missing reference frame for motion prediction.

For client/server streaming, the video is assumed to be transmitted over a single path. Thus, the video sequence is encoded into a single description substream (i.e., MDC when $M = 1$), and this method is denoted as SDC.

In general, the probability of receiving n frames followed by a lost frame is $P_{S0} P_{00}^{n-1} P_{01}$, and the frames' dropout rate for receiving n frames followed by a lost frame is $\frac{T-n}{T} P_{S0} P_{00}^{n-1} P_{01}$, where T is the length of the GOP. The mean frame loss rate, ε_{SDC}, is shown in (15.10). The first term indicates the probability that the I-frame is lost (i.e., the video frames for the entire GOP is not reconstructable), and the second term represents I- and P-frames are partially received before a lost P-frame (i.e., a number of video frames can be reconstructed, followed by non-reconstructable video frames until the end of the GOP).

$$\varepsilon_{\text{SDC}} = P_{S1} + P_{S0} \sum_{n=1}^{T-1} \frac{(T - n) P_{00}^{n-1} P_{01}}{T}$$

$$= P_{S1} + \frac{P_{S0} (1 - P_{00})}{T} \left(T \cdot \frac{P_{00}^{T-1} - 1}{P_{00} - 1} - H \right), \tag{15.10}$$

where

$$H = \sum_{n=1}^{T-1} n P_{00}^{n-1}$$

$$= \frac{1}{(P_{00} - 1)^2} (T P_{00}^{T} - T P_{00}^{T-1} - P_{00}^{T} + 1) \tag{15.11}$$

substituting H back to (15.10) yields

$$\varepsilon_{\text{SDC}} = P_{S1} + P_{S0} \frac{T + P_{00}^T - TP_{00} - 1}{T(1 - P_{00})}$$

$$= 1 - \frac{(P_{11} - 1)(P_{00}^T - 1)}{T(P_{00} + P_{11} - 2)(P_{00} - 1)}. \tag{15.12}$$

15.4.2 Packet Loss Analysis in Centralized P2P Streaming

In centralized P2P streaming, the server and the peer-nodes possess different loss attributes. The server is a reliable source and the peer-nodes are non-reliable sources. Hence, the server should have a higher good state probability compared to the peer-nodes. To simplify the analysis, the peers are assumed to have identical loss attributes, and hence, identical steady state probabilities will be used for all peers. In this section, the steady state probabilities in (15.8) and (15.9) are used for servers and peers, respectively. For the server, the two states of Gilbert model are denoted as $(S0, s)$ (good) where the packets are received correctly and timely, and $(S1, s)$ (bad) where the packets are assumed to be lost. The state transition probabilities from $(S0, s)$-to-$(S1, s)$ and $(S1, s)$-to-$(S0, s)$ are denoted as $P_{01,s}$ and $P_{10,s}$, respectively. The probabilities of the remaining in the same state are denoted as $P_{00,s}$ and $P_{11,s}$ where $P_{00,s} = 1 - P_{01,s}$ and $P_{11,s} = 1 - P_{10,s}$. $P_{x,s} \in R$ and $0 < P_{x,s} < 1, \forall x \in \{00, 01, 10, 11\}$. Similarly, the steady state probabilities and the transmission probabilities for the peers are denoted as $P_{S0,p}$, $P_{S1,p}$, $P_{x,p} \in \mathbf{R}^+$ and $0 < P_{x,p} < 1, \forall x \in \{00, 01, 10, 11\}$, respectively. The steady state probabilities of successful and unsuccessful packet transmissions from the server are

$$P_{S0,s} = \frac{P_{11,s} - 1}{P_{00,s} + P_{11,s} - 2}, \tag{15.13}$$

$$P_{S1,s} = \frac{P_{00,s} - 1}{P_{00,s} + P_{11,s} - 2}. \tag{15.14}$$

Similarly, the steady state probabilities of successful and unsuccessful packet transmissions from the peers are

$$P_{S0,p} = \frac{P_{11,p} - 1}{P_{00,p} + P_{11,p} - 2}, \tag{15.15}$$

$$P_{S1,p} = \frac{P_{00,p} - 1}{P_{00,p} + P_{11,p} - 2}. \tag{15.16}$$

For centralized P2P streaming with M MDC substreams transmitted over M independent paths, output video can be reconstructed upon receiving any substream. With MDC, the video frames cannot be reconstructed only if all substreams are lost.

Let γ_i and ρ_i denote the probability of transmitting $i - 1$ frames followed by a frame drop from the server and the peer-nodes, respectively. Therefore, γ_i and ρ_i are

$$\gamma_i = \begin{cases} P_{S1,s} & \text{when } i = 1, \\ P_{S0,s} P_{00,s}^{i-2} P_{01,s} & \text{when } i > 1, \end{cases} \tag{15.17}$$

$$\rho_i = \begin{cases} P_{S1,p} & \text{when } i = 1, \\ P_{S0,p} P_{00,p}^{i-2} P_{01,p} & \text{when } i > 1. \end{cases} \tag{15.18}$$

For each MDC stream, a lost frame will make the remaining frames unreconstructable, which is known as the drifting error. The probability that at least one channel transmits the video at and before $i = k$ and all the channels have lost a frame at and before $i = k + 1$ is

$$\left(\sum_{i=1}^{k+1} \rho_i \right)^{M-1} \left(\sum_{i=1}^{k+1} \gamma_i \right) - \left(\sum_{i=1}^{k} \rho_i \right)^{M-1} \left(\sum_{i=1}^{k} \gamma_i \right). \tag{15.19}$$

Let $w(n) = \sum_{i=1}^{n} \rho_i$ and $v(n) = \sum_{i=1}^{n} \gamma_i$, the mean frame loss rate $\varepsilon_{\text{CP2P}}$ for the multi-path transmission scheme can be expressed as

$$\begin{aligned} \varepsilon_{\text{CP2P}} &= \frac{T}{T} [w(1)^{M-1} v(1)] \\ &+ \frac{T-1}{T} [w(2)^{M-1} v(2) - w(1)^{M-1} v(1)] \\ &+ \frac{T-2}{T} [w(3)^{M-1} v(3) - w(2)^{M-1} v(2)] \\ &+ \vdots \\ &+ \frac{1}{T} [w(T)^{M-1} v(T) - w(T-1)^{M-1} v(T-1)] \\ &= \frac{1}{T} \left(\sum_{k=1}^{T} w(k)^{M-1} v(k) \right) \\ &= \frac{1}{T} \left[\sum_{k=1}^{T} x^{M-1} y \right], \end{aligned} \tag{15.20}$$

where $x = P_{S1,p} - P_{S0,p}(P_{00,p}^{k-1} - 1)$ and $y = P_{S1,s} - P_{S0,s}(P_{00,s}^{k-1} - 1)$. Finally, substitute (15.13)–(15.16) into (15.20) and the frame loss rate for multi-path transmission can be simplified as

$$\varepsilon_{\text{CP2P}} = \frac{1}{T} \sum_{k=1}^{T} \alpha^{M-1} \beta, \tag{15.21}$$

where $\alpha = 1 - \frac{(P_{11,p}-1)P_{00,p}^{k-1}}{P_{00,p}+P_{11,p}-2}$ and $\beta = 1 - \frac{(P_{11,s}-1)P_{00,s}^{k-1}}{P_{00,s}+P_{11,s}-2}$.

15.4.3 Packet Loss Analysis in Decentralized P2P Streaming

Consider a video sequence divided into M MDC substreams, and transmitted over M-independent paths. To simplify the analysis, assume each path has an identical loss attribute, and therefore, contains identical state transition parameters in the Gilbert model.

For multiple-description coding with M independent substreams, output video can be reconstructed from any substream. Under MDC, the video frames cannot be reconstructed if all streams are lost. Let T denote the GOP period and ρ_i denote the probability of successfully transmitting $i - 1$ frames followed by a frame drop. Then, ρ_i is represented by the following sequence:

$$\rho_i = \begin{cases} P_{S1} & \text{when } i = 1, \\ P_{S0} P_{00}^{i-2} P_{01} & \text{when } i > 1. \end{cases} \tag{15.22}$$

The probability that one channel loses a frame before or at $i = k$ is $\sum_{i=1}^{k} \rho_i$, and the probability that all the channels lose a frame before or at $i = k$ is $\left(\sum_{i=1}^{k} \rho_i\right)^M$. Similarly, the probability that all the channels have lost a frame before or at $i = k+1$ is $\left(\sum_{i=1}^{k+1} \rho_i\right)^M$. The probability that at least one channel transmits the video at and before $i = k$ and all the channels have lost a frame at $i = k+1$ is

$$\left(\sum_{i=1}^{k+1} \rho_i\right)^M - \left(\sum_{i=1}^{k} \rho_i\right)^M. \tag{15.23}$$

The mean frame loss rate for the M multi-channel transmission scheme, therefore, is

$$\begin{aligned} \varepsilon_{\text{MDC}} = \;& \frac{T}{T} \rho_1^M \\ &+ \frac{T-1}{T}\left[\left(\sum_{i=1}^{2} \rho_i\right)^M - \left(\sum_{i=1}^{1} \rho_i\right)^M\right] \\ &+ \frac{T-2}{T}\left[\left(\sum_{i=1}^{3} \rho_i\right)^M - \left(\sum_{i=1}^{2} \rho_i\right)^M\right] \\ &+ \vdots \\ &+ \frac{1}{T}\left[\left(\sum_{i=1}^{T} \rho_i\right)^M - \left(\sum_{i=1}^{T-1} \rho_i\right)^M\right]. \end{aligned} \tag{15.24}$$

Equation (15.24) can be simplified as

$$\varepsilon_{\text{MDC}} = \frac{1}{T} \sum_{k=1}^{T} \left(\sum_{i=1}^{k} \rho_i \right)^M$$

$$= \frac{1}{T} \sum_{k=1}^{T} \left(P_{S1} + P_{S0} P_{01} \sum_{j=2}^{k} P_{00}^{j-2} \right)^M$$

$$= \frac{1}{T} \sum_{k=1}^{T} [P_{S1} - P_{S0}(P_{00}^{k-1} - 1)]^M. \tag{15.25}$$

Finally, by substituting (15.8) and (15.9) into (15.25), the frame loss rate may be obtained for multi-path transmission ε_{MDC} where

$$\varepsilon_{\text{MDC}} = \frac{1}{T} \sum_{k=1}^{T} \left[1 - \frac{(P_{11} - 1) P_{00}^{k-1}}{P_{00} + P_{11} - 2} \right]^M. \tag{15.26}$$

15.4.4 Single Path Transmission vs. Multi-Path Transmission

This subsection demonstrates that the frame loss rate of multi-path transmission is always equal to or lower than that of single path transmission. Two cases are considered: $M = 1$ and $M > 1$. When $M = 1$,

$$\varepsilon_{\text{MDC}} = \frac{1}{T} \sum_{k=1}^{T} \left[\frac{P_{00} - 1 + P_{11} - 1 - (P_{11} - 1) P_{00}^{k-1}}{P_{00} + P_{11} - 2} \right]^1$$

$$= 1 - \frac{P_{11} - 1}{T(P_{00} + P_{11} - 2)} \sum_{k=1}^{T} P_{00}^{k-1}$$

$$= 1 - \frac{P_{11} - 1}{T(P_{00} + P_{11} - 2)} \frac{P_{00}^T - 1}{P_{00} - 1}$$

$$= \varepsilon_{\text{SDC}}.$$

For $M > 1$, consider M-path transmission and $(M - 1)$-path transmission. The difference in frame loss rate between M-path transmission and $(M - 1)$-path transmission is $\Delta \varepsilon_{\text{MDC}}$, which could be expressed as

$$\Delta \varepsilon_{\mathrm{MDC}} = \frac{1}{T} \sum_{k=1}^{T} \left[1 - \frac{(P_{11} - 1) P_{00}^{k-1}}{P_{00} + P_{11} - 2} \right]^{M}$$

$$- \frac{1}{T} \sum_{k=1}^{T} \left[1 - \frac{(P_{11} - 1) P_{00}^{k-1}}{P_{00} + P_{11} - 2} \right]^{M-1}$$

$$= \frac{1}{T} \sum_{k=1}^{T} \frac{-(P_{11} - 1) P_{00}^{k-1} A^{M-1}}{[(P_{00} - 1) + (P_{11} - 1)]^{M}}, \tag{15.27}$$

where $A = P_{00} - 1 + (P_{11} - 1)(1 - P_{00}^{k-1})$. In (15.27), $0 < P_{00} < 1$ and $0 < P_{11} < 1$, $P_{00} - 1 + (P_{11} - 1)(1 - P_{00}^{k-1}) < 0$, $(P_{00} - 1) + (P_{11} - 1) < 0$, and $(P_{11} - 1) P_{00}^{k-1} < 0$. Therefore, $\Delta \varepsilon_{\mathrm{MDC}} < 0, \forall M > 1$. Thus, the frame loss rate of multi-path transmission is equal to (when $M = 1$) or lower than (when $M > 1$) than single-path transmission.

In this chapter, scenarios where the MDC substreams have aligned I-frames, such as the example illustrated in Fig. 15.6, are studied. For audiences who are interested in scenarios for unaligned I-frames, the work was disseminated in [14].

15.5 Analysis

Frame lost rates for centralized P2P streaming with different number of MDC streams, and under different network conditions, are examined in Fig. 15.8a and Fig. 15.8b, respectively. Figure 15.8a examines the frame loss rate by evaluating (15.21) with $P_{00,p} = 0.9$, $P_{11,p} = 0.2$, $P_{00,s} = 0.95$ and $P_{11,s} = 0.15$. These parameters indicate that the server is more reliable than each individual peers. The frame loss rate increases with a larger GOP length due to drifting error. In Fig. 15.8b, different transition probabilities are applied, with $M = 4$, $P_{00,s} = P_{00,p} + 0.05$ and $P_{11,s} = P_{11,p} - 0.05$. By increasing the transition probability for success transmissions ($P_{00,p}$) and decreasing the transition probability for failure transmissions ($P_{11,p}$), lower frame loss rates are observed.

Figure 15.9a and Fig. 15.10b examine the performance of decentralized P2P streaming with different number of MDC streams and different GOP lengths. The frame loss rate of the single video stream transmission and the MDC transmission using the Gilbert model is shown in (15.12) and (15.26), respectively. The frame loss rate is a function of length of GOP (T), number of MDC substreams (M) and Gilbert model transition probabilities (P_{01} and P_{10}). To highlight the performance gain of multi-path transmission using MDC over SDC, identical Gilbert model transition probabilities are chosen for Figs. 15.9a and 15.10b, with $P_{00} = 0.9$ and $P_{11} = 0.2$. As shown in Fig. 15.9a, the frame loss rate increases with T due to a higher drifting error associated with a larger T value. Under all T values, MDC outperforms single stream transmission (the lower the frame loss rate, the higher the perceived video quality). Figure 15.9b examines the number of MDC substreams and their impacts

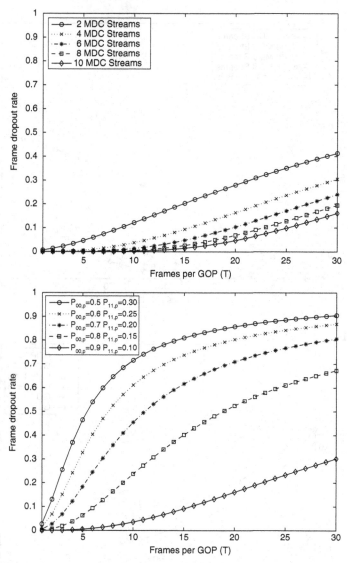

Fig. 15.8 Frame loss rates for centralized P2P streaming

on the frame loss rate. It is observed that the higher the number of MDC substreams, the lower the frame loss rate.

Observations of the frame loss rate as a function of the number of MDC substreams (M) and the GOP length (T) lead to an assumption that there exists a combination of M and T that yields a consistent frame loss rate. That is, by increasing M results in a reduced frame loss rate, and by increasing T results in an increased frame loss rate. By increasing both M and T together, it is possible to yield a consistent frame loss rate. Figure 15.10b examines different

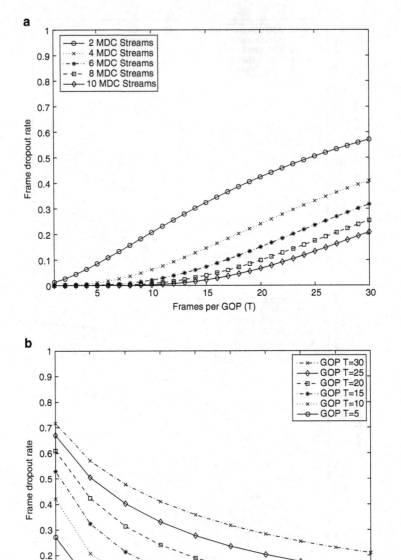

Fig. 15.9 Frame loss rates for decentralized P2P streaming with (**a**) different MDC substreams and (**b**) group of picture (GOP) lengths

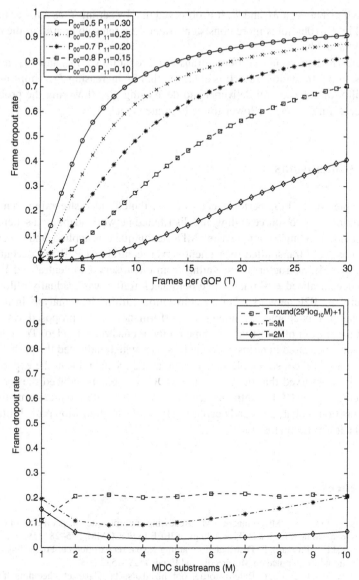

Fig. 15.10 Frame loss rates for decentralized P2P streaming

relationships between M and T. It is observed that by setting T as a linear multiple of M, Fig. 15.10b yields more consistent frame loss rates compared to the ones in Figs. 15.9a and b.

Figure 15.10a compares different transition probabilities, P_{00} and P_{11}, and their impacts on the frame loss rate. It is observed that by increasing P_{00} (improving the probability of a successful delivery) and decreasing P_{11} (lowering the probability of a successful delivery), a lower frame loss rate is yield.

15.6 Conclusions

This chapter studied the performance of a distributed video streaming framework, which utilized video source coding and distributed network adaptation schemes. An efficient video coding technique using MDC technique was applied, and the encoded substreams were transmitted over client/server, centralized P2P and decentralized P2P network infrastructures. Escalating from client/server to centralized P2P and then to decentralized P2P phases, the bottleneck traffic was gradually offloaded to under-utilized P2P networks. Unlike conventional traffic loss analysis in networking research, this chapter examined the performance of the proposed system and studied the impact of a lost video frame on the reconstructed video. The perceived quality was measured in terms of frame loss rate, which indicated the probability of receiving a non-reconstructable video frame at the receiver. From the experimental results, it is observed that increasing the MDC substreams reduced the frame loss rate, increasing the GOP length increased the frame loss rate and increasing the good state transition probabilities and decreasing the bad state transition probabilities also yielded a lower frame loss rate.

References

1. Byers, J., Luby, M., Mitzenmacher, M.: Accessing multiple sites in parallel: using tornado codes to speed up downloads. Proceedings of IEEE INFOCOMM, 275–283 (1999)
2. Chakareski, J., Frossard, P.: Distributed streaming via packet partitioning. Proceedings of IEEE International Conference on Multimedia and Expo, 1529–1532 (2006)
3. Chakareski, J., Frossard, P.: Rate-distortion optimized distributed packet scheduling of multiple video streams over shared communication resources. IEEE Transactions on Multimedia 8(2), 207–218 (2006)
4. Chow, A.L., Golubchik, L., Lui, J.C., Lee, W.J.: Multi-path streaming: optimization of load distribution. Performance Evaluation 62, 417–438 (2005)
5. Cui, Y., Li, B., Nahrstedt, K.: oStream: asynchronous streaming multicast in application-layer overlay networks. IEEE Journal on Selected Areas in Communications 22(1), 91–106 (2004)
6. Goyal, V.K.: Multiple description coding: compression meets the network. IEEE Signal Processing Magazine 18(5), 74–93 (2001)
7. Jeon, W.J., Nahrstedt, K.: Peer-to-peer multimedia streaming and caching service. Proceedings of IEEE International Conference on Multimedia and Expo, 57–60 (2002)

8. Kim, J., Mersereau, R.M., Altunbasak, Y.: Distributed video streaming using multiple description coding and unequal error protection. IEEE Transactions on Image Processing **14**(7), 849–861 (2005)
9. Lee, I., Guan, L.: A scalable video codec design for streaming over distributed peer-to-peer network. Proceedings of IEEE Global Telecommunications Conference **1**, 539–543 (2002)
10. Lee, I., Guan, L.: Centralized peer-to-peer streaming with layered video. Proceedings of IEEE International Conference on Multimedia and Expo, 513–516 (2003)
11. Lee, I., Guan, L.: Centralized peer-to-peer streaming for pfgs video. Proceedings of IEEE Pacific-Rim Conference on Multimedia, 131–138 (2004)
12. Lee, I., Guan, L.: Reliable video communication with multi-path streaming. In: Proceedings of IEEE International Conference on Multimedia and Expo, Amsterdam, Netherlands (2005)
13. Li, W.: Overview of fine granularity scalability in mpeg-4 video standard. IEEE Transactions on Circuits and Systems for Video Technology **11**, 301–317 (2001)
14. Ling, Z., Lee, I.: Adaptive multi-path video streaming. In: Proceedings of IEEE International Symposium on Multimedia, San Diego, CA (2006)
15. Nguyen, T., Zakhor, A.: Distributed video streaming over the internet. Proceedings of SPIE Conference on Multimedia Computing and Networking, 186–195 (2002)
16. Tran, D.A., Hua, K.A., Do, T.T.: Zigzag: an efficient peer-to-peer scheme for media streaming. Technical Report, University of Central Florida (2002). URL http://citeseer.nj.nec.com/534591.html
17. Wu, D., Hou, Y.T., Zhu, W., Lee, H.J., Chiang, T., Zhang, Y.Q., Chao, H.J.: On end-to-end architecture for transporting mpeg-4 video over the internet. IEEE Transactions Circuits and Systems for Video Technology **18**(6), 977–995 (2000)
18. Wu, D., Hou, Y.T., Zhu, W., Zhang, Y.Q., Peha, J.M.: Streaming video over the internet: approaches and directions. IEEE Transactions on Circuits and Systems for Video Technology **11**(3), 282–300 (2001)
19. Wu, F., Li, S., Zhang, Y.Q.: A framework for efficient progressive fine granularity scalable video coding. IEEE Transactions on Circuits and Systems for Video Technology **11**(3), 332–344 (2001)
20. Yee, J.R., Weldon, E.J.: Evaluation of the performance of error-correcting codes on a gilbert channel. IEEE Transactions on Communication **43**, 2316–2323 (1995)

Chapter 16
QoE in Pervasive Telecommunication Systems

Florence Agboma and Antonio Liotta

Abstract The concept of offering pervasive telecommunication services, i.e., services that are available anytime, anywhere and from any terminal, is very appealing. Providing pervasive services to users has been the ultimate goal of telecommunication systems for many years. We introduce pervasive systems and services from the telecommunication perspective. We also look at the enabling technologies and different pervasive services that are currently being provided to users. In view of this, we emphasize on why quality of experience (QoE) in telecommunication systems is important. Next, we elaborate on the different requirements needed to provide pervasive services from the user's perspective. A case study is presented, illustrating how the sensitivity of different network parameters (such as bandwidth, packet loss and delay) for a pervasive service can affect QoE. The chapter then concludes with what the current status is, and the shortcomings in providing QoE in a truly pervasive service.

16.1 Introduction

A pervasive system is formed by the convergence of different networks to provide services that are made available anywhere, anytime and from any terminal to users. Like any other industry, the primary aim of the telecommunication industry is to increase the average revenue per user (ARPU) while still maintaining a competitive edge. The commoditization of voice services has led service providers and network operators to look for other strategies of providing non-voice services in order to increase ARPU, and to differentiate their service offerings from other competitors. This convergence of different networks such as circuit switched networks

F. Agboma (✉)
Department of Computing and Electronic Systems, University of Essex, Wivenhoe Park, Colchester, CO4 3SQ, UK
e-mail: Fagbom@essex.ac.uk

A.-E. Hassanien et al. (eds.), *Pervasive Computing: Innovations in Intelligent Multimedia and Applications*, Computer Communications and Networks, DOI 10.1007/978-1-84882-599-4_16, © Springer-Verlag London Limited 2009

and IP networks enables more value-added services such as video sharing, mobile TV, triple play services, mobile internet, peer-to-peer applications, etc. to be easily deployed and accessed by the end users. An example of an enabling platform that allows for this convergence in telecommunication systems is the IP multimedia sub-system (IMS), an architectural framework that has been standardized by the third generation partnership project (3GPP). IMS is seen as a service centric framework for providing rich and personalized services over a multi-access network. Examples of these access technology networks are cellular networks (2G, GPRS, 3G and 4G), wireless networks (WLAN, Bluetooth, Wimax,) and wired networks.

The deployment of pervasive systems and services is not just about the technologies used in implementing them. The deployment of such services involves issues, such as end user expectations and experiences. The perceived usefulness brought to the users for using the services, coupled with the users' experience, should be the major focal point of any service deployment activity. This is necessary for service providers if they want to maintain competitive edges within the highly dynamic telecommunication industry.

A user's quality of experience[1] (QoE) is considered an important issue since it relates to the perception of the user about the quality of a particular service or network [5]. It is a measure of perception that determines whether users will adopt a given service or not. QoE strongly depends on the expectations the users have about the offered service. Customers do not care about how service quality is achieved. What matters to them most is how well a service meets their expectations in terms of the service availability and reliability, ease of use when interacting with the service, interoperability, etc. The combination of these factors influences the challenge of delivering high QoE. In this chapter, we discuss the requirements for pervasive services from the users' perspective. Then, by means of a case study, we introduce the issues and methods relating to the assessment and delivery of QoE-enabled pervasive services.

16.2 QoE Requirements for Pervasive Services

In this section, we discuss the requirements of pervasive services in relation to QoE delivery.

16.2.1 Mobility

In providing pervasive services, the mobility of users is not always limited to the same access technology since they may hop across different networks. Ensuring

---

[1] Another term for this is known as the user perception of Quality of Service.

a continuous service quality at the boundaries of heterogeneous networks (e.g., UMTS to WLAN or vice versa) becomes quite challenging as their characteristics suddenly change in terms of service capabilities such as data rate, transmission range, access cost, etc. There have been a number of studies on service quality over heterogeneous networks, some of which can be found in [9, 16, 20, 24]. A user on the move should be able to have a continuous service experience without having to worry about service failure or service interruptions due to network issues (service mobility). An additional essential requirement is the ability of the terminal itself to be capable of accessing services irrespective of its location (terminal mobility). Thus, there is the need for new generation of terminals that can support multimode access technologies. A seamless service delivery needs to be achieved by an integration of these heterogeneous networks in a way that is hidden from the user in order to provide a satisfactory user experience.

16.2.2   Cost

If the cost of using a service is perceived to be expensive and the users' expectations are not met, it may cause the users to stop using the service. The initially slow uptake of multimedia messaging service (MMS) observed in cellular network providers was due to its high cost of using the service, coupled with interoperability issues among the handsets. The price the user is willing to pay for a seamless continuous service quality as it moves across networks using different access technologies (e.g., UMTS to WLAN or vice versa) is crucial for mass-market acceptance. Another issue regarding cost will be the price of the new generation of terminals that support multimode access technologies.

16.2.3   Display Characteristics

There are multitudes of pervasive access devices such as mobile phones, pagers, PDAs, laptops, etc. possessing varying display screen sizes and device capabilities. An application may be intended to run on several devices having different capabilities and characteristics, e.g., a web page that displays on a desktop computer may also need to be displayed on a mobile phone. This poses several challenges for designers of pervasive services. An example to this challenge was observed with the introduction of WAP services, where users experienced difficulties in navigating to specific parts of the service due to its poor design. It was time-consuming even in accomplishing the simplest tasks on these WAP services. The consequence was a commercial failure.

Knowing the users' preferences will facilitate the development of acceptable services. For example, web pages on the Internet should be transcoded to match the capabilities of both the handset and the type of network. Methods for reformatting web pages to match small form-factor wireless devices are discussed in [6].

In one of our previous studies on addressing user expectations in mobile content delivery systems [1], it was found that media adaptation onto any mobile device cannot be achieved by merely re-broadcasting existing traditional TV materials to a mobile TV environment. Doing so would hardly satisfy the user watching a football match, for example, on the mobile phone. This is because the different shot types and textual detail usually found suitable for traditional TV viewing may not be suitable for a small screen. The loss of visual details and the difficulty in identifying players or in detecting ball movements are bound to substantially decrease user satisfaction. Contents must be edited specifically (e.g., larger text size for smaller screen size) for the type of terminal that will be used to access the content. This is a further level of optimization that can make a significant difference to the end user's viewing experience.

16.2.4 Integration of Services

Network operators have realized that the traditional use of the "walled garden model" (closed portals where customers are restricted to use only those services that are provided by the network operators) will not be a sustainable strategy as users are increasingly demanding for personalized services and enhanced communication. The ability of the network operators and service providers to rapidly create new attractive services is essential in order to maintain a competitive edge. What is required is a secure open service platform that allows the interoperability of applications/services developed by third party service providers and other network operators, as this will provide all the benefits of a service-centric approach.

From the network operator's perspective, the user is central to the development of pervasive services. Thus, customer access to third party services is needed. This will create new business models and generate more revenue both for the third party service providers and the network operators. The user also benefits from more choice of value added services, enhanced personalization and increased user experience.

16.2.5 Usability Issues

The user friendliness of both the device and the services is of paramount importance to the user. This user friendliness will have a major impact on QoE. If the design of the device interface lacks the ability to properly provide the service, it will result in users abandoning the service. The device used to access a service plays a major role on the user experience as this dictates the interaction between the user and the service. In [10], usability is defined as "the extent to which a product can be used by specified users to achieve specified goals with effectiveness, efficiency and satisfaction in a specified context of use."

A survey carried out by [17] found that 55% of first time users abandoned the value added service of mobile data offered by mobile operators because of usability problems. These problems include difficulty in navigating through the menus, inability to find downloaded content and confusion in terminologies like "streaming" and "download." This reflects the need to have service applications that are easy to use and do not require thorough understanding of the service logic [18]. If the user's interaction with the service is poor, the consequence will be a decline in the use of the service.

16.2.6   Security and Privacy

Inter-working across heterogeneous environments to provide seamless services poses entirely new challenges to the user's security and privacy because different access technologies have different implementations of their security schemes. The composition of two secure architectures (e.g., 3G and WLAN) may produce an insecure result [22]. This can occur because of differing, possibly contradictory security assumptions. A solution to this is to invoke a dynamic security system with sufficient intelligence to prevent security breaches [3]. Security breaches could include the misuse of users' data confidentiality and integrity by a malicious user. Users will not adopt pervasive services until they are convinced that the application or infrastructure is secured and reliable. Thus, service provisioning should be secure, and users' privacy should be protected.

16.2.7   Quality of Service Assurance

Different types of traffic demand different network-level QoS (NQoS) requirements. Real-time streaming applications impose more stringent delay constraints compared to e-mail and Internet browsing applications. Defining QoS requirements entails applying policies, which can be used to differentiate and prioritize the transmission of mixed traffic.

An example is seen in the delivery of triple play services (video, voice and data). Traffic prioritization and the guaranteeing of QoS requirements become extremely important in providing acceptable service quality. Real-time streaming services such as voice or video are sensitive to packet losses, delays, jitter and bandwidth variations, and are further exacerbated by the presence of mobility. The effects of jitter and end-to-end delay in streaming services (e.g., mobile TV and P2P TV) can, to some extent, be mitigated by adding a playout buffer on the receiver's device. The playout buffer stores the received video packets until its playout time. The use of these playout buffers also makes the retransmission of lost packets possible, though this is not well suited for real-time conversational video applications because of its high delay constraint.

The QoS level will change as a user moves across networks with different service capabilities, i.e., a reduction in link quality from WLAN to UMTS. Also, during this handover process, delays and packet losses might occur. Video packet losses or corrupted video streams greatly affect the user's viewing experience. Thus, maintaining the required QoS should be a top priority for network operators, especially in the transmission of multimedia contents. Resource management in a pervasive system must be adaptive to changes in context and their resultant effect on QoS [23].

16.3   Case Study on QoE in a Pervasive Service

Peer-to-peer (P2P) technologies support the provisioning of globally pervasive services. Its architecture serves as a common platform on which new pervasive services can be easily deployed. Examples are seen in the delivery of audio streams, video-on-demand services and television programmes. A good background literature on P2P systems can be found in [14]. P2P systems offer scalability, i.e., an unlimited number of users (peers) can be added to the network, since each peer contributes resources (e.g., bandwidth, storage capacity and computing power) to the network. The primary goal of P2P technologies is to share content directly between peers. Given its non-centralized design, it provides more robustness to central failures by adapting to changes in users' behaviour, access patterns and location. This paradigm is already attracting network operators and service providers in the telecommunication industries. Operators are interested in leveraging their infrastructure using the P2P concept to reduce transmission costs, thereby increasing their service offerings. However, little information is available on users' QoE on P2P systems. In this section, we introduce P2P television and discuss factors affecting QoE for P2P television systems. Next, we discuss the general problems behind the QoE analysis of P2P streaming, and then illustrate a case study that introduces a method for assessing a user's QoE on P2P television systems.

16.3.1   P2P Television Systems

In P2P television systems, each peer acts both as a client and a server, i.e., while a peer is downloading a video stream as a client, it is simultaneously serving that video stream to requesting peers on the network, thereby contributing to the overall network bandwidth. P2P television systems support both linear and non-linear television channels, and the growing demand of user generated contents. P2P pervasive television service offers television channels from across the world, where users' terminals collaborate with the purpose of making the television channel distribution process more efficient by reducing the number of client-server interactions to the minimum. Examples of P2P television systems are PPLive[2] [8], SopCast[3] [21], Joost[4] [7, 12], AnySee[5] [13] and CoolStreaming[6] [25].

16.3.2 Factors Affecting QoE for P2P Television

The factors contributing to P2P television QoE from the user's perspective are:

The start-up delay: This is the total time taken in connecting to the system until video playback starts. This start-up time relies on the availability of peers and video content. During this initial start-up delay period, peer registration on the network and searches for other peers to download video packets from are carried out. Video packets are quickly stored in a playout buffer before their playback deadline, allowing for a smooth viewing experience when playback starts. Depending on the size of this buffer, the playout delay is typically between 5 and 15 s, which is acceptable for most video streaming applications [19].

Channel switching delay: This is the time it takes for the system to respond to a channel change request from a user. During this time, searches are quickly made for the availability of peers that host the video requested, and the video packets are buffered before rendering on the screen. The channel switch time for digital broadcast services (traditional TV) is about 1–1.5 s [4]. The channel switching time delay incurred by P2P television is considerably longer than those in traditional television. The ultimate challenge will be to provide a similar match to that presently experienced in traditional TV viewing.

The media (video and audio) quality: This is perceived as a significant factor affecting the user's QoE. In P2P television systems, the media quality can be affected by degradations caused by the media coding, peer churn and also the network parameters (delay, jitter, bandwidth and packet loss), which are unpredictable and dynamic. Packet losses are mainly caused by transmission over unreliable channels, network congestion and random peer departures and they severely degrade the media playback performance. The lack of service quality guarantees at the QoS level infers that the user may experience a longer delay and frozen pictures due to the intermittent buffering. The user's QoE of P2P television is crucial for its large-scale service acceptance.

---

[2] www.pplive.com

[3] www.sopcast.org

[4] www.joost.com

[5] www.anysee.net

[6] www.coolstreaming.us

16.3.3 QoE Analysis of a Peer-to-Peer Television System

Carrying out QoE analysis on pervasive systems such as a P2P streaming application is challenging because such systems involve heterogeneous networks and are
usually large, i.e., they span a large geographical area, involving a large number
of peers (users). Thus, their performances are considerably affected by the user's
behaviour and the statuses of the sub-networks making up the system. The user behaviour and network statuses are unpredictable, thereby making them difficult to
parameterize and model in simulation software.

Because of the above features of P2P systems, the experiments carried out on
them on a small scale (e.g., in a laboratory) are often meaningless as these small-
scale P2P systems do not adequately reflect the real-life P2P systems. Experiments
carried out on a large scale require a large-scale deployment and user base. The
latter approach is hard to follow since many P2P systems are proprietary and also,
it is often too late to identify their major architectural limitations since the system
would already have been deployed.

The key starting point to resolve this problem is an assessment based on existing QoE subjective methods. However, carrying out QoE analysis requires some
reverse engineering in order to understand and gather sufficient knowledge about
the system itself. It also requires an investigation into which network parameters are
most sensitive to the system, and how these parameters affect the user's QoE. We
introduce a method of assessing P2P television systems by starting with an analysis
of the most sensitive network parameters that affect QoE, and leading to the QoE
subjective study itself.

16.3.4 Experimental Methods

We present here the main experimental methods required to assess QoE in P2P television system Joost, which, at the time of writing, represents the most up to date
commercial P2P television system. Joost, originally known as The Venice Project,
was created by the founders[7] of Skype and KazaA. Joost is a P2P streaming application that provides licensed non-linear television channels to users over the Internet.
Joost video servers are the original source root of all television materials. A first
time user of Joost is required to download and install the client software from the
website (www.joost.com). After installation, the user can select and watch a channel
they are interested in. At the time of writing, there were only few studies of the Joost
P2P system available in the public domain [7, 11, 12]. To the authors' knowledge,
no studies have focused on the user's QoE experiments on P2P television systems.
Carrying out QoE experiments on Joost requires an in-depth knowledge of its architecture, protocols and mechanisms. But these are not readily available since it is

---

[7] Niklas Zennström and Janus Friis.

a proprietary system. We present below two experimental methods used. The first method enables to understand the Joost architecture and how it works. The second method (a subjective study) enables the identification and isolation of the network parameters that the system was most sensitive to.

16.3.4.1 Measurement Methodology

The first thing to do is to carry out measurements on the application to better understand its underlying architecture and mechanisms. This is necessary as most pervasive systems are proprietary. The output of this first part of the study is to understand which parameters are most sensitive and which one impacts QoE the most. In the case study under scrutiny, Joost (Beta version 1.04) is inspected at its packet level in order to resolve its network architecture and communication protocols. By running its client software, it is possible to measure start-up delay and channel switching delay to get an insight into its internal working mechanisms.

In a study carried out in our lab, we collected traces of Joost packets within two different settings – a university campus and a residential environment. The PCs used with both environments were Windows XP based and had processor speeds of at least 2.4 GHz. Each PC (peer) ran Wireshark[8] Version 0.99.8 (a network protocol analyzer) to capture all inbound and outbound traffic of Joost.

In order to determine the sensitivity of the system to changes in the network parameters, we followed an initial experimental assessment based on traffic analysis to obtain the experimental QoS matrix, which is depicted in Table 16.1. This provided a basis for identifying and isolating the network parameters that were sensitive to the Joost P2P system. Figure 16.1 shows a basic diagram of the experimental testbed. A network emulator was used to reproduce each network parameter.

The sensitivity of the delay parameter was determined. Between the values of 200 and 700 ms, no significant observations were noticed. At a delay of 1,300 ms and above, it took longer to buffer video packets before playback commenced. But once video playback started, the playback continuity was smooth.

Next, the sensitivity of the bandwidth parameter was determined. The system could not support video playback at bandwidth lower than 600 kbps. Between the values of 600 and 700 kbps, the system would connect and begin rendering the

Table 16.1 Initial experimental QoS matrix

Delay (ms)	Bandwidth (kbps)	Packet loss (%)
200	600	0
700	700	14
1,300	750	18
2,200	800	25
3,000	900	31

---

[8] www.wireshark.org

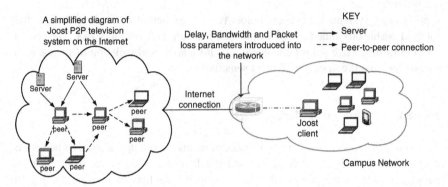

Fig. 16.1 Experimental testbed

Table 16.2 Final QoS matrix

Test conditions	Packet loss (%)
1	0
2	14
3	18
4	25

video, but there were recurrent freezes in the video playback due to buffer starvation (lack of video packets in the buffer). At 800 kbps and above, the video playback was smooth.

Packet loss was the final network parameter to be studied. At an ideal rate of 0%, the video playback was smooth. At packet loss rates between 14 and 25%, video playback was constantly interrupted with the system needing to buffer video packets. The system could not tolerate packet loss rates above 31%.

From this initial experimental assessment based on traffic analysis, it was seen that the negative effects of the delay parameters were mitigated by the buffer implementation. Also, the variations in the effects caused by the bandwidth values in the range 600–700 kbps were negligible.

The Joost P2P system was still sensitive to packet losses, in spite of the buffer implementation and the use of packet loss recovery technique (FEC) to mitigate this effect. We concluded that packet loss rate was the only parameter that was sensitive to the system. Hence, we only focused on the packet loss rate parameter. Table 16.2 shows final QoS matrix. We chose a monotonic degradation of the packet loss rate at 0, 14, 18 and 25%. This rate of packet loss is realistic for a wireless networks, which are more susceptible to losses compared to wired line networks. A packet loss rate of 31% was excluded from the subjective assessment since from the initial experimental assessment based on traffic analysis, it was noticed that the Joost system could not tolerate packet loss rates at 31% and above. This stimulates some concerns, since pervasive systems operate in different network clouds such as wireless, ad hoc, satellite, etc., which are very noisy and have high packet loss rates.

16.3.4.2 Subjective Assessment Methodology

Subjective assessment methods produce quality ratings as perceived by the user. The QoS matrix defined above (Table 16.2) was put forward to our subjects to generate QoE responses that can be used for evaluating its performance and identifying architectural limitations of the system. The QoE responses can also be used in understanding the user perceptions of content delivery systems.

Packet losses over the Internet are unpredictable and dynamic, and can follow this monotonic degradation trend. The plan was to determine at what packet loss rate the viewing experience became unacceptable for our subjects. This methodology of monotonic degradation of quality, when used with the qualitative response received from a subject, gives useful information about the user's QoE.

From the experimental testbed (see Fig. 16.1), the network emulator acted as a proxy server and was used in introducing packet losses over the network. The Joost client software was installed on computer "A." A PHP Application Server software ran on the same computer to enable the Joost client to run within the web application used in conducting our study.

The web application was implemented as a collection of PHP scripts that enabled the Joost client to be embedded and started within a web page. The other pages in the application had forms that enabled the collection of the user's information (i.e., name, age, gender, email address, details about previous experience with Internet and P2P streaming, etc.) and the user's responses regarding the streaming quality. The PHP script structure is shown in Fig. 16.2.

- The scripts "1_intro.php, 2_confirm.php and 3_welcome.php" implemented the web page forms where the users' information were collected and also provided instructions for the user.
- The scripts "4_conditions.php and 5_timer.php" implemented the functionality where a packet loss rate was introduced into the network.

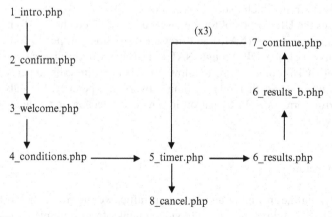

Fig. 16.2 Diagram of the script structure

- The script "5_timer.php" was used in limiting each test condition to 4 min.
- The scripts "6_results.php and 6_results_b.php" were used in collecting the user ratings (i.e., acceptable or unacceptable) at the end of each test condition.
- The pages looped a total of three times from "4_conditions.php" to "7_continue. php" in order to set the four different test conditions and collect the results. Every time a new test condition begins, the Joost cache was cleared in order to avoid biased results.
- After the four test conditions are executed, the script "8_cancel.php" automatically shut down the Joost client to mark the end of the experiment.

The total duration of the experiment for each user was approximately 20 min. The experiment was performed without the users having any knowledge of the packet loss parameters. Figure 16.3a–c shows the screenshot of the test environment.

16.3.5 Results

The results from our experimental measurements and subjective assessment are presented below.

16.3.5.1 Results from the Experimental Measurements

Basic Operation of Joost

At initialization, a peer initiated encrypted handshakes with three servers at the following IP addresses: (89.251.4.178), (89.251.4.175) and (89.251.2.85). Next, the peer sent an HTTP GET request to the site (89.251.2.87) to check for the current version of the Joost software. Finally, the peer contacted some super nodes at the sites (89.251.4.71), (89.251.0.17) and (89.251.0.16) in order to obtain lists of the available peers from which to download video chunks.

Joost uses the UDP protocol for the distribution of video chucks. To bypass network address translators (NATs) and firewall restrictions on peers, Joost uses the simple transversal of UDP through NAT (STUN) and interactive connectivity establishment (ICE) protocol [15] to allow peers behind firewalls to participate in a P2P streaming systems, thereby providing network transparency. Joost also uses the forward error correction (FEC) packet loss recovery technique to handle live peer packet losses [15].

Joost Architecture

After analyzing the incoming and outgoing traffic, we inferred that Joost belongs to a mesh-based architecture. It pulls video chunks from multiple video sources, thereby providing more resilience to churn rate as compared to the tree-based

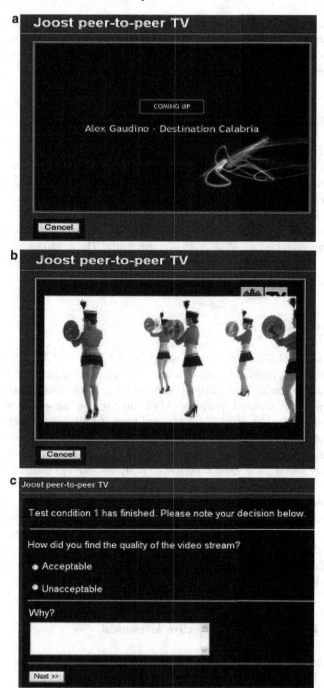

Fig. 16.3 Screen shots of the test environment. (**a**) PHP script initializing joost start-up; (**b**) An example of joost playing a popular channel; and (**c**) Qualitative feedback form for collecting subjects' ratings

system, where peers can only receive video packets from a single source at a given time. However, a disadvantage of a mesh-based architecture is the extra processing time in re-ordering the video chunks at the receiving peer, since these video chunks are received from multiple sources.

Start-up Delay

We measured the start-up delay, i.e., the delay from when a peer gets connected to Joost until video playback started. By taking the average over several trials (each time, clearing the local video cache in order to eliminate biases), we determined the start-up delay of a popular Joost channel on the campus settings to be 25 s, with minimum and maximum values of 16 and 25 s, respectively.

For the residential settings, the average start-up delay was 28 s, with minimum and maximum values of 15 and 38 s, respectively. These values are still higher than those experienced in client-server architectures, which are typically between 5 and 15 s.

Channel Switching Delay

We also measured the channel switching delay for Joost P2P TV. To measure the channel switching delay, a random channel was left running until the video stream was considered stable. Then navigating through the "Joost Channel Explorer," another channel was selected. We recorded the time it took the system to respond to this request. Taking the average over several trials, for different selection of channels, we observed the average channel switching delay to be 5 s, with minimum and maximum values of 4 and 6 s, respectively. The channel switching delays are significantly longer than those experienced in traditional TV, which are between 1 and 1.5 s.

From the experimental measurements, it can be seen that the user's QoE in current P2P streaming systems is still not comparable to the digital broadcast systems (traditional TV). Users are used to traditional TV, and thus, will always compare the performance of a P2P TV service to that of traditional TV. The ultimate challenge for P2P television systems will be to improve its performance to provide users with a similar viewing experience to that in digital broadcast systems.

16.3.5.2 Results from the Subjective Assessment

Twenty-four university students (13 males and 11 females) participated in this experiment. The age range was between 20 and 22 years. Our sample size included those who had previous experience in using Internet streaming and/or P2P streaming applications. Before the subjective assessments began, subjects were given information to explain what the experiment was all about, in addition to a feedback form

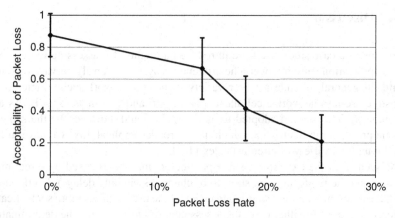

Fig. 16.4 Subjects acceptance of packet loss rate at 95% confidence interval

which the subjects had to fill up. A training session was also given to make sure that the subjects' understood what was required. From Sect. 16.3.4.1, it was explained that the negative effect of the delay and bandwidth parameters were mitigated by Joost's buffer implementation. From our initial study (Sect. 16.3.4.1), it was noticed that the Joost system was particularly sensitive to packet losses. Hence, this was the only parameter that was used in the subjective assessment.

From the subjective assessment, the user's acceptability of the Joost service at a packet loss rate is depicted in Fig. 16.4. Acceptability in this context refers to the proportion of our subjects who found the viewing experience at a given packet loss rate acceptable all the time. As can be seen from the graph, our users were relatively accurate in acknowledging when there was degradation in service quality, i.e., their acceptability decreased as the packet loss rate increased. From our observations, we noticed that the subjects who had previous experience on Internet streaming and/or P2P streaming had a higher acceptability threshold because they had a general idea of what to expect. They perceived the P2P services as free (i.e., they were not paying for it) on the Internet, so they were more tolerant to poor service qualities.

However, at a packet loss rate of 25%, the majority of our subjects said viewing quality was unacceptable. The qualitative responses from our subjects suggested that at higher packet loss rates, the incurred longer start-up delays and the lack of smooth continuity during video playback significantly affected their viewing experience. The error bars were quite large due to our small sample size (this project is still ongoing at the time of writing). It is clear that a larger number of subjects with more diverse ages and a lower granularity of packet loss between 0 and 14% will be needed in future studies.

A method for assessing the user's experience on P2P television systems is essential in order to improve the user's QoE. Although P2P television offers a cheap platform for providing video services, understanding the user's QoE in such systems could increase their popularity and has the potential to revolutionize this evolving technology.

16.4 Discussion

By means of a case study, we have introduced a method for assessing QoE in pervasive application (running over a heterogeneous system). A truly pervasive system would, in general, include a larger variety of access network technologies (e.g., infrastructure-less networks, cellular and wireless) and terminals (e.g., PDAs and cell phones). The method adopted to assess QoE would, however, be the same as the one presented in Sect. 16.3, which has a broader applicability. We have in fact tested it under a variety of circumstances [1, 2].

As seen from the case study, some parameters may be assessed by direct measurement on the platform (e.g., start-up or channel switching delays). On the other hand, the assessment of the quality perceived by the user requires more sophisticated subjective studies. In either case, the assessment of QoE requires the determination of the sensitivity of the various factors in relation to the architectural and functional properties of the platform. We have seen, for instance, how buffering mechanisms reduce the sensitivity to delay. On the other hand, packet loss is more critical, though thanks to the mesh-based approach there is a good level of resilience.

The significance of the results obtained in this case study can be further increased by extending the study to a larger user population, which will allow a more fine-grained assessment of the relationship between network quality and user's experience. This, in turn, will lead to QoS-to-QoE mapping algorithms that can considerably improve overlay management. P2P streaming is still at its infancy and the subject of intensive studies aimed at improving overlay management algorithms, resilience and the ability to work in a dynamic environment.

Extending the assessment of P2P streaming to a mobile environment may unveil interesting unexpected findings. QoE subjective studies will also help taking into account psychological factors. For instance, users may have lower expectations if they connect with an inexpensive (or low-power) terminal. Very little progress has been done in the area of QoE-based assessment of P2P streaming, which is the subject of this case study and the general theme of this chapter.

16.5 Conclusions

In this chapter, we discussed pervasive systems and services, highlighting the paramount importance of QoE in service deployment. We have argued that the QoE approach is a major tool in understanding user perceptions of services, since the user's QoE is central to the commercial success of the services offered by these systems. The Internet protocol has undoubtedly paved the way towards making telecommunications systems pervasive. Applications and services are no longer localized within strict boundaries. Instead applications or services are becoming available anywhere and at anytime. An example is P2P television, where television channels can be made available to anyone, anywhere in the world.

Despite the availability of the service enabling technologies and the huge improvements of pervasive devices, the future of seamless fixed-mobile convergence in providing truly pervasive services still requires certain issues to be addressed. Some of these issues include mobility management, QoS assurance and security mechanisms. In addition, the efficient collaboration between the different entities (networks and service providers, access technologies, terminals manufacturers, etc.) involved in the service provisioning chain is needed. Standardization bodies such as 3GPP, open mobile alliance (OMA), European Telecommunications Standards Institute (ETSI), Parlay Group and World Wide World Consortium (W3C) are working towards the development and deployment of pervasive services.

A major effort will be required to develop general methods and models that allow mapping QoS parameters of pervasive systems directly to QoE factors. Suitable QoS-to-QoE prediction models will enable advanced, QoE-based management of pervasive systems, whereby network and computing resources are harmonized in such a way as to maximize the user's experience, regardless of their heterogeneous and dynamic context. We anticipate that QoE-management will become an essential element of pervasive systems, complementing the more rudimentary QoS-management mechanisms used today.

References

1. Agboma, F., & Liotta, A. (2007). Addressing user expectations in mobile content delivery. *Mobile Information Systems, 3*, 153–164.
2. Agboma, F., & Liotta, A. (2008). QoE for mobile TV services. In *Multimedia Transcoding in Mobile and Wireless Networks*.
3. Ahamed, S. I., & Haque, M. (2006). Security in pervasive computing: Current status and open issues. *International Journal of Network Security, 3*(3), 203–214.
4. Benham, D. (2005). Video service to network linkages. In *IP Implementation and Planning Guide, United States Telecom Association*. USA.
5. David, S., Man, L., & Renaud, C. (2006). *QoS and QoE Management in UMTS Cellular Systems*. Wiley, New York.
6. Gordon, M. M., & Agbinya, J. I. (2004). Vertical handover. In *Cellular Communication Networks*. Paper presented at the South African Telecommunication Networks and Applications.
7. Hall, Y. J., Piemonte, P., & Weyant, M. (2007). *Joost: A Measurement Study: Tech. Rep.* Carnegie Mellon University, Pittsburgh, PA.
8. Hei, X., Liang, C., Liang, J., et al. (2007). A measurement study of a large-scale P2P IPTV system. *IEEE Transactions on Multimedia, 9*(8), 1672–1687.
9. Isaksson, L., & Fiedler, M. (2007). *Seamless Connectivity in WLAN and Cellular Networks with Multi Criteria Decision Making*. Paper presented at the 3rd Conference on Next Generation Internet Networks.
10. ISO 9241–11. (1998). Ergonomic requirements for office work with visual display terminals (VDTs) – Part 11: Guidance on usability.
11. Krieger, U. R., & Schwessinger, R. (2008). *Analysis and Quality Assessment of Peer-to-Peer IPTV Systems*. Paper presented at the IEEE International Symposium on Consumer Electronics, 2008. ISCE 2008.
12. Lei, J., Shi, L., & Fu, X. (2007). *An Experimental Analysis of Joost Peer-to-Peer VoD Service Tech. Rep. IFI-TB-2007–03*, Institute for Computer Science, University of Göttingen, Germany.

13. Liao, X., Jin, H., Liu, Y., et al. (2006). *AnySee: Peer-to-Peer Live Streaming*. Paper presented at the INFOCOM 2006, 25th IEEE International Conference on Computer Communications. Proceedings. pp. 1–10.

14. Liu, Y., Guo, Y., & Liang, C. (2008). A survey on peer-to-peer video streaming systems. *Peer-to-Peer Networking and Applications, 1*(1), 18–28.

15. Maccarthaigh, M. (2007). *Joost Network Architecture*.

16. Massimo, B., Filippo, C., Raffaele, C., et al. (2005). *Adaptive Streaming on Heterogeneous Networks*. Paper presented at the Proceedings of the 1st ACM Workshop on Wireless Multimedia Networking and Performance Modeling, Canada.

17. Olista. (2007). Live trials by Olista with European mobile operators demonstrate common barriers for mobile data services. Press Release.

18. Raatikainen, P. (2005). On developing of networking technologies and pervasive services. *Wireless Personal Communications, 33*, 261–269.

19. Salkintzis, A. S., & Passas, N. (2005). *Emerging Wireless Multimedia Services and Technologies*. Wiley, New York.

20. Sattari, N., Pangalos, P., & Aghvami, H. (2004). *Seamless Handover Between WLAN and UMTS*. Paper presented at the 29th IEEE Vehicular Technology Conference.

21. Sentinelli, A., Marfia, G., Gerla, M., et al. (2007). Will IPTV ride the peer-to-peer stream?. *Communications Magazine, IEEE, 45*(6), 86–92.

22. Shin, M., Ma, J., Mishra, A., et al. (2006). Wireless network security and interworking. *Proceedings of the IEEE, 94*(2), 455–466.

23. Yuping, Y., & Williams, M. H. (2006). *Handling Dynamic QoS Requirements in a Pervasive System*. Paper presented at the Networking, International Conference on Systems and International Conference on Mobile Communications and Learning Technologies.

24. Zahariadis, T. B., Vaxevanakis, K. G., Tsantilas, C. P., et al. (2002). Global roaming in next-generation networks. *Communications Magazine, IEEE, 40*(2), 145–151.

25. Zhang, X., Liu, J., Li, B., et al. (2005). *CoolStreaming/DONet: A Data-driven Overlay Network for Peer-to-Peer Live Media Streaming*. Paper presented at the 24th Annual Joint Conference of the IEEE Computer and Communications Societies.

Chapter 17
Agents Based e-Commerce and Securing Exchanged Information

Raja Al-Jaljouli and Jemal Abawajy

Abstract Mobile agents have been implemented in e-Commerce to search and filter information of interest from electronic markets. When the information is very sensitive and critical, it is important to develop a novel security protocol that can efficiently protect the information from malicious tampering as well as unauthorized disclosure or at least detect any malicious act of intruders. In this chapter, we describe robust security techniques that ensure a sound security of information gathered throughout agent's itinerary against various security attacks, as well as truncation attacks. A sound security protocol is described, which implements the various security techniques that would jointly prevent or at least detect any malicious act of intruders. We reason about the soundness of the protocol using Symbolic Trace Analyzer (STA), a formal verification tool that is based on symbolic techniques. We analyze the protocol in key configurations and show that it is free of flaws. We also show that the protocol fulfils the various security requirements of exchanged information in MAS, including data-integrity, data-confidentiality, data-authenticity, origin confidentiality and data non-repudiability.

Keywords Mobile agents · Security properties · Formal methods · Security protocols · Security techniques · Electronic commerce

17.1 Introduction

Mobile agents are autonomous programs that act on behalf of users and have some level of intelligence [6]. The agent is able to choose what to do and in which order according to the external environment and user's requests. They control where they execute and can run in heterogeneous environments. They traverse the Internet from one host to another through various architectures and platforms to access remote resources or even to meet, cooperate and communicate with other programs and

R. Al-Jaljouli (✉)
School of Engineering and Information Technology, Deakin University, Australia
e-mail: ralj@deakin.edu.au

A.-E. Hassanien et al. (eds.), *Pervasive Computing: Innovations in Intelligent Multimedia and Applications*, Computer Communications and Networks, DOI 10.1007/978-1-84882-599-4_17, © Springer-Verlag London Limited 2009

agents to accomplish their tasks. Agents can remain stationary filtering incoming information or become mobile searching for specific information across the Internet and retrieving it.

Mobile agents have been proposed for e-commerce applications such as shopping applications [32]. They can be employed to search the Internet for offers, negotiate the terms of agreements or even purchase goods or services. As mobile agents transport from one host to another through insecure channels and may execute on non-trusted hosts, they are vulnerable to direct security attacks from intruders and non-trusted hosts. The attacks might result in release of sensitive data, erroneous credits or money fritter induced by the truncation of offers of competing traders.

Security is a major obstacle that prevents mobile agent technology from being widely adopted. Several protocols have been presented in the literature that assert the security properties of mobile agent's execution results, such as integrity, confidentiality and authenticity in the presence of malicious hosts and intruders [7, 13, 17, 18, 21, 22, 33]. However, most of these approaches fail to prevent or at least detect one or more of the following security breaches [16]: (a) truncation of collected data, (b) alteration of the data which a host has formerly provided, in case the host co-operates with a succeeding malicious host in the agent's itinerary, (c) impersonating the genuine initiator and hence, breach the privacy of collected data, (d) sending others data under the private key of a malicious host and (e) replacing the collected data with data of a similar agent or a protocol run. For mobile agents to be viable in security-aware applications, mechanisms to make mobile agents resistant to or at least detect these security attacks are needed.

In this chapter, we discuss major security threats to data gathering mobile agents. A survey of countermeasures that the exiting security protocols implemented and the flaws detected is presented. We propose a set of new security techniques that would boost security of exchanged information in MAS and develop error-free security protocols. The techniques include: (a) utilizing co-operating agents, (b) jumbling collected offers, (c) instructing a visited host to clear its memory of any results before dispatching the agent to the next host, (d) carrying out verifications at the early execution of the agent at a visited host on the identity of the genuine initiator and (e) encrypting a collected offer for the verified genuine initiator. A new security protocol is described that asserts integrity, confidentiality, authenticity, origin confidentiality and non-repudiability of exchanged information in MAS. The protocol implements the proposed security techniques. The protocol is verified formally and is free of security flaws of concern.

The rest of the paper is organized in the following manner. Section 17.2 presents the background concepts, defines the security properties, and describes the security threats to which data gathering mobile agent are susceptible. Section 17.3 discusses the security protocols presented in the literature and the security flaws revealed in the corresponding protocols. In Section 17.4, we describe the robust security techniques and the new security protocol that implements the techniques. In Section 17.5, we analyze the protocol regarding security and efficiency. We use Symbolic Trace Analyzer (STA) to model the protocol, specify its properties, analyze the protocol formally, verify the security properties of concern and show that the protocol is free of the flaws. In addition, we reason the correctness of a general model of the protocol. In Section 17.6, we summarize the security problem, the robust security techniques and the new security protocol.

17.2 Background

The principal scheme of the data gathering agent is that it is initiated by host i_0 and then it is sent out to a set of n hosts called visiting hosts. We assume that the channels are insecure and the agent has no prior knowledge of whether it is executing on non-trusted hosts. As in [29], we use anonymous connections that hide the identity of the previously visited host. The agent has code and static and dynamic data. The code and the static data are denoted as Π. Each host has a private and public keys.

Figure 17.1 shows the agent's itinerary. A visited host is denoted as i_j for $(1 \leq j \leq n)$. The agent gets executed at each of the visited hosts in the agent's itinerary. The agent stores the result of execution at host i_j as m_j for $(1 \leq j \leq n)$. The execution results are modelled as a chain of $m_1, m_2, \ldots, m_n$, which is stored within the agent and returned to the initiator i_0. The returned chain is expressed as $m'_1, m'_2, \ldots, m'_n$.

The problem is that the returned execution results $m'_1, m'_2, \ldots, m'_n$ might differ from the genuine execution results m_j for $(1 \leq j \leq n)$ due to tampering acts of adversaries. Tampering with the already stored execution results m_j for $(1 \leq j \leq n)$ could occur either during the migration of the agent or during its execution at visited hosts.

The problem of interest to us is how to prevent tampering with the already stored execution results or at least enable the initiating host to detect tampering upon the agent's return. The execution results would be validated if the following security properties are preserved [10, 22]:

- Data confidentiality: The chain of execution results $m_1, \ldots, m_j, \ldots, m_n$ stored within the agent can only be read by the initiator i_0.

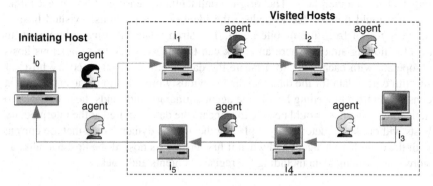

Fig. 17.1 Agent's itinerary

- Data non-repudiability: The initiator i_0 can build a proof about the identity of host i_j that added the execution result m'_j $(1 \leq j \leq n)$ to the chain of results $m'_1, m'_2, \ldots, m'_n$.
- Data authenticity: Upon the agent's return, the initiator i_0 can determine for sure the identity of host i_j that appended m'_j to the chain of execution results $m'_1, m'_2, \ldots, m'_n$.
- Origin confidentiality: The identity of host i_j for $(1 \leq j \leq n)$ that generated and added the execution result m_j to the chain $m_1, \ldots, m_n$ can only be known at host i_0.
- Data integrity: The data integrity requires that the chain of execution results $m'_1, m'_2, \ldots, m'_n$ which is returned to the initiator i_0 matches the genuine chain of execution results $m_1, m_2, \ldots, m_n$.

The data integrity property refers to the following classes of protection:

1. Insertion resilience: Data can only be appended to the chain $m_1, \ldots, m_j$ for $(j < n)$.
2. Deletion resilience: Deletion of an execution result m_j for $(1 \leq j \leq n)$ from the chain of results $m_1, \ldots, m_n$ is prevented, or at least is detected upon the agent's return to the initiator. If an execution result m_j is deleted and the chain of execution results reduces to $m_1, \ldots, m_{j-1}, m_{j+1}, \ldots, m_n$, then the initiator i_0 has a proof that an execution result is deleted from the chain of results.
3. Truncation resilience: Truncation of the chain $m_1, \ldots, m_j, \ldots, m_n$ at host i_j and reducing it to the chain $m_1, \ldots, m_j$ for $(j < n)$ are prevented, or at least are detected upon the agent's return to the initiator i_0. The computed verification terms, e.g., message authentication code, would indicate inconsistency with the returned chain of execution results.
4. Strong forward integrity: None of the execution results in a chain can be modified. The property necessitates that the returned execution result m'_j matches m_j for $(1 \leq j \leq n)$.
5. Strong data integrity: Requires the four classes of protection: insertion resilience, deletion resilience, truncation resilience and strong forward integrity.

The data authenticity property ensures that an adversary should not be able to impersonate another host. The origin confidentiality ensures that an executing host i_k should not be able to deduce the identity of a previously visited host i_j for $(1 \leq j < k)$ from the mobile agent. The strong data integrity is important to avoid colluding attacks where an attack can take place when two malicious hosts co-operate with each other to truncate the data acquired at intermediary hosts or substitute new data for the data they had previously provided to the agent. If a host conspires with a preceding host in the agent's itinerary and sends the agent back to it, the preceding host would be able to truncate the data acquired at the intermediary hosts without being detected by replacing the agent's dynamic data that are current with the data that the agent had when it first visited its host, if the host had already stored the dynamic data including the register contents and stack.

17.3 Literature Review

Cryptographic protocols are used to secure the data aggregated by mobile agents. The protocols presented in the literature [7, 13, 17, 18, 21, 22, 33] build a proof on the security of the aggregated data, particularly the integrity of the data based on the implementation of one or more of the following security techniques: public key encryption, digital signature, message authentication code, backward chaining, one-step forward chaining and code-result binding. The common thread among the existing approaches is that they fail to accomplish the desirable security properties discussed in Section 17.2. Table 17.1 summarizes the security breaches revealed in the existing security protocols, which the initiator i_0 would not be able to detect upon the agent's return [16]. The "Targeted State Protocol" [17] is based on encrypting the data that should only be available to a trusted host using the public key of the host. The "Append Only Container Protocol" [17] is proposed so that new objects can be appended to a container of objects in an agent, but any later modification or deletion of an already contained object can be detected upon the agent's return. Also, the insertion of a new object within the contained objects can be detected. The security of protocol is based on an encrypted checksum. The "Multi-hops Protocol" [7] has the same purpose as the Append only Container Protocol. The protocol binds the static data and program code to the execution results. The "Publicly Verifiable Chained Digital Signature Protocol" [18] uses a hash chain and a chain of encapsulated execution results. The hash chain binds the encapsulated execution result at the preceding host to the identity of the next host in the agent's itinerary. The "Chained Digital Signature Protocol with Forward Privacy" [18] enhances the security techniques implemented in the "Publicly Verifiable Chained Digital Signature Protocol." It proposes the execution results at a visited host to be firstly signed by the host and then encrypted with the public key of the initiator. The "Publicly Verifiable Chained Signature Protocol" [18] uses temporary key pairs (private signing key and the corresponding verification key) and a chain of encapsulated execution results. Each host generates a pair of keys (private and public). The "Configurable Mobile Agent Data Protection Protocol" [22] is based on: (a) securely storing the addresses of next hosts to be visited and (b) binding the program code and static data to a chain of encapsulated execution results at hosts in the agent's itinerary. The "Mobile Agent Integrity Protocol" [13, 21] is based on the chain of execution results, a message integrity code and hash chain of a nonce. The message integrity code binds the execution result and the hash chain computed at the current host to the message integrity code computed at the preceding host. The "Improved Forward Integrity Protocol" [33] enhances the "Publicly Verifiable Chained Signature Protocol" [18]. It involves the preceding and the succeeding hosts of a particular host in signing its offer. A host constructs a joint private key for signing its offer using a one-time private key generated by the preceding host and its long-term private key. We propose a set of new security techniques that would truly hinder or at least detect the security breaches the existing protocols failed to detect.

Table 17.1 Security breaches in the existing mobile agent security protocols

Security protocol	Aimed properties	Failed property	Type of security breach
• Append only container protocol	Authenticity integrity	Authenticity integrity	— Returned data are erroneously authenticated — Co-operating hosts can truncate collected data — Adversary can append fake data. Hence, returned data may not belong to agent of concern
• Multi-hops protocol	Integrity authenticity	Integrity	— Cooperating hosts can truncate collected data. — Adversary can append fake data. Hence, returned data may not belong to agent of concern
• Improved forward integrity protocol	Integrity	Integrity	— Cooperating hosts can truncate collected data
• Targeted state protocol	Confidentiality	Confidentiality	— Adversary can breach privacy of collected data
• Publicly verifiable chained digital signature protocol	Integrity confidentiality	Integrity	— Co-operating hosts can truncate collected data — Adversary can append fake data. Hence, returned data may not belong to agent of concern
• Chained digital signature protocol with forward privacy protocol	Integrity confidentiality forward privacy	Integrity	— Co-operating hosts can truncate collected data — Adversary can append fake data. Hence, returned data may not belong to agent of concern
• Improved forward integrity protocol	Integrity	Integrity	— Co-operating hosts can truncate collected data
• Chained MAC protocol	Integrity confidentiality forward privacy	Integrity	— Co-operating hosts can truncate collected data — Adversary can append fake data. Hence, returned data may not belong to agent of concern
• Publicly verifiable chained signature protocol	Integrity confidentiality	Integrity	— Co-operating hosts can truncate collected data — Adversary can append fake data. Hence, data may not belong to agent of concern
• Mobile agent integrity protocol	Integrity	Integrity	— Co-operating hosts can truncate collected data — Adversary can append fake data. Hence, returned data may not belong to agent of concern
• Configurable mobile agent data protection protocol	Confidentiality authenticity integrity non-repudiation forward privacy	Confidentiality integrity	— Adversary can breach privacy of collected data — Cooperating hosts can truncate collected data

17.4   Robust Security Techniques

Figure 17.2 describes the sequence of processes carried out during the agent's life-time. The protocol uses two agents (a secondary agent, SA, and a major agent, MA) as shown in Fig. 17.2. Generally, the agents carry static and dynamic data, while the initial verification terms are stored in the initiator's host memory. The initiators carry out verifications upon the agent's return based on data that are stored within the agent and in its memory. The problem with this approach is that the data, both in the agent and the initiator's host memory, are susceptible to tampering. To avoid these problems, we utilize two co-operating agents where the initial verification terms are securely stored within a SA that resides at the initiator and co-operates with a MA that traverses the Internet.

It is assumed that it is possible to deduce the identity of the signer from a signa-ture.[1] Table 17.2 summarizes the common notations used in describing protocols. The protocol requests the initiating host to create two agents (i.e., SA and MA) and initialize them with appropriate value before proceeding with the dispatching.

The initiator executes the Agent_Initialization algorithm shown in Fig. 17.3. The algorithm accepts SA and MA as inputs, initializes the MA agent, computes and stores verification data in the SA agent.

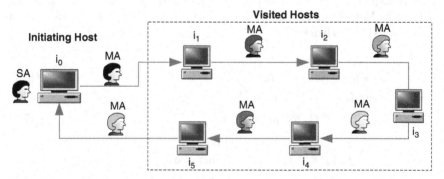

Fig. 17.2 System architecture

---

[1] When a host adds a signature to a message, it uses a digital certificate that is attached to the message and vouches for the authenticity of the message, or supplies a verifiable signature. The digital certificate consists of identifying information: public key of the person being certified, name and address of the person being certified, and issue and expiration dates that are signed by a trusted third party.

Table 17.2 Common notations in protocol's description

Notation	Description
Π	Program code and the static data
$i_0, i_1, i_2, \ldots, i_n, i_0$	Itinerary of a terminating agent initiated by initiating host i_0
$i_j \rightarrow i_k : m$	Transfer of data m from host i_j to host i_k
$s_{i_j}^{-1}(m)$	Signing data m with the private key of host i_n
$\{m\} k_{i_j}^+$	Encrypting data m with the public key of host i_n
$h(m)$	Hashing data m
P_0	Agent's initial itinerary
P_n	Set of new hosts added to agent's initial itinerary
d_n	Execution result at a host
T	Timestamp that uniquely identifies a protocol run

Fig. 17.3
Agent_initialization algorithm

Algorithm **Agent_Initialization**
INPUT: SA, MA
BEGIN
1. MA $\leftarrow$ (Π , i_0 , i_1 , P_0 , t)
2. Compute the terms: Π_0, Π_1, C_n, D_n and M_n
3. SA $\leftarrow$ (Π , t , i_0 , i_1)
4. Update MA $\leftarrow$ (Π_0 , Π_1 , M_0)
END **Agent_Initialization**

The first step the algorithm performs is to set the values of the terms: Π, i_0, i_1, P_0 and t in the MA. It then computes the terms: Π_0, Π_1, C_n, D_n and M_n as given in (17.1)–(17.3) shown below.

$$i_n \rightarrow i_{n+1} : \Pi_{n+1}, \{M_0, \ldots, M\} \tag{17.1}$$

$$\text{where } \Pi_{n+1} = \left\{ \{\Pi, t\} S_{i_0}^{-1} \right\} K_{i_{n+1}}^+ \tag{17.2}$$

$$M_n = D_n \parallel C_n \text{ for } (0 \leq n \leq k) \tag{17.3}$$

$$D_n = \begin{cases} P_0 & \text{if } i_n = i_0 \\ \{d_n\} k_{i_0}^+, P_n & \text{otherwise} \end{cases}$$

$$C_n = \begin{cases} (P_0, \Pi_0, i_1) S_{i_0}^{-1} & \text{if } i_n = i_0 \\ \left\{ (d_n, P_n, \Pi_0, C_{n-1}, i_{n+1}) S_{i_n}^{-1} \right\} k_{i_0}^+ & \text{otherwise} \end{cases}$$

where, $\Pi_0 = h(\Pi, t, h(i_0))$

The initial verification terms that are stored within the SA are: (a) the timestamp t which uniquely identifies a particular protocol run, (b) the static part Π and (c) the identity of the first host in the agent's itinerary i_1. Upon the agent's return, the SA communicates the terms to the major agent and then the major agent verifies that the communicated terms match the terms returned with the migrating agent to check if the gathered data belong to the agent and protocol run of concern. The initiator then dispatches the MA agent to gather data/offers from hosts in agent's itinerary. In order to prevent malicious hosts from tampering with the agent's dynamic data, the MA agent requests an executing host to clear its own memory from any data acquired as a result of executing the agent before the host sends out the agent to the succeeding host in the agent's itinerary. An executing host has also to create and sign a trace of the execution of the agent, and to store it at its host so as to be forwarded to the initiator upon request as recommended in [31]. Upon agent's return, the winning host or the most competing hosts would be asked to send execution trace's to the initiator before the final decision is made on the collected offers. If a trace does not show that the host responded to the clearing memory request, it implies that the host might impose a truncation attack on gathered offers. We recommend execution traces can be limited to the requests of clearing the memory of executing hosts, otherwise traces would be extremely long and require large amounts of storage resources at the executing hosts. Moreover, it would overburden the communication channels as traces are transmitted to the initiator.

Figure 17.4 shows the pseudo-code of the verification algorithm that is performed at each of the visited host and at the initiator host. The host i_{n+1}, where $(1 \leq n \leq k)$, decrypts the cipher Π_{n+1} with its private key having Π'_{n+1}. Then, it deduces the identity of the signer of the agent (initiator) and decrypts it with the signature verification key of the signer. Next, it deduces the terms: Π, and t. Then the host computes Π_0 as a hash of the tuple $(\Pi, t, h(i_0))$ and then verifies it with the corresponding term enclosed within C_0. If the verification passes, it confirms that the agent is signed by the genuine initiator and hence, MA uses the public key of the initiator in computing the terms D_n and C_n of the offer of the executing host. Whereas if the verification fails, it implies that an adversary is impersonating the genuine initiator. Hence, the execution of the agent is terminated. The host encrypts Π'_{n+1} with the public key of the succeeding host i_{n+2} just to be readable at the next host in the agent's itinerary and to prevent an adversary that intercepts the agent and attempts to decrypt Π_{n+1} and sign it with its private key so as to impersonate the genuine initiator and be able to breach the privacy of data to be gathered. The agent requests the host to clear its memory from any data acquired as a result of executing the agent, and then dispatches the agent to the succeeding host.

The second verification is performed upon agent's return to the initiator host. The initiating host deduces the initial verification terms: Π, t and i_0 from Π_n and the term i_1 from C_0, which are enclosed within the migrating agent upon its return. The initiating host compares the deduced initial verification terms with the corresponding terms stored within the SA. The initiating host computes the cipher Π_0 using the terms stored with the SA and then verifies the cipher with the corresponding cipher enclosed in the term C_n for $(0 \leq n \leq k)$. If all the verifications pass, then it implies that the data were generated for the genuine initiator and for the agent's code and timestamp of concern.

The protocol has an advantage over the existing protocols: it verifies that the data were generated for the agent's code of concern as it compares the computed Π_0 using the terms (SP, T) stored with the SA with those enclosed within C_n for $(0 \leq n \leq k)$. In brief, it is able to detect if the agent's code has been tampered with.

Algorithm **Verification**
INPUT: MA, i_{n+1}

$\quad\quad\quad\quad i_{n+1}$: Identity of the current host
$\quad\quad\quad\quad d_n$: Data provided by the current host i_n
$\quad\quad\quad\quad P_n$: New hosts added to the initial agent's itinerary P_0
$\quad\quad\quad\quad eKi_{n+2}$: Encryption public key of the current host i_{n+2}
$\quad\quad\quad\quad eKi_x$: Encryption private key of the initiator i_x
$\quad\quad\quad\quad dKi_{n+1}$: Decryption private key of the succeeding host i_{n+1}
$\quad\quad\quad\quad dSKi_{n+1}$: Digital signature private key of the current host i_{n+1}
$\quad\quad\quad\quad S_vKi_x$: Signature verification public key of the agent signer i_x

BEGIN

1. $\Pi'_{n+1} \leftarrow$ Decrypts (Π_{n+1}, dKi_{n+1})
2. Deduces the identity of the signer i_x from the sender's digital certificate
3. Learns the signature verification public key of the signer S_vKi_x from the sender's digital certificate and then use it in the next step
4. $\{\Pi, t\} \leftarrow$ Decrypts (Π'_{n+1}, S_vKi_x)
5. $\{P_0, \Pi_0, i_1\} \leftarrow$ Decrypts (C_0, S_vKi_x)
6. IF ($i_{n+1} \in P_n$) THEN
   - Computes h(i_x)
   - $\Pi'_0 \leftarrow$ h(Π, t, h(i_x))
   - IF ($\Pi_0 ==$ $\Pi'0$) THEN
     . $\Pi_{n+2} \leftarrow$ Encrypts (Π'_{n+1}, eKi_{n+2})
     . $D_{n+1} \leftarrow$ Encrypt (d_{n+1}, eKi_x), P_{n+1})
     . $C_{n+1} \leftarrow$ Encrypt (Sign ((d_{n+1}, P_{n+1}, Π_0, C_n, i_{n+2}), $dSKi_{n+1}$), eKi_x)
     . MA requests the current host to clear its memory from the agent's execution results
     . Dispatches the agent to the succeeding host i_{n+2}
   - ELSE Terminates execution of the agent

   ELSEIF ($i_{n+1} == i_x$)
   1. Compares the terms: Π, t, i_1, and i_0 stored in MA with the corresponding terms stored in SA
   2. Computes the cipher Π_0 using the terms stored in SA
   3. For (n = 0; n < = k ; n++)
   4. Decrypts C_n
   5. Deduces identity i_n of the signer of C_n
   6. Learns the identity of succeeding host i'_{n+1}
   7. IF (cipher Π_0 enclosed within C_n == computed Π_0) THEN
   8. IF ($C_n == C_n$ enclosed within C_{n+1}) THEN Next n
   9. Assemble agent's itinerary I_a using identities deduced in step 5
   10. Assemble agent's itinerary I'_a using identities deduced in step 6
   11. IF ($I_a == I'_a$) THEN RETURN pass
   12. ELSE RETURN fail
   13. END **Verification**

Fig. 17.4 Data verification algorithm

Also, it can detect if the returned data belong to the protocol run of concern, which is identified by a timestamp.

The executing hosts encrypt the data they provide using the public key of the signer of the agent. In order to avoid impersonation of the genuine initiator host, the MA carries a cipher that has the identity of the genuine initiator host. The MA performs verifications on the identity of the genuine initiator at the early execution of the agent at a visited host and would only encrypt the offer an executing host provides if the verification passes. Otherwise, the MA execution terminates. Another problem with existing approaches is that gathered results are typically arranged in the order of visits to executing hosts in the agent's itinerary and are transmitted as a chain of offers. This enables a malicious host to infer the data that belong to the preceding host and may tamper with it. To address this problem, we jumble the gathered data within the chain to mislead an adversary trying to truncate the offer of the preceding host.

17.5   Protocol Analysis

In this section, we discuss formal methods of verification and show the formal verification of the protocol. The formal methods have been successfully employed in the verification of the security properties of mobile agent protocols [2, 11–14, 19, 20, 23, 24]. We employ STA [4, 27, 28], a tool for automatic verification of security protocols. STA has the following advantages: (a) avoids the state explosion problem [3, 4, 9], (b) does not need to model the intruder explicitly [4, 5, 25], (c) does not require expert guidance [2, 8] and (d) the verification is automatic [8]. In STA, the protocol can be specified using four kinds of declarations: identifiers, processes, configurations and properties. The declarations of STA are explained in Table 17.3.

The syntax of STA is depicted in Table 17.4. It follows closely the syntax of Spi-calculus [1] with a few minor differences. The notations used in the declarations

Table 17.3 STA declarations

Identifiers	
Names	DecName $ $K1, K2, \ldots, Km$ $
Variables	DecVar $ $x1, x2, \ldots, xr$ $
Labels	DecLabel $ $a1, a2, \ldots, an$ $
Processes	Val $Pr = P$
Configuration	Val Conf $= (L @ Pr)$
Properties	Val Prop $= (A \leftarrow B)$

Table 17.4 Syntax of STA

$A! M$	Output action
$A? x$	Input action
Stop	Terminated process
$\gg$	Sequence of actions
K new_in	Fresh name K
$P1 \parallel P2$	Parallel composition of the processes $P1$ and $P2$
$(M)^\wedge + K$	Encrypting the term M with the public key K
$(M)^\wedge + \text{sig}K$	Signing digitally the term M with the signing key $\text{sig}K$
$(M \text{ is } N)$	Equality test of the terms M and N
$(M1, M2)$	Pairing of the terms $M1$ and $M2$
hsh(M)	Hash of the term M
M pkdecr$(-K, x)$	Decrypting the variable x with the private key $-K$ to get the plain message M
M pkdecr$(-\text{sig}K, x)$	Decrypting the variable x with the signature verification key $-\text{sig}K$ to get the plain term M

Table 17.5 Notations used in STA script of the verified protocols

Notation	Actual term
I, A, B, C	Identities of the initiator, and the three participants hosts
T	Timestamp
SP	Static part (program code and static data)
$P0$	Agent's initial itinerary
$P1$, $P2$, $P3$	New hosts appended to the agent's initial itinerary at hosts A, B, and C
$X1$, $X2$, $X3$	Data acquired at hosts A, B, and C respectively
$+sigI$, $+sigA$, $+sigB$, $+sigC$	Digital signature of hosts: I, A, B, and C respectively
$+KI$, $+KA$, $+KB$, $+KC$	Public key of hosts: I, A, B, and C respectively
$-sigI$, $-sigA$, $-sigB$, $-sigC$	Signature verification keys of hosts I, A, B, and C respectively
$i1$	Output action that sends initial verification data to the secondary agent
$i2$	Output action that sends initiating data to the first host in the agent's itinerary
$i3$	Input action that receives the data gathered by the mobile agent upon its return to the initiator
$i4$	Input action that receives the data stored within the secondary agent
$a1$, $a2$	(I/O) actions at host A
$b1$, $b2$	(I/O) actions at host B
$c1$, $c2$	(I/O) actions at host C
$hsh(m)$	Hashing of data m
S	Denotes Π_{n+1}
D	Denotes Π_0
IE	Denotes $\{\Pi, t\} S_{i_j}^{-1}$
Accept!	Output action at host I that outputs the gathered data that pass all the necessary security verifications
guard?	Input action "guardian" that can detect if the environment learns some piece of confidential data
disclose!	Output action that leaks some sensible data to the environment

are shown in Table 17.5. In STA, variables notations begin with x, y, z or w. For example, a name $P0$ is transmitted from host I to host A and is then received at A as a variable $wP0$. The command used to verify a property is in the form of: CHECK *Conf Prop*, where *Conf* is the configuration of the system and *Prop* is the property to check.

17.5.1 Protocol Formal Verification

The verification is carried out for an instance of the protocol susceptible to the various malicious acts of intruders, especially the colluding attacks. Though the instance is of a limited number of participants, as execution slows down as the number of

val iI = T new_in P0 new_in SP new_in
    i1!(((SP,T)^+sigI)^+kI) >>
      i2!(((SP,T)^+sigI)^+kA), P0, ((P0,hsh(SP,T,hsh(I)),A)^+sigI) >>
      i3?wS,wP0,((wP0,wD,A)^+sigI), (wX1)^+kI,wP1,
      ((wX1,wP1,xD, ((wP0,xD,A)^+sigI),B)^+sigA)^+kI,
      (wX2)^+kI,wP2,((wX2,wP2,yD,((wX1,wP1,yD,
      ((wP0,yD,A)^+sigI),B)^+sigA)^+kI,C)^+sigB)^+kI,
      (wX3)^+kI,wP3,((wX3,wP3,zD,((wX2,wP2,zD,((wX1,wP1,zD,
      ((wP0,zD,A)^+sigI),B)^+sigA)^+kI,C)^+sigB)^+kI,I)^+sigC)^+kI >>
      (wS pkdecr (wIE, -kI)) >>
    i4?xSP >> (xSP pkdecr (wSP, -kI)) >> (wIE is wSP) >>
      (xD is hsh(SP,T,hsh(I))) >> (yD is hsh(SP,T,hsh(I))) >>
      (zD is hsh(SP,T,hsh(I))) >> (wD is hsh(SP,T,hsh(I))) >>
      Accept!((A,X1), (B,X2), (C,X3)) >> stop;
val rA = X1 new_in P1 new_in
    a1?xS, xP0, ((xP0,xD,A)^+sigI) >> (xS pkdecr (xIE, -kA)) >>
      (xIE pkdecr (xID, -sigI)) >> (xD is hsh(xID, hsh(I))) >>
    a2!(xIE)^+kB, xP0, ((xP0,xD,A)^+sigI),
      (X1)^+kI, P1, ((X1,P1,xD,((xP0,xD,A)^+sigI),B)^+sigA)^+kI >> stop;
val Sys = KI new_in KA new_in KB new_in KC new_in iI || rA || rB || rC || guard?y >> stop;
val Conf = ([disclose!(SPold, Told, I, A, B, C, T,+KI, +KA, +KB, +KC, -SigI, -SigA, -SigB,
    -SigC, ((xSP,xT)^+SigI, xP0, (xP0,(xSP,xT)^+SigI,A,+SigI)))] @Sys);

Fig. 17.5 Declarations of roles of hosts I and A of the protocol in STA

participants and the associated number of identifiers increase. The instance we considered is of three executing hosts A, B, and C and the initiator I.

Due to space limitations, we merely present the roles of hosts I and A, and the declarations of both the *Sys* and *Conf* of the new protocol are expressed in the syntax of STA in Fig. 17.5. The full modelling and specifications of the protocol can be found in [15].

We analyze the protocol for key configurations that would generate a system susceptible to the most common and critical attacks, which existing protocols fail to hinder or even detect. The configurations are as follows.

- Configuration (1): Single run with the presence of an intruder.
- Configuration (2): Single run with the presence of a malicious host.
- Configuration (3): Single run of the protocol with two co-operating malicious hosts.
- Configuration (4): Two parallel runs of the protocol with two different initiators.

The induced security threats associated with the configurations are explained below:

- Threat (1): Breach of privacy and/or erroneous authentication.
- Threat (2): Data truncation or replacement.
- Threat (3): Replacing of the gathered data with the data of a similar agent.

Here, only the verifications of data $X1$ acquired at host A are explained and shown expressed in STA. The verifications are of two types as follows:

1. At the early execution of the agent at host A, the host checks the identity of the genuine initiator. It decrypts the term xS it receives with its private decryption key and binds the result to variable xIE, and then it deduces the identity of the signer of xIE. Next, it decrypts xIE with the signature verification key of the host from which its identity is deduced. It would then bind the result to variable xID. If the decryption passes, it computes Π'_0 as hsh(xID, hsh(I)) and then compares it with the corresponding term Π_0 enclosed with C_0, which is received as variable xD. If the verification passes, it would ensure that the deduced identity is the identity of the genuine initiator and would encrypt the data it provides to the agent with the public key of the genuine initiator. The verification is given in (17.4).

$$(xS \text{ pkdecr } (xIE, \ -KA)) \gg (xIE \text{ pkdecr } (xID, \ -sigI))$$
$$\gg (xD \text{ is hsh } (xID, \ \text{hsh } (I))) \gg \qquad (17.4)$$

2. Upon the agent's return, the initiator performs the two verifications given in (17.5) and (17.6).

   - Verifies that the offer of host A was generated for the genuine initiator.

$$(xD \text{ is hsh } (SP, T, \text{hsh } (I))) \qquad (17.5)$$

   - Verifies that the returned data were generated for the agent's code and timestamp of concern. It checks the static part of the agent, which is securely stored with the SA and would be communicated to it through the input action $a4?$, with the corresponding term returned with the agent.

$$(wSis \, xSP) \qquad (17.6)$$

We used STA tool to check the security properties of the gathered data. The security properties of the protocol are expressed in STA as given in Fig. 17.6. Due to space limitations, we only explain the verification of the data $X1$ acquired at host A as follows:

1. Verify the authenticity of the data $X1$ acquired at host A and returned with the agent as given in (17.7).

$$\text{val Auth1} = (a2!X1 \leftarrow i3?wX1); \qquad (17.7)$$

2. Verify that host A sends out the static part, which was originally signed by the genuine initiator, intact to host B as given in (17.8).

$$\text{val Auth 4} = \left(i2! \left((SP,T)^\Lambda + sigI \right) \leftarrow a2! \, (xIE) \right); \qquad (17.8)$$

Fig. 17.6 Declarations of
security properties of the
protocol in STA

```
val Auth1 = (a2!X1 <-- i3?wX1);
val Auth2 = (b2!X2 <-- i3?wX2);
val Auth3 = (c2!X3 <-- i3?wX3);
val Auth4 =  (i2!((SP,T)^+sigI) <-- a2!(xIE));
val Auth5 =  (i2!((SP,T)^+sigI) <-- b2!(yIE));
val Auth6 =  (i2!((SP,T)^+sigI) <-- c2!(zIE));
val Auth7 =  (i2!hsh(SP,T,hsh(I)) <-- i3?(xD));
val Auth8 =  (i2!hsh(SP,T,hsh(I)) <-- i3?(yD));
val Auth9 =  (i2!hsh(SP,T,hsh(I)) <-- i3?(zD));
val Auth10 =  (i2!hsh(SP,T,hsh(I)) <-- i3?(wD));
val Auth11= (a2!(xIE)^+kB <-- b1?yS);
val Auth12= (b2!(yIE)^+kC <-- c1?zS);
val Auth12= (c2!(zIE)^+kI <-- i3?wS);
val Auth13 = (i2!P0 <-- i3?wP0);
val Auth14 = (a2!P1 <-- i3?wP1);
val Auth15 = (b2!P2 <-- i3?wP2);
val Auth16 = (c2!P3 <-- i3?wP3);
val Secrecy1 = (Absurd <-- guard?X1);
val Secrecy2 = (Absurd <-- guard?X2);
val Secrecy3 = (Absurd <-- guard?X3);
```

3. Verify that the data $X1$ acquired at host A were generated for the genuine initiator, and for the agent's code and timestamp of concern as given in (17.9).

$$\text{val Auth } 7 = (i\,2!\text{hsh}\,(SP,T,\text{hsh}\,(I)) \leftarrow i\,3\,(xD)); \qquad (17.9)$$

4. Verify that an intruder would not be able to tamper with the static part, which was originally signed by the genuine initiator, during the agent's move from host A to host B as given in (17.10).

$$\text{val Auth } 11 = \left(a2!\,(xIE)^\Lambda + kB \leftarrow b1?yS\right); \qquad (17.10)$$

5. Verify that the set of new hosts that host A appended to the agent's initial itinerary are maintained intact during the agent's lifecycle as given in (17.11).

$$\text{val Auth } 14 = (a2!P1 \leftarrow i3?wP1); \qquad (17.11)$$

6. Verify the secrecy of the data $X1$ acquired at host A as given in (17.12).

$$\text{val Secrecy } 1 = (\text{Absurd} \leftarrow \text{guard}?X1); \qquad (17.12)$$

We analyzed the protocol in four key configurations for the instance of three executing hosts and an initiator. The runs are: (1) A single run with an intruder, (2) A single run of the protocol with host A as a malicious host, (3) A single run with hosts A and C as conspiring hosts and (4) Two parallel runs of the protocol, each with an initiator and a particular static part Π_0.

Table 17.6 Results of the analysis of the protocol for different runs

Protocol's configuration	Results of analysis
A single run with an intruder	No attack was found, 328 symbolic configurations reached
A single run of the protocol with host A as a malicious host	No attack was found, 67 symbolic configurations reached
A single run with hosts A and C as conspiring hosts	No attack was found, 18 symbolic configurations reached
Two parallel runs of the protocol, each with an initiator and a particular static part: agent's code, and timestamp	No attack was found, 986413 symbolic configurations Reached

The analysis of the security properties of the data that are gathered by mobile agents using STA shows that the protocol is free of attacks, particularity the attacks revealed in the existing protocols as shown in Table 17.6. The results of verifications in the key configurations provide a motivation for a proof of correctness of the proposed security techniques.

17.5.2 Security Reasoning

We are concerned with the security of a general model of the protocol. We consider the critical attacks that the existing protocols failed to prevent or detect and carefully reason the correctness of a general model of the protocol. The reasoning is given in Table 17.7.

In addition, we reason the correctness of the protocol against the various attacks of an intruder [34] that may intercept, delete, insert, append messages or spy out confidential data as follows:

Security threat (1): Breach the privacy of the collected offers.

Security technique: A visited host signs its offer digitally and then encrypts it with the encryption key of the initiator. Next, it encrypts the agent's execution results with the public encryption key of the succeeding host in the agent's itinerary.

Security threat (2): Impersonate the genuine initiator.

Security technique: At the early execution of the agent at a visited host, the host decrypts the term Π_{n+1} using its decryption key and deduces the identity of the signer of the decrypted term. Then, it decrypts the term using the decryption verification key of the signer. Next, it computes a hash of $(\Pi, t, h(i_0))$ and then it verifies that the computed hash is the same as Π_0 enclosed within C_0, otherwise the agent execution terminates.

Security threat (3): Impersonate the genuine provider of an offer.

Security technique: The offer C_n is digitally signed with the private key of host, i_n and then encrypted with the public key of the initiator. Hence, an adversary would not be able to read the offer or send the offer under its private key.

Table 17.7 Verifying a system of arbitrary size

Attack	Protocol's security techniques
Malicious host tries to truncate the gathered data and alter the data it has provided to the agent at an earlier time, by replacing the agent's current dynamic part with the part that the agent had when it first visited it	The host has to have the dynamic part of the agent when the agent first visited it. The host does not have the part, since the protocol requests the current executing host to clear its memory from any data acquired as a result of executing the agent, before it dispatches the agent to the succeeding host. The denial of request would be revealed in the execution trace it should store and forward to the initiator upon request
Intruder intercepts the agent and tries to impersonate the genuine signer of the static part of the agent	The static part is encrypted with the public key of the succeeding host in the agent's itinerary, and can only be decrypted with a key that is private to the succeeding host

Security threat (4): Append arbitrary or fake offer.

Security technique: A host should sign the offer it provides with its private key. Hence, an adversary would not append an arbitrary offer for which it is held responsible and cannot repudiate it.

Security threat (5): Replace the collected data with data of a similar protocol run.

Security technique: Upon agent's return, the initiator verifies that M_n for $(1 \leq n \leq k)$ are provided for the protocol run identified with a timestamp t. If checks fail, then the attack took place. Hence, the protocol detects the attack.

Security threat (6): Replace the collected data with data of a similar agent.

Security technique: Upon agent's return, the initiator verifies that the terms $(\Pi, P_0, i_0$ and $i_1)$ stored within the agent upon its return are verified with the corresponding terms stored within the SA. The verification would fail if the attack took place.

Security threat (7): Truncate data – delete the initial offer M_0.

Security technique: Upon the agent's return, the initiator calls the initial offer M_0, which is securely stored within the SA. Next, it checks the availability of the same data within the data returned with the agent. The unavailability of the data implies that the attack took place.

Security threat (8): Truncate data – delete the offer M_1.

Security technique: Upon the agent's return, the initiator checks that the first host in the assembled agent's itinerary is host i_1. The identity is securely stored within the SA. If the check fails, it implies that the attack took place.

Security threat (9): Truncate data – delete the offers M_1 and M_0.

Security technique: Upon the agent's return, the initiator does two verifications as follows:

–   Calls the initial offer M_0, which is securely stored within the SA. Next, it checks the availability of the same data within the data returned with the agent. The unavailability of the data implies that the attack took place.

–   Checks that the first host in the assembled agent's itinerary is host i_1. If the checks fail, it implies that the attack took place.

Security threat (10): Truncate data – delete the offer of the preceding host.

Security technique: Collected offers are jumbled so the initial offer M_0 is placed at the end of the collected offers to conceive an adversary trying to delete the offer of the preceding host.

Security threat (11): Delete the offer M_n.

Security technique: Three countermeasures are implemented as follows:

- Upon the agent's return, the initiator decrypts the terms C_n for $(0 \leq n \leq k)$ and deduces the partial agent's itineraries, where each signed term C_k includes the identity of the succeeding host i_{n+1}. Next, it checks that the partial agent's itineraries are consistent. If assembled agent's itinerary indicates a missing connection, it implies that the attack took place.
- Upon the agent's return, the initiator verifies that the term C_{n-1} enclosed within the term C_n for $(0 \leq n \leq k)$ is among the standalone terms. If a term is missing, it implies that the offer of that host has been deleted.
- Terms that are necessary to replace a previous offer with a new valid offer are assumed to be cleared from the memory of the host during the first visit of the agent to the host and just before the host dispatches the agent to the succeeding host. Hence, the attack is not possible. If a malicious host did not clear its memory from the terms, the next check would detect the attack if it took place.

Security threat (12): Replace its previous offer C_n with a new offer C'_n so as to substitute d'_n for d_n.

Security technique: The succeeding host stores the term C_{n-1} within the term it provides C_n. Upon agent's return, the initiator would check if the term C_{n-1} stored within C_n matches the corresponding term provided by host i_{n-1}. If the check fails, it implies that the attack took place.

Security threat (13): illegitimately insert or append offer/s.

Security technique: The intruder needs to run the agent. But the agent's code is encrypted with the public key of scheduled succeeding host in the agent's itinerary. Hence, the intruder would not be able to insert or append offer/s.

The reasoning shows that the security scheme of the protocol has sufficient measures that would make it capable of preventing or at least detecting the various attacks which the existing protocols fail to prevent or detect.

17.5.3 Protocol Efficiency

The protocol is efficient as having the following advantages:

1. Effective verification at the early execution of the agent at the visited hosts:
   The protocol carries out an instant verification on the identity of the genuine initiator at the early execution of the agent at a visited host. In case the verification fails, the agent execution terminates. Hence, it saves time and costs of running

the protocol. The cost of running the protocol includes costs of cryptographic operations, communications, verifications and executions, etc.

2. Effective verifications of returned data: The protocol carries out three preliminary and instant checks upon the agent's return to check the following:

(a) The returned data belong to the protocol run of concern
(b) The returned data have been generated for the genuine initiator

The checks are based on the static part, timestamp, identity of the genuine initiator and identity of the first scheduled host in the agent's itinerary. The three instant checks would save time and costs of verifications.

3. Effective utilization of time and money: The results of running the protocol are accurate and thus, time and money are utilized effectively. Whereas the results of running the existing protocols are not totally accurate and thus, time and money are not utilized effectively and are wasted. The decision taken in the existing protocols on the returned data might be in favour of a particular host due to data truncation/alteration. The existing protocols would not be able to detect the attack as a malicious host might be storing the terms necessary to compute a new valid offer and thus, would be able to truncate the offers of competing hosts visited following the first visit of the agent to its host and to replace its previous offer with a valid and competing offer leaving no signs on truncation/alteration of data. In the proposed protocol, the decision taken on the returned data would not be in favour of a particular host in case a malicious host has truncated/altered the gathered data to win over competing hosts. The protocol prevents data truncation/alteration, provided that the visited hosts respond to the request of clearing their memories from any data acquired as a result of executing the agent.

17.6 Conclusions

Mobile agents are vulnerable to security attacks of malicious hosts and intruders. The literature presents several data gathering mobile agent security protocols that aim to hinder or at least prevent the security attacks. In this chapter, we discussed the security techniques implemented in the security protocols and the revealed security deficiencies. We showed the need for a security protocol that is capable of preserving the security properties, particularly strong data integrity. We described a set of new security techniques that can effectively prevent or at least detect any tampering with gathered information and overcome deficiencies in security protocols of data gathering mobile agents. The security techniques are: (1) Utilization of co-operating agents where the initial verification terms are securely stored within a secondary agent (SA) that resides at the initiator and co-operates with a migrating agent (MA) that traverses the Internet, (2) Jumbling the collected offers to mislead an adversary trying to truncate offers collected at the recently visited host/s, (3) Instructing an executing host to clear its memory from any data acquired as a result of executing the agent before it dispatches the agent to the succeeding host in the agent's itinerary so as to prevent data truncation or alteration, (4) Running verifica-

tion on the identity of the genuine initiator at the early execution of the agent at a
visited host as a provision to the execution of the agent at the host and (5) Encrypting
a collected offer for the verified genuine initiator.

A new security protocol that aims to preserve data authenticity, data confidentiality and particularly strong data integrity is proposed. The proposed security
techniques are implemented to the protocol. The protocol runs an intermediate verification on the identity of the genuine initiator at a visited host and a final verification
upon agent's return on data-integrity and data-authenticity.

We used Symbolic Trace Analyzer (STA), an infinite-state exploration formal
method, to analyze the security properties of the protocol. We analyzed a reasonably
small instance of the security protocol in four key configurations that would generate the common attacks. The verification with STA reported no security flaw and
hence, would guarantee that the protocol is secure as regard the modelled instance
and configurations. The results of verification provide a motivation for a proof of
correctness of the protocol for a general model. Moreover, we reasoned about the
security of a general model of the protocol and showed that the protocol is capable of preventing or at least detecting the malicious acts that the existing protocol
fails to prevent or at least detect. Moreover, we discussed the efficiency of the new
security techniques as compared to the existing techniques.

The STA analyzes execution traces of security protocols based on symbolic techniques. The symbolic model is finite because each input action should be preceded
by the corresponding action for every generated trace, whereas the analysis of execution traces in model checkers [25] suffers from state-explosion problem and the
testing equivalences between processes in process algebra [26, 30] suffers from the
infinite universal quantifications as having infinitely many such processes [8]. It
takes less than half an hour to write the STA script of a protocol run. The execution
is automatic, though it slows down as the number of participants and consequently
the number of associated terms increases. According to Fiore and Abadi [9], the
symbolic analysis is proven sound and complete. Detecting an attack on the symbolic model would imply that an attack exists in the infinite standard model and
vice versa.

The new security techniques can be implemented to the existing security protocols to amend revealed defects. The adequacy of the security techniques can be
verified using STA or other formal methods, such as model checking and theorem proving. The implementation would test the soundness of the proposed security
techniques, which assert data confidentiality, data authenticity and strong data integrity of mobile agents.

References

1. Abadi M, Gordon A D (1999) A calculus for cryptographic protocols: The Spi-Calculus. Information and Computation 148(1): 1–70.
2. Aziz B, Gray D, Hamilton G, Oehil F, Power J, Sinclair D (2001) Implementing protocol verification for E-commerce. In: Proceedings of the 2001 International Conference on Advances in

Infrastructure for Electronic Business, Science, and Education on the Internet (SSGRR 2001), L'Aquila, Italy.

3. Boreale, M (2001) Symbolic trace analysis of cryptographic protocols. In: Proceedings of ICALP'01, Lecture Notes in Computer Science, vol. 2076, Springer, Berlin.

4. Boreale M, Buscemi M (2002) Experimenting with STA, a tool for automatic analysis of security protocols. ACM Symposium on Applied Computing 2002, ACM Press.

5. Boreale M, Gorla D (2002) Process calculi and the verification of security protocols. In: Journal of Telecommunications and Information Technology – Special Issue on Cryptographic Protocol Verification JTIT, Warsaw, Poland.

6. Bradshaw J M (1997) An Introduction to software agents. In: Software Agents, J.M. Bradshaw (ed), Chap. 1, pp. 3–46, AAAI Press.

7. Corradi A, Montanari R, Stefanelli C (1999) Mobile agents protection in the Internet environment. In: The 23rd Annual International Computer Software and Applications Conference (COMPSAC'99), pp. 80–85.

8. Durante L, Sisto R, Valenzano A (2000) A state-exploration technique for spi-calculus testing equivalence verification. In: Proceedings of the IFIP International Joint Conference on Formal Description Techniques for Distributed Systems and Communication Protocols (FORTE XIII) and Protocol Specification, Testing and Verification (PSTV XX), Kluwer Academic Publishers, Dordrecht, pp. 155–170.

9. Fiore M, Abadi M (2001) Computing Symbolic models for verifying cryptographic protocols. In: Proceedings of the 14th IEEE ComputerSecurity Foundations Workshop (CSFW 2001), IEEE Computer Society Press, Washington, DC, pp. 160–173.

10. Fischer L (2003) Protecting integrity and secrecy of mobile agents on trusted and non-trusted agent places. Diploma Dissertation, University of Bremen, Germany. http://www.hackercontest.de/pages/dipl/docs/finished/fischer_diplom.pdf. Accessed 5 Mar 2007.

11. Formal Systems (Europe) Ltd (2000) Failures divergence refinement. FDR2 User Manual. http://www.fsel.com/documentation/fdr2/fdr2manual.pdf. Accessed 20 Mar 2007.

12. Fournet C, Gonthier G, Lévy J J, Maranget L, Rémy D (1996) A calculus for mobile agents. In: Proceedings of the 7th International Conference on concurrency Theory (CONCUR'96), Lecture Notes in Computer Science, vol. 1119, pp. 406–421, Springer.

13. Hannotin X, Maggi P, Sisto R (2001) Formal specification and verification of mobile agent data integrity properties: A case study, LNCS 2240: pp. 42–53, Springer.

14. Jaljouli R (2005) Boosting m-Business using a truly secured protocol for information gathering mobile agents. In: Proceedings of the 4th International Conference on Mobile Business, IEEE Computer Society Press.

15. Jaljouli R (2005) Formal methods in the enhancement of the data security protocols of mobile agents. Technical Report TR 520, University of New South Wales, School of Computer Science and Engineering, http://cgi.cse.unsw.edu.au/~reports. Asccessed 15 Mar 2007.

16. Jaljouli R (2006) A Proposed security protocol for data gathering mobile agents. Thesis Dissertation, University of New South Wales, School of Computer Science and Engineering, Australia.

17. Kanik N, Tripathi A (1999) Security in the Ajanta mobile agent system. Technical Report TR-5-99, University of Minnesota, Minneapolis.

18. Karjoth G, Asokan N, Gülcü C (1998) Protecting the computation results of free-roaming agents. In: K. Rothermel and F. Hohl (ed), Proceedings of the 2nd International Workshop on Mobile Agents, Lecture Notes in Computer Science, vol. 1477: pp. 195–207, Springer.

19. Lowe G (1997) Casper: A compiler for the analysis of security protocols. In: Proceedings of the 10th Computer Security Foundation Workshop (PCSFW), IEEE Computer Society Press.

20. Ma L, Tsai JJP (2000) Formal verification techniques for computer communication security protocols. In: Handbook of Software Engineering and Knowledge Engineering, vol. 1. ftp://cs.pitt.edu/chang/handbook/12.pdf. Accessed 10 Apr 2007.

21. Maggi P, Sisto R (2001) Experiments on formal verification of mobile agent data integrity properties. http://citeseer.ist.psu.edu/hannotin01formal.html. Accessed 16 Mar 2007.

22. Maggi P, Sisto R (2003) A configurable mobile agent data protection protocol. In: Proceedings of AAMAS'03, ACM Press, New York, pp. 851–858.

23. Meadows C (1994) Formal verification of cryptographic protocols: A survey. In: Advances in Cryptography – ASIACRYPT'94, pp. 135–150.
24. Milner R, Parrow J, Walker D (1992) A calculus for mobile processes (part I and II). In: Information and Computation, 100:1–77.
25. Mitchell J C, Mitchell M, Stern U (1997) Automated analysis of cryptographic protocols using Murφ. In: Proceedings of Symposiums on Security and Privacy, IEEE Computer Society Press, pp. 141–153.
26. Sangiori D (1992) Expressing mobility in process algebra: first order and higher order paradigms, Ph.D. Thesis, University of Edinburgh.
27. STA Documentation. http://www.dsi.unifi.it/~boreale/documentation.html. Accessed 15 Mar 2007.
28. STA: a tool for trace analysis of cryptographic protocols (2001). ML object code and examples. http://www.dsi.unifi.it/~boreale/tool.html. Accessed 5 Apr 2007.
29. Syverson P F, Goldschlag M, Reed M G (1997) Anonymous connections and onion routing. In: IEEE Symposium on Security and Privacy, pp. 44–54, Oakland, California.
30. Vitek J, Gastagna G (1999) Seal: A framework for secure mobile computations. In: Internet Programming Language ICCL'98 Workshop, Lecture Notes in Computer Science, vol. 1686: pp. 47–77, Springer.
31. Vigna G (1998) Cryptographic traces for mobile agents. In: Mobile Agent Security, G. Vigna, (ed), Lecture Notes in Computer Science, vol. 1419: pp. 137–153, Springer.
32. Wang T, Guan S, Chan T (2002) Integrity protection for code-on-demand mobile agents in e-commerce. In: Systems and Software, 60(3): 211–221.
33. Yao M, Foo E, Peng K, Dawson E (2003) An improved forward integrity protocol for mobile agents. In: Proceedings of the 4th International Workshop on Information Security Applications (WISA 2003) Lecture Notes in Computer Science, vol. 2908: pp. 272–285, Springer.
34. Yao Y, Dolev D (1983) On the security of public key protocols. In: IEEE Transactions on Information Theory, 29(2): 198–208.

Chapter 18
Neighbor Selection in Peer-to-Peer Overlay Networks: A Swarm Intelligence Approach

Hongbo Liu, Ajith Abraham, and Youakim Badr

Abstract Peer-to-peer (P2P) topology has a significant influence on the performance, search efficiency and functionality, and scalability of the application. In this chapter, we investigate a multi-swarm approach to the problem of neighbor selection in P2P networks. Particle swarm share some common characteristics with P2P in the dynamic socially environment. Each particle encodes the upper half of the peer-connection matrix through the undirected graph, which reduces the search space dimension. The portion of the adjustment to the velocity influenced by the individual's cognition, the group cognition from multi-swarms, and the social cognition from the whole swarm, makes an important influence on the particles' ergodic and synergetic performance. We also attempt to theoretically prove that the multi-swarm optimization algorithm converges with a probability of 1 towards the global optima. The performance of our approach is evaluated and compared with other two different algorithms. The results indicate that it usually required shorter time to obtain better results than the other considered methods, specially for large scale problems.

Keywords P2P swarming networks · Neighbor selection · Particle swarm · Genetic algorithm · Undirected graph

18.1 Introduction

Peer-to-peer (P2P) computing has recently attracted great interest and attention of the computing industry and gained popularity among computer users and their networked virtual communities [1, 2], since it allows the implementation of large distributed repositories of digital information. Many peer-to-peer systems also have emerged as platforms for users to search and share information over the Internet [3].

A. Abraham (✉)
Norwegian Center of Excellence, Center of Excellence for Quantifiable Quantity of Service,
Norwegian University of Science and Technology,
Trondheim, Norway
e-mail: ajith.abraham@ieee.org, http://www.softcomputing.net/

A.-E. Hassanien et al. (eds.), *Pervasive Computing: Innovations in Intelligent Multimedia and Applications*, Computer Communications and Networks, DOI 10.1007/978-1-84882-599-4_18, © Springer-Verlag London Limited 2009

In essence, a P2P system can be characterized as a distributed network system in which all participant computers/nodes have symmetric capabilities and responsibilities. In the system, numerous nodes of equal roles are connected through an arbitrary network and exchange data or services directly with each other. All participants in a P2P system act as both clients and servers to one another, thereby surpassing the conventional client/server model and bringing all participant computers together with the purpose of sharing resources such as content, bandwidth, CPU cycles [4]. P2P networks are applied to many fields, which includes communication and collaboration, distributed computing, Internet service support, database system, and content/data distribution, even service platform for public welfare (e.g., providing processing power to fight cancer) [5–10]. More specifically, P2P file sharing systems set up a network or pool of peers on Internet and provide facilities for searching and transferring files between them. Since these systems provide a economical platform for data-sharing that is highly scalable and robust, a great number of commercial and academic projects have been developed using this technology. However, it is reported in a recent survey that P2P applications generate one-fifth of the total Internet traffic, and it is believed that it will continue to grow [11, 12].

In pure P2P systems, individual computers communicate directly with each other and share information and resources without using dedicated servers. A node cannot realistically keep the addresses of all other peers, so an overlay network need be constructed where each node keeps addresses of a few other peers (called its neighbors) at the application level. These connections may be directed, may have different weights and are comparable to a graph with nodes and vertices connecting these nodes. Defining how these nodes are connected affects many properties of an architecture that is based on a P2P topology, which has a significant impact on application properties such as the performance, search efficiency, reliability and scalability of a system. The virtual topology also determines the communication costs and efficiency associated with running the P2P application, both at individual hosts and in the aggregate. A common difficulty in the current P2P systems is caused by the dynamic membership of peer hosts. The neighbor-selection (NS) mechanism and topology control become very important topics in P2P networks [13].

On the other hand, the performance and availability of these systems relies on the voluntary participation of their users, and so they may be highly variable and unpredictable, which results in a large proportion of the participants (20–40% of Napster and almost 70% of Gnutella peers) share few or no files [14]. This phenomenon is known as free-loading: peers that consume more resources than they contribute. One of the reasons for this problem is that those users, called free-riders, benefit largely from contributions of other users but reduce the system performance for contributing users. And self-interested behavior of the peers had no taken into account at the design stage. In fact, the P2P system's users act rationally trying to maximize the benefits obtained from using the system's shared resources. Therefore, it will be necessary to find mechanisms that provide incentives and encourage cooperative behavior between the peers.

Particle swarm optimization (PSO) algorithm is inspired by social behavior patterns of organisms that live and interact within large groups. In particular, PSO incorporates swarming behaviors observed in flocks of birds, schools of fish, or swarms of bees, and even human social behavior, from which the swarm intelligence (SI) paradigm has emerged [15]. It could be implemented and applied to solve various function optimization problems, or the problems that can be transformed to function optimization problems. As an algorithm, the main strength of PSO is its fast convergence, which compares favorably with many global optimization algorithms [16]. In this chapter, we explore the NS problem based PSO for P2P Networks. We introduce the crossover neighborhood organization mechanism from the social networks to improve the swarm algorithm, which results in more mutual trust, mutual benefit, equality and cooperation among the participants.

This chapter is organized as follows. We introduce the problem and formulate the objective in Sect. 18.3. Our approach based on particle swarm algorithm is presented in Sect. 18.4. In this section, the issues about the algorithm design, dynamic chaotic characteristics, and convergence theoretical analysis are also discussed. In Sect. 18.5, experiment results and discussions are provided in detail, followed by some conclusions in Sect. 18.6.

18.2 Related Research Work

P2P comprises peers and the connections between these peers. A common difficulty in the current P2P systems is caused by the dynamic membership of peer hosts. This results in a constant reorganization of the overlay topology [17–20]. As the size of distributed systems keeps growing, no entity has a global knowledge of the system. As much as this property is essential to ensure the scalability, monitoring the system under such circumstances is a complex task [21]. Meo and Milan [22] investigated the design of content management at the nodes. They proposed criteria for the QoS design of content management policies. And they evaluated its performance by an analytical model based on a Markovian approach. In the application system, finding the desired resource and constructing the efficient topology are the critical issues in peer-to-peer networks. Risson and Moors [23] surveyed the search methods about finding the resource in the recent research towards robust P2P networks. In this chapter, we pay more attentions on peer selection, since it offers a unique opportunity for P2P networks to tackle both the free-riding and the quality-of-service (QoS) challenges [24].

Lo et al. [25] defined the supernode selection problem which has emerged across a variety of P2P applications. Supernode selection involves selection of a subset of the peers to serve a special role. The supernodes must be well-dispersed throughout the P2P overlay network, and must fulfill additional requirements such as load balance, resource needs, adaptability to churn, and heterogeneity. The supernode selection problem must meet the additional challenge of operating within a huge, unknown and dynamically changing network. They describe three generic supernode selection protocols. They developed for P2P environments: a label-based scheme for structured overlay networks, a distributed protocol for coordinate-based overlay networks, and a negotiation protocol for unstructured overlays. Kothapalli and Scheideler presented a general methodology for designing supervised P2P systems [26]. It can be seen as being between server-based systems and pure P2P systems. The supervisor has to store a constant amount of information about the system at any time and needs to send a small constant number of messages to integrate or remove a peer in a constant amount of time. Koulouris et al. [27] presented a framework and an implementation technique for a flexible management of P2P overlays. The framework provides means for self-organization to yield an enhanced flexibility in instantiating control architectures in dynamic environments, which is regarded as being essential for P2P services to access, routing, topology forming, and application layer resource management. In these P2P applications, a central tracker decides about which peer becomes a neighbor to which other peers.

A peer randomly choosing logical neighbors without any knowledge about the underlying physical topology causes topology mismatch between the P2P logical overlay network and physical underlying network. In unstructured P2P systems, there exists a serious topology mismatch problem between physical and logical network. Liu et al. [28] analyzed the relationship between the property of the overlay and the corresponding message duplications incurred by queries in a given overlay, and prove that computing an optimal overlay with global knowledge is an NP-hard problem. Leung and Kwok [29] proposed a greedy server-peer selection algorithm to decide from which peer should a client download files so that the level of fairness of the whole network is increased and expected service life of the whole file sharing network is extended. Mastronarde et al. [30] proposed a distributed and efficient framework for resource exchanges that enables peers to collaboratively distribute available wireless resources among themselves based on their quality of service requirements, the underlying channel conditions, and network topology. The resource exchanges are enabled by the scalable coding of the video content and the design of cross-layer optimization strategies, which allow efficient adaptation to varying channel conditions and available resources. They compare the designed low complexity distributed resource exchange algorithms against an optimal centralized resource management scheme and show how their performance varies with the level of collaboration among the peers. They measure system utility in terms of the multimedia quality and show that collaborative approaches achieve 50% improvement over non-collaborative approaches. Additionally, their distributed algorithms perform within 10% system utility of a centralized optimal resource management scheme.

Fenner et al. [31] presented a stochastic model for a social network, where new actors may join the network, existing actors may become inactive and, at a later stage, reactivate themselves. The model captures the evolution of the network, assuming that actors attain new relations or become active according to the preferential attachment rule. They derived the mean-field equations for this stochastic model and shown that, asymptotically, the distribution of actors obeys a power-law distribution. The result illustrated that the distribution of user accesses was asymptotically a power-law distribution. Sacha et al. [32] proposed and evaluated a search algorithm. The results indicated that it achieved significantly better performance than random walking. The approach can be used by certain classes of applications to improve the availability and performance of system services by placing them on the most stable peers, as well as to reduce the amount of network traffic required to discover and use these services. They demonstrated the design of a naming service on the gradient topology.

Bisnik et al. [33] developed a model for random walk-based search mechanisms in unstructured P2P networks. The model is used to obtain analytical expressions for the performance metrics of random walk search in terms of the popularity of the resource being searched for and the random walk parameters. Simulation results illustrated that the performance of the equation-based adaptive search was significantly better than the non-adaptive random walk and other straightforward adaptive mechanisms. Kersch et al. [34] defined a loose and stochastic long-range connection maintenance mechanism, which can significantly reduce maintenance overhead in large networks with high churn rates without affecting routing performance. They used Kleinberg's small worlds model to describe and (re)construct long-range connections. The maintenance method scale logarithmically with the system's size, which is the theoretical lower bound for maintenance traffic to ensure connectivity of the network.

Researchers have also considered clustering close peers based on their IP addresses (e.g., [35, 36]) or probed distances [37]. Xu [38] presented a decentralized and fault tolerant protocol called Alpha-Beta Cluster-based protocol, for ABC. In ABC, a cluster of nodes work together to offer efficient greedy routing and the size of each cluster can vary between an upper bound (Alpha) and a lower bound (Beta). The flexible cluster scheme helps to maintain the stability of the system. Ramaswamy et al. [39] described a Connectivity-based Distributed Node Clustering scheme (CDC). The scheme presented a scalable and efficient solution for discovering connectivity-based clusters in peer networks. To cope with the typical dynamics of P2P networks, they provided mechanisms to allow new nodes to be incorporated into appropriate existing clusters and to gracefully handle the departure of nodes in the clusters. These mechanisms enable the CDC scheme to be extensible and adaptable in the sense that the clustering structure of the network adjusts automatically as nodes join or leave the system. Their experiments shown that utilizing message-based connectivity structure can considerably reduce the messaging cost and provide better utilization of resources, which in turn improved the quality of service of the applications executing over decentralized P2P networks. Huang et al. [3] proposed a cluster-based P2P system, called PeerCluster, for sharing data over the Internet. In PeerCluster, all participant computers are grouped into various interest clusters, each of which contains computers that have the same interests. The intuition behind the system design was that by logically grouping users interested in similar topics together, it can improve query efficiency. To efficiently route and broadcast messages across/within interest clusters, a hypercube topology was employed. In addition, to ensure that the structure of the interest clusters is not altered by arbitrary node insertions/deletions, they have devised corresponding JOIN and LEAVE protocols. The experimental results shown that PeerCluster outperformed previous approaches in terms of query efficiency, while still providing the desired functionality of keyword-based search. Tewari and Kleinrock [40] provided mechanisms for modeling clustering in file popularity distributions and the consequent non-uniform distribution of file replicas. They derived relations shown the effect of the number of replicas of a file on the search time and on the search cost for a search for that file for the clustered demands case in such networks for both random walk and flooding search mechanisms. The derived relations were used to obtain the optimal search performance for the case of flooding search mechanisms. The potential performance benefited that clustering in demand patterns affords was captured by our results. Interestingly, the performance gains ware shown to be independent of whether the search network topology reflects the clustering in file popularity (the optimal file replica distribution to obtain these performance gains, however, does depend on the search network topology).

Empirical studies have shown free-riding (consuming resources without contributing) to be prevalent in P2P file-sharing networks. Contributors to the system are rewarded with flexibility and choice in peer selection, resulting in high quality streaming sessions. Free-riders are given limited options in peer selection, if any, and hence receive low quality service. Idris and Altmann [5] proposed an incentive scheme for P2P networks that motivates users to collaborate within the system. The solution has an impact on the topology formation of a P2P network. Using the market-managed topology formation algorithm (IUTopForm) for P2P networks, contributing users would be clustered within clubs that are different to clubs of free-riders. The differentiation was possible because of a reputation system, which considers users' past contributions. The effect of this approach was that service requests of free-riders will take longer to be answered (if at all) than service requests of resource-contributing users. The results shown that their approach improved the overall utility of the system. Habib and Chuang [24] proposed an incentive mechanism that provides service differentiation in peer selection for P2P streaming based on relative contribution of the peers. The incentive mechanism follows the characteristics of rank-order tournaments theory that considers only the relative performance of the players, and the top prizes are awarded to the winners of the tournament. The simulation and wide-area measurement results illustrate that the approach can provide near optimal streaming quality to the cooperative users until the bottleneck shifts from the streaming sources to the network. To solve the neighbor discovery problem and network organization problem in practical wireless P2P networks, Leung and Kwok [29] proposed a topology control protocol, which consists of two components, namely, Adjacency Set Construction (ASC) and Community-Based Asynchronous Wakeup (CAW). The protocol is able to enhance the fairness and provide an incentive mechanism in wireless P2P file sharing applications. It is also capable of increasing the energy efficiency.

Kurmanowytsch et al. [41] developed the P2P middleware systems to provide an abstraction between the P2P topology and the applications that are built on top of it . These middleware systems offer higher-level services such as distributed P2P searches and support for direct communication among peers. The systems often provide a pre-defined topology that is suitable for a certain task (e.g., for exchanging files). Gupta et al. [42] discussed the system architecture, functionality, and applications of the CompuP2P architecture. They had implemented a Java-based prototype, and the results shown that the system was light-weight and can provide almost a perfect speedup for applications that contain several independent compute-intensive tasks. Zeinalipour-Yazti et al. [43] presented the peer fusion (pFusion) architecture that aims to efficiently integrate heterogeneous information that was geographically scattered on peers of different networks. The approach built on work in unstructured P2P systems and uses only local knowledge. Our empirical results, using the pFusion middleware architecture and data sets from Akamai's Internet mapping infrastructure (AKAMAI), the active measurement project (NLANR), and the text retrieval conference (TREC) show that the architecture we propose is both efficient and practical.

Ghanea-Hercock et al. [44] presented an algorithm based on P2P agent application in which each agent has a goal to maintain a preferred number of connections to a number of service providing agents. The agents updated a weight value associated with each connection, based on the perceived utility of the connection to the corresponding agent. This utility function can be a combination of several node or edge parameters, or frequency of the message response from the node. The weight is updated using a set of Hebbian-style learning rules, such that the network as a whole exhibits adaptive self-organizing behavior. The result was the finding that by limiting the connection neighborhood within the overlay topology, the resulting P2P network can be made highly resilient to targeted attacks on high-degree nodes, while maintaining search efficiency.

To get some insights into the performance of different peer organization strategies, Biersack et al. [45] analytically three different distribution models: linear chain architecture, tree architecture, and forest architecture. The results indicated that the service capacity of these systems grew exponentially with the number of chunks a file consists of. Therefore, several heuristics and meta-heuristics have been proposed to solve the problems within the feasible runtime. Koo et al. [19] investigated the NS process in the P2P networks, and proposed an efficient NS strategy based on genetic algorithm (GA).

Networks seem to be the natural way chosen by nature to organize individuals, resources and interactions in an effective and robust structure. Studies about natural networks focused on the central role of emerging structures in distributed environments, and pointed out some properties such as small-world effect and communities which are of the most importance to guarantee a fast and efficient communication among nodes. Carchiolo et al. [46] proposed a model for P2P networks which mimics behaviours of peers in social and biological networks and naturally evolves to a robust graph of peers with some interesting properties, including small-world effect and community decomposition. Zhuge and Li [47] proposed three improved gossip mechanisms by mapping links into metric space and dynamically adapting the number of selected neighbors to disseminate messages. Experiments and comparisons shown that these mechanisms can improve the performance of gossip in P2P networks. It was the effect of mapping a network into a metric space that differentiates nodes and links according to linking characteristics and controlling local information flow with knowing such differences. An intrinsic rule is found by experimental comparisons and analysis: The performance of a P2P network can be improved by designing an appropriate mapping from the network into metric space or semantic space. These research works indicated the NS in P2P would be improved further by matching social characteristics of P2P system.

18.3   NS Problem

In a P2P system, all participating peers form a P2P network on top of an underlying physical network. A P2P network is an abstract, logical network called an overlay network. Based on existing research [4,11,28,44,48], we formulate the NS problem for P2P overlay networks in this section. As given by Liu et al. [28], a P2P network can be modeled based on the following assumptions:

- An overlay connection between a pair of peering nodes consists of a number of physical links which form a shortest path between the pair of end nodes in the physical topology, and Internet paths are relatively stable.
- The same size packets traversing the same physical link in a short period of time will have similar delay, as assumed by many other measurement applications.

18.3.1   Modeling P2P Networks

The P2P overlay networks can be modeled by an undirected graph $G = (V, E)$ where the vertex set V represents units such as hosts and routers, and the edge set E represents physical links connecting pairs of communicating unit. And $f : V \rightarrow \{1, \ldots, n\}$ be a labeling of its nodes, where $n = |V|$. For instance, G could model the whole or part of the Internet. Given an undirected graph $G = (V, E)$ modeling an interconnection network, and a subset $X \subseteq V(G)$ of communicating units (peers), we can construct a corresponding weighted graph $D = (V, E)$, where $V(D) = X$, and the weight of each $uv \in E(D)$ is equal to the length of a shortest path between peer u and peer v in G. D includes the connected edges, and is referred to as the distance graph of G. Usually we start with a physical network G (perhaps representing the Internet), and then choose a set of communicating peers X. The resulting distance graph D is the basis for constructing a P2P overlay graph $H = (V, E)$, which is done as follows. The vertex set $V(H)$ will be the same as $V(D)$, and edge set $E(H) \subseteq D(G)$. The key issue here is how to select $E(H)$. If $E = [e_{ij}]_{n \times n}$ is such that $e_{ij} = 1$ if $(i, j) \in E$, and 0 otherwise, i.e., E is the incidence matrix of G, then the NS problem is to find a permutation of rows and columns which brings all non-zero elements of E into the optimal possible interconnection around the diagonal.

18.3.2   Metrics

In P2P file sharing, an interested file is divided into many fragments. The size of each fragment ranges from several hundred kilobytes to several megabytes. When a new peer joins the network, it begins to download fragments from other peers.

As long as it obtains one fragment of the file, the new peer can start to serve other peers by uploading fragments. Since peers are downloading and uploading at the same time, when the network becomes large, although the demands increase, the service provided by the network also increases [49]. Given N peers, a graph $G = (V, E)$ can be used to denote an overlay network, where the set of vertices $V = \{v_1, \ldots, v_N\}$ represents the N peers and the set of edges $E = \{e_{ij} \in \{0, 1\}, i, j = 1, \ldots, N\}$ represents their connectivities: $e_{ij} = 1$ if peers i and j are connected, and $e_{ij} = 0$ otherwise. For an undirected graph, it is required that $e_{ij} = e_{ji}$ for all $i \neq j$, and $e_{ij} = 0$ when $i = j$. Let C be the entire collection of content fragments, and $\{c_i \subseteq C, i = 1, \ldots, N\}$ denotes the collection of the content fragments each peer i has. The disjointness of contents from peer i to peer j is denoted by $c_i \setminus c_j$, which can be calculated as:

$$c_i \setminus c_j = c_i - (c_i \cap c_j), \tag{18.1}$$

where $\setminus$ denotes the intersection operation on sets. This disjointness can be interpreted as the collection of content fragments that peer i has but peer j does not. In other words, it denotes the fragments that peer i can upload to peer j. Moreover, the disjointness operation is not commutative, i.e., $c_i \setminus c_j \neq c_j \setminus c_i$. Let $|c_i \setminus c_j|$ denote the cardinality of $c_i \setminus c_j$, which is the number of content fragments peer i can contribute to peer j. In order to maximize the disjointness of content, we maximize the number of content fragments each peer can contribute to its neighbors by determining the connections e_{ij}'s. Define ϵ_{ij}'s to be sets such that $\epsilon_{ij} = C$ if $e_{ij} = 1$ and $\epsilon_{ij} = \emptyset$ (null set) otherwise.

In an overlay network, every node is a potential neighbor of each other node since the network's topology is a logical one. So the full connection is an ideal solution for the peer's connectivity. For the networks, we have to consider some constraints [20, 48]:

- based on the underlying network characteristics, i.e., delay or capacity of actual links
- based on location of data and services
- based on the nodes's capabilities of managing peers, e.g., the number of direct neighbors a node can maintain. Some peers are tied down since they possess relative more content fragments. This resource constraint can be independent of the underlying network

In the environment, the maximum number of each peer need to be considered, i.e., each peer i will be connected to a maximum of d_i neighbors, where $d_i < N$. Therefore we have the following optimization problem:

$$\max_{E} \sum_{j=1}^{N} \left| \bigcup_{i=1}^{N} (c_i \setminus c_j) \cap \epsilon_{ij} \right| \tag{18.2}$$

subject to

$$\sum_{j=1}^{N} e_{ij} \leq d_i \quad \text{for all } i,$$

$$\sum_{i=1}^{N} e_{ij} \leq d_j \quad \text{for all } j. \tag{18.3}$$

18.4 Particle Swarm Heuristic for NS

For applying the particle swarm algorithm successfully for any problem, one of the key issues is how to map the problem solution to the particle space, which affects its feasibility and performance [50]. The constraint conditions have to be satisfied, and the particle would search the solutions in as efficient a search space as possible. In this section, a new approach to the problem space mapping is depicted for PSO with reference to the NS problem. For solving the problem, the upper half of the peer-connection matrix through the undirected graph is encoded to the particle's position, which reduces the search space dimension significantly. Since particle swarm shares some common characteristics with P2P in the dynamic socially environment, a multi-swarm interactive pattern is introduce to match the corresponding mechanism. We analyze the dynamic characteristic of the single particle in the swarm, and then illustrate theoretically the convergence of our algorithm.

18.4.1 Algorithm Design

Given a P2P state $S = (N, C, M, f)$, in which N is the number of peers, C is the entire collection of content fragments, M is the maximum number of the peers which each peer can connect steadily in the session, f is to goal the number of swap fragments, i.e., to maximize (18.2). It is to be noted that the routing and connection between peers must satisfy the constraint in (18.3) because of bandwidth, etc. To apply the particle swarm algorithm successfully for the NS problem, one of the key issues is the mapping of the problem solution into the particle space, which directly affects its feasibility and performance. Usually, the particle's position is encoded to map each dimension to one directed connection between peers, i.e., the dimension is $N * N$. But the neighbor topology in P2P networks is an undirected graph, i.e., $e_{ij} = e_{ji}$ for all $i \neq j$, and $e_{ij} \equiv 0$ for all $i = j$. To reduce the space complexity, we set up a search space of D dimension as $N * (N-1)/2$. Accordingly, each particle's position is represented as a binary bit string of length D. Each dimension of the particle's position maps one undirected connection. The domain for each dimension is limited to 0 or 1.

The particle swarm model consists of a swarm of particles, which are initialized with a population of random candidate solutions. They move iteratively through the D-dimension problem space to search the new solutions, where the fitness f can be measured by calculating the number of swap fragments in the potential solution. Each particle has a position represented by a position-vector $\mathbf{p}_i$ (i is the index of the particle), and a velocity represented by a velocity-vector $\mathbf{v}_i$. Each particle remembers its own best position so far in a vector $\mathbf{p}_i^\#$, and its j-th dimensional value is $p_{ij}^\#$. The best position-vector among the swarm so far is then stored in a vector $\mathbf{p}^*$, and its j-th dimensional value is p_j^*. When the particle moves in a state space restricted to zero and one on each dimension, the change of probability with time steps is defined as follows:

$$P(p_{ij}(t) = 1) = f(p_{ij}(t-1), v_{ij}(t-1),$$
$$p_{ij}^\#(t-1), p_j^*(t-1)), \tag{18.4}$$

where the probability function is (Fig. 18.1)

$$\text{sig}(v_{ij}(t)) = \frac{1}{1 + e^{-v_{ij}(t)}}. \tag{18.5}$$

At each time step, each particle updates its velocity and moves to a new position according to (18.6) and (18.7):

$$v_{ij}(t) = wv_{ij}(t-1) + c_1 r_1(p_{ij}^\#(t-1) - p_{ij}(t-1))$$
$$+ c_2 r_2(p_j^*(t-1) - p_{ij}(t-1)), \tag{18.6}$$

$$p_{ij}(t) = \begin{cases} 1 & \text{if } \rho < \text{sig}(v_{ij}(t)); \\ 0 & \text{otherwise}, \end{cases} \tag{18.7}$$

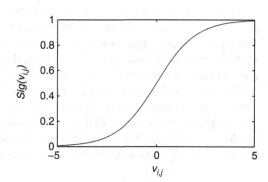

Fig. 18.1 Sigmoid function for PSO

where c_1 is a positive constant, called as coefficient of the self-recognition component, c_2 is a positive constant, called as coefficient of the social component. r_1 and r_2 are the random numbers in the interval $[0, 1]$. The variable w is called as the inertia factor, which value is typically setup to vary linearly from 1 to near 0 during the iterated processing. ρ is random number in the closed interval $[0,1]$. From (18.6), a particle decides where to move next, considering its current state, its own experience, which is the memory of its best past position, and the experience of its most successful particle in the swarm. The particle has a priority levels according to the order of peers. The sequence of the peers will be not changed during the iteration. Each particle's position indicates the potential connection state.

The particle swarm algorithm can be described generally as a population of vectors whose trajectories oscillate around a region which is defined by each individual's previous best success and the success of some other particle. Some previous studies have discussed the trajectory of particles and its convergence [51–54]. It has been shown that the trajectories of the particles oscillate as different sinusoidal waves and converge quickly, sometimes prematurely. Various methods have been used to identify some other particle to influence the individual. Eberhart and Kennedy called the two basic methods as "gbest model" and "lbest model" [55]. In the gbest model, the trajectory for each particle's search is influenced by the best point found by any member of the entire population. The best particle acts as an attractor, pulling all the particles towards it. Eventually all particles will converge to this position. In the lbest model, particles have information only of their own and their nearest array neighbors' best (lbest), rather than that of the whole swarm. Namely, in (18.6), gbest is replaced by lbest in the model. The lbest model allows each individual to be influenced by some smaller number of adjacent members of the population array. The particles selected to be in one subset of the swarm have no direct relationship to the other particles in the other neighborhood. Typically lbest neighborhoods comprise exactly two neighbors. When the number of neighbors increases to all but itself in the lbest model, the case is equivalent to the gbest model. Some experiment results testified that gbest model converges quickly on problem solutions but has a weakness for becoming trapped in local optima, while lbest model converges slowly on problem solutions but is able to "flow around" local optima, as the individuals explore different regions [56]. Some related research and development during the recent years are reported in [57–60].

As mentioned above, one of the most important applications is to share files, distribute content in corporate networks by the dynamic membership of peer hosts. Those users usually share some common interests in some virtual spaces. They are apt to cluster into different groups. Sometime they are also the members of several groups at the same time [61]. To match the social characteristics, we introduce a multi-swarm search algorithm for NS problem in P2P networks. In the algorithm, all particles are clustered spontaneously into different sub-swarms of the whole swarm. Every particle can connect more than one sub-swarm, and a crossover neighborhood topology is constructed between different sub-swarms. The particles in the same sub-swarm would carry some similar functions as possible and search their optimal.

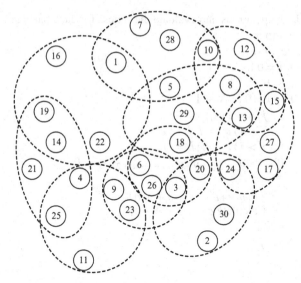

Fig. 18.2 A multi-swarm topology

Each sub-swarm would approach to its appropriate position (solution), which would be helpful for the whole swarm to keep in a good balance state. Figure 18.2 illustrates a multi-swarm topology. In the swarm system, a swarm with 30 particles is organized into ten sub-swarms, which one consists of 5 particles. Particles 3 and 13 have the maximum membership level, 3. During the iterated process, the particle updates its velocity following by the location of the best fitness achieved so far by the particle itself and by the location of the best fitness achieved so far across all its neighbors in all sub-swarms it belongs to. The process makes an important influence on the particles' ergodic and synergetic performance.

Since the positions of all the particles indicate the potential assigned solutions, the binary bit strings of length D can be "decoded" to the feasible solution. "1" denotes the two corresponding peers are selected in the neighborhood. On the contrary, "0" denotes the two corresponding peers are disconnected. The position may violate the constraint (18.3) after some iterations. We scan each column and row before the decoding procedure. The latest binary bits are set to "0" if $\sum_{j=1}^{N} e_{ij} > d_i$ or $\sum_{i=1}^{N} e_{ij} > d_j$. The scan direction are reversed after each scan. The pseudo-code for the multi-swarm search algorithm is illustrated as follows:

Step 1. Initialize the size of the particle swarm n, and other parameters. Initialize the positions and the velocities for all the particles randomly.

Step 2. Multiple sub-swarms n are organized into a crossover neighborhood topology. A particle can join more than one sub-swarm. Each particle has the maximum membership level l, and each sub-swarm accommodates default number of particles m.

Step 3. Decode the positions and evaluate the fitness for each particles.

3.01 For $s = 1$ to n

3.02   If ($reverse$)

3.03   For $i = 0$ to $N - 1$

3.04 $e = 0$

3.05   For $j = 0$ to $N - 1$

3.06   If ($j == i$) $e_{ij} = 0$;

3.07   If ($j < i$) $a = j; b = i$;

3.08   If ($j > i$) $a = i; b = j$;

3.09   If ($e > d_j$) $p_{[a*N+b-(a+1)*(a+2)/2]} = 0$

3.10   else

3.11   If ($p_{[a*N+b-(a+1)*(a+2)/2]}$),

3.12   Calculate $c_i \setminus c_j$; $e + +$;}

3.13   End if

3.14   Next j

3.15   Next i

3.16   else

3.17   For $i = N - 1$ to 0

3.18 $e = 0$

3.19   For $j = N - 1$ to 0

3.20   If ($j == i$) $e_{ij} = 0$;

3.21   If ($j < i$) $a = j; b = i$;

3.22   If ($j > i$) $a = i; b = j$;

3.23   If ($e > d_j$) $p_{[a*N+b-(a+1)*(a+2)/2]} = 0$

3.24   else

3.25   If ($p_{[a*N+b-(a+1)*(a+2)/2]}$),

3.26   Calculate $c_i \setminus c_j$; $e + +$;}

3.27   End if

3.28   Next j

3.29   Next i

3.30   End if

3.31   Calculate $f = f + \left| \bigcup_{i=1}^{N}(c_i \setminus c_j) \cap \epsilon_{ij} \right|$;

3.32   If ($rand(0, 1) < 0.5$) $reverse = 0$

3.33   else $reverse = 1$;

3.34 Next s

Step 4. Find the best particle in the swarm, and find the best one in each sub-swarms. If the "global best" of the swarm is improved, $noimprove = 0$, otherwise, $noimprove = 1$. Update velocity and position for each particle at the iteration t.

4.01 For $m = 1$ to $subs$

4.02 $\mathbf{p}^* = argmin_{i=1}^{subs_m} (f(\mathbf{p}^*(t - 1)), f(\mathbf{p}_1(t)),$

4.02 $f(\mathbf{p}_2(t)), \cdots, f(\mathbf{p}_i(t)), \cdots, f(\mathbf{p}_{subs_m}(t)))$;

4.03   For $ss = 1$ to $subs_m$

4.04 $\mathbf{p}_i^\#(t) = argmin(f(\mathbf{p}_i^\#(t - 1)), f(\mathbf{p}_i(t)))$;

4.05   For $d = 1$ to D

4.06   Update the d-th dimension value of $\mathbf{p}_i$ and $\mathbf{v}_i$

4.06   according to (18.6) and (18.7);
4.07   Next d
4.08   Next ss
4.09 Next m

Step 5. If $noimprove = 1$, goto Step 2, the topology is re-organized. If the end criterion is not met, goto Step 3. Otherwise, output the best solution, the fitness.

18.4.2 Dynamic Ergodic Characteristics

Clerc and Kennedy have stripped the particle swarm model down to a most simple form [51,54]. If the self-recognition component c_1 and the coefficient of the social-recognition component c_2 in the particle swarm model are combined into a single term c, i.e., $c = c_1 + c_2$, the best position $\mathbf{p}_i$ can be redefined as follows:

$$\mathbf{p}_i \leftarrow \frac{(c_1\mathbf{p}_i + c_2\mathbf{p}_g)}{(c_1 + c_2)}. \tag{18.8}$$

Then, the update of the particle's velocity is defined by:

$$\mathbf{v}_i(t) = \mathbf{v}_i(t-1) + c(\mathbf{p}_i - \mathbf{x}_i(t-1)). \tag{18.9}$$

The system can be simplified even further by using $\mathbf{y}_i(t-1)$ instead of $\mathbf{p}_i - \mathbf{x}_i(t-1)$. Thus, the reduced system is then:

$$\begin{cases} \mathbf{v}(t) = \mathbf{v}(t-1) + c\mathbf{y}(t-1), \\ \mathbf{y}(t) = -\mathbf{v}(t-1) + (1-c)\mathbf{y}(t-1). \end{cases}$$

This recurrence relation can be written as a matrix-vector product, so that

$$\begin{bmatrix} \mathbf{v}(t) \\ \mathbf{y}(t) \end{bmatrix} = \begin{bmatrix} 1 & c \\ -1 & 1-c \end{bmatrix} \cdot \begin{bmatrix} \mathbf{v}(t-1) \\ \mathbf{y}(t-1) \end{bmatrix}.$$

Let

$$\mathbf{P}_t = \begin{bmatrix} \mathbf{v}_t \\ \mathbf{y}_t \end{bmatrix}$$

and

$$A = \begin{bmatrix} 1 & c \\ -1 & 1-c \end{bmatrix}$$

we have an iterated function system for the particle swarm model:

$$\mathbf{P}_t = A \cdot \mathbf{P}_{t-1}. \tag{18.10}$$

Fig. 18.3 Norm of A

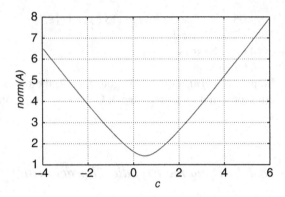

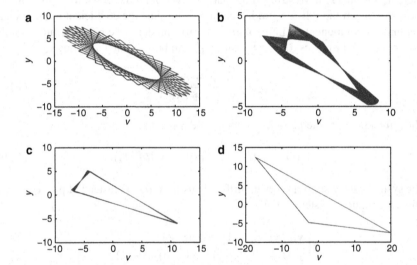

Fig. 18.4 Trajectory of the particle (**a**) $c = 2.9$, (**b**) $c = 2.999$, (**c**) $c = 2.999$, and (**d**) $c = 2.9999$

Thus, the system is completely defined by A. Its norm $\|A\|_2$ (also written $\|A\|$) is determined by c. The relationship of A and its dependence on c is illustrated in Fig. 18.3.

IFS is sensitive to the values of c. It is possible to find different trajectories of the particle for various values of c. Figure 18.4(a) illustrates the system for a torus when $c = 2.9$; Fig. 18.4(b), a hexagon with spindle sides when $c = 2.99$; Fig. 18.4(c), a triangle with spindle sides when $c = 2.999$; Fig. 18.4(d), a simple triangle when $c = 2.9999$. As depicted in Fig. 18.4, the iteration time step used is 100 for all the cases. Another system sensitivity instance is illustrated in Fig. 18.5. It is to be noted that Figs. 18.4 and 18.5 illustrate only some 2-dimensional representations of the iterated process. In multi-dimensional search space, the particle displays the characteristics of ergodicity, which will be analyzed theoretically in Sect. 18.4.3.

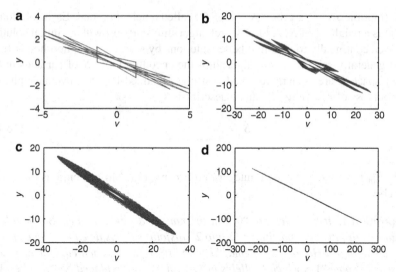

Fig. 18.5 Trajectory of the particle (**a**) $c = 3.7321$, (**b**) $c = 3.8$, (**c**) $c = 3.9$, and (**d**) $c = 3.999$

18.4.3   Convergence Analysis of Multi-Swarm Algorithm

For analyzing the convergence of the multi-swarm algorithm, we first introduce the definitions and lemmas [62–64], and then theoretically prove that the algorithm converges with a probability 1 or strongly towards the global optimal.

Xu et al. [65] analyzed the search capability of an algebraic crossover through classifying the individual space of GAs, which is helpful to comprehend the search of GAs such that premature convergence and deceptive problems [66] could be avoided. In this subsection, we also attempt to theoretically analyze the performance of the multi-swarm algorithm with crossover neighborhood topology. For the sake of convenience, let crossover operator $|_c$ denote the wheeling-round-the-best-particles process.

Consider the problem (P) as

$$(P) = \min\{f(\mathbf{x}) : \mathbf{x} \in D\}, \tag{18.11}$$

where $\mathbf{x} = (x_1, x_2, \ldots, x_n)^T$, $f(\mathbf{x}) : D \rightarrow R$ is the objective function and D is a compact Hausdorff space. Applying our algorithm the problem (P), it can be transformed to P' as

$$(P') = \begin{cases} \min f(\mathbf{x}), \\ \mathbf{x} \in \Omega = [-s, s]^n, \end{cases} \tag{18.12}$$

where Ω is the set of feasible solutions of the problem. A swarm is a set, which consists of some feasible solutions of the problem. Assume S as the encoding space of D. A neighborhood function is a mapping $\mathcal{N} : \Omega \rightarrow 2^\Omega$, which defines for each solution $S \in \Omega$ a subset $\mathcal{N}(S)$ of Ω, called a neighborhood. Each solution in $\mathcal{N}(S)$ is a neighbor of S. A local search algorithm starts off with an initial solution and then continually tries to find better solutions by searching neighborhoods [67]. Most generally said, in swarm algorithms the encoding types S of particles in the search space D are often represented as strings of a fixed-length L over an alphabet. Without loss of generality, S can be described as

$$S = \underbrace{z_m \times \cdots \times z_m}_{L}, \tag{18.13}$$

where z_m is a finite field about integer number mod m. Most often, it is the binary alphabet, i.e., $m = 2$.

Proposition 1. *If k alleles are "0"s in the nontrivial ideal Ω, i.e., $L - k$ alleles are uncertain, then θ_Ω partitions Ω into 2^k disjoint subsets as equivalence classes corresponding to Holland's schema theorem [68, 69], i.e., each equivalence class consists of some "1"s which k alleles in Ω with "0" are replaced by "1"s. Let $A \in S/\theta_\Omega$, then there is an minimal element m of A under partial order $(S, \vee, \wedge, \neg)$, such that $A = \{m \vee x \mid x \in \Omega\}$.*

Theorem 1. *Let A, B, C are three equivalence classes on θ_Ω, where θ_Ω is the congruence relation about Ω. $\exists\, x \in A$, $y \in B$, and $x \mid_c y \in C$, then $C = \{x \mid_c y \mid x \in A, y \in B\}$.*

Proof. Firstly, we verify that for any $d_1, d_2 \in \Omega$, if $x \mid_c y \in C$, then $(x \vee d_1) \mid_c (y \vee d_2) \in C$. In fact,

$$\begin{aligned}
(x \vee d_1) \mid_c (y \vee d_2) &= (x \vee d_1)c \vee (y \vee d_2)\bar{c} \\
&\quad (xc \vee y\bar{c}) \vee (d_1 c \vee d_2 \bar{c}) \tag{18.14} \\
&\quad (x \mid_c y) \vee (d_1 c \vee d_2 \bar{c}).
\end{aligned}$$

Obviously, $(d_1 c \vee d_2 \bar{c}) \in \Omega$, so $(x \vee d_1) \mid_c (y \vee d_2) \equiv (x \mid_c y)(\mathrm{mod}\ \theta_\Omega)$, i.e., $(x \vee d_1) \mid_c (y \vee d_2) \in \Omega$.

Secondly, from Proposition 1, $\exists\, m, n, d_3, d_4 \in \Omega$ of A, B, such that $x = m \vee d_3$, $y = n \vee d_4$. As a result of analysis in (18.14), $x \mid_c y \equiv (m \mid_c n)(\mathrm{mod}\ \theta_\Omega)$, i.e., $m \mid_c n \in C$.

Finally, we verify that $m \mid_c n$ is a minimal element of C and $(m \mid_c n) \vee d = (m \vee d) \mid_c (n \vee d)$. As a result of analysis in (18.14), if $d_1 = d_2 = d$, then $m \mid_c n \vee d = (m \vee d) \mid_c (n \vee d)$. Therefore $m \mid_c n$ is a minimal element of C.

To conclude, $C = \{(m \mid_c n) \vee d \mid d \in \Omega\} = \{x \mid_c y \mid x \in A, y \in B\}$. The theorem is proven.

Proposition 2. *Let A, B are two equivalence classes on θ_Ω, and there exist $x \in A$, $y \in B$, such that $x \mid_c y \in C$, then, $x \mid_c y$ makes ergodic search C while x and y make ergodic search A and B, respectively.*

Definition 1 (Convergence in terms of probability). Let ξ_n a sequence of random variables, and ξ a random variable, and all of them are defined on the same probability space. The sequence ξ_n converges with a probability of ξ if

$$\lim_{n\to\infty} P(|\xi_n - \xi| < \varepsilon) = 1 \qquad (18.15)$$

for every $\varepsilon > 0$.

Definition 2 (Convergence with a probability of 1). Let ξ_n a sequence of random variables, and ξ a random variable, and all of them are defined on the same probability space. The sequence ξ_n converges almost surely or almost everywhere or with probability of 1 or strongly towards ξ if

$$P\left(\lim_{n\to\infty} \xi_n = \xi\right) = 1; \qquad (18.16)$$

or

$$P\left(\bigcap_{n=1}^{\infty} \bigcup_{k \geq n} [|\xi_n - \xi| \geq \varepsilon]\right) = 0 \qquad (18.17)$$

for every $\varepsilon > 0$.

Theorem 2. *Let $\mathbf{x}^*$ is the global optimal solution to the problem (P'), and $f^* = f(\mathbf{x}^*)$. Assume that the clubs-based multi-swarm algorithm provides position series $\mathbf{x}_i(t)$ $(i = 1, 2, \ldots, n)$ at time t by the iterated procedure. $\mathbf{p}^*$ is the best position among all the swarms explored so far, i.e.,*

$$\mathbf{p}^*(t) = \arg\min_{1 \leq i \leq n} (f(\mathbf{p}^*(t-1)), f(\mathbf{p}_i(t))). \qquad (18.18)$$

Then,

$$P\left(\lim_{t\to\infty} f(\mathbf{p}^*(t)) = f^*\right) = 1. \qquad (18.19)$$

Proof. Let

$$D_0 = \{\mathbf{x} \in \Omega \,|\, f(\mathbf{x}) - f^* < \varepsilon\}, \qquad (18.20)$$
$$D_1 = \Omega \setminus D_0$$

for every $\varepsilon > 0$.

While the different swarm searches their feasible solutions by themselves, assume Δp is the difference of the particle's position among different club swarms at the iteration time t. Therefore $-s \leq \Delta p \leq s$. $Rand(-1, 1)$ is a normal distributed random number within the interval $[-1, 1]$. According to the update of the velocity and position by (18.6)~(18.7), Δp belongs to the normal distribution, i.e., $\Delta p \sim [-s, s]$. During the iterated procedure from the time t to $t + 1$, let q_{ij} denote that $\mathbf{x}(t) \in D_i$

and $\mathbf{x}(t+1) \in D_j$. Accordingly the particles' positions in the swarm could be classified into four states: q_{00}, q_{01}, q_{10} and q_{01}. Obviously $q_{00} + q_{01} = 1, q_{10} + q_{11} = 1$. According to Borel-Cantelli Lemma and Particle State Transference [59], proving by the same methods, $q_{01} = 0$; $q_{00} = 1$; $q_{11} \leq c \in (0, 1)$ and $q_{10} \geq 1 - c \in (0, 1)$.

For $\forall \varepsilon > 0$, let $p_k = P\{|f(\mathbf{p}^*(k)) - f^*| \geq \varepsilon\}$, then

$$p_k = \begin{cases} 0 & \text{if } \exists T \in \{1, 2, \ldots, k\}, \mathbf{p}^*(T) \in D_0, \\ \bar{p}_k & \text{if } \mathbf{p}^*(t) \notin D_0, t = 1, 2, \ldots, k. \end{cases} \tag{18.21}$$

According to Particle State Transference Lemma,

$$\bar{p}_k = P\{\mathbf{p}^*(t) \notin D_0, t = 1, 2, \ldots, k\} = q_{11}^k \leq c^k. \tag{18.22}$$

Hence,

$$\sum_{k=1}^{\infty} p_k \leq \sum_{k=1}^{\infty} c^k = \frac{c}{1-c} < \infty. \tag{18.23}$$

According to Borel-Cantelli Lemma,

$$P\left(\bigcap_{t=1}^{\infty} \bigcup_{k \geq t} |f(\mathbf{p}^*(k)) - f^*| \geq \varepsilon\right) = 0. \tag{18.24}$$

As defined in Definition 2, the sequence $f(\mathbf{p}^*(t))$ converges almost surely or almost everywhere or with probability 1 or strongly towards f^*. The theorem is proven.

18.5 Algorithm Performance Demonstration

To illustrate the effectiveness and performance of the PSO algorithm, we illustrate an execution trace of the algorithm for the NS problem. A file of size 7 MB is divided into 14 fragments (512 KB each) to distribute, 6 peers download from the P2P networks, and the connecting maximum number of each peer is 3, which is represented as $(6, 14, 3)$ problem. In some session, the state of distributed file fragments is as follows:

$$\begin{bmatrix} 1 & 0 & 0 & 4 & 0 & 6 & 7 & 8 & 0 & 10 & 0 & 12 & 0 & 14 \\ 0 & 0 & 0 & 4 & 5 & 0 & 7 & 0 & 9 & 0 & 11 & 0 & 13 & 0 \\ 0 & 2 & 0 & 0 & 0 & 6 & 0 & 0 & 0 & 0 & 11 & 12 & 0 & 14 \\ 0 & 2 & 3 & 4 & 0 & 6 & 0 & 0 & 0 & 0 & 11 & 0 & 0 & 0 \\ 0 & 2 & 0 & 0 & 0 & 0 & 7 & 8 & 0 & 10 & 0 & 12 & 0 & 14 \\ 1 & 2 & 0 & 0 & 5 & 0 & 0 & 0 & 9 & 10 & 11 & 0 & 13 & 14 \end{bmatrix}.$$

The optimal result search by the multi-swarm algorithm is 31, and the NS solution is illustrated below:

$$
\begin{array}{c@{\;}c}
 & \begin{array}{cccccc} 1 & 2 & 3 & 4 & 5 & 6 \end{array} \\
\begin{array}{c} 1 \\ 2 \\ 3 \\ 4 \\ 5 \\ 6 \end{array} &
\left(\begin{array}{cccccc}
0 & 0 & 0 & 1 & 1 & 1 \\
0 & 0 & 0 & 0 & 1 & 1 \\
0 & 0 & 0 & 1 & 1 & 1 \\
1 & 0 & 1 & 0 & 0 & 0 \\
1 & 1 & 1 & 0 & 0 & 0 \\
1 & 1 & 1 & 0 & 0 & 0
\end{array}\right)
\end{array}.
$$

We also tested other three representative instances (problem (25, 1400, 12), problem (30, 1400, 15), problem (35, 1400, 17) and problem (100, 1400, 20)) further. In our experiments, the algorithms used for comparison were mainly SPSO (standard PSO) ([55]) and GA ([70]). These algorithms share many similarities. GA is powerful stochastic global search and optimization methods, which are also inspired from the nature like the PSO. GAs mimic an evolutionary natural selection process. Generations of solutions are evaluated according to a fitness value and only those candidates with high fitness values are used to create further solutions via crossover and mutation procedures. Both methods are valid and efficient methods in numeric programming and have been employed in various fields due to their strong convergence properties. The considered algorithms were repeated 4 times with different random seeds. Each trial had a fixed number of 50 or 80 iterations. Other specific parameter settings of the algorithms are described in Table 18.1, where D is the dimension of the position. The average fitness values of the best solutions throughout the optimization run were recorded. The average and the standard deviation were calculated from the 4 different trials.

Figures 18.6–18.9 illustrate the performances during the search processes using the considered algorithms to solve the NS problems. The best values, mean values, the standard deviations for 4 trials are shown in Table 18.2. As evident, the multi-swarm algorithm obtained better results much faster than other algorithms, especially for large scale problems. The multi-swarm algorithm offered the advantages of steady performance, since it has the least standard deviations.

Table 18.1 Parameter settings for the algorithms

Algorithm	Parameter name	Value
	Size of the population	(even)(int)$(10 + 2 * \mathrm{sqrt}(D))$
GA	Probability of crossover	0.8
	Probability of mutation	0.01
	Swarm size	(even)(int)$(10 + 2 * \mathrm{sqrt}(D))$
	Self coefficient (c_1)	$0.5 + \log(2)$
PSO(s)	Social coefficient (c_2)	$0.5 + \log(2)$
	Inertia weight (w)	0.91
	Clamping coefficient (ρ)	0.5

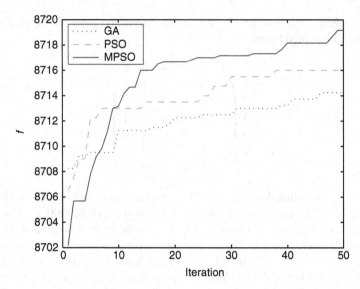

Fig. 18.6 Performance for the NS (25, 1400, 12)

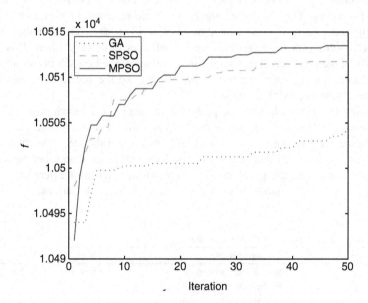

Fig. 18.7 Performance for the NS (30, 1400, 15)

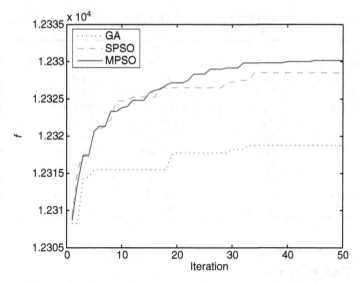

Fig. 18.8 Performance for the NS (35, 1400, 17)

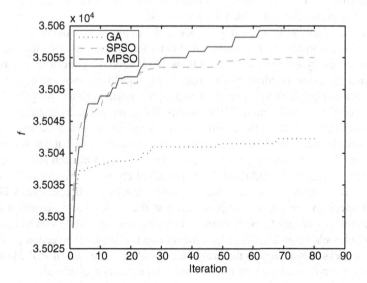

Fig. 18.9 Performance for the NS (100, 1400, 20)

Table 18.2 Performance comparison of the three algorithms

Instance	Item	GA	SPSO	MPSO
	Best	8716.00	8717.00	8721.00
(25, 1400, 12)	Mean	8.714.30	8716.00	87192.00
	Std. dev.	1.7078	1.1547	1.3292
	Best	10513.00	10514.00	10515.00
(30, 1400, 15)	Mean	10504.00	10512.00	10514.00
	Std. dev.	6.3443	1.2990	1.2910
	Best	12321.00	12332.00	12332.00
(35, 1400, 17)	Mean	12319.00	12329.00	12330.00
	Std. dev.	1.7078	2.5166	1.1690
	Best	35047.00	35057.00	35061.00
(100, 1400, 20)	Mean	35042.25	35055.00	35059.25
	Std. dev.	3.6996	1.2247	1.0897

18.6 Conclusion

In this chapter, we investigated to solve the class of the neighbor-selection problem in peer-to-peer (P2P) networks by using a swarm intelligence approach. We encoded the particles using the upper half matrix of the peer connection through the undirected graph, through which we accomplished the mapping between the problem and the particle. It is feasible to reduce the dimension of the particle's search space. Since particle swarm shares some common characteristics with P2P in the dynamic socially environment, a multi-swarm interactive pattern was introduced to match the corresponding mechanism. We designed a crossover neighborhood multi-swarm algorithm based on discrete particle swarm optimization (PSO) for the neighbor-selection problem in P2P networks. We analyzed the dynamic characteristic of the single particle in the swarm. The multi-swarm algorithm performance was illustrated theoretically that it converges with a probability of 1 towards the global optimum. We evaluated the performance of the proposed approach and compared it with genetic algorithm (GA) and SPSO (standard PSO). The results indicated that multi-swarm approach usually obtained better results much faster than GA and SPSO, specially for large scale problems and the multi-swarm algorithm offered the advantages of steady performance. The crossover neighborhood multi-swarm algorithm could be an ideal approach for solving the neighbor-selection problem in P2P networks. Compared to the previous algorithms proposed in P2P file sharing systems, the proposed algorithm has a low communication overhead.

Acknowledgment The authors would like to thank Drs. Shichang Sun, Mingyan Zhao for their scientific collaboration in this research work. This work is supported partially by NSFC Grant 60873054 and DLMU Grant DLMU-ZL-200709.

References

1. Lua E K, Crowcroft J, Pias M, Sharma R and Lim S (2005) A Survey and Comparison of Peer-to-Peer Overlay Network Schemes. IEEE Communications Surveys & Tutorials, 7(2):72–93
2. Kwok S (2006) P2P Searching Trends: 2002-2004. Information Processing and Management, 42:237–247
3. Huang X, Chang C and Chen M (2006) PeerCluster: A Cluster-Based Peer-to-Peer System. IEEE Transactions on Parallel and Distributed Systems, 17(10):1110–1123
4. Belmonte M V, Conejo R, Díaz M and Pérez-de-la-Cruz J L (2006) Coalition Formation in P2P File Sharing Systems, Lecture Notes in Artificial Intelligence, CAEPIA'05, vol. 4177, pp. 153–162
5. Idris T and Altmann J (2006) A Market-managed Topology Formation Algorithm for Peer-to-Peer File Sharing Networks, Lecture Notes in Computer Science, vol. 4033, pp. 61–77
6. Cho H (2007) An Update Propagation Algorithm for P2P File Sharing over Wireless Mobile Networks, Lecture Notes in Computer Science, ICCS'07, vol. 4490, pp. 753–760
7. Pianese F, Perino D, Keller J and Biersack E W (2007) PULSE: An Adaptive, Incentive-Based, Unstructured P2P Live Streaming System. IEEE Transactions on Multimedia, 9(8):1645–1660
8. Sigurdsson H M, Halldorsson U R and Hasslinger G (2007) Potentials and Challenges of Peer-to-Peer Based Content Distribution. Telematics and Informatics, 24:348–365
9. Yang S and Chen I (2008) A Social Network-based System for Supporting Interactive Collaboration in Knowledge Sharing Over Peer-to-Peer Network. International Journal of Human-Computer Studies, 66:36–50
10. Kim J K, Kim H K and Cho Y H (2008) A User-oriented Contents Recommendation System in Peer-to-Peer Architecture. Expert Systems with Applications, 34:300–312
11. Sen S and Wang J (2004) Analyzing Peer-to-Peer Traffic Across Large Networks. IEEE/ACM Transactions on Networking, 12(2):219–232
12. Leung A and Kwok Y (2005) An Efficient and Practical Greedy Algorithm for Server-Peer Selection in Wireless Peer-to-Peer File Sharing Networks, Lecture Notes in Computer Science, MSN'05, vol. 3794, pp. 1016–1025
13. Ardizzone E, Gatani L, La Cascia M, Lo Re G and Ortolani M (2007) Enhanced P2P Services Providing Multimedia Content. Advances in Multimedia, 1–12
14. Androutsellis-theotokis S and Spinellis D (2004) A Survey of Peer-to-Peer Content Distribution Technologies. ACM Computing Surveys, 36(4):335–371
15. Clerc M (2006) Particle Swarm Optimization, ISTE Publishing Company, London
16. Abraham A, Guo H and Liu H (2006) Swarm Intelligence: Foundations, Perspectives and Applications. Swarm Intelligent Systems, Studies in Computational Intelligence, 3–25
17. Schollmeier R (2001) A Definition of Peer-to-Peer Networking for the Classification of Peer-to-Peer Architectures and Applications, Proceedings of the First International August Conference on Peer-to-Peer Computing, pp. 101–102
18. Ghosal D, Poon B K and Kong K (2005) P2P Contracts: A Framework for Resource and Service Exchange. Future Generation Computer Systems, 21:333–347
19. Koo S G, Kannan K and Lee C S (2006) A Genetic-algorithm-based Neighbor-selection Strategy for Hybrid Peer-to-Peer Networks. Future Generation Computer Systems, 22:732–741
20. Surana S, Godfrey B, Lakshminarayanan K, Karp R and Stoica I (2006) Load Balancing in Dynamic Structured Peer-to-Peer Systems. Performance Evaluation, 63:217–240
21. Merrer E, Kermarrec A, and Massoulié L (2006) Peer to Peer Size Estimation in Large and Dynamic Networks: A Comparative Study, Proceedings of 15th IEEE International Symposium on High Performance Distributed Computing, pp. 7–17
22. Meo M and Milan F (2008) QoS Content Management for P2P File-sharing Applications. Future Generation Computer Systems, 24:213–221
23. Risson J and Moors T (2006) Survey of Research Towards Robust Peer-to-Peer Networks: Search Methods. Computer Networks, 50:3485–3521
24. Habib A and Chuang J (2006) Service Differentiated Peer Selection: An Incentive Mechanism for Peer-to-Peer Media Streaming. IEEE Transactions on Multimedia, 8(3):610–623

25. Lo V, Zhou D, Liu Y, GauthierDickey C S and Li J (2005) Scalable Supernode Selection in Peer-to-Peer Overlay Networks, Proceedings of the Second IEEE International Workshop on Hot Topics in Peer-to-Peer Systems, pp. 18–27

26. Kothapalli K and Scheideler C (2005) Supervised Peer-to-Peer Systems. Proceedings of the 8th International Symposium on Parallel Architectures, Algorithms and Networks, pp. 188–193

27. Koulouris T, Henjes R, Tutschku K and de Meer H (2004) Implementation of Adaptive Control for P2P Overlays, Lecture Notes in Computer Science, vol. 2982, pp. 292–306

28. Liu Y, Xiao L, Esfahanian A and Ni L M (2005) Approaching Optimal Peer-to-Peer Overlays, Proceedings of the 13th IEEE International Symposium on Modeling, Analysis, and Simulation of Computer and Telecommunication Systems, pp. 407–414

29. Leung A K and Kwok Y (2008) On Localized Application-Driven Topology Control for Energy-Efficient Wireless Peer-to-Peer File Sharing. IEEE Transactions on Mobile Computing, 7(1):66–80

30. Mastronarde N, Turaga D S and van der Schaar M (2007) Collaborative Resource Exchanges for Peer-to-Peer Video Streaming Over Wireless Mesh Networks. IEEE Journal on Selected Areas in Communications, 25(1):108–118

31. Fenner T, Levene M, Loizou G and Roussos G (2007) A Stochastic Evolutionary Growth Model for Social Networks. Computer Networks, 51:4586–4595

32. Sacha J, Dowling J, Cunningham R and Meier R (2006) Discovery of Stable Peers in a Self-Organising Peer-to-Peer Gradient Topology, Lecture Notes in Computer Science, vol. 4025, pp. 70–83

33. Bisnik N and Abouzeid A A (2007) Optimizing Random Walk Search Algorithms in P2P Networks. Computer Networks, 51(6):1499–1514

34. Kersch P, Szabo R, Cheng L, Jean K and Galis A (2007) Stochastic Maintenance of Overlays in Structured P2P Systems. Computer Communications, doi:10.1016/j.comcom.2007.08.017

35. Krishnamurthy B and Wang J (2001) Topology Modeling via Cluster Graphs, Proceedings of the 1st ACM SIGCOMM Workshop on Internet Measurement, pp. 19–23

36. Padmanabhan V N and Subramanian L (2001) An Investigation of Geographic Mapping Techniques for Internet Hosts, Proceedings of the ACM Conference on Applications, Technologies, Architectures, and Protocols for Computer Communications, pp. 173–185

37. Nakao A, Peterson L and Bavier A (2003) A Routing Underlay for Overlay Networks, Proceedings of the ACM Conference on Applications, Technologies, Architectures, and Protocols for Computer Communications, pp. 11–18

38. Xu X (2007) ABC: A Cluster-based Protocol for Resource Location in Peer-to-Peer Systems. Journal of Parallel and Distributed Computing, doi:10.1016/j.jpdc.2005.02.004

39. Ramaswamy L, Gedik B and Liu L (2005) A Distributed Approach to Node Clustering in Decentralized Peer-to-Peer Networks. IEEE Transactions on Parallel and Distributed Systems, 16(9):814–829

40. Tewari S and L. Kleinrock L (2007) Optimal Search Performance in Unstructured Peer-to-Peer Networks With Clustered Demands. IEEE Journal on Selected Areas in Communications, 25(1):84–95

41. Kurmanowytsch R, Kirda E, Kerer C and Dustdar S (2003) OMNIX: A topology-independent P2P middleware, Proceedings of the 15th Conference on Advanced Information Systems Engineering, pp. 47–56

42. Gupta R, Sekhri V and Somani A K (2006) CompuP2P: An Architecture for Internet Computing Using Peer-to-Peer Networks. IEEE Transactions on Parallel and Distributed Systems, 17(11):1306–1320

43. Zeinalipour-Yazti D, Kalogeraki V and Gunopulos D (2007) pFusion: A P2P Architecture for Internet-Scale Content-Based Search and Retrieval. IEEE Transactions on Parallel and Distributed Systems, 18(6):804–817

44. Ghanea-Hercock R A, Wang F and Sun Y (2006) Self-Organizing and Adaptive Peer-to-Peer Network. IEEE Transactions on Systems, Man, and Cybernetics – Part B: Cybernetics, 36(6):1230–1236

45. Biersack E W, Rodriguez P and Felber P (2004) Performance Analysis of Peer-to-Peer Networks for File Distribution, Lecture Notes in Computer Science, QofIS'04, vol. 3266, pp. 1–10

46. Carchiolo V, Malgeri M, Mangioni G and Nicosia V (2007) Emerging structures of P2P networks induced by social relationships, doi:10.1016/j.comcom.2007.08.016
47. Zhuge H and Li X (2007) Peer-to-Peer in Metric Space and Semantic Space. IEEE Transactions on Knowledge and Data Engineering, 19(6):759–771
48. Wang S, Chou H, Wei D and Kuo S (2007) On the Fundamental Performance Limits of Peer-to-Peer Data Replication in Wireless Ad hoc Networks. Journal on Selected Areas in Communications, 25(1):211–221
49. Qiu D and Sang W (2007) Global Stability of Peer-to-Peer File Sharing Systems. Computer Communications, doi:10.1016/j.comcom.2007.08.012
50. Salman A, Ahmad I and Al-Madani S (2002) Particle Swarm Optimization for Task Assignment Problem. Microprocessors and Microsystems, 26:363–371
51. Clerc M and Kennedy J (2002) The Particle Swarm – Explosion, Stability, and Convergence in a Multidimensional Complex Space. IEEE Transactions on Evolutionary Computation, 6(1):58–73
52. Cristian T I (2003) The Particle Swarm Optimization Algorithm: Convergence Analysis and Parameter Selection. Information Processing Letters, 85(6):317–325
53. van den Bergh F and Engelbrecht A P (2006) A Study of Particle Swarm Optimization Particle Trajectories. Information Sciences, 176:937–971
54. Liu H, Abraham A and Clerc M (2007) Chaotic Dynamic Characteristics in Swarm Intelligence. Applied Soft Computing, 7:1019–1026
55. Kennedy J and Eberhart R (2001) Swarm Intelligence. CA: Morgan Kaufmann Publishers
56. Liu H, Li B, Ji Y and Sun T (2006) Particle Swarm Optimisation from lbest to gbest. Applied Soft Computing Technologies: The Challenge of Complexity, 537–545
57. Grosan C, Abraham A and Nicoara M (2005) Search Optimization Using Hybrid Particle Subswarms and Evolutionary Algorithms. International Journal of Simulation Systems, Science & Technology, 6(10):60–79
58. Jiang C W and Etorre B (2005) A Hybrid Method of Chaotic Particle Swarm Optimization and Linear Interior for Reactive Power Optimisation. Mathematics and Computers in Simulation, 68:57–65
59. Liu H and Abraham A (2007) An Hybrid Fuzzy Variable Neighborhood Particle Swarm Optimization Algorithm for Solving Quadratic Assignment Problems. Journal of Universal Computer Science, 13(7):1032–1054
60. Liang J J, Qin A K, Suganthan P N and Baskar S (2006) Comprehensive Learning Particle Swarm Optimizer for Global Optimization of Multimodal Functions. IEEE Transactions on Evolutionary Computation, 10(3):281–295
61. Elshamy W, Emara H M and Bahgat A (2007) Clubs-based Particle Swarm Optimization, Proceedings of the IEEE International Conference on Swarm Intelligence Symposium, vol. 1, pp. 289–296
62. Guo C and Tang H (2001) Global Convergence Properties of Evolution Stragtegies. Mathematica Numerica Sinica, 23(1):105–110
63. He R, Wang Y, Wang Q, Zhou J and Hu C (2005) An Improved Particle Swarm Optimization Based on Self-adaptive Escape Velocity. Journal of Software, 16(12):2036–2044
64. Weisstein E W (2007) Borel-Cantelli Lemma, From MathWorld – A Wolfram Web Resource, http://mathworld.wolfram.com/Borel-CantelliLemma.html
65. Xu Z, Cheng G and Liang Y (1999) Search Capability for an Algebraic Crossover. Journal of Xi'an Jiaotong University, 33(10):88–99
66. Whitley L D (1991) Fundamental Principles of Deception in Genetic Search. Foundation of Genetic Algorithms. CA: Morgan Kaufmann Publishers, pp. 221–241
67. Mastrolilli M and Gambardella L M (2002) Effective Neighborhood Functions for the Flexible Job Shop Problem. Journal of Scheduling, 3(1):3–20
68. Holland J H (1975) Adaptation in Natural and Artificial Systems. Ann Arbor: University of Michigan Press
69. Goldberg D E (1989) Genetic Algorithms in Search, Optimization and Machine Learning. Reading, MA: Addison-Wesley
70. Abraham A (2005) Evolutionary Computation. Handbook for Measurement Systems Design, pp. 920–931

Chapter 19
Analysis of Pervasive Mobile Ad Hoc Routing Protocols

Nadia N. Qadri and Antonio Liotta

Abstract Mobile ad hoc networks (MANETs) are a fundamental element of pervasive networks and therefore, of pervasive systems that truly support pervasive computing, where user can communicate anywhere, anytime and on-the-fly. In fact, future advances in pervasive computing rely on advancements in mobile communication, which includes both infrastructure-based wireless networks and non-infrastructure-based MANETs. MANETs introduce a new communication paradigm, which does not require a fixed infrastructure – they rely on wireless terminals for routing and transport services. Due to highly dynamic topology, absence of established infrastructure for centralized administration, bandwidth constrained wireless links, and limited resources in MANETs, it is challenging to design an efficient and reliable routing protocol. This chapter reviews the key studies carried out so far on the performance of mobile ad hoc routing protocols. We discuss performance issues and metrics required for the evaluation of ad hoc routing protocols. This leads to a survey of existing work, which captures the performance of ad hoc routing algorithms and their behaviour from different perspectives and highlights avenues for future research.

Keywords Mobile Ad hoc Networks · Routing Protocols · Pervasive Computing · Proactive Routing · Reactive Routing · Hybrid Routing · Performance Analysis · Protocols Comparison

19.1 Introduction

Mobile ad hoc networks (MANETs) are a fundamental element of pervasive networks and therefore, of pervasive systems that truly support pervasive computing, where users can communicate anywhere, anytime and on-the-fly. In fact, future advances in pervasive computing rely on advancements in mobile communication,

N.N. Qadri (✉)
Department of Computing and Electronics Systems, University of Essex, Wivenhoe Park, Colchester CO4 3SQ, UK
e-mail: nnawaz@essex.ac.uk

A.-E. Hassanien et al. (eds.), *Pervasive Computing: Innovations in Intelligent Multimedia and Applications*, Computer Communications and Networks, DOI 10.1007/978-1-84882-599-4_19, © Springer-Verlag London Limited 2009

which includes both infrastructure-based wireless networks and non-infrastructure-based MANETs. The traditional infrastructure-based communication model is not adequate for today's user requirements. In many situations the communication between mobile hosts cannot rely on any fixed infrastructure. The cost and delay associated with installation of infrastructure-based communication model may not be acceptable in dynamic environments such as disaster conditions, battle field, intervehicular communications, etc. MANET would be an effective solution in these scenarios.

MANETs introduce a new communication paradigm, which does not require a fixed infrastructure – they rely on wireless terminals for routing and transport services. A MANET is characterized as "the art of networking without a network" [1]. The network topology of such a system is changeable and unpredictable; therefore, the traditional wired network routing protocols are not applicable for these networks. The special features of a MANET bring about great opportunities together with severe challenges. Due to their highly dynamic topology, the absence of an established infrastructure for centralized administration, bandwidth constrained wireless links, and limited resources, MANETs are hard to design in terms of efficient and reliable routing.

A robust and flexible routing approach is required to efficiently use the limited resources available, while at the same time being adaptable to the changing network conditions, such as network size (scalability), traffic density and mobility. The routing protocol should be able to provide efficient route establishment with minimum overhead, delay and bandwidth consumption, along with a stable throughput. Furthermore, the possibility of asymmetric links, caused by different power levels among mobile hosts and other factors such as terrain conditions, makes routing protocols more complicated than in other networks.

For this purpose, a wealth of innovative protocols has been introduced and authors of each proposed protocol claim that the algorithm proposed by them brings in enhancements and improvements over a number of different strategies under different scenarios and network conditions. However, only few protocols have actually been implemented (beyond the simulation stage) and not all of these have been assessed in depth. Many articles have provided a protocol assessment which is specific and often does not allow drawing general conclusions. Therefore, it is difficult to determine which protocols may perform better under different network scenarios.

To address these shortcomings, this chapter reviews the key studies carried out so far on the performance of mobile ad hoc routing protocols. First, we introduce taxonomy of a wide variety of different protocols based on mechanisms including route construction, maintenance and update, topology formation, network configuration and exploitation of specific resources. An overview of the most significant protocols presented and widely used in literature is given. Then we discuss the requirements of Mobile ad hoc routing protocols and performance metrics required for the evaluation of ad hoc routing protocols. This leads to a survey of existing work, which captures the performance of ad hoc routing algorithms and their behaviour from different perspectives. A critical discussion of the state-of-the-art will yield the identification of the key areas that require further research. We conclude with discussion and our view on this topic.

19.2 Taxonomy of Mobile Ad Hoc Routing Protocols

Mobile ad hoc routing protocols can be classified in many ways depending upon their route construction and maintenance mechanisms, route selection strategy, topology formation, update mechanism, utilization of specific resources, type of cast, etc. [2]. Here we have classified them using few characteristics – the bases of classification are discussed below. Taxonomy of routing protocols is shown in Fig. 19.1. In this section, we focus on those that will be discussed in the later part of this chapter.

19.2.1 Approaches Based on Route Construction, Maintenance and Update Mechanisms

These protocols can be described as the way the route is constructed, updated and maintained and route information is obtained at each node and exchanged between the nodes. Based upon these characteristics, routing protocols can be divided broadly into three categories.

19.2.1.1 Proactive (Table-Driven) Routing

In proactive or table-driven routing protocols, each node consistently maintains up-to-date routing information for all known destinations. These types of protocols keep routing information in one or more tables and maintain routes at each node by periodically distributing routing tables (RTs) throughout the network or when the topology changes. Each node keeps information of all the routes, regardless of weather or not these routes are needed. Therefore, control overhead in these protocols would be significantly high, especially for large networks or in a network where nodes are highly mobile. However, the main advantage of these protocols is that the routes are readily available when required and end-to-end delay is reduced during data transmission in comparison to the case in which routes are determined reactively, which introduces a latency to discover a route to the destination.

19.2.1.2 Reactive (On-Demand) Routing

In Reactive or on-demand routing protocols, the routes are discovered only when they are actually needed. These protocols consist of route discovery and route maintenance processes. The route discovery process is initiated when a node wants to send data to a particular destination. Route discovery usually occurs by flooding the network with route-request packets. When a destination node or node holding a route to destination is reached, a route-reply is sent back to the source node by

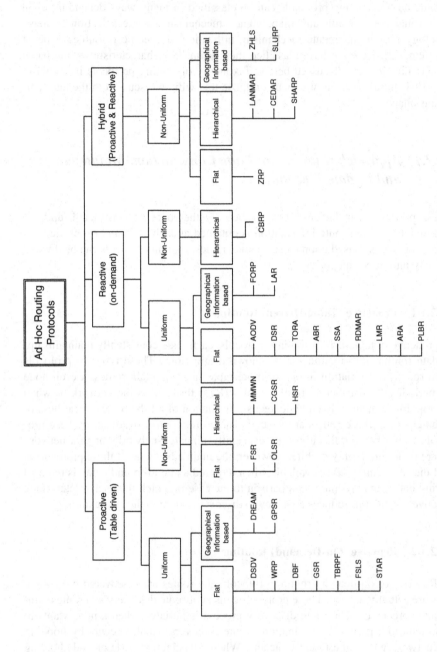

Fig. 19.1 Taxonomy of mobile ad hoc routing protocols (for abbreviations please refer list of abbreviations)

instantiating routing information at the appropriate intermediate nodes. Once the route reply reaches the source, the data can be sent to the destination. The route maintenance process deletes failed routes and re-initiates route discovery in case of topology change. The advantage of this approach is that overall overhead is likely to be reduced compared to proactive approaches. However, as the number of sessions increases, the overhead generated by route discovery became high and may exceed that of proactive protocols.

19.2.1.3 Hybrid Routing

The hybrid routing protocols combine the advantages of both proactive and reactive routing. These protocols usually divide the network in zones such that each node sees the network in number of zones. The routes to nodes close to each other or within a particular zone are proactively maintained and the routes to far-away nodes are determined reactively using a route discovery strategy.

19.2.2 Approaches Based on Logical Organization, Network Configuration, and Utilization of Specific Resources

19.2.2.1 Uniform Routing

In uniform routing, all nodes are equal and each node participates in route computations. Each node generates routing control messages and replies to routing control requests in the same way. So, every node accomplishes exactly the same functionality as the other. Uniform protocols can be sub-divided into Flat and Geographical Information-based routing protocols. The geographical information-based protocols proposed to date are mostly uniform except for the zone-based hierarchical link state (ZHLS) [3] and scalable location update routing protocol (SLURP) [4] routing protocols, which are nonuniform routing protocols.

Flat Uniform Routing

In flat routing, nodes do not form a specific structure or hierarchy. Each node has similar roles. Nodes that are within the transmission range of each other form a connection, where the only limitations are determined by connectivity conditions or security constraints. The major advantage of this routing structure is that there are multiple paths between source and destination, which reduce traffic congestion and traffic bottlenecks in the network. Single points of failure in case of cluster head could lead to larger control overheads arising from network reconfiguration. Nodes in flat routing require significantly lower power for transmission in comparison to cluster heads [5].

Geographical Information Based Uniform Routing

In these types of protocols, the location of the nodes can be obtained by utilizing global positioning system (GPS); alternatively, the relative coordinates of nodes can be obtained by calculating the distance between the nodes and exchanging this information with neighbouring nodes. The distance between nodes can be estimated on the basis of incoming signal or time delays in direct communications [6]. The main advantage of this approach is that the protocols can improve routing performance and reduce control overheads by effectively utilizing location information. All the protocols in this category assume that all nodes know their positions and the network topology of nodes corresponds well with the geographical distance between them. The drawback of this approach is that its above mentioned assumptions are often not acceptable and location information may not be accurate at all times [7,8].

19.2.2.2 NonUniform Routing

In Nonuniform routing, the way of generating and/or replying to routing control messages may be different for different groups of nodes. In these protocols, only few nodes are involved in route computation. For instance, some nodes shall broadcast received routing requests, others shall not. Nonuniform protocols attempt to reduce routing overhead by reducing the number of nodes involved in route computation. Moreover, they have a cost introduced for maintaining a high-level structure complexity and use of complex algorithms. Nonuniform protocols can be logically sub-divided into Flat (based on neighbour selection) and Hierarchical routing.

Flat NonUniform Routing

In this routing approach, each node selects some subset of its neighbours to take a distinguished role in route computation and/or traffic forwarding. Each node makes its selection independently, and there is no negotiation between nodes to attain nodes consensus and the node's selection is not affected by nonlocal topology changes [9].

Hierarchical NonUniform Routing

In hierarchical routing protocols, the nodes organize themselves into groups, called clusters. Within each cluster, a cluster head or gateway node is selected which coordinates all the traffic in and out of their clusters. Routing between two nodes from different clusters is usually performed by their cluster heads. The depth of the network can vary from single to multiple levels depending upon the number of hierarchies. The advantage of this approach is that each node maintains route to its cluster head only, which means that routing overheads are much lower compared to flooding routing information through the network. However, these protocols require complex algorithms for the creation and reconfiguration of clusters in case of single point of failure by cluster heads. Along with that, there are significant overheads associated with maintaining clusters [5].

19.3   An Overview of the Most Common Ad Hoc Routing Protocols

In this section we give an overview of the protocols that are most widely and frequently used in existing work, illustrating key strength and weaknesses as indicated by the reviews described in [2,10,11]. The analysis of these protocols will be further discussed in Sect. 19.5.

19.3.1   Destination Sequence Distance Vector (DSDV)

Destination sequence distance vector (DSDV) is a proactive, uniform routing protocol [12]. It is an improved version of distributed Bellman-Ford (DBF) routing algorithm, which guarantees loop free routes. Each node maintains a RT that contains routes for and number of hops to all possible destinations in the network [9]. The path to destination is selected using the shortest path distance vector algorithm and each node periodically broadcasts RT updates throughout the network in order to maintain table consistency. Each entry is tagged with sequence number assigned by the destination in order to indicate the freshness of route and avoid the formation of routing loops. Sequence numbers are incremented each time a node sends an update. A route is considered to be more favourable if its sequence number is higher or in case of the routes with same sequence number, the one with shortest path would be considered. The availability of routes to all destinations at all times is the main advantage of this protocol as less delay will be involved in the route setup process. However, periodic updates and updates due to broken links in high mobility lead to a large amount of overhead. Therefore, this protocol will not scale well in large networks; even a small network with high mobility can block the network.

19.3.2   Wireless Routing Protocol (WRP)

Wireless routing protocol (WRP) is a proactive uniform type protocol [13]. It is an advanced version of DBF and also guarantees loop-free routing similar to DSDV, but differs from DSDV in terms of table maintenance and update mechanisms.

WRP requires each node to maintain four RTs, i.e., distance table (DT), RT, link cost table (LCT) and a message retransmission list (MRL). This requires a significant amount of memory and greater processing power from each node for the maintenance of these tables. In contrast to DSDV, WRP periodically exchanges a simple HELLO packet, rather than exchanging the whole table even when there is no link change. In case of link changes, only information that reflects the updates is sent. To improve reliability, every neighbour is required to send acknowledgements with respect to update packet received. Retransmissions are sent if no positive acknowledgements are received within a given timeout period. This avoids temporary loops by using predecessor information [14]. When there is no recent packet transmission, hello messages are exchanged between nodes. This requires each node to stay active all the times (i.e., they cannot enter into sleep mode to save their power), which consumes a large amount of bandwidth and battery power. Control overheads involved in WRP are comparable to those of DSDV, which makes it unsuitable for highly dynamic and large networks.

19.3.3 Source Tree Adaptive Routing (STAR)

Source tree adaptive routing (STAR) is a proactive, uniform routing protocol [15]. It is a variation of other table-driven routing protocols that attempt to provide feasible paths that are not guaranteed to be optimal, but involve much less control overhead using the least overhead routing approach (LORA). This approach reduces the average control overhead as compared to other proactive protocols by eliminating the periodic updating procedures, making update dissemination conditional. In STAR, every node maintains source-tree information, which consists of a set of wireless links of preferred paths to destination used by nodes [2]. STAR can scale very well due to its reduced consumption of bandwidth by routing updates. However, maintaining source tree information at each node may result in significant memory and processing overheads in large and highly dynamic networks, since the source tree may change frequently as the neighbours keep reporting different source trees.

19.3.4 Distance Routing Effect Algorithm for Mobility (DREAM)

Distance routing effect algorithm for mobility (DREAM) is a proactive, location-based routing protocol [16]. In DREAM, the data are partially flooded to nodes laying in the direction of destination, using location information to limit the flood of data packets to a small region. Nodes are required to periodically broadcast their physical location to inform all other nodes. Nearby nodes are updated more frequently than far away nodes. The RT maintains the co-ordinates of the nodes instead of route vectors. Therefore, it consumes significantly less bandwidth than exchanging complete link-state or distance-vector information. DREAM adjusts to network dynamics by making the frequency at which update messages are disseminated proportional to mobility and to the distance effect. Therefore, stationary nodes do not need to send any update messages, which results in reduced routing overhead.

19.3.5 Fisheye State Routing (FSR)

Fisheye state routing (FSR) is a proactive, non-uniform routing protocol [17, 18], employing a link-state routing algorithm. To reduce the overhead incurred by periodic link-state packets, FSR modifies link-state routing in the following three ways:

1. Link-state packets are no longer flooded – instead, only neighbouring nodes exchange the topology table information
2. The link-state exchange is solely time-triggered and not event-triggered
3. Instead of periodically transmitting the entire link-state information, FSR uses different exchange intervals for different types of entries in the topology table

Link-state entries corresponding to nodes within a predefined distance (scope) are propagated to neighbours more frequently (intra updates) than entries of nodes outside the scope (inter updates). FSR is suitable for large and highly mobile network environments as it triggers no control messages on link failures. Broken links will not be included in the next link state message exchange. This means that a change on a far away link does not necessarily cause a change in the RT. However, scalability comes with a price of reduced accuracy because as mobility increases, the route to remote destinations becomes less accurate.

There are the four following configuration parameters for FSR, the value of which depends on factors, such as mobility, node density and transmission range:

1. Size of the scope: This parameter specifies the scope radius of a node in number of hops.
2. Time-out for the neighbouring nodes: If a node does not hear from a neighbour specified by this value, the neighbour node will be deleted from the neighbour list.
3. Intra scope update interval: Update interval of sending the updates of the nodes within the scope radius.
4. Inter scope update interval: Update interval of sending the updates of the nodes outside the scope radius.

19.3.6 Ad Hoc On-Demand Distance Vector (AODV)

The ad hoc on-demand distance vector (AODV) routing protocol is a type of on-demand (reactive) protocol based on DSDV [19, 20]. AODV and DSDV share the same on-demand characteristics of DSR and use the same discovery process to find routes when required. AODV uses the periodic beaconing and sequence numbering procedure of DSDV, but minimizes the number of required broadcasts by creating routes on demand, as opposed to maintaining a complete list of routes as in DSDV [2].

There are two major differences between AODV and DSR. AODV uses a traditional RT with one entry per destination, whereas DSR maintains multiple route cache entries for each destination. Another difference is that AODV relies on RT entries to propagate route replies back to the source and subsequently to route data packets to their destination. Along with that, AODV uses sequence numbers carried by all routing packets to determine the freshness of routing information and prevent routing loops. Therefore, its connection setup delay is smaller.

One of the disadvantages of AODV is that intermediate nodes can lead to inconsistent routes if the source's sequence number is very old and the intermediate nodes have a higher (but not the latest) destination sequence number, thereby having stale entries. Also multiple RouteReply packets in response to a single RouteRequest packet can lead to heavy control overheads, thereby introducing extra delays as the size of network increases. Another shortcoming is that periodic beaconing leads to unnecessary bandwidth consumption.

19.3.7   Dynamic Source Routing (DSR)

Dynamic source routing (DSR) is an on-demand routing protocol based on the concept of source routing [21–23]. Mobile nodes are required to maintain route caches that contain the source routes of which the mobile is aware. The route cache entries are continually updated as new routes are learned. The protocol consists of two main phases: route discovery and route maintenance. When a node wants to send a packet to destination, it first checks its route cache to determine whether it already has a valid route to the destination. If it has a valid route to the destination, it will use that route to send the packet. Otherwise, it initiates a route discovery process by broadcasting a route request packet.

Maintaining a route cache is highly beneficial for networks with low mobility as in this way, routes will be valid for a longer period. In addition, the route cache information can also be utilized by intermediate nodes to efficiently reduce control overheads. However, the broken links are not locally repaired by route maintenance mechanism, which is a disadvantage of this protocol. Along with that, stale route cache information could also result in variations during the route reconstruction phase. The connection setup delay is higher than in table-driven protocols. The protocol performs better with static nodes and slow moving nodes, but its performance degrades rapidly with increase in mobility. Also, due to the source routing mechanism, adapted in DSR results in considerable routing overhead.

19.3.8   Temporally Ordered Routing Algorithm (TORA)

Temporally ordered routing algorithm (TORA) is a reactive, uniform routing protocol [24]. It is highly adaptive, loop-free distributed routing algorithm based on a link reversal algorithm. TORA is specially designed to discover routes reactively, provides multiple routes to a destination, establish routes quickly and minimize communication overheads by localizing algorithmic reaction to topological changes when possible. Route optimality (shortest path routing) is considered to be of secondary importance, and longer routes are usually used to avoid the overhead of discovering newer routes [25]. This increases the reliability of the protocol. Nodes use a "height" metric to establish a directed acyclic graph (DAG) rooted at the destination during route creation and maintenance phases. The process of establishing a DAG is similar to the query/reply process used in light-weight mobile routing (LMR) [26]. Also, the link reversal and route repair procedures are the same as in LMR. The advantage of TORA is that it supports multicasting. One of its disadvantages is that it may produce temporary invalid routes.

19.3.9   Associativity-Based Routing [5]

Associativity-based routing (ABR) is a uniform source initiated-based reactive routing protocol [27]. In ABR, routes are established based on the degree of association stability of the mobile nodes. Here association is referred to a spatial, temporal and connectivity relationship of a mobile host with its neighbours. Associativity is measured by recording the number of control beacons received by a node from its neighbours. For each beacon received, the associativity tick of the current node with respect to the beaconing node is incremented. Associativity ticks are reset when the neighbours of a node or the node itself move out of proximity [28]. The advantage of ABR is that routes tend to live longer. Therefore, fewer route reconstructions are needed and hence, more bandwidth remains available for data transmission. The disadvantage of this protocol is that it requires periodic beaconing to determine the associativity of the links; therefore, all nodes are required to be alive all the time, which may result in additional power consumption. Another disadvantage is that alternative routes are not readily available as ABR does not maintain multiple routes or route caches. However, its localized route discovery procedure compensates to some degree for not having multiple routes.

19.3.10   Location Aided Routing [29]

Location aided routing (LAR) is analogous to on-demand routing protocols such as DSR, but it uses location information to reduce routing overheads [30, 31]. LAR assumes that each node knows its physically location by using GPS. GPS information is used to restrict the flooded area of route request packets. In [31], two different schemes are proposed. In Scheme 1, the source defines a circular area in which the destination may be located. The position and size of the circle are decided based on the location, speed and time instance of the destination. The smallest rectangular area that includes this circle and the source is the request zone. This information is attached to a route request by the source and only nodes inside the request zone propagate the packet. In Scheme 2, the source calculates the distance between the destination and itself. The source includes the distance and location of destination in route request and sent it to neighbours. When neighbour nodes receive this packet, they compute their distance to the destination and relay the packet only if their distance to destination is less than or equal to the distance indicated by the packet. When forwarding the packet, the node updates the distance field with its distance to destination. In both schemes, if no Route Reply is received within the timeout period, the source retransmits a route request via pure flooding [14]. The major advantages of LAR are an efficient use of geographical position information, reduced control overhead and increased utilization of bandwidth. The disadvantage is that each node must support GPS.

19.3.11 Cluster-Based Routing Protocol (CBRP)

Cluster-based routing protocol (CBRP) is an on-demand, hierarchical nonuniform routing protocol [32]. In CBRP, nodes are organized in a hierarchy and form clusters. Each cluster has a cluster-head that knows the addresses of its cluster members. Cluster head co-ordinates the data traffic within the cluster and with/to other clusters. Broadcasting route requests to the cluster head are equivalent to broadcasting route requests to every node in the network. Each node is required to keep the cluster adjacency table and neighbour table, which also contain link type. CBRP uses a simple cluster formation strategy in which the cluster diameter is only two hops, with a cluster-head in each cluster. Clusters can overlap, but each node must be a part of at least one cluster [33]. The advantage is that only cluster heads exchange routing information and therefore, the control overhead is much less than the traditional flooding methods. However, there are overheads associated with cluster formation and maintenance. Another disadvantage is that in CBRP, some nodes may have inconsistent topology information due to long propagation delay, which may result in routing loops.

19.4 Mobile Ad Hoc Routing Protocol Requirements and Performance Evaluation Metrics

Due to the highly dynamic nature of MANETs, designing suitable ad hoc routing protocols are a challenging issue. The ultimate goal of an ad hoc routing protocol is to provide proper, efficient and effective route establishment among nodes, so that messages may be delivered in a reliable and timely manner. Route construction and maintenance should be done with minimum overhead and bandwidth consumption.

Many routing protocols have been proposed since the conception of MANETs, mainly focusing on solving specific issues and under particular ad hoc scenarios. To achieve the required efficiency, routing protocols for MANETs must satisfy special characteristics. Important characteristics are identified by the Internet engineering task force (IETF) MANET Charter in RFC 2501 [34]. These will be discussed in the next subsection.

The research goal of the IETF MANET charter group is to concentrate on standardization of functionalities of routing protocols for both static and mobile wireless applications. Several IETF MANET Internet drafts have been produced so far, but only two proactive routing protocols, namely optimized link state routing (OLSR) [35] and topology dissemination based on reverse-path forwarding (TBRPF) [36] and two reactive routing protocols, namely AODV and DSR, have reached a reasonable level of development in terms of analytical studies and prototyping [37]. In the following two subsections, the requirements of an ideal ad hoc routing protocol and some common metrics to evaluate a performance of an ad hoc routing protocol identified by the IETF MANET charter group will be discussed, which can give a better understanding of strengths and weakness of a protocol.

19.4.1   Characteristics of Ad Hoc Routing Protocols

The fundamental characteristics of mobile ad hoc routing protocols are exemplified below.

- *Distributed routing*: Routing protocols must be fully distributed, as this approach is more fault tolerant than centralized routing.
- *Adaptive to topology changes*: Routing must adapt to frequent topological and traffic changes that result from node mobility and link failure.
- *Proactive/reactive operation*: The routing algorithm may intelligently discover the routes on demand. This approach will be useful to efficiently utilize the bandwidth and energy resources, but comes with the cost of additional delay. However, in certain conditions, the delay incurred by on-demand operation would be unacceptable.
- *Loop free routing*: Routes free from loops and stale paths are desirable. Perhaps to increase robustness, multiple routes should be available between each pair of nodes.
- *Robust route computation and maintenance*: The smallest possible number of nodes must be involved in the route computation and maintenance process, to result in minimum overhead and bandwidth consumption.
- *Localized state maintenance*: To avoid propagation of overheads, localized state maintenance is desirable.
- *Optimal usage of resources*: The efficient utilization and conservation of resources such as battery power, bandwidth, computing power and memory are required.
- *Sleep mode operations*: To reduce energy consumption, the routing protocol should be able to employ some form of sleep mode operation. Nodes that are inactive should switch to "sleep mode" for arbitrary periods.
- *Quality of Service*: Routing algorithms are required to provide certain levels of QoS in order to meet specific application requirements.

- *Security*: Some form of security protection is desired to prevent disruption due to malicious modifications of protocol operations.

In the next subsection, we will discuss the metrics that can analyze the performance of protocols with respect to the characteristics mentioned above.

19.4.2 Performance Evaluation Metrics

To evaluate the performance of a routing protocol, it is necessary to have some common metrics to assess the level of efficiency, scalability and adaptability. These metrics should be independent of the context. A protocol can be evaluated in different ways and from various angles, depending on the metrics adopted. Effective metrics identified by IETF MANE charter group are listed below:

- Packet delivery ratio/packet loss rate.
- End-to-end throughput.
- End-to-end delay.
- Routing/control overhead (can be measured in number of bits or packets).
- Hop Count.
- Route Acquisition time.

These metrics can be evaluated in terms of the following changing network conditions. Changing any of these factors can affect the protocols' behaviour:

- Mobility – node speed expressed in metres per second (m/s).
- Network size – number of nodes.
- Traffic flow/traffic patterns – the rate at which packets are transmitted, measured in packets per second (pkts/s).
- Network connectivity – average node degree, i.e., the average number of neighbours of a node.
- Topological rate of change – the speed at which network topology changes.
- Link capacity – bandwidth, measured in bits per second (bps).
- Traffic load – number of sources and average traffic injected by each source.
- Fraction and frequency of sleeping nodes – percentage of sleeping and awakening nodes.

In Sect. 19.5, we will look at the work done in literature to assess different protocols (defined in Sect. 19.3) performance with some of the metrics discussed above.

19.5 Performance Analysis Based on Existing Literature

In recent years, a variety of routing protocols for MANETs have been proposed. However, the analysis of existing systems is often restricted to specific scenarios and fails to identify the protocol limitations and causes. A good review is provided in [10, 11]. Many other articles provide a protocol assessment, which is specific and often does not allow drawing general conclusions. For brevity we mention below the most significant articles, dividing them into three groups.

19.5.1   Approaches Based on Varying Pause Time and Traffic Load

The first attempt to analyze the performance of ad hoc routing protocols was made by Samir et al. in which DSDV, AODV, DSR and TORA were evaluated over a network of 30 nodes in an area of $1,000\,\text{m} \times 1,000\,\text{m}$, considering varying number of conversations per node (traffic flow) and speed in two different scenarios. In lower speed scenario, the speed was uniformly distributed between 0.4 and 0.6 m/s. At higher speed scenario, speed was uniformly distributed between 3.0 and 4.5 m/s. The evaluation was based on packet delivery ratio, end-to end delay and routing load. The mobility model adopted was based on a discrete-event framework. Each node chooses a direction, speed and distance of move based on a predefined distribution and then computes its next position accordingly.

The authors found that DSDV provides excellent performance by delivering almost 100% packets at around 6 ms delay. However, this is countered by a high routing overhead. AODV and DSR performance was comparable in all scenarios. However, at lower speeds, DSR introduces a smaller routing load than AODV. Per contra, at higher speeds, the result was reversed [38, 39].

Broch et al. investigated packet delivery ratio, routing overhead and path optimality of DSDV, AODV, DSR and TORA in a network of 50 and 60 nodes, considering varying pause time from 0 to 900 s, speeds of 1, 10 and 20 m/s, and an area of $1,500\,\text{m} \times 300\,\text{m}$ [25]. Similar work was done by Jiang et al. who investigated the amount of data delivered, control overhead and average latency of AODV, STAR and DSR over varying pause time in the range of 0–900 s and a network of 40 nodes with constant speed of 20 m/s, in an area of $4,000\,\text{m} \times 4,000\,\text{m}$ and $5,000\,\text{m} \times 3,000\,\text{m}$ [8]. The mobility model used in both cases was the random way point mobility model [40].

In the first case, the performance of DSR was better than all other protocols, for all values of pause time and mobility speed. This was achieved at the expense of higher routing overheads. AODV performs almost the same as DSR, but incurs lower routing overheads. DSDV performance is good at higher pause time between 100 and 900 s and lower mobility, but fails to converge as node mobility increases. TORA performance was the worst in all scenarios.

In the latter case in [8], the performance of all the protocols were almost similar in all scenarios and only minor differences were observed. However, STAR introduces less control overheads than others. The performance of all the protocols degrades at higher pause times, making them unable to delivery any data packet for values greater than 600 s.

Other work results from the same simulation setup, but analyzes different protocols. In [41] the authors investigate packet delivery fraction, average end-to-end delay, normalized routing load and normalized medium access control (MAC) load of DSR and AODV. On the other hand, Boukerche considers AODV, CBRP, DSR, DSDV and preemptive AODV (PAODV) [33]. The author adopts throughput, average end-to-end delay and routing overheads as evaluation metrics.

In both works, the simulation model was based on two different groups of experiments. The simulation model has 50 nodes over a 1,500 m × 300 m area in the first group of experiments and 100 nodes over 2,200 m × 600 m area in the second group of experiments, with varying pause time in the range of 0–800 s, constant speed of 20 m/s, along with number of sources varying from 10 to 40. The random way point mobility model was used for the simulations.

In [41], DSR outperforms AODV in terms of delay and throughput, but with smaller number of nodes and at a lower load and/or mobility speed, and generates less routing load. However, AODV outperforms DSR at higher load and mobility, but with a slightly higher routing overhead.

Whereas in [33], CBRP and DSR outperform all others in terms of higher throughput, but introduce higher delay. AODV comes next, but with a lower delay. However, DSR produces less routing overheads than CBRP and AODV. DSDV performance was worst among all. PAODV performance was slightly better than AODV.

This first group of works carries out a performance comparison between proactive and reactive protocols by varying pause time or mobility at invariable network size. The pause time is varying in the range of 0–900 s, which reflects low mobility because after 100 s of pause-time, nodes become almost stationary.

It is worth noting that most of the above mentioned analyses were performed on high-density networks. An exception is represented by [8] in which nodes are sparsely connected. The results observed from all above research papers were slightly contradictory for few protocols. This is due to different scenario setups.

Overall, in some cases, DSDV performs better at higher pause time (more static conditions), but introduces larger overheads. DSR performance was satisfactory at lower mobility and load conditions. However, AODV performance was better under highly dynamic conditions with lower delay, but with more routing overhead. STAR performance was moderate. The performance of TORA observed was worst among all of these scenarios.

19.5.2 Approaches Based on Varying Mobility and/or Traffic Flow

In the second group of work, Johansson et al. focus on the evaluation of delay, throughput and routing overheads of DSDV, AODV and DSR in a network of 50 nodes, varying speed from 0 to 3.5 m/s and varying traffic flow from 5 to 20 pkts/s, in an area of 1,000 m × 1,000 m and a constant pause time of 1 s. The mobility model used in this case was proposed by the authors. Both AODV and DSR perform quite well in almost all scenarios, but DSDV performance degrades with the increase in mobility. However, DSR performs better than AODV at low traffic flow; at higher traffic flow, AODV was better [29].

A similar simulation setup was adopted by Camp et al., but with varying speed from 0 to 20 m/s [42], in which DSR, DREAM and LAR were analyzed by evaluating packet delivery ratio, average end-to end delay, data overhead, control overhead and total number of packets transmitted per data packets delivered. In this case, DSR and LAR achieve higher packet delivery ratio (at lower speeds), which decreases when speed increases.

DREAM was quite stable with increases in mobility. Similar results were observed at delay and at overheads for DREAM; at low mobility, these were higher than others, but remain constant with the increase in mobility. Delay introduced by DSR was higher than LAR and overheads generated by both were almost similar.

Lee et al. investigate five different protocols, WRP, FSR, DSR, LAR and DREAM on 50 nodes, varying speed from 0 to 20 m/s and an area of 750 m × 750 m. These protocols were evaluated by analyzing the packet delivery ratio, hop count, data overhead, control overhead, total number of packets transmitted per data packets delivered and varying traffic load. The results were observed in two different mobility models (random way point and group mobility model).

In case of random way point, DREAM performance was more promising at increasing speed, but with slightly higher overhead than LAR and DSR. LAR and DSR performance was better, but slightly degraded with mobility. FSR was found to be sensitive to mobility and its performance decreased with the increase in speed. WRP was unable to reach the same level of efficiency at higher mobility, as performance degraded significantly. Along with that, the overheads generated by FSR and WRP were also the highest among all. However, in the case of group mobility model, most performance factors gave comparable results, with the exception of DREAM. In the case of WRP, packet delivery ratio increased with mobility, instead of decreasing. LAR and DSR were still the best performing protocols [14, 28].

In almost all the work mentioned in this group, overall DSR, LAR and AODV outperform than others. DREAM performance was contradictory in different papers, but overall it was considered a reliable one. FSR comes next, performing better than WRP.

19.5.3   Approaches Based on Varying Number of Nodes

In the third group, Layuan et al. evaluate packet delivery ratio, end-to-end delay, data throughput, routing load, jitter and number of broken links in DSDV, AODV and TORA, by varying the number of nodes [43]. The nodes were randomly placed in a 1,000 m × 1,000 m area with constant speed of 40 m/s and pause time of 0 s. The throughput for AODV and DSR was higher and it was increasing with the number of nodes. Then comes DSDV which performed better than TORA, which was unaffected by changing number of nodes, but lower among all. The routing load for all protocols was increasing with the increase in number of nodes except for TORA. Delay produced by DSR was much higher with more nodes than any other protocol. However, the delay introduced by AODV and DSDV was very low than TORA.

In [44], we have made a comparison between AODV, DSR, FSR and LAR1. We evaluated the packet delivery ratio, average end-to-end delay, throughput and routing overhead by varying network size (from 10 to 50 nodes), mobility (from 1 to 21 m/s) and traffic flow (20–100% sources). The nodes were randomly placed in a 1,400 × 1,400 area. We placed particular care in choosing simulation parameters and their ranges to obtain four scenarios that complement existing studies.

The study shows that the performance of LAR was promising in almost all scenarios, but with a high end-to-end delay varying between 10 and 100 s. AODV was the second best performing protocol, but resulted to be more sensitive than the others to network size and traffic load. AODV performance is better than DSR for dynamic changing conditions. However, FSR performance was poor in all scenarios, which mainly depends on the scope of fisheye and the frequencies at which updates are sent.

19.6 Discussion

From the above discussion, it is clear that some protocols perform better under specific scenarios, but also exhibit significant drawbacks when simulation conditions vary considerably. In fact, the analysis of the same protocols performed by different authors often leads to contradictory results. In many cases, this is due to different simulation setups, the adoption of different mobility models or even the use of different simulation environments.

Some work is based on random node placements. Others adopt a uniform model with continuously moving nodes. In either cases, the topology changes randomly and unpredictably, which makes it difficult to replicate experiments and produce comparable results.

The analytical studies presented in the literature so far take into consideration mainly mobility, pause time, traffic flow, traffic load and network size. However some other evaluation network conditions are equally important, as identified by IETF MANET charter. The ones discussed in this chapter include network connectivity, link capacity, topological rate of change and fraction of sleeping nodes. An in-depth analysis based onthese factors should be the subject of future investigations, as this will most probably unveil new, noticeable effects on protocol behaviour. Referring back to Fig. 19.1, we see that a broad variety of protocols has been proposed to date. Nevertheless, only few of them have been studied in depth and very few have actually been prototyped, beyond the simulation stage. Addressing these shortcomings should be a priority in future work, along with a greater effort to achieve interoperability among different systems and eventually, some level of standardization.

19.7   Conclusion

This chapter provides a detailed analysis of different MANET routing protocols. We present a taxonomy that extends existing ones, identifying also key parameters, metrics and mechanisms for the classification and evaluation of routing in MANETs. After that, we use this classification to capture the state-of-the-art in the performance evaluation of the most significant routing approaches. This review leads to the identification of promising research issues beyond the study of new protocols. We come to the conclusion that there is also a need to improve simulation environments, design and assessment methodologies, allowing for the study of protocols under a broader range of parameters, factors and scenarios.

Abbreviations

ABR	Associativity-based routing
AODV	Ad hoc on-demand distance vector
CBRP	Cluster-based routing protocol
DAG	Directed acyclic graph
DBF	Distributed Bellman Ford
DREAM	Distance routing effect algorithm for mobility
DSDV	Destination sequence distance vector
DSR	Dynamic source routing
FSR	Fisheye state routing
GPS	Global positioning system
IETF	Internet engineering task force
LAR	Location aided routing
LMR	Light-weight mobile routing
LORA	Least overhead routing approach
MANET	Mobile ad hoc network
OLSR	Optimized link state routing
SLURP	Scalable location update routing protocol
STAR	Source tree adaptive routing
TBRPF	Topology dissemination based on reverse-path forwarding
TORA	Temporally ordered routing algorithm
WRP	Wireless routing protocol
ZHLS	Zone-based hierarchical link state

References

1. Jiang, S., et al., Provisioning of adaptability to variable topologies for routing schemes in MANETs. *IEEE Journal on Selected Areas in Communications* 2004;22(7):1347–1356.
2. Murthy, C.S.R. and B.S. Manoj, *Ad Hoc Wireless Networks, Architecture and Protocols*. Upper Saddle River, NJ: Prentice-Hall; 2004.

3. Joa-Ng, M. and I. Lu, A peer-to-peer zone-based two-level link state routing for mobile ad hoc networks. *IEEE Journal on Selected Areas in Communications* 1999;17(8):1415–1425.

4. Woo, S.-C.M. and S. Singh, Scalable routing protocol for ad hoc networks. *Wireless Networks* 2001;7(5):513–529.

5. Haas, Z.J. and S. Tabrizi, On some challenges and design choices in ad-hoc communications. In *Proceedings of IEEE Military Communications Conference (MILCOM 98)*. Boston, MA; 1998.

6. Stojmenovic, I., Position-based routing in ad hoc networks. *IEEE Communications Magazine* 2002;40(7):128–134.

7. Wu, J. (Ed.), *Handbook on Theoretical and Algorithmic Aspects of Sensor, Ad Hoc Wireless, and Peer-to-Peer Networks*. Boca Raton, FL: Auerbach Publications; 2006.

8. Jiang, H. and J.J. Garcia-Luna-Aceves, Performance comparison of three routing protocols for ad hoc networks. In *Proceedings of IEEE Twelfth International Conference on Computer Communications and Networks (ICCCN)*. Phoenix, Arizona; October 15–17, 2001.

9. Feeney, L.M., A taxonomy for routing protocols in mobile ad hoc networks. *SISC Technical Report*; 1999.

10. Royer, E.M. and C.-K. Toh, A review of current routing protocols ad hoc mobile wireless networks. *IEEE Personal Communications* 1999;6(2):46–55.

11. Abolhasan, M., T. Wysocki, and E. Dutkiewicz, A review of routing protocols for mobile ad hoc networks. *Ad Hoc Networks* 2003;2:1–22.

12. Perkins, C.E. and P. Bhagwat, Highly dynamic destination-sequenced distance-vector routing (DSDV) for mobile computers. In *Proceedings of ACM SIGCOMM's Conference on Communications Architectures, Protocols and Applications*. London; 1994.

13. Murthy, S. and J.J. Garcia-Luna-Aceves, An efficient routing protocol for wireless networks. *Mobile Networks and Applications* 1996;1(2):183–197.

14. Lee, S.J., et al., Selecting a routing strategy for your ad hoc network. In *Symposium on Applied Computing, Proceedings of the 2007 ACM symposium on Applied Computing*. Seoul, Korea: Elsevier; 2002.

15. Garcia-Luna-Aceves, J.J. and M. Spohn, Source-tree routing in wireless networks. In *Proceedings of the Seventh Annual International Conference on Network Protocols*. IEEE Computer Society; 1999.

16. Basagni, S., et al., A distance routing effect algorithm for mobility (DREAM). In *Proceedings of the 4th Annual ACM/IEEE International Conference on Mobile Computing and Networking*. Dallas, TX: ACM; 1998.

17. Pei, G., M. Gerla, and T.-W. Chen, Fisheye state routing: a routing scheme for ad hoc wireless networks. In *Proceedings of the IEEE International Conference on Communications*. New Orleans, LA; 2000, pp. 70–74.

18. Pei, G., M. Gerla, and T.-W. Chen, *Fisheye state routing: a routing scheme for ad hoc wireless networks*. IETF internet draft 2002. Available from: URL http://tools.ietf.org/html/draft-ietf-manet-fsr-03.

19. Perkins, C.E., E.M. Royer, and S.R. Das, *Ad hoc on demand distance vector (AODV) routing*. IETF Internet Draft 2003. Available from: http://www.ietf.org/rfc/rfc3561.txt.

20. Perkins, C.E. and E.M. Royer. Ad hoc on-demand distance vector routing (AODV). In *Proceedings of the 2nd IEEE Workshop on Mobile Computing Systems and Applications*. New Orleans, LA; 1999.

21. Johnson, D.B., D.A. Maltz, and J. Broch, DSR the dynamic source routing protocol for multihop wireless ad hoc networks. In C.E. Perkins (Ed.). *Ad Hoc Networking*. Reading, MA: Addison-Wesley; 2001.

22. J. Broch, D. Johnson, and D. Maltz. *The dynamic source routing protocol for mobile ad hoc networks*. IETF Internet draft 2003. Available from: http://www.cs.cmu.edu/~dmaltz/internet-drafts/draft-ietf-manet-dsr-09.txt.

23. Johnson, D.B. and D.A. Maltz, Dynamic Source Routing (DSR) in adhoc wireless networks. In K. Imielinski (Ed.). *Mobile Computing*. Dordrecht: Kluwer Academic Publishers; 1996.

24. Park, V.D. and M.S. Corson, A highly adaptive distributed routing algorithm for mobile wireless networks. In *Proceedings of the INFOCOM '97. Sixteenth Annual Joint Conference of the IEEE Computer and Communications Societies. Driving the Information Revolution*. IEEE Computer Society; 1997.

25. Broch, J., et al., A performance comparison of multi-hop wireless ad hoc network routing protocols. In *Proceedings of the 4th Annual ACM/IEEE International Conference on Mobile Computing and Networking*. Dallas, TX; 1998.
26. Corson, M.S. and E. Anthony, A distributed routing algorithm for mobile wireless networks. *Wireless Networks* 1995;1(1):61–81.
27. Chai-Keong, T., Associativity-based routing for ad hoc mobile networks. *Wireless Personal Communication* 1997;4(2):103–139.
28. Lee, S.-J., M. Gerla, and C.-K. Toh, A simulation study of table-driven and on-demand routing protocols for mobile ad hoc networks. *IEEE Network* 1999;13(4):48–54.
29. Johansson, P., T. Larsson, and N. Hedman, Scenario-based performance analysis of routing protocols for mobile ad-hoc networks. In *International Conference on Mobile Computing and Networking, Proceedings of the 5th Annual ACM/IEEE*. Seattle, Washington, DC: ACM; 1999, pp. 195–206.
30. Ko, Y.B. and N.H. Vaidya. Location-Aided Routing (LAR) mobile ad hoc networks. In *Proceedings of ACM/IEEE MOBICOM '98*. Dallas, TX; 1998.
31. Ko, Y.B. and N.H. Vaidya, Location Aided Routing (LAR) in mobile ad hoc networks. *Wireless Networks* 2000;6(4):307–321.
32. Jiang, M., J. Li, and Y. Tay, Cluster Based Routing Protocol (CBRP) Functional Specification. In *Internet Draft, draft-ietfmanet-cbrp-spec-00.txt*; 1998.
33. Boukerche, A., Performance evaluation of routing protocols for ad hoc wireless networks. *Mobile Networks and Applications* 2004;9(4):333–342.
34. Corson, S. and J. Macker, *Mobile Ad hoc Networking (MANET): Routing Protocol Performance Issues and Evaluation Considerations*. RFC Editor; 1999.
35. Clausen, T. and P. Jacquet, Optimized Link State Routing Protocol (OLSR). In *RFC 3626, IETF Network Working Group*; 2003.
36. Ogier, R., F. Templin, and M. Lewis, *Topology Dissemination Based on Reverse-Path Forwarding (TBRPF)*. RFC Editor; 2004.
37. Chakeres, I. and J. Macker. *IETF MANET working Group*. Available from: http://www.ietf.org/html.charters/manet-charter.html.
38. Das, S.R., R. Castañeda, and J. Yan, Simulation based performance evaluation of routing protocols for mobile ad hoc networks *Mobile Networks and Applications*. Springer Netherlands 2000;5(3):179–189.
39. Das, S.R., et al., Comparative performance evaluation of routing protocols for mobile ad hoc networks. In *Proceedings of 7th International Conference on Computer Communications and Networks (IC3N)*; 1998.
40. Christian, B., R. Giovanni, and S. Paolo, The node distribution of the random waypoint mobility model for wireless ad hoc networks. *IEEE Transactions on Mobile Computing* 2003;2(3):257–269.
41. Perkins, C.E., et al., Performance comparison of two on-demand routing protocols for ad hoc networks, *IEEE Personal Communication* 2001;8(1):16–28.
42. Camp, T., et al., Performance comparison of two location based routing protocols for ad hoc networks. In *Proceedings of IEEE INFOCOM 2002 (Twenty-First Annual Joint Conference of the IEEE Computer and Communications Societies)*; 2002, pp. 1678–1687.
43. Layuan, L., L. Chunlin, and Y. Peiyan, Performance evaluation and simulations of routing protocols in ad hoc networks. *Computer Communications* 2007;30(8):1890–1898.
44. Qadri, N.N. and A. Liotta, A comparative analysis of routing protocols for MANETs. In *IADIS International Conference on Wireless Applications and Computing (WAC 2008)*. Amsterdam, Netherlands; 2008.

Index

A

Actor-critic (AC), 16–18, 22–23
Adaptive, 3–25, 62, 107, 136–139, 147,
    152, 182, 185, 223, 265, 313–337,
    342, 370, 409, 411, 440, 442, 445
Ad hoc networks, 138, 433
Adversary, 386, 391, 393, 398–401
Agent, 20, 21, 107, 136, 138, 158, 163,
    181–197, 217, 223, 231–256, 259–284,
    383–402, 411
Algorithm, 15, 16, 18, 23, 30, 34, 41, 45,
    50–52, 55, 58, 71, 79, 82–86, 89, 94,
    109, 137, 140, 203, 204, 206–211, 213,
    223, 228, 244–251, 253, 254, 271, 273,
    279–281, 290–292, 303, 305–307, 309,
    313–316, 324–328, 331, 335, 337, 342,
    343, 380, 389–392, 406–408, 410, 411,
    414–419, 421–428, 434, 438–443, 445
Ambient, 181–197, 259
Analysis, 11, 29, 30, 41, 60, 98, 102–105, 147,
    159, 184, 223, 227, 235, 237–239, 241,
    242, 244, 245, 261, 313, 314, 337, 343,
    347, 352–362, 370, 372–374, 393–402,
    407, 411, 421–424, 433–451
Animation, 106, 107
Annotated BPEL, 292, 302
Annotated CTL, 292, 305
Annotated STS, 302
Annotation, 86, 90, 94, 289–310
Approximation spaces, 19–20
Architectures, 9, 10, 52, 91, 92, 94, 99, 107,
    128, 136, 140–147, 152, 158, 161–164,
    167, 173, 177, 178, 181–183, 185, 187,
    188, 197, 203–205, 211, 222, 231–256,
    259–284, 314, 315, 337, 343, 369, 370,
    373, 376–378, 383, 389, 406, 410, 411
Artificial, 82, 84, 158, 167, 210, 236, 317
Assertion, 291, 292, 295–307
Assurance, 369–370, 381

Asymmetric, 322–324, 434
Augmented, 97–113, 136, 139, 141
Augmented reality, 97, 106, 107, 136
Authenticity, 384, 386, 389, 396, 402
Automatic, 4–11, 13, 14, 31, 49, 158, 160, 162,
    166, 170, 172–174, 179, 182, 189, 190,
    202, 203, 207, 217, 228, 238, 243, 256,
    260, 261, 273, 274, 276, 281, 282, 289,
    292, 309, 310, 321, 336, 393, 402, 409
Automotive, 173–176

B

Bandwidth, 48, 49, 53, 55–58, 60, 61, 66, 72,
    138, 139, 148, 150, 151, 166, 179, 202,
    203, 206–210, 212, 213, 226, 341, 343,
    345, 347, 369–371, 373, 374, 379, 406,
    414, 434, 440, 442–446
Bayesian networks, 158, 167–169, 174, 178,
    207
Behavior, 3, 138, 139, 406–407, 411
B-frames, 350
Binarization, 79, 87, 89
Biologically-inspired, 3, 4, 6, 16
Body machine interface, 99, 112
Breach of privacy, 395
Broadcast, 48, 53, 79, 80, 82, 86, 90, 92, 94,
    165, 204, 211, 212, 216–218, 228, 345,
    368, 371, 378, 409, 439–442, 444
Browser, 163, 172–174
Browsing, 77–84, 369
Business Process Execution Language (BPEL),
    290–295, 298, 300–302, 309, 310

C

Categorization, 207, 333
CAVELib, 106

Centralized, 51, 60, 62, 161, 224, 225, 238, 343–349, 354–356, 358, 359, 362, 408, 434, 445

Checksum, 387

Classifier, 228, 234, 240, 243–251, 254–256

Client, 4, 6, 9, 11, 13, 23, 52–54, 140–148, 150–151, 161, 172, 174, 234, 242, 275, 342–347, 349, 353–354, 362, 370–373, 375, 376, 378, 406, 408

Coding, 51, 137, 138, 238, 342, 343, 345, 349–352, 356, 362, 371, 408

Cognitive impairments, 3

Coindesigner, 106, 107

Collected offers, 384, 391, 398, 400–402

Colluding attack, 386, 394

Communication, 48, 118, 124, 129, 131, 138, 144, 163, 178, 181–183, 185, 186, 188–190, 192, 202, 203, 206–211, 216, 218–221, 226, 228, 232, 233, 235, 238–242, 260–263, 265–268, 270–274, 276, 277, 279, 282, 283, 341, 342, 373, 391, 401, 406, 410, 411, 428, 433, 434, 438, 443

Competing host, 391, 401

Computational intelligence, 9, 50

Computation Tree Logic (CTL), 291–293, 303, 305, 306, 310

Computing, 3–25, 98, 117–133, 135–152, 158, 201–229, 236, 262, 289–310, 314, 316, 320, 330, 433

Concept assertion, 295, 296, 298, 301, 303

Confidentiality, 232, 234, 235, 264, 369, 384–386, 402

Configuration, 8, 33, 34, 36, 70, 103, 142, 143, 190, 240, 250, 393–395, 397, 398, 402, 437–439, 441

Congestion controllers, 58–60, 72

Content, 49, 77, 78, 82, 90, 94, 101, 108, 118, 129, 133, 144, 158, 160, 162, 167, 172–174, 176–178, 241, 264, 342, 345, 349, 368–371, 375, 386, 406–408, 413, 414, 416

Context, 6, 12, 15, 16, 18, 78, 80, 86, 98, 158–174, 176, 178, 182, 208, 228, 262–264, 266, 273, 283, 309, 314–317, 319–324, 330, 332–335, 369, 370, 379, 381, 446

Context-aware, 157–179, 183, 185, 188–190, 193, 265, 278, 314

Control, 4, 7, 13, 29–73, 98, 100–102, 107, 109–113, 125, 126, 137, 138, 162, 166, 174, 186, 190, 192, 202, 203, 205, 207, 210–213, 216, 217, 220, 224–226, 228, 234–236, 240, 248, 260, 265, 273,

274, 276, 278, 280–282, 290, 292, 324, 327, 342, 343, 345, 347, 349, 383, 406, 408, 410, 437, 438, 440–444, 446–449

Convergence, 214, 248, 283, 365, 366, 381, 407, 414, 416, 421–424

Cooltown, 160

Co-operating agents, 20, 384, 389, 401

Creativity, 118–120, 133

D

Databases, 88, 143, 160, 166, 186, 231–256, 261, 275, 279, 406

Data-fusion, 105, 224, 316

Decentralized, 289, 343–349, 356–358, 360–362, 409

Decisions, 21, 22, 50, 138, 147–148, 151, 152, 188, 209, 232, 254, 256, 391, 401

Deformation, 101–103, 202, 204, 207, 220

Degree of freedom (DOF), 8, 29–33, 35, 37–39, 41, 42, 99, 101, 103, 109, 110

Description logic, 290–292, 295, 301, 303

Descriptors, 163–165

Destination, 212, 214, 347, 435, 437, 439–444

Detecting, 81, 92, 224, 231–256, 280, 368, 400, 402

Detection vector, 87

Digitized, 342

Direct, 48, 137, 168, 194, 196, 252, 275, 296, 380, 384, 410, 413, 416, 438

Distance, 15, 31, 83, 106, 113, 144, 206, 210, 213, 214, 327, 335, 336, 409, 412, 438–441, 444, 447

Distractors, 11–13, 15

Distributed, 47, 135, 137–139, 152, 161, 162, 181–197, 203, 232–235, 238–240, 251, 252, 255, 261, 265, 266, 283, 289, 342, 343, 345, 362, 405–411, 423, 424, 439, 442, 445, 447, 451

Domotics, 173–176

Drift, 109, 222, 343, 350, 351, 353, 355, 358

Dynamic data, 385, 386, 389, 391

E

Efficiency, 79, 85, 145, 158, 168, 184, 186, 190, 193, 197, 206, 207, 211, 232, 251, 256, 260, 262, 350, 369, 384, 400–402, 406, 409–411, 444, 446, 449

Elastometer, 101

Engine, 91, 107, 108, 143, 146, 164, 165, 171, 173, 174, 304, 314, 315, 317, 324–327, 345

Environment, 3–25, 31, 41, 98–101, 105–108,
    111, 112, 118, 123, 127, 128, 135–152,
    157–179, 181–185, 188–190, 193, 197,
    201–203, 206–208, 210, 211, 213, 215,
    216, 220–222, 225, 231–233, 235, 236,
    238, 240, 243, 251, 252, 256, 259–267,
    269, 272–274, 277–284, 292, 313, 314,
    319, 320, 330, 343, 368, 369, 373, 376,
    377, 380, 383, 407, 408, 413, 414, 428,
    434, 441, 450
Erroneous credit, 384
Ethical approval, 109
Ethogram, 3, 4, 6, 15–17, 21, 22
Ethology, 3, 6, 15–16
e-Vital, 261
Executing host, 391–393, 395, 401
Execution result, 384–387, 398
Execution trace, 391, 402, 424
Extraction text, 79, 86–90

F
Fabric, 101
Failure, 123, 124, 137, 188, 209–211, 215, 217,
    239, 241, 291, 295, 300–302, 305–307,
    342, 358, 367, 370, 437, 439, 441, 445
Filter, 165–166
Fisheye state routing (FSR), 441, 449, 450
Formal verification, 394–398
Frames, 16, 42–44, 49–54, 62, 63, 65, 80, 84,
    87, 89, 213, 215, 343, 349–362
Funnel, 121, 122, 133
Fuzzy, 49–52, 63, 64, 66, 70, 71, 89, 314, 315,
    317–319, 323, 324, 330, 336, 337
Fuzzy logic, 47–73, 314, 315, 317–319, 337

G
Game, 4, 6–8, 11–14, 16, 19, 23, 24, 136–138,
    146–152
Genetic, 79, 81–86, 94, 137, 271, 411, 428
Genetic algorithm (GA), 82, 83, 85, 86, 94,
    137–138, 271, 411, 425, 428
Geochemical, 202
Geophysical, 202
Global positioning system (GPS), 202, 204,
    207, 209, 220–224, 438, 443, 444
Grounding, 290–292, 305–309

H
Hierarchical modeling, 108
Heuristic, 137, 138, 316, 317, 320, 321, 323,
    324, 333, 411, 414–424

Home care, 259–284
Hosts, 62, 342, 371, 383–387, 389–402, 406,
    407, 412, 416, 434, 443
Hotel rooms, 118, 119, 130–131
Hybrid, 107, 132, 259–284, 437
Hydrogen, 161

I
Identification, 131, 190, 235, 243, 260, 266,
    272–274, 278, 282, 284, 373, 434, 451
Impersonation, 392
Incremental, 79, 82, 120–121
Indexation, 86–91, 94
Inference, 158, 166, 167, 171, 172, 176, 303,
    314, 315, 317, 321, 324, 328, 335–337
Initiating host, 385, 389, 391
Initiator, 384–387, 389–392, 395–402
Innovation, 117, 119–121, 123–124, 133
Integrity, 186, 232, 252, 369, 384, 386, 387,
    401, 402
Intelligence, 9, 50, 82, 98, 114, 153, 158, 167,
    180–197, 210, 236, 259, 260, 283, 369,
    383, 405–428
Intelligent, 29–46, 79, 117–133, 136, 181–185,
    231, 241, 259–261, 265, 266, 313, 314,
    337, 445
Intelligent multimedia, 117–133
Intelligent systems, 79, 131–132, 183
Intelligent video summarization, 79
Interaction, 99–101, 105, 110, 113, 137–139,
    142, 147, 150–152, 158, 159, 173, 179,
    181, 188, 192, 193, 197, 212, 213,
    238–240, 261, 262, 267, 272, 279, 293,
    368, 369
Interfaces, 8, 62, 90, 91, 98, 99, 106, 136, 139,
    141, 161, 165, 172, 179, 189, 192–195,
    211, 213, 222, 236, 240, 252, 261, 270,
    290, 292, 293, 295, 309, 368
Interoperability, 91, 106, 137, 185, 265, 289,
    366–368, 450
Intruder, 384, 393–395, 397, 398, 400, 401
Itinerary, 384–387, 390, 391, 393, 397–401

K
Key-frames, 80

L
Learning, 3, 4, 6, 9, 14–23, 79, 107, 182, 210,
    233, 236–239, 243, 245, 248, 255, 337, 411
Lightweight, 192, 204, 208, 313, 324, 327, 335
Linguistic, 54, 55, 317, 323
Lycra, 101

M

Major agent, 389, 390

Malicious host, 384, 386, 391, 393, 395, 397, 400, 401

Malicious tampering, 391

Management, 50, 108, 137, 139, 158, 161, 164–165, 168, 169, 202–208, 211–213, 215, 226, 234–236, 260, 266, 267, 269, 278, 282–284, 345, 370, 380, 381, 407, 408

Manipulators, 29–46

Man-machine, 97

Markovian Gilbert model, 352

Matlab, 34, 64, 92, 100, 101

Memory maps, 98

Middleware, 158, 163, 207, 208, 410, 411

Migrating agent, 390, 391

Mining, 184, 234, 271, 277, 313–315, 324–329, 335–337, 413

Mismatch, 171, 408

Mitsubishi Movemaster manipulator, 35, 38, 40

MoBe, 157, 162–166, 172, 173, 177

Mobile, 29–46, 49, 50, 61, 72, 78, 100, 126, 131, 135–152, 157, 158, 162–165, 167, 170–174, 176–179, 182, 184, 186, 188, 189, 192, 193, 231–233, 236, 238–242, 251, 260–262, 264, 266, 267, 270, 274–279, 282, 313–315, 326, 337, 366–381, 383, 384, 386–388, 393, 394, 398, 401, 402, 433–451

Mobile agent, 158, 184, 239, 241, 242, 383, 384, 386–388, 393, 401, 402

Mobility, 30, 41, 48, 113, 137, 182, 183, 189, 190, 233, 238, 262, 366–367, 369, 381, 434, 439–442, 445–450

Model checking, 292, 293, 305–308, 402

Modeling, 51, 107, 108, 409, 412

Money fritter, 384

Monitoring, 132, 162, 166, 183, 184, 190, 195, 197, 201–229, 235, 237, 251, 260, 261, 277, 282, 283, 314, 316, 327, 336, 337, 407

Motion, 7, 8, 10, 11, 29, 31, 41, 43, 45, 49, 53, 56, 57, 72, 124, 131, 137, 273, 314, 350, 353

Motion sensor, 8, 10, 314

MPEG-4, 108

MPEG7, 90–91, 94

Multiagent, 232, 233, 238–242, 251, 255, 256, 259–284

Multicast, 212, 218, 272, 342, 345, 443

MultihopLQI, 213–215, 217

Multimedia, 49, 58, 60, 61, 65, 90, 91, 99, 108, 117–133, 138, 158, 162, 168, 173, 176–179, 262, 341, 342, 345, 346, 366, 367, 370, 408

Multimedia data, 99, 346

Multiple-access, 49, 62, 206

Museum, 162, 176

N

National Instruments, 100–102

Navigation, 98, 100, 105, 109–111, 141–144, 146, 150, 151

Neighbor, 405–428

Network, 4, 25, 47–73, 88, 135, 136, 138–144, 146, 147, 150, 152, 158, 159, 161, 164–171, 174–176, 178, 184, 190, 192, 202–213, 215–218, 220, 221, 223–225, 229, 232, 233, 237, 239, 240, 242–245, 247, 248, 250, 251, 253, 254, 256, 260–266, 271, 272, 277, 314, 341–343, 345–347, 349, 358, 362, 365–376, 380, 381, 405–428, 433–435, 437–442, 444, 446–448, 450

Networking, 48, 139, 225, 434

Neural, 88, 138, 233, 237, 239, 240, 243–251, 253, 254, 256, 271

Neural network, 88, 138, 233, 239, 240, 243–251, 253, 254, 256, 271

News broadcast, 79, 80, 82, 86, 90, 92, 94

Notation, 17, 18, 326, 389, 390, 393, 394

NuSMV, 293, 305, 307, 308

O

Object-movement, 24

Ontologies, 9, 158, 171, 178, 290–292, 295–297, 300–302, 304, 309

Open inventor, 107

Open inventor scene graphs (OISG), 106, 108

Optimization, 31, 137, 138, 209, 218–220, 342, 368, 405–408, 413, 425, 428

Optimized, 202, 212, 213, 227, 303, 305, 362, 445

P

Packet, 48–53, 56–58, 60, 62–69, 72, 100, 203–205, 208–210, 212–217, 219, 220, 223, 225, 341–343, 352–354, 356–357, 369–371, 373–376, 378–380, 412, 435, 440–444, 446–450

Parameterized, 314, 315

Participants, 8, 99–101, 103, 105, 108, 109, 111–113, 283, 394, 395, 402, 406, 407, 409
Particle swarm optimization, 406, 407, 414, 415, 424, 425, 428
Patients, 4, 8–11, 19, 24, 102, 182–185, 193–197, 251, 261, 262, 274, 277, 279–284, 316, 335, 336
Perceptual granule, 3
Personalization, 166, 263, 264, 368
Pervasive, 3–25, 49, 97–113, 117–133, 135–152, 158, 173, 176–179, 201–229, 236, 262–264, 289–310, 314, 316, 317, 319, 320, 330, 365–381, 433–451
Pervasive computing, 3–25, 98, 117–133, 135–152, 158, 201–229, 236, 262, 289–310, 314, 316, 320, 330, 433
P-frames, 350, 353
Pictorial summaries, 78–80, 83, 86
Pipelined, 218–220
P2P, 341–362, 369–376, 378–380, 405–412, 414, 416, 424, 428
Preceding host, 386, 387, 393, 400
Prediction, 141, 145, 146, 150, 233, 237, 239, 243, 254, 256, 350, 353, 381
Preventing, 231–256, 400, 402
Principal component (PC), 92, 101, 109–111, 179, 192, 373
Prioritization, 207–210, 212, 213, 369
Privacy, 130, 158, 171, 179, 234, 369, 384, 387, 391, 395, 398
Processes, 86, 90, 118, 123, 132, 133, 143, 164, 178, 219, 228, 267–271, 273, 274, 289–310, 389, 393, 402, 425, 435
Program code, 387
Projection system, 105, 106
Protocol, 48, 51, 58–60, 62, 100, 181, 189, 192, 203, 206, 210, 211, 213, 214, 216–218, 221, 222, 236, 242, 260, 261, 265, 266, 270–272, 345, 347, 349, 372, 373, 376, 380, 384, 385, 387–402, 407–410, 433–451
Prototype, 4, 41, 42, 98, 101, 109, 122, 141, 142, 144, 146–148, 172–174, 176, 179, 203, 220, 233, 251, 410, 450
Puma 560 manipulator, 33–38

Q

Quality, 17, 48, 50, 51, 53, 54, 66, 69, 70, 72, 82, 94, 133, 136, 137, 145, 148, 150, 182, 183, 195, 204, 207, 211, 213, 215, 221, 237, 260, 264, 269, 272, 274, 277, 309, 342, 343, 346, 347, 351, 358, 362, 366, 367, 369–371, 375, 379, 380, 407–410, 445
Quality of experience (QoE), 365–381

R

Radical, 120–121
Rapid application development (RAD), 107
Real-time, 47, 50–52, 60, 101, 105, 110, 137–139, 152, 202–204, 206–208, 220–223, 267, 272, 313–315, 337, 341–343, 345, 349, 369, 370
Real-time streaming, 369
Real-time video streaming, 47
Reasoning, 158, 182, 185, 186, 188, 192, 193, 233, 237, 238, 246, 261, 278, 279, 282, 290, 292, 305, 309, 310, 314–317, 319–324, 329–331, 333–335, 337, 398–400
Reduction, 9, 71, 113, 196, 207, 213, 216, 283, 347, 370
Reinforcement, 4, 17–21
Reliable, 69, 72, 123, 183, 201, 202, 212, 216–218, 267, 345, 354, 369, 434, 444, 449
Remapping of the brain, 98
Rendering, 136, 139–141, 147, 148, 150–152, 371, 373
Resource, 47–73, 90, 121, 122, 137–139, 147, 148, 150–152, 158, 165, 166, 173, 184, 186–190, 197, 202, 208–210, 213, 216, 219–222, 224, 226, 235, 238, 239, 242, 265, 266, 279, 289, 314, 315, 324–330, 336, 337, 342, 370, 381, 383, 391, 406–411, 413, 434, 435, 437–439, 445
Resource-aware, 47–73, 324, 326–330
Retrieval, 81, 90, 92, 158, 160, 163, 165–166, 174, 179, 236, 262, 303, 411
Rheumatoid arthritis (RA), 4, 9–11, 13, 14, 19, 20, 24
Robotics, 30, 34, 41, 42, 45, 52, 107, 108, 131, 132, 182, 184
Robotics Interface Multi-agent System (RIMS), 107
Role assertion, 291, 292, 295–299, 301, 302, 304, 306, 307
Rough coverage, 16, 21–22
Rough sets, 19–21
Routing, 48, 202–204, 210–218, 270, 349, 408, 409, 414, 433–451
Rule-based, 158, 167–169, 174, 178

S

Scalable, 202, 203, 211, 270, 272, 275, 341–362, 406, 408, 409, 437
Scenario, 7, 142, 143, 158, 174, 176, 184, 206, 208, 214, 232, 251, 252, 261, 293, 300, 314, 335, 347, 349, 447, 448
Scene graph nodes, 108–109
Scene graphs, 108

Scheduling, 51, 60, 137, 138, 140, 184, 193,
    203, 206–209, 251, 262, 362
Search, 78, 86, 92, 137, 138, 164, 165, 173,
    178, 239, 293, 300–302, 384, 405–411,
    414–417, 420–422, 425, 428
Secondary agent, 389, 401
Security, 131, 132, 158, 179, 184, 186, 189,
    196, 197, 232–238, 240, 242, 251, 253,
    264, 266, 268–270, 273, 279, 281, 345,
    369, 381, 384, 385, 387–393, 395–402,
    437, 446
Security attack, 384, 401
Security breaches, 369, 384, 387, 388
Security properties, 384, 387, 393, 396–398,
    401, 402
Security tampering, 385
Security techniques, 384, 385, 387, 389–393,
    398–402
Segmentation, 87, 89
Selection, 17, 72, 79–82, 118, 131, 138, 166,
    207, 273, 289–292, 302, 304, 307, 309,
    378, 405–428, 435, 438
Self-organizing, 211, 212, 216, 411
Semantic, 9, 10, 81, 86, 94, 171, 213, 235, 238,
    241, 265, 289–310, 411
Semantic annotation, 289–310
Sensorized garment, 97–113
Sensors, 8–10, 42, 51, 97–113, 131, 132,
    136, 158, 162, 164, 165, 167, 168, 171,
    173, 174, 176, 186, 190, 192, 202–217,
    220–229, 236, 239, 241, 260–264, 266,
    270–272, 274, 277, 279–281, 283, 313,
    314, 316, 317, 319–322, 324, 333, 337
Sensor shirt, 100–105, 112, 113
Sequenced, 21, 72, 78–81, 92, 214, 219, 293,
    302, 303, 350, 355, 356, 369, 416, 423,
    424, 439, 441, 442
Server, 52, 53, 139–141, 143, 145–148, 151,
    163–165, 170, 174, 236, 238, 242, 261,
    342–347, 349, 353–355, 358, 362, 371,
    375, 378, 406, 408
Services, 8, 41, 48, 51, 117, 125–127,
    130–132, 136, 138, 151, 158, 160, 172,
    182–186, 188–190, 192, 197, 207, 210,
    211, 213, 227, 228, 234, 260–278, 280,
    282, 283, 289–310, 341, 342, 345, 347,
    349, 365–381, 384, 406–411, 413, 445
Signals, 7, 8, 48, 49, 51, 53, 54, 69, 98–103,
    109, 110, 137, 151, 190, 212, 213, 217,
    219, 220, 222, 223, 227, 261, 274, 345, 438
Simulation, 139, 141, 143–147, 272, 372, 409,
    410, 434, 448–451
Singular value decomposition (SVD), 31–34
Situation-aware, 313–337

Smart, 98, 99, 125, 136, 162, 202–205, 217,
    220, 221, 226, 240, 261, 263, 272, 313, 314
Social, 27, 120, 136, 137, 139, 159, 173,
    176–179, 233, 238, 251, 406–408, 411,
    416, 419
Source tree adaptive routing (STAR), 440, 447,
    448
Space tourism, 128–129
Sparkle, 161
Stability, 98, 100, 102–105, 137, 409, 443
State transition system (STS), 291–293, 296,
    298, 301, 302, 304–307
Static data, 385, 387
Stick-e Notes, 160
Stories, 69, 80–86, 90–94, 120, 123, 130
Streaming, 47–73, 79, 82, 221, 226, 341–362,
    369–372, 375, 376, 378–380, 410
Streams, 48–52, 56–58, 70, 72, 138–141, 146,
    165, 227, 313–337, 342, 343, 345, 347,
    349, 350, 355, 356, 358, 370, 378
Subgraphs, 108, 109
Succeeding host, 387, 391, 398, 400, 401
Supervised learning, 79
Swarming, 407
Symmetric, 321–324, 406
Synchronized, 53, 66, 72, 205, 207, 221–223

T
Telecommunications, 48, 50–52, 233, 365–381
Telegaming, 3–25
Telemedicine, 261
Television, 124, 370–372, 378–380
Text detection, 87–88
Text segmentation, 79, 89
Threat, 118, 232–238, 255, 384, 395, 398–400
Time, 13–17, 21, 47–54, 58, 60, 62, 63, 65–67,
    72, 78–81, 90, 98, 101–103, 105, 106,
    109, 110, 112, 123, 126, 127, 129, 135,
    137–139, 146, 148–152, 158–162, 166,
    170, 174, 177, 182, 184, 186, 188, 190,
    193, 195, 197, 202–204, 206–209, 212,
    214–217, 219–223, 225, 228, 231, 234,
    236, 237, 239, 240, 251, 253, 260, 267,
    269, 272, 274, 275, 277–280, 282, 283,
    290, 303, 304, 313–315, 321, 324, 327,
    328, 336, 337, 342, 343, 345, 349, 352,
    367, 369–372, 376, 378, 379, 387, 389,
    400, 401, 408, 410, 412, 413, 415, 416,
    420, 423, 434, 438, 439, 441, 443, 446–450
Tiny-dynamic, 208
Topology, 55, 56, 72, 202, 203, 206, 211–220,
    345, 406–414, 416, 417, 419, 421, 434,
    435, 437, 438, 441, 444–446, 450

Tourist, 176–178
Tracking, 4–11, 14, 57, 71, 101, 113, 132, 137, 166, 178, 217, 274, 345
Transmission, 48, 50, 51, 53, 62–65, 68, 72, 205, 206, 209, 210, 213, 215–217, 220, 221, 223, 236, 264, 342, 343, 345, 349, 353–358, 367, 369–371, 435, 437, 441, 443
Truncation attack, 391
Trusted host, 387
Type-2 fuzzy, 48, 52, 70–72
Type-2 logic, 48, 52, 70–73

U
Ubiquitous, 127, 129, 130, 132, 133, 157–179, 181, 182, 193, 197, 231–256, 260, 264, 266, 267, 313, 314, 337
Unauthorized disclosure, 383
Undirected graph, 412–414, 428
Unified datagram protocol (UDP), 100
United Nations, 98
Upper limbs, 102, 111

V
Video, 4, 6–11, 16, 19, 24, 47–73, 77–94, 138, 160, 176, 177, 260, 272, 341–362, 366, 369–374, 376, 378, 379, 408
Video games, 3, 4, 6–11, 16, 19, 24
Video streaming, 47–73, 341–362, 371
Virtual, 8, 50, 51, 97–113, 135–152, 158, 160, 164, 184, 272, 283, 297, 405, 406, 416
Virtual reality (VR), 8, 97–113, 136, 139
Virtual Reality Modeling Language (VRML), 108

Visited host, 384–387, 391, 392, 398, 400–402
Volcano, 201–229

W
Wearable computing, 98, 99
Web, 9, 47, 136, 158, 160, 163, 172–174, 178, 185, 202, 203, 205, 211, 226–228, 236, 238, 265, 270, 275, 289–310, 367, 368, 375
Web Service Definition Language (WSDL), 265, 291–293, 295–297, 300, 309
Web Service Modelling Language (WSML), 291, 295–297, 299, 300
Web Service Modelling Ontology (WSMO), 290, 291, 297, 309, 310
Web services, 136, 185, 265, 270, 289–310
Wi-Fi, 61, 164, 165, 190, 192, 197, 266
Winning host, 391
Wireless, 3–25, 47–73, 98, 125, 129, 131, 133, 136, 138–142, 150–152, 164, 186, 190, 192, 202–210, 216, 217, 220, 232, 234, 236, 239, 240, 251, 260–262, 264, 266, 273, 341, 366, 368, 374, 380, 408, 410, 434, 439–440, 445
Wireless networks, 47–73, 136, 139, 141, 150, 164, 190, 205, 208, 209, 216, 217, 232, 266, 366, 434
WorldViz, 98, 106

X
XML, 91, 165, 228, 268, 269, 291, 295, 298
XPath, 292, 295, 296, 298
XQuery Engine, 91